STUDIES IN BAPTIST HISTORY AND THOUGHT
VOLUME 9

The Search for a Common Identity

The Origins of the Baptist Union
of Scotland 1800-1870

STUDIES IN BAPTIST HISTORY AND THOUGHT

A full listing of all titles in this series
appears at the close of this book

STUDIES IN BAPTIST HISTORY AND THOUGHT
VOLUME 9

The Search for a Common Identity

The Origins of the Baptist Union of Scotland 1800-1870

Brian R. Talbot

Eugene, Oregon

Wipf and Stock Publishers
199 W 8th Ave, Suite 3
Eugene, OR 97401

The Search for a Common Identity
The Origins of the Baptist Union of Scotland 1800–1870
By Talbot, Brian R.
Copyright©2003 Paternoster
ISBN: 1-59752-762-9
Publication date 6/8/2006
Previously published by Paternoster, 2003

This Edition Published by Wipf and Stock Publishers
by arrangement with Paternoster

Paternoster
9 Holdom Avenue
Bletchley
Milton Keyes, MK1 1QR
Great Britain

STUDIES IN BAPTIST HISTORY AND THOUGHT

Series Preface

Baptists form one of the largest Christian communities in the world, and while they hold the historic faith in common with other mainstream Christian traditions, they nevertheless have important insights which they can offer to the worldwide church. *Studies in Baptist History and Thought* will be one means towards this end. It is an international series of academic studies which includes original monographs, revised dissertations, collections of essays and conference papers, and aims to cover any aspect of Baptist history and thought. While not all the authors are themselves Baptists, they nevertheless share an interest in relating Baptist history and thought to the other branches of the Christian church and to the wider life of the world.

The series includes studies in various aspects of Baptist history from the seventeenth century down to the present day, including biographical works, and Baptist thought is understood as covering the subject-matter of theology (including interdisciplinary studies embracing biblical studies, philosophy, sociology, practical theology, liturgy and women's studies). The diverse streams of Baptist life throughout the world are all within the scope of these volumes.

The series editors and consultants believe that the academic disciplines of history and theology are of vital importance to the spiritual vitality of the churches of the Baptist faith and order. The series sets out to discuss, examine and explore the many dimensions of their tradition and so to contribute to their on-going intellectual vigour.

A brief word of explanation is due for the series identifier on the front cover. The fountains, taken from heraldry, represent the Baptist distinctive of believer's baptism and, at the same time, the source of the water of life. There are three of them because they symbolize the Trinitarian basis of Baptist life and faith. Those who are redeemed by the Lamb, the book of Revelation reminds us, will be led to 'fountains of living waters' (Rev. 7.17).

Series Editors

Anthony R. Cross, Fellow of the Centre for Baptist History and Heritage, Regent's Park College, Oxford, UK

Curtis W. Freeman, Research Professor of Theology and Director of the Baptist House of Studies, Duke University, North Carolina, USA

Stephen R. Holmes, Lecturer in Theology, University of St Andrews, Scotland, UK

Elizabeth Newman, Professor of Theology and Ethics, Baptist Theological Seminary at Richmond, Virginia, USA

Philip E. Thompson, Assistant Professor of Systematic Theology and Christian Heritage, North American Baptist Seminary, Sioux Falls, South Dakota, USA

Series Consultant Editors

David Bebbington, Professor of History, University of Stirling, Scotland, UK

Paul S. Fiddes, Professor of Systematic Theology, University of Oxford, and Principal of Regent's Park College, Oxford, UK

Stanley J. Grenz, Pioneer McDonald Professor of Theology, Carey Theological College, Vancouver, British Columbia, Canada

Stanley E. Porter, President and Professor of New Testament, McMaster Divinity College, Hamilton, Ontario, Canada

*To Derek Murray whose lectures in Baptist History
inspired the writing of this book*

Contents

Foreword xiii
Acknowledgements xv
Abbreviations xvii

Chapter 1 Introduction 1

Chapter 2 The Scotch Baptists, 1765-1842 29
   2.1 Origins of the Scotch Baptists 29
   2.2 Distinctive Church Principles of the Scotch Baptists ... 31
   2.3 The Relationship of Scotch Baptists with other
British Baptists 45
   2.4 The Causes of Disunity amongst the Scotch Baptists 53
      An External Cause of Division 55
      Internal Causes of Division 57

**Chapter 3 The Haldanes and the Haldaneite Baptists,
1794-1851** 73
   3.1 The Early Years 73
   3.2 The Influence of Prominent Ministers in England ... 74
   3.3 The Work of The Society for the Propagation of the
Gospel at Home 78
   3.4 Robert Haldane's Catholic Christianity 83
   3.5 James Haldane's Ecclesiological Principles 86
   3.6 The Causes of the Divisions in Scottish Independent
Ranks 89
   3.7 Some Important Colleagues of the Haldanes 98
   3.8 The Work of Theological Education 106
   3.9 Haldaneite Attitudes to the 1827 Baptist Union 110

Chapter 4 The 'English' Baptists, 1796-1852 115
   4.1 The Distinctive Beliefs of 'English' Baptists 115
   4.2 The Earliest 'English' Baptist Churches in Scotland 118
   4.3 Prominent 'English' Baptist Leaders 120
      Donald McArthur 120

		Dugald Sinclair	121
		Alexander McLeod	124
		Sinclair Thomson	126
		George Barclay	127
		Christopher Anderson	132
		Jonathan Watson	144
	4.4	'English' Baptists and Theological Education	147

Chapter 5		The Baptist Home Missionary Society: A Substitute Union, 1827-1868?	153
	5.1	The Earliest Efforts in Home Evangelisation by Scottish Baptists	153
	5.2	The Formation of the Baptist Home Missionary Society for Scotland	158
	5.3	The Geographical Spread of BHMS Agents	159
	5.4	Financial Support for the BHMS	161
	5.5	The Wider Ministry of BHMS Agents	165
	5.6	Training and Provision of Home Missionaries	166
	5.7	Reasons why the BHMS did not become a 'Substitute Union'	169
	5.8	BHMS Activities that went beyond the Boundaries of a Baptist Union	184

Chapter 6		The Attempts to Form a Baptist Union of Scotland, 1827-1842	191
	6.1	The Formation and Demise of the 1827 Baptist Union	191
		The Process of Establishing the Baptist Union	191
		The Reasons for the Failure of this Baptist Union...	206
	6.2	The Formation and Establishment of the SBA, 1835-1842	212
	6.3	The Importance of Ministerial Training in Uniting Scottish Baptists	215
	6.4	Reasons for the Lack of Success of the SBA	220

Chapter 7		The Third Attempt to Form a Baptist Union of Scotland, 1843-1856	229
	7.1	The Religious Revolution in Scotland in the Early 1840s	229

Contents

7.2	The Importance of Francis Johnston in the 1843-1856 Baptist Union	231
7.3	The Significance of the Temperance Movement.........	240
7.4	The Place of Theological Education	246
7.5	The One Opportunity to Unite Scottish Baptists in the 1840s	247
7.6	Reasons for the Failure of the Johnstonian Baptist Union..	252
	Thomas Milner and the Churches of Christ	262
7.7	Francis Johnston: His Methods and Theology	265

Chapter 8 The Genesis of the 1869 Baptist Union 277
    8.1   Obstacles that had Hindered Attempts at Union ... 278
    8.2   Factors that Assisted the Formation of a Union of Churches 287
           The Importance of the SBA Leadership............... 287
           The Importance of Outside Influences 293
           English Particular Baptist Influences, with Special Reference to the London Baptist Association and the Pastor's College 300
    8.3   From the SBA to the Baptist Union of Scotland 307
    8.4   Union for the Provision of Theological Education ... 312

Chapter 9 Conclusions 319
    9.1   The Wider Social and Religious Context within Scotland 326
    9.2   Developments amongst Baptists in England, Wales and Ireland 335
    9.3   The Contribution of Scottish Baptist Historians, in particular the Work of Derek Murray 338

Appendices 344
    Appendix 1   The Attitude to Baptist Church Union amongst Haldaneite Baptists 344
    Appendix 2   Scottish Baptists sent from Scotland to Horton Baptist College by 1837 345
    Appendix 3.1 Location of Baptist Home Missionaries in Scotland, 1800-1870 346

Appendix 3.2	The Number of Baptist Missionaries Employed in Scotland, 1800-1879	348
Appendix 3.3	Total Income of the Baptist Home Missionary Society in Scotland	350
Appendix 3.4	Total Income of the BHMS, 1829-1870	351
Appendix 3.5	BHMS Subscription Income from Scotland ...	352
Appendix 3.6	The Trends in BHMS Subscription Income using a Four-Year Moving Average	353
Appendix 4.1	The Baptist Union of Scotland, 1827	354
Appendix 4.2	The Proportion of Churches Affiliated to the Scottish Baptist Association or the Baptist Union of Scotland, 1827-1879	356
Appendix 4.3	The Scottish Baptist Association, 1835-1842 ...	358
Appendix 5.1	The Baptist Union of Scotland, 1843-1856 ...	360
Appendix 5.2	Scottish Baptist Churches, Ministers and Lay-Leaders involved in the Total Abstinence Cause before 1842	362
Appendix 6.1	English Baptist Colleges and Scotland	364
Appendix 6.2	The Pastor's College Former Students involved in the Scottish Baptist Association or Baptist Union of Scotland by 1870	365
Appendix 6.3	The Baptist Union of Scotland, 1869	366
Appendix 6.4	The Baptist Union of Scotland, 1879	368

Bibliography 371

Index 395

Foreword

During the nineteenth century Scotland was a divided country. The Lowlands, which contained the flourishing capital Edinburgh and the immensely prosperous Glasgow, differed from the Highlands, which were generally backward, undergoing depopulation and suffering the decline of the ancient Gaelic language. The Highlands, although part of the United Kingdom, seemed a mission field. In the early years of the century there were as many as three Baptist missionary societies devoted to the evangelisation of the Highlands. Their number reflected another kind of division, one that afflicted the Baptists of Scotland, for each of the missions represented a different party. Although Scottish Baptists were not numerous – only some one per cent of churchgoers at the 1851 census – they were by no means united. Apart from small local communities that had distinctive origins, there were as many as four distinct strands of Baptist life.

First there were the Scotch Baptists, who drew much of their inspiration from the Glasites, an eighteenth-century sect believing that New Testament church order should be rigorously reproduced. Archibald McLean, originally a bookseller, was deeply influenced by the Glasites, but, unlike them, was convinced of the truth of believer's baptism. McLean's writings set out the guiding principles of the Scotch Baptists, who insisted that each church must possess several elders rather than a single minister. Their punctilious requirement of unanimity in church decisions paradoxically led to frequent schisms in their ranks. Today only a handful of Scotch Baptist churches survive, and they are in Wales.

Another Baptist movement consisted of the followers of Robert and James Haldane, gentry from the Airthrey estate near Stirling. After their conversion, they sold their property, organised home missions and set up congregations in many parts of Scotland. They were at first pragmatic independents, but in 1808 adopted Baptist convictions, carrying a minority of their adherents with them. Like most Scots, they were Calvinist in their theology and, like a growing proportion of Presbyterians, they were dedicated to the spread of the gospel.

There were also, in the third place, Calvinistic, or Particular, Baptists indistinguishable in principle from their English counterparts. Indeed, because their churches, unlike those of the Scotch Baptists, were each led by a single minister, they were usually described as being of the 'English order'. A representative figure was Christopher Anderson, minister of Charlotte Chapel, Edinburgh, from 1806. Trained at Bristol Academy, the leading centre of Baptist intellectual life, he was actively involved in a variety of ventures such as supporting William Carey, the celebrated missionary to India. The 'English' Baptists were typically more concerned for a learned ministry than the other branches of Baptist life.

The fourth strand, arising only in the 1840s, consisted of those who reacted against the Calvinism that was the common property of the other three groups. The American Charles Finney exerted an influence over certain Scots, inducing them to abandon the traditional insistence on the limitation of salvation to a few. Like the Evangelical Union, which was a non-Baptist denomination, a group of Baptists held, with increasing vehemence around mid-century, that Christ died for all. Their existence added a fresh element of fragmentation to Baptist life.

The sheer heterogeneity meant that co-operation in a single Baptist organisation proved impossible for the first two-thirds of the century. It is the achievement of Brian Talbot to have disentangled the threads of Baptist diversity in Scotland in order to reveal why no successful denominational structure was created until 1869. He has examined almost all the existing evidence, manuscript as well as published, that casts light on his theme. The fruit of his painstaking research is set out clearly in this volume, the fullest history of the denomination in nineteenth-century Scotland written so far. The eventual launching of the Baptist Union, he shows, was a sign of another Baptist trait that has often kept their tendency to division in check: the imperative to mission. Eventually a desire to spread the gospel led to the triumph of co-operation over disintegration.

David Bebbington
University of Stirling
April 2003

Acknowledgements

I am grateful to the librarians and staff members of numerous archives and libraries in the United Kingdom. I would like to acknowledge, in particular, the helpfulness and kindness of Mrs Susan Mills, the Librarian, and Mrs Jennifer Thorpe, the Archivist, at the Angus Library, Regent's Park College, Oxford; the staff at the Inter-Library Loans department of Stirling University; the Librarians at New College, Edinburgh; the Librarians at St Andrews University; the Librarian of Bristol Baptist College and the Rev. Dr Ian Randall and staff at Spurgeon's College, London. In addition, the willingness on the part of numerous Scottish Baptist Churches to allow access to their records has proved invaluable. Particular acknowledgement needs to be given to Mr Ian Docherty of St Andrews Baptist Church; Miss Francis Manley of Adelaide Place Baptist Church, Glasgow; Dr Ian Balfour and Mr Angus Ferguson of Charlotte Baptist Chapel, Edinburgh; Miss Christine Lumsden of Bristo Baptist Church, Edinburgh and Mrs Ann Tennyson of Elgin. I am grateful to Mr Owain Jones of Mold, Clywd, for placing his collection of Scotch Baptist MSS in the National Library of Scotland. Generous assistance with computer technology has been given by Mr Stanley Johnson and the Rev. Richard Tuckley. Heartfelt thanks is also due to the Rev. Eric Worton and Mr John Longridge for the production of maps and graphs. I also want to thank the Rev. Dr Derek Murray, Prof. Donald Meek, and Mr J.S. Fisher for advice on historical matters relating to the thesis. Gratitude must also be warmly expressed to the Dr Williams Trust, and the Checkland Memorial Fund for financial assistance.

Dr David Bebbington, my doctoral superviser, has provided considerable help and encouragement with this project over the last decade. His stimulating questions and helpful advice have ensured that this book is considerably better than it might otherwise have been.

I am also grateful to the editorial committee of Paternoster Press which accepted this book for publication, in particular to Jeremy Mudditt and Anthony Cross for their encouraging comments at various stages along the way.

My wife Kathryn is owed a special debt of appreciation for her encouragement and support. First of all, when this work was begun as a doctoral thesis in 1993 and then in the processes leading to publication as a book in the Studies in Baptist History and Thought Series. To my children Helen, Benjamin and Rachel who patiently accepted that 'Daddy was in the study again' on many occasions when I was working on research for this book. I am also especially thankful to my parents Herbert and Elizabeth Talbot, for their constant love and support in many ways over the years. I am also grateful for the encouraging comments from the members of Cumbernauld Baptist Church and other Scottish Baptist colleagues, including the members of the Scottish Baptist History Project, who heard and commented on early drafts of some of the material in this book.

Abbreviations

BES	Baptist Evangelical Society
BFBS	British and Foreign Bible Society
BHMS	Baptist Home Missionary Society
BMS	Baptist Missionary Society
BQ	Baptist Quarterly
BUGBI	Baptist Union of Great Britain and Ireland
BUS	Baptist Union of Scotland
DEB	Blackwell Dictionary of Evangelical Biography, 1730-1860
EU	Evangelical Union
LBA	London Baptist Association
MS Letters	Manuscript Letters relating to the Scotch Baptist Churches
NBES	Northern Baptist Education Society
PCM	The Primitive Church Magazine
SBA	Scottish Baptist Association
SIS	Scotch Itinerant Society
SPGH	The Society for the Propagation of the Gospel at Home
STL	Scottish Temperance League
TAS	Total Abstinence Society
UPC	United Presbyterian Church
WSTU	West of Scotland Temperance Union
YMCA	Young Men's Christian Association

CHAPTER 1

Introduction

Since the modern inception of their cause in the mid-eighteenth century, Baptists have been a very small proportion of the church-going population of Scotland. In the mid-eighteenth century the overwhelming majority of the population claimed at least a nominal attachment to the Established Church. It was estimated in 1766 that around 89% of the people associated with the Church of Scotland. There were also 100,000 Presbyterian Dissenters and 20,000 Roman Catholics, with a similar number of Episcopalians.[1] It is unlikely that there were more than about one hundred Scottish Baptists in that year in Keiss and Edinburgh.[2] It is known from the census in 1801 that the population of Scotland had risen to 1,608,000 people.[3] There were two Baptist groups that were operating by 1800, the 'English' Baptists with approximately forty-two members and up to one hundred hearers,[4] and the Scotch Baptists with around 400 members and approximately 1000 hearers.[5] The community of Scottish Baptists, including hearers, comprised a mere 0.1% of the population. The limited size of their constituency, however, did not prevent them from focusing more on their differences than on the things that united them, especially in the first three decades of the nineteenth century. This study of the developments in the life of the Baptist community will concentrate on the issue of relationships between the different Baptist streams, and, in particular, the moves to establish a national union of churches

It is important to note that Baptists have a very different church polity from some of the other Christian churches that emphasise a central authority or hierarchical structure. For Baptists the authority is vested in the church meeting of the members of a local congregation. There are no outside parties, whether national officials, syn-

---

1 C.G. Brown, *Religion and Society in Scotland since 1707*, (Edinburgh: Edinburgh University Press, 1997), p. 46.
2 D.B. Murray, 'The Seventeenth and Eighteenth Centuries', in D.W. Bebbington (ed.), *The Baptists in Scotland: A History*, (Glasgow: Baptist Union of Scotland, 1988), pp. 15-16.
3 *Parliamentary Papers*, 6, 1801, cited by T.C. Smout, *A History of The Scottish People 1560-1830*, (London: Fontana, 1985), p. 241.
4 Chapter four, p. 119.
5 J. Rippon (ed.), *Baptist Annual Register*, 1795, pp. 373-374.

ods, councils or assemblies, that can over-rule in the affairs of a local church. The relationship between any two or more Baptist congregations is strictly on a voluntary basis. The emphasis on the autonomy of the local church, however, does not preclude the possible importance of district associations and national unions of churches. There were, however, some ecclesiological differences between the Scotch and 'English' Baptists. Scotch Baptists took a more literalistic approach to biblical interpretation than their 'English' colleagues. They affirmed the necessity of a plurality of elders and deacons in contrast to the sole pastor and deacons model of the 'English' Baptists. It was also mandatory in their circles for elders to be present at the celebration of the Lord's Supper in the context of weekly Sunday worship. The churches in their ranks attempted to observe uniformity of practice in their congregations as a basis for fellowship. Scotch Baptists, therefore, would not have sought formal fellowship with 'English' Baptists at the beginning of the nineteenth century. Chapter two will list more of their distinctive views. 'English' Baptists in Scotland, on the other hand, viewed themselves as part of a wider Baptist movement in the United Kingdom. They were in fellowship with the English Particular Baptists. These English Baptists reciprocated the desire for fellowship and co-operation in ministry by supporting, for example, home mission activities in Scotland. This book will seek to elucidate the evolution within the Baptist community in Scotland from a number of disparate groups to a consolidated union of churches and ministers in the last quarter of the nineteenth century.

There had been a Baptist presence in Scotland since the 1650s during the Cromwellian era.[6] Persecution by the authorities and disapproval by the strongly homogeneous Presbyterian populace had caused them apparently to disappear by the end of the seventeenth century.[7] The re-emergence of the Baptist witness in Scotland during the eighteenth century occurred in a most unlikely place, Keiss in Caithness. Sir William Sinclair[8], the laird of Dunbeath estate, had been influenced by Baptists outside Scotland and had brought his

---

6   J. Nicoll, *Diary of Public Transactions, 1650-1659*, (ed.) D. Laing, (Edinburgh: no publisher stated, 1836), pp. 38-39, 106.

7   P. Waugh, 'The New Dawn and the Rise of the Scotch Baptists', in G. Yuille (ed.), *History of the Baptists in Scotland*, (Glasgow: Baptist Union of Scotland Publications Committee, 1926), p. 36.

8   An excellent introduction to the life and religious beliefs of Sir William Sinclair is found in C. Lumsden, 'The Life of Sir William Sinclair' (unpublished paper presented to the Scottish Baptist History Project, Keiss, May 6 2000).

new faith back to his native land. Debts incurred by his father had caused Sinclair to sell all his patrimony by 1765. In his later years the Caithness knight lived in Edinburgh, but continued to maintain contact with the Keiss church until his death in 1768.[9] Although a Baptist congregation had been established in the capital city by 1765 there is no record of Sinclair having any association with it.[10] The earliest Edinburgh Baptist congregation held to the Scotch Baptist opinions that will be discussed in the next chapter. The Scotch Baptists were led by Archibald McLean, an elder in the Edinburgh church from 1768 until his death in 1812. His inspiring leadership and great learning dominated his connexion for over forty years. In the late eighteenth century almost all the eleven Baptist congregations in Scotland were linked to that connexion.[11] The only exception was the 'English'-style congregation of Frederick McFarlane that had commenced in Edinburgh in 1796, details of which are given in chapter four. In 1800 the Baptist community in Scotland was dominated by the Scotch Baptist tradition, but within a decade a much more complex picture had emerged. The developments that occurred within the period 1800 to 1810 amongst Scottish Baptists laid the foundation on which this study will be based.

The decision by Robert and James Haldane, two members of the Scottish gentry, to accept believer's baptism in 1808 marked their entrance into Baptist ranks.[12] The Independent network of churches to which they had belonged was deeply divided, with some pastors and congregations following their patrons into Baptist circles whilst others retained their paedobaptist convictions. Chapter three will examine the impact of the Haldanes, especially considering the impact they and their followers had on the existing Baptist congregations in Scotland. The Baptist constituency had grown rapidly in the years following their adoption of Baptist principles and, by 1810, 48% of the congregations were associated with the Haldane brothers.[13] Their background and the number of colleagues under their patronage and influence would ensure that the opinions of

---

9   Murray, 'Seventeenth and Eighteenth Centuries', pp. 15-16.
10 P. Wilson, *The Origin and Progress of the Scotch Baptist Churches*, (Edinburgh: Fullarton And Co., 1844), pp. 3-5.
11 D.B. Murray, 'The Social and Religious Origins of Scottish Non-Presbyterian Protestant Dissent from 1730-1800' (PhD thesis, St Andrews University, 1976), p. 68.
12 A. Haldane, *The Lives of Robert and James Haldane*, (Edinburgh: Banner of Truth Trust, 1990 [1853]), pp. 359-360.
13 Chapter three, p. 112.

these two men would be highly significant in the decades to come.

The third sector of the Baptist community in Scotland was known as the 'English' Baptists. The reason for the name with which their tradition was associated was their preference for a single pastor in charge of a congregation. This individual was normally to be supported financially by the members.[14] Scotch Baptists, as will be seen in chapter two, firmly supported the plurality of elders in leadership with the majority of that number retaining their secular occupation alongside their pastoral responsibilities. In the early part of the nineteenth century the 'English' Baptists were numerically the smallest group of Scottish Baptists, but due to their energetic vision for evangelism both at home and overseas, the number of their congregations grew so that they became the dominant force by the 1830s. Chapter four provides details of the rise and progress of this stream of Baptist witness.

Scottish Baptists recognised that there was a need to co-operate with each other, and with Baptists in England, in the work of overseas mission. The Particular Baptist Missionary Society (BMS) established by ministers such as Andrew Fuller and William Carey received wholehearted support from their Scottish brethren, as well as from some Presbyterian congregations.[15] Archibald McLean, leader of the Scotch Baptists, was the first Scottish minister to advocate, in 1798, support for the BMS.[16] Robert and James Haldane were also inspired by reading the accounts of the work of the BMS in India. They considered offering themselves for service overseas, but the obstacles blocking their progress were too large. It was no surprise that these men and the colleagues associated with them joined the 'English' Baptists in offering support for the missionary work in Bengal.[17] If it was beneficial to associate in the work of evangelism in other lands, questions would naturally be raised about the need for a united missionary society at home.

Each of the three streams of Baptists in Scotland was committed to the evangelisation of their home country. Scotch Baptists had been active from the 1790s, especially in Aberdeenshire and Banff, where the ministry of James Watt resulted in the formation of a number of congregations.[18] 'English' Baptists too had been active in

---

14 H. Anderson, *The Life and Letters of Christopher Anderson*, (Edinburgh: W.P. Kennedy, 1854), pp. 64-65.
15 J. Belcher (ed.), *The Complete Works of the Rev. Andrew Fuller*, (3 Vols; Harrisonburg, Virginia: Sprinkle Publications, 1988 [1845]), I, p. 69.
16 Chapter two, pp. 51-52.
17 Chapter three, p. 82.
18 Chapter two, pp. 41-42.

Introduction 5

the same areas through the work of a Baptist minister, William Ward, who was based at Old Deer, and a man called Paterson whose itinerant labours were centred on Stonehaven. The two 'English' evangelists received financial assistance from 'The Baptist Society in London for the Encouragement and Support of Itinerant Preaching' after the BMS secretary Andrew Fuller had sought assistance for his Scottish friends.[19] This link with English Particular Baptists is significant in that it was the first of many ties between England and Scotland for the 'English' Baptists in Scotland. Co-operation between Baptists north and south of the border had had practical benefits, and it would be no surprise that it was from this tradition that moves began in the process towards union between Baptist churches in Scotland.

The Haldanes had had an even greater impact on their native land in the 1790s through the work of the Society for Propagating the Gospel at Home (SPGH). This home evangelisation society had never intended to set up a new denomination. Its aim had been to use men of different ecclesiastical traditions who shared the same evangelical faith to itinerate wherever they found opportunities.[20] This desire to build bridges between Christians who shared a common faith remained with the Haldanes even after the collapse of the SPGH in 1808. It was, therefore, no surprise that the Scottish Baptist home missionary societies had combined their organisations and efforts in 1827. Details of the merger and related events will be given in chapter five. The ranks of Scottish Baptists by the late 1820s were growing in terms of the numbers of members and churches. If home missionary activities could be carried out under a common banner it was only to be expected that closer union between congregations might also receive further consideration.

The Baptist Union of Scotland was set up in 1869. This organisation has continued its work to the present day. There were, however, three previous attempts to unite the churches which had ended in failure. This book aims to examine the factors that favoured a merger of the different Baptist traditions and those obstacles which hindered union in the years leading up to the establishment of the Union. Scottish Baptists did not work in a vacuum, however, and so their operations have to be seen in the light of the changing ecclesiastical context. In the nineteenth century Scotland passed through a period of great change in its religious expression from a tendency towards fissiparity in the earlier decades to a greater desire for

---

19   Chapter five, p. 153-154.
20   Chapter three, pp. 78-80.

unions and mergers between denominations in the later years. The Secession Church is a good example of both tendencies. In 1799 and 1806 its two main branches split into four groups over whether to maintain adherence in full to the Westminster Confession. Some members of each of the two branches in 1799 and 1806 wished to reject some of the apparently persecuting principles in the Confession and became known as 'New Light' Burghers and Antiburghers. In 1820 there was a modest reversal of this trend with the union of the two 'New Light' groups to form the United Secession Church.[21] In 1843 a minority of the United Secession Church adopted universal views of the atonement and left to form the Evangelical Union denomination. 1843 saw the most significant secession in nineteenth-century church history with the formation of the Free Church of Scotland, due to a minority of the Established Church refusing to accept the spiritual dependence of the church upon the state. In this same year Francis Johnston launched the second Baptist Union of Scotland which survived for thirteen years.[22] After a half-century of largely fissiparous tendencies the next five decades were mainly marked by unions amongst different Presbyterian groups. The Relief Church and the United Secession Church merged in 1847 to form the United Presbyterian Church. The bulk of the Reformed Presbyterian Church joined with the Free Church in 1876 and in 1900 the main body of the Free Church and the United Presbyterian Church became the United Free Church. There were some minor Presbyterian schisms in this period, but the general trend was in the direction of consolidation and union.[23] The Congregational Union of Scotland, after a minor schism in 1843 to 1845 over the extent of the atonement, also followed the trend towards union through closer ties with the Evangelical Union from the 1860s. Their co-operation led to a merger in 1896 with the new body retaining the name the Congregational Union of Scotland.[24] The Baptists in Scotland, after similar theological tensions over the atonement in their ranks in the 1850s,[25] united to form the (third) Baptist Union of Scotland in 1869. This new body soon gained the support of almost all Scottish Baptists.[26] Scottish Baptists in the first

---

21 K.R. Ross, 'Secessions', in N.M. de S. Cameron (ed.), *Dictionary of Scottish Church History and Theology*, (Edinburgh: T. & T. Clark, 1993), pp. 764-765.
22 Chapter seven, pp. 233-240.
23 Ross, 'Secessions', p. 765.
24 H. Escott, *A History of Scottish Congregationalism*, (Glasgow: Congregational Union of Scotland, 1960), pp. 107-115.
25 Chapter seven, p. 260.
26 Chapter eight, pp. 311-312.

Introduction 7

half of the nineteenth century appeared to share the common tendencies to fissiparity amongst Scottish Churchmen and the same trends towards union in the second half of the century.

The moves towards union in 'New Light' Secession churches, in the second decade of the nineteenth century, arose due to the growing co-operation between churches in home and overseas evangelism, Bible societies and other religious causes. This fellowship led to the formation of the United Secession Church in 1820.[27] The new denomination continued its missionary activities, developing ever closer ties to the Relief Church in the next two decades.[28] One of the spurs towards the uniting of these bodies was ironically victory for the Relief Church in the 'Campbeltown Case', an action in the civil courts to determine whether Scottish law allowed the judicial authorities 'to transfer ownership of church property on the grounds that the present occupiers of the church had altered the doctrines for whose propagation the property had been erected'. In this case James Smith, the minister, wished to take the church property with him into the Established Church. The courts after a long battle from 1835 to 1839 found in favour of the Relief Church.[29] Gavin Struthers, the author of *The History of the Rise, Progress and Principles of The Relief Church*, produced his book in the light of this judgement with a view to promoting further unions between Presbyterian denominations.[30] He noted that:

> The Campbeltown decision has removed one barrier to the union of different dissenting churches, that are agreed about the great doctrines and ordinances of the gospel…Undoubtedly this process for a time served to retard the union between the Secession and Relief churches; but as the way is now legally clear, it is to be hoped that it will be pushed forward with vigour.[31]

In the same manner John McKerrow's *History of the Secession Church* was reissued in 1845 to reveal to the general public that the principles of the Secession Church were remarkably similar to those of the Free Church. It was stated that the reasons for the secessions

---

27 I. Hamilton, 'United Secession Church', in Cameron (ed.), *Scottish Church History and Theology*, p. 841.
28 S.D. Gill, 'United Presbyterian Church', in Cameron (ed.), *Scottish Church History and Theology*, pp. 839-840.
29 N.R. Needham, 'Campbeltown Case (1835-9)', in Cameron (ed.), *Scottish Church History and Theology*, p, 131.
30 'Sketch of the late Rev. Dr Struthers', *United Presbyterian Magazine*, 2, (1858), pp. 458-459.
31 G. Struthers, *The History of the Rise, Progress and Principles of The Relief Church*, (Glasgow: A. Fullarton & Co., third edition, 1843), p. 546.

from the Established Church in the eighteenth century were, in essence, the same as those promoted in 1843. The underlying agenda was to educate the church-going public with a view to promoting union with the Free Church.[32] The United Secession Church and the Relief Church united to form the United Presbyterian Church (UPC) in 1847. Informal negotiations between the UPC and the Free Church began soon after 1847, though only formally in 1863. Differing views over the establishment principle caused negotiations to falter in 1873, due to a strong minority of Free Church members opposing the merger. The union between the two bodies was finally effected in 1900,[33] to form the United Free Church, a body which had, at least by 1906, become an evangelical non-confessional church.[34] There are clear similarities here with developments during the nineteenth century in Scottish Baptist circles. The initial uniting focus for Scottish Baptists was support for mission at home and overseas. Scottish Baptists all accepted the need for a united body, but different ecclesiological opinions between Scotch and 'English' Baptists and later differences over Morisonian doctrines ensured that significant difficulties had to be overcome prior to a successful merger. The 1869 Baptist Union, like the later United Free Church, was an evangelical body that chose not to possess a creed or confession that would serve as a means of admission to the membership of a local church. The old battles over Calvinist versus Arminian sentiments were formally relegated from official pronouncements to issues of private debate.

It will be appropriate to ask whether the developments in Scottish Baptist circles were theologically in step with other denominations or whether there was a significant contrast in approaches to the changing world. For example, did the splits over Arminianism in the Secession Church and the Congregational denomination have any parallels in Baptist ranks ? On social questions such as the temperance crusade, did Scottish Baptists support it as enthusiastically as the Evangelical Union or was it not particularly important among them ? On a wider stage how did the changes amongst Scottish Baptists compare with developments experienced by English Baptists ? Was there any cross-fertilisation of ideas or sharing of activities that aided or hindered union attempts ? These questions are amongst those to be considered in this study of a small Scottish denomination.

---

32 J. McKerrow, *History of the Secession Church*, (Glasgow: A. Fullarton & Co., third edition, 1845), p. v.
33 Gill, 'United Presbyterian Church', p. 840.
34 N.R. Needham, 'United Free Church', in Cameron (ed.), *Scottish Church History and Theology*, pp. 838-839.

Introduction

The first attempt to produce a history of one of the Baptist streams in Scotland occurred in 1844. Patrick Wilson's book, *The Origins and Progress of the Scotch Baptist Churches 1765-1835*, was produced 'in order to rescue from oblivion the origin of this society'.[35] Scotch Baptists, after disastrous divisions over the question of the necessity of elders at the Lord's Table in 1834, were fatally weakened as a connexion. The once dominant body of Scottish Baptists was now destined to play only a minor role in future Scottish Baptist history.[36] Wilson, an Edinburgh architect,[37] was concerned to emphasise that the dire circumstances in which his fellow-Scotch Baptists now found themselves were very different from the era when Archibald McLean was alive. The first major history of the whole Baptist movement in Scotland was edited by George Yuille in 1926. This book, *History of the Baptists in Scotland*, is a rich resource of information, particularly on the lives of local congregations, though there is also material about the wider work in the Baptist constituency. The main weaknesses of this book are a lack of attention to detail and the absence of references to identify primary sources. There is also a tendency to interpret past events such as the moves towards union in the light of later theological views. For example, the endeavours of Francis Johnston in the late 1840s and early 1850s were described as 'benignant activities'. Johnston, however, despite all his enthusiasm for union, was primarily a source of division rather than union. It was he who persuaded the Baptist Union Executive to reject a comprehensive union of Scottish Baptists in December 1845, despite the enthusiasm for this proposal by the majority of union members.[38] Laudatory reference was made in the *History of the Baptists in Scotland* to *The Evangelist* magazine,[39] a periodical used from January 1850 to promote militant Morisonianism. This policy would only serve to reduce the Union's influence and cause its circulation to decline.[40] In the late nineteenth and early twentieth centuries Arminian theological opinions were predominant in the Baptist Union of Scotland, thus identifying with Johnston, but in the 1850s such views were held only by a minority and caused serious divisions, hindering the moves towards union.

---

35 Wilson, *Scotch Baptist Churches*, p. 4.
36 Chapter two, pp. 67-72.
37 *Post Office Annual Directory for 1843-1844*, (Edinburgh: Ballantyne and Hughes, 1843), p. 132.
38 Chapter seven, pp. 252-253.
39 P. Waugh, 'The "Scotch Baptists" and the First Baptist Union', in Yuille (ed.), *Baptists in Scotland*, p. 236.
40 Chapter seven, pp. 259-262.

The standard reference work was edited by D.W. Bebbington in 1988 and is entitled *The Baptists in Scotland: A History*. It is notably superior to the Yuille book in its acknowledgement of the wider social and economic context of the Baptist movement.[41] There is plenty of useful information on the seventeenth, eighteenth and twentieth centuries,[42] but the importance of the nineteenth century, especially over the moves towards the formation of the Baptist Union of Scotland, is understated.[43] Even more recently a popular history was *Impelled by Faith* produced by J.S. Fisher in 1996. This short paperback is especially strong in its coverage of Baptist work in the Highlands of Scotland. The various printed articles of D.E. Meek such as 'Evangelical Missionaries in the Early Nineteenth Century Highlands'; 'The Independent and Baptist Churches of Highland Perthshire and Strathspey'; 'Evangelicalism and Emigration'; 'The Fellowship of Kindred Minds'; ' "The Glory of the Lamb: The Gaelic Hymns of Peter Grant'; and 'Dugald Sinclair' provide valuable information about the Highland and Island churches and home missionaries, enabling a clear picture to be drawn of the nature and extent of Baptist work in the north and west of Scotland. Further work needs to be done, however, on the Baptist preachers who served in urban centres such as Aberdeen and Dundee and in rural areas in other parts of Scotland that are not covered in the Meek articles.

The Independent (now Congregational) churches in Scotland have had a similar theological and ecclesiological framework to the Baptists. Their founders, though accepting that the Established Church held to an orthodox Reformed theology, believed that it had failed to engage adequately in home evangelisation. The primary purpose of these new movements was to attempt to remedy this deficiency. In addition, both Independents and Baptists shared a belief in the autonomy of local congregations, though not excluding district or national associations of churches. Harry Escott's *A History of Scottish Congregationalism* traces their origins in the 1790s when the Haldanes were amongst the most prominent leaders in the early stages of that movement. Escott's book was written, in part, to emphasise the supreme role within this body of Greville Ewing, the main architect of the union of Congregational churches.[44] It is, though, an institutional history concentrating on the broad sweep of events in the national body, with less space allocated to cover

---

41 For example, pp. 17-19, 28-30, 48-54, 67-70.
42 Chapter one and most of chapters four to eighteen.
43 Chapter two, pp. 40-42; Chapter three, pp. 57-59.
44 Escott, *Scottish Congregationalism*, p. vi.

Introduction

regional and local developments. Escott shows in this book the development not only of the Congregational Union of Scotland and its member churches, but also the history of the Evangelical Union denomination and how the two bodies were eventually united in 1896. It will be instructive to analyse the similarities between that process towards union and the merger between the Johnstonian (Morisonian) and the mainstream Calvinistic Baptists leading up to the Baptist Union in 1869.

A Church History of Scotland by J.H.S. Burleigh concentrates almost exclusively on the Presbyterian churches, and primarily on the Church of Scotland. Burleigh has no interest in developments amongst Scottish Baptists and incorrectly assumes that the first indigenous Baptist group emerged after Robert and James Haldane adopted Baptist principles in 1808;[45] rather than as early as the 1650s, and securely established from the 1760s. The major Scottish church history produced in recent years was A.L. Drummond and J. Bulloch's three-volume work, *The Scottish Church 1688-1843*, *The Church in Victorian Scotland 1843-1874* and *The Church in Late Victorian Scotland 1874-1900*. Scottish Baptists receive no mention at all in the first volume. In the second volume no reference is given to either the Scotch or 'English' Baptists, with the assumption that it was the Haldanes who 'virtually created the Baptists as a denomination'.[46] The wider Baptist movement is completely ignored in all three volumes. The third volume appears to indicate that this series was produced with the view of portraying the Church of Scotland in a more favourable light, in the nineteenth century, at the expense of the Free Church. To compare Principal Robert Rainy, the leading Free Church minister in the late nineteenth century, with the Pope and General Franco and to describe Carnegie Simpson's biography of him as 'tendentious and uncritical' reveals the bias of the authors.[47] A thorough multi-volume ecclesiastical history of Scotland that would adequately reveal the Baptist contribution to Scottish church life still remains to be written. *The People of the Great Faith: The Highland Church 1690-1900* by Douglas Ansdell provides a fair account of the work of 'English' and Haldaneite Home Missionaries in the north west of Scotland, though it fails to mention the Scotch Baptists and the 'Baptist Highland Mission'. It also

---

45   J.H.S. Burleigh, *A Church History of Scotland*, (London: Oxford University Press, 1960), p. 313.
46   A.L. Drummond & J. Bulloch, *The Church in Victorian Scotland*, (Edinburgh: The St Andrew Press, 1975), pp. 52-53.
47   A.L. Drummond & J. Bulloch, *The Church in Late Victorian Scotland*, (Edinburgh: The St Andrew Press, 1978), pp. 308-309.

makes no mention of the Baptist Union or moves towards union in this period. John MacInnes produced *The Evangelical Movement in the Highlands of Scotland 1688-1800* in 1951. This book aimed to examine the attempt by the Church of Scotland to promote Presbyterianism in the Highlands. It is a thorough study of not only Presbyterian preachers, but also some Baptists such as Peter Grant (1783-1867), who was strictly speaking outside the period of this book.[48] There was, though, no reference to the labours of Dr James Watt, a Baptist evangelist in the north of Scotland in the last decade of the eighteenth century. The Scottish Baptists in the Presbyterian histories of the nineteenth century appear to be marginalised due to their limited numbers of members and adherents.

The Transforming of the Kirk by A.C. Cheyne suggests that there was a religious revolution in Victorian Scotland. It naturally focuses primarily on the Presbyterian denominations as they comprised the majority of churchgoers, but the issues raised are relevant to each religious tradition. Cheyne notes persuasively the dramatic changes in Presbyterian church life in the nineteenth century, but overstates his case by simplifying the evidence,[49] for example, over the liberalising trend of the 'Biblical Revolution'. James Orr, Professor of Systematic Theology and Apologetics at the United Free Church College, Glasgow, 1900 to 1913 was clearly a prominent conservative biblical critic.[50] The liberal triumph was less complete in the late-Victorian period than Cheyne appears to suggest. It is, therefore, natural to ask if the changes in Scottish Baptist circles in this period, for example in attitudes towards a national union of churches, were revolutionary, or were they more evolutionary in nature ? *Religion and Society in Scotland since 1707* by Callum Brown examines the social impact of religion on Scottish society over the last three centuries. This book can be used to work out the statistical significance of Baptists in the religious life of the nation, to analyse the changes in beliefs and practices and the tendencies either to fissiparity or union in the period 1800 to 1870. Scottish Baptists cannot be considered without reference to the ecclesiastical and social milieu in which they operated, though Brown appears to give excessive weight to social and economic developments. For example,

---

48 J. MacInnes, *The Evangelical Movement in the Highlands of Scotland 1688-1800*, (Aberdeen: Aberdeen University Press, 1951), pp. 59, 151, 264-265, 270, 291.

49 A.C. Cheyne, *The Transforming of the Kirk*, (Edinburgh: The St Andrew Press, 1983), p. 57,

50 G.C. Scorgie, 'Orr, James (1844-1913)', in Cameron (ed.), *Scottish Church History and Theology*, pp. 638-639.

Introduction

in reference to the Disruption, Brown states, 'In different regions and different types of community it was the product of varied social tensions and segregation'. He places emphasis on the middle-class origins of many of their leaders, suggesting, in part, issues of class struggle.[51] It is most unlikely that the majority of participants would have given other than religious reasons as their primary motivation for seceding from the Established Church. Allan MacLaren's *Religion and Social Class: The Disruption Years in Aberdeen*, provides a Marxist analysis of the Disruption in one Scottish city. It is not surprising that this book appears to underestimate the religious motivation of participants, or that the class contrasts between middle- and working-class members is overstated. The description of the Baptist churches in Aberdeen in the 1840s and 1850s reveals both their weakness and their lack of unity, providing a typical insight into the difficulties faced by those individuals seeking to unite Scottish Baptists into a national union of churches in this period.[52] Scottish Baptists could not fail to be affected by social and ecclesiastical changes in national life, but their limited numbers and often insular outlook would have modified any potential influence. It was only major events such as the Disruption in 1843 that had a decisive influence over Baptist congregations, in this case primarily in the Highlands, because a large majority of people had identified with the Free Church in many local communities.[53]

T.C. Smout's *A History of the Scottish People 1560-1830* and *A Century of the Scottish People 1830-1950* form a masterly overview of Scottish history in this period. The discussion of religion in Scotland, though, is lacking accurate understanding of some key individuals. The influence of the Haldanes is minimised, even in the 1790s when it is probable that the labours of the SPGH created a religious revolution in Scotland. Robert Haldane is dismissed as a 'former midshipman', a description that takes no account of his ancestry in a family that possessed the free barony of Gleneagles.[54] The second volume covering 1830-1950 uses the same 'broad brush' approach to address the issue of 'Churchgoing'. The problem of excessive generalisation mars the narrative. 'The destruction of the literal interpretation of the Bible', was deemed well underway in

---

51 Brown, *Religion and Society in Scotland*, pp. 25-28.
52 A.A. MacLaren, *Religion and Social Class: The Disruption Years in Aberdeen*, (London: Routledge & Kegan Paul, 1974), pp. 32-33, 41.
53 Chapter five, pp. 171-175.
54 T.C. Smout, *A History of The Scottish People 1560-1830*, (London: Fontana, 1985 [1969]), p. 217. Chapter three, pp. 73-74.

the 1850s and 1860s, for example, and almost complete by the end of the century.[55] This viewpoint concentrates on prominent occupants of university chairs, but it was far from assumed in this era in the churches. Scottish Baptist ministers such as P.W. Grant, John Urquhart and James Culross, for example, were representative of their denomination in maintaining what Smout refers to as 'the literal interpretation of the Bible'.[56] The three-volume history, *People and Society in Scotland* (1760-1990), of which the first two volumes refer to the period covered by this book, concentrates on social history. The article in the first volume on 'Religion and Social Change' correctly distinguishes between Scotch and 'English' Baptists in Scotland and notes correctly that Baptist churches prior to 1830 offered almost all seats gratis to the public.[57] There is, though, a failure to note that Baptists, in line with Presbyterians and Roman Catholics, attempted to provide Gaelic-speaking congregations in the Lowlands for Highland immigrants at this time,[58] a point also missed by C.W.J. Withers' *Urban Highlanders: Highland-Lowland Migration and Urban Gaelic Culture, 1700-1900*.[59] The general trend of Scottish denominations in the nineteenth century to move from divisiveness to union is seen to be in line with similar developments in England and Wales.[60] Scottish Baptists in their moves towards the successful church union of 1869, therefore, appeared to be in line with contemporary trends that reached across denominational barriers. William Ferguson's *Scotland 1689 to the Present*, makes very few references to the smaller denominations such as the Baptists. His discussion of Baptist origins repeats the old myth that the Haldane brothers were the real founders of the Scottish Baptist movement, dismissing without evidence Yuille's claim to the contrary. Ferguson is aware of the 'Old Scotch Baptists' [sic], but describes them as 'of very limited significance'.[61] As the overwhelming major-

---

55 T.C. Smout, *A Century of The Scottish People* 1830-1950, (London: Collins, 1986), pp. 193-195.
56 Bebbington (ed.), *Baptists in Scotland*, p. 56.
57 T.M. Devine and R. Mitchison (eds), *People and Society in Scotland: Volume I, 1760-1830*, (Edinburgh: John Donald, 1988), pp. 151, 153.
58 Devine and Mitchison, *People and Society*, I, p. 157. Chapter five, pp. 180-182.
59 C.W.J. Withers, *Urban Highlanders: Highland-Lowland Migration and Urban Gaelic Culture, 1700-1900*, (East Linton: Tuckwell Press, 1998), pp. 160-198.
60 W.H. Fraser and R.J. Morris (eds), *People and Society in Scotland: Volume II, 1830-1914*, (Edinburgh: John Donald, 1990), p. 318.
61 W. Ferguson, *Scotland 1689 to the Present*, (Edinburgh: Mercat Press, 1968), pp. 230-231.

ity of Baptists in Scotland in 1800 belonged to this stream his case is untenable. In fact Scotch Baptists remained a force in Baptist circles in Scotland until their division over the presence of elders at the Lord's Table in 1834 resulted in their numerical decline and the fragmentation of their connexion.[62] Ferguson appears also to be unaware of the 'English' Baptists, associated with English Particular Baptists, who were the most prominent stream of Baptists in Scotland by the 1830s.[63] Michael Lynch in his *Scotland: A New History* appears to marginalise the place of the smaller denominations in his account of the history of the nation. The one reference to Scottish Baptists is less than flattering as he deems them to be outside the ranks of conventional churches.[64] Ecclesiastical developments amongst Scottish Baptists in the nineteenth century have received little coverage in the works of recent major historians. The one exception to this rule relates to the Scottish Highlands where MacInnes and Ansdell do provide an indication of the presence of Baptist missionaries. The pioneering work of Baptist historians, Murray and Meek in particular, have rescued from oblivion the Baptist contribution to Scottish church history in this period and provided the framework on which this book can build.

One of the major themes of ecclesiastical development in the nineteenth century was the decline in adherence to the Calvinistic faith of the Reformed Churches. This phenomenon was found not only in Scotland, but also in other parts of the English-speaking world, for example New England. The adaptation of Reformed theology in this part of America came to influence a significant proportion of Scottish Christians through the revivalist and theologian Charles Finney. Jonathan Edwards (1703-1758), an American Congregational minister, had been the most prominent of the New England theologians in the eighteenth century. He had been influential in guiding the thought of Scottish Presbyterian ministers such as James Robe of Kilsyth and William McCulloch of Cambuslang as well as English Baptist leaders Andrew Fuller and John Sutcliff.[65] Fuller and Sutcliff were to become advisers to the 'English' Baptists in Scotland that emerged at the beginning of the nineteenth century.[66] The followers of Edwards in New England gradually departed

---

62 Chapter two, pp. 67-70.
63 Chapter four, p. 150.
64 M. Lynch, *Scotland: A New History*, (London: Pimlico Publishing, 1992), p. 403.
65 M.A. Noll, 'Edwards, Jonathan (1703-58)', in Cameron (ed.), *Scottish Church History and Theology*, p. 286.
66 Chapter four, pp. 118-125.

from his theological position culminating in the transition to a more liberal viewpoint as propounded by Nathaniel W. Taylor of Yale College.[67]

One of the Presbyterian ministers most strongly influenced by Taylor was the revivalist Charles Finney. This former lawyer held to the governmental theory of the atonement, the doctrine of general atonement and argued strongly for the freedom of the will and the active participation of man in regeneration.[68] Finney's influence on the Scottish churches came through his 1835 *Lectures of the Revival of Religion*. Copies of this book circulated in Scotland. James Morison, a United Secession Church minister, was convinced by the new theology. In a letter to his father, Robert Morison, in 1838, he urged the reading of Finney's book and the copying of his methods.[69] Morison and his supporters were expelled from their denomination in 1841 and founded their own body, the Evangelical Union, to propagate the new theology that was formally Arminian, though it had been derived from a modified Calvinism.[70] This new theology entered Scottish Baptist circles through Francis Johnston, the main leader of the Baptist Union of Scotland in the 1840s and 1850s, but also through William Landels and Thomas Milner, former members of the Evangelical Union, later prominent leaders in that Baptist Union.[71] The Baptist Union became a strictly Morisonian body in January 1850, leading to its collapse by 1853.[72] The successful Baptist Union that was launched in 1869 had been preceded by a Scottish Baptist Association that sought to welcome all evangelical Baptist ministers into its ranks. When the 1869 body was constituted its membership was open to both Calvinists and Arminians.[73] The earlier ascendancy of Calvinism was now over. An era in which evangelical Arminianism predominated was now about to take place in the last quarter of the nineteenth century.

The majority of British Baptists in the nineteenth century were to be found in England. It would, therefore, be surprising if they had had no influence on the life and work of their colleagues in Scot-

---

67 J. Haroutunian, *Piety Versus Moralism: The Passing of the New England Theology*. (New York: Harper & Row, 1960 [1932]), pp. xxx-xxxii. F.H. Foster, *A Genetic History of the New England Theology*, (Chicago: The University of Chicago Press, 1907), pp. 467-468.
68 Foster, *Genetic History*, p. 453.
69 Chapter seven, pp. 267-268.
70 Chapter seven, pp. 229-231.
71 Chapter seven, pp. 232-233, 252, 262-263.
72 Chapter seven, pp. 264-265.
73 Chapter eight, p. 308.

Introduction 17

land. In fact in the previous century there had been contact between Scotch and English Particular Baptists and especially with Andrew Fuller on behalf of the Baptist Missionary Society.[74] Raymond Brown's *The English Baptists of the Eighteenth Century* accurately covers the history of the Particular (Calvinistic) and General (Arminian) Baptist denominations in this period. There is, however, a significant dependence for General Baptists on the minutes of General Assemblies. This national picture might helpfully have been supported by the greater use of local church records. In addition the focus on leading ministers could have been supplemented by additional information about the ordinary members and their social context. *The English Baptists of the Nineteenth Century* by J.H.Y. Briggs helpfully analyses the changes and developments in both the General and Particular Baptist denominations leading up to their merger in 1891. Briggs chooses a thematic approach to cover his field which some readers unfamiliar with Baptist history might find difficult to fit into the overall chronology of the Baptist witness in this era. His judgement on Robert Haldane, as an advocate of 'a closed sectarian evangelicalism',[75] does appear somewhat harsh. This opinion was undoubtedly true of aspects of his career, for example in the first decade of the nineteenth century, but less so in his ecumenical ministry in Continental Europe in 1817 to 1819.[76] The Baptists of the two theological traditions in Scotland had merged in 1869, twenty-two years earlier than their counterparts south of the border, though ties between the Particular and General bodies had grown closer in England since the early 1830s.[77] The Particular Baptists had commenced their first Baptist Union in 1813, followed by a reconstituted body in 1832. It will be important to determine if there are any parallels with the earlier associations of churches in Scotland. An attempt will be made to consider the differences and the similarities between the two situations. *The Baptist Union: A Short History* by E.A. Payne is the institutional history of the Baptist Union of Great Britain and Ireland (BUGBI). This work would have been improved by fuller references in the text. Payne incorrectly states, for example, that in 1872 the Welsh and Scottish Baptist Unions chose to be recognised as affiliated to the Baptist Union of Great Britain and Ireland (BUGBI), but lists no primary source as evidence. The Scottish

---

74 Chapter two, pp. 48-52.
75 J.H.Y. Briggs, *The English Baptists of the Nineteenth Century*, (A History of English Baptists, 3; Didcot: Baptist Historical Society, 1994), p. 43.
76 Chapter three, pp. 84-86, 91-96.
77 Chapter six, pp. 212-213.

Union had decided not to affiliate to BUGBI in 1872, thus declining the offer made by the larger body.[78] This is just one of many examples lacking primary references found in the text. This important book, though, provides insights into the strengths and weaknesses of the united Baptist work and witness amongst churches associated with BUGBI.

It is important to note the developments towards union amongst the Welsh and Irish Baptists as well as in the English ranks. T.M. Bassett's *The Welsh Baptists* contains a mass of accurate though concentrated information, but it lacks tables, diagrams, pictures and maps to assist readers unfamiliar with the intricacies of Welsh Baptist life. The Baptist Union of Wales was formed in 1866. Associations had been in existence in the eighteenth as well as the nineteenth centuries, long before any attempts to form a national body. The difficulties that hindered union in Wales prior to 1866 were both linguistic and theological. The Welsh-speaking churches tended to join the Union, whereas many English-speaking churches and their associations affiliated to the BUGBI. The theological issue in dispute was the debate over open versus closed communion. Churches in fellowship with the Baptist Union of Wales tended to be closed communion whereas those associated with BUGBI in Wales were usually open communion. The support for the Welsh Union was less than wholehearted until all the Welsh-speaking associations had affiliated in the 1880s.[79] In line with Scotland where the strongest churches were amongst the last to desire Union affiliation,[80] it was the strongest associations that applied last to join the Welsh Baptist Union. Baptists in Wales, like their Scottish counterparts, guarded their independence carefully.[81]

The Baptist Union of Ireland did not come into existence until 1895. The history of this body is contained in Joshua Thompson's *Century of Grace: The Baptist Union of Ireland: A Short History 1895-*

---

78 E.A. Payne, *The Baptist Union: A Short History*, (London: Carey Kingsgate Press, 1959), p. 104. The proposal was approved by the BUGBI Annual Assembly, April 22 1872, Minutes of the Baptist Union of Great Britain and Ireland, Angus Library, Regent's Park College, Oxford. The Baptist Union of Scotland Assembly, October 24 1872, agreed to exchange Assembly delegates, but declined to affiliate to the larger body, Baptist Union of Scotland Minute Book, 1869-1880, Scottish Baptist History Archive, Baptist House, Glasgow.
79 T.M. Bassett, *The Welsh Baptists*, (Swansea: Ilston House, 1977), pp. 337-341. Payne, *Baptist Union*, pp. 103-104.
80 Chapter eight, pp. 283-284.
81 Bassett, *Welsh Baptists*, p. 340.

Introduction 19

1995. This brief history of the Irish Union presents the bare facts of union developments, but it would have been improved by providing some additional information on the social and political context of the Irish churches. There is also a lack of maps and tables to assist the assimilation of information provided. The separate identity of Irish Baptists had been crystallised by the Downgrade controversy in BUGBI. The Irish Baptists were strongly conservative in theology and had actively supported Charles Spurgeon in his battle against apparently encroaching liberalism in Union ranks. The BUGBI annual Assembly of 1888 had agreed to pass control of the Irish mission to the Irish Baptist Association, a body that had re-formed in 1862, the date of its formal affiliation to BUGBI. It was felt by many Irish Baptists that their separate identity would be better served as a distinct union of churches rather than by continuing as an association in fellowship with the larger body.[82] This evolution of a union structure has some similarities to the Scottish Baptists who formally considered affiliating to BUGBI in 1872, only after their Baptist Union had been established in 1869 – in essence, from a position of strength rather than of weakness. They decided, like the Irish, to maintain a separate Baptist Union, though in the case of Scotland in 1872 there were, by contrast, no doctrinal reasons for their rejection of the proposal.[83]

This book will, however, be primarily comparing and contrasting its findings with the work of the pre-eminent Scottish Baptist historian Derek Murray. His studies have laid the foundation for the critical study of the Baptist community covering the last three centuries. Murray was the first modern historian to attempt to produce work on Scottish Baptist history. He also chaired, from 1978, the Scottish Baptist History Project to provide a forum for the presentation of new work on denominational history. He produced the general outline of Scottish Baptist history on which later historians build. His major studies, listed in the bibliography, that are relevant to this book include 'Baptists in Scotland before 1869', 'The Scotch Baptist Tradition in Great Britain', *The First Hundred Years- The Baptist Union of Scotland 1869-1969* and an article jointly written with D.E. Meek, 'The Early Nineteenth Century' in Bebbington's *Baptists in Scotland*. Murray identified three streams of Baptist witness in Scotland prior to 1869, namely the Scotch, Haldaneite and 'English' Baptists. This study will suggest that there were actually four identifiable groups

---

82   J. Thompson, *Century of Grace. The Baptist Union of Ireland: A Short History 1895-1995*, (Belfast: Baptist Union of Ireland, 1995), pp. 6-8.
83   Briggs, *English Baptists of the Nineteenth Century*, p. 219. See also note 78 above.

within the Baptist community. It will be seen that the Haldaneite and 'English' Baptists merged around 1827, but that a new stream of Morisonian Baptists emerged under the leadership of Francis Johnston in the late 1840s. There were, though, only three networks of Scottish Baptist churches in existence at any one time between 1800 and 1870. Murray has proposed that the Baptist Union of Scotland, begun in 1827, was an abortive attempt at union, and that the 1835 to 1842 Baptist Association was also limited in its effect. The value of his assessment will be examined in an attempt to give greater clarity to our understanding of the events that took place in those years. The priority treatment in attempts at union, indeed pride of place, is given by Murray to Francis Johnston and the Baptist Union of 1843 to 1856. Johnston is seen as the primary architect of moves to bring Scottish Baptists closer together and the individual most worthy of credit for the eventual establishment of the union of churches in 1869. This judgement will be challenged as there is evidence to suggest that Johnston's role in the Baptist community in Scotland in the 1840s and 1850s was not as helpful as is portrayed in the standard accounts of this period. At the time of Johnston's leadership of the Baptist Union he was involved in a number of serious controversies with fellow Baptist leaders and with leaders of other denominations in Scotland. Murray appears to take the side of Johnston, giving him the benefit of the doubt if the picture is unclear. Evidence has emerged that enables us to gain greater insight into those events and, therefore, to reassess Johnston's role in the proceedings. If Johnston was not as dominant in Scottish Baptist circles as has been suggested, it is important to consider which other individuals might have provided the necessary leadership skills to have moved forward the process towards union.

There is a range of primary materials that can assist us in our studies of this period of Scottish Baptist history. The materials on Scotch Baptists primarily consist of two manuscript collections. The National Library of Scotland in Edinburgh holds a series of letters and documents dating mainly from 1820 to 1850 entitled 'Manuscript Letters relating to the Scotch Baptist Churches'. This collection had been held by the family of J. Idwal Jones, a leading Scotch Baptist elder in North Wales in the twentieth century.[84] Its origin was probably from the personal papers of James Everson, the prominent Scotch Baptist elder in Beverley during the first half of

---

84 For further information on J. Idwal Jones see D.W. Bebbington, 'Baptist Members of Parliament in the Twentieth Century', *Baptist Quarterly*, 31.6 (April, 1986), p. 269.

the nineteenth century. The Baptist Union of Scotland holds the 'Waugh Papers', a series of manuscripts collected by the late Percival Waugh, secretary of the Baptist Home Missionary Society for Scotland c.1900-1930,[85] in which are contained documents relating to the three main Baptist traditions and also unique materials on the 1827 attempt to form a union of churches. In addition to the manuscript collections, certain periodicals illuminate Scotch Baptist life. William Jones, a Scotch Baptist pastor in London, edited a number of Baptist magazines promoting his strongly conservative perspective on religious issues, together with the works of Archibald McLean. These titles included *The Christian Advocate, The New Evangelical Magazine, The Theological Repository* and *The New Theological Repository*.

Alexander Haldane in the middle of the nineteenth century produced *The Lives of Robert and James Haldane*. This biography of two of the most prominent Baptist leaders in Scotland was written by a family member who sought to place their actions in the best possible light. Alexander Haldane sets the scene for their ministries both at home and overseas. It helps to place in their context the many books and articles written by the two brothers that reveal the developments in their thinking over this period of time. In addition, the author provides valuable assistance to modern researchers in his summary of the arguments of some of James Haldane's works that have apparently not survived. The most valuable of these, for the purposes of this study, was *On Christian Union*, produced in 1846, in which the elder statesman of Baptists in Scotland reiterated his understanding of this subject.[86] The book on this same subject, *Remarks on Christian Union*, by his colleague William Innes, who held very similar opinions to James Haldane, provides an opportunity to gain access to Haldane's understanding of church union. *The Baptist Home Missionary Society Reports*, produced annually, not only provide information about the activities of the Baptist preachers in the Highlands and Islands, but also comment on the theological views held by these men. There is, though, a far from complete set of surviving annual reports for the period after 1829, with the major gap between 1868 and 1898, and reports from 1847, 1851, 1865 and 1867 also apparently lost. The man most responsible for the contents of the reports was one of its secretaries, James Haldane. These materials and other items listed in the bibliography help to provide an assessment of the Haldanes' contributions to Baptist life in Scotland.

---

85   Information stated in the 'Waugh Papers', Scottish Baptist History Archive, Baptist House, Glasgow.
86   Chapter three, pp. 89-90.

Hugh Anderson's biography of Christopher Anderson, *The Life and Letters of Christopher Anderson*, is a chronological record of his life rather than a critical assessment of his career. It provides the backdrop to the work and witness of the most prominent 'English' Baptist in Scotland. The *Journal of Itinerating Exertions in some of the more destitute parts of Scotland*, produced in six volumes from 1814 to 1817, gives details of the home missionary activities of Anderson and his colleagues from 1808 to 1814. Anderson, the editor, is conscious, though, of presenting the reports in a manner that would encourage supporters to continue to pledge their finances for future ministry. It outlines the constant financial strains upon the work, but also highlights an enthusiasm for home evangelisation.[87] The pages of *The Baptist Magazine*, the periodical associated with English Particular Baptists, make a point of including information relevant to the progress of uniting the churches in Scotland. It is especially valuable for information relating to events in the 1830s that took place north of the border.

The organ of the Johnstonian Baptist Union was *The Evangelist*. This denominational periodical which was produced from 1846 to 1853 reveals the changes in emphasis of the leadership of that union, especially after 1850. Unfortunately no copies have apparently survived from 1848 or 1849. This loss of two years' issues is highly important because there were probably articles, especially in late 1849, that prepared the way for a momentous change of direction in editorial policy in January 1850.[88] The private letters to his son William by Peter Grant, Baptist pastor at Grantown-on-Spey, provide a Highland perspective on the controversies that took place during Francis Johnston's time as secretary of the Union. The recent rediscovery of Johnston's major work, *The Work of God and the Work of Man in Conversion*, produced in 1848, provides confirmation of his adoption of formal Arminian sentiments. The two books of his colleague Thomas Milner, *The Gospel Guide* and *The Messiah's Ministry*, reveal not only similar views to Johnston, but also more radical sentiments that are in line with Milner's decision in the mid-1850s to join the then recently constituted Churches of Christ.

There were to be three attempts to bring Scottish Baptist churches together prior to the successful union of 1869. The documents relating to the 1827 Union are to be found in the 'Waugh Papers'. Unfortunately very little material has survived, but there are sufficient documents and letters from the papers of Archibald Smith, the

---

87 Chapter four, pp. 140-141.
88 Chapter seven, pp. 259-261.

Introduction

secretary of an obscure Edinburgh Scotch Baptist congregation, Clyde Street Hall, to give some insights into this Baptist Union. The Scottish Baptist Association of 1835 to 1842 produced minutes that are now kept by Bristo Baptist Church, Edinburgh, together with minutes for annual meetings of the Baptist Union of Scotland, 1843 to 1847, and minutes of the executive committee of the same body from 1843 to 1847. The 'Minute Book of the Executive Committee of the Baptist Union of Scotland and Theological Academy', September 1850 to August 1855, is stored in the History Archive in Baptist House, Glasgow. Once again the crucial documentary evidence from 1848 to 1849 has apparently not survived. There is, however, sufficient material to make a critical reappraisal of the contribution of Francis Johnston and his colleagues to the cause of Baptist union in Scotland in the middle of the nineteenth century.

The importance of the attitudes of Calvinistic Baptists towards union in Scottish Baptist ranks has been overlooked with reference to the 1850s. As they were to be denied access to the life of the Johnstonian Baptist Union, a significant proportion of them associated with English Particular Baptist colleagues in the little known Baptist Evangelical Society. This organisation produced *The Primitive Church Magazine*, a periodical that sought to promote strict communion amongst Particular Baptists. Insight into the activities of this group of mainly English Baptists has been provided by Geoffrey Breed's booklet *The Baptist Evangelical Society* and his thesis, 'Strict Communion Organisations amongst the Baptists in Victorian Britain'.[89]

There are apparently no surviving minutes from The Scottish Baptist Association of 1856 to 1869. Records of proceedings can, though, be gleaned from the summary presented in the pages of *The Freeman*, the British weekly Baptist newspaper, a periodical committed to building closer ties between British Baptists.[90] In addition *A Manual of the Baptist Denomination* produced annually by Baptists in England from 1845 to 1859, followed by *The Baptist Handbook*, 1861 to 1879, from the same source, provides valuable statistical evidence that can compensate for some of the missing Scottish materials. *Baptist Union of Scotland Annual Reports* after 1869 and the *Scottish Baptist Magazine* from 1875 also provide useful information and

---

89 G. Breed, *The Baptist Evangelical Society*, (Dunstable: The Fauconberg Press, 1988). G. Breed, 'Strict Communion Organisations amongst the Baptists in Victorian England', (M.A. thesis, Keele University, 1991). This thesis was published as *Particular Baptists in Victorian England*, (Didcot: Baptist Historical Society, 2003).

90 Chapter eight, pp. 293-294.

interpretations of events leading up to the formation of the union in 1869. The majority of articles describing the events leading up to the successful union are almost exclusively from Johnstonian Baptists who, especially William Landels, are not above providing an extremely partisan interpretation of that history.[91]

The picture presented in official histories of Scottish Baptist life in the period 1800 to 1870 has been necessarily limited by a lack of key primary materials that can help to provide an adequate interpretation of events such as the moves towards the formation of the Baptist Union. The re-discovery of some of the materials used in this study alongside a fresh evaluation of existing documents can provide new insights into the factors that contributed to the events that shaped the co-operative ventures of Scottish Baptist churches in this period.

It is important first of all to examine the first three streams of Baptist witness that were active in the early years of the nineteenth century. Each of these sectors of the Baptist constituency had separate origins and possessed distinct identities, especially the Scotch Baptists. This group of Scottish Baptists were the most conservative sector of the Baptist movement. Chapter two will look at their strengths and weaknesses in particular, focusing on their attitudes towards Baptists with differing beliefs and practices. The way in which such challenges were handled within their ranks gave clear indications as to their responses when invited to co-operate with Baptist groups holding to different opinions. The nineteenth century in Scotland provided the occasion for the rise of a number of new denominations, one of which was the Churches of Christ. This new organisation raised some serious theological questions about the nature of the Christian church which had particular relevance to this sector of the Baptist constituency. Most important of all, the Scotch Baptists after being the dominant Baptist tradition in 1800 had weakened significantly by the 1830s in comparison with the other Baptist groups. The impact of this change in their fortunes will be assessed to evaluate its significance for the attempts at union after 1827.

The Haldaneite Baptists entered the ranks of their new tradition from Independent circles, in particular from the churches associated with Robert and James Haldane and the SPGH. Some of these

---

91 W. Landels, 'Past and Present', *Scottish Baptist Magazine*, 2.3 (March, 1876), pp. 37-40. 'Denominational Reminiscences by an Old Baptist I', (March, 1886), pp. 71-75. 'Denominational Reminiscences by an Old Baptist II', (June, 1886), pp. 152-156. 'Denominational Reminiscences by an Old Baptist III', (October, 1886), pp. 267-269, are examples.

men, like their patrons, may have been associated with Independent churches by virtue of being unwelcome in the Church of Scotland, whilst others may have been Independent by theological conviction. The theological heritage they had retained had major similarities with that of the Scotch Baptists, but their greater flexibility in ecclesiology caused tensions to arise in discussions between the two parties. In addition the informal nature of their association through their wealthy patrons made collective-decision making very difficult. This book will reveal that it was members of this network of churches in the second decade of this century that had felt most acutely the need for a more co-ordinated approach to home mission work, and that had articulated in the 1830s the greatest need for a union of Baptist churches.[92] The opinions of Robert and James Haldane on the question of Christian union are of crucial importance. Did they provide support for the attempts at union or were their hopes for a wider alliance of evangelical Christians? Chapter three will assess the contribution of this group of Baptists in the moves to unite the different congregations of this religious tradition.

The 'English' Baptists identified with the Particular Baptists in England with whom they shared a common set of beliefs and church practices. Opportunities to unite with Scotch Baptists in the first decade of the nineteenth century had been offered and rejected on both theological and practical grounds.[93] Chapter four will discuss the reasons for this early rejection of merger proposals and then examine the influence of this tradition in the process of uniting Scottish Baptists in home evangelism and in the work of a wider union. The discovery in this thesis that the first attempt to persuade Scottish Baptist churches to belong to a formal denomination of autonomous congregations in 1827 came from an 'English' Baptist congregation raises questions about the nature of their wider vision. Did they wish this union to be associated with the barely functioning British Baptist Union or was it to be a separate and distinct body? George Barclay and Christopher Anderson, their leading ministers, though not as prominent in Scottish ecclesiastical circles as the Haldane brothers, nevertheless played a crucial role in developing the Scottish Baptist identity in the early nineteenth century. The impact of these men on the merger proposals provides an integral part of chapter four. It is, therefore, very important to identify the leading participants in Scottish Baptist ranks before their impact on union proposals can be assessed.

---

92   Chapter five, pp. 155-156; Chapter six, pp. 213-214.
93   Chapter four, pp. 141-142.

One focus for Scottish Baptist identity in this era was the BHMS. The extraordinary success of this body will be described in chapter five. In comparison with the equivalent society in England it had captured the affections of a high proportion of its small constituency.[94] Chapter five will examine to what extent the home missionary society functioned as a substitute union for some Scottish Baptists. Did this society fufil the aspirations of a significant proportion of its constituency or was there always a realisation that an additional organisation was required to co-ordinate the work amongst Scottish Baptists? Once the role of the BHMS is clarified it will then be appropriate to look in closer detail at the various attempts at union.

Chapters six to eight will assess the three bodies set up by Scottish Baptists in order to strengthen their witness. Chapter six will challenge the prevailing opinion that the first Baptist Union of Scotland was insignificant and that it had little impact in its constituency. It will be compared with the British Particular Baptist Union established nearly two decades earlier to see if there was any interaction between the two constituencies. The contribution of the three streams of Baptist witness will be evaluated to assess the attitudes taken by Scottish Baptists to this innovative proposal. The lessons concerning its subsequent failure will be noted to indicate possible difficulties that might impede future attempts at union. The 1835 to 1842 Scottish Baptist Association, which will also be discussed in chapter six, was very different in character from the preceding Baptist Union. The limited scope of its appeal to Scottish Baptists and its slow progress will raise questions about the corporate vision of the members of this constituency. Consideration will be given to a comparison with the reconstituted Baptist Union in England to see if there are any common factors in the approaches taken by these new bodies. Then an evaluation will be made of the major developments affecting the life of Scottish Baptists in the 1830s that will indicate the possible direction in which the moves towards uniting the churches might have subsequently taken.

Chapter seven covers the Johnstonian Baptist Union that existed from 1843 to 1856. Previous studies of the work of this union have tended to concentrate on its strengths while ignoring its weaknesses. This research has uncovered new evidence that will throw fresh light on crucial events in the life of this organisation, in particular, the growing polarity in the 1840s between Arminian and Calvinistic Baptists. The recognition of the deterioration in relationships prior to the controversies in these years will provide the basis for

---

94   Chapter five, pp. 161-165.

Introduction 27

reassessing the place of Francis Johnston in the overall process of uniting Scottish Baptists in the nineteenth century.

Chapter eight will look at the genesis of the 1869 Union, commencing with the work of the Scottish Baptist Association (SBA) in 1856. This body was instituted in order to unite individual Scottish Baptist leaders. It was to play a vital role in preparing the way for the eventual re-formation of the Baptist Union of Scotland in 1869. The various factors that led to the success of the 1856 SBA will be drawn out in order to highlight the main reasons for the eventual unification of the overwhelming majority of Scottish Baptist churches.

The final chapter of this book will draw together the threads of the arguments produced in the preceding chapters. It will reveal in more detail the contribution made by the different groups of Scottish Baptists to the process of uniting the churches than previous studies in this field. It will give a new focus for explaining the roles of key individuals and for interpreting a number of important decisions made by the most prominent leaders. In short it will explain why the first three attempts at union did not achieve their objectives, but why they led in due course to the overwhelming success of the final merger in 1869.

CHAPTER 2

The Scotch Baptists, 1765-1842

2.1 Origins of the Scotch Baptists[1]

The Scotch Baptists were the oldest of the three streams of Baptist life in Scotland. They started their first society in 1765 in the city of Edinburgh. At the end of the eighteenth century Scotch Baptist churches contained around 400 members and 1000 adherents.[2] This stream of Baptist witness could claim the allegiance of approximately 90% of Baptists in Scotland at the start of the nineteenth century.[3] The name 'Scotch Baptist' was given to them to distinguish between those individuals who had adopted Baptist principles in Scotland and the Particular Baptists in England. It was not merely a national distinction because these Scottish Baptists differed from their Particular colleagues in their understanding of the constitution of a church of Christ. The reason for the differences between the two Baptist traditions arose in part from the distinctive origins of the Scotch Baptists. The name 'Scotch' is not an anachronistic description of a group of Scottish Christians. There were, by the end of the eighteenth century, churches in fellowship with their connexion in England and Wales.[4] In addition, congregations of this tradition were formed in the nineteenth century in Canada.[5] The first Scottish historian of this Baptist stream, Patrick Wilson, noted that many of their ecclesiological ideas were influenced by John Glas, the leader of the Glasite movement, a group of independent Protestant churches that had begun in Scotland in 1730.[6] Scotch Baptists, though, were even closer in theological ties to another Christian

---

1   Some material used in this chapter has been published in B.R. Talbot, 'Unity and Disunity: The Scotch Baptists, 1765-1842', in R. Pope (ed.), *Religion and National Identity Wales and Scotland c.1700-2000* (Cardiff: University of Wales Press, 2001), pp. 221-241.
2   J. Rippon (ed.), *The Baptist Annual Register*, (London, 1795), pp. 373-374.
3   See Chapter 4, p. 150.
4   D.B. Murray, 'The Scotch Baptist Tradition in Great Britain', *Baptist Quarterly*, 33.4 (October, 1989), pp. 188-189.
5   E.R. Fitch, *The Baptists of Canada*, (Toronto: The Standard Publishing Company Limited, 1911), p. 106.
6   D.B. Murray, 'Glas, John (1695-1773)', in N.M. de S.Cameron (ed.), *Dictionary of Scottish Church History and Theology*, (Edinburgh: T. & T. Clark, 1993), p.364.

denomination, the Old Scotch Independents. They were 'with the exception of baptism...nearly allied in sentiment to the Old Scotch Independents – the followers of Mr David Dale', the industrialist from New Lanark. It was from the latter group that many of the earliest members of this connexion emerged to play a prominent part in shaping the future direction of the wider Baptist life and witness in Scotland in the first four decades of the nineteenth century.[7] This chapter will examine the contribution made by the Scotch Baptists in their attempts to promote closer fellowship within their own ranks, and especially to the early moves towards uniting the different Baptist congregations in Scotland

The earliest leaders in their connexion, Robert Carmichael and Archibald McLean, had originally left Presbyterian denominations, the Antiburghers and the Established Church respectively, after reading John Glas's *Testimony to the King of Martyrs* in the late 1750s. Glas's book had persuaded these men that a national or state church was inconsistent with the New Testament concept of a gathered church, or an association of churches. After a year in fellowship with the Glasite church in Glasgow both McLean and Carmichael, a former Antiburgher minister from Cupar, Angus, seceded in 1763 as a result of the apparently unjust exercise of church discipline in that congregation. A small independent congregation in Edinburgh invited Carmichael to serve as their minister in that year, a proposal he accepted. McLean and Carmichael exchanged correspondence in 1764 on the subject of baptism, in particular examining whether infant baptism could be deduced from the scriptures. The debate between the two men was lengthy and took in excess of twelve months before Baptist convictions were adopted. After the ordinance had been administered to Carmichael, and five other people in Edinburgh, they constituted themselves as a Baptist church in Scotland's capital city.[8] This congregation, under the leadership of McLean after 1768, was the first of ten societies set up by Scotch Baptists in Scotland in the eighteenth century.[9]

---

7   P. Wilson, *The Origin and Progress of the Scotch Baptist Churches from their Rise in 1765 to 1834*, (Edinburgh: Fullarton And Co., 1844), pp. 3-4.
8   W. Jones (ed.), *The Works of Mr Archibald McLean*, (London: William Jones, 1823), VI, pp. xvix-xxii.
9   D.B. Murray, 'The Social and Religious Origins of Scottish Non-Presbyterian Protestant Dissent from 1730-1800' (PhD thesis, St Andrews University, 1976), p. 68.

2.2 Distinctive Church Principles of the Scotch Baptists

The reason for examining first the Scotch Baptist contribution to the cause of union, or disunity, amongst Scottish Baptists arises as a result of their distinctive ecclesiastical origins. The other two Baptist streams held to doctrinal and ecclesiological views that had much more in common with the English Particular Baptists. It is, therefore, easier to compare the Haldaneite and 'English' Baptist traditions with this, the earliest group of Scottish Baptists, after the doctrinal opinions and contribution to moves for unity from the Scotch stream have been discussed. The Scotch Baptists saw themselves as a different sector of the Baptist family in comparison to the Particular Baptists in England, and later also to the members of that same 'English' tradition in Scotland.[10]

> The appellation *Scotch* Baptists is assumed merely to distinguish them from the two classes of Baptists in England, known as *General* or Arminian; and *Particular* or Calvinistic Baptists; with neither of which have they any communion; as they differ materially from both the bodies above named in their views of the Gospel, and especially in regard to church order.[11]

The clear distinctives that set apart their congregations from those of the other Baptist traditions provided a focus for their unity. This group of British Baptists was careful to ensure that the basic principles at the heart of their identity were maintained, even if it guaranteed that their numerical strength would never rise above a few thousand individuals. This chapter will first consider the factors that promoted unity within their ranks. Secondly, the ties between them and other British Baptists will be evaluated, before assessing the reasons for the disunity that led to their numerical decline in the period leading up to 1842. Discussion of these issues will help to elucidate the form of contribution made by the Scotch Baptists to the process of uniting Baptist churches in Scotland.

It is important to note the beliefs and practices that united this association of Baptist congregations. William Jones, a leading Scotch Baptist elder in Liverpool, described their opinions in his monthly magazine, *The Theological Repository*, in two articles in March and April 1808. The first article was concerned with a defence of believer's baptism. It was of particular significance in Scotland as Scotch Baptists were the only Christian denomination in that part of Britain who held to that belief. The second article discussed the other tenets

---

10 Wilson, *Origin and Progress*, p. 37.
11 J. Everson, 'The Scotch Baptist Churches', *The Christian Advocate and Scotch Baptist Repository*, 1.1 (March, 1849), p. 1.

of their faith. The opening section referred to beliefs held in common with other Calvinistic Baptists regarding the Godhead and salvation. It was, however, the second section of Jones's article which revealed the distinctive features of their position.

> They also hold it their indispensable duty to follow entirely the *pattern* of the primitive apostolic churches, as recorded in the New Testament, and to attend to all the directions given them, which they consider to be inseparably connected with genuine love to the truth, and steadfastness and liveliness in the faith and hope of the gospel...[12]

In practice, the New Testament was believed to teach that each congregation of believers should have a plurality of elders and deacons. 'English' Baptists, by contrast, could accept a plurality of deacons, but normally preferred a sole elder or pastor. Church discipline had to be exercised 'on all proper occasions'. Scotch Baptists were not unique in advocating this principle, but its use was probably more rigorous than in other Baptist circles. It was stated that 'the Rule of forbearance *is divine revelation*, and not the fancies of men' and, therefore, a command to be obeyed. This rule was, however, qualified in the statement that 'no precept given by Christ can be a matter of indifference, they act upon this principle, that his authority can never clash with itself by giving laws, and at the same time a dispensation to neglect them'. In addition, 'they consider it their duty to be all of one mind in every thing that regards their faith and practices as a body, agreeably to the unanimity which was exemplified in the Church in Jerusalem and is most solemnly inculcated upon other churches'. The observance of this principle was in due course to be the cause of damaging conflicts which drained their enthusiasm for evangelism and weakened the ties between their congregations. This issue will be discussed in more detail later in this chapter. At the time when Jones wrote his article, in 1808, Scotch Baptists could have foreseen only benefits from the promulgation of this teaching, for example, in the successful resolution of the Socinian disputation over the deity of Christ, considered later in chapter two. The weekly observance of the Lord's Supper, regular participation in 'the feast of charity', the fellowship meal each Sunday, and the abstinence from 'eating of blood, and things strangled' were other practices observed by this group of Christian believers.[13] Jones was correct in laying the emphasis on their 'order and practices'. It was the church order of Scotch Baptists that marked them

---

12 'A Compendious Account of the Principles and Practices of the Scottish Baptists', *The Theological Repository*, 4.23 (April, 1808), pp. 199-200.
13 'Compendious Account', pp. 200-205.

apart from other British Baptists. It is ironic that the Baptist tradition with which they shared this excessive biblical literalism in ecclesiological matters, the Old Connexion of English General Baptists, differed from them, more than the other Baptist traditions, in doctrinal matters, holding to an Arminian rather than a Calvinistic theological perspective.

There were only a few theological opinions resulting from a strict adherence to New Testament language that marked them out from other Calvinistic Baptists. One such belief, promulgated by Archibald McLean, their leader, was the necessary denial of the eternal sonship of Jesus on the grounds that such terminology could not be found in the Bible. McLean probably held this opinion as a result of his association with the Old Scotch Independents. James Smith, former parish minister of Newburn, Fife, and one of the founders of this new body, taught that Jesus in the scriptures 'is never said to be eternally begotten'.[14] McLean concluded his discussion of that subject by declaring:

> Christ is eternal, but not as the Christ; the Son of man is eternal but not as the Son of man. Emmanuel is eternal; but not as Emmanuel; even so the Son of God is eternal in his divine person, but it does not follow that he is so as a Son.[15]

The impact of such a viewpoint in the other Baptist streams would have been modest, due to the willingness to tolerate a measure of theological diversity within a conservative theological framework. The Scotch Baptists, by contrast, long after McLean's death, used this doctrinal shibboleth as a test of orthodoxy for aspiring church members.[16] Detailed examples on this subject will be considered later in this chapter, but here it is significant to note that the Scotch Baptists had set out a clear statement of their opinions regarding beliefs and practices to which allegiance must be given by all who sought to remain within their ranks.

It is necessary also to note the relationship between the views of the Scotch Baptists and the Glasites or Sandemanians, an independent paedobaptist denomination founded by John Glas of Tealing in 1730. The Glasites took a strict biblicist view of beliefs and church practices. They were convinced that a clear blueprint for church life

---

14 'The Case of James Smith, late minister at Newburn and Robert Ferrier, late minister at Largo, truly represented and defended' (Glasgow, 1816 [1768]), cited by H. Escott, *A History of Scottish Congregationalism*, (Glasgow: Congregational Union of Scotland, 1960), p. 25.
15 Jones (ed.), *Works of Archibald McLean*, I, p.451.
16 J. Williamson, *Some Reminiscences of The Old Baptist Church Pleasance*, (Edinburgh: John Anderson, 1901), p. 15.

in all its details was to be found in the New Testament. Weekly communion, the principle of unanimity in all decisions in the church, and the plurality of the eldership were major features of life in their congregations. Although believing in a Calvinistic understanding of soteriology, Glas and his followers, including his son-in-law Robert Sandeman, promoted a novel understanding of faith. They defined it as a bare belief in, or assent to (*assensus*), the facts of the gospel, and excluded any affections or fruits.[17] Scotch Baptists, led by McLean, adopted many of the practices of the Glasites though they did not hold to the narrow sectarian outlook that characterised the followers of John Glas:

> they acknowledge none as Christians who are not connected with them; and have the keenest opposition to such as make the nearest approach to their principles, unless they agree with them in every particular…This contracted spirit leads men to lay greater stress on the peculiarities which distinguish them from other Christians, than on the things wherein all Christ's people are one.[18]

McLean certainly exercised a more benevolent form of leadership within Scotch Baptist circles than did John Glas in his churches, but the requirement for unanimity in belief in both traditions ensured a similar outcome for any dissidents who challenged accepted teaching.

The Scotch Baptist leader adopted a similar understanding of faith to that of the Glasites in contrast to the views of other Baptists, for example Andrew Fuller. McLean in his literary disputation with the Kettering minister wrote:

> Every body knows that faith or belief, in the ordinary sense of the word, is the CREDIT which we give to the truth of any thing which is made known to us by report or testimony, and is grounded either on the veracity of the speaker, or on the evidence by which his words are confirmed.[19]

McLean was careful to exclude any notion that confused the fact of justification and its effects, in contrast, he believed, to Fuller. He was, though, to go beyond the Glasites in accepting that faith is an exercise of the mind which does not include either the affections or the will.[20] Fuller's reply entitled *Strictures on Sandemanianism* reaffirmed the traditional Calvinistic understanding of faith as *fiducia* meaning 'trust', that included the exercise of both the will and the

---

17 Murray, 'Social and Religious Origins', pp. 138-138.
18 Jones (ed.), *Works of Archibald McLean*, VI, p. xlix.
19 Jones (ed.), *Works of Archibald McLean*, I, p. 74.
20 Jones (ed.), *Works of Archibald McLean*, I, pp. 74-76; VI, pp. lxi-lxii.

affections.[21] The Scotch Baptist leader could claim with some justification that it was not entirely fair to denote the Scotch Baptists as Sandemanian Baptists, but the similarity between these two Christian traditions was sufficient to ensure that not all Christians would be persuaded by his protests.[22]

The presence of this Edinburgh elder overshadowed all other leaders in the Scotch Baptist connexion in his lifetime. McLean was undoubtedly the main focus for unity within their ranks. In the first 44 years of Scotch Baptist witness his pronouncements on an issue served as a definitive statement of their beliefs or practices. These declarations on such issues as the Socinian controversy, concerning the nature of the Godhead, discussed later in this chapter, tended to reinforce his authority within the movement. There were individuals who departed for other denominations, such as Charles Stuart and George Grieve, but the vast majority of Scotch Baptists accepted the guidance he offered to them.[23] The whole connexion was often called the McLeanite Baptists.

It is important to consider next the other factors that contributed to the internal cohesion of this movement. Unity in doctrine and church practices was assumed amongst the Scotch Baptists. This issue was nearly as important to the maintenance of harmony in the connnexion as was their leader Archibald McLean. It was a policy that provided the essential framework for relationships between the local congregations. They had no doubts in their minds that unity, even unanimity, was essential in their ranks. A church wishing to be received into fellowship faced a process that was lengthy and thorough. Samuel Swan, an elder of the Leeds congregation, Wellington Road, Wortley, near Leeds, made this clear in a letter, in 1835, to James Everson, one of the pastors of the Beverley Church. 'I admit the independent right of each church to judge, but surely when a number of churches are associated, *none* ought to be received into the association without the concurrence of the whole...'[24] This had been practised by the Scotch Baptist churches when Haggate Baptist Church sought fellowship with them in 1834.The correspondence between Swan and Everson that year records in great detail

---

21 A. Fuller, 'Strictures on Sandemanianism, in Twelve Letters to a Friend', in J. Belcher (ed.), *The Complete Works of the Rev. Andrew Fuller*, (3 Vols; Harrisonburg, Virginia: Sprinkle Publications, 1988 [1844]), II, pp. 561- 646.
22 Jones (ed.), *Works of Archibald McLean*, VI, pp. xxxiii-li.
23 Wilson, *Origin and Progress*, pp. 19-23.
24 Samuel Swan, Leeds, to James Everson, Beverley, February 15, 1835. MS Letters relating to the Scotch Baptist Churches, National Library of Scotland, Edinburgh.

the process by which approval was granted. The initial contact was between the Leeds and Haggate churches and involved the exchanging of statements of faith and practices for mutual inspection.

> We deemed it our duty to open correspondence with them with a view to fellowship. We gave them a brief statement of our faith and practice requesting one from them in return. The subjoined letter No 1 is a copy of their statement which we hand for your inspection and approval. The question they propounded led to an explanation on both sides and the whole correspondence was brought to a favourable issue by the reception of the following letter No.2.
>
> We received them with greater confidence from the report of one of our brethren who visited them last July and who was perfectly satisfied with what he saw and heard amongst them.[25]

Swan noted that in reply to a letter from his church the Haggate friends had declared: '...with respect to what is said of the Institutions of Christ our views exactly agree with yours...Indeed we can truly say that we agree with every sentence in your letter.'[26] This outcome was remarkable considering that the Leeds letter contained a very full statement of their beliefs and practices. The Haggate church had been accepted as a sister church at the end of this process, but there was still one other matter to be sorted out. This issue was the practice of infant dedication services. Swan told Everson, in a letter dated November 1834, that he had written to the Edinburgh church for confirmation of his view that this practice ought to cease. The grounds for his disapproval were twofold: firstly that some people might see it as infant baptism by another name; secondly that it was a ceremony that was not accepted in the other churches. Unity and uniformity appeared to go together amongst Scotch Baptists. Swan did, however, show some charity when he declared: 'I consider that there is need for forbearance with them for some time as we all know that old customs are not so easily changed.'[27] It is hard to escape the conclusion that men like Swan appeared more ready to criticise than to accept other believers. The maintenance of such exact conformity could not be expected to continue indefinitely.

It is not easy to understand exactly where Scotch Baptists stood with respect to statements of faith. This issue, though, does appear

---

25 Swan to Everson, October 7, 1834, MS Letters.
26 Haggate Letter sent by John Hudson to Samuel Swan dated April 6 1834, cited in Swan to Everson, October 7, 1834, MS Letters.
27 Swan to Everson, November 18, 1834, MS Letters.

to have been less important to them than the unanimity of practices and deference to the opinions of McLean. They prided themselves on the belief that they had no human doctrinal standards in contrast to the English Particular Baptists. This issue appears to be made plain in the article 'A Short Account of the SCOTS BAPTISTS' in John Rippon's *Baptist Annual Register* for 1795. Rippon based the article upon material produced by Archibald McLean in that year.[28]

> As to their principles, they refer us to no human system as the unexceptionable standard of their faith. They think our Lord and his apostles used great plainness of speech in telling us what we should believe and practice; and hence they are led to understand a great many things more literally and strictly than those who seek to make the religion of Jesus correspond with the fashion of the times.[29]

This quotation appears to rule out the use of doctrinal standards as the basis for unity between Baptist churches. McLean, however, seems to take a different approach on this issue when he gives his reasons for seeking to persuade his fellow Scotch Baptists to support the Particular Baptists in their missionary work in India. He begins by making it plain that there are differences between the English Particular Baptists and Scotch Baptists, but because they hold certain doctrines in common there is no reason why they cannot work together in mission.

> Though we of the Baptist denomination in Scotland differ in some things from those of the same denomination in England, and have no intention to depart from those principles by which the order and government of our churches have hitherto been regulated; yet being satisfied upon the whole that they preach the faith of the gospel, and, as they declare 'maintain the important doctrines of Three equal Persons in the Godhead; eternal and personal election; original sin; particular redemption; free justification by the righteousness of Christ imputed; efficacious grace in regeneration; the final perseverance of the saints; the resurrection of the dead; the general judgement at the last day; and the life everlasting,' we have considered it as our duty to assist their missionary society.[30]

McLean in his quotation of the articles of faith of the 1812 Particular Baptist Union appears to suggest that all Scotch Baptists could assent to them.[31] This understanding of their position was easy to

---

28 Wilson, *Origin and Progress*, p. 4.
29 Rippon, *Baptist Annual Register*, 1795, p. 374.
30 Rippon, *Baptist Annual Register*, 1795, pp. 379-380.
31 E.A. Payne, *The Baptist Union: A Short History*, (London: Carey Kingsgate Press, 1959), p. 24.

maintain while a strong leader like McLean dominated their connexion, but having an 'unwritten creed' was a potential source of problems for the future.

Scotch Baptists insisted that they held no creed or confession as authoritative, but they conducted their relationships with each other, and with other types of Baptists, as if they did hold to a fixed doctrinal statement. The problem for them was that their unwritten creed was much more restrictive in practice than any Calvinistic Baptist confession. Usually, the writings of Archibald McLean were the standards which they followed. If he rejected a doctrine that was normally considered orthodox, such as the eternal generation of the Son, then he was followed by other Scotch Baptists. The section on the causes of disunity within Scotch Baptist ranks will give examples of the dominance of McLean in the settlement of controversial issues. Those who would not accept the party line were forced out of the connexion.

The churches were in theory independent, but in practice closely dependent upon each other. The nature of their connexionalism in the era of McLean bears some degree of comparison to Wesleyan Methodism in the time of Jabez Bunting, one of their most prominent ministers, though Scotch Baptist churches were by contrast independent. A strong leader was required to ensure the effective operation of their corporate activities. Methodism between the eras of the leaders noted above showed fissiparous tendencies which paralleled those amongst Scotch Baptists once McLean's influence began to fade near the end of his life.[32] There was, however, no figure of similar stature within their midst to take Archibald McLean's place after his death in 1812. The balance between the observance of everything that Christ has commanded and forbearance with fellow Scotch Baptists on issues over which there had been disagreement was almost impossible to maintain. One of the most remarkable features of life amongst Scotch Baptists was the maintenance of unity within their ranks from 1765 to 1810, the year in which the first division over the place of elders at the Lord's Table took place.

The volume of correspondence, the visits and the exchange of preachers and members ensured that each church was carefully watched by the others. At the time of ordination of elders, representatives of other churches were usually present. On some other occasions, statements of faith were sent for the consideration of another fellowship with the unwritten intention of checking that

---

32 D.A. Gowland, *Methodist Secessions*, (Manchester: The Chetham Society, 1979), pp. 1-19.

they had not strayed from the truth.[33]

The Beverley church sent its statement of faith to all its sister churches in 1837 and received many letters of approval. The elders of Argyle Square Church, Edinburgh, William Pattison and John Horsburgh, sent a letter strongly approving the request for continued fellowship.

> The church agreed unanimously and heartily to accede to your desire to be united with us and our sister churches in the fellowship of the Gospel...we only regret that it has not taken place sooner...we know that the church in Dundee and the church in Glasgow have agreed unanimously as we have done.[34]

This congregation was one of the strictest Scotch Baptist churches. If its members were in favour of a doctrinal statement then it was likely to command common assent in the rest of the constituency.

Great care was taken before accepting someone as a new member of a Scotch Baptist church. The candidate's previous church was required to give its support for such a transfer of membership. The case of Andrew Bruce may be exceedingly thorough, but it illustrates the extremely diligent consideration given to requests for admission to the membership of a congregation. Complications arose over his request to join the Clyde Street congregation in Edinburgh. Clyde Street records show that correspondence was entered into with the Tabernacle Church, Edinburgh, where Bruce had been an adherent; Thurso Baptist Church where he had been a member; Thurso magistrates; and various other individuals in different parts of Scotland of whom some were ministers or elders.[35] This example was not an isolated case of extraordinary thoroughness in considering an application for membership. Samuel Swan sought to demonstrate the care of his own fellowship in such matters, in a letter to James Everson in November 1834. This dealt with the case of a William Thomson:

> with respect to Mr Thomson we think we acted very cautiously. Mr [William] Jones of London was so kind to apprise us of the part he had taken in the dispute concerning the appropriation of the fellowship and said that unless he promised to conduct himself in a peaceable manner it was at our peril to receive him. We also, by Thomson's request, wrote to one of the Deacons of the

---

33 The correspondence of James Everson, Beverley, for example, with various leaders in other Scotch Baptist congregations, MS Letters.
34 William Pattison and John Horsburgh, Edinburgh, to James Everson, Beverley, September 24, 1837, MS Letters.
35 Andrew Bruce's Case, July 14 1828, Clyde Street Hall, Bundle 9, Waugh Papers, Baptist House, Glasgow.

London Church, a Mr Malcolm Ross, and received for an answer a narrative of the whole affair drawn up by Mr Jones and signed on behalf of the church by the deacons which narrative was sent to Edinburgh. Moreover we wrote to Edinburgh to know how he conducted himself while a member with them and the answer was very satisfactory. As Thomson had not been separated from the church in London and professed his readiness to forbear and not to disturb the peace of the church by obtruding his peculiar views concerning the fellowship, and, after being repeatedly faithfully admonished concerning the crime of causing divisions and strifes in the church of Christ which admonitions appeared to have considerable effect upon his mind, we unanimously received him and as yet we are perfectly satisfied with his conduct.[36]

It is surprising that anyone was willing to endure such an ordeal, but it did indicate the seriousness with which Scotch Baptists took the links with their sister churches. Even a visit to a town in which one of their congregations was located, by a member on private business, could be the occasion of a letter assuring that church of his good character. In one particular case the visit was midweek and the man in question had no plans to attend a service, but should he come into contact with any members of that church they would be aware of his commendation by his own fellowship.[37]

Scotch Baptists also sought to be united in evangelistic efforts. The significance of this factor is seen in that the periods of greatest mission activities were also those of harmony in the connexion, for example, in the late 1790s.[38] The 1830s, by contrast, the era of the greatest disunity in the ranks, saw little co-operative efforts in evangelism. The Bristo Place Church, Edinburgh, sent annual letters to its sister churches in this period with a view to increasing evangelistic activity, though with little success.[39] It was only to be expected that the Edinburgh Church, later the Bristo Church, would take the lead in urging the churches to co-operate together in raising funds, and in sending out workers as home missionaries, as it had done earlier in support of the work of the Particular Baptist Missionary Society. After the 1834 division in the ranks of Scotch Baptists, discussed later in this chapter, the small breakaway group that moved

---

36 Swan to Everson, November 17, 1834, MS Letters. For fuller details of the Thomson case see D.M. Thompson, *Let Sects And Parties Fall*, (Birmingham: Berean Press, 1980), pp. 27- 28.
37 Letter to a church in Kendal, Cumbria, January 16, 1838, concerning John McNeil from Clyde Street Hall, Waugh Papers.
38 For Example, *Edinburgh Quarterly Magazine*, I, (1798), pp. 68-73.
39 For Example, 'From the Church meeting in Bristo Street, Edinburgh, to the Church in [Beverley]', a Circular Letter, Edinburgh, February 9, 1838.

to Minto House took the lead in directing the affairs of the stricter party in the constituency. The problem, however, that Scotch Baptists faced was that as the network of churches with which they associated grew smaller, so the amount of evangelistic activity they could accomplish also diminished.

> A letter was sent out from the Edinburgh congregation to the churches signed by the elders Archibald McLean, William Braidwood and Henry Inglis, dated November 18 1798.[40] The stimulus for this call to evangelise came from the labours of the Haldanes and their Independent colleagues. Scotch Baptist rejoicing, however, was qualified by the statement that there was regret that many of these efforts would fail to realise their full potential because part of Jesus' mandate was being ignored. This partial commendation referred to the words 'teach them to observe all things that I have commanded you' (Mt.28.20). The significance of these words of Jesus was believed to have been taken more seriously within their own constituency. They hoped, though, that the mission work might be successful. The letter stated: We hope the Lord will bless their labours, so far as they declare the truth; but from such partial and defective teaching we have little cause to expect a revival of primitive Christianity, or that anything like the first churches of the saints will be the result of their exertions.[41]

'Primitive Christianity' referred to the distinctive tenets of the Scotch Baptist stream of the Baptist denomination, in contrast to the opinions of other evangelical Christians, including other types of Calvinistic Baptists. In this context the reference was made to Scottish evangelicals holding to either Independent or Presbyterian opinions.

The challenge from Edinburgh was for churches to form a fund to pay the expenses of those individuals involved in evangelistic labours and to release elders and other preachers to spearhead the work. One of those who had already taken up the challenge was James Watt, who had evangelised extensively in Aberdeenshire and Banff in 1797. Watt, a former Anti-Burgher Secession minister had been suspended from the ministry of that body in 1796 due to doubts he had expressed about some of their practices. Following his adoption of Baptist views he had joined the Edinburgh Scotch Baptist congregation, the cause which had commissioned his itinerant work.[42] His ministry led to small fellowships springing up in

---

40 Wilson, *Origin and Progress*, pp. 41-47.
41 Wilson, *Origin and Progress*, p. 44.
42 *Edinburgh Quarterly Magazine*, I (1798), pp. 68-73.

Balmaud (1797), New Pitsligo (1803), Aberchirder (1808), St Fergus (1809), and Fraserburgh (1810). There were also home groups at Banff, Portsoy and Inchture.[43] Watt's ministry was an encouragement to other Scotch Baptists to undertake this kind of work. The success of Edinburgh's appeal was seen in the establishment of an itinerant fund, in 1804, to cover the costs of Highland missionaries and elders on preaching tours. The contributors to the fund included the churches at Edinburgh and Glasgow, Paisley and Dunfermline. Edinburgh administered the fund and sent out two of its elders, McLean and Inglis, to promote the cause. Edward Mackay in Thurso, David Macrae in Fortrose, and A. Fraser, first in Huntly and then in Dundee, were employed in itinerant ministry for some years beginning in 1805.[44] The value of this emphasis on evangelism not only enabled the numbers of people in their connexion to grow, but also allowed Scotch Baptists to be more outward-looking and united in their vision.

The important place of evangelism in Scotch Baptist circles was undermined by their internal wrangles, though it continued to be prominent in their thinking. Henry Dickie of Edinburgh wrote a letter in December 1829 to John Selly, a grocer and a leader in the Beverley Scotch Baptist Church, expressing his hopes for the coming year:

> You are aware of the desire which has been often expressed and is I believe participated in by all the churches that some more active exertions could be made by us as a body for the spread of the Gospel and of the knowledge of primitive Christianity...Could Mr [John] Charlton or any qualified brother among you undertake a tour from Beverley to London and Nottingham or to some of the churches in Scotland ? If so I am desired to express on the part of this church our readiness to join with the other churches in defraying the expenses... We have some hopes that one of the parties at Aberdeen and one from Dundee (where there are now three) will be able to itinerate for a short time in the north this summer.[45]

These hopes were not realised in northern Scotland in 1830. A circular sent to the churches of the connexion in the name of the Glas-

---

43 P. Waugh, 'The Converging Streams 1800-1850', in Yuille (ed.), *Baptists in Scotland*, p. 53. J.S. Fisher, *Impelled by Faith*, (Stirling: Scottish Baptist History Project, 1996), p. 8.
44 P. Waugh, 'Home Mission and the Highlands', in Yuille (ed.), *Baptists in Scotland*, p.68 [and note p. 276]. Fisher, *Impelled by Faith*, p.8.
45 H.D. Dickie, Edinburgh, to John Selly, Beverley, December 18, 1829, MS Letters.

gow congregation, in October 1830, urged the brethren to attend to the needs of their smaller fellowships in the north. Andrew Liddel, a member of the Glasgow Church, while on a business trip to Elgin, had had some encouraging conversations with local people and was urging the connexion to send some elders to Elgin to take advantage of this opportunity. The circular also hinted at difficulties in relationships between some churches but stressed the need to overcome them for the sake of 'Christian union for the Truth's sake'.[46] Those churches involved in evangelistic outreach were unlikely to be involved in protracted internal wrangling. Co-operation in mission would strengthen the links between the churches.

Circulars on the subject of united evangelistic efforts were sent out to their fellow Scotch Baptists by the Edinburgh Church in October 1833 and April 1834. Bristo Baptist Church, the largest section of the Edinburgh Church after the 1834 division, continued this practice with circulars in September 1836 and February 1838. In the 1838 circular a comment was passed on the impact of the three previous letters to the churches. Evangelistic outreach was described as:

> a matter of much importance which has long been the subject of correspondence amongst the churches, while little comparatively has been done…In our last [circular] we expressed a hope that we should obtain the use of the gifts and time of one or two of our brethren, to accomplish in some measure the important objects referred to in our letters…We considered it our duty to endeavour to exemplify that which we had recommended to your consideration.

Bristo Baptist Church commissioned Daniel Kemp, one of its members, to work in the Chester area. James Stephen, another member, was 'requested to relinquish his business, and to devote himself to that work'. Stephen was commissioned to itinerate as a travelling evangelist in Scotland and the north of England. Andrew Arthur, from the Kirkcaldy Scotch Baptist Church, was called to work full-time with Bristo Baptist Church in Edinburgh in association with three other pastors of the church. These decisions revealed a renewed dedication to itinerant evangelism in this church of 175 members. The 1838 circular also noted that the Aberdeen church employed two members as city missionaries.[47]

One other though less important factor in maintaining union amongst Scotch Baptists was the determination to work diligently

---

46 Printed Circular Glasgow Church to Beverley Church, October 4, 1830, MS Letters.
47 Printed Circular Bristo Baptist Church, Edinburgh, to Beverley Church, February 9, 1838, MS Letters.

to overcome problems that arose between the churches. The detailed interest in the affairs of each other's congregations was bound to throw up issues which caused profound disagreement, but this was not allowed to be an excuse for failing to maintain 'the unity of the Spirit in the bond of peace' (Eph.4.3). Andrew Duncan, an elder of the Glasgow congregation, described in a letter to John Charlton, an elder of the Beverley Church, how a reconciliation had been achieved between his own congregation and another smaller Scotch Baptist church in the city in 1825.

> We had a baptism last Saturday morning and a small church attended who were formerly in fellowship with us, but who withdrew from us on a matter of discipline. They have again applied for admission to our communion. After some correspondence it was effected last Lord's Day...[48]

Scotch Baptists have been noted for their divisions in the nineteenth century. It is important to record a balanced picture that includes some successful reunions such as what happened in Glasgow. The achievement in healing a local division led the Glasgow Church to attempt to bring about a reunion with Scotch Baptist churches that had left the connexion for various reasons in the preceding decades. They lamented the fact that some churches appeared resigned to being outside the connexion in perpetuity.

> It is truly melancholy to see the disorder prevailing among the Baptists in various places, so far as respects affectionate Christian union for the Truth's sake, no scriptural principle of union pervading them as one body; but everyone disjointed from his neighbour, as if the Great Head of the church had not provided for – had not commanded – and prayed for – their union in the faith, hope, and holiness of the gospel.[49]

This circular received replies from ten of the thirteen churches to which it was sent in the next two months. In December 1830 a follow-up circular was sent indicating that further work was needed to persuade all the churches to agree that immediate action was required.[50] The importance of these circulars is that the churches thought it important to work out how to achieve greater harmony within their midst.

This desire to implement Christian unity was to receive a serious

---

48 Andrew Duncan, Glasgow, to John Charlton, Beverley, September 7, 1825, MS Letters.
49 Printed Circular Glasgow Church, to Beverley Church, October 4, 1830, MS Letters.
50 Printed Circular Glasgow Church, to Beverley Church, December 20, 1830, MS Letters.

setback in 1834, a matter that will be considered later in this chapter, but it did not prevent genuine attempts to heal the wounds. The Glasgow church refused to take sides with either party in Edinburgh and in its February 1835 circular urged its sister churches outside Edinburgh to follow their example.[51] The problem that constantly afflicted Scotch Baptists was that fissiparous tendencies undermined genuine desire for united efforts.

2.3 The Relationship of Scotch Baptists with other British Baptists

The second area for consideration concerns the relationship between Scotch Baptists and other British Baptists. Scotch Baptists were in touch with events outside their connexion through the literature produced by other Baptists. There were many Scotch Baptists who read the magazines and books produced by the Haldanes. Andrew Liddel, of Glasgow, in a letter to James Everson, of Monmouth, in 1832, made the following references to James Haldane's writings:

> I have delayed sending this same day in expectation of getting from Edinburgh a copy of the magazines edited by Mr Haldane of which I spoke to you. Two numbers are published, if they come in time, I will enclose them...Thursday night. I must close the parcel without the magazines referred to. They have not come though I ordered them a week ago. I have however enclosed a few old Scripture magazines edited also by Mr Haldane.[52]

James Wallis, a prominent member of the Nottingham Church, in an undated letter sent to Everson, in late 1836 or early 1837, made a passing reference to Haldane's magazines circulating in that congregation.[53] John Hine, another member of the Nottingham Church, in a letter largely taken up with personal matters, told Everson in October 1836 that amongst other magazines a set of Haldane's magazines was being sent.[54] It is worth noting that Hine was soon to leave Scotch Baptist circles for the newly formed Churches of Christ, along with his colleague James Wallis. The growing rigidity of views that Wallis and Hine had on such matters as baptism and

---

51 Printed Circular Glasgow Church, to Beverley Church, February 12, 1835, MS Letters.
52 Andrew Liddel, Glasgow, to James Everson, Monmouth, August 1, 1832, MS Letters.
53 James Wallis, Nottingham, to James Everson, Beverley, n.d. (1837?), MS Letters.
54 John Hine, Nottingham, to James Everson, Beverley, October 2, 1836, MS Letters.

the nature of true faith did not prevent them from reading and circulating items of very different, though baptistic, persuasion. This meant that even in the most narrow minded of Baptist circles other viewpoints were still being taken into consideration.

It must not be assumed that all Scotch Baptists approved of such varied reading matter. Robert Anderson, an elder in Bristo Baptist Church, when invited to comment in 1836 on an article in *The Baptist Magazine*, showed his unfamiliarity with that particular publication.'I do not read the Baptist Magazine: so therefore your letter surprised me much and certainly made me enquire for the number referred to'. A lengthy discussion of the letter's contents, dealing with the subject of forbearance, was followed by these remarks:

> I should inform you that after discovering the author of the paper referred to I gave him my opinion of the step he had taken in publishing such views, and though I do not think I convinced him of his error, yet I do expect he will not appear again on that subject, and I rather think he would not have appeared at all there, if the misstatements of an English Baptist at Greenock in the magazine had not excited him. I am very far from thinking either that we should excommunicate him or that he ought to withdraw from us.[55]

Everson was informed that the letter writer was not representing the church's views in his letter and thus his error ought to be overlooked. Anderson's moderate outlook on this matter was probably a minority view in his connexion.

One unexpected contribution to unity with other types of Baptists in Scotland came with the adoption of Baptist practices by members of churches in the Tabernacle connexion. These churches were independent and paedobaptist. They lost a steady stream of members to the Baptists in Scotland in the first decade of the nineteenth century. One example of this occurred in Glasgow when a small Tabernacle connexion church, with forty members, joined with the Scotch Baptist church, of two hundred members, led by James Watt, David Smith and James Duncan. The Scotch Baptist church accepted the two elders of the smaller fellowship, David McLaren and James Buchan, thus increasing its own eldership to five members. No date is recorded for this event but it must have been prior to the summer of 1808, as this was the time when the information was published.[56] These new members brought fresh ideas about church life into the Scotch Baptist churches. There

---

55 Robert Anderson, Edinburgh, to James Everson, Beverley, December 8, 1836, MS Letters.
56 *Theological Repository*, 5, New Series, (July-December 1808), p. 346.

would probably have been occasions when the new ideas were rejected, but equally others when new thinking was influential. The significance of this is that though the influx of new members probably contributed to the tensions that lay behind the divisions in Scotch Baptist circles in 1810, which will be discussed later in this chapter, there was also probably influence exerted in the direction of bridge-building with other Baptists. It is notable, as chapter six will record, that nearly all the Scotch Baptists who participated in the 1827 Baptist Union had had a previous involvement in one of the churches associated with the Haldanes. David McLaren, mentioned above, is one example of this phenomenon.

The most prominent area of united effort amongst Scottish Baptists was in evangelism, both at home and overseas. The willingness of all three streams of Baptist witness to unite in the work of home mission will be discussed in chapter five. It is, however, important to refer to this co-operation in evangelistic work here as it was the most important factor in uniting Scotch Baptists with the other Baptists in Scotland. Scotch Baptist support for the work of William Tulloch in Aberfeldy (1816-1819), and later in Blair Atholl (1819-1861), is a good example of co-operative evangelism. Tulloch was one of the evangelists (agents) trained and supported by Robert and James Haldane. All these agents, until the Haldanes changed their views, were required to hold Independent (Congregational) theological opinions. Tulloch embraced Baptist principles in 1808. The financial support required to continue in his work was now no longer guaranteed for all the former agents by the Haldanes. Chapter three will examine the work of the Haldanes and the churches associated with them. Tulloch and other colleagues in Highland Perthshire appealed to fellow Baptists for assistance. As a result of this appeal the Baptist Highland Mission was eventually formed in 1816. The leadership of this mission came from three of the elders of a Glasgow Scotch Baptist Church, James Watt, James Buchan and David McLaren, and three members of the Perth Baptist Church, John Stalker, Robert Pullar (the treasurer) and Isaac Nicol. The Perth Scotch Baptist Church had received a big influx of members from Christians who had formerly been associated with the Tabernacle connnexion church in the town.[57] They had been accompanied by two of their three pastors.[58] It is not difficult to understand why the named individuals supported this mission. Watt had shown by his own example an enthusiasm for home mission with his tours in the

---

57 Waugh, 'Converging Streams', p. 59.
58 B. Robertson, *Perth Baptist Church: The History, The People*, (Perth: Strath Fleet Publishing Company, 1994), p. 33.

north-east of Scotland. The other leaders from his own congregation had been associated with the Haldanes. It is possible that Tulloch and his colleagues who were supported through the Baptist Highland Mission had existing links to members of the Glasgow and Perth churches. Scottish Baptists were beginning to realise the potential benefits of associating for the work of home evangelism.

The Scotch Baptists had enjoyed good relationships with several English Particular Baptist churches in the late eighteenth century, for example those in Hexham and Newcastle. The closest links, however, were between the Scot David Fernie, a Particular Baptist preacher based in Bishop Auckland, and the Edinburgh congregation, until he emigrated to America in 1771.[59] The pastor of Whitehaven Particular Baptist Church, William Graham, who was ordained in 1787, was influenced by Scotch Baptist views. He sought to introduce such practices as weekly communion and the exhortation of the brethren into his congregation. This move split the church into two groups, of which one remained with him. After Graham left the area, the two groups reunited and called George Jamieson as the new pastor. Jamieson had been associated with the Haldanes in Edinburgh. He was accepted by both parties and restored harmony in the church.[60] It is possible that this development was facilitated by the adoption of many Glasite practices by the Haldanes. James Haldane's book *Views of Social Worship*, published in 1805, was well known and discussed both in Scotland and England. It is equally important to note that Robert Haldane and his friend William Ballantyne, pastor of the Tabernacle in Elgin, made a tour of the north of England and London to promote these practices.[61] The significance of James Haldane's book and his brother's conduct will be discussed in the next chapter. It is probable that in matters of ecclesiology many Haldaneites and Scotch Baptists were coming closer together in their views in the first decade of the nineteenth century. This assumption would explain the ease with which such interchanges took place.

Archibald McLean had established a friendship with Andrew Fuller, one of the leading English Particular Baptists. They entered into regular correspondence and had opportunities for fellowship on Fuller's visits to Scotland on behalf of the Particular Baptist Missionary Society (BMS).[62] Fuller received support from all the Baptist

---

59 D. Douglas, *History of the Baptist Churches of Northern England*, (London: Houlston and Stoneman, 1846), pp. 190-198.
60 Douglas, *Baptist Churches of Northern England*, p. 285.
61 A. Haldane, *The Lives of Robert and James Haldane*, (Edinburgh: Banner of Truth, 1990 [1853]), p. 357.

streams in Scotland in his attempts to raise funds for the BMS. There was only one occasion when he was temporarily refused access to a Baptist pulpit. This event occurred in Glasgow in September 1802. The members of this Baptist church had wanted Fuller to confirm his soundness in theological matters before being allowed to conduct public worship in their midst. It was not surprising that he refused to accept such a demand. A church meeting overturned the original condition and invited him to preach in its pulpit on the following evening. Fuller, afterwards, recorded some of the details in a letter to his wife from Liverpool on September 25:

> I learnt that the refusal of their pulpit was against the will of the church, except two members; that the church at P[aisley], with which they are in connexion, had sent deputies to oppose my being admitted to preach and commune with them; and these, with the two members, carried their point; but on Lord's day noon, the church were so hurt at my being refused, that they resolved to invite me. The two deacons were deputed to request that I would look over the affair of the Lord's day, and consider them as one with us. Accordingly I preached there in the evening.[63]

Fuller would not have expected access to every Baptist pulpit in Scotland, but gratefully accepted those that were offered to him. It is difficult to identify the two churches involved in this incident with any degree of certainty. One possibility is that the church in Paisley was the 'Pen Folk' independent Baptist Church and the church in Glasgow, its sister church. An extract from the 'Pen Folk' church records that has survived from 1798 records the following information:

> The church being thus left without a shepherd [after the pastor David Wylie and some of the members left to join Storie Street Scotch Baptist Church in Paisley] from November to December, they connected themselves with a church in Glasgow, of which George Begg was the pastor. The church in Glasgow being fewer in number than the church in Paisley, it was agreed upon by the churches mutually that George Begg should remove to Paisley, and act there in the character of pastor. This was carried into effect in that same month of December, 1798.[64]

---

62 In 1796 they exchanged letters on the different forms of church discipline in 'English' and Scotch Baptist churches. Belcher (ed.), *Andrew Fuller*, III, pp. 478-479.
63 Belcher (ed.), *Andrew Fuller*, I, pp. 77-78.
64 D. Gilmour, *Reminiscences of The Pen' Folk*, (Paisley: Alex Gardner, 1889), p. 41.

George Begg had been an elder of the main Scotch Baptist Church in Glasgow. The above extract confirms that he had left that church prior to 1798. It is probable that it was one of many divisions within Scotch Baptist circles over disciplinary matters. The prickly nature of relationships between some Scottish Baptist congregations in this period, even when of very similar ecclesiologies, ensured that the Kettering minister would inevitably be out of favour with some of the churches.

It is also possible to ascertain how the Pen Folk congregation viewed the Scotch Baptist Church in Paisley.

> For several years the members roll of the 'Pen' gradually enlarged, during which period they would neither 'pick nor dab' with others, 'because', in the words of an old Penite, 'frae the vera beginnin' the Storie Street Baptists were tainted with the heresy o' free will, contrair tae the hale tenour o' Scripture, seestu;' whereas the Pen Folk were, to state it kindly, as pure as Kilmeny in that respect.[65]

Gilmour, a former member of the Pen Church, attributes the exclusiveness of this Baptist congregation to the fact that almost all their members had been drawn from the Oakshaw Street Antiburgher Church, where Dr William Ferrier was the minster from 1787-1835.[66] Ferrier, 'a person of high intellectual endowments'[67] had apparently turned out a greater number of clever men, and qualified more lay preachers, than any other minister of the Associate body'. His congregation, though, was perceived by some other churches in Paisley as having 'assumed a superiority over other bodies, and its members gathered up, as it were, their garments to prevent defilement from other Christians when they passed.'[68] If this perception of Ferrier's congregation is accurate then it is unsurprising that some of the same characteristics were found in an offshoot of this body. This incident illustrates the insular nature of the life of some churches at the start of the nineteenth century in Scotland. It is, though, important to state that these two hybrid Baptist churches, in Paisley and Glasgow, were not under

---

65 Gilmour, *Pen' Folk*, pp. 42-43.
66 Gilmour, *Pen' Folk*, p. 48. I am grateful to Dr Derek Murray for providing information about Dr William Ferrier that confirmed the identity of the Dr Ferrier described in Gilmour's book. More information about this Antiburgher congregation under Dr Ferrier's ministry is found in R. Small, *History of the Congregations of the United Presbyterian Church from 1733-1900*, (Edinburgh: David M. Small, 1904), Vol.1, pp. 514-516.
67 McKerrow, *Secession Church*, p. 926
68 Gilmour, *Pen' Folk*, pp. 48-49.

the influence of McLean. He, therefore, had no way of swaying them in favour of Fuller and the work of the BMS.

Overseas mission work conducted by Particular Baptists in India came to McLean's attention while on his regular journeys to England.[69] Support for evangelistic activities in other countries was not as important as home evangelism in uniting Scottish Baptists, but it played its part in widening their horizons, especially those of Scotch Baptists. In his *Memoir* of McLean, William Jones, an elder of the Windmill Street Scotch Baptist Church in London, stressed the lively interest of McLean in this subject:

> This indeed was only the legitimate consequence of his own views of the nature of the Gospel, and of our Lord's Commission to 'Go into all the world, and preach (or proclaim) it to every creature'...He considered it to be his duty to assist the society which had been established for the support of the mission, to the utmost of his ability.[70]

McLean was probably the first minister in Scotland to announce publicly the need to obey the 'Great Commission' of Matthew 28.19-20. At the end of 1798 he delivered a stirring discourse to his Edinburgh congregation based on Psalm 22.27-28. He persuaded them to support the Particular Baptist Missionary Society. This was soon followed by his *An Address to the People of God in Scotland, on the Duty of Using Means for the Universal Spread of the Gospel of Christ* which affirmed the need to engage in evangelism in Scotland. McLean had no difficulty in persuading fellow Scotch Baptists to follow the lead from Edinburgh. They responded generously to his appeal. McLean was able to reveal the level of this generosity to Fuller in a letter sent in April 1796:

> Sir, enclosed you have a banker's bill for £151.11.0 for your missionary society, to be applied to the purpose of propagating the gospel among the heathen. It was collected as follows:
>
> | | |
> |---|---:|
> | From the church at Edinburgh | £58.04.0 |
> | From the hearers at Edinburgh | £19.10.0 |
> | | £77.14.0 |
> | From the church and hearers at Glasgow | £41.00.0 |
> | From the church and hearers at Dundee | £10.06.0 |
> | From the church and hearers at Paisley | £10.10.0 |
> | From the church and hearers at Largo | £05.05.0 |
> | From some brethren at Wooler | £04.11.0 |
> | From a few brethren at Galashiels | £02.05.0 |
> | | £151.11.0 |

---

69 Wilson, *Origin and Progress*, p. 29.
70 Jones (ed.), *Works of Archibald McLean*, VI, p. lxxiii.

Since the above collections were made, we have received about £24 more, and having published two small pamphlets on the subject, if any thing comes from the sale of them it shall be appropriated to the same use.[71]

Scotch Baptists were consistent not only in their continued support for the Baptist missionary work in India but also in other Baptist work overseas. James Everson, a printer and publisher in Beverley, published news from Particular Baptist churches and showed interest in the work of Frederick Crowe in Honduras, where strict communion churches were being set up. Johann Oncken's work in Germany was commended, although not all Everson's readers agreed. One correspondent was very critical of the Argyle Square Baptist Church in Edinburgh because it allowed its members to attend a meeting in support of the German mission alongside members of other Baptist churches in the city.[72] A minority of Scotch Baptists chose to be extremely insular in their thinking and practices. These individuals who offered no support for home and overseas Baptist mission outside their own connexion would certainly have no desire for a wider Baptist union. Other Scotch Baptists who had seen the benefits in such evangelistic activities would be more likely to consider offering support to achieve the cause of wider Baptist union in Scotland.

Scotch Baptists showed great caution in their relationships with other Baptists. There were some who were quick to associate, but others, like the correspondent above, that appeared to want almost no contact at all. The majority of church members would have been somewhere in the middle between these two positions. It is likely that many of them would have agreed with the sentiments expressed by Robert Anderson, nephew of Christopher Anderson and elder of Bristo Baptist Church alongside Henry Dickie, in a letter sent to James Everson in 1836:

> I feel as you do, that in general our conduct should be such as to make it appear that we remain separate from the English Baptists from principle. At the same time I think that opportunities of preaching the Gospel in any of their churches or elsewhere occasionally may be embraced consistent with strict Scriptural views.[73]

Unity with fellow Scotch Baptists was the first priority of those within that particular connexion. There were, however, varying degrees of willingness to work with other Baptists in Scotland.

---

71 W. Jones (ed.), *The New Evangelical Magazine*, II, (1816), p. 76.
72 Murray, 'Scotch Baptist Tradition', p. 194.
73 Anderson, Edinburgh, to Everson, Beverley, March1, 1836, MS Letters.

Scotch Baptists were involved in the 1827 Baptist Union of Scotland, a matter to be considered in chapter six, but the primary focus regarding union was to preserve it within their own ranks.

2.4 The Causes of Disunity amongst the Scotch Baptists

The problem of disunity within Scotch Baptist ranks regularly engaged their attention. It was not surprising that those individuals who set such high standards for the maintenance of church purity in doctrine and practice should fail to live up to them. This issue greatly affected their ability to relate to other types of British Baptists. Chapter six will discuss the particular reasons involved in the failure of early attempts to encourage Baptists in Scotland to join a union of churches. Here it is important to consider the causes of disunity within Scotch Baptist circles.

One factor for consideration was the social composition of the churches. The Edinburgh congregations of this Baptist stream will be assessed to ascertain if this issue contributed to the cause of union or disunity within their ranks. The majority of these Scotch Baptists were poor and working-class. There was, initially, in the eighteenth century only one man of means, a surgeon called Robert Walker, in the sole Edinburgh Church. The account in the *Baptist Annual Register* by John Rippon records the following information about him:

> [Robert] Walker was...eminently useful in the Baptist church at its first erection, and for several years after, particularly in liberality; for as the members were then very few, and in mean circumstances, the greater part of the necessary expense attending the public profession fell to his share.[74]

In 1778 another man of means entered into membership of the church, namely Dr Charles Stuart. He was the son of a Lord Provost of Edinburgh and himself a former minister of the Parish of Cramond. He inherited the Dunearn estate in Fife on the death of his father and owned a house in George Square in Edinburgh.[75] William Braidwood who joined the church in 1778 and became an elder alongside McLean was also a prominent citizen. He was admitted Burgess and Guild Brother of Edinburgh through his father's interest in 1797, and was described as an ironmonger.[76] Braidwood later became the first manager of the Caledonian Insurance Company.

74　Rippon, *Baptist Annual Register*, 1795, p. 363.
75　*The Book of the Old Edinburgh Club for the years 1946 and 1947*, XXVI, (Edinburgh: T. and A. Constable Ltd, 1948), p. 164.
76　Scottish Records Society, *The Burgesses and Guild Brethren of Edinburgh 1761-1841*, (ed.), C.B. Boag-Watson, (Edinburgh: J. Skinner and Company, 1948), p. 22.

He lived from 1822 to the end of his life at 23 George Square in Edinburgh.[77] A citizen of Edinburgh who lived in George Square was of high social rank and would have been considered as wealthy by many of his contemporaries. Henry David Inglis was also a distinguished member of the church. Inglis qualified as an advocate in 1794 and had a prominent ministry to prisoners.[78] There were others who were former Presbyterian ministers such as Robert Carmichael, a former Antiburgher minister from Coupar Angus,[79] and George Grieve from Wooler in Northumberland, who worked in later years as a doctor.[80] In each case the above named men had prominent positions in the church, but this was on merit, not because of their wealth. The wealth, or poverty, of individual members was not a primary influence on church decisions regarding doctrine or practices. Robert Walker and Charles Stuart both left the church after theological disputations regarding disciplinary matters.[81] When Walker seceded in 1774, the congregation was unable to pay for the use of Magdalen Chapel and had to find a new home.[82] Here there was no doubt that wealth had not been a determining factor in the decision of the church meeting, because the overwhelming majority of the congregation had opposed the viewpoint held by Robert Walker.[83]

In 1837 the results of a government enquiry into church accommodation were published. This survey contained a substantial amount of information about church life and the people that made up a local congregation.[84] An analysis of the Edinburgh Scotch Baptist Churches' social composition from this survey reveals the following information about them. There were two churches officially described as Scotch Baptist churches. Niddry Street congregation had an average attendance of 450 and three-quarters of its member-

---

77 *Book of the Old Edinburgh Club*, XXVI, p. 146.
78 Murray, 'Social and Religious Origins', p. 99.
79 Wilson, *Origin and Progress*, p. 5.
80 Wilson, *Origin and Progress*, p. 18.
81 Wilson, *Origin and Progress*, pp. 18-19.
82 Murray, 'Scotch Baptist Tradition', p. 189.
83 Rippon (ed.), *Baptist Annual Register*, 1795, p. 364.
84 *Report of the Commission of Enquiry into the Opportunities of Public Religious Worship, and means of Religious Instruction, and the Pastoral Superintendence afforded to the people of Scotland*, (9 Vols; London: House of Commons, 1837-1839). Discussion of these volumes is found in B.R. Talbot, 'Baptists and the Scottish Commission of Enquiry on Religion, 1836-1838', *Baptist Quarterly*, 39.8 (2002), pp. 368-386; and in two articles by D.B. Murray,'Scotch Baptist Tradition', p. 193, and 'Baptists in Scotland before 1869', *Baptist Quarterly*, 23.6 (1970), pp. 258-260.

ship were poor and working-class. The Argyle Square Church, a breakaway group from Niddry Street Church in 1834, had an average attendance of 160, with most of its members engaged in business and only 'a few' described as poor. The Clyde Street Church, a congregation constituted in 1824, comprised former members of the Haldane Tabernacle. It operated as a Scotch Baptist church and had an average attendance of 120, of whom two-thirds to three-quarters of the members were poor and working class.[85] It is important to be cautious about what inferences can be drawn from such a small number of churches, but there are indications that those individuals of limited income were more inclined towards union than their richer colleagues. Clyde Street Hall, the poorest of the three congregations, was to be a committed supporter of the 1827 Baptist Union of Scotland, discussed in chapter six.[86] Niddry Street Church with a mixed congregation took a cautious line over union. Its elders would be supportive of the Baptist Home Missionary society, but chose to hold back from any formal union of churches.[87] The Argyle Square congregation with its wealthier members held aloof from the co-operative ventures outside its own conservative Scotch Baptist circles.[88] The sample of churches here is small, but it is possible to suggest that amongst Edinburgh Scotch Baptists the social composition of a congregation did influence their approach to the issue of wider Baptist union. The church members of limited means were more aware of their dependence on fellow-worshippers and were, therefore, more inclined towards union with other Scottish Baptists. Social differences would have contributed to the tensions within these congregations, but this factor would be significant only in association with other causes of disunity.

An External Cause of Division

There was one major external cause that produced divisions amongst the followers of Archibald McLean, that is, the rise of the Campbellites. This new denomination came into being through the preaching of Alexander Campbell. This Ulsterman, in association with his father Thomas, launched their first congregation at Brush Run in America in 1813. Campbell aimed to restore 'the ancient order of things', that is, a return to the original pattern of church life

---

85 *Commission of Enquiry*, I, 1837, pp. 88-91, 96-99, 124-127.
86 Bundle 8, Waugh Papers, 'Correspondence over proposals to form a union of Baptist churches in Scotland.'
87 Bundle 8, Waugh Papers.
88 Yuille (ed.), *Baptists in Scotland*, p. 121.

found in the New Testament. He argued for congregational autonomy, the weekly observance of the Lord's Supper, a plurality of elders and deacons in each congregation, and a simple pattern of worship. New Testament preaching began with a testimony to the gospel facts; this testimony, without any other supernatural agency, produced faith.[89] It was abundantly clear that there were marked similarities between Campbell's teaching and the opinions of the Scotch Baptists. William Jones, the London Scotch Baptist elder, introduced Campbell's writings to Scotch Baptists in 1835 after reading some of his magazine articles. Jones published them in a new magazine, *The Millennial Harbinger and Voluntary Church Advocate*, designed to promote Campbell's views in Great Britain. Soon, however, Jones began to doubt the wisdom of promoting the works of Alexander Campbell.[90] In 1837 he produced a book entitled *Primitive Christianity* with a view to counteracting the new opinions.[91] Jones objected to Campbell's dismissal of all human creeds and confessions and voluntary associations of churches.[92] He also took exception to Campbell's view that the Lord's Supper could be observed without the presence of elders, and to the Ulsterman's doubts over the orthodox interpretation of the Trinity and the personality of the Holy Spirit.[93] Scotch Baptists faced this new challenge from the followers of Alexander Campbell at a time when their connexion was at its weakest. It was, therefore, an additional threat to the internal unity of the Scotch Baptist movement.

The damage had been done and division and disharmony became an even greater part of the experience of Scotch Baptist congregations. Scotch Baptists in Edinburgh, Glasgow, Liverpool and Manchester had invited the Campbellite leader in England, James Wallis, to meet with them in 1839. There were even some whole churches that parted company with the Scotch Baptists, such as the Saltcoats congregation in 1842. A similar decision was taken by the Stevenson church, Ayrshire, in that same year. Divisions in the Dunfermline and Kilmarnock congregations resulted in the establishment of other Campbellite churches.[94] William Jones became highly

---

89 C.L. Allen, 'Alexander Campbell', in D.M. Lewis (ed.), *The Blackwell Dictionary of Evangelical Biography 1730-1860* (DEB), (Oxford: Blackwell, 1995), I, pp. 188-189.
90 W. Jones, *Autobiography*, (edited by his son; London: John Snow, 1846), pp. 124-125.
91 Thompson, *Let Sects and Parties Fall*, pp. 20-21.
92 Allen, 'Alexander Campbell', p. 188.
93 Thompson, *Let Sects and Parties Fall*, pp. 20-21.

unpopular in his own connexion as a result of his involvement with Alexander Campbell, and for a time was out of fellowship with the churches in Scotland. John Gilbert, a member of the Dundee Church, in a letter to James Everson in 1838, thanked God that his church had come through the various controversies of the 1830s, including that for which William Jones had been responsible. He did, however, hope that fellowship between Jones and the Scottish churches could be restored. 'The subject of Mr Jones being out of our fellowship shall not rest... It was before our Church and we are to make any apology necessary for our conduct in the matter. I hope other Churches will follow...'[95] D. Gordon, in a letter written to Everson three months later, from the same church in Dundee, included this comment in an otherwise personal letter: 'There is sorrow indeed to hear that there is no likelihood of the matter between William Jones and the Churches in Scotland being healed.'[96] Scotch Baptists were learning the hard way that it is easy to break relationships but much harder to restore fellowship.

Internal Causes of Division

The external threat posed by the Campbellites had caused serious difficulties for Scotch Baptists, but it did not compare to the challenge posed by internal divisions. The principal problem was raised by Andrew Liddel in a letter to James Everson dated March 1836. Officially Scotch Baptists believed both in forbearance and unanimity in belief and church order. Such a position could be maintained only in principle but not in practice. This letter majored on the theme of the futility of compromise on doctrinal and ecclesiological issues. Liddel spent the first part of his letter recording his grief at the divisions caused in Scotch Baptist ranks in the 1830s over the issue of whether elders are required at the Lord's Table to celebrate communion. He saw that forbearance on this issue would lead to acceptance of an open table and then an open membership amongst Baptist churches. He stated: 'It cannot now be denied, I think, that the sentiment about the Lord's Supper, the avowed cause of division, leads into other and more evident disorders. From this I humbly think that the most timorous might see that such a sentiment and practice cannot be of God.'[97] Liddel was correct to discern the

---

94 Thompson, *Let Sects and Parties Fall*, pp. 26-27.
95 John Gilbert, Dundee, to James Everson, Beverley, May 5 1838, MS Letters.
96 D. Gordon, Dundee, to James Everson, Beverley, August 7 1838, MS Letters.

likely direction of compromises between churches in order to strengthen or to establish unity between them. He was, however, only thinking what others had perceived many years earlier. James Haldane had published two pamphlets on *Mutual Forbearance in Matters of Church Order* in 1811 and 1812 in which he argued for an open table and an open membership in Baptist churches. This position was never adopted by the Leith Walk Tabernacle during Haldane's ministry. Elder Street Church, in Edinburgh, however, had an open table and an open membership under William Innes and Jonathan Watson.[98] James Haldane did try to change the constitution to allow unbaptised believers to become church members. The occasion when this incident took place, probably in 1819, was during Haldane's attempt to persuade the congregation to allow his brother Robert's wife to join the church without previously being immersed.[99] Archibald Smith, an elder alongside James Haldane at the Tabernacle, clinically exposed the weakness of Haldane's position in a paper prepared for a church meeting in March 1819. After speaking concerning baptism, Smith argued:

> Do you admit that forbearance can be extended to any commandment of Christ? e.g. Can we admit one who denies Salutation to be an Ordinance – or the exhortation of the brethren? Or where is the Scripture warrant for making any one institution, or doctrine, or precept, a matter for forbearance, in preference to another? Does the Word of God leave it at our option or discretion to determine what we shall forbear with or what not ?[100]

The issue was never resolved in the church. It was no surprise when Smith and some other members left the Tabernacle in 1824 to form Clyde Street Hall Church on Scotch Baptist lines.[101] Unfortunately for Smith the issue of forbearance was to cause him as many problems, in the mid-to-late 1830s, as it had done for Haldane in the Tabernacle Church. Smith had been negotiating, in 1836 to 1837, with Henry Dickie and Robert Anderson concerning a possible merger between the Bristo Place and Clyde Street congregations. The negotiations, though, were in difficulties because the Bristo eld-

---

97 Andrew Liddel, Sheffield, to James Everson, Beverley, March 12 1836, MS Letters.
98 A.B. Thomson, *Sketches of Some Baptist Pioneers*, (Glasgow: W. Asher, 1901), p.13.
99 R. Balmain, *Reminiscences of Clyde Street Hall*, (Edinburgh: Private publication, 1893), p. 5.
100 Archibald Smith, 'Discourse on the Issue of Forbearance', March 15 1819, Bundle 4, Waugh Papers.
101 Murray, 'Baptists in Scotland before 1869', p. 259.

ers were unwilling to forbear, despite Smith's appeal, with some of the Clyde Street members who held to Arminian sentiments.[102] At the same time a conflict arose in Clyde Street Hall over whether forbearance ought to be exercised over open versus closed communion. Smith and a small number of other members favoured open communion, but having lost the vote were forced to leave the congregation. Ill health brought about Smith's death within a few months of having to leave his church.[103]

It was easier to remain within the safety of one's own ecclesiastical circles. Robert Anderson, of Bristo Baptist Church, took this viewpoint in his letters, in the mid-1830s, to James Everson. In March 1836 he wrote:

> We are endeavouring to prevail (in conjunction with other churches of our connexion) with some others around us who are much assimilated to us to give up the practice of receiving into occasional fellowship such persons, though themselves baptised, [who] are members of free communion Churches.[104]

Later that year in reply to a letter from Everson, dated October 20, Anderson was quick to deny that his church was serious about uniting with 'English' Baptists. Everson was making it plain that should this be the case they would be dis-fellowshipped by the Beverley Church. 'You are mistaken' [said Anderson] 'in supposing we are hankering after Union with the English Baptists as presently constituted, or throwing down the things which distinguish us from them'.[105] Schism within Scotch Baptist ranks had been extremely painful for all concerned. The inability to exercise forbearance with each other over one or two issues of doctrine or church practice was a fatal flaw in their bond of union. It also had resulted in the fragmentation of a once united body.

These letters by Anderson were written at the time of the second attempt at forming a union of Baptist churches in Scotland, a topic discussed in chapter six. The letters reveal that memories of the first failed attempt were still strong amongst Scotch Baptists. Everson, and others in the stricter party of Scotch Baptists, became staunch defenders of Sandemanian theology after the 1834 split which will be discussed later in this chapter.[106] This was a definite hardening of Everson's position, as he had previously made no comment on

---

102 Correspondence between Smith, Dickie and Anderson, 1836-1837, Bundle 10, Waugh Papers.
103 Balmain, *Reminiscences of Clyde Street Hall*, pp. 24-25.
104 Anderson, Edinburgh, to Everson, Beverley, March 1 1836, MS Letters.
105 Anderson, to Everson, December 8 1836, MS Letters.
106 Murray, 'Scotch Baptist Tradition', p. 194.

Scotch Baptist churches participating in the attempts at union in Scotland. Everson, in addition, was to begin publishing and promoting Sandemanian theological books in the late 1830s.[107] This conservative policy isolated the stricter party amongst the Scotch Baptists to an even greater extent than before. After Everson's death George Chesser, an agent in Aberdeen who sold the items published by Everson, wrote to his widow expressing his condolences and making, in addition, the following remarks:

> ...Christians who endeavour to follow the churches of Judea which were in Christ are laughed at and nicknamed as Sandemanians and Glasites – but we must not be discouraged on this account, remembering that the disciples of Christ have since the dispersion been but a despised few, only a scattered remnant among the nations.[108]

The barriers between the more conservative Scotch Baptists and other Baptists in Scotland were continuing to grow in the 1830s. One illustration of this concerns the removal of James Blair, a full-time elder in the Saltcoats Scotch Baptist Church, to an 'English' church, Ayr Baptist Church, where he held the position of sole pastor. Blair had not sought this position, but the invitation from a wealthy Baptist lawyer, 'a Mr Garrett, who was a judge in the East India Company', though now resident in Ayr, had offered to provide both a stipend for him and cover any expenses incurred in his itinerant labours. Blair had understood this opportunity as God's guidance for the next phase of his ministry.[109] The George Street Scotch Baptist Church in Glasgow, that had supported Blair's ministry until he resigned from the Saltcoats Church in mid-February 1837, was deeply unhappy with his conduct.[110] Andrew Duncan, an elder of the church, gave his opinion in a letter to his friend James Everson.

> Have you heard what has happened at Saltcoats ? Mr Blair, the only pastor of the church there, and the first to join Mr [H.D.] Dickie in his novelties, has had *a call* from a few individuals in Ayr connected with the English Baptists which he has accepted and announced to the church, that he leaves them to join his new connections in Ayr in a few months. The church were confounded

---

107 D. Gordon, Aberdeen, to James Everson, Beverley, August 7 1838, MS Letters.
108 G. Chesser, Aberdeen, to Mrs Everson, Beverley, November 30 and December 7 1853, MS Letters.
109 *The Scottish Evangelist The Life and Labours of the Rev. James Blair*, (Glasgow: George Gallie, 1860), pp. 44-47.
110 Murray, 'Scotch Baptist Tradition', p. 193.

at this unexpected intimation. They took the matter into their consideration, and having remonstrated with Mr Blair on the indecency of his leaving them unprovided and going to join men with whom they were not connected in Christian fellowship proceeded on the second Sabbath to separate him from their communion as an offender against the laws of Christ. Such are the effects flowing from these new views and in no one instance have they been productive of harmony and concord but of confusion and disorder.[111]

James Blair and Henry Dickie, and other more liberal Scotch Baptists, had joined the Baptist Home Missionary Society in association with the Haldaneite and 'English' Baptists in Scotland. The more conservative members of their party were not in favour of any kind of co-operation with other Scottish Baptists even in the work of home evangelism. The Scotch Baptist connexion was in a serious state of disorder in the 1830s. It was split into numerous factions each suspicious of the others and even less inclined to consider union with other Baptists. Some of the details of the divisions in 1810 and 1834 will be explained later in this chapter. Any Scotch Baptist Church co-operating with 'English' Baptists in this decade was doing so in its own name and not in the name of the wider constituency.

The biggest problem that Scotch Baptists faced was not caused by outsiders, but from within their ranks. This was the persistent problem of mutual mistrust. It was, ironically, their own insistence on mutual exhortation, that is the opportunity for any male member to bring a sermon or contribution in worship services without prior approval from the eldership, that left them vulnerable to strange ideas being put forward. As early as March 1774 a group within the church in Edinburgh persistently challenged the official line on a number of points. One individual argued that only real Christians had a duty to pray to God; that the office of elder was not a special position, but that the work of ruling, public teaching, and dispensing the ordinance belonged equally to all the brethren; that neither the apostolic prohibition of blood-eating, nor the observation of the first day of the week were binding upon Christians. This party of eight people appear to have been more interested in drawing attention to themselves than in presenting a considered theological position. After they had left the church they began to advance even more radical ideas including a denial of the deity of Christ.[112] The

---

111 Andrew Duncan, Glasgow, to James Everson, Beverley, February 24 1837, MS Letters.
112 Wilson, *Origin and Progress*, pp. 10-11.

regular presentation of contrasting opinions in congregational worship cannot have assisted either with the harmony or edification of the membership.

These problems were an irritation to the Edinburgh congregation. Other problems were much more serious, especially the doctrinal errors advanced by Neil Stuart, an elder of the Glasgow congregation. He had been promoting the Sabellian belief that there are no personal distinctions in the Godhead. Glasgow Scotch Baptist Church accepted Stuart's ideas as correct doctrine in the spring of 1776. Archibald McLean received news of this development and requested clarification of their beliefs concerning the doctrine of the Trinity. The written response duly arrived and received an even quicker reply from McLean. In his reply McLean quoted extracts from Stuart's letter including this description of the Trinity:

> You say 'That the three names Father, Son (or Word) and Holy Ghost, are not expressive of *three distinct subsistences* in the same Godhead; but of the one undivided Godhead dwelling bodily in the man Christ Jesus – and thus acts in all the characters, relations, and offices implied in these and in every other appellation which he condescends to bear for our complete salvation and consolation.'[113]

McLean using the scriptures recommended by Stuart convincingly destroyed the case that he advanced. The church at Glasgow recognised the strength of McLean's case and changed their view to Socinianism, admitting that the Father and the Son are distinct persons, but affirming that the Godhead is the person of the Father, and the manhood of Christ is the person of the Son. The logic of their case forced them to deny that the Son of God was a divine person or had any existence at all prior to his conception in the virgin Mary.

A conference was organised in Edinburgh to sort out this matter. George Begg and Neil Stuart, the Glasgow elders, committed a breach of a previously agreed protocol by visiting the churches at Dundee and Montrose prior to the conference to argue their case, with a view to gaining their support in Edinburgh. It appears that they had some measure of success because 'they were not altogether disappointed, for they unsettled the minds of several of the brethren at both places, and not a few were entirely subverted'.[114]

When they arrived in Edinburgh, the elders were allowed to state their case. McLean countered the arguments presented with a convincing refutation.

---

113 Letter III 'On Sabellianism', Jones (ed.), *Works of Archibald McLean*, III, (pp. 497-508), p. 499.
114 Rippon, *Baptist Annual Register*, 1795, pp. 365-366.

Neil Stuart exposed himself sufficiently by such arbitrary and unnatural glosses as flatly contradicted the plain sense and scope of the sacred text; but, being closely pressed with these and similar passages, he found himself shut up and was at last sunk into silence.[115]

George Begg later admitted the error of his ways, as did many of the other members of the Glasgow Church. The Dundee and Montrose churches also regained most of the members who had adopted the views of Neil Stuart. In the end there were only three people, one of whom was Stuart, who remained outside the connexion after the resolution of this controversy.[116]

Another doctrinal controversy that arose in the Edinburgh congregation in 1777 was over the nature of Christ's Sonship. Was Christ the eternal Son of God or just the Son of the eternal God? Robert Walker advanced the view that Christ was the eternal Son of God – but to no avail. The influence of McLean was decisive. He insisted that Christ was not the Son until He appeared in the flesh. His congregation dutifully accepted the position he propounded.[117] This view was maintained by Scotch Baptists long after McLean's death. James Williamson in his reminiscences of life in the Pleasance Church from the 1820s recorded the interview of a friend who had made an application for church membership.

> An old Aberdonian weaver, Mr T. – always took the 'opportunity' of putting the question, 'What did the candidate think of the "pairson" [person] and "dig-nae-tee" [dignity] of Christ ?' This was a poser to a chum of mine, Walter Wilson, who having been brought up a Presbyterian, answered, that He was the 'eternal Son of God'. This answer was quite heterodox, according to McLean theology; so Walter, like Apollos, had to be instructed in the way more perfectly.[118]

This unfortunate episode between McLean and Walker deprived the church of the valuable services of their elder Robert Walker who continued to hold firmly to his beliefs. He published a *Defence of the Doctrine of the Trinity and Eternal Sonship of Christ* in 1787. McLean replied to this by publishing his *Letter on the Sonship of Christ*, which was written at the time of the dispute in the church. He added to it a review of Walker's arguments as presented in the former elder's book. McLean, to his credit, had offered to forbear on this subject if Robert Walker had also agreed to remain silent, both in the pulpit

---

115 Wilson, *Origin and Progress*, p. 13.
116 Wilson, *Origin and Progress*, pp. 14-17.
117 Wilson, *Origin and Progress*, pp. 17-18.
118 Williamson, *Old Baptist Church Pleasance*, p. 15.

and in the press. The difficulty Scotch Baptists encountered on many occasions was that on an issue that one person believed was suitable for forbearance, another person held that it was too vital to compromise, resulting in an inevitable division.

One very important issue and probably the 'Achilles heel' of Scotch Baptists was the question of the relationship between the Lord's Supper and the eldership. The answers to the following questions were sought very carefully, especially over the situation at Newburgh, in the period 1780 to 1810: Is an elder required for an act of communion to take place ? What number of people are required to constitute a church for this purpose ? Is a church set in order if there is only one elder ? These were important issues, not merely academic questions, as they had a practical bearing upon life in the churches. Small societies not set in church order were permitted to receive communion only at the Edinburgh church. Naturally the distance was a major obstacle to attendance in Edinburgh on Sundays. So the question began to be raised, why could Christians observe every part of divine worship in their locality except communion ?

William Hynd, a member at Newburgh, claimed that it was the duty of disciples to observe the Lord's Supper wherever two or three of them could meet together, although they were not furnished with elders or set in church order. There were several people in Newburgh that were convinced by his arguments; others, though, were persuaded that there was a need to examine this matter. As a result of this discussion in Newburgh a letter was sent to the Edinburgh church for its deliberation. At the Edinburgh church meeting Charles Stuart and George Grieve, two members who were former ministers, argued that the position of Hynd was weak, but in any case it ought to be a matter of forbearance. A local church had the responsibility to make up its own mind on this matter. This flexible approach was similar to that which Andrew Fuller had recommended in his exchange of letters with McLean in 1796.[119] McLean and the rest of the church, however, maintained that the Lord's Supper belonged only to a regular constituted church. The decision was strongly contested by those who held the opposing viewpoint. Hynd was ordered on three occasions to come to Edinburgh and argue his case but he refused to accept the invitations. As a result he was excommunicated by a majority vote of the Edinburgh church. Charles Stuart and one other person were also put out for objecting forcefully to the decision to expel Hynd. George Grieve then withdrew from the church because he felt the whole situation had been

---

119 Belcher (ed.), *Andrew Fuller*, III, p. 480.

unwisely handled. It appeared as though the matter was now settled in the connexion. The departure of some valuable members, whom they could hardly afford to lose, appeared to be the only long-term consequence of this controversy. This vexatious affair was concluded in April 1784.[120] J. Idwal Jones, a twentieth-century Scotch Baptist elder in North Wales, discussed the various arguments put forward in Scotch Baptist journals and concluded that a great deal of energy was wasted on futile attempts to insist that the Bible spoke conclusively in favour of either case.[121]

Scotch Baptists in this era were quick to censure other Baptists, but were equally swift in paying attention to the perceived failings of their brethren. There is no doubt that personality clashes were at the heart of some of the divisions, such as the one in the Nottingham church in the summer of 1827, at least according to Andrew Scott, a member of the Niddry Street Church, in Edinburgh, who attempted to reconcile the parties but without success.[122] Other tensions were caused by eccentric individuals, such as William Clark from Bath. He led a controversy over the use of Bible commentaries and theological books, both in his own congregation and in the connexion. He claimed that it was man's wisdom that was the cause of all the troubles in the church. William Jones, one of the targets of Clark's criticism, was quick to point out the inconsistencies in his argument in a letter sent to Clark in 1830.

> Where would you yourself have been in all human probability at this moment, had it not been for human writings on the faith and obedience of the Gospel... You had been drenched up to the ears in the dregs of Methodism but by the blessing of God your attention was called to the Holy Scriptures – and they were eminently useful in freeing you from the doctrine and commandments of men – as you yourself have repeatedly acknowledged to me.[123]

Clark had been followed by sixteen other members of the Bath church in this controversy. Everson, who was a long-suffering recipient of his letters, was solemnly rebuked for being part of a society that promoted a perverted gospel. This tirade increased after Ever-

---

120 Wilson, *Origin and Progress*, pp. 19-23.
121 J. Idwal Jones, 'Essay on Early Doctrinal Differences amongst Scotch Baptists mainly in the period 1780-1810 and largely revolving around the question of the Celebration of the Lord's Supper', MS Letters.
122 Andrew Scott, Manchester, to John Charlton, Beverley, September 3 1827, MS Letters.
123 Cited by William Clark, Bath, to James Everson, Monmouth, April 1 1830, MS Letters.

son had suggested, very politely, that Clark was being rather narrow-minded. It was ironic, in view of the nature of the controversy, that the remedy that Clark had for Everson's difficulties was as follows: 'I have sent you the book I named :- two hours' attention to it every day for three months will have removed the principal difficulties...'. Clark, a classics teacher, was recommending a book on Greek grammar, but it was without doubt produced by man's wisdom! In his letter to Everson dated May 1827 Clark's closing words sum up the situation that he and many other Scotch Baptists faced: 'I beg my warmest respects to the few friends among you who are like minded...'[124]

Another problem that Scotch Baptists seemed unable to handle was church discipline. There appeared to be conflicting opinions as to whether it was right to become involved in the problems of other churches. A dispute in the London church in the mid-1830s was the context in which Andrew Duncan from Glasgow and William Pattison of Edinburgh tried to effect a resolution. William Jones, an elder of the London church, was extremely unimpressed by Duncan and Pattison's motives and actions. He told James Everson: 'he [Andrew Duncan] and William Pattison are too proud to acknowledge their error in meddling with our discipline as they did...'[125] It is clear that on occasions the disciplinary measures meted out were too severe. An example of this took place in the Haggate church in 1839. There was a church split over some unnamed matter which resulted in both sides appealing to the Beverley and Glasgow churches. The Glasgow church had no hesitation in condemning the eighteen individuals for leaving the church but reserved its main criticism for the rest of the church for their unduly harsh disciplinary measures.[126]

Scotch Baptists entered the nineteenth century in Scotland expecting to make significant progress in the propagation of their principles and practices. It was, ironically, as a result of church growth that the fatal difficulty arose upon which they were to founder. This can be illustrated from the life of the Perth church. In April 1808 James Murray and John Macfarlane were appointed elders of a church consisting of only twelve members. The church grew rapidly in the next few years by additions from the Old Scotch Independents and the Tabernacle connexion church in the town. In 1810

---

124 William Clark, Bath, to James Everson, Monmouth, May 24 1827, MS Letters.
125 William Jones, London, to James Everson, Beverley, September 12 1837, MS Letters.
126 Andrew Duncan, Andrew Liddel & Richard Duncan, Glasgow, to James Everson, Beverley, May 21 1839, MS Letters.

the church had eighty members, four elders, four deacons, and two preachers. These incomers were now convinced of believer's baptism but not necessarily of all the other views of Scotch Baptists. This mixture of theological backgrounds was an explosive mixture with the potential for a violent eruption. In 1810 trouble arose over the question of whether elders were essential to the observance of the Lord's Supper, chiefly instigated by individuals who had joined the Scotch Baptists from Haldaneite churches.[127] William Jones in his *Memoirs* blames the Haldane brothers for the havoc this controversy had brought in 1810, and again in 1834. He criticised them because they had set up their own churches rather than joining existing Scotch Baptist churches, and because, 'they had broached several novel principles amongst which was the sentiment that the Elder's Office was not essential to the organisation of a Church of Christ...that the Lord's Supper was competent to the lowest plurality'.[128] Jones' criticism was excessive, but it revealed that Scotch Baptists were already struggling to adapt to the changing religious climate. Other churches were modifying their theological positions in line with the growing tolerance for a diversity of opinions within a denominational framework. One example of this trend was the Baptist Union of Great Britain and Ireland which changed its constitution in 1832 from an exclusively Calvinistic one to a more inclusive evangelical position to allow evangelical General Baptists to affiliate.[129] Scotch Baptists in contrast to this trend revealed a growing rigidity in their outlook that hindered both their ability to work with each other and any opportunities for wider union with other Scottish Baptists. In a context where Scotch Baptists were the only Baptist stream it was easier to maintain their distinctive theological position. The presence of Baptists with other sentiments joining their congregations provided an unwelcome test regarding the limits of their willingness to exercise forbearance. It was an ominous sign for the future of the connexion.

The result of this controversy in 1810 was minor in Edinburgh, as on the previous occasion when this issue flared up in 1784 and had resulted in the expulsion of William Hynd of Newburgh from the connexion, but elsewhere the story was very different. In Glasgow 160 members left the church with James Watt to form a new congregation, because they could not accept the Edinburgh church's view that elders had to be present in order for the Lord's Supper to

---

127 Wilson, *Origin and Progress*, p. 56.
128 William Jones, *Autobiography*, p.36.
129 J.B. Pike and J.C. Pike (eds), *A Memoir and Remains of the late Rev. John Gregory Pike*, (London: Jarrold And Sons, 1855), p. 247.

be observed. The churches in Dundee and Aberdeen also each split into two societies. The churches in Paisley, Dunfermline, Liverpool and a few other places embraced the new views and had no further fellowship with their more conservative brethren. An annual circular of 1822 giving statistics of the recognised Scotch Baptist churches reveals the extent of the 1810 division. The returns are accurate up to August 1821. There were thirty Scotch Baptist churches known to have been founded by 1821. The names of only seventeen of these appear on the list, implying that almost half of the churches favoured the new sentiments and as a result had left the connexion. The remaining churches were Beverley, Dundee, Edinburgh, Ford Forge, Galashiels, Glasgow, Kirkcaldy, Largo, London, Musselburgh, Newburgh, Nottingham, Perth, Stirling, Wooler, Aberdeen and Allerdean. The aggregate membership of these churches was given as 991. The churches that had left still regarded themselves as Scotch Baptists. As they had adopted more flexible practices the prospect of union with other types of Baptists had become a more realistic proposition. In fact, the withdrawal of the opportunities for fellowship with a connexion they had valued appeared to make it more likely that these liberal Scotch Baptists would seek to build bridges towards Haldaneite and 'English' Baptists in Scotland.[130] The members of the churches that remained in the main body faced a great deal of discouragement. In the next twenty years only two new churches, Leeds in 1833 and Haggate in 1834, joined the connexion. However, an attempt was made to heal the breach when the Edinburgh and Paisley churches attempted to resume normal relations. This proposal in 1831 fell through as each wished to retain its theological differences and was unwilling to exercise forbearance with the other church.

It was ironic that it was the reunion of the two Aberdeen churches in 1834 that was to cause the fatal blow to unity amongst the Scotch Baptists. These two small societies had felt that it was foolish to stand apart from each other. The basis of union, however, was that members of both churches could maintain their links with the respective groups of churches to which they had formerly belonged. If both had agreed to be in fellowship with only one connexion then they would have had no problems. Their decision, instead of producing harmony amongst the churches, re-awakened controversy over the whole question of communion and the place of elders in the church. This re-opening of debate on these controversial matters

---

130 T.W. Davies, 'A Scotch Baptist Circular', *Transactions of the Baptist Historical Society*, 5, (1916-1917), pp. 251-257.

should not be taken to mean that there had been no discussion of these issues between 1810 and 1834. William Jones had stirred up the controversy in an anonymous article in the *New Evangelical Magazine* in 1816 in which he strongly defended the conservative position. He had conveniently ignored the fact that he had argued for the more liberal position in the *Theological Repository* in 1807-1808. 'Let Christians, therefore, beware of casting one another out of their charity merely on the grounds of a difference of sentiment respecting it [the need for elders at the Lord's Table]'. J. Idwal Jones concluded that in the period after this article William Jones' attitude hardened until the impression was given that it had become an obsession. If Scotch Baptists, including the London elder, had heeded Jones' plea for tolerance in 1807 then the divisions might have been less painful or have been avoided altogether on this issue.[131]

The church in Edinburgh was divided over this matter for the first time in 1834. The majority of members led by elder Henry Dickie remained in the church. A minority of members led by elders William Pattison and John Horsburgh left to organise a new church that was to meet in Minto House in Edinburgh. The differences between them were set out in the printed circulars which both parties sent out to the churches that had been in fellowship with Edinburgh. The manifesto of the majority party stated:

> We desire it to be understood, that we do not approve of the practice of eating the Lord's supper without the presence of an elder, – all we plead for, is forbearance with those churches who think they may do lawfully, and with such of our brethren as may find themselves at liberty to do so when assembled with such churches.

The circular reaffirmed the traditional understanding of what constituted a church set in order and the importance of elders within the church and of the Lord's Supper as exclusively a church ordinance. The issue of forbearance was again the dividing line. The chaos in Edinburgh was replicated in other parts of the connexion. The churches in Glasgow and Dundee divided, with one party adhering to either side in Edinburgh. The churches in Kirkcaldy, Anstruther, Saltcoats, Nottingham and Leeds remained in fellowship with the majority group in Edinburgh. The churches in Newburgh, Largo, Stirling, Galashiels, Wooler, Beverley and Haggate supported the minority party.[132]

---

131 *Theological Repository*, 5, 1807, p. 229. *New Evangelical Magazine*, 2, 1816, pp. 238-241. J. Idwal Jones, 'Essay in Early Doctrinal Differences', MS Letters.
132 Wilson, *Origin and Progress*, pp. 79-80.

A letter of William Jones sent to James Everson in June 1836 aptly summarises the situation. Jones gives a quotation from a letter he had recently received from Andrew Liddel who was a member of the Glasgow church.

> The late uncalled for division seems to have paralysed the energies of both parties. Some of those who were most forward in bringing on the discussion ... are now heartily vexed at seeing the results that have followed particularly the disorders that prevail amongst the churches in connexion with Mr Dickie of Edinburgh.

It was unfortunate that Liddel had no remedies to suggest for the resolution of this problem. He proceeded in his letter to give vent to his anger at the person whom he perceived as the major cause of the Scotch Baptist division.

> Well! this is just what I anticipated – fools must be whipped to teach them wisdom. Except Dr [James] Watt of Glasgow there has not arisen a more mischievous person amongst the Scotch Baptists, from their commencement than Henry Dickie of Edinburgh!!![133]

Henry Dickie, one of the elders of the Edinburgh church, had persuaded the majority of that congregation to adopt a more tolerant position than his conservative critics would accept, in line with the liberal position taken by James Watt in the 1810 division. Andrew Liddel and his friends could offer trenchant criticism of the Edinburgh elder, but no practical alternative approach to rescue Scotch Baptists from their difficulties.

Scotch Baptists were ensnaring themselves deeper and deeper in the mires of division. They appeared to be more interested in criticising each other than in getting on with the normal work and tasks at the heart of life in a local congregation. The 1834 division in this connexion led to the more liberal party, led by the Bristo Church, Edinburgh, to draw closer to the other Baptist streams in Scotland. The stricter party, led by the Minto House congregation, withdrew into even more restrictive opinions. The ranks of this later group diminished in the decades that followed leading to the closure of some churches and the merger of others with the congregations from which they had seceded, for example the two Edinburgh congregations in 1875.[134]

In the period from 1765 to 1834 the Scotch Baptists had made considerable progress. They had appeared to lay a strong foundation for the future by their constant measures aimed at maintaining

---

133 William Jones, London, to James Everson, Beverley, June 24 1836, MS Letters.
134 Yuille (ed.), *Baptists in Scotland*, p. 121.

union between the churches in the connexion. Archibald McLean, an elder in the Edinburgh congregation, was the major bond of union between the different congregations. Great care was taken over the reception of new members into local congregations and over churches into their wider fellowship. Archibald McLean sought to broaden the horizons of the churches by urging them to co-operate in evangelism in Scotland and by supporting the English Particular Baptist Mission in India. Scotch Baptists in Glasgow had gone further than McLean had done when they united with some Baptists who had Haldaneite connections to form the Baptist Highland Mission in 1816. This co-operative venture in home evangelism pointed forward to the greater unity amongst Baptists in Scotland that would become a reality in the next decade. There had been problems in and between the churches but it did appear that the difficulties were being overcome prior to 1834.

There were many obstacles that prevented Scotch Baptists from uniting with other Baptists in Scotland. The most important reason was an inability to exercise forbearance on almost any matter by a large minority of the connexion. It is ironic that the same factor was the most significant issue in tearing their own union asunder in 1834. This unresolved problem had been raised on a number of occasions without a satisfactory answer. It was not too difficult for the connexion to stand firm against Socinianism, but the mistake was made in assuming that all other contentious matters could also be brought to a swift conclusion. In the 1830s some Scotch Baptists were keen to work with the 'English' Baptists in Britain whilst others were drawn to the even more conservative Churches of Christ. This led to a loss of identity within the movement as different sections of it were pulling in opposing directions. The inevitable result was division between Baptists who no longer had 'all things in common'. The final blow to any pretence of unity amongst Scotch Baptists came with the division in 1834, officially, over the necessity of elders presiding at the Lord's Table. It was, in reality, an acknowledgement that their basis of union could not survive in an era of changing theological opinions. Scotch Baptists had been imprisoned by their past and had consequently been unable, as a body, to come to terms with a changing religious environment in Britain. There were some conservative Scotch Baptists like John Cowan, an elder of the Galashiels church, who had come to regret the opportunities that the connexion had failed to grasp in earlier years. He stated:

> Our churches will never be what they have been, I fear – if indeed they long survive. Other connexions are occupying the fields which I am convinced we might have occupied had we been

properly alive to our duty. But let us not despair nor faint in the Lord's work. His end will be secured independently of man.[135]

The Baptists who had striven hardest to maintain fellowship with one another ended up losing the grounds of their own unity. The Scotch Baptist tradition had contributed much to Baptist life in Scotland. It was, however, destined to play only a minor part in the future due to disunity within its own ranks.

---

135 John Cowan, Galashiels, to James Everson, Beverley, December 11 1848, MS Letters.

CHAPTER 3

The Haldanes and the Haldaneite Baptists, 1794-1851

3.1 The Early Years

The Haldaneite Baptists were the third Baptist stream to emerge in Scotland. This group of men was identified by its links with Robert and James Haldane. There were some individuals such as George Barclay and Christopher Anderson who accepted Baptist principles earlier than the Haldane brothers, but the major turning point occurred in 1808 when the two gentlemen became convinced of Baptist principles. It is from that point onwards that a distinctive Haldaneite grouping of Baptists emerged to play an important role in the wider Scottish Baptist constituency. This chapter will compare and contrast the views of Robert and James Haldane regarding Baptist union, in relation to the men associated with, and in some cases dependent on, their patrons. There will then be an attempt to evaluate why the Haldaneites showed a greater desire for a union of churches than either of the two leaders of their network.

Robert Haldane was born on February 28 1764 in his father's house in London. His younger brother James Alexander Haldane was born four years later in Dundee, on July 14 1768, within two weeks of the death of his father, Captain James Haldane of Airthrey. The two brothers were descended through both parents from an ancient Perthshire family that possessed the free barony of Gleneagles. The loss of their mother, Catherine Duncan, only six years later resulted in their being placed under the guardianship of her brothers Lieutenant-Colonel Alexander Duncan of Lundie, and Adam, Viscount Duncan. After education at Edinburgh High School the two brothers chose careers at sea. Robert entered the Royal Navy and James the East India Company, where he rose to the rank of captain. The older brother left the navy in 1783 and resumed his studies at Edinburgh University before settling on his estate at Airthrey, near Stirling, for over ten years prior to his evangelical conversion in 1794.[1] Early plans, while still a teenager, to train as a Church of Scotland minister had been dismissed after others in his

---

1   A. Haldane, *The Lives of Robert and James Haldane*, (Edinburgh: Banner of Truth, 1990 [1853]), pp. 1-45.

social circles explained that a man of his wealth and standing ought not to consider a career in the church.² The decision to enter the navy and later to give attention to his estate appeared to indicate that Christian beliefs would not play a prominent place in his future career.

Robert, as an adult, had paid little attention to religious matters until the French Revolution caused him to think deeply about the future direction of his own life. Conversations with William Shirreff and William Innes, evangelical clergymen in the Established Church in Stirling, led him in 1794 to 'accept the truth as it is in Jesus'.³ In the same year whilst in command of the 'Melville Castle', a ship in the East India fleet, James Haldane also accepted the Christian faith and resolved to leave his command.⁴ The younger brother and his wife eventually purchased a house in George Square, Edinburgh. At that time they attended the Canongate Parish Church where Dr Walter Buchanan was the minister.⁵ This Edinburgh clergyman was a significant influence in the promotion of the evangelical cause in the capital city and of preaching tours throughout Scotland. Charles Simeon, the prominent Anglican evangelical clergyman from Cambridge, said of Buchanan that 'it [was] one of the greatest blessings of my life ever to have known [him]'.⁶ The conversion to evangelical Christianity was the turning point in the lives of these two brothers. The spreading of their new-found faith would in future take precedence over other career goals.⁷

3.2 The Influence of Prominent Ministers in England

The future Christian service performed by Robert and James Haldane, and their opinions regarding denominational structures, including schemes for Baptist union, were profoundly influenced by a number of prominent ministers based in England. David Bogue met the Haldane brothers during their time of naval service in the late 1770s and 1780s. Bogue, born in Berwickshire and edu-

---

2   Haldane, *Robert and James Haldane*, p. 22.
3   R. Haldane, *Address to the Public concerning Political Opinions and Plans lately adopted to Promote Religion in Scotland*, (Edinburgh: J. Ritchie, 1800), pp. 7-13.
4   R. Kinniburgh, *Fathers of Independency in Scotland*, (Edinburgh: A. Fullarton & Co., 1851), pp. 456-457.
5   Haldane, *Robert and James Haldane*, p. 74. For details on Buchanan's career see D.F. Kelly, 'Buchanan, Walter (1755-1832)', in Cameron (ed.), *Scottish Church History and Theology*, p. 108.
6   W. Carus, *Memoirs of The Life of the Rev. Charles Simeon M.A.*, (London: J. Hatchard & Son, 1847), p. 112.
7   Haldane, *Robert and James Haldane*, pp. 97-98.

cated in Edinburgh for the Church of Scotland ministry, accepted a call in 1777 from an Independent congregation in Gosport, Hampshire.[8] Gosport was the headquarters of Admiral Lord Duncan between 1779 and 1787. When granted shore leave, Robert and James often stayed with their uncle, and during those visits attended Bogue's church.[9] Bogue was a man of vision involved in many projects designed to promote the Christian faith. In 1780 he established a new seminary for the training of ministers for Independent churches. The course of study closely related evangelistic labours at home to the academic curriculum. The Gosport minister in 1781 helped found the Hampshire Association of Independent Churches, the first of its kind, in order to promote systematically itinerant mission activities in the county. In addition, Bogue, inspired by the Baptist work in Bengal, was one of the earliest paedobaptist ministers to promote the cause of overseas mission, and was one of those individuals instrumental in the establishment of the London Missionary Society in 1795. He was also responsible in the 1790s for the preparation of missionaries for overseas service.[10] The importance of Bogue for the future development of the Haldanes' thinking is clear in each of these areas. He encouraged Robert Haldane in the proposals for service in Bengal, a plan that also included, amongst others, Greville Ewing, the assistant minister of Lady Glenorchy's Chapel, Edinburgh, and William Innes.[11] His establishment of an academy for training preachers was the inspiration for the training classes established later by the Haldanes in Scotland, in both their Independent and their Baptist circles.[12] The Hampshire Association was also the model used by the Haldanes for their own Scottish society for home evangelism, the Society for Propagating the Gospel at Home (SPGH) in 1797.[13]

There were also two Church of England clergymen that played an important part in shaping the future direction of the ministries of Robert and James Haldane, namely Charles Simeon, minister of Holy Trinity Church, Cambridge, and Rowland Hill, minister of Surrey Chapel, London, a proponent of a non-denominational 'catholic' Christianity. The significance of this influence was to lead the Haldanes to place a lower priority on the importance of denom-

---

8 S. Piggin, 'Bogue, David (1750-1825)', in Cameron (ed.), *Scottish Church History and Theology*, p. 83.
9 Haldane, *Robert and James Haldane*, p. 32.
10 J.H.Y. Briggs, 'Bogue, David', in Lewis (ed.), *DEB*, I, p. 115.
11 Haldane, *Robert and James Haldane*, pp. 97-123.
12 Haldane, *Robert and James Haldane*, p. 233.
13 Haldane, *Robert and James Haldane*, p. 193.

inational unity, and greater emphasis on the wider evangelical sphere. In their correspondence Hill and Simeon played down church unions, preferring to concentrate on the work of evangelism. Charles Simeon, in a letter from Cambridge dated April 1798, included these lines on this subject:

> As for more union among the different parties of Christians, I do not expect to see it. "Every man", said Luther, "has a Pope in his own belly". People of different sentiments may coalesce for a time, but there are few who will not be endeavouring to proselyte others.[14]

Simeon endeavoured to avoid causing offence to his fellow Christians during his preaching tours in Scotland. The proclamation of the gospel was the priority, church order was of secondary importance. Simeon declared: 'I officiated precisely as they do in the Kirk of Scotland: and I did so upon this principle; Presbyterianism is as much the established religion in North Britain, as Episcopacy is in the South'.[15] A similar policy, to be discussed later in this chapter, was adopted by Robert Haldane in his relations with continental Protestants.[16]

The influence of Rowland Hill was to be felt primarily in the network of churches that would be established by the Haldanes in the first decade of the nineteenth century. He urged them to promote an undenominational Christianity that was not limited by sectarian boundaries. It is likely that James Haldane's preference for an open table and open membership in the Tabernacle Church, Edinburgh, was linked to this vision of reducing the divisions between evangelical Christians.[17] Hill's venture into print in the autumn of 1797 was a mixed blessing. This booklet was his 'Journal' written while on a recent tour of Scotland, and was dedicated primarily to Robert Haldane, but also included a letter to his brother James. In this letter Hill expressed support for the younger Haldane's work, in his own unmistakable style:

> Go on, my dear Sir, be the maul of bigotry, and of every sectarian spirit among all denominations; declare vengeance against the unscriptural innovations of narrow-minded bigots, who, finding the Word of God uncompliant to designs like theirs, have combined together to support their dogmas, according to certain

---

14   Haldane, *Robert and James Haldane*, p. 198.
15   Carus, *Charles Simeon*, p. 113.
16   Haldane, *Robert and James Haldane*, pp. 460-461, 483.
17   'Some Baptist Pioneers in Scotland during the Eighteenth Century and the early years of the Nineteenth', *Scottish Baptist Yearbook* (Glasgow: W. Asher, 1902), p. 20.

modes of their own creating; and all these as contrary to the sacred designs of God, that all should be brethren and love as such, as the designs of Christianity can be to those of Mahomet, the Pope, or the devil.[18]

Hill proceeded to criticise in a most blunt manner the bigotry of the different denominations in Scotland, castigating them all for their faults. This was hardly a means of winning friends and influencing people, nor was it likely to be beneficial to his friend's cause. His model clergyman was 'The Right Rev. Bishop Bunyan, the apostle of Cambridgeshire and Bedfordshire [who] though a Baptist admitted all to communion with him whom he believed to be the children of God'.[19] The itinerant labours of Rowland Hill in Scotland had occurred as a result of the invitations sent to him by Robert Haldane.[20] It is probable that Haldane had hoped that his visitor's presence would increase support for the work of non-denominational evangelism, but Hill's dogmatic style almost certainly proved more of a hindrance than a source of assistance.

The key part of the journal considered Hill's advice regarding the advancement of the cause of Christ in Scotland.

> If [he says] in Edinburgh another place of worship should be built, what should be its glory? Let it embrace all who love the Lord Jesus, and be the centre of union among them who are now disunited. Let it, then, be called the Union Church, and let her prove she deserves the name. Let her pulpit be open to all ministers who preach and love the Gospel, and her communion equally open to all who love the Lord Jesus in sincerity. I would allot at least half the area of the church to the poor, that they may attend it with as much freedom as they attend a field preaching.

It was Hill who inspired Robert Haldane to open a series of independent Tabernacles for the unfettered preaching of the gospel in various towns and cities in Scotland.[21] In the light of this advice it is significant to note the similarities between the opinions expressed by Hill and a statement made by James Haldane, when the first Tabernacle was opened in Edinburgh, in February 1799. Haldane stated:

> It was, in fact, no separation from the Establishment. It was

---

18 W. Jones, *Memoirs of the Life, Ministry, and Writings of the Rev. Rowland Hill, M.A.*, (London: John Bennett, 1834), pp. 57-59.

19 'Review of *Journal through the North of England, and parts of Scotland; with remarks on the present state of the Established Church of Scotland, and the different secessions therefrom*, by Rowland Hill, *The Missionary Magazine*, 38 (June, 1799), p. 271.

20 Jones, *Rowland Hill*, p. 46.

21 Haldane, *Robert and James Haldane*, pp. 226-231.

merely opening another place of worship for preaching the Gospel without regard to forms of external arrangement or church order, and where the pastor and many of the members showed their catholic spirit by going to the sacrament in the Established Church. Add to this, that the preaching was almost entirely addressed to the people of the world.[22]

The advice received by the Haldane brothers from their Anglican visitors confirmed their catholicity, as modern historians affirm.[23] This undenominational vision of the future for evangelical Christianity, in the late 1790s, may have appeared to be naive, but it was sincerely held and earnestly promulgated. It ensured that when Robert and James Haldane became Baptists their main focus was on evangelical Christian unity more than union amongst Scottish Baptists.

3.3 The Work of The Society for the Propagation of the Gospel at Home

An excellent example of the Haldanes' vision of Christian work in Scotland is seen in the work of the SPGH.[24] This society was set up in 1797 to engage in itinerant evangelism throughout Scotland, especially in those areas where the evangelical witness was at its weakest. The inspiration for this organisation had come from David Bogue, with whom the Haldanes had maintained contact ever since their first visits to his church in Gosport. William Ballantyne, John Cleghorn and Joseph Rate, colleagues with whom James Haldane itinerated in Scotland, were trained under Bogue in Gosport.[25] The SPGH was constituted on December 20 1797. It had twelve directors, all of whom were laymen, and nine of them engaged in secular pursuits. It was a deliberate policy decision not to have any ministers on the committee so as to ensure its inter-denominational character. 'It is not our design to form or to extend the influence of any sect. Our sole intention is to make known the Evangelical Gospel of our Lord Jesus Christ.'[26] The SPGH committee members

---

22 Haldane, *Robert and James Haldane*, p. 354.
23 J. MacInnes, *The Evangelical Movement in the Highlands of Scotland 1688 to 1800*, (Aberdeen: Aberdeen University Press, 1951), p. 128. C.G. Brown, *Religion and Society in Scotland since 1707*, (Edinburgh: Edinburgh University Press, 1997), p. 88.
24 A recent paper on the SPGH by D.W. Lovegrove is 'A set of men whose proceedings threaten no small disorder': The Society for Propagating the Gospel at Home, 1798-1808', *The Scottish Historical Review*, 79.207 (April, 2000), pp. 61-81.
25 *The Edinburgh Quarterly Magazine*, I (1798), p. 160.

were aware that some denominations required their ministers to preach either solely within their parish or within licensed church premises. Itinerant preachers for this society were expected to take the Christian message to wherever the people could be found. Presbyterian or Episcopalian clergymen might have objected to their strategy had any of them been on the committee. Charles Simeon, in a private letter to James Haldane, dated April 1798, sought to encourage him in his itinerant work, but regretted that as an Anglican minister he had to preach only in Presbyterian and Episcopalian pulpits on his forthcoming visit to Scotland.[27] The wholly lay character of the SPGH was unusual in Scotland. The long-established Society in Scotland for Propagating Christian Knowledge had always had a significant clerical presence on its committee. The Edinburgh and Glasgow Missionary Societies had also allowed ministers a place on their governing body.[28] It is noticeable, though, that apart from Walter Buchanan, its clerical secretary, the Edinburgh Missionary Society had twenty-one laymen as its other named committee members and directors in 1799.[29] The employees of the SPGH were deliberately chosen from a variety of denominational backgrounds. The sole determining factor was their commitment to evangelical Christianity. A very similar model of a society entirely composed of lay-leaders from different ecclesiological backgrounds was also adopted by the British and Foreign Bible Society (BFBS) in 1803-1804.[30] The first catechist employed by the SPGH was a member of the Antiburgher Synod, in Orkney, called Magnus

---

26 Haldane, *Robert and James Haldane*, p. 193. See also D.M. Thompson, *Denominationalism and Dissent, 1795-1835: A Question of Identity*, (London: Dr Williams Trust, 1985), pp. 10-11, for further comments on the significance of laypeople serving as leaders in the management of interdenominational societies.

27 Haldane, *Robert and James Haldane*, pp. 198-199.

28 D.W. Lovegrove, 'Unity and Separation: Contrasting elements in the thought of Robert and James Alexander Haldane', in K. Robbins (ed.), *Protestant Evangelicalism: Britain, Ireland, Germany and America c.1750 – c.1950*, (Oxford: B. Blackwell, 1990), p. 155. The 'Baptist Society in London for the Encouragement and Support of Itinerant and Village Preaching', formed in February 1797, had no official rules about the composition of its committee, but the majority of its members were laymen, for example, in 1799 there were nineteen laymen and ten pastors on the committee, revealing a stronger clerical presence than in these Scottish bodies. R.P. Roberts, *Continuity and Change London Calvinistic Baptists and The Evangelical Revival 1760-1820*, (Wheaton, Illinois: Richard Owen Roberts Publishers, 1989), p. 206.

29 *Missionary Magazine*, (April 1799), p. 188.

Anderson. The next worker engaged, Hugh Ross, was a Gaelic-speaking catechist who was based in Perthshire. He had gathered a large Sabbath school at Dunkeld. As an itinerant, however, he was unable to attend as regularly as the Dunkeld congregation desired so the Society asked the Relief Church to take responsibility for the work.[31] The named individuals who had offered to receive subscriptions for the work of the SPGH included Andrew Duncan, a Scotch Baptist bookseller from Glasgow, and George Cowie, the Antiburgher minister in Huntly.[32] It must be noted that the leaders of the SPGH were members of the Church of Scotland. Even in the earliest days of this society, therefore, the Haldanes and their colleagues were demonstrating that they held to a 'catholic' view of Christianity.

This understanding of the Haldanes' approach to ministry was confirmed by the private correspondence of James Haldane with his son who was based in London. In 1822, James wrote:

> I see plainly...that, although at present there are many defects in all parties, we ought to love all who love the Lord Jesus Christ, and that our love to them ought to abound in proportion as we see the great features of the kingdom of God, righteousness and peace and joy in the Holy Ghost, abounding in them; and when these are observed, it ought to enable us to throw a mantle of love over their defects.

This extract from a letter came from an era after the Haldane brothers had hardened their stance on matters of church order and government.[33] It is, therefore, clear confirmation of the spirit that had motivated their earlier ministry.

This 'catholic' Christianity was not confined to Scotland. In England inter-denominational co-operation in evangelism was also taking place in the late 1790s.[34] One of the best known examples of this kind of venture took place in Bedfordshire with the establishment

---

30 R.H. Martin, *Evangelicals United: Ecumenical Stirrings in Pre-Victorian Britain 1795-1830*, (Metuchen, New Jersey: The Scarecrows Press, 1983), p. 86.
31 *An Account of the Proceedings of The Society for Propagating the Gospel at Home from their commencement, December 28, 1797, to May 16, 1799*, (Edinburgh: J. Ritchie, 1799), pp. 15-20.
32 *Account of the Proceedings of The Society for Propagating the Gospel*, 1799, p. 96.
33 W. Landels, 'In the days of the Haldanes', in N.L.Walker (ed.), *Religious Life in Scotland from the Reformation to the present Day*, (London: T. Nelson and Sons, 1888), p. 165.

of 'The Bedfordshire Union of Christians'.³⁵ This organisation was certainly not one of the earliest of its kind, but it is probably the scheme that lasted the longest, even if in the twentieth century only the Baptists and Congregationalists retained their involvement. There had been initially Anglican, Methodist and Moravian participation as well in this itinerant ministry throughout Bedfordshire.³⁶ Even in this apparently 'golden era' of interdenominational activity there were problems to overcome. Samuel Clift, a dissenting leader, sent an apologetic letter to the Bishop of Salisbury with a view to reassuring his lordship that Anglican ministers were not being encouraged to engage in itinerant work at the expense of parish commitments.³⁷ The Haldanes had risen to prominence in evangelical Christian circles at a time when 'catholic' Christianity was predominant. This approach to Christian service was held by the church leaders whom they most highly respected, for example David Bogue of Gosport.³⁸ It was not surprising, therefore, that they tended to adopt this same philosophy of ministry. As a result they would in later decades place a lower priority on plans for establishing a union of Baptist churches than some other Baptist leaders in Scotland.

The willingness of Christians from different traditions to work together in home evangelism had been inspired by united efforts in overseas mission. In an article in the *Missionary Magazine*, in February 1797, a plan was proposed for the setting up of the SPGH. The society was hoping to involve all Christians in Scotland who were concerned for the evangelisation of their country.

> As this also is a liberal, as well as a disinterested scheme, so every lover of the name of Jesus ought to engage in it. Let the names

---

34 D.W. Lovegrove, *Established Church Sectarian People*, (Cambridge: Cambridge University Press, 1988), p. 35. Roberts, *Continuity and Change*, pp. 141-146, noted support for this cause amongst London Particular Baptists who had been influenced by the eighteenth-century revival.
35 *Missionary Magazine*, (October 1797), pp. 478-480.
36 W.R. Ward, *Religion and Society in England 1790-1850*, (London: B.T. Batsford, 1972), pp. 48-49.
37 S. Clift, *An Incidental Letter, Addressed to the Lord Bishop of Sarum, August the 9th, 1798, the day of his Visitation held at Chippenham, Wilts, with some Observations and Reflections in Favour of Village Preaching*, (Chippenham: n.p., n.d. [1798]), p.20, cited by Lovegrove, *Established Church*, p.110.
38 W.M. Kirkland, 'The Impact of the French Revolution on Scottish Religious life and thought with special reference to Thomas Chalmers, Robert Haldane and Niel Douglas', (Ph.D. thesis, Edinburgh University, 1951), p. 89. Haldane, *Robert and James Haldane*, p. 123.

Establishment, Antiburgher, Burgher, Relief, &c, be lost in preaching the Gospel to poor sinners:…We are the more bold to speak, as we have before us, in the present day, such liberal institutions, as the Missionary Societies, both in England and Scotland, for propagating the Gospel abroad. We wish no more than a similar institution for converting the Heathen at home.[39]

The SPGH account of its work in 1798-1799 refers in its introductory pages to the inspiration given to its leaders by those Christians who had been sufficiently concerned about the salvation of people in other lands to set up missionary societies. The challenge was given to its readers to the effect that if concern was legitimate for the souls of the heathen in other lands, then it was equally so for the spiritually destitute in Scotland.[40] Robert Haldane had been profoundly influenced by reading the first accounts of the Baptist work in India. It had raised in his mind the great need for overseas missionaries. His aspirations to be involved in overseas ministry led to the plan, in 1795-1797, for a group of men, including the Haldanes, to go to Bengal as missionaries. The East India Company had refused to grant permission, which resulted in the two brothers turning their attention to home mission.[41] This change of focus was in line with work undertaken by Baptists in England. The BMS, in 1796 and 1797, had sponsored two itinerant preachers working in Cornwall.[42] The benefit to Scottish Baptist life and witness came first when the Haldanes set up their own Baptist home missionary society after 1808 through the Tabernacle Church, Edinburgh, to support workers in the north of Scotland.[43] This initiative culminated, in 1827, in the establishment of the Baptist Home Missionary Society for Scotland.

The work of the SPGH was not universally welcomed in Scotland, especially on the part of the Established Church. In a 'Pastoral Admonition' sent out to all the parish churches by William Moodie, Moderator of the General Assembly in 1799, the opposition to the

---

39 *Missionary Magazine*, (February 1797), pp. 49-56.
40 *Account of the Proceedings of the Society for Propagating the Gospel*, 1799, pp. 7-11.
41 Haldane, *Robert and James Haldane*, pp. 98-120.
42 Baptist Missionary Society, *Periodic Accounts*, (Clipstone: J.W. Morris, 1800), 1.3, pp. 263-271, and 1.4, pp. 358-360. For more details on this home evangelisation in Cornwall see B.R. Talbot, 'John Saffery (1763-1825)', in M.A.G. Haykin (ed.), *The British Particular Baptists 1638-1910*, III, (Springfield, Missouri: Particular Baptist Press, 2003), pp. 61-70.
43 P. Waugh, 'Home Mission and the Highlands', in Yuille (ed.), *Baptists in Scotland*, pp. 72-73.

new society was made plain. After a lengthy attack upon the promoters of the French Revolution, the letter turned to a source of concern within Scotland.

> It is much to be lamented, that, while we are assaulted by false principles imported to us from abroad, there shall of late have arisen among ourselves, a set of men, whose proceedings threaten no small disorder to the country. We mean those, who, assuming the name of Missionaries from what they call the Society for Propagating the Gospel at Home, as if they had some special commission from Heaven, are at present going through the land;... Much reason there is to suspect, that those who openly profess their enmity to our Ecclesiastical Establishment, are no friends to our Civil Constitution, and that the name of liberty is abused by them, as it has been by others, under a cover for secret Democracy and Anarchy.[44]

It is ironic that it was Moderates in the Church of Scotland such as Prof. John Robison of Edinburgh who had urged the Haldanes and their colleagues to 'win over the infidels among ourselves' rather than look to serve overseas in Christian mission.[45] Once the challenge had been taken up through the work of the SPGH, it was criticised on the grounds of the unorthodox means used in the propagation of the faith. The restrictions that the General Assembly sought to impose on these evangelists were shackles from which they became free when many of them chose to separate themselves from the Church of Scotland at the end of the eighteenth century. In future years they would be promoting the cause of Independent, or later Baptist in some cases, home missionary endeavours.

3.4 Robert Haldane's Catholic Christianity

Robert Haldane in 1798 to1799 established a series of Tabernacles, or preaching centres, based on the Whitefieldite Tabernacles in London. In these churches in Glasgow, Edinburgh, Perth, Dundee and Caithness the intention was for a series of ministers to give evangelistic addresses, in rotation, to the unchurched masses, who could gain admission to the meetings without charge.[46] It was soon realised that, though their original intention had been to remain inside the Church of Scotland, other Christians would perceive the

---

44 *Missionary Magazine*, 38, (July, 1799), pp. 289-293. A reply to the 'Pastoral Admonition' by the SPGH was given in the *Edinburgh Quarterly Magazine*, 2 (1800), pp. 77-88.
45 Haldane, *Address to the Public*, p. 62.

growing network of churches as a new denomination of Independent congregations. As early as December 1798 fourteen of the leading members of the SPGH and the Edinburgh Circus congregation had met to consider the wisdom of forming themselves into an Independent church. The elder Haldane brother recognised that there needed to be some grounds of association between these newly Independent congregations. In his 1800 *Address to the Public* he confirmed that 'if they [the Tabernacles] conformed to the same strict and Scriptural discipline, they might be united, as far as Congregational principles admit.'[47] In 1800, therefore, Robert Haldane was in favour of a union of autonomous congregations in line with the model that would later be adopted by the 1827 Baptist Union of Scotland, discussed in chapter six.

In the period 1816 to 1817 Robert Haldane expounded his well-known lectures on Romans to theological students in Geneva. It is important to note that his mission was restricted to the preaching of the gospel, without any reference to ecclesiastical polity, rite or ceremony. One of his students called Louis Gaussen, a Reformed pastor in Satigny, Geneva, from 1816 to 1828,[48] described his theological lectures in this way:

> His wisdom at Geneva was indicated by the sobriety of his language and by the pre-eminence he assigned to all that was essential. He was himself a Baptist, but never did I hear him utter a word on the subject. I have been told that our brother, M.[Emil] Guers, at that time also a Baptist, wrote to him, 'We have baptised two persons', and that your uncle replied, 'I should have been better pleased had you written that you had converted two persons'.[49]

The position Robert Haldane adopted, both in Geneva, Switzerland, and Montauban in France, where he preached and lectured

---

46 Haldane, *Address to the Public*, pp. 69-82. 'Tabernacle', an article explaining the purposes of the Tabernacles was published in the *Edinburgh Quarterly Magazine*, 2 (1800), pp. 59-61.
47 Haldane, *Address to the Public*, p. 82.
48 J.B. Raney, 'Gaussen, Louis', in Lewis (ed.), *DEB*, I, pp. 431-432.
49 Haldane, *Robert and James Haldane*, pp. 460-461. It is probable, however, that Haldane did discuss baptism in private conversations with individuals who sought his counsel on this subject and that a few of his student hearers in Geneva adopted Baptist principles, including Henry Pyt and Emil Guers. *The Christian Repository*, 3 (May, 1818), pp. 309-311. See also A. Bost, *Memoirs Pouvant Servir a L'Histoire du Reveil Religieux*, (3 Vols; Paris), 1854, I, p. 379, cited in K.J. Stewart, 'Restoring the Reformation: British Evangelicalism and the 'Reveil' at Geneva 1816-1849' (PhD thesis, Edinburgh University, 1992), p. 160.

from 1817 to 1819, was to concentrate on encouraging evangelical believers in the Reformed churches in these countries, and in seeking to proclaim the importance of the evangelical view of Christianity to those of more liberal persuasions. This policy guaranteed a greater acceptance of his ministry than would otherwise have been the case. There were, not surprisingly, few of his European supporters who adopted his baptistic outlook.[50] Haldane also had no difficulty in joining with evangelical Presbyterians in France when the Lord's Supper was administered in the form to which they were accustomed.[51]

It seems likely that Robert's continental experience had led him to change the emphasis of his ministry. In the first decade of the nineteenth century he had been extremely enthusiastic in promoting new ideas in church practices, even if it caused controversy. Now it appeared that he was wiser and more careful in evaluating his course of action. He was to maintain an interest in the European Reformed Churches, through the Continental Society that was founded in London in 1818, though he never felt the need for another extended tour of the European mainland.[52] This decision ensured that though the elder Haldane remained in Scotland his outlook

---

50 A contemporary continental account of the significance of Robert Haldane's work is provided in C. Malan, *The Life, Labours and Writings of Caesar Malan*, London: James Nisbet & Co., 1869, pp. 40-55. See also C. Malan, *The Conventicle of Rolle*, (Geneva, 1821), English translation London, 1865, pp. 114-115, cited by Stewart, "Reveil' at Geneva', pp. 156-157. English Independent minister Josiah Conder, in a lengthy discussion of the apparently low state of spiritual life in Geneva in the early nineteenth century, described Haldane's ministry there in this way: 'Mr Haldane, from whose design nothing seems to have been more remote than any project of a sectarian character.'*Eclectic Review*, New Series 9 (January, 1818), p. 13. A fuller picture and assessment of Robert's work in Switzerland and France is given in T.C.F. Stunt, *From Awakening to Secession: Radical Evangelicals in Switzerland and Britain, 1815-1835*, (Edinburgh: T. & T. Clark, 2000), pp. 25-49, 239-246. Older articles that are also helpful include A.L. Drummond, 'Robert Haldane at Geneva (1816-1817)' *Records of the Scottish Church History Society*, 9 (1947), pp. 69-83, and D.W. Lovegrove, '"The Voice of Reproach and Outrage": The Impact of Robert Haldane on French-Speaking Protestantism', in D.W.D. Shaw (ed.), *In Divers Manners*, (St Andrews: St Mary's College, St Andrews University, 1990), pp. 73-83.
51 Haldane, *Robert and James Haldane*, p. 483. Haldane, however, did have too low an estimation of the level of evangelical orthodoxy amongst the ministers at Montauban and could have worked more closely with the theological faculty in that place. See Stewart, "Reveil' at Geneva', pp. 163-169.

went far beyond it. His priority at this time was the production of theological literature that included some of the most influential Christian books of the nineteenth century. His book *The Evidence and Authority of Divine Revelation* had been produced in 1816 on the continent; now he added to that notable works such as *On the Inspiration of Scripture* in 1828 and *Exposition of The Epistle to the Romans* in 1835. Robert was now focusing mainly on issues that commanded substantial agreement amongst evangelicals, rather than on issues that produced disagreement and disunity.[53] This understanding was confirmed by his decision in September 1840 to refuse to support the Baptist Bible Society in America. His letter to them dated September 25 stated that he 'altogether disapproved of any external ordinance being made a bond of union instead of faith in Christ and sound doctrine.' The term 'Baptist' was 'quite inappropriate as prefixed to the Society's name.'[54] For Robert Haldane, unlike some other Scottish Baptists, the question of the formation of an association or union of Baptist churches was not one to which he would give much future consideration.

3.5 James Haldane's Ecclesiological Principles

James Haldane, like his brother Robert, did not appear to give a high priority to union amongst Scottish Baptists. There is, however, a measure of consistency in his books and pamphlets on the subject of union amongst Christians. His major title, *A View of the Social Worship and Ordinances*, had revealed his understanding, in 1805-1806, of a range of ecclesiological subjects. In the fifth chapter of that book he dealt with the nature of Christian churches. He had argued that New Testament churches were single independent churches. He had found no reference to the word 'church' being used in the sense of a denomination.'But in any intermediate sense', he explains, 'between a single congregation and the whole community of Christians, not one instance can be brought of the application of the word in sacred writ'.[55] An open letter to the church of Christ at Leith Walk, published in 1807, retained the same position.[56] A further and more substantial publication, *Observations on the Association of Believers*, published in 1808, had a section entitled 'Of a

---

52 Stewart, "Reveil' at Geneva', pp. 296-324, discusses the rise and fall of the Continental Society.
53 Haldane, *Robert and James Haldane*, pp. 495-496, 598-604.
54 Haldane, *Robert and James Haldane*, p. 625.
55 J.A. Haldane, *A View of the Social Worship and Ordinances observed by the First Christians drawn from the Sacred Scriptures alone*, (Edinburgh: Ogle & Aikman and Guthrie and Tait, 1806 [second edition]), p. 125.

Church of Christ'. Haldane discussed the manner in which believers could unite in worship and witness, but avoided all references to denominations, or any form of wider associations of churches beyond the local congregation.[57] The Edinburgh Tabernacle pastor, in the first decade of the nineteenth century, had been working through his understanding of the internal operations of a local congregation. It appears likely that limited mutual co-operation for such tasks as home evangelism was the extent of his vision for a wider association of Christians. It is also probable, however, that such co-operation, after 1808, in his mind at least, would not have been limited to Scottish Baptists. The pan-evangelical pattern of the SPGH at its inception had been retained even if it was a theoretical vision after the divisions of 1808. There is every likelihood that the involvement of Robert and James Haldane in the later united Baptist Home Missionary Society for Scotland, established in 1827, was based on such aspirations.

In his early years as a Baptist pastor James Haldane had spent a considerable amount of time reflecting on the need for mutual forbearance within evangelicalism, with respect to issues upon which Christians could not agree. His 1811 publication, *Observations on Forbearance*, was in part a critique of the narrower views of this subject which he believed were held by Scotch Baptists. This book received a swift reply from the Scotch Baptist Samuel Jones, who in his book made some important criticisms of Haldane's opinions.

> The title of Mr Haldane's book, viz, 'Observations on Forbearance', affords no distinct notion to what extent he would plead for its application; nor, which is most a matter of surprise, have we even in the body of the work any clear and explicit avowal of the length to which he would carry his favourite sentiment.[58]

Haldane did not satisfactorily answer this criticism in his 1812 response to Jones. His reply consisted of repeating the same points in a similar form of words.[59] His first book on forbearance, however, does make some pertinent points relevant to the subject of Christian union. At the beginning of that book he states a point of princi-

---

56 J.A. Haldane, *An Address to the Church of Christ Leith Walk Edinburgh*, (Edinburgh: J. Ritchie, 1807).
57 J.A. Haldane, *Observations on The Association of believers; Mutual Exhortation; The Apostolic Mode of Teaching; Qualifications and Support of Elders; Spiritual Gifts*, (Edinburgh: J. Ritchie, 1808).
58 S. Jones, *A Review of Mr J.A. Haldane's Late Publication entitled 'Observations on Forbearance'*, (London: W. Jones, 1812), p. 3.

ple.

> In entering on this subject, it may be necessary to observe, that there is no doubt of our being laid under the strongest obligations to obey God in all things. Nothing is more fallacious than the idea, that we are at liberty to set aside any part of the will of Christ for the sake of union. This is the wisdom of the world which cometh to nought.[60]

James Haldane wanted to explain why, in his view, the Glasite and Scotch Baptist churches were too narrow-minded in their understanding of forbearance. Haldane used the example of the insistence of these groups to require the presence of elders before the Lord's Supper could be celebrated. He believed that scripture did not warrant that regulation.[61] The purpose of his arguments concerning forbearance, especially with regard to Baptists in Scotland, was that their mutual witness was being hindered in their native land. Fellowship between different types of Baptist churches was largely non-existent even in a single town.

> What has been the consequence? The more that knowledge has increased, the more have divisions multiplied. In few towns is there one Baptist church, without two or three others who can have no fellowship together. This is easily accounted for. Each is convinced they ought not to give up anything which Christ has enjoined. So far it is well; but they also imagine that they must reject all who differ from them in any respect: and thus separations among the disciples of Christ, of which we find no example in the New Testament, are multiplied without end, and the way of truth is evil spoken of.[62]

It was a practical issue, co-operation in itinerant evangelism in Scotland, that lay behind Haldane's concern about forbearance. He held out no hope of resolving the differences between the different types of Baptist ecclesiologies. These differences, however, should be set on one side for the sake of the gospel. The consistent position James Haldane held over forbearance in the first two decades of the nineteenth century gave a clear pointer to his future conduct in the attempts that would be made in the 1820s for a united Baptist home missionary society and a union of churches. As later chapters will reveal, his involvement in the former and endorsement of the latter

---

59 J.A. Haldane, *Remarks on Mr Jones's Review of Observations on Forbearance*, (Edinburgh: J. Ritchie, 1812).
60 J.A. Haldane, *Observations on Forbearance*, (Edinburgh: J. Ritchie, 1811), p. 12.
61 Haldane, *Observations on Forbearance*, pp. 18,42,76.
62 Haldane, *Observations on Forbearance*, p. 53.

movement should not have caused surprise to any informed observer.

One important question that has to be asked is this: Did James Haldane maintain this position on church union and co-operation until his death in 1851? This question can be answered, though not as conclusively as it might have been, due to no copies apparently surviving of his 1846 volume *On Christian Union*. This issue is, however, discussed in his biography. A letter written to a friend dated June 1845 includes this section on Christian unity:

> I went last night, to a meeting to promote unity [leading to the formation of the Evangelical Alliance]. Sir Andrew Agnew was in the chair. Mr [Octavius] Winslow [Baptist], from Leamington Spa, spoke; also D'Aubigne and Monod [Continental Reformed Churches]; Guthrie, of the Free Church; Drummond and Crowther, Episcopalian; and Candlish concluded. I came away before Dr Candlish spoke, which I regretted, for I understood it was the best speech of the evening. He disclaimed presuming to judge between essentials and non-essentials, and said in regard to what God has revealed and commanded we were bound to obey in all things, but still to exercise forbearance with each other. On every question on which I have heard him, he always takes high ground. He is decidedly the leader of the Free Church.

Alexander Haldane, James's biographer, went on to record:

> These were always his views on Christian union, and he shortly afterwards published a little treatise on the subject, in which he cites, in embodying his mature opinions, what he had written more than forty years before, in his book on Social Worship.[63]

James Haldane had maintained a consistent position with respect to Christian union in his ministry. His opinions on this subject were shared by his friend and colleague William Innes, who had in turn been influenced by their adoption of Baptist principles in the years that followed and ironically, was one of the few Scottish Baptist ministers of that period to adopt an open table and open membership, as commended in James Haldane's book *A View of the Social Worship and Ordinances*.[64] Innes published his *Remarks on Christian Union* in 1811. This booklet expresses clearly his thoughts on this subject, and they are remarkably similar to those of James Haldane, namely that the real issue to grapple with was not Baptist but Christian union.[65]

3.6 The Causes of the Divisions in Scottish Independent Ranks

It is important next to consider how the developing opinions of the

---

63 Haldane, *Robert and James Haldane*, pp. 658-659.
64 'Baptist Pioneers in Scotland', 1902, p. 20.

Haldane brothers and their Independent colleagues weakened the ties of fellowship between them in the first decade of the nineteenth century. The impact of the conflicts that arose during this period of time had a formative influence on the attitudes to union that Robert and James Haldane carried with them into Scottish Baptist circles. The newly Independent churches, formed by individuals associated with the Haldanes in the SPGH, had retained many of the forms of Presbyterian worship. The two major differences, adopted in 1800, consisted in the weekly observance of the Lord's Supper and the 'weekly meeting', in which an opportunity was given for the mutual exhortation of the brethren. This meeting was also the forum for the conducting of church business and matters of discipline within the fellowship. Disciplinary matters were only heard, however, after the hearers had withdrawn from the gathering.[66] These innovations were in line with the practices of the Glasites, the Old Scotch Independents and the Scotch Baptists.[67] Greville Ewing, minister of the Glasgow Tabernacle, drew up in 1800 a formal statement of the guidelines adopted in his church in order to offer guidance to the other Independent churches.[68] The Glasgow minister did not view his document as a 'human standard' for the churches, because 'subscription to human standards' had been one of Ewing's differences with respect to the Established Church, while he had previously been associated with it. He noted that:

> They were printed, not as any authority distinct from that of Scripture, but merely to save trouble, in answering the questions of individuals, till their practices should be sufficiently known and understood; and accordingly, the circulation of them was soon discontinued.[69]

The new connexion of congregations had sought to establish its ecclesiological identity in the first decade of the nineteenth century. The brief statement of Ewing, however, was not the end, but rather the beginning, of theological reflection regarding the future beliefs and practices of the Independent churches.

James Haldane, who had spent some time working out his own

---

65 W. Innes, *Remarks on Christian Union*, (Edinburgh: Oliphant, Waugh & Innes, 1811). W. Innes, *Reasons for Separating from the Church of Scotland*, (Dundee: Chalmers, Ray & Co., 1804).
66 J.J. Matheson, *A Memoir of Greville Ewing*, (London: John Snow, 1843), pp. 235-240.
67 J. Ross, *A History of Congregational Independency in Scotland*, (Glasgow: James Maclehose & Sons, 1900), pp. 76-80.
68 'Copy of the Regulations of the Church in Jamaica Street, Glasgow', cited in Matheson, *Greville Ewing*, pp. 647-649.
69 Matheson, *Greville Ewing*, pp. 236-237.

vision of the future, accepted the guidelines of his Glasgow colleague, but he intended to develop those ideas with respect to other church practices. He sought, in particular, to promote during Sunday worship services the mutual exhortation of the brethren and the discipline of church members that had been formerly reserved for week-night meetings. It was, though, as Haldane stated in the 1806 preface to his book *A View of the Social Worship and Ordinances*, important to note that 'this book is not intended as a standard for the order of any church of Christ. Should it be adopted as such, the views of the writer would therefore be completely defeated.'[70] The Edinburgh and Glasgow Tabernacle pastors had unwittingly started an open debate within Independent ranks on ecclesiological issues that would eventually cause division in the connexion. It was, though, other leaders such as William Ballantyne, pastor of the Elgin Tabernacle, and Robert Haldane whose zeal for reformation exceeded their desire for the unity of the Independent movement. The two men began to practise some of the ecclesiological innovations advocated by James Haldane as early as 1805. The occasion was a preaching tour that year in which they had sought to promote the new ideas in Newcastle and London. Alexander Haldane, the Haldanes' biographer, who sought to defend James on this matter, had to concede with respect to Robert, whose convictions were very similar to his brother's, that he was 'less disposed to delay the experiment of carrying them into operation'.[71] The small group of people that took part in the trip to England consisted of Ballantyne, Robert Haldane, their wives and servants. The Sunday worship services that they conducted were not in association with any congregation, yet this company of believers mutually exhorted each other, and dispensed the Lord's Supper each Sunday morning. Greville Ewing, upon hearing of these new developments, was alarmed at the desire for what he considered to be novelties. Ewing was convinced that unless such behaviour was checked it could undermine the entire Independent movement.[72] The Glasgow pastor had correctly foreseen the necessity for decency and order in church affairs, if their Independent connexion was to continue to prosper in Scotland. Robert Haldane, in particular, appeared to be unaware of the wider pastoral consequences of the ecclesiological changes he had been promoting.

---

70 Haldane, *View of the Social Worship*, preface, p. v.
71 Haldane, *Robert and James Haldane*, pp. 357-358.
72 G. Ewing, *Facts and Documents Respecting the Connections which have subsisted between Robert Haldane Esq. and Greville Ewing*, (Glasgow: M. Ogle and J.A. Duncan, 1809), pp. 247-248.

The controversy emerged into the open in 1807 with the publication of a *Treatise on the Elder's Office* by William Ballantyne, who advocated a plurality of elders in each congregation. The Elgin minister stated his opposition to theological seminaries, and to the regular preaching of ordained pastors. Ballantyne was, in effect, proposing views later taken up by the Brethren movement. In that year the elder Haldane brother and Ewing were engaged in a serious debate about the future direction of Independency. The decision of the financial backer of the movement to incline towards the views of the author of this treatise brought the conflict within the connexion to the point of no return.[73] Ewing, an Independent by conviction, had found it increasingly difficult to remain in fellowship with a patron whose theological convictions were continually under review.

The decision by both Robert and James Haldane in 1808 to adopt Baptist principles was the occasion of the formal parting of the ways between those Independents who retained paedobaptist convictions and those who joined their patrons as Scottish Baptists. The Edinburgh Tabernacle pastor had consistently sought to maintain the principle of forbearance regarding issues over which evangelical Calvinists had disagreed. He had already expressed his doubts over the scriptural authority for infant baptism as early as 1804. James Haldane had intimated to his congregation by February 1808 that Baptists and paedobaptists should be able to worship in the same congregation on the basis of mutual forbearance. He declared his position in a letter written in April 1808 to John Campbell, minister of Kingsland Chapel, London.

> If we are all acting on conviction and both desiring to know the will of Jesus in this and in all other respects, I have no apprehension of disunion. Of one thing I am sure...if it be improper for Baptists to be in fellowship [with paedobaptists] in the same church, it must be equally improper to have occasional fellowship in private.[74]

If a change of sentiment over the ordinance of baptism had been the only grounds for disagreement between the Haldanes and many of their colleagues then the union might have survived, but a division in Scottish Independent ranks had already become inevitable.

Gavin Struthers, the historian of the Relief church, claimed:

> everything externally augured abundant success. But there was a

---

73 Ross, *Congregational Independency*, p. 85.
74 Haldane, *Robert and James Haldane*, pp. 359-360.

worm at the root, which afterwards displayed itself, and which was the source of many troubles, and great bitterness of spirit. It was engendered rather by the rapid concoction of the system than by anything bad in the men.[75]

The debate over minutiae regarding the details of church polity was the fault line that was exposed in the Scotch Baptist connexion in 1810, discussed in chapter two. It had already caused serious problems amongst the Glasites and Old Scotch Independent churches.[76] It was now also undermining the vitality of the Haldaneite Independent congregations. Another parallel may also be drawn with the Scotch Baptists, namely, that when evangelism was the primary focus of their attention, the connexion was at its most harmonious. By contrast, when their thoughts were focused on internal matters of faith and church order, divisions emerged that led to a separation and an inevitable parting of the ways between paedobaptist and Baptist Independents.

The baptismal controversy had caused a damaging split throughout the whole Scottish Independent movement. This impact was typified by events in the Edinburgh Tabernacle. A letter of Robert Haldane indicated that some people had rejoined the Established Church, others attended John Aikman's Independent church in North College Street, Edinburgh, and a further group of one hundred people formed an Independent congregation in West Thistle Street, to which William Innes of Dundee was soon called as pastor. Another section of the congregation joined Archibald McLean's Scotch Baptist church in Niddry Street, though about half the members stayed loyal to James Haldane.[77] It is easy to suggest new church practices and commend them to others, but the outcome in the life of a local congregation can result in a serious undermining of its vitality. After 1808 both the paedobaptist and the Baptist Haldaneites faced difficult years. The 'honeymoon' period of success amongst church-goers in Scotland was now clearly at an end.

The most acrimonious separation was that between Greville Ewing and Robert Haldane. The lengthy controversy was debated in minute detail by both men in printed volumes.[78] Differences of opinion between these two determined individuals had emerged as early as 1802. The initial reason for this had been the removal of the seminary class from Glasgow to Edinburgh, because Haldane had

---

75 G. Struthers, *The History of the Rise, Progress and Principles of The Relief Church*, (Glasgow: A. Fullarton And Co., 1843), p. 391.
76 Ross, *Congregational Independecy*, p. 85.
77 Haldane, *Robert and James Haldane*, p. 360.

been unhappy at the pronounced Independent ecclesiology being taught in Ewing's lectures. Haldane's action was appropriate in that context because the SPGH had gone to great lengths at its inception to maintain strict neutrality on matters that divided evangelical Christians. If individuals associated with the SPGH had been allowed to promote party positions then the society would have been in difficulties, due to the variety of ecclesiastical positions held by its supports and workers. The prompt action taken by the elder Haldane enabled the society to continue its work for a further six years. Alexander Campbell, in later years one of the leaders of the Churches of Christ denomination, was a house-guest of Ewing at the time of greatest controversy in 1808. He noted that the removal of the classes from under Ewing's tuition by Robert Haldane in no way implied any diminution of Christian regard for Ewing with whom he still wished to maintain close fellowship.[79] Robert Haldane had not departed from the principle of desiring to hold together evangelical Christians in fellowship. It is evident, however, from Robert Haldane's actions in 1802 that by preventing Greville Ewing from attempting to turn the SPGH into an Independent denomination he was unlikely to be enthusiastic about establishing a union of Baptist churches in Scotland on any future occasion.

The relationship between Haldane and Ewing had deteriorated to a point of complete breakdown in 1808. Ewing by this time, even before Haldane had demanded the return of the Tabernacle property in Glasgow, had refused to meet him without the presence of witnesses. Ewing records in his account of the conflict a 'meeting' with Robert Haldane on June 8 1808. Robert Haldane had travelled to Glasgow to speak to Ewing in private about the future of the Tabernacle. The encounter consisted of a blank refusal by Ewing to have any meaningful conversation with his visitor. It was now inevitable that a confrontation would take place.[80] The division of the SPGH into two groups, Baptist and Independent, at the instigation of the Independents, meant that it had always been likely that Robert Haldane as a Baptist would cease supporting Independent causes. Greville Ewing, however, was the only one of the leading Independent ministers to find his course of action to be totally unreasonable. William Innes, pastor of the Tabernacle Church, Dundee, voluntari-

---

78 Ewing, *Facts and Documents*. R. Haldane, *An Answer to Mr Greville Ewing's Pamphlet entitled Facts and Documents*, (Edinburgh: J. Ogle and A. Johnstone, 1810).
79 R. Richardson, *Memoirs of Alexander Campbell*, (2 Vols; Philadelphia: J.P. Lippincott & Co.,1868 and 1870), I, p. 175.
80 Ewing, *Facts and Documents*, pp. 121-122.

ly relinquished his claim to financial support.[81] In the Tabernacle Church, Perth, the Independents expected to have to leave their premises to those of the congregation who had become Baptists.[82] The Nairn congregation and its minister James Dewar were united in retaining Independent views. The members of that church were unable to pay back to Robert Haldane the money owed to him. After having made every effort to raise a reasonable proportion of the sum Dewar requested a meeting with him in Edinburgh. Dewar's honesty and personal integrity so impressed his host that the remainder of the debt was waived. Kinniburgh, the Scottish Independent minister and historian, referred to Haldane, in the context of settling debts after the division, as a 'good man with a generosity seldom to be met with'.[83] Alexander Campbell, Ewing's friend, had expected to take his side in the conflict, but having heard an account of the proceedings from Ewing became convinced that it had been Robert Haldane who had taken the more honourable course.[84] It was no surprise that the elder Haldane turned his attention, in the next decade, to his work on the European mainland and the development of his new estates at Auchingray near Airdrie.[85] The bitterness of the conflict with Greville Ewing ensured that he would approach ecclesiastical affairs in the future with great caution.

Public reconciliation with Ewing was never achieved despite numerous attempts by Haldane to achieve it.[86] In his reply to Ewing's charges Robert Haldane had seemed to have changed his views on a range of ecclesiological matters. He stated:

> The Tabernacles and the bonds [legal agreements stating the relationship between R. Haldane and the congregation who benefited from his generosity] were a worldly establishment, in a different form from the one we had left. The education of men for the office of pastors was another violation of the laws of the kingdom of Christ, which tended to keep up the distinction of clergy and laity, and also to continue a mode of procedure in the assemblies of believers on the Lord's Day; very different from what was instituted by the apostles, and practised by the first churches.[87]

The conflict with Ewing had become very intense. Robert Hal-

---

81 Haldane, *Robert and James Haldane*, p. 369.
82 Kinniburgh, *Fathers of Independency*, p. 127.
83 Kinniburgh, *Fathers of Independency*, pp. 307-308.
84 Richardson, *Alexander Campbell*, I, p. 175.
85 Haldane, *Robert and James Haldane*, pp. 382-384.
86 Haldane, *Robert and James Haldane*, pp. 374-375.

dane soon modified his theological opinions from the views expressed above. His conduct amongst continental Reformed Churches in the second decade of the nineteenth century, and his involvement amongst Scottish Baptists revealed that these statements were not his considered sentiments. It is probable, however, in the heat of the moment that both Haldane and Ewing advanced lines of argument that lacked considered judgement. The patron of Independency in particular had sought to institute too many changes in the connexion without either careful planning or the necessary persuasion of his colleagues.

At the heart of the dispute between the elder Haldane and Greville Ewing was a fundamental disagreement over ecclesiology. The Independent minister was a Congregationalist by conviction, not by circumstances, unlike Robert and James Haldane.[88] The damaging disputes within Independent ranks over baptism in 1808 had left many of the newly formed congregations in very difficult circumstances, due to a loss of both members and money. In November 1812 the Congregational Union of Scotland was formed in Edinburgh. The aims of this new body were as follows:

> The relief of Congregational churches in Scotland, united in the faith and hope of the Gospel; who, from their poverty, the fewness of their numbers, or from debt upon their places of worship, are unable to provide for the ministration of the word of God, in that way which would tend most to their own edification, and the eternal happiness of those around them.

This new body was in effect a home missionary society with the principal aim of evangelising Scotland.[89] There was, however, a second aim, the provision of financial aid to the churches in greatest need of assistance. This Union in 1812 attracted the support of fifty-five Congregational churches. Opposition to the new body was strong within some Independent churches in 1812,[90] but its membership had increased to seventy-two by 1822. According to the foundation dates of Congregational churches in H. Escott, *A History of Scottish Congregationalism*, there were only seventy-three in existence in 1822.[91] There was, therefore, a strong desire for union expressed by the overwhelming majority of ministers and church members by the early 1820s. This conviction of the need for a cor-

---

87 Haldane, *Answer to Mr Greville Ewing's Pamphlet*, p. 350.
88 J.C.G. Binfield, 'Congregationalism', in Cameron (ed.), *Scottish Church History and Theology*, pp. 206-208. H. Escott, *A History of Scottish Congregationalism*, (Glasgow: The Congregational Union of Scotland, 1960), pp. 88-90.
89 Matheson, *Greville Ewing*, pp. 392-393.
90 Escott, *Scottish Congregationalism*, p. 95.

porate body to unite this paedobaptist denomination was in contrast to the attitudes of Baptists in Scotland. It was only in 1869 that as many as 50% of the Baptist congregations agreed to join the Baptist Union of Scotland.[92] It must not be overlooked, however, that a Baptist Home Missionary Society for Scotland was formed in 1827.[93] This Baptist mission agency appeared to share many of the characteristics of the Congregational Union of Scotland, and may, therefore, have reduced the desire for a union of churches within the Scottish Baptist constituency in a proportion of the churches. In 1808 to 1812, though, Greville Ewing appeared to articulate the opinions of Scottish Congregationalists regarding church union. The Haldane brothers, by contrast, in their caution regarding formal unions were expounding views in line with those of many Scottish Baptists at that time.

The sentiments expressed by Robert Haldane in his conflict with Ewing appeared to have some similarities with the opinions of John Walker, a former episcopal clergyman from Dublin.[94] The difference, however, was that Walker had held such opinions consistently since 1803 whereas the older Haldane brother held his anti-clerical sentiments only briefly towards the end of his conflict with Greville Ewing in 1810 to 1811. Walker, the leader of a small group of separatists in southern Ireland, engaged in fierce literary debates with advocates of a variety of theological opinions. In 1821, at the request of a continental friend, Walker summarised the sentiments his connexion had held since their formation in 1803. The document included the following statements:

> They have therefore no such thing among them as any men of the clerical order; and abhor the pretensions of the clergy of all denominations considering them to be official ringleaders in maintaining the antichristian corruptions with which Europe has been overspread under the name of Christianity...
>
> they conceive the office of elders to be nothing like that of administering ordinances to the brethren; but mainly....called to be examples and guides to the rest in that course which the divine word prescribes alike to all....
>
> Belonging to a kingdom that is not of this world, they can have no connection with any of the various religions of the world.[95]

Walker had held firmly to a separatist position for eighteen years.

---

91 Escott, *Scottish Congregationalism*, pp. 337-375.
92 Chapter eight, pp.311-312.
93 Chapter five, pp. 158-159.
94 G. Carter, 'Evangelical Seceders from the Church of England c.1800-1850', (PhD thesis, Oxford University, 1990), pp. 131-163.

His public comments were considered opinions, in contrast to the hastily published views of Robert Haldane at the end of the first decade of the nineteenth century. The mentality expressed by his connexion was clear from his own description of it. 'They are a very small sect, very little known, and less liked; nor do they expect to be numerous or respectable on earth'.[96] The Dublin separatist engaged in debate with Scotch Baptists,[97] Scottish Independents,[98] and James Haldane.[99] The leader of these mainly Irish separatists appeared to have no conception of Christian forbearance, and, as a result, he isolated himself from Christians who held to different opinions.[100] Robert Haldane had travelled only briefly down the separatist pathway. An assumption that he had retained this mentality would be inaccurate.

An initial reading of the Haldane document of 1810 could imply that Robert Haldane had been approaching a proto-Brethren position in his views of the church. This understanding of his thinking would be at best partially true because both the approach taken by the elder Haldane in his relations with continental Reformed churches and his later involvement in Scottish Baptist activities imply a drawing back from this 'advanced' position. It would, however, allow the conclusion to be drawn that Robert Haldane would have little interest in formal denominational structures amongst Baptists or any other association of Christians, due to his protracted disputes with Greville Ewing.[101]

3.7 Some Important Colleagues of the Haldanes

It is appropriate next to consider the opinions of the leading Scottish Baptists that were associated with Robert and James Haldane.

---

95 J. Walker, 'A Brief Account of the people called Separatists'[London, 1821], in W. Burton (ed.), *Essays and Correspondence, chiefly on Scriptural subjects by the late John Walker*, (Dublin: E. Maddens and R.M. Tims, 1846), pp. 556-560.
96 Walker, 'people called Separatists', p. 557.
97 J. Walker, 'Observation on a letter Addressed to the Author in reply to his pamphlet entitled 'Thoughts on Baptism' [Dublin, 1809], in Burton (ed.), *Essays and Correspondence*, pp. 256-309.
98 J. Walker, 'Remarks on Certain Questions proposed for the serious Consideration of Disciples of Christ, connected with the Congregational Churches in Scotland' [Dublin, 1810], in Burton (ed.), *Essays and Correspondence*, pp. 310-331.
99 J. Walker, 'A Sufficient Reply to Mr Haldane's late stricture upon the author's letters on Primitive Christianity' [London, 1821], in Burton (ed.), *Essays and Correspondence*, pp. 432-506.
100 Walker, 'Remarks on Certain Questions', pp. 310-311.
101 Haldane, *Robert and James Haldane*, pp. 363-366.

Amongst the Haldaneite Baptists there were a number of prominent men whose understanding of their Baptist identity, and attitude to union between the local congregations, need to be considered. William Innes, who lived from 1770 to 1855, was the son of James Innes, the parish minister of Yester, near Haddington, from 1760 to 1821. Innes Senior was an evangelical preacher who had an influential ministry in his district of Scotland. William Innes also entered, in 1792, the ministry of the Established Church receiving the second charge of Stirling in August 1793. He was appointed chaplain of the garrison at Stirling Castle of which James Haldane's father-in-law was then the acting governor. His powerful preaching and consistent character had a marked impact on some of the prominent local citizens, including Robert and James Haldane, whose conversions owed a great deal to this Stirling minister. Innes joined the Haldane brothers in their proposed scheme for serving as missionaries in Bengal, and, after its failure, in the work of the SPGH in Scotland. When Independent Tabernacles were set up to provide preaching centres in the major urban centres, Innes agreed to take charge of the congregation in Dundee, where he served for eight years as minister of the church in North Tay Street. The Dundee minister was probably one of the few men within the Haldaneite Independent movement who would have been regarded as socially or spiritually on the same level as its patrons. The views of William Innes, therefore, are of particular importance.

In 1808 Innes became the pastor of an Independent congregation in West Thistle Street, Edinburgh, formed after a division in the Edinburgh Tabernacle Church that resulted from the adoption of Baptist principles by James Haldane. It was, though, only two years later that Innes too became a Baptist, and as a consequence had to leave his pastorate. A Baptist congregation under his leadership was formed in 1811, settling in 1813 in a church in Elder Street, Edinburgh.[102] Innes, like the Haldanes, had patronised a wide variety of evangelical interdenominational societies throughout his ministry in Scotland's capital city. He was particularly prominent in 1850, for example, serving as President of the 'Edinburgh Association in aid of Moravian Missions', an 'Examiner' of the Edinburgh City Mission and a member of the committee of the Edinburgh subdivision of the Evangelical Alliance. The Elder Street minister also served on the committee of the Edinburgh Medical Missionary Society. The most important interdenominational society with which he was associated, for the purposes of this study, was the Edinburgh

---

102 'Baptist Pioneers in Scotland', 1902, pp. 16-24.

Auxiliary Bible Society.[103] In 1827 the Edinburgh auxiliary of the BFBS was outraged at the parent body's apparent reluctance regarding the printing of Bibles containing the metrical Psalms for Scotland, while at the same time producing copies of the Bible that included the Apocrypha for their continental agents. The majority of the Edinburgh BFBS supporters had no hesitation in withdrawing their affiliation to the national organisation, forming in its place the Edinburgh Bible Society, but William Innes, unlike Haldane, retained his link with the BFBS.[104] In 1850 Innes served as Depository for the Edinburgh Auxiliary Bible Society.[105] His conciliatory and catholic spirit towards Christians of different sentiments revealed the likelihood of an affirmative response by him to any attempts to unite Baptists in Scotland.

Innes was an active member of the committee of the BHMS, which was formed in August 1827 by the merger of the three Scottish Baptist home missionary organisations, a topic to be discussed in chapter five.[106] The Edinburgh pastor was also a leading member of the 'Baptist Academical Society for Scotland', an organisation established to provide a theological training for prospective Scottish Baptist ministers, either in their native land or in England.[107] It would have been no surprise to his fellow Baptists that it was the Elder Street Chapel that was chosen as the venue for the meeting called to consider the formation of a union of Baptist churches in Scotland, discussed in chapter six. When a committee was formed in May 1827 to co-ordinate the launch of the new union, William Innes was the sole minister within its ranks, though other ministers were added to this body at the formal launch in June of that year.[108] The Scottish Baptist Association, 1835 to1842, a much more modest organisation compared to the previous Baptist Union, also received the support of the Elder Street pastor.[109] This leading member of the

---

103 *New Edinburgh Almanac and National Repository for the year 1850*, (Edinburgh: Oliver & Boyd, 1850), pp. 506-509.

104 [21st and 24th] *Annual Report of the British and Foreign Bible Society*, for a comparison of Scottish patronage in 1825 and 1828, cited by Martin, *Evangelicals United*, p. 131.

105 *New Edinburgh Almanac*, 1850, pp. 506-509.

106 *Address by the Committee of the Baptist Home Missionary Society for Scotland*, October 2 1827, Edinburgh, MS ref. 1950.69 (20), National Library of Scotland, Edinburgh.

107 *The First Report of the Committee of the Baptist Academical Society for Scotland*, (Edinburgh: R. Marshall, n.d. [1839]).

108 *Circular from the Committee of Proposed Baptist Union*, May 4 1827, Bundle 8, Waugh Papers.

Haldaneite Baptists was clearly committed to the cause of both Baptist and wider evangelical union.

William Innes in 1811 set out his views on Christian union in a pamphlet entitled *Remarks on Christian Union*. At the heart of Christian union was the principle of forbearance. It was recognised that genuine Christians will disagree on theological issues, but that this fact should not call into question the profession of faith of another believer.

> You will remark that I take it for granted that the points on which I differ from those I would receive into communion, are not such that a particular view of them is to be considered as essential to a man's Christianity.[110]

If forbearance was to be adopted within or between congregations then it was 'to be equally exercised on both sides'. The example of believer's baptism was used to illustrate the author's point. He noted that infant baptism was not found in any of the apostolic churches, but in a different age this issue had arisen for our attention. Christians, according to Innes, in such circumstances ought to forbear with one another 'in keeping with the general spirit of the gospel'. There was

> no consistency in person's acknowledging as Christians in private life, those who differ from them, while they refuse to admit them to their communion in public. To be consistent, such persons should refuse to treat those of this description as Christians at all. In addition, we sometimes find churches very willing to receive occasionally into their communion persons who differ from them, while they would decidedly object to doing it in general. Surely their procedure is more the result of prejudice, or, to give it a gentler name, of expediency, than of a principle distinctly understood and consistently maintained.[111]

Proof of the similarity of the views of Innes and James Haldane can be seen by comparing the above comments with the opinion of the Edinburgh Tabernacle pastor.[112] The Elder Street pastor, however, chose to practise these principles in a more thorough manner. Innes' support for a union of Baptist churches and the BHMS were very clear, but he also believed that it was equally important to grapple with the issue of wider Christian union.

Lachlan Mackintosh, born in Badenoch, Inverness-shire, was con-

---

109 Minutes of the Scottish Baptist Association, 1836, p. 3, MS in the possession of Bristo Baptist Church, Edinburgh.
110 Innes, *Christian Union*, p. 2.
111 Innes, *Christian Union*, pp. 22-24.
112 Chapter three, p.92.

verted through the preaching of James Haldane in Perth during 1803.[113] Mackintosh was accepted for training from 1803 to 1805 in Robert Haldane's theological classes, which will be discussed later in this chapter. He served as a preacher for the Independent congregation in Badenoch during the summer of 1804, prior to succeeding John Reid in 1805 as the pastor of the Independent Church at Rothiemurchus.[114] This congregation was divided for geographical reasons later that year, which resulted in two separate congregations, one at Kingussie under William Hutchison and the other at Grantown under Lachlan Mackintosh. After three years of ministry in Grantown-on-Spey its pastor adopted Baptist principles. He was baptised by immersion in 1808 in the Scotch Baptist Church, Edinburgh. It was on this visit to Edinburgh that Mackintosh discussed his change of sentiments regarding baptism with the Tabernacle pastor. It is probable that the Grantown minister was instrumental in confirming James Haldane's decision to adopt Baptist principles only a month later.[115] The Strathspey congregation gave its full support to their minister's change of views and reconstituted the church in 1808, in line with the new understanding of the ordinance of baptism. This church under the leadership of Mackintosh from 1808 to 1826 became the largest and most influential Baptist church ever established in the Gaelic-speaking Highlands.[116] The personal friendship of Mackintosh with the Edinburgh Tabernacle pastor and his dynamic influence within the Strathspey area in spreading the evangelical message made him an influential leader amongst the Haldaneite Baptists in the Highlands of Scotland.

In 1827 due to a lack of finance in the church to support his growing family, Mackintosh left Grantown under the auspices of the BHMS, with a view to planting a new Baptist congregation in Dundee, probably amongst Highland immigrants.[117] This new position was combined with serving in a part-time capacity as the first travelling agent of the BHMS.[118] In addition to his ongoing work with this society, the former Grantown minister was called

---

113 D.E. Meek, 'The Independent and Baptist Churches of Highland Perthshire and Strathspey', *Transactions of the Gaelic Society of Inverness*, (61, 1991), p. 282.
114 W.D. McNaughton, *The Scottish Congregational Ministry 1794-1993*, (Glasgow: Congregational Union of Scotland, 1993), p. 92.
115 Yuille (ed.), *Baptists in Scotland*, pp. 58, 95.
116 Meek, 'Independent and Baptist Churches', p. 282.
117 P. Grant, 'Sketch of my own Life and Times and A History of the Baptist Church, Grantown, and the progress of Religion in Strathspey from the beginning of the nineteenth century', Grantown, 1844, private MS.

in 1829 to the pastorate of Orangefield Baptist Church, Greenock, where he served in this post until 1832.[119] The Greenock congregation was a Gaelic-speaking body composed of immigrant Highlanders. The combination of pastoral duties and itinerant labours for the BHMS, though, proved to be unsatisfactory for both the church and the society.

> It has therefore been determined [recorded the Society], with the full concurrence of the church, that Mr Mackintosh shall in future be entirely devoted to the service of the Society. His time will be fully occupied in visiting the stations, in making the plans of the Society more extensively known in England and Scotland, and in preaching the gospel both in Gaelic and English, as he may have opportunity.[120]

The success of Mackintosh's work in collecting funds for the BHMS resulted in the employment of more than twenty full-time home mission agents each year after 1827, principally in the Highlands and Islands. The extent of his travels can be seen in his annual report, for example the one published by the society in 1843, in which Mackintosh refers to two extended visits to England and a tour of Ireland, as well as the promotion of the cause in many parts of his native land.[121] The former Grantown pastor, though, was not interested exclusively in the work of home evangelisation. He was also associated with the 1827 Baptist Union of Scotland. Mackintosh wrote a letter in June 1827, on behalf of the home mission church in Dundee, to offer support for this new venture.[122] In an aided congregation it was not surprising that they valued the ties with fellow Baptists. Mackintosh could see the need to strengthen the links between Scottish Baptist congregations and played his part in seeking to promote the cause.

William Tulloch was the first agent employed by the BHMS in 1827. He was also the oldest of its agents at his death in service at Blair Atholl aged 85. He had been born in 1776 in Rothiemurchus, growing up in the district and working initially in the timber trade.[123] He was converted at a communion service through the ministry of Lachlan Mackenzie, the evangelical parish minister of Lochcarron. A short time later Tulloch met James Haldane during

---

118 *Report of the Baptist Home Missionary Society (BHMS Report)*, (Edinburgh: J. & D. Collie, 1829), pp. 38-39.
119 Yuille (ed.), *Baptists in Scotland*, p. 199.
120 *BHMS Report*, (Edinburgh: J. & D. Collie, 1831), pp. 13-14.
121 *BHMS Report*, (Edinburgh: Thornton & Collie, 1843), pp. 22-23.
122 *To the Baptist Churches in Scotland*, printed Circular for the Baptist Union of Scotland, June 13 1827, Bundle 8, Waugh Papers.

one of the Edinburgh minister's preaching tours of the Highlands. As a result of a conversation between the two men Tulloch was persuaded to attend the training classes established by Robert Haldane in Edinburgh. After completing his studies, the Strathspey preacher was associated first with the Independent church at Killin from 1801 to 1803, and then with the congregation at Lawers from 1808 to 1815. In 1808 while minister at Lawers, Tulloch adopted Baptist principles and was followed by the great majority of the congregation.[124] The financial constraints for his family in Lawers led Tulloch to resign his pastorate and move for a period of twelve months to Renfrew. North Portland Street Scotch Baptist Church, Glasgow, however, recognised his evangelistic and pastoral skills and invited him to consider returning to the Highlands to work in Aberfeldy, in particular to resume his itinerant labours.[125] A journal was published of his work from September 1817 to August 1818. It was used to draw attention to the labours of Tulloch, Lachlan Mackintosh, Walter Munro of Fortrose, and John Anderson of Tullymet. Three years of work in Aberfeldy from 1816 to 1819 followed by a move to Kilmavionaig, Blair Atholl, where Tulloch was based for the rest of his ministry until 1861. This Strathspey preacher was responsible for calling Scottish Baptists to recognise the importance of co-operating in home evangelisation. His labours under the auspices of the Baptist Highland Mission were the first to unite Baptists from two different traditions, as Tulloch, a Haldaneite Baptist, was supported primarily by a Scotch Baptist Church in Glasgow, but also by the Baptist church in Perth.

Tulloch had worked hard to persuade his fellow Baptists to associate in the work of home evangelisation. It was no surprise, therefore, that he and his Kilmavionaig congregation were in favour of the 1827 Baptist Union of Scotland.[126] The failure of this first Baptist Union by around 1830, and the demise of 'The Association' of Scottish Baptist leaders, led by James Haldane, probably around four or five years later,[127] led to calls for a new body to take its place. This new association, to be discussed in chapter six, received strong backing from the Perthshire churches including that of William Tulloch.[128] The Blair Atholl minister prominent in the work of home mission was equally so in the cause of establishing closer ties

---

123 D.E. Meek, 'Tulloch, William', in Lewis (ed.), *DEB*, II, p. 1124.
124 *BHMS Report*, (Edinburgh: D.R. Collie & Son, 1861), pp. 19-20.
125 Yuille (ed.), *Baptists in Scotland*, pp. 70-72.
126 *To the Baptist Churches in Scotland*, 13 June 1827.
127 W. Tulloch, 'President's Address', *The Fourteenth Annual Report of the Baptist Union of Scotland*, (Glasgow: Baptist Union of Scotland, 1882), p. 40.

between Scottish Baptist congregations in a wider union.

Peter Grant (1783-1867) was born at Ballintua, Strathspey. He was of small-farming stock and was the precentor in his local parish church when the Haldaneite preachers began promoting evangelical religion in the Highlands of Scotland. Grant attended meetings conducted by Lachlan Mackintosh and this led to his conversion and baptism, followed by an itinerant preaching ministry in the district. When Mackintosh left Grantown to become an agent for the BHMS Peter Grant was called, in 1827, to the pastorate of the church.[129] His evangelistic gifts were evident in the growth of the church to a membership of almost 300. The Grantown pastor for many years, though, received no salary from the church. He needed, therefore, to support himself through his farm at Ballintua.[130] He received some financial assistance through the BHMS, probably in 1828 or 1829, with reports of his work in the district being published in the society's annual reports after 1829.[131] Peter Grant followed in Lachlan Mackintosh's footsteps in his commitment to the work of Scottish Baptist home mission.

The Grantown minister was also, like his predecessor, a strong supporter of moves to establish a union of Scottish Baptist churches. When the first Baptist Union was constituted in June 1827, a letter of support was received from the Grantown church through its minister.[132] The next attempt at forming a union of Baptist churches, the 1835 to 1842 Scottish Baptist Association, was also supported wholeheartedly by this congregation and its pastor.[133] In a letter dated March 1846 that was sent to his son William, a student in Edinburgh, the eminent Strathspey pastor made plain his support for the Johnstonian Baptist Union.[134] Grant was convinced of the importance of a strong union of Scottish Baptist churches and hoped for its success, even though he acknowledged that Johnston's theology was not entirely consistent with Calvinistic principles.[135] This Strathspey minister was one of the first Scottish Baptist ministers to recognise that for the union of churches to prosper it must be

---

128 Minutes of the Scottish Baptist Association, 1836, p. 7.
129 Yuille (ed.), *Baptists in Scotland*, p. 95.
130 Grant, 'Sketch of my own Life and Times', p. 9.
131 *BHMS Report*, 1829, pp. 9-20.
132 *To the Baptist Churches in Scotland*, June 13 1827.
133 Minutes of the Scottish Baptist Association, 1836, p. 7.
134 Peter Grant, Grantown, to William Grant, Edinburgh, March 7, 1846, private MS, location of original unknown.

willing to allow a degree of theological diversity within its ranks, though from within an evangelical framework. This viewpoint, which emerged from within the Haldaneite Baptist constituency, proved to be the basis on which the 1869 Baptist Union of Scotland would be established.

3.8 The Work of Theological Education

One issue of great importance in uniting the Haldanes and their supporters was the work of theological education. The inspiration for the Haldaneite theological classes in Scotland had come from Nonconformist theological education in England. There were some Dissenting academies in the late eighteenth and early nineteenth centuries whose standards were very high indeed, possibly surpassing the provision available in the English universities, where degrees could be obtained only by members of the Church of England.[136] These academies, for example Philip Doddridge's in Northampton, required entrants to have a good knowledge of the classics, and aimed to produce scholarly ministers from the ranks of those individuals who otherwise would have attended one of the English universities.[137] There were, though, other academies that had more modest objectives. One such institution was established by a London banker George Welch, and the noted preacher William Jay of Bath. Jay in his *Autobiography* described the motivation behind that project:

> it was desirable immediately to search out, and educate, a number of young men of gifts and grace for the ministry, and place them in a kind of domestic academy...not...in opposition to any larger and higher establishments, but rather in addition to them. They were to give these young men a less literary training, but a more theological and practical one; or with a fuller reference principally, though not exclusively, to divinity and preaching. These students were to be placed...where they could be, even during their tuition, employed in teaching the poor and ignorant...and while employed, to be...actually prepared for their work.[138]

---

135 Peter Grant, Ballintua, to William Grant, Edinburgh, November 17, 1846, private MS.

136 E.A. Payne, 'The development of Nonconformist Theological Education in the nineteenth century, with special reference to Regent's Park College', in E.A. Payne (ed.), *Studies in History and Religion*, (London: Lutterworth Press, 1942), pp. 229-231. D.A. Johnson, *The Changing Shape of English Nonconformity 1825-1925*, (Oxford: Oxford University Press, 1999), p. 16.

137 I. Parker, *Dissenting Academies in England*, (New York: Octagon Books, 1969 [1914]), pp. 50-55.

This description could equally have been made of the principles and methods of the Trevecca College established by Selina, Countess of Huntingdon, in 1768, the first example of this kind of seminary. Welch and Jay placed students under three tutors, including from 1789 David Bogue in Gosport, whose church in that naval town had been planted by a Trevecca student, Thomas English.[139] Robert Haldane shared the same convictions regarding theological education in preparation for Christian ministry. In a letter to John Campbell, dated October 1798, he stated, 'I intend to give one year's education to 10 or 12 persons of any age that may fit it, under Mr Bogue, with a view to the ministry'. James Garie, Independent minister in Perth, and Greville Ewing, persuaded the intended patron of the Bogue seminary to reconsider his decision in the light of Bogue's liberal political views. As a result the first Scottish students were placed under the tutorship of Greville Ewing in Edinburgh during January 1799.[140] There were nine classes of students trained in Edinburgh, Glasgow and Dundee in the period from January 1799 to December 1808, with a pre-seminary preparatory class in Elgin under the care of William Ballantyne from 1804 to 1805. The total number of students that passed through these training courses came close to 300 men.[141] The form of training offered in Haldaneite seminaries had followed the pattern established at Trevecca, in the promotion of a practical evangelical faith that laid less emphasis on denominational distinctives, concentrating on producing itinerant preachers and pastors rather than academics and scholars.

The conviction of the necessity of training itinerant preachers continued long after the Haldanes had adopted Baptist principles. Various seminary classes were held in Scotland, for example at Grantown-on-Spey, for several years from 1820 under Lachlan Mackintosh. The Grantown pastor trained four men for the Christian ministry including his successor, Peter Grant, James McQueen, later minister at Broadford, Skye, William Fraser who served at Uig, Skye, and one other unknown man.[142] This practice of recognising

---

138 G. Redford & J.A. James (eds), *The Autobiography of William Jay*, (Edinburgh: Banner of Truth Trust, 1974 [1854]), pp. 424-425.
139 G.F. Nuttall, *The Significance of Trevecca College 1768-91*, (London: Epworth Press, 1968), p. 17.
140 R.F. Calder, 'Robert Haldane's Theological Seminary', *Transactions of the Congregational History Society*, (13, 1937-1939), p. 60.
141 R. Kinniburgh, 'A Historical Survey of Congregationalism in Scotland', in *The Jubilee Memorial of the Scottish Congregational Churches*, (Edinburgh: A Fullarton & Co., 1849), pp. 67-72.

the importance of a theological education continued after many Haldaneites had become Baptists, and strengthened the conviction in Scottish Baptist circles of the necessity of training prior to Christian ministry. This influence countered the conviction held by some Scotch Baptists, discussed in the previous chapter, that formal preparation for Christian service was inappropriate.

It is important to note the continuing financial input from Robert Haldane after 1808. In the period 1799-1807 he had invested between £50,000 and £60,000 in support of the seminary classes, the payment of salaries to itinerant preachers, and the purchase and preparation of various buildings that were set up as Independent Tabernacles.[143] Lindsay Alexander, a prominent Scottish Independent minister in the mid-nineteenth century, acknowledged that one of the chief reasons for the success of Independency in Scotland had been the generous financial support of Robert Haldane. 'The chief of these extrinsic causes of prosperity, however, was, beyond all question, liberal pecuniary aid afforded to the party by Mr Robert Haldane'.[144] The extent of Robert Haldane's contribution to Christian ministry in Scotland was said to have exceeded £70,000 by 1810.[145] It is legitimate to presume that most of the additional money from the period after 1808 was spent in support of Baptist churches and ministers. Details of how the money was allocated have apparently not survived.[146]

It is important to note those individuals, both staff and students, associated with the Haldane theological classes who adopted Baptist principles, and who combined that understanding with support for academic training for other men as well. Three of the eight tutors became Baptists. They were William Innes, Thomas Wemyss and William Stephens. Innes was a tutor from 1800 to 1802.[147] His support for the provision of training for prospective ministers has already been noted. Thomas Wemyss was the classical tutor from 1802 until his change of viewpoint over the mode of baptism in 1805.[148] William Stephens had begun his adult life as an actor before becoming a powerful and popular preacher.[149] He had been minister of George Street Independent Church, Aberdeen, prior to his call to

---

142 Grantown-on-Spey Baptist Church records, information supplied by Mr J.S. Fisher of Inverness.
143 Haldane, *Robert and James Haldane*, p. 366.
144 Haldane, *Robert and James Haldane*, p. 362.
145 Haldane, *Robert and James Haldane*, p. 367.
146 P. Waugh, 'The Converging Streams 1800-1850', in Yuille (ed.), *Baptists in Scotland*, p. 56.
147 McNaughton, *Scottish Congregational Ministry*, p. 283.

the Tabernacle, in 1804, to work alongside James Haldane. He became a tutor in the Edinburgh seminary from 1804 to 1806.[150] After his espousal of the Baptist position he resigned his charge, moving to Rochdale, where he pastored a Baptist church for many years until his death.[151] Other Baptist leaders put out of the Tabernacle connexion at the beginning of the nineteenth century included Christopher Anderson, the minister of Rose Street Baptist Chapel, Edinburgh, who had been excluded from Haldane's church in March 1801 after accepting believer's baptism.[152] George Barclay, Anderson's friend, a graduate of the Haldanes' seminaries, left to found a Baptist church at Kilwinning in 1803. A further colleague, Donald McVicar, an itinerant preacher, also trained by the Haldanes, founded Bellanoch Baptist Church in Argyll in 1805.[153] Dugald Sinclair, the well known agent of Anderson's Baptist Itinerant Society, an organisation that will be discussed in the next chapter, was originally from the Tabernacle Church in Edinburgh. Andrew Fuller, was reported to have stated in his diary in 1805 that nine or ten of the Haldane agents had become Baptists, including in 1805, Edward Mackay of Thurso and John Young of Paisley, who later baptised James Haldane. Lachlan Mackintosh from Grantown-on-Spey was baptised in Edinburgh in February 1808.[154] The Haldane brothers became Baptists in 1808 followed by other co-workers including William Tulloch and Archibald Cameron of Lawers, and William Hutchison, the pastor of Kingussie Baptist Church.[155] The practical emphasis in the training for Christian ministry, following a pattern already adopted in Wales and England, and the placement of these pastors in these newly established causes was a unique development in the context of Scottish theological education. The Baptist movement had gained a good number of well trained 'English' pastors that enabled its cause to begin to prosper in the second decade of the nineteenth century. In addition, the cooperation they had experienced within the Haldaneite movement

---

148 McNaughton, *Scottish Congregational Ministry*, p. 283.
149 Richardson, *Memoir of Alexander Campbell*, I, p. 171.
150 Kinniburgh, *Fathers of Independency*, p. 464.
151 Richardson, *Memoir of Alexander Campbell*, I, p. 171.
152 D.B. Murray, 'Christopher Anderson and Scotland', in D.E. Meek (ed.), *A Mind for Mission*, (Edinburgh: The Scottish Baptist History Project, 1992), p. 4.
153 D.E. Meek, 'The Missionary Theology of Christopher Anderson', in Meek (ed.), *Mind for Mission*, p. 12.
154 Waugh, 'Converging Streams', pp. 51-53.
155 D.E. Meek, 'Independent and Baptist Churches', p. 284. J. Scott, 'The Baptists in Scotland', (PhD thesis, Glasgow University, 1927), pp. 54-56.

was lacking in Scottish Baptist circles at that time, and as a result, a number of them including Anderson and Barclay looked to the ties that united the 'English' Baptists across the border in England. This point will be explored further in the next chapter.

3.9 Haldaneite Attitudes to the 1827 Baptist Union

The final issue for consideration is to note the extent of Haldaneite involvement with the movement towards a union of Baptist churches in Scotland in 1827. In this chapter comment will only be passed on the significance of the response of the Haldaneites to this venture. The limited endorsement of James Haldane, and the lack of support from Robert his brother, implied that a mixed response might have been expected from some of those individuals who had been associated with them. According to a survey recorded in 1844, there were sixty-two Scottish Baptist churches in existence in 1827.[156] The number of churches in favour of union peaked at twenty-eight in the autumn of 1827. A further six churches wrote letters to indicate their disapproval of the planned venture, with no response from the other thirty-two churches.[157] There were sixteen out of the thirty pastors and churches that had indicated a response to the union proposal that had some kind of link with the Haldanes. The connections include former members of the Tabernacle Church, Edinburgh; former students of the Haldaneite academies; or preachers and churches that had received financial support from the Haldanes. There were thirteen pastors or churches in favour of union and three officially against it. The probable positions are set out in Appendix One.

The three churches that voted against the proposed union did so for the following reasons.

The Airdrie congregation was the home church of Robert Haldane. He had never forgotten his conflict with Greville Ewing. Haldane's influence in the congregation was probably sufficient to ensure that a negative letter was returned to the committee for proposed union. In addition, though, this congregation was a joint Independent-Baptist body and this reason was most likely to be the principle one for not participating in moves towards a union of Baptist congregations.[158] Anstruther Baptist Church in 1827 was a weak body whose pastor had recently resigned due to age and infirmity. It was also in the process of uniting with the Independent church in

---

156 *First Yearly Report of the Baptist Union of Scotland*, (Cupar: G.S. Tullis, 1843), pp. 18-24.
157 *To the Baptist Churches in Scotland*, June 13 1827.

the town, a temporary merger that commenced in 1828. Local issues, therefore, were more important than a national initiative amongst its fellow Baptists.[159] The third congregation and pastor to decline the invitation to take part in the union was Thurso Baptist Church and its pastor Edward MacKay, a former SPGH agent. The reason for this Caithness church's response was due to the fact that its pastor's salary was paid out of the Itinerant fund of the Scotch Baptist Church in Edinburgh. The Scotch Baptists who had had no links with the Haldanes all declined even to respond to the invitation to consider a proposed union.[160] There were, therefore, special reasons for all the exceptions, but the overwhelming feeling was in favour of the new venture.

The Haldaneites in favour of the 1827 Baptist Union probably had a variety of reasons for supporting the new venture. There were some rural congregations such as Grantown and Kilmavionaig in the Highlands that valued formal fellowship with other Baptists from the central belt of Scotland. The Perthshire churches,[161] like the Highland congregation at South Portland Street Baptist Church, Glasgow, were very poor.[162] Any assistance, therefore, that fellow Baptists could provide was an encouragement to them. It was no surprise that Perthshire churches provided the core membership of both James Haldane's 'Association' in the early 1830s,[163] and the Scottish Baptist Association that commenced in 1835.[164] There were also some Scotch Baptists represented in this body. Alexander Kirkwood (Berwick)[165], Adam Kirk (Dunfermline)[166] and Archibald Smith (Clyde Street)[167] had been pastors in Haldaneite Independent churches prior to serving as elders in the Scotch Baptist connexion. Unlike many of the Scotch Baptists who had never shared fellowship with other types of Scottish Baptists, these men already knew some of their colleagues in other Baptist streams, and so joining

---

158 Yuille (ed.), *Baptists in Scotland*, p. 214. *Report of the Commission of Enquiry into the Opportunities of Public Religious Worship*, (8, Appendix), pp. 144-145.
159 *The Christian Herald*, (8, December 1828), p. 419, cited by W.D. McNaughton in private correspondence.
160 Yuille (ed.), *Baptists in Scotland*, p. 68.
161 Peter Grant to William Grant, December 4 1846, private letter, copy obtained from Mrs Ann Tennyson of Elgin.
162 Chapter four, p. 125.
163 Chapter six, pp. 211-212.
164 Chapter six, pp. 212-214.
165 D. Douglas, *History of Baptist Churches in the North of England*, (London: Houlston & Stoneman, 1846), p. 249.
166 *The Evangelist*, (1.2, August 1846), p. 41.
167 Balmain, *Clyde Street Hall*, pp. 5-7.

together with them in a union of autonomous churches was not seen as such a momentous step. Anderson, Barclay and Sinclair were 'English' Baptists who were familiar with the Particular Baptist associations in England. The establishment of a Scottish union or association, for them, would have been a natural progression.[168] The BHMS-sponsored church in Dundee would naturally have recognised its dependence on the financial support of other sister congregations. William Innes as the first prominent Baptist minister in Scotland to declare active support for the 1827 union by joining its planning committee, gave the new cause confidence to believe that other ministers might follow the example of the esteemed Edinburgh pastor.[169] In addition, the issue of financial security, or the lack of it, does explain in part the different attitudes to union shown by the Haldaneites compared with the Haldanes. The self-financing patrons of this Baptist stream were immune from the real hardships faced by many of their colleagues. It was, therefore, no surprise that the Haldaneites had a greater desire for the proposed union than either Robert and James Haldane.

The influence of the Haldanes in Scotland in the first half of the nineteenth century was pervasive. In their vision for the spread of evangelical Christianity, assisted by ministerial friends from England, an extraordinary transformation of Scottish church life was achieved within a few short years. Their financial contribution to Independent and Baptist church life had been without parallel in recent Scottish church history. An unfortunate desire for constant innovation, especially by Robert Haldane in 1804 to 1807, had caused serious tensions within Independent ranks that had begun to undermine the effectiveness of its work. The split in Independency, in 1808, as a result of the Haldanes' change of sentiments on a number of issues, principally baptism, had led to a dramatic increase in the number of Baptist churches in Scotland. In 1810 there were forty-eight Baptist churches, of which twenty-three dated their origins to the years 1808-1810.[170] This point alone indicates the dramatic impact made upon Baptist life in Scotland by the two brothers. Robert Haldane's disputation with Greville Ewing had caused him to reduce his public ministry in Scotland, after 1810, and to have a suspicion of any kind of formal bonds between Christians or churches. Robert Haldane, therefore, provided no inspiration to those Baptists who desired a union of churches in Scotland. His

---

168 Chapter four, pp. 134-135.
169 *Circular from the Committee of Proposed Baptist Union*, May 4 1827, p. 2.
170 *First Yearly Report of the Baptist Union*, pp. 18-22.

vision was of co-operation between evangelical Christians to further the cause of Christ's kingdom. The formation of the Evangelical Alliance in 1846 probably would have caused his heart to rejoice far more than any Baptist scheme for union. It was appropriate that it was John Angell James, one of the students of Bogue's academy, whom he had sponsored, who was the first President of the Alliance.[171]

James Haldane provided a greater influence on Scottish Baptists than his brother. The Tabernacle Church in Edinburgh, of which he was minister, provided generous support for many Highland Baptist pastors at a time when their future was uncertain in the second decade of the nineteenth century. He strove to develop a spirit of forbearance amongst the different groups of Baptists. This effort was to bear fruit in the establishment of the united Baptist Home Missionary Society for Scotland in 1827. The support of the Haldane brothers for this body resulted in them serving as office-bearers in the remaining years until their deaths. Details of the work of this society will be given in chapter five.

The changing theological climate in Scotland in the 1840s was not appreciated by the younger Haldane brother. The Calvinistic pan-evangelical consensus of former decades was beginning to break down with no sign of what might take its place. His prognosis for the future was gloomy. Some words from James Haldane's commentary on Paul's epistle to the Galatians published in 1848 sum up not only his feelings but also those of his brother and many of their colleagues.

> We may form evangelical alliances, we may cherish love to believers who differ from us – and such, no doubt, is our duty; but there can be no real union among believers, which is not based upon truth. However we may 'agree to differ', and however well this amiable principle may appear for a time to work, offences will come, irritation will be gendered, and then the hollowness of our union will become apparent.[172]

It may be fairly stated that the Haldane brothers contributed a great deal to the development of Baptist life in their native land, but it was not in the area of encouraging the formation of a Baptist union of churches in Scotland. It is ironic that their greatest contribution to the development of this process of union was in the training of men who were to see it to fruition in later years. The Hal-

---

171 D. Reeves, 'The Interaction of Scottish and English Evangelicals 1790-1810', (M.Litt. thesis, Glasgow University, 1973), p. 152.
172 J.A. Haldane, *An Exposition of the Epistle to the Galatians*, (Edinburgh: William Whyte and Co., 1848), p. vii.

daneites William Innes, Lachlan Mackintosh, William Tulloch and Peter Grant all worked hard to unite their fellow Baptists in a home missionary organisation and in a union of churches. The evidence of Haldaneite support for the 1827 Baptist Union makes plain their conviction that far more could be achieved by united efforts than in separate ventures. The recipients of the Haldanes' financial aid were naturally reminded that team working and a common purse strengthened both the work of the local church and the wider connexion. It is, therefore, not surprising that the Haldaneites not only believed in Christian and Baptist co-operation in line with their patrons, but went beyond them in working hard to establish a union of Baptist churches in Scotland.

CHAPTER 4

The 'English' Baptists, 1796-1852

4.1 The Distinctive Beliefs of 'English' Baptists

The 'English' Baptists at the beginning of the nineteenth century were a small and weak minority within the ranks of Scottish Baptists. The Scotch Baptists, by contrast, had begun to experience a period of growth and seemed likely to be predominant in Scotland in the near future, yet within three decades it was the 'English'-style churches that had become stronger and more numerous. The Scotch tradition had placed a definite emphasis on unity within their ranks, but, as has been noted in chapter two, had made little effort to build relationships outside their own constituency.'English Baptists, the subject of this chapter, were also conscious of the need for fellowship, but approached this subject from a different perspective. This chapter will look at the leaders within this stream of Baptist church life with special reference to George Barclay, pastor of Kilwinning Baptist Church, Ayrshire, and Christopher Anderson, pastor of Charlotte Chapel, Edinburgh, its two most influential figures. The relationship of 'English' Baptists in Scotland with their fellow-Christians and fellow-Baptists both at home and in England will be examined in order to cast light on their contribution to the process of uniting Scottish Baptists in their work and witness.

It is appropriate to note, first of all, the distinguishing beliefs and practices that separated the 'English' from their Scotch Baptist colleagues. There is evidence noted in chapter two that the Scotch party saw other types of British Baptists as members not of a variant branch of their own denomination but of a sister denomination with whom they could co-operate under certain circumstances, for example, in overseas missionary work in Bengal through the Particular Baptist Missionary Society. In 1846 Christopher Anderson gave an address to his congregation explaining why the church had come into existence during November 1806 when there were already other Baptist churches in Edinburgh.[1] The particular focus of his address was centred on the differences between the 'English' and Scotch Baptist principles. Anderson insisted that at the time of the

---

1   H. Anderson, *The Life and Letters of Christopher Anderson*, (Edinburgh: William P. Kennedy, 1854), p. 70.

constitution of his congregation only one 'English' Baptist church was fully operational in Scotland. This church, pastored by George Barclay, was in Kilwinning.[2] The Edinburgh pastor had made plain his ecclesiastical position in letters to friends in 1806, but now in 1846 a formal public statement was made to his congregation. A comparison of the private correspondence with his formal address indicates that Anderson had maintained over these decades the same objections to Scotch Baptist practices and principles. An extract from an 1806 letter sets out his opinions of the followers of 'good old Father McLean'.

> The doctrines and principles of Mr McLean's Church I do in general and always did approve of...I long to see [them show] more zeal for the glory of God, and more diligence in devising and using means for gathering in the ordained unto eternal life. If they would address the conscience as well as the understanding of men, or be more frequent and pointed in their addresses, and speak with a little more life, it is likely that the Lord's Day evening they have begun would be more easily gathered and kept together. Their sentiments also respecting the pastoral office are a great deal too low. From the height of clerical dignity they have run to the opposite extreme, and seem to imagine a man can attend to the Church of God, his family, and a worldly calling, and do justice to all, at least their practice seems to warrant this opinion. Not that I think a Church should be without a pastor until they can support him, or that two or three years at a university is necessary for the office; – far from it. A pastor may be chosen and labour with his own hands till the Church can support him.[3]

The 1846 sermon notes record the following points:

> With the body known as Scotch Baptists, we could not unite for two reasons:-
>   1. As to the nature and ordinances of a Church.
>   2. As to the work of the ministry.
> There was considerable difference too, as to doctrine, but in passing this -
> First. We saw no ordinances, save baptism and the Lord's Supper.
> Second. We thought it was the privilege and duty of every Church to support its own pastor; that he ought to give himself not to any business but to study and prayer and the ministry [of the Word].[4]

Anderson provided an accurate description of the views promulgated by the stricter party amongst the Scotch Baptists typified by

---

2   Anderson, *Christopher Anderson*, p. 418.
3   Anderson, *Christopher Anderson*, pp. 64-65.
4   Anderson, *Christopher Anderson*, p. 418.

their revered leader Archibald McLean. The more liberal Scotch Baptist elders, however, such as Dr James Watt of Glasgow and Henry Dickie of Bristo Place Baptist Church, Edinburgh, could not have been faulted for a lack of evangelistic zeal or for inflexibility in their style of Christian ministry. The differences between 'English' and Scotch Baptists, though, regarding the status of their pastors, the manner of the observance of the Lord's Supper, the style of preaching in their services, and the ability to handle changes in their practices separated the two constituencies. The inherent conservatism within Scotch Baptist circles allied with their emphasis on obedience to decrees from the mother church in Edinburgh was to prove unworkable even within their own ranks. It was, therefore, no surprise that Anderson preferred the greater freedom exhibited within English Particular Baptist circles.

The Calvinistic Baptists in England, with whom Anderson and the 'English' Baptists in Scotland had identified, had emerged from the Independent congregations of London in the 1630s. They held that the visible church of Christ was composed of gathered congregations of believing men and women, and practised baptism of believers by immersion. The Bible, for them, was the sole authority for church life and practice, including worship, fellowship and church discipline. In line with the Independents, these English Baptists shared a common Calvinistic framework to their beliefs, that were described in the 1677 Confession of Faith.[5] These Particular Baptist congregations normally had a sole pastor in charge, in contrast to the requirement of a plurality of elders in the Scotch churches. The articles of faith of the Glasgow 'English' Baptist Church, written in 1801, give a clear indication of its ecclesiological position. After a series of doctrinal points the document includes the following statements:

13. A company of believing persons are warranted to form a church; and for this purpose should meet, when convenient, to try their own gifts and tempers, and from themselves (when it can be done) to choose men who may be ordained to the office of pastor and deacon..........
15. When any seek admission into the church, they profess their faith publicly, are baptised by the pastor in the name of the Sacred Three, and receive the right-hand of fellowship....... from all the members.
16. The church, when the commanded rule of admonition has been

---

5 B.R. White, *The English Baptists of the Seventeenth Century*, (A History of English Baptists, 1; Didcot: The Baptist Historical Society, second edition, 1996), pp. 6-13.

taken, can exclude from her communion any member for error in doctrine, or immorality in practice.

17. Churches, though not subordinate to any one, and complete in themselves, are bound, when one in faith and order, to hold frequent and intimate communion; pastors to assist each other by preaching and administering the ordinances; members to exhort and communicate with each other; and all to advise and pray for each other, and to separate from any church that corrupts the doctrine or order of Christ.[6]

'English'-style Baptist churches in Scotland shared many opinions in line with their Scotch friends, but their acceptance of sole pastors in charge of a congregation and the recognition of the autonomy of local churches gave them greater flexibility in the prosecution of their labours.

4.2 The Earliest 'English' Baptist Churches in Scotland

It is important to emphasise the difficulties that 'English' Baptists had at the beginning of the nineteenth century in establishing their identity in Scotland, in contrast to on-going links between Scotch Baptist Churches. The members of the first 'English' Baptist Church in Glasgow went to great lengths to identify with English Particular Baptists. They had sent a copy of their constitution and the order of service from their opening meeting for consideration and approval from Andrew Fuller, the esteemed secretary of the Baptist Missionary Society.[7] He had approved their principles and passed on the documents with a view to publication to John Rippon, a London Baptist minister and editor of *The Baptist Annual Register*. This periodical had been established to unite 'those whose names adorn the following sheets with a desire of promoting an universal interchange of kind offices among them'.[8] The members of this Glasgow congregation, led by its minister James Lister and deacon James Deakin, had stated in their letter, 'You may reckon us then as one of your churches'.[9] Lister did note, however, that there were two points of difference in church practice between his congregation and their English brethren:

> We are willing to be one with you, if you can be one with us. Our weekly communion of the Supper, and the exhortations of the brethren, seem to be our only points of difference. The latter may possibly be confined to week-nights; and we consider both as

---

6   Rippon, *Baptist Annual Register*, 1801-1802, pp. 677-680.
7   Rippon, *Baptist Annual Register*, 1801-1802, pp. 677-680.
8   Rippon, *Baptist Annual Register*, 1790, dedication, n.p.
9   Rippon, *Baptist Annual Register*, 1801-1802, p. 678.

objects of forbearance.[10]

This small congregation was concerned about its own survival and the establishment of fellowship with like-minded Baptists in England. This church, though it had fears about its own viability, sought to engage in evangelism, especially in the Highlands of Scotland. It is probable that the interest in spreading the Christian gospel in the north of their country had developed as a result of the influx of Highland people into the church. In 1803 two members of the church, Christopher Anderson and the deacon James Deakin, went to Bellanoch, near the Crinan canal, to assist in the constitution of a Baptist church under the pastoral leadership of Donald McVicar. McVicar had begun his labours in the area in 1801. He was probably a native of Mid-Argyll. McVicar had attended a Haldane training class in Glasgow with the intention of future employment in the service of the SPGH, but his adoption of Baptist principles ensured the need for an alternative form of support. It is probable that he turned at this time for assistance to the 'English' Baptist Church in Glasgow.[11] This congregation had thirty members in 1802.[12]

Andrew Fuller received regular updates on their progress. In 1805 he wrote in his diary the following comments after his visit to the Glasgow church:

> They are a poor people, and but few in number; yet they collected about eight pounds. This little church also supports a mission in the Highlands of Scotland, where a new society has lately been formed.

After also noting that McVicar had written to him, Fuller recorded McVicar's assessment of the church at Bellanoch: 'We have raised a little church here; the number of our members is only twelve'.[13] The weakness of these two churches was clear for all to see, but it was not used as an excuse to avoid the demands of evangelism in Scotland. There was, therefore, a need for 'English' Bap-

---

10 Rippon, *Baptist Annual Register*, 1801-1802, p. 678.
11 D.E. Meek, 'Dugald Sinclair', *Scottish Studies*, (30, 1991), p. 64.
12 'Baptist Pioneers in Scotland', 1905, p. 152. It was the 'English' Baptist single-pastor model of leadership that was to prosper in the Highlands, as it was closer to the Presbyterian model, in contrast to the unpaid plurality of elders found in Scotch Baptist churches. I am grateful to Prof. Donald Meek for drawing my attention to this point in a private communication in May 1999.
13 J.W. Morris, *Memoirs of the Life and Writings of the Rev. Andrew Fuller*, (London: J.W. Morris, 1816), pp. 140-141.

tists in Scotland to identify and build up their own constituency before there could be any possibility of a union of churches in association with the Scotch Baptists.

The fragility of the earliest 'English' Baptist Churches can be seen in the limited duration of their existence. The first church of this type in Scotland was formed in Skinner's Hall, Edinburgh, in the late eighteenth century by Frederick McFarlane, a former Anti-Burgher minister in Montrose.[14] Christopher Anderson made reference to this congregation in a letter written in 1806: 'Mr McFarlane's Church...- I know little or nothing about it, they are still going on in the same monastic style...'[15] McFarlane, whose address is listed in the *Post Office Directory* as Venal, [sic] West Port, probably started his congregation in 1796, but no other information has survived about the life of this congregation or its minister.[16] This congregation declined in numbers after McFarlane had emigrated to America in 1807,[17] and was dissolved during 1809.[18] One of the potential weaknesses of an 'English'-style congregation was revealed through this church. The departure of its pastor on whom church members had been over-reliant had resulted in its demise. The viability of the 'English' model of pastoral ministry amongst Baptists in Scotland had still to be established in the first decade of the nineteenth century.

4.3 Prominent 'English' Baptist Leaders

Donald McArthur

It was in McFarlane's congregation that Donald McArthur, a powerful Gaelic-speaking evangelist, was ordained in 1804 and as a result became pastor of a congregation which he had established at Port Bannatyne, Bute, which had grown by 1810 to 170 members. McArthur had both worked as a shoe-maker in the winter and engaged in the herring fishing and coastal trade in the summer season, prior to abandoning his secular calling.[19] In 1801 he had built up a congregation in the parish of Strachur to which he had acted as a pastor, but there is no evidence of its formal constitution.[20]

---

14 Anderson, *Christopher Anderson*, p. 65. Yuille (ed.), *Baptists in Scotland*, p. 63.
15 Anderson, *Christopher Anderson*, p. 65.
16 *The Edinburgh and Leith Directory*, (Edinburgh: Thomas Aitchison,1796), p. 83.
17 Yuille (ed.), *Baptists in Scotland*, p. 63.
18 J. Brown, *A Sketch of the Life of the late Robert Primrose*, (Glasgow: William Gilchrist, 1861), p. 10.

Other Gaelic-speaking congregations were formed in the first decade of the nineteenth century as a result of his preaching ministry, at Millport, Isle of Cumbrae, and in Greenock, the latter composed of Highland immigrants.[21] The congregations he had directly established, though, faded away in the decades following his emigration in 1812 to Thompkins County, New York, USA.[22] McArthur had taken the decision to emigrate after persistent opposition from the authorities to his ministry.[23] His withdrawal from ministry in Scotland had fatally weakened the cause of the churches with which he had been associated. Strong leadership had been required from others to take the work forward but it was in short supply. 'English' Baptists in this part of Scotland were concentrating all their energies on survival, leaving little scope for consideration of a wider vision.

Dugald Sinclair

Dugald Sinclair was another 'English' Baptist leader in Scotland in the first three decades of the nineteenth century. It is known that he had become an evangelical Christian by 1801. It is probable that he had been influenced by the itinerant preachers sent out by the SPGH into his native Kintyre in the late eighteenth and early nineteenth century.[24] An entry in his journal dated June 1810 that was written in the neighbourhood of Caolside, near Clachan, Kintyre, makes reference to his conversion while living in that locality.

> June 19, Detained today through a very heavy rain, the first for nine or ten weeks in this place. Find very little comfort in this quarter, saving the few moments of retirement that I have, to call to my recollection the abundant riches of the grace of Jesus, that delivered me from the thraldom under which I groaned when I resided here. O that some of my former acquaintances were now brought to that deep concern of soul, which then pressed down my spirit![25]

---

19   D.E. Meek, 'The Preacher, the Press-gang and the Landlord: the impressment and vindication of the Rev. Donald McArthur', *Records of the Scottish Church History Society*, (25.2, 1994), p. 264.
20   Meek, 'Donald McArthur', p. 269.
21   'History of the Baptist Church in Greenock', *Scottish Baptist Magazine*, (August, 1877), pp. 120-121.
22   P.R. Wilson, 'Church and Community: Old School Baptists in Ontario, 1818-1901', in D.T. Priestley (ed.), *Memory and Hope Strands of Canadian Baptist History*, (Waterloo, Ontario: Wilfrid Laurier University Press, 1996), p. 84.
23   *Scottish Baptist Magazine*, (April 1876), pp. 58-59.
24   Meek, 'Dugald Sinclair', p. 62.

Sinclair had moved by the beginning of 1801 to Glasgow. His baptism as a believer by James Lister in the 'English' church had taken place in March of that year. He may have gone to the Lowlands as did many Highlanders in search of employment. His removal to Glasgow was a pointer to the future links that were to be established by Baptists in the Scottish Lowlands to the Highland communities they had left behind. The Highland Baptist Church, Glasgow, founded by 1820, which met in the Old Grammar School, Glasgow,[26] later known as South Portland Street Baptist Church,[27] had been established to cater for Highland immigrants and had a Gaelic-speaking pastor. It was in this congregation that the future Mrs Christina Sinclair had been baptised by immersion after she had moved to Glasgow in 1820.[28] Dugald Sinclair had preached in a lay capacity, probably in his native mid-Argyll,[29] prior to entering the Horton Baptist College, near Bradford, in 1805.[30] Sinclair, like William Tulloch, the Haldaneite Baptist preacher,[31] provided a prominent link between the Highlands and Baptists in the Scottish Lowlands, ensuring that the spiritual needs of the Highlanders were not forgotten.

Sinclair returned to his native land in March 1810 to serve as an itinerant evangelist with the Scotch Itinerant Society (SIS). This society had been set up by Christopher Anderson and George Barclay in 1808 in order to engage in evangelistic work in the rural, especially Highland, districts of Scotland. The Horton College Annual Report for the year 1809-1810 includes this reference to Sinclair.

> Mr Dugald Sinclair is employed as an Itinerant in his native country of Scotland, under the patronage of a Society lately formed in that Kingdom for the spread of evangelical religion, in which department he is likely to be extensively useful.[32]

---

25 D. Sinclair, *Journal of Itinerating Exertions in Some of the More Destitute Parts of Scotland*, (6 Vols; Edinburgh: Andrew Balfour, 1814-1817), I (covering 1808-1810), p. 8.
26 *The Post Office Annual Directory for 1834-35*, (Glasgow: John Graham, 1834), Appendix, p. 48.
27 Yuille (ed.), *Baptists in Scotland*, p. 282.
28 James Kilgour, 'Obituary of Mrs Dugald Sinclair', *The Christian Standard*, (September 29 1888), cited by Meek, 'Dugald Sinclair, p. 63.
29 Edmund Sheppard, 'Obituary of Dugald Sinclair', *The Christian Standard*, (November 5 1870), cited by Meek, 'Dugald Sinclair, p. 62. Sinclair, *Journal of Itinerating Exertions*, I, p. 9.
30 *Northern Baptist Education Society Report 1805-1806*, (NBES) (Bradford : J. Hartley, 1806), p. 57.
31 Chapter three, pp. 103-105.

Sinclair was formally set apart for his work as an itinerant evangelist in the Kilwinning Baptist Church in June 1810. The service was conducted by the pastor of that church, George Barclay, in association with Christopher Anderson and Peter McFarlane.[33] McFarlane had entered the Horton College at the same time as Sinclair but did not return to his native land for pastoral ministry. He had served from 1809 to 1815 in Rawdon Baptist Church in Yorkshire, followed by his final pastorate in Trowbridge, Wiltshire, from 1815 to his death in 1826.[34] Sinclair accepted the pastorate of the Lochgilphead Baptist Church in 1815, formerly located at Bellanoch, filling the vacancy left by the emigration to Canada of its former pastor Donald McVicar.[35] The depopulation of Bellanoch due to emigration and the growth in size of Lochgilphead revealed the wisdom of this change of location. Emigration continued from this district and led to Sinclair's decision to go to Canada with sixteen out his twenty-nine members in 1831.[36] In Canada he founded a church in Lobo township, Ontario, now called Poplar Hill. Sinclair's opinions changed while in Canada and led him to become associated with the Disciples of Christ.[37] The life and ministry of Dugald Sinclair reveal a growing confidence amongst 'English' Baptists in Scotland. He was one of the first men sent to Horton College in England to train for his future service and the second evangelist employed by the Scotch Itinerant Society. Sinclair was one of the leaders present at the formation of the 1827 Baptist Union of Scotland, discussed in chapter six. On that occasion he was the official representative of the churches at Lochgilphead and Tiree.[38] His emigration to Canada cut short his ministry in his native land. It did, however, reveal a man with a vision for the future of united Baptist work and witness in Scotland. These future developments, though, were left in the hands of other 'English' Baptist ministers in Scotland.

---

32 *NBES Report 1809-1810*, (Bradford: J. Hartley, 1810), pp. 162-163,169.
33 Sinclair, *Journal of Itinerating Exertions*, I, p. 3.
34 *NBES Reports 1809-1826. The Baptist Magazine*, 19.1 (January, 1827), pp. 1-6; 19.2 (February, 1827), pp. 49-66.
35 R. Butchart, 'Early History of the Disciples of Christ in Ontario.' Paper read at Wellington County Convention at Guelph, October 1933, with emendations to the year 1951, Archives of the Disciples of Christ History Society, Nashville, Tennessee, cited by Meek, 'Dugald Sinclair', p. 77.
36 *BHMS Report*, 1831, pp. 6-7.
37 R. Butchart, *The Disciples of Christ in Canada since 1830*, (Toronto: Canadian Headquarters' Publications Churches of Christ, 1949), pp. 67-68, 139-140.
38 *To the Baptist Churches in Scotland*, June 13 1827.

Alexander McLeod

Alexander McLeod was another prominent 'English' Baptist minister. He began his ministry in association with the Haldanes, serving as pastor of the Independent Tabernacle in Dunkeld from 1804 to 1807. At that time there had been controversy over the form of baptism which had led to McLeod and some of his congregation adopting Baptist principles. The internal debates on this subject continued in that congregation until its temporary dissolution in 1813.[39] This controversy was probably stirred up by the presence of Scotch Baptist preachers known to have been in the area prior to 1807. The Scotch Baptists had established small fellowships in Killin and Lawers in that year.[40] McLeod needed to raise a new source of support if he was to continue with his work in Perthshire. He had considered the possibility of seeking to collect money for his work in England but was dissuaded in February 1807 from taking this course of action by Dr Charles Stuart, a prominent Edinburgh Baptist associated with the Haldanes.[41] It must, therefore, be assumed that an alternative form of funding was under consideration to support McLeod. Christopher Anderson and George Barclay decided in 1808 to raise funds to support McLeod's itinerant ministry in Perthshire from that year. In a letter to Anderson dated May 1808, Andrew Fuller encouraged him to apply to the London Itinerant Baptist Society for money to support evangelistic work in Scotland.[42] The records of 'The Baptist Society in London for the Encouragement and Support of Itinerant Preaching' in 1808 do indicate that letters requesting financial assistance were received from George Barclay on behalf of the Scotch Itinerant Society.[43] McLeod was certainly still based in Edinburgh in January 1808 as he took part there in the induction of Christopher Anderson as the first pastor of the 'English' Baptist congregation that assembled in Richmond Court Chapel, Edinburgh.[44] Two years of itinerant ministry based at Perth were followed by ten more years spent raising a con-

---

39 Escott, *Scottish Congregationalism*, p. 281.
40 Yuille (ed.), *Baptists in Scotland*, pp. 284-285.
41 Anderson, *Christopher Anderson*, p. 72.
42 Anderson, *Christopher Anderson*, p. 102. More information on the work of this society and its leadership can be found in Roberts, *Continuity and Change*, pp. 203-209.
43 Minutes of the Proceedings of The Baptist Society in London for the Encouragement and Support of Itinerant Preaching, 1797-1812, July 12 1808 to December 13 1808, MS in Angus Library, Regents Park College, Oxford, n.p.

gregation in Crieff. This congregation, however, foundered shortly after McLeod moved to Glasgow. It must, therefore, have been a small group of people totally dependent on their pastor for leadership.[45] McLeod's experience of the weakness of small isolated 'English' congregations, such as Crieff Baptist Church, would have induced him to support co-operative ventures amongst Scottish Baptists, both in home evangelisation and towards wider church union.

In 1820 McLeod accepted a call to pastor the Gaelic-speaking Highland congregation that met in the Old Grammar School, Glasgow. There is a possibility that members of his Highland congregations had migrated to Glasgow and thus facilitated the call made to him to accept that pastoral charge. This congregation was very poor and struggled to pay the rent on its property. There was in 1836 still no possibility that a pastor's stipend could be paid, though the congregation had agreed that should funds allow a salary would be paid sometime in the future.[46] The congregation had moved to new premises on the north side of St George's Place, Glasgow, by 1842.[47] It was installed by 1846 in the Baronial Hall, South Portland Street, Glasgow.[48] McLeod remained as pastor of this congregation until his death in 1869. He, like Sinclair, valued the support of colleagues in order to work effectively in Scotland. It was no surprise that McLeod was to be prominent in the attempts in 1827 to establish a union of Baptist churches of Scotland. He was appointed in June 1827 to the interim committee of the Baptist Union, a position to be ratified at the September committee meeting that year.[49] McLeod was a man of strong Calvinistic convictions. He was one of the Scottish Baptists who joined the Baptist Evangelical Society, an organisation committed to promoting strict communion principles, discussed in chapter seven, in order to identify publicly with Particular Baptists in England. It was unfortunate for McLeod that his desire for an established union of Baptist Churches was not realised until the year of his death in 1869. He had seen clearly that a united effort was required to engage in Highland evangelism in order to provide the

---

44 Anderson, *Christopher Anderson*, pp. 79-80.
45 Anderson, *Christopher Anderson*, pp. 101,116. Yuille (ed.), *Baptists in Scotland*, pp. 70,165.
46 Anderson, *Christopher Anderson*, p. 62.
47 *The Post Office Glasgow Annual Directory for 1842-43*, (Glasgow: John Graham, 1842), Appendix, p. 22.
48 *Glasgow Post Office Directory 1847-1848*, (Glasgow: William Collins & Co., 1847), Appendix, p. 57.
49 *To the Baptist Churches in Scotland*, June 13 1827, p. 2.

required financial assistance. Greater union had also been seen by this stalwart Baptist minister as necessary to cement the bonds of fellowship and establish a more effective framework for Baptist witness in Scotland in the nineteenth century.

Sinclair Thomson

Sinclair Thomson, known as the Shetland Apostle, was an 'English' Baptist based in the Shetland Isles. He had been brought up in the Church of Scotland and was a faithful attender in his local congregation. His attention was drawn to an evangelical understanding of the Christian faith by a small group of Independents based in Lerwick.[50] It was through his own private study of the scriptures that he became convinced of the need to be baptised as a believer. Thomson's attempts to go to Edinburgh in order to be baptised came to nothing, but his hopes were fulfilled when Daniel Bain, a Shetlander himself, though a member of James Haldane's congregation in Edinburgh, came to visit his native island. During August 1815 Bain baptised Thomson in Spiggie Loch, a location only a few hundred yards from his own home.[51] Dunrossness Baptist Church was founded with twenty-four members in 1816. Other churches founded as a result of his itinerant labours were at Burra Isle (1820), Lunnasting (1836), Lerwick (1840), Sandsting (1843) and Scalloway (1850).

Poverty was widespread in the Shetland Isles and native Baptists could not have raised the funds needed to build the required premises. Thomson took it upon himself to obtain the necessary funds by preaching tours in mainland Britain and by published appeals. In a letter dated April 1864 Thomson made reference to his appeals being highlighted in *The Baptist Magazine*, *The Freeman* and *The Primitive Church Magazine*.[52] The former title was a monthly magazine amongst English Particular Baptists. The second title was a weekly newspaper devoted to the same constituency. The third magazine was committed to strict communion principles and served that part of the same denomination in England. Thomson and his Shetland colleagues could not afford the cost of travelling to

---

50 J.A. Smith, *Sinclair Thomson: The Shetland Apostle*, (Lerwick: Lerwick Baptist Church, 1969 [1867]), p. 17.
51 Smith, *Sinclair Thomson*, p. 37.
52 *The Baptist Magazine*, 55.9 (September 1864), p. 626. *Primitive Church Magazine*, New Series 2.1 (January, 1845), pp. 30-32; 7.4 (April, 1850), pp. 113-115; 9.11 (November, 1852), p. 353; 12.12 (December, 1855), p. 384; *The Freeman*, 2 (May 14, 1856), p.266.

central Scotland for meetings to promote union amongst Scottish Baptists. In an age of basic communications it was assumed that such gatherings would be limited to those representatives of churches located closer to Glasgow or Edinburgh. This problem did not, however, prevent Thomson from receiving the Particular Baptist periodicals and contributing to their pages. His appeals for money from his brethren in England revealed his assumption of union with them in doctrine and practice. Union amongst Baptists in Shetland could be taken for granted as Thomson had both founded and set in order all of the churches on the 'English' model. Although there did appear to be some similarities to the Methodist-style circuit, the Spiggie Church pastor and his fellow Baptists had very little contact, if any, with the Methodists, or any other denomination. If Thomson had been influenced by Methodist practices it was almost certainly unintentional.[53] There had been no Scotch Baptists in the Shetlands. There was, therefore, in the islands an assumption of the value of practical unity amongst British Particular Baptists.

George Barclay

George Barclay was born in Kilwinning, Ayrshire, on 12 March 1774. His parents were devout Christians who belonged to the Anti-Burghers. He became an apprentice at the age of thirteen to a cabinet-maker with whom he completed his seven-year period of training. At the age of twenty he considered training for the Anti-Burgher ministry but the cost of another seven-year period of preparation was beyond his resources. Barclay was able, however, to train in the Haldane Academy in Dundee for a year under the supervision of William Innes,[54] and then in the Glasgow Academy for fifteen months under Greville Ewing. After concluding his studies he was sent by the SPGH to Kilwinning to work alongside a small group of Independent believers. A discussion with a friend over the subject of baptism led him to adopt the Baptist position, and as a result he was baptized by Dr Charles Stuart in Edinburgh during October 1803. In December that year twelve people united with him to form the Baptist Church in Kilwinning.[55] As a result of contacts made between members of James Haldane's congregation in Edinburgh and English Baptist students at the university there was a small number of members from the congregation who had

---

53   Smith, *Sinclair Thomson*, pp. 41-45.
54   Calder,'Robert Haldane's Theological Seminary', pp. 60-61.

accepted the need for believer's baptism.[56] Barclay went to Edinburgh in 1805 to baptise two of these people, friends of Christopher Anderson, who had recently embraced Baptist principles. They had joined others already baptised in a newly formed fellowship that met in the Cordiners' Hall, Edinburgh. One of the two baptismal candidates was Archibald Smith, later an elder at Clyde Street Hall, Edinburgh, and one of the leaders of the 1827 Baptist Union of Scotland.[57] It was in this fellowship, in Edinburgh, that the young Christopher Anderson developed his preaching and pastoral gifts.[58] Barclay had seen what could be achieved in evangelistic labours through his brief association with the Haldanes' SPGH. His observation of the benefits of input from English Particular Baptists in Edinburgh, resulting first in the formation of the Cordiners' Hall fellowship, and in 1808 Anderson's congregation in Richmond Court, Edinburgh, would have opened his eyes to the potential benefits of more extensive co-operation in the future.

Evidence to support this understanding of his ministry can be seen in his attempts to build up the Baptist cause in Ireland. Barclay and Anderson in 1808 had launched the first Baptist home missionary society in Scotland – the Scotch Itinerant Society, that will be discussed in chapter five. In that same year August and September was spent in Ireland preaching the gospel, encouraging evangelical churches and seeking to draw an accurate picture of the state of religion in Ireland. The main intention of the report from the visit was to stir up interest from mainland Particular Baptist preachers to volunteer to work as itinerants in Ireland.[59] Barclay returned to Ireland in 1813 in the company of John Saffery, Particular Baptist minister in Salisbury. Saffery provided a report of the work undertaken for *The Baptist Magazine* that included some comments as to the purpose of the time spent in Ireland:

> The public will therefore be expecting some account of an engagement, the object of which was to visit our Churches, collect for the Mission [BMS], and itinerate as much as possible. This we cheerfully furnish; the more so as we indulge a hope that our communication will increase the concern already excited, and that something more may be done by our denomination in that part of the United Kingdom.

It had been the committee of the BMS that had asked Barclay and

---

55   *The Baptist Magazine*, 29.2 (February, 1839), p. 47.
56   Anderson, *Christopher Anderson*, pp. 9-11.
57   'Baptist Pioneers in Scotland', 1902, p. 29.
58   'Baptist Pioneers in Scotland', 1907, p. 147.
59   Anderson, *Christopher Anderson*, pp. 102-106.

Saffery to undertake their trip to Ireland.[60] The Baptist churches in Ireland were isolated independent units that needed outside support in order to make an impact on the communities in which they were located. The report ventured the opinion that the absence of a formal link to fellow Baptists was detrimental to their labours. 'They have, however, no connexion with our churches'. The main concerns expressed about the churches were as follows:

> The Baptist Churches are few and small. They are in danger of Arminianism on the one hand, and Sandemanianism on the other; so that there is much to deplore; yet there are those in their communion who are desiring and praying for better days.

The remedy suggested for the assistance of their Irish colleagues was also stated plainly:

> In connexion with the exertions of our brethren who reside in Ireland, a visit annually by some of our ministers of reputation from England or Scotland, who would labour, is desirable.[61]

The evidence considered above reveals some important points about the relationships between Baptists in the United Kingdom. First of all, Particular Baptists in England and Scotland were considered to belong to the same denomination and as such could be expected to work together. Secondly, the want of a union in Ireland was a hindrance to the effective prosecution of their endeavours. Thirdly, the work was undertaken under the auspices of the BMS, a body that was supported by Scotch as well as 'English' Baptists. It is probable that the more open-minded of the Scotch Baptist preachers would have been acceptable had they volunteered as labourers. It is certain, though, that some of the more conservative of the Scotch Baptists who were suspected of having an intellectualist view of the Christian faith, indicative of Sandemanianism, would have been rejected. Barclay in his work in Ireland gives a clear impression that he wished to build on the unity of Baptists in the United Kingdom in order to render in a more effective manner their service for God. It is, therefore, no surprise that this pattern of behaviour was repeated in other types of Baptist activities in which he was engaged.

There is no better example of Barclay's conciliatory skills than was exhibited in his work with the BMS during his time in Kilwinning. Andrew Fuller preached for the first time in Kilwinning in 1805 during his third collecting tour in Scotland. He appears to have

---

60 J. Belcher and A.G. Fuller (eds), *The Baptist Irish Society: Its Origins, History and Prospects*, (London: Houlston and Stoneman, 1845), p. 2.
61 *The Baptist Magazine*, 5.10 (October 1813), pp. 432-434.

highly esteemed George Barclay, and on the two succeeding visits in 1808 and 1813 he was accompanied by him when preaching and collecting funds for the society in the south-western counties of Scotland.[62] Christopher Anderson had introduced Barclay to some of the leading supporters of the BMS in England, in particular Andrew Fuller. This friendship was maintained until Fuller's death in 1815. Barclay's involvement in the work at Serampore was summed up by his son-in-law and successor as pastor in the church at Irvine, John Leechman:

> He was also the correspondent of [William] Carey, and [Joshua] Marshman, and [William] Ward...and in all the trials and triumphs of the Baptist Mission he ever took the deepest interest. The Serampore brethren especially shared his confidence and regard; and as several of his own family were privileged to reside for a season at that loved spot, where the 'first three' lived, and laboured and died....in that spot his interests and attachments, in his later years, were so concentrated that he seemed to live as much at Serampore as he did in Irvine.[63]

In 1831 Barclay's youngest and only surviving son, William Carey, joined his illustrious colleagues at Serampore. He had been trained as a printer, but was also used as a preacher after showing remarkable fluency in the Bengali language. The young Barclay's career was cut short in June 1837 by his untimely death on the missionfield. There was, however, another link between Barclay and the work in Serampore. John Leechman, who had studied at Bristol Baptist College and later as a Ward student at Glasgow University, was commissioned for missionary service by Christopher Anderson in July 1832 at Charlotte Chapel, Edinburgh. Leechman was an able scholar and well suited to the post of lecturer in the Serampore College. In India during 1833 he married Mary Barclay, daughter of George and brother of W.C. Barclay. The climate in India had an adverse effect upon Mary Leechman's health and after consultation with their colleagues the Leechmans returned to Britain for good in 1837.[64] The Leechmans also wished to assist the attempts in Britain to resolve the conflicts between the Serampore missionaries and the BMS home committee. George Barclay had been a faithful partner, fund-raiser and activist in the work of the BMS. It was, however, in the resolution of conflicts between 1815 and 1837 within the BMS in which he would make his greatest contribution.

The controversy within the BMS arose in 1815 after the death of

---

62 'Baptist Pioneers in Scotland', 1902, p. 29.
63 *The Baptist Magazine*, 29.2 (February 1839), p. 48.
64 'Baptist Pioneers in Scotland', 1902, pp. 30-31.

its secretary Andrew Fuller. Details of the controversy are complex but have been explained elsewhere.[65] The key point was that traditional supporters in the Northamptonshire Association and Scotland wanted existing arrangements to continue, whereas influential London Baptists, for example Joseph Gutteridge, wanted to control BMS operations through the new committee in the metropolis. It was a recipe for a disastrous confrontation. William Carey in October 1817 gave a warning about the dangers of this situation in a letter to John Ryland, a Baptist minister and a senior member of the BMS committee. 'I beseech you not therefore to attempt to exercise a power over us to which we shall never submit'.[66] After twelve uneasy years the partnership was broken in 1827 and reconciliation was not effected until December 1837. The burden of raising funds in this interval primarily fell upon the shoulders of Anderson and Barclay in Scotland and Samuel Hope, a Liverpool banker known for his philanthropic activities. Hope had been described by John Dyer, the BMS secretary, as 'the great stay of the Serampore mission'.[67] Tireless work by these men to bring about a resolution of the conflict between the missionaries and the home committee finally began to bear fruit in 1837. The last major public event in which Barclay participated before his death was the BMS committee meeting in London during December 1837. The reunion of the two parties had been a pressing goal for this stalwart supporter of the Bengal mission. John Leechman, Barclay's son-in-law, emphasised this point in the obituary written for his father-in-law.

> To accomplish this desirable object he visited London in December 1837, as one of the deputation to the Society; and none rejoiced more than he at the amicable agreement that was thus, in the Providence of God, so happily brought about. He considered it a peculiar honour to have been instrumental in any degree, in helping forward this auspicious event. The writer recollects with what pleasure he frequently quoted the words of Isaiah, and applied them to this subject, 'And thou shalt be called, The Repairer of the breach, The Restorer of paths to dwell in;' and often did he rejoice that they were applicable to him and others, who were honoured to promote this union.[68]

It has been suggested that Barclay was the leader in bringing about the work of reconciliation.[69] This opinion is plausible due to

---

65 B. Stanley, *The History of the Baptist Missionary Society 1792-1992*, (Edinburgh: T. & T. Clark, 1992), pp. 57-67.
66 Carey to Ryland, October 1 1817, cited by Stanley, *Baptist Missionary Society*, p. 59.
67 'The Necrologies of John Dyer', *Baptist Quarterly*, 23.7 (1950), p. 309.

Barclay's strong relationship with the Serampore missionaries, especially through his family ties, that put him in a unique position to negotiate an appropriate settlement with the London BMS committee. He had believed that strength lay in unity rather than in division and had sought to demonstrate it through his Christian ministry both at home and elsewhere in the Baptist cause. It was, therefore, natural that his conciliatory skills should be utilised in the resolution of this conflict.

In his native land Barclay was involved in the attempts to establish a society to promote ministerial education amongst Baptists in Scotland. He had been grateful for the provision for his own training by Robert Haldane and sought to provide opportunities for the next generation of ministers. This process had attracted not only 'English' Baptists in Scotland but also some of their Scotch colleagues. The society that was later set up will be considered in chapter six. Once again his vision of uniting Baptists in the service of a common cause was seen in this project in the 1830s.

The Baptist Union of Scotland established in 1827 was also patronised by the Irvine minister. Barclay was present at the crucial meeting held in the Elder Street Chapel, Edinburgh, in June 1827. He was not only the official delegate of his congregation but also the presiding minister for the session of assembly in which the Baptist Union was officially constituted. This position of great symbolic importance probably reflected the respect of his colleagues for their senior member, but also for his contribution to the cause of Baptist unity in Scotland. There is no doubt that a man who, along with John Saffery of Salisbury, had lamented in 1813 the lack of ties of union amongst Baptists in Ireland, would equally have desired to promote greater union amongst the Baptist parties in Scotland.

Christopher Anderson

Christopher Anderson was the most prominent of the 'English' Baptists in Scotland in the first half of the nineteenth century. This status is due principally to the breadth of his friendships and activities compared to his colleagues.[70] He was brought up to attend with his family the Old Scotch Independent Church that met in the Candlemakers' Hall in Edinburgh. The Anderson brothers when they came of age chose alternative places of worship with the full blessing of their father. The majority of his brothers attended the Scotch

---

68 *The Baptist Magazine*, 29.2 (February, 1839), p. 49.
69 'Baptist Pioneers in Scotland', 1902, pp. 30-31.
70 'Baptist Pioneers in Scotland', 1902, pp. 24-31; 1907, pp. 149-159.

Baptist Church that met in Richmond Court, Edinburgh, though Christopher preferred the Circus, where James Haldane was the main preacher. It was under Haldane's preaching that Christopher was converted at the age of seventeen. Anderson appreciated the variety of preachers that supplied the Circus pulpit on a regular basis, including the colourful Anglican clergyman Rowland Hill from London and David Bogue, an Independent minister from Gosport in Hampshire. Another regular preacher was John Campbell, later the well-known minister of Kingsland Independent Chapel, London. Campbell, at the time of Christopher's baptism, came across the road from his shop to Christopher's father's shop to talk with him about the baptism. He had come, in fact, 'to condole with him on the apostasy of his children', as he called it, four out of the five having become Baptists. 'No, Johnnie,' said the good man, 'rejoice with me rather that all my sons are now the sons of God.'[71] A tolerance towards the views of others and the ability to work with people who shared only some of his views can be traced in embryo to the wise nurture of Christopher Anderson's parents.

In 1799 Anderson considered offering himself for service with the BMS in India, but had by 1808 committed himself to pastoral ministry in his native city of Edinburgh.[72] Preparation for that ministry began in 1805 with his visit to England to spend time with Baptist minister John Sutcliff in Olney and subsequently at the academy in Bristol. Time was also spent in visiting some of the major figures amongst English evangelicals, such as Rowland Hill and John Newton, and some leading London Baptists, for example, Abraham Booth. His study arrangements were very flexible and he appeared to take preaching appointments or make visits to other places on a regular basis. The entries in his journal make it plain that he wished to look at styles of worship and structures of churches with a view to his future service. The breadth of his interest is revealed by the two places of worship chosen on Christmas Day, 1805, in Bristol.

> Went to the Catholic Chapel with Mr Pearson. Saw high mass performed.... went to Temple Church in the evening. The service was interspersed with music vocal and instrumental;...performed by a full band...trumpet, drum &c![73]

His travels to England had been primarily, though not exclusively, for study at Olney. This had been revealed by Christopher in a letter to his brother Charles in either late December 1805 or early

---

71 Anderson, *Christopher Anderson*, pp. 1-18.
72 'Baptist Pioneers in Scotland', 1907, p. 159.
73 Anderson, *Christopher Anderson*, p. 46.

January 1806.

> Independent of all other advantages, I feel sensibly the effect which travelling has in enlarging the mind. I have now in some respects a more adequate idea of what the world can offer its votaries; have seen the Lord's people in different places and in various concerns....In the event of my settling in Edinburgh or Scotland for life, I shall by no means regret my visit to England.[74]

The importance of these visits must be seen in the context of Baptist life in Scotland. At this period of time the successful and established churches were of the Scotch variety which Anderson had already rejected as a model for his future ministry. He needed to formulate clearly in his own mind the structure of the church he had anticipated forming in Edinburgh.

Anderson was deeply impressed by the strength of the Western Association of Baptist Churches when he attended their annual meeting in June 1805 at Kingsbridge in Devon. At this meeting nearly fifty churches in the west and south of England were represented. He was impressed by their 'vigour, fervour and animation'. He also made a point of attending the annual meeting of the Northamptonshire Association that same month at Dunstable, but was disappointed to find that the zeal for association was not as hearty there as in the Western Association. At this early stage of his Christian experience the principle of churches co-operating for the sake of mission and mutual support was taken for granted. This gives some insight into his possible future response to developments of this kind in Scotland.[75]

Anderson's exploration of ecclesiological issues must be seen in the context of the rapidly changing views of the Haldane brothers and some of their colleagues in Presbyterian Scotland. In addition, the instability and flexible practices of the two Baptist churches he had identified with in Scotland, namely James Lister's church in Glasgow and the Cordiners' Hall Church that met in Horse Wynd, Edinburgh, had left Anderson seeking a more secure basis of union for an 'English' Baptist church.[76] His rejoicing at the annual meeting of the Western Association, where the churches were united around the 1689 Particular Baptist Confession of Faith, had confirmed his belief in the need for a theological confession as the basis for union amongst churches.[77] His belief in statements of faith was a practical one with a view to being enabled to concentrate on Christian serv-

---

74 Anderson, *Christopher Anderson*, p. 55.
75 Anderson, *Christopher Anderson*, pp. 32-33. 'Baptist Pioneers in Scotland', 1907, p. 150.
76 Anderson, *Christopher Anderson*, pp. 66-67.

ice during his ministry rather than in doctrinal controversies. Anderson's sadness at the transformation of life in the Cordiners' Hall fellowship during his time in England had led him in October 1806 to resign his membership of that society. The summary of the problems listed by his biographer reveals the heart of the problems.

> He [Anderson] was soon mortified to find that their freedom from the disputatious spirit which was wasting the Tabernacle Church, was at an end, and with it, their zeal for the preaching of the gospel to sinners. 'Mutual exhortation of the brethren', as an ordinance of the New Testament, had been introduced, and this, with some other observances which Mr Anderson disapproved of as unscriptural in their authority, were prejudicial to the furtherance of the gospel, in their effects, were insisted on being attended to, not only in their private, but in their public meetings on the Lord's day. To this he could not assent.[78]

He believed that his home congregation had transformed itself into a Scotch Baptist society rather than the 'English' form it had taken when first constituted. The changes in this Edinburgh congregation in 1806 were in line with similar developments in the Haldane Tabernacle in that city during 1805.[79] Anderson had taken a conscious decision not to join the Scotch Baptists several years earlier. He had, therefore, no choice but to attempt to raise a totally new congregation in Edinburgh with a small group of his supporters.

The doctrinal statement of his congregation at Charlotte Chapel has been preserved in a Trust Deed of 1837. This summary of evangelical belief is remarkably similar to the 1813 doctrinal statement of the General Union of Particular Baptist Churches in England.[80] It is, however, no surprise because Anderson had always identified himself with the English Particular Baptists. In addition to this, the doctrinal statement of the 1827 Baptist Union of Scotland, though in different words, covers essentially the same theological points. The link in this context to Anderson's church can be established because the first committee of this Union was composed solely of members of his congregation, a point discussed in chapter six. The only differences between the Charlotte Chapel statement and the equivalent of the Baptist Union are two additional points made in the 1827 document, 'the Influence of the Holy Spirit' prior to regeneration and 'the sufficiency of the Scriptures'.[81] The former point could be relat-

---

77 R. Hayden, 'Evangelical Calvinism among Eighteenth-Century British Baptists', (PhD thesis, Keele University, 1991), p. 13.
78 Anderson, *Christopher Anderson*, p. 69.
79 Chapter three, pp. 86-89
80 Meek, 'Missionary Theology of Christopher Anderson', p. 10.

ed to the controversy discussed in chapter seven over whether the influence of the Holy Spirit is required in the salvation of sinners. The second point is almost certainly related to the apocrypha controversy that had been raging in Edinburgh during 1827.[82] The Edinburgh auxiliary of the BFBS had been outraged by the parent society's conduct, but it had been split in two over whether to secede from the BFBS. June 1827 saw the establishment of two Bible Society auxiliaries in Edinburgh, the very month in which the Baptist Union of Scotland had been established.[83] Anderson had no time for theological controversies. He did, however, wish to construct a basis for the constitution of his future church that would stand the test of time and in this he appeared to have been successful.

Anderson was a bridge-builder who had an ability to bring together people of contrasting opinions in order to promote a common cause. His work for the Irish people reveals this sensitivity, especially in relation to the Roman Catholic community. Anderson and George Barclay had been involved with attempts to promote Baptist work and witness in Ireland in the early years of the nineteenth century. The Baptist Irish Society had been established in 1814. The committee declared in its first public statement that 'while they teach the Irish language they will exclude every kind of "Catechism" so that it would be easier for Roman Catholics to send their children to the schools'. Anderson, a man who preferred to stay out of the limelight and consequently never joined its committee, would have been wholeheartedly behind this wise decision. It is possible that behind the scenes he had promoted this approach to education in Ireland. He was also supportive of the work in Ireland of other denominations. In 1826 he was present in the Assembly Rooms in Edinburgh, with others including Robert Haldane, in order to form an auxiliary to the Society of Irish Church Missions. This was a practical expression of the view he had stated in his book *Historical Sketches of the Native Irish and their Descendants*:

> The author…would rather appeal to the benevolent feeling of many intelligent minds, resident in various parts of…Ireland – in various parts of Britain. He has no mere party purpose whatever to serve, and he thinks the reader will watch in vain for any expression throughout these pages indicative of mere party feeling.[84]

---

81 *To the Baptist Churches in Scotland*, June 13 1827, p. 2.
82 Martin, *Evangelicals United*, pp. 99-147.
83 [21st and 24th] *Annual Report of the British and Foreign Bible Society*, for a comparison of Scottish patronage in 1825 and 1828, cited by Martin, *Evangelicals United*, p. 131.

This approach he had consistently adopted from the time he had first ventured into print in aid of this cause. In 1815 his first publication on this subject, *Memoir on behalf of the Native Irish*, produced an encouraging response from 'almost all denominations' and part of its success was that no-one could 'learn from the pamphlet itself to what section of Protestantism its author belonged.'[85] Many of his strongest supporters in this work belonged to the Established Church in Ireland and there was an extensive correspondence between them, especially with the authoress known as 'Charlotte Elizabeth', whose full name was Charlotte Elizabeth Browne Phelan Tonna (1790 – 1846).[86] 'Charlotte Elizabeth' was one of the first writers of her era to use the religious novel not only to promote Evangelical virtues but also to combat perceived Tractarian vices. She used the genre of fiction to speak powerfully to evangelical young people in the mid-nineteenth century about the major religious issues of the day.[87] 'Charlotte Elizabeth' and Anderson exchanged letters over a number of years, yet her letter of September 18 1830 reveals that she did not know his ecclesiastical position. It contained a discussion about Protestant divisions and in it she remarked that he might be 'a bishop for aught I know', a comment that revealed the circumspect nature of his letters to her.[88] His breadth of vision in carefully promoting the needs of the Irish people without offending any section of opinion is a great achievement revealing the care taken in his work to avoid unnecessary conflict. Anderson had the ability to see what the major issues were in a situation and to deal with them rather than attempt to solve all the problems. A man who refused to follow a party line in the wider church was also a man who had the ability to help overcome divisions amongst his fellow Scottish Baptists.

When the work of the BMS in its earliest years is considered, few today would recall the name of Christopher Anderson as one of the major figures, yet this Scottish Baptist played an important role in setting it on a firm footing as it entered the second generation. It is instructive to be aware that the uniting of Baptists for overseas mission work led to a greater degree of unity on the home front and led to calls for a formal union of Particular Baptist churches in Britain.

---

84 C. Anderson, *Historical Sketches of the Native Irish and their Descendants*, (Edinburgh: Oliver & Boyd, 1830, 2nd edition), p. 21.
85 Anderson, *Christopher Anderson*, p. 137.
86 E. Jay, *The Religion of the Heart*, (Oxford: Clarendon Press, 1979), p. 12.
87 M. Maison, *Search Your Soul Eustace*, (London: Sheed and Ward, 1961), pp. 93-94.
88 Anderson, *Christopher Anderson*, p. 152.

This point was true of other groups of Christians as well, for example the Congregationalists. Josiah Conder, one of their leading lay men, looking back over the earlier years of the nineteenth century, stated:

> The London Missionary Society (though not strictly confined to the denomination) has been substantially a Congregational Union, and the Baptist Missionary Society a Baptist Union; and out of these annual assemblies or convocations the Unions appear to have naturally arisen.[89]

There is no doubt that the 'English' Baptists in Scotland felt a particular responsibility to support the work of the BMS because it was the society of their own denomination. They were aided, however, by the Scotch Baptists who, following the lead of their patriarch Archibald McLean, gave generously to the cause, as has been seen in chapter two. In the *Brief Narrative of the Baptist Mission in India*, published in 1819, it is illuminating to note that 'English' Baptists dominate the list of those individuals willing to receive subscriptions for the BMS in Scotland. Subscribers listed under Edinburgh were the predictable Christopher Anderson alongside Dr Charles Stuart, a man whose name appears as a donor to many societies in the city and who had links with all the Baptist groups, and William Innes, the brother-in-law of Robert and James Haldane and minister of Elder Street Baptist Church. The person named in Glasgow was James Deakin, treasurer to the Glasgow Auxiliary Society. He had been the sole deacon of the 'English' Baptist church in the city during the ministry of James Lister, 1801 to 1803, and from then until the church had closed in 1806. Deakin was now associated with the Albion Street Baptist Church that was to call the former St Ninian's Parish Church minister William Shirreff, from Stirling, as its minister in 1823.[90] George Barclay of Kilwinning was the other Scottish contact listed in the Report.[91] Anderson saw the *Periodical Accounts* of the BMS as not merely a record of events in India, but as a means of strengthening relationships with the Scotch Baptists at home. In a letter to Fuller dated June 1809 he requested the inclusion of an account of the restoration of an Indian believer to the church to 'enhance the Mission in the esteem of the godly', meaning the Scotch Baptists as the following quotation confirms.

I hope you will certainly publish the case of the restoration to the

---

89 J. Conder, *The Eclectic Review*, New Series, 1 (February, 1837), p. 181.
90 Anderson, *Christopher Anderson*, pp. 383-385.
91 C. Anderson, *Brief Narrative of the Baptist Mission in India*, (London: Button and Son, 1819, 5th edition), introduction, n.p.

church, that of poor Deep Chundra, and Brother Carey's address to him when re-admitted. It is not only very affecting and calculated to do good to backsliders in general but it will show the Scotch what sort of discipline we have got among us.[92]

Anderson was convinced that improved relationships between Baptists in England had come about through their co-operation in the work of overseas mission and that it had led to the formation of a union of Baptist churches. He hoped that closer ties would also emerge between Scotch and 'English' Baptists in Scotland as a result of partnership in evangelistic activities. His ability to see the 'big picture' rather than get bogged down in detail revealed his long-term strategy.

This ability to grasp a wider perspective on many issues than some of his colleagues explains his reaction to the launch of *The Baptist Magazine*. In January 1812 Anderson wrote a letter to Andrew Fuller in response to information from Fuller that several English Baptists had withdrawn their support for *The Evangelical Magazine* in order to promote *The Baptist Magazine* as a self-consciously denominational periodical. Anderson's comments were unusually forceful, indicating his strength of feeling:

> Well [James] Hinton [Oxford Baptist minister] and the magazine; if you and Dr Ryland [Jr] take part in it, do, I entreat, let us have another title. The present is to me almost odious, at least I seldom hear the name of it pronounced by any who are not in our communion without almost blushing. This is not a little matter. The world is ruled by names; and it is a great pity if we most unwisely have bound a name to ourselves as a crown, which has been given to us by our foes. Had it been Christian, that worthy name by which our denomination had been most accurately described, how much better had it been for us.[93]

The principle held by Anderson, and already discussed regarding his work in Ireland, was that more effective work can usually be accomplished when Christians unite across the denominational boundaries than when they work in isolation. Anderson,[94] like most of the other first generation of BMS leaders,[95] shared the 'catholic' vision of evangelical Christianity that played down denominational identities in the late eighteenth and early nineteenth century.[96] If

---

92 Anderson to Fuller, June 30, 1809, cited by Anderson, *Christopher Anderson*, pp. 189-190.
93 Fuller to Anderson, January 27, 1812; Anderson to Fuller, February 1812, cited by Anderson, *Christopher Anderson*, pp. 196-200.
94 Anderson, *Baptist Mission in India*, pp. 2-3.
95 Fuller to Anderson, November 9, 1812, cited by Anderson, *Christopher Anderson*, pp. 212-213.

an inter-denominational society in which Baptists were participants was working effectively, as was the case with *The Evangelical Magazine*, then it was inappropriate to set up a rival denominational alternative. Anderson could see a need for separate home missionary societies and denominational structures but duplication of resources beyond this boundary was unnecessary.

The same principle was evident in his conduct with respect to other Baptist societies. In Scotland before Anderson and Barclay in 1808 had set up the SIS there had been no Scottish Baptist home missionary society. In the following years a principally Scotch Baptist society and one associated with the Haldanes had been established to do essentially the same kind of work. Chapter five will discuss these societies and explain how they united in 1827 to form a more effective organisation. Anderson was a pioneer who saw a need and remained committed to a cause until others could take the helm. He and George Barclay maintained the Scotch Itinerant Society through its difficult existence until 1824 when a merger was arranged with the Haldanes' society for Highland evangelism. Once the union of the two societies had been established Anderson withdrew in order to promote other causes with which he had been associated. A brief statement of accounts for the SIS has survived for the years 1808 to 1815, revealing the unpredictable levels of income during those years. In the earliest years of the SIS, as revealed by Table 4.1, income and expenditure were largely comparable, but from 1811 to 1814 the deficits began to mount. 1815 was the last financial year in which donations to the cause exceeded the minimum figure required to balance the books. After seven years of generous support for this cause Christopher Anderson felt obliged to indicate that his resources were insufficient to meet the existing need. The extract of accounts shown in Table 4.1 indicates that Anderson was expecting other subscribers to provide the funds to reclaim more than fifteen pounds that he had loaned to the SIS to cover existing debt.

---

96 Anderson, *Baptist Mission in India*, p.67. See Martin, *Evangelicals United*, and W.R. Ward, *Religion and Society in England 1790-1850*, (London: B.T. Batsford, 1972).

Table 4.1 Scotch Itinerant Society Abstract of Accounts to the End of 1815.

Income £ s d	Year	Expenditure £ s d
44 2 0	1808	49 9 0
42 11 0	1809	43 19 0
105 13 5	1810	101 13 5
83 14 1	1811	95 4 9
39 4 1	1812 & 1813	74 15 3
159 2 3	1814	110 9 4
67 19 0	1815	82 6 8
15 10 11	Balance in advance by Mr A[nderson]	
557 17 5		**557 17 5** [sic]

[Source: Sinclair, *Journal of Itinerating Exertions*, (6, 1817), p. 40.]

The finances of the Society fell deeper and deeper into debt, the greater part of which, if not all of it, was owed to Anderson, who had taken personal responsibility not only for the itinerant evangelists but also for the church-planting work at Falkirk and Aberdeen. The amount owed to him for itinerating work in the period 1816-1824 was £147; a further £92 or £93 was incurred as expenses in Falkirk and Aberdeen. This admission revealed that Anderson had personally contributed approximately 25% of the income for the mission.[97] Anderson once again had initiated a project but when it had established itself he had withdrawn to promote some of his other interests in the wider Christian community. The importance of recognising the way in which the Charlotte Chapel minister engaged in generous support for mission provides a clear perspective from which to interpret his involvement in the 1827 Baptist Union of Scotland.

The 1827 Baptist Union was not the first attempt to promote union amongst Baptist churches of different ecclesiologies in Scotland. The first attempt, ironically, was initiated in 1806 by the Edinburgh Scotch Baptist Church led by Archibald McLean. It invited the small fellowship of 'English' Baptists that met in Cordiners' Hall, after their expulsion from the Tabernacle due to having accepted believer's baptism, to enter into full fellowship with them. James Young and Archibald Smith, who had risen to prominence in Anderson's absence, sent a letter in August 1806 in reply to the overtures they had received, two days prior to Anderson's return to Scotland. The letter, addressed to McLean and William Braidwood, the church elders, explained why the union proposal had to be turned down. The

---

97 Anderson, *Christopher Anderson*, pp. 118-119.

reasons given included a variety of Scotch Baptist characteristics: a lack of emphasis on evangelism, the engagement of pastors in secular pursuits, and the prohibition of the celebration of the Lord's Supper without elders. All these reasons were in line with the declared convictions of Anderson that have already been considered earlier in this chapter. The Cordiners' Hall fellowship re-united its members with the Tabernacle Church after James Haldane had been baptised in 1808 by James Young, a step in itself of Baptist union.[98] The proposed union that had been offered by the Baptist tradition most secure in its identity was declined, in part because the 'English' Baptist congregation was insecure about its own priorities and identity. In addition, the invitation offered by the Edinburgh Scotch Baptists was in effect an opportunity to bring about a 'merger' of the two congregations. This event, therefore, was of a different character from the 1827 Baptist Union of Scotland in which the autonomy of each participating congregation was safeguarded.

Christopher Anderson recognised that separate denominations would remain in existence for the foreseeable future. This point was made in a letter to Serampore Baptist missionary John Marshman in June 1845: 'in our present condition the question called "the church" never will be, never can be settled'.[99] What could be achieved in terms of Christian union amongst Baptists? This subject was addressed by Anderson in a letter in 1822 to William Turnbull and Thomas Swan, two students training for the Baptist ministry at Bristol Baptist College. Turnbull, a native of Edinburgh, had been converted under Anderson's ministry in 1818, and as a result had been received into fellowship after baptism in the following year. He had been sent out as an evangelist by the church in various districts of Edinburgh during the period 1819 until 1821, when he was sent to train in Bristol. He died aged 28 in December 1823 after becoming ill while supplying 'a destitute church in Glasgow'.[100] Swan, likewise, had been a member of Anderson's congregation and had been sent to Bristol in preparation for taking up the post of divinity tutor at Serampore College in India.[101] He was to serve for three years at Serampore, 1826 to 1829, before accepting the pastorate of Cannon Street Baptist Church, Birmingham, until his death in 1857. It is highly significant to note that during his ministry in

---

98 'Baptist Pioneers in Scotland', 1902, p. 27; 1907, pp. 149, 155-156.
99 Anderson to John Marshman, June 12 1845, cited by Anderson, *Christopher Anderson*, pp. 328-329.
100 *The Baptist Magazine*, 16.3 (March, 1824), pp. 97-103.
101 S. Hall, 'The Scottish Connections with Bristol Baptist College', p. 2. A copy of this MS is held by the author of this book.

Birmingham Swan was President of the Baptist Union of Great Britain and Ireland in 1839.[102] It is possible that the influence of his pastor during his formative years in Edinburgh had contributed to his devotion to the affairs of this Baptist Union. In his letter to his two young members, Anderson stated:

> I know that in order to much good being done, co-operation, the result of undissembled love, is absolutely necessary; and I think that if God in His tender mercy would take me as one of but a very few whose hearts He will unite as the heart of one man – since all the watchmen cannot see eye to eye – might I be one of a little band of brothers who should do so, and who should leave behind them a proof of how much may be accomplished in consequence of the union of only a few on earth in spreading Christianity, oh how should I rejoice and be glad.[103]

Anderson had seen the benefits of union amongst Particular Baptists in England, but there is no indication that any attempts at union amongst Scottish Baptists had been undertaken before the time of his letter in 1822. His views, however, had been made plain, revealing that he would be in favour of the attempts at union in 1827.

The 1827 attempt at forming a Baptist Union of Scotland appeared to take place without the involvement of Christopher Anderson, as his name does not appear on any of the lists of individuals participating in the various committee and public meetings. It is, however, equally important to note that all the members of the initial committee formed to promote this body came from his congregation, as will be explained in chapter six. What are the possible explanations for this anomaly? One possible suggestion is that Anderson may have felt that overtures to the Scotch Baptists might have been better received from lay leaders in his congregation rather than an ordained minister, given the opposing sentiments on the pastoral office. Another possibility is that he believed that the body of opinion in favour of a Baptist union of churches was so strong that his personal presence at the committee meetings and public gatherings was unnecessary, especially considering his own heavy workload. It is certain, though, that all the 'English' Baptist churches which responded to the invitation to consider a proposed union were in favour of union.[104] It is probable, however, that the

---

102 A.S. Langley, *Birmingham Baptists Past and Present*, (London: The Kingsgate Press, 1939), p. 36.
103 Anderson to Swan and Turnbull, September 7 1822, cited by Anderson, *Christopher Anderson*, pp. 378-381.

second suggestion is the better explanation of his actions.

Jonathan Watson

It is appropriate to consider next Jonathan Watson, the founding pastor of Cupar Baptist Church, who was the principal 'English' Baptist contributor to union amongst Scottish Baptists in the period prior to 1869. He had the unique distinction of having been associated with all but one of the joint endeavours amongst Scottish Baptists in those years, a record surpassed by no other member of his denomination. The one exception was the Johnstonian Baptist Union of Scotland, 1843 to 1856, from which he had been excluded despite a request for association in 1845, discussed in chapter seven. Watson, a druggist by trade, had come to Cupar in 1814 from Montrose where his brother James was the pastor of the local Baptist Church.[105] In Cupar two years of public lectures in a room in the Lady Wynd, known as the Weaver's Hall, had resulted in the formation of a properly constituted Baptist Church. Watson was inducted to the pastorate by Robert Aikenhead of Kirkcaldy, his brother-in-law,[106] and William Innes of Edinburgh. The significance of the presiding ministers is vital in view not only of the nature of his congregation but also of Watson's own opinions as a factor promoting union amongst Scottish Baptists. Innes was the pastor of an open membership Baptist Church in Edinburgh, a status unique amongst Baptist churches in Scotland's capital city. All the other Baptist congregations required candidates for church membership to have previously been baptised by immersion.[107] Robert Aikenhead was the minister of an Independent Church in Kirkcaldy. In 1835 Aikenhead's congregation had agreed to exercise 'mutual forbearance' with him on the subject of baptism after he had become convinced of the Baptist understanding of this ordinance.[108] Cupar Baptist Church was founded as an open membership congregation of whom three out of the original twenty-three members were pae-

---

104 *To the Baptist Churches in Scotland*, June 13, 1827, p. 2.
105 Cupar Baptist Church Minute Book, September 1916, n.p., the MS is in the possession of Cupar Baptist Church.
106 *Historical Notes and Reminiscences* of Cupar, (Cupar, 1884), p. 126, cited by W.D. McNaughton, 'The Congregational Church in Kirkcaldy and other Congregational Churches in Fife, from their beginning to 1850', (ThD thesis, The American Congregational Centre, Ventura, California, 1989), p. 172.
107 'Baptist Pioneers in Scotland', 1902, p. 20.
108 Kinniburgh, *Fathers of Independency*, p. 430.

dobaptists, including the pastor's wife! Jonathan Watson, though he was a convinced Baptist, had agreed to exercise forbearance over the ordinance of baptism.[109] The constitution of Watson's church was in line with the extraordinary degree of co-operation in ministry between the Baptists and Independents in Fife in the early nineteenth century. In 1825 'The Fife Home Missionary Association or Itinerating Society' was established to co-ordinate evangelistic activities in the kingdom. All seven of the Independent and probably seven of the eight Baptist congregations, including Cupar Baptist Church, were participants in this venture.[110] Watson's willingness to seek an inclusive basis of fellowship in his own congregation had prepared him for his role in future years of seeking an inclusive basis for union amongst the various groups of Scottish Baptists.

An example of Watson's ecumenical spirit was seen in his relationship with the Independent Church in St Andrews and with its minister William Lothian. Watson had encouraged Baptists in St Andrews to associate with the Independent Church and not to seek the establishment of another cause as long as they had been given the full privileges of membership. Mutual forbearance, he argued, should be exercised upon the ordinance of baptism in line with the situation in his own congregation. There was growth in correspondence between Watson and Lothian in 1841 after the Independent minister had asked the Baptist brethren in his congregation to refrain from discussing the nature of this ordinance, to avoid divisions within the fellowship, especially as the church had adopted a clear paedobaptist position in its constitution. The Cupar pastor protested at this attempt to stifle debate on the grounds that it was a secondary rather than a primary issue of the faith. If the form of baptism had been essential to salvation then the proposed course of action was essential, but as this was not the case mutual forbearance was the only appropriate pathway to follow. Watson concluded a letter in April 1841 by stating:

> forbearance properly understood implies an equality of rights and privileges among Christians. As the brethren have shown no wish to invade yours and if left alone will rejoice to walk together in love and unity of the faith, I sincerely hope that you will see the necessity and consistency of swaping off [removing] this remnant

---

109 *A Brief History of Cupar Baptist Church*, (Cupar: Cupar Baptist Church, 1936), pp. 8-9.

110 The seven Baptist Churches were Cupar, Kirkcaldy, Auchtermuchty, Ferry-Port-on-Craig, Dunfermline, Anstruther and Kinghorn. Newburgh Baptist Church, a small Scotch Baptist group, was the one non-participating body, cited by McNaughton, 'Congregational Church in Kirkcaldy', p. 347.

of intolerance and of embracing in the arms of affection as aforetimes all who love the Lord Jesus Christ in sincerity.[111]

The valiant attempts to prevent a division in the St Andrews Independent Church did not succeed. As a result a separate Baptist congregation had been formed in the town.[112] The importance of this correspondence is seen in Watson's attempts to act as a conciliator between parties who had deemed their divisions to be too great to overcome. On this occasion the Cupar pastor had been unable to effect a reconciliation, but it had revealed the spirit with which he would seek to build bridges between Baptists of differing convictions in Scotland. His principles regarding forbearance were not only maintained, but held with greater conviction in the later years of his ministry in Dublin Street Baptist Church, Edinburgh. In an address on this subject to his congregation in 1867, Watson made the following point regarding baptism:

> Baptism is an ordinance of God, but it is, I have remarked, too frequently insisted upon by our Denomination, the result of which is just to produce a contrary effect from what was intended...At any rate, it is, as appears to me, becoming more and more obvious to all classes, that to attempt to coerce the conscience by withholding privileges to which Christ's disciples are entitled, is as foreign to the spirit of the New Testament as it is opposed to the common sense of mankind.[113]

This message proclaimed at the time of the concluding efforts of the process of establishing a union of Baptist churches in Scotland confirms that Watson had maintained a consistent position from the 1820s to the 1860s regarding forbearance amongst believers with respect to secondary issues upon which they could not agree.

Jonathan Watson had been present at the 1827 meetings called to unite Baptist churches in Scotland. The opening meeting of the group proposing union in April 1827 took place in Elder Street Chapel, Edinburgh. Three 'English' Baptist ministers Alexander McLeod of Glasgow, John Gilmour of Aberdeen and Jonathan Watson, took responsibility for leading the main session. Watson was invited to preside and to deliver the main address, implying that he had played a significant role in the proceedings of the movement for unity amongst Scottish Baptists.[114] The formal launch of the Bap-

---

111 Watson to Lothian, April 9 1841, MSS of correspondence in the possession of St Andrews Baptist Church.
112 I.G. Docherty, *'Something Very Fine' A History of St Andrews Baptist Church 1841-1991*, St Andrews: St Andrews Baptist Church, 1991, p. 7.
113 J. Watson, 'Observations suggested by a Pastorate of upwards of fifty years', private MS, Bundle 1, Waugh Papers.

tist Union of Scotland took place at the same venue in June 1827 at which Watson and Robert Murdoch, one of the Cupar deacons who had been a part of the church since its inception in 1816, were present.[115] The senior men from within 'English' Baptist circles took the most prominent roles on that occasion, as will be noted in chapter six, but the young pastor from Cupar made a notable contribution. He was one of only six, out of fifteen, Baptists from outside the capital city of Scotland who were invited to serve on the committee of the union.[116] Watson's zeal for union was clearly evident in his practical support for this venture in the late 1820s.

The 1835 to 1842 Scottish Baptist Association, discussed in chapter six, also attracted the support of the Cupar minister. Minutes of the 1835 annual meetings state that Watson and James Paterson of Glasgow had been appointed preachers for the following year's Association meetings. Watson's support for this Association was assured though he did not adopt as high a profile as in the late 1820s. His zeal for union, however, was not in question as Watson, like Christopher Anderson, appeared to be content to avoid the limelight if other colleagues were willing to take projects forward.[117]

4.4 'English' Baptists and Theological Education

The most important and enduring contribution by the 'English' Baptist tradition in Scotland to the process of fostering union amongst Scottish Baptists was in their promotion of the cause of theological training for prospective ministers and evangelists. This factor, which will be considered in more detail in chapters six, seven and eight, underlies each of the attempts at Baptist union after 1835. This development in Scotland was in line with the notable advance in educational interest amongst the various Nonconformist bodies in England, including the Particular Baptists.[118] The 'English' Baptists were the first to use a theological college south of the border for the training of its ministers. The first students, Peter McFarlane and Dugald Sinclair, were sent in 1806 to Horton Baptist College, Bradford.[119] In the period from 1806 to 1837 'English' Baptists sent twenty-two men to Horton College.[120] The John Street Baptist Church, Aberdeen, considered setting up a facility to train men for

---

114 *Circular from Committee of Proposed Baptist Union*, May 4 1827, p. 2.
115 *To the Baptist Churches in Scotland*, June 13 1827, p. 1.
116 *To the Baptist Churches in Scotland*, June 13 1827, p. 1.
117 Minutes of the Scottish Baptist Association, July 1835, p. 2.
118 Payne, 'Nonconformist Theological Education, pp. 229-231.
119 *NBES Report*, 1805-1806, p. 57.

the ministry in that city. The members of the church approached Benjamin Godwin, a tutor at Horton, in February 1837 with a view to asking him to superintend this work, but he declined their invitation.[121]

Appendix Two lists the names of the candidates sent for training in Bradford. William Steadman, the College Principal, was a passionate supporter of Baptist union. In his 1807 Address to the Lancashire and Yorkshire Association, he declared:

> But that which constitutes the chiefest benefit of associations, and warmly pleads for their necessity is, that without them we cannot conceive of any effectual means of ministers and churches uniting their endeavours and concentrating their strength for the farther advancement of the interest of Christ in the world. Individual efforts, though laudable, are generally weak, and ineffectual, but what one or a few cannot do, many may accomplish.[122]

Steadman showed by his practical exertions a clear commitment to Baptist union in England. He was, for example, the only northern Baptist minister at the annual meeting of the Baptist Union of Great Britain and Ireland in June 1832.[123] The importance of the Bradford College, under Steadman's principalship, in influencing the Scottish students in favour of a union of Baptist churches can be seen in the conduct of those individuals who returned to their native land to take up pastoral duties. Appendix Two lists twenty-two Scots who entered Horton College with a view to Baptist ministry. There were eleven men who settled outside Scotland and a further two men who failed to complete the course, leaving nine men who returned to their native land. One man, John McMillan, served as an evangelist with the Scotch Itinerant Society, based in Inveraray from 1825 until his early death in 1829.[124] There were eight men who settled in pastoral charges, each one of them supporting moves for union during their ministries. Dugald Sinclair, John Gilmour, and William Fraser, prior to entering Horton in 1828,[125] were involved in the 1827 Baptist Union of Scotland.[126] Robert Thomson, Donald

---

120 *NBES Reports*, 1805-1806 to 1837 – 1838.
121 Minutes of the Proceedings of the Church assembling in the Crown Terrace Chapel, Aberdeen, 1821-1868, February 17 1837. This MS is in the possession of Crown Terrace Baptist Church, Aberdeen.
122 W. Steadman, *The Utility of Associations*, (Bradford: J. Nicholson, 1807), p. 14.
123 Proceedings of the Baptist Union 1812-1870, Wednesday June 20, 1832, I, pp. 1-2. MS in the possession of Angus Library, Regents Park College, Oxford.
124 *NBES Report*, 1828-1829, (Idle: J. Vint, 1829), p. 60.

Thomson, Alexander Stalker and Francis Johnston joined the Scottish Baptist Association that operated from 1835 to 1842.[127] Francis Johnston, Robert Thomson and David McKay[128] were involved in the 1843 to 1856 Johnstonian Baptist Union.[129] Robert Johnstone, brought up in the Orangefield Baptist Church, Greenock,[130] pastored the union-affiliated St Andrews Baptist Church from 1856 to 1862.[131] Theological training at Horton College under William Steadman provided key Scottish students with a vision of what a union of Baptist churches could achieve in their native land. The influence of their College Principal played a significant part in helping to shape their vision of Scottish Baptist life in the future, including, of necessity, a national association of Baptist congregations.

It was this stream of Scottish Baptists that demonstrated the necessity for college-based ministerial training and their efforts were rewarded when a consensus in favour of this cause began to emerge in the 1830s. When meetings were called to discuss the inadequate situation regarding training for Baptist ministerial candidates at this time, 'English' Baptists were prominent in their espousal of the cause. The Baptist Academical Society, discussed in more detail in chapter six, that had been set up as a result of those meetings had a committee and corresponding members that included a high proportion of 'English' Baptists. Christopher Anderson's congregation was represented by Archibald Wilson, a wine and spirits dealer, in Edinburgh.[132] Other 'English' Baptists included James Paterson, minister of Hope Street Baptist Church, Glasgow, together with three of his members; George Barclay of Irvine, Jonathan Watson from Cupar and John McIlvain of Orangefield Baptist Church in Greenock.[133] In order to be motivated to engage in union with Baptists from other traditions, Scottish Baptists needed practical and visible evidence of the value of their co-operation; it was on this subject that united action was agreed with the least effort. The lim-

---

125 *NBES Report*, 1828-1829, p. 17.
126 *To the Baptist Churches in Scotland*, June 13 1827.
127 Minutes of the Scottish Baptist Association, 1835-1842.
128 *A Manuel of the Baptist Denomination for the Year 1846*, (London: Houlston and Stoneman, 1846), p. 36.
129 Baptist Union of Scotland Minutes of Annual Meetings 1843-1847. MS in the possession of Bristo Baptist Church, Edinburgh.
130 *NBES Report*, (Bradford: E. Keighley, 1831-1832), p. 64.
131 Yuille (ed.), *Baptists in Scotland*, p. 288.
132 *The Post Office Annual Directory for 1833-1834*, (Edinburgh: Ballantyne and Co., 1833), p. 97.
133 *First Report of the Committee of the Baptist Academical Society for Scotland*, (Edinburgh: R. Marshall, 1840), p.1.

ited results obtained in the 1820s and 1830s made them even more determined to work together to obtain a better system for training their ministers in future years. It was largely out of this shared commitment to theological education that there emerged a successful Baptist Union of Scotland.

The 'English' Baptists had been a small, even insignificant group of people at the start of the nineteenth century with a mere forty-two members, and possibly up to a hundred adherents.[134] The Scotch Baptists by contrast had around 400 members, with probably around 1000 adherents.[135] These statistics indicate that only approximately 10% of Baptist church members were associated with the 'English' stream at the start of the nineteenth century. The growth in 'English' ranks in the next four decades brought them to the forefront of Baptist life in Scotland. In 1843 Francis Johnston, Secretary of the Baptist Union of Scotland, published details of the approximate membership figures of the different Baptist churches in the country. Scotch Baptist Churches had a combined membership that had increased to 1974, but 'English' congregations had grown at a much faster rate to reach 3550 members, giving a total of 5524 in Scottish Baptist churches.[136] 'English' Baptists now comprised 64% of the constituency. They had replaced the Scotch Baptists as the dominant Baptist ecclesiological tradition by the 1830s.

The earlier 'English' Baptist leaders in Scotland, Frederick McFarlane, James Lister, Donald McVicar and Donald McArthur, laid the foundations for this style of Baptist ministry in Scotland. The next group of leaders was able not only to build a local congregation but also to engage in wider ministry and evangelism in Scotland. Itinerant evangelists Dugald Sinclair and Alexander McLeod combined ministries with the Scotch Itinerant Society and pastoral charges in their distinguished Christian service. They were both involved in the 1827 Baptist Union of Scotland, recognising that considerably more could be achieved by united efforts than solitary ventures. Sinclair by his departure to Canada had left a void in the Highlands that was never adequately filled. He had been the most successful of the Highland itinerants. Sinclair Thomson, the Shetland Apostle, was prevented by his geographical isolation and poverty from playing a fuller part in wider Baptist work in Scotland. His sterling efforts in church-planting in the far north of his native land did not cause him to be unmindful of what was happening in other places. His familiarity with the Baptist periodicals of his day and the suc-

---

134 Chapter four, pp. 119-120.
135 Rippon, *Baptist Annual Register*, 1795, pp. 373-374.
136 *First Yearly Report of the Baptist Union*, (Cupar: G.S. Tullis, 1843), pp. 18-22.

The 'English' Baptists, 1796-1852   151

cess of his fund-raising tours amongst the wider Particular Baptist community in Britain showed the value he placed on his union with other Calvinistic Baptists.

There is no doubt, though, that two men stand at the forefront of this tradition in Scotland, George Barclay and Christopher Anderson. Barclay was to some extent part of the pioneer generation who established the 'English' Baptist presence in Scotland. His contribution to the process of uniting Baptists in Scotland covered a wide range of activities including the establishment of the links with English Baptists in the work in Ireland under the auspices of the BMS; the fund-raising efforts for the BMS in his native land; and the resolution of the divisions in the BMS in 1837-1838, which has been called his greatest achievement. Barclay was the first 'English' Baptist minister to send ministerial students to train at Horton Baptist College, a decision that was eventually to set in motion a process that resulted in the formation of the Baptist Academical Society for Scotland, a body that would include Baptists from all three strands of Baptist life in Scotland. Barclay was a prominent member of that society in the last year of his life. He also had the honour of presiding at the constitution of the 1827 Baptist Union of Scotland in recognition of his services to Baptist life in his own land. Christopher Anderson was the most distinguished of the 'English' Baptists in Scotland in the first half of the nineteenth century, in part due to his wide and varied interests and activities in both Baptist and wider ecclesiastical circles. Anderson was a wise leader who carefully planned out his life's work. His travels in England in 1805 to 1806 enabled him to see the successful operation of the English Baptist Associations which provided a model for the future constitution of his church and also possibly the 1827 Baptist Union of Scotland. Anderson, together with Barclay, was prominently involved in the British Baptist work in Ireland, though he also was involved with the efforts of other denominations in that island. The BMS was always prominent in his thinking and it was upon his shoulders that the burden of the Serampore missionaries principally rested in the difficult years, especially in the area of financial support. Anderson was a proponent of 'catholic' Christianity who did not see the need to set up distinctive denominational bodies where an undenominational society or periodical was engaged in an effective ministry. He was the co-founder with Barclay of the first Scottish Baptist home missionary society and was involved in the process of uniting the three societies in 1825 to 1827. He was not listed among the prominent individuals who served on the committee of the 1827 Baptist Union but there was no doubt that he had been in favour. The evidence for this is seen especially in the prominence of his church's members on the original Baptist Union committee.

Jonathan Watson had been content to focus his energies in Baptist work and witness in his native land. His pastorates in Cupar and Dublin Street, Edinburgh, alongside his promotion of united efforts amongst Scottish Baptists, had been the extent of his labours. It is possible that this restriction of his activities enabled his influence amongst his colleagues to be greater than those of more prominent 'English' Baptists such as Barclay and Anderson who had been involved in a range of projects outside Scotland. The pinnacle of his career, which will be referred to in chapter eight, was to come in 1869 with the invitation to become the first President of the Baptist Union of Scotland. The granting of this honour was to be a recognition of his contribution to the process of uniting Scottish Baptists in a union of churches.[137]

The most important contribution, though, by 'English' Baptists to the process of uniting Scottish Baptists was in the field of theological education. It was the establishment of an adequate theological training system that brought Baptists from the three traditions together in the 1830s. This process developed over time and was at the heart of the third and the final attempts to form a Baptist Union of Scotland in the 1840s to the 1860s. The importance of the vision for Baptist union promulgated by the Horton principal William Steadman was passed on to his ministerial students, a body that included a number of Scots. Overall, 'English' Baptists had made the most significant contribution to the process of uniting Scottish Baptists in the first five decades of the nineteenth century.

---

137 Yuille (ed.), *Baptists in Scotland*, p. 239.

CHAPTER 5

The Baptist Home Missionary Society: A Substitute Union, 1827-1868?

5.1 The Earliest Efforts in Home Evangelisation by Scottish Baptists

The Baptist Home Missionary Society (BHMS) was formed in August 1827 from the two existing Baptist evangelistic agencies.[1] In this chapter it is appropriate first to set the scene by charting the progress of the various Baptist home missionary organisations towards the united body that they became in 1827, before attempting to examine the role played by this organisation. Secondly, the factors that promoted the possibility of the BHMS being seen as a substitute union will be considered. Thirdly, the evidence from home missionary reports that suggested a need for a formal union of Baptist churches will be assessed.

There were originally three groups involved in Highland mission work connected with the three streams of Baptist church life in Scotland. Itinerant evangelism by 'English' Baptists appeared to commence in Scotland at the beginning of the nineteenth century with the labours of William Ward in Aberdeenshire. Ward had been the minister of an Episcopal Church in Old Deer, Aberdeenshire. Discussions with a Roman Catholic priest on the subject of infant baptism led him to question his position, resulting in the adoption of Baptist principles during a visit to England in 1797. He returned to Old Deer, but was expelled from his clerical office.[2] The Old Deer minister offered his services to the SPGH in 1798 and was accepted as an itinerant preacher under their auspices in Aberdeenshire.[3] Ward then, in July 1800, sought assistance from The Baptist Society in London for the Encouragement and Support of Itinerant Preach-

---

1 *Address by the Committee of the Baptist Home Missionary Society for Scotland*, October 2 1827, p. 1.
2 *Scottish Baptist Magazine*, 5.7 (July, 1879), pp. 105-107.
3 R. Kinniburgh, 'A Historical Survey of Congregationalism in Scotland from its rise in 1798 to 1812', in *The Jubilee Memorial of the Scottish Congregational Churches*, (Edinburgh: A Fullarton & Co., 1849), p. 52.

ing, at which he was awarded £10. His itinerant labours had been completed in Aberdeenshire no later than 1805.[4] Ward, a graduate of Queen's College, Cambridge, had returned to his native East Anglia as pastor of Diss Baptist Church, Norfolk.[5] The second applicant to request support from the London society was a Mr Paterson from Stonehaven. He had first made contact with it in 1804 and had been granted £5 to assist with his expenses in itinerant preaching in Aberdeenshire.[6] Paterson's applications to this body for financial assistance continued at least until the autumn of 1810.[7] His identity has not been satisfactorily resolved. One view that has been suggested indicates that he was a Scotch Baptist preacher from Montrose.[8] Harry Escott in *A History of Scottish Congregationalism* refers to Adam Paterson, one of Robert Haldane's students, who was the first minister of the Independent Church at Bervie, Kincardineshire. At some point in 1803 or 1804 the minister and a large part of the congregation adopted Baptist opinions.[9] The timing of this change of views appears to suggest that Adam Paterson may be the person in question that applied to the London society, but the evidence is inconclusive. These applications for assistance from Scotland led the society in 1806 to review its constitution regarding home missionary work outside England and Wales. The deliberations took some time, but especially after written support for the Scots from Andrew Fuller it was decided to treat Scots on the same basis as English applicants.[10] As a result of this important decision 'English' Baptists in Scotland began to consider a more permanent structure to organise the work of itinerant evangelism in their native land.

The first 'English' Baptist organisation to be established was the

---

4   Minutes of the Proceedings of the Baptist Society in London for the Encouragement and Support of Itinerant Preaching, July 24 1800, January 22 and April 23 1801, May 13 1806; MS in the Angus Library, Regents Park College, Oxford. K. Dix, *Strict and Particular: English Strict and Particular Baptists in the Nineteenth Century*, (Didcot: Baptist Historical Society, 2001), p. 123, has suggested 1802 as the date for the commencement of the Diss ministry. Unfortunately there is insufficient evidence to fix this date with precision. Dix also notes on page 123 of his book that Ward resigned from the Diss pastorate in 1822 'after adopting anti-Trinitarian views'.
5   J. Browne, *History of Congregationalism and Memorials of the Churches in Norfolk and Suffolk*, (London: Jarrold and Sons, 1877), p. 556.
6   The Baptist Society in London Minutes, July 24 1805 and August 12 1805, n.p..
7   The Baptist Society in London Minutes, October 11 1810, n.p..
8   Private communication by Mr J.S. Fisher of Inverness.
9   Escott, *Scottish Congregationalism*, p. 267.
10 The Baptist Society in London Minutes, October 20 1808, n.p..

SIS. Christopher Anderson and George Barclay set up this society in 1808. Andrew Fuller had prepared the way for their applications for funds. The London committee's minutes for July 21 1808 refer to Fuller's intervention:

> they had received a letter from Mr Fuller in which he says 'the Baptist Itinerant Society if they wish to do good and their plans be not confined to England cannot at this time do better than by giving some assistance to Anderson and Barclay. I need not say to you they are men of God and men that will do much with a little money. That which renders it more important at this time is the fierce disputes amongst the Scotch Independents about discipline and the performance of ordinances has occasioned the dissolution of their Society for Propagating the Gospel at Home.' They had thereupon resolved that a letter be written to Mr Fuller informing him that if Messrs Anderson and Barclay will make personal application that the committee will attend to their cases.[11]

George Barclay received regular donations of money (usually £5 each time) and in addition, according to the extant minutes from 1808 to 1812, the London Society sent tracts and copies of the New Testament.[12] It is probable that this aid continued in the following years, but the minutes apparently have not survived. The SIS employed three full-time missionaries. The first of these was Alexander McLeod who had been the minister of the Haldane Tabernacle in Dunkeld, Perthshire, from 1804 to 1807. He had become a Baptist by 1807. McLeod's change of views had caused a controversy in that church which had resulted in his resignation from the pastorate. He was employed by the SIS to itinerate in Perthshire.[13] David Gibson, a member of the Kilwinning church, was employed to work in Kirkcudbrightshire, and Dugald Sinclair, upon the completion of his studies at the Bradford Academy, was appointed to serve in Argyllshire.[14] Anderson and Barclay had been given encouragement from the London Society regarding financial support when the SIS was formed in 1808. This aid from Particular Baptists south of the border was the incentive needed for 'English' Baptists in Scotland to launch their itinerant evangelistic activities.

The Haldane brothers, Robert and James Alexander, did not form a Baptist home mission organisation to support their Baptist colleagues who had formerly served with the SPGH.[15] They chose, instead, to

---

11 The Baptist Society in London Minutes, July 21 1808, n.p..
12 The Baptist Society in London Minutes, July 21 1808 – April 9 1812, n.p..
13 Meek, 'Independent and Baptist Churches', p. 283. Additional details of McLeod's career are given in Chapter four, pp. 124-126
14 Anderson, *Christopher Anderson*, pp. 101-102.

work with a more loosely connected group of agents whom they financed. There is much information about their involvement with Baptist home missionaries that has not survived. It is clear, however, that they had retained a commitment to many Highland pastors. James Haldane's congregation, the Tabernacle Church, Leith Walk, Edinburgh, supported several men including Lachlan Mackintosh of Grantown; Alexander Grant of Tobermory; William Hutchison of Kingussie and Walter Munro of Fortrose.[16] In 1823 their loose network of agents was merged with the operations of the SIS to form the Baptist Evangelical Society. The SIS probably would not have survived on its own much longer due to mounting debts. It had been funded principally by Christopher Anderson who had been owed £147 from debts incurred in itinerating work over the period from 1816 to 1824 and a further £92 or £93 incurred as expenses in church-planting work in Aberdeen and Falkirk.[17] In the new society, called the Home Missionary Society for Scotland after 1824, its gifted workers would have a financially secure future that would enable them to continue the work they had begun.

George Barclay was appointed as the secretary of the new society. He wrote a letter to *The Baptist Magazine* in May 1825 explaining the reasons for the setting up of this new mission agency and the additional work that it would undertake. It was stated that the principal reason for its emergence was the great need for more evangelists in the Highlands and Islands of Scotland. The most significant step forward was the employment of four additional Gaelic-speaking missionaries who would work on a full-time basis in Lewis, Skye (two missionaries), and Islay, Jura and Colonsay (one altogether). Other missionaries were employed on the understanding that all their expenses would be met on their preaching tours. The size of the committee and its support base were also enlarged.[18] The success of the Home Missionary Society for Scotland through its stronger financial base and increased team of missionaries was undoubtedly the major factor in bringing together the two remaining evangelisation societies in 1827. It appeared to be evident that itinerant evangelism could be carried out more effectively through the combined efforts of Scottish Baptists than through much smaller separate societies.

The other body engaged in Highland evangelism during this

---

15 See Chapter three, pp. 78-80, 94-95, for details on the work of the SPGH.
16 Yuille (ed.), *Baptists in Scotland*, pp. 72-73.
17 Anderson, *Christopher Anderson*, p. 118.
18 G. Barclay, *The Baptist Magazine*, 17.5 (May, 1825), p. 216.

period of time was the Baptist Highland Mission. It had been constituted in 1816 by three Scotch Baptist pastors in Glasgow, James Watt, James Buchan and David McLaren, and by three members of the Baptist Church in Perth, John Stalker, Robert Pullar (the treasurer) and Isaac Nicol. This society had been formed to support some of the former agents of the SPGH who had not received financial assistance since the demise of that Independent organisation, in particular William Tulloch. After his adoption of Baptist principles in 1808, Tulloch had become the pastor of Lawers Baptist Church, but the absence of pecuniary aid forced him to travel to the Lowlands for paid employment. He had settled briefly in Renfrew. At this time Tulloch came into contact with the Scotch Baptist pastors from Glasgow who invited him to work as their agent in Aberfeldy.[19] Tulloch served in the town from 1816 to 1819 before moving to Blair Atholl, where he remained until 1861.[20]

The establishment of the Baptist Highland Mission in 1816 by the liberal party in the constituency, after the 1810 divisions amongst Scotch Baptists, was not the first venture of the Scotch Baptists into Highland evangelisation.[21] The Edinburgh Scotch Baptist Church had sent one of its members in 1797 to work as an itinerant evangelist. James Watt (1762-1821), a former Antiburgher minister from Aberdeenshire, had been invited to return to his former sphere of service, a ministry he was eager to undertake. He had been based at Balmaud but travelled all over Aberdeenshire and Banffshire before moving to Glasgow in 1802. In Glasgow Watt worked as a doctor. He also became a pastor in a Scotch Baptist congregation.[22] Watt's labours had resulted in the formation of Baptist churches in Balmaud (1797) and Old Deer (1800). His hearers were responsible for other Baptist churches constituted in the area at New Pitsligo (1803), Aberchirder (1807), Silver Street, Aberdeen (1807), St Fergus (1809) and Fraserburgh (1810).[23] The impact of his own ministry in Highland evangelism was undoubtedly a catalyst behind his support for the establishment of the Baptist Highland Mission in later years.

The success of Watt's labours had stimulated the Edinburgh

---

19 Yuille (ed.), *Baptists in Scotland*, pp. 71-72.
20 'Memoir of the late William Tulloch by his son', *BHMS Report*, (Edinburgh: D.R. Collie & Son, 1861), pp. 19-24.
21 Chapter two, pp. 41-42.
22 *Scottish Baptist Yearbook*, Glasgow: W. Asher, 1900, p. 14. Wilson, *Origin and Progress*, pp. 39-40.
23 J.S. Fisher, 'The North East', in D.W. Bebbington (ed.), *The Baptists in Scotland A History*, Glasgow: Baptist Union of Scotland, 1988, p. 262.

Scotch Baptist church in November 1798 to issue a general call in its connexion to support Highland mission.[24] A fund was established by 1804 to which the churches in Glasgow, Paisley, Edinburgh, Dunfermline and a few others contributed. This new fund administered by the Edinburgh congregation covered all the costs of a number of their elders on itinerant tours as well as full-time support for Edward Mackay in Thurso, David Macrae in Fortrose, and A. Fraser in Huntly and then in Dundee from 1805 to 1810. Scotch Baptist divisions in 1810 seriously affected this fund, but the Edinburgh congregation endeavoured to continue financing home missionary work that was maintained within the stricter party of the Scotch Baptists.

5.2 The Formation of the Baptist Home Missionary Society for Scotland

There was, however, in the mid-1820s a general mood in the Baptist constituency that favoured greater united effort. In the first half of 1827 there were several well-attended meetings that aimed to create a union of Baptist churches in Scotland.[25] The earliest Baptist Union of Scotland, as we shall see, was established in June 1827.[26] It was the first time that Baptists from all three groups in Scotland had agreed to work together on a formal basis. Once this was acknowledged, there was a significant increase in momentum towards the amalgamation of the mission agencies. The marriage of the Home Missionary Society for Scotland and the Baptist Highland Mission duly took place in August 1827.[27] The desire for unity and co-operation between the men who led the Baptist Union and the Home Missionary Society can be seen from the large proportion of ministers and Scotch Baptist elders who were prominently associated with both bodies: William Innes (Elder Street, Edinburgh); George Barclay (Irvine); David Souter (who had been minister in Perth but was now in Aberdeen); Jonathan Watson (Cupar); David McLaren (North Portland Street, Glasgow); Peter Grant (Stirling); Charles Arthur (Kirkcaldy); and David Dewar (Dunfermline).[28] In the case of the Scotch Baptist church in Dunfermline, the other pastor Adam Kirk attended meetings of the Baptist Union of Scotland on behalf

---

24 Wilson, *Origin and Progress*, pp. 40-47.
25 Chapter six, pp. 192-201.
26 *To the Baptist Churches in Scotland*, June 13 1827.
27 *Address by the Committee of the Baptist Home Missionary Society for Scotland*, October 2 1827, p. 1.
28 *Address by the Committee of the Baptist Home Missionary Society for Scotland*, October 2 1827, p. 3.

of the church.[29] In the late summer of 1827 it appeared that the question under consideration in this chapter would be irrelevant due to the successful launch of the two national Baptist organisations. The Baptist Union, however, was not to survive though the date of its demise, probably circa 1830, is unknown.[30] At the end of the third decade of the nineteenth century it appeared that the BHMS had a secure future, but the vision of a formal union of churches had failed to secure the assent of the wider Baptist constituency.

5.3 The Geographical Spread of BHMS Agents

There were a number of factors indicating that in some measure the BHMS was taking over the role of substitute 'Union' in the following decades. The first of these and the most important of all was apparent in the astonishing success achieved by the Highland missionaries and this agency that supported them. Scottish Baptists were a tiny minority in a largely Presbyterian land. In 1843 Francis Johnston indicated that there were only 5,000 Scottish Baptists and lamented the slow growth in numbers compared to England and Wales.[31] As late as 1863 James Paterson, minister of Hope Street Baptist Church, Glasgow, indicated that there were no more than 8-10,000 Scottish Baptists.[32] In the light of the numerical base on which to support their work, the geographical spread of the BHMS's operations, illustrated in Appendix 3.1, is truly astonishing.

There were at least seventy-two places in Scotland where full-time or part-time (in terms of income) agents were based between 1800 and 1870. This list does not include preaching stations or locations regularly visited by itinerant preachers. The home missionaries were moved by the sending agencies if their prospects for success were poor or because the society had inadequate income. There were, however, many stations occupied for a lengthy period of time resulting in the establishment of churches. The topographical range of the work was from the Orkney and Shetland Isles, together with Caithness in the north of Scotland, to Dumfries and Galloway in the south. In the west the Hebrides were well served, as was Argyll. In the centre and east of the country Perthshire and Aberdeenshire, for example, had been provided with a consistent supply of Baptist preachers. Stonehaven and Dundee further south also had resident

---

29 *Address by the Committee of the Baptist Home Missionary Society for Scotland*, October 2 1827, p. 1.
30 Chapter six, p. 210.
31 F. Johnston, *An Inquiry into the means of advancing the Baptist Denomination in Scotland*, (Cupar: G.S. Tullis, 1843), pp. 6-7.
32 *The Freeman*, 9 (May 27, 1863), p. 331.

missionaries for a time. The central belt of Scotland received a smaller proportion of missionaries than its population merited, but agents were stationed at Stobhill (Glasgow), Stirling, Tullibody, Grahamston, Falkirk and Edinburgh. The south-east of Scotland had no resident home missionaries, but this is probably due to their being comparatively well served with Baptist churches. If the BHMS was able to co-ordinate evangelistic outreach activities effectively throughout Scotland then there was less need to establish a parallel union of churches. It appeared that the home mission strategy in the late 1820s and early 1830s did include significant attempts to reach the urban masses, in addition to the primary work in the Highlands and Islands. There was, therefore, at that time no significant evangelistic role for a Baptist Union to play, a situation that would change by the 1840s.[33]

The number of communities served by the Baptist preachers was much greater than the total of the stations to which they had been posted. Mr Paterson, the agent supported in part by the Baptist Itinerant Society in London in the first decade of the nineteenth century, indicated in a report in 1807 that 'he had itinerated to Kinnef, Aberdeen, Glen(t?)son, Marykirk, Laurencekirk, Fettercairn and Skaetrow besides his stated places.'[34] A report from Alexander McLeod to the same society in January 1809 described the preaching stations that he visited on a regular basis from Perth.

> He has preached at the following amongst other places: At Stanley 7 miles from Perth...At Stormont Fields 5 miles...At Methven 6 miles...At Chapel Hill 9 miles...At Buchany 12 miles...At Auchtergaven 8 miles...At Springfield 2 miles...At Ruthven Fields 3 miles...At Pitcaithly Hills 5 miles....At Abercraigie 7 miles...and at several other more distant places the names of which are not stated.[35]

The wide-ranging ministries of these Baptist preachers continued throughout this period. James Miller, the home missionary based on Islay, was a typical example from the 1850s. The 1856 *BHMS Report* presented a clear description of his work.

> Besides labouring at all the stations in the island, he has, in the course of the year visited Lismore, Oban, Muckairn, Loch-awside, Craignish, Lochgilphead, and Colonsay; and these are no journeys of pleasure and of ease.He (and it is much the same with the other Missionaries,) says: 'When on these tours, I am of opinion that I travel from twenty-five to thirty miles a week, and

---

33 Chapter seven, p. 234.
34 The Baptist Society in London Minutes, July 23, 1807, n.p..
35 The Baptist Society in London Minutes, January 19, 1809, n.p.

preach at least five sermons each week, besides three on the Lord's day, and visiting from house to house...' Their journeys are on foot, through mosses and muirs and over mountains, and crossing ferries in open boats, at all seasons of the year.[36]

It is probable that after 1827 a high proportion of the towns and villages of Scotland were visited in the course of any given year by one of the BHMS agents. This evidence indicates that the influence of these Baptist evangelists was probably far greater than would have been suggested by the numbers of Scottish Baptists. Appendix 3.2 reveals the growth in the numbers of itinerant evangelists serving communities under the auspices of the home missionary societies.

In the first decade of the nineteenth century there was only a handful of full-time agents, with a greater number of ministers and laymen making extended preaching tours during the summer months. The formal establishment of Baptist Highland evangelistic societies after 1808 resulted in a 100% increase in the numbers of missionaries employed. Once all three streams of Scottish Baptists had combined their efforts to form the BHMS in 1827, there was a further increase in the number of agents. In the period 1813 to 1822 the annual total was either nine or ten agents; the late 1820s recorded the regular employment of twenty-one or twenty-two itinerant evangelists; in the following decades there was a slight increase in the number engaged, but it is evident that there was no possibility of employing more workers unless the support base were significantly enlarged. The maintenance of financial assistance for so many agents in the period 1827-1880 is a record of high achievement, and the wise use of the resources at the disposal of the BHMS committee. The growth in the numbers of agents employed by the society continued until it reached its peak in 1840. The steady increase in the numbers of evangelists employed in the 1820s and 1830s may have led some Scottish Baptists to conclude that an effective mission strategy for the whole nation could be organised under the auspices of the BHMS.

5.4 Financial Support for the BHMS

The raising of financial support for the work of home missions in Scotland was a constant challenge throughout the nineteenth century. In this respect it was similar to the difficulties experienced by the English BHMS whose own income fell short of its expectations. The Scottish home missionary society, however, never encountered the

---

36 *BHMS Report*, (Edinburgh: D.R. Collie & Son, 1856), pp. 9-10.

depths of crises that its English counterpart experienced. It may have depended to an unhealthy degree on income from legacies in the late 1850s and early 1860s, but its independence and operations were secure. In England during 1826 money for agents' wages had to be borrowed for six months until five generous donors cleared the debt.[37] The situation became critical in the 1850s with the English home missionary society relying almost exclusively on generous gifts or bequests to pay its debts.[38] As a result of the continuing financial difficulties, the English BHMS was merged with the better supported Baptist Irish Society in 1865 and renamed as the 'British & Irish Baptist Home Mission'.[39] Even this approach failed to satisfy the demands for additional income and after protracted negotiations the home mission was amalgamated with the Baptist Union of Great Britain and Ireland in the autumn of 1882.[40] The strength of the position of the Scottish BHMS is seen in its resistance to formal amalgamation with the Baptist Union until as late as 1931.[41] It is clear that in comparison with the English BHMS the Scottish society was more generously supported, even if its income was approximately only one third or one half of that received by its neighbour. One example will illustrate this point. The income of the English BHMS in 1835 amounted to less than £2,000;[42] by contrast the equivalent income received in Scotland was £1,067.[43] When the sizes of the Baptist constituency in England and Scotland are compared, the contrast in incomes becomes even clearer. In 1843 though there were 1630 Baptist churches in England, Wales and Ireland, Scottish Baptist Churches numbered only ninety-four.[44] The evidence indicates that Scottish Baptists demonstrated a greater commitment to the work of their BHMS than their English counterparts. The strength of the home mission in Scotland, as opposed to any kind of Baptist union of churches prior to 1869, indicates that in the affections of

---

37 D.J. Tidball, 'English Nonconformist Home Missions 1796-1901', (PhD thesis, Keele University, 1982), pp. 126-127.
38 Tidball, 'Home Missions', p. 144.
39 Tidball, 'Home Missions', p. 147.
40 Tidball, 'Home Missions', p. 152.
41 D.B. Murray, *The First Hundred Years: The Baptist Union of Scotland*, (Glasgow: The Baptist Union of Scotland, 1969), pp. 84-85. *Scottish Baptist Yearbook*, 1932, pp. 178-179.
42 C. Brown, *The Story of Baptist Home Missions*, (London: Veale, Chifferiel & Co., 1897), p. 32.
43 *BHMS Report*, (Edinburgh: J. & D. Collie, 1836), p. 55.
44 *The First Yearly Report of the Baptist Union of Scotland*, (Cupar: G.S. Tullis, 1844), p. 23.

many Baptists the BHMS was in effect a substitute union.

It is helpful to consider the sources of funding for the Scottish BHMS, and to note the changes in the patterns of contributions in the forty years from 1830 to 1870. Appendices 3.3 to 3.6 illustrate the level of support for this work. One important detail to emerge from any analysis of financial contributions to its work is the dependence upon English subscribers. Even though most of the funds was raised in Scotland, there were some records of annual accounts in which income from England was greater (see Appendix 3.3). In the majority of these years the English contributions provided between 35 and 50% of the funds. Appendix 3.4 records the actual amounts of money raised in Scotland and England during this period. The total income received by the society in Scotland was more marked by peaks and troughs due to the occasional giving of additional donations, and, much more important, legacies from deceased supporters. The English income was consistently derived from its annual subscribers.[45] The regular provision of over one third of the money collected for the home mission by English Baptists indicates a sense of loyalty and commitment to their Scottish brethren. It is likely that some English Particular Baptists may have regarded the 'English' Baptists in Scotland as part of their denomination, in line with the known views of men such as Anderson and Barclay.[46] If this understanding is correct then it would help provide a basis for explaining the high English contributions to the work of home missions in Scotland. It is also probable that English supporters of the BHMS regarded the Scottish Highlands and Islands as a missionfield, in a similar category to the work done overseas by the BMS.

The support of English Baptists for the BHMS in Scotland was actively encouraged by the appointment of Lachlan Mackintosh as the travelling representative of the society. Mackintosh had been moved from his post in Dundee to Greenock in order to use the steam-boats to visit the different home mission stations and to make trips to England. His role as an itinerant fundraiser was initially combined with pastoral duties in Greenock when invited to his post in 1828.[47] The request for funds from England was only a continuation of the practice employed by the separate Baptist Highland Missionary societies. There was, however, a difference in that the previous societies had relied on written appeals to ministers in England to take collections for them or on occasional visits to England.[48]

---

45 The details of BHMS income for the years 1865 and 1869 are incomplete. No data has survived apparently from 1847 and 1851.
46 Chapter four, pp. 118-119, 128-129, 135.
47 *BHMS Report*, 1829, pp. 38-39.

It became evident that Mackintosh was needed as the full-time travelling representative of the BHMS.[49] In addition the members of the home mission's committee also realised their dependence upon funds from England. The 1833 Report made this clear:

> After remaining two months in Scotland, Mr Mackintosh again set out for England, where he is at present. With all the exertions which are made in Scotland, the committee find it absolutely necessary to apply to their friends in England, and hitherto their application has not been in vain. The number of preachers employed, although the strictest economy is studied, necessarily requires considerable funds.[50]

There were occasional slumps in the money donated from England, for example in 1843, but this was due to the depressed state of the economy in England, as is made clear in the Report from Lachlan Mackintosh that year:

> My first journey was to Newcastle-upon-Tyne, North and South Shields, and Sunderland, where I met with the same kindness as formerly; but owing to the depressed state of trade...the collections were considerably diminished.[51]

Economic as well as spiritual factors were important in determining the level of financial backing for evangelistic activities in Scotland.

The graphs in Appendices 3.3 to 3.6 record the pattern of financial giving from the accounts throughout the period under consideration. Appendix 3.3 that deals with all income is distorted in a number of years by the contributions made from legacies, but because all were from Scottish supporters of the BHMS the general trends of the giving are clear. Appendix 3.5 removes the occasional donations and concentrates on the annual subscription income from supporters of the Society. In the first twenty years of the united Society it was only in the years of economic hardship in England, for example 1831, 1842 and 1843, or Scotland, for example 1849, that the figures of money raised differed greatly in the two countries.[52] Financial contributions from England did fall in the late 1850s and the early 1860s which forced the Scottish subscribers to replace the lost income. It was, though, legacies that provided the additional funds that enabled the accounts to be settled in the difficult years. It

---

48 G. Barclay in *The Baptist Magazine*, 17.5 (May, 1825), p. 216.
49 *BHMS Report*, 1829, pp. 38-39.
50 *BHMS Report*, (Edinburgh: J. & D. Collie, 1833), p. 25.
51 *BHMS Report*, (Edinburgh: Thornton & Collie, 1843), p. 22.
52 *BHMS Report*, (Edinburgh: J. & D. Collie, 1831), p.13. (Edinburgh: Thornton & Collie, 1842), p. 26.

is, however, likely that the growing sense of unity and purpose amongst Scottish Baptists in the late 1860s stimulated English supporters to increase their giving substantially in the next decade.

It is to the credit of the English supporters that they contributed so consistently to the work of Highland mission in Scotland. Appendix 3.6 uses the same data as Appendix 3.5, but takes a four-year moving average to give a better indication of the general trends in giving from 1830 to 1870. Here the picture emerges of typical giving in Scotland of between 50 and 60% in the first thirty years of the BHMS with the English contribution to the total subscription income of between 40 and 50%. It is probable that some of the donations to the work of the BHMS from England came from Scots living south of the border. The data confirms that the fundraising capability of the BHMS through their travelling agent, was consistently productive in generating sufficient income in England to finance considerably more missionaries and churches than it could have done in Scotland alone. The Society was acknowledged in England as comparable in its work to the much larger BHMS in that country, and by contrast to its English counterpart generously funded.[53]

5.5 The Wider Ministry of BHMS Agents

A further feature of the BHMS to be noted was the role of its missionaries in the ordination and induction of ministers in local congregations. This practice was not unique to Scotland, though in England it was common for the county Baptist Association to oversee ordinations and inductions, as in the Essex Baptist Association.[54] One example from Scotland concerned the ordination of William Fraser as the pastor of the Baptist Church at Uig on Skye on July 27 1828. The 1829 *BHMS Report* records this account of the proceedings:

> On the 27th, Mr Fraser was solemnly set apart to the pastoral office by prayer, with fasting. Mr [Dugald] Sinclair [Lochgilphead] addressed him from Acts xx.28. Mr [Walter] Munro addressed the church from I Thess. v. 12,13. Mr [Alexander] Grant [Tobermory] concluded the service by prayer; and preached in the evening from Psalm ii.12.[55]

Here three ministers connected with the BHMS ordained and

---

53 D.C. Sparkes, *The Home Mission Story*, (Didcot: Baptist Historical Society, 1995), pp. 2-5.
54 Essex Baptist Association Minute Book, 1805-1864, introductory notes, BU. MSS., Angus Library, Regents Park College, Oxford, cited by Lovegrove, *Established Church Sectarian People*, p. 57.

inducted William Fraser to the pastorate of Uig Baptist Church on behalf of the wider Baptist constituency. Fraser had been placed as a missionary of the BHMS at Uig in 1826, two years prior to the confirmation of the call by ordination to the pastorate. The church grew rapidly under his ministry until he took the decision to emigrate to Breadalbane, Glengarry County, Ontario, Canada in 1831.[56] The next example occurred in 1836.

> It was judged proper that the brethren in Ross [on Mull] should meet as a church of Christ; and brethren Duncan Macintyre and Duncan Ferguson were unanimously chosen to be their elders. They were ordained on Monday, May 31, with fasting, prayer, and laying on of hands. We were all heartily thankful that Providence brought our much esteemed brother Lachlan Mackintosh to assist [Alexander Grant of Tobermory] on this occasion.[57]

The third recorded example in the minutes of the annual reports of the BHMS took place in 1838 at Broadford on the island of Skye. Here two of the ministers from Mull, Alexander Grant and Duncan Ferguson, were present to perform the ordination and induction ceremony for James McQueen.[58] In each of these three cases men who were linked to the BHMS conducted services in the name of the wider fellowship of churches. It was the home mission that functioned as the corporate body for many Scottish Baptists in this period. In all of these cases the ordination took place during the time of the existence of a national union or Baptist association.

5.6 Training and Provision of Home Missionaries

The most important contribution of the BHMS was the provision of missionaries for the churches and mission stations under its superintendence. In England, by contrast, the driving force behind home evangelisation was the associations. The Western Association as early as May 1775 had established a fund to support the work of itinerant evangelism. The Northamptonshire Baptist Association followed suit in 1779 in its support for village preaching.[59] In 1796 the Essex Baptist Association had engaged its first itinerant.[60] Ten years later an evangelistic association was formed for Shropshire as

---

55 *BHMS Report*, 1829, p. 33.
56 Meek, 'Independent and Baptist Churches', p. 334. For more details of Fraser's work in Canada see M.A.G. Haykin, 'Voluntarism in the Life and Ministry of William Fraser (1801-1883)' in W.H. Brackney (ed.), *The Believers Church: A Voluntary Church*, (Kitchener, Ontario: Pandora Press, 1998) pp. 25-50.
57 *BHMS Report*, 1836, pp.11-12.
58 *BHMS Report*, (Edinburgh: D.R. Collie, 1838), pp. 13-14.

an offshoot of the much older Midland Association.[61] In some parts of England where Baptists were few in numbers they joined with Independent colleagues to form evangelistic associations for their counties. An example of this was the association set up in 1798 for the four most northerly counties in England where Charles Whitfield, the Baptist minister in Hamsterley, County Durham, joined James Hill,[62] his Independent contemporary at Ravenstonedale, Westmoreland, with other Dissenting ministers and laymen.[63] In Scotland the BHMS was almost exclusively the only Baptist organisation providing evangelists to work in the rural and to a lesser extent the urban centres of the country. The one exception to this rule was The Fife Home Missionary Association or Itinerating Society, a body that united Baptists and Independents in Fife in missionary activities.[64] The English BHMS was engaged in work similar to that carried out under the auspices of county associations and by other more localised initiatives. It is for this reason that the Scottish BHMS played a more important role in the Scottish Baptist constituency than its English counterpart. At the formation of the BHMS in 1827 it had adopted the six missionaries of the Baptist Highland Mission and the thirteen employed by the Home Missionary Society for Scotland.[65] The combined society attracted greater financial support than the two previous agencies and was able by 1839 to employ thirty agents and in addition provide financial assistance to several churches.[66] It was not to exceed this number of full-time employees in the next thirty years, principally as a

---

59 The minutes and accounts of the Northamptonshire association meetings were published annually with the circular letter to member churches. These are extant from 1768 onwards. See especially minutes for 1779. Records of the Baptist Western Association in the years 1733-1809, minutes of annual meetings and accounts, BBC. MSS G98, Bristol Baptist College, Bristol, cited by Lovegrove, *Established Church*, p. 32.

60 Essex Baptist Association minute book, 1805-1864, introductory notes, BU. MSS, Angus Library, Regent's Park College, Oxford, cited by Lovegrove, *Established Church*, p. 32.

61 Shropshire and Cheshire Baptist Association, Circular Letter, 1815, cited by Lovegrove, *Established Church*, p. 32.

62 Information about James Hill can be found in A.P.F. Sell, *Church Planting A study of Westmoreland Nonconformity*, (Eugene, Oregon: Wipf and Stock, 1998 [1986]), pp. 67, 75-76.

63 This body, officially designated 'The Evangelical Association for propagating the Gospel in the villages of Cumberland, Durham, Northumberland and Westmoreland', cited by Lovegrove, *Established Church*, p. 33.

64 Chapter four, p. 145.

result of the churches being able to bear part of the costs for their preachers. The 1864 *BHMS Report* listed twenty-four missionaries employed by the society, but significantly ten were supported on a part-time basis, including all five ministers in the Shetland Isles.[67] The society was fortunate to have available to them a good number of dedicated and able preachers who committed their lives to working in the Highlands and Islands of Scotland. It was the ministry of these men that was the BHMS's greatest contribution to the establishing and maintaining of Baptist churches in rural Scotland.

The provision of training for potential missionaries occupied a significant part of the BHMS committee's attention in 1855 and 1856. A letter was sent out to the churches enquiring whether there were any young men with appropriate gifts who were willing to be trained as missionaries for future service in Scotland. The church at Elgin put forward two young men who were sent with recommendations to the Baptist Academies at Bristol and Bradford for further preparation. A different scheme of training was set up for Duncan Macfarlane, a merchant, who was a member of Tobermory Baptist Church on Mull. He was an older man with experience of church work. He had decided to give up his business and devote himself full-time to missionary work in the Highlands. Macfarlane came to Glasgow to work as an assistant to John Shearer, a Baptist minister, with whom he received further experience and instruction before returning to work under the society in Tobermory with the commendation of both Alexander Grant and John Shearer. It is clear that formal training was valued by the BHMS, though it recognised that potential candidates had to be sent to established institutions in England as there was no Baptist Academy in Scotland. There was also flexibility in its approach, with a wise decision taken regarding the training needs of Duncan Macfarlane. The importance of training at an evangelical seminary for itinerant ministry was also grasped by Nonconformists in England and Wales. In contrast to the formal training of the older Dissenting academies, seminaries had a practical emphasis with a view to preparing men for work as itinerant evangelists as well as pastoral ministry. Trevecca College in Wales made a major contribution in this work in the paedobaptist constituency,[68] whilst the work of William Steadman at the Bradford Academy was an excellent model for Baptist evangelists. Steadman, alongside John Saffery and Samuel Pearce, English Par-

---

65 *Address by the Committee of the Baptist Home Missionary Society for Scotland*, October 2 1827.
66 *BHMS Report*, (Edinburgh: Thornton & Collie, 1839), p. 5.
67 *BHMS Report*, (Edinburgh: D.R. Collie & Son, 1864), p. 25.

ticular Baptist ministers, laid the foundations for the recognition of the necessity for itinerant evangelists in England in addition to the needs of the foreign mission-field.[69] This function of providing, or at least obtaining, ministerial training for suitable candidates reveals the BHMS acting as a national co-ordinating body for Scottish Baptist churches.

The BHMS also undertook to employ ministers from outside Scotland where this was seen as necessary for a local church or churches. The society was asked in 1855 by the small Baptist churches in Forfarshire and Kincardinshire for a preacher. Archibald Livingstone, who had been working in Dunfanaghy in the north-west of Ireland, was approached with a view to accepting the call. He took up his new work in Scotland in February 1856.[70]

5.7 Reasons why the BHMS did not become a 'Substitute Union'
The information presented above indicates that the case for the BHMS being seen as a 'substitute union' has significant strength. It is important now to consider the evidence that prevented many Baptists from taking this viewpoint, before attempting to assess the relative weight of the two positions. There was no particular issue that influenced some Baptists to desire the formation of a Baptist Union of Scotland in addition to the Home Missionary Society. It was the combination of several factors. The BHMS was not as successful as many had hoped. One reason for a reduction in attendances at home mission-linked Baptist Churches was the provision of new parish churches in areas where there had been a desperate need. A good example to illustrate this issue was the situation in Lochgilphead in the 1820s. The Baptist church had been built in 1815 when there was no established church between Kilmichael and Inverneill, a distance in excess of eight miles. There were, therefore, additional reasons, not simply a denominational preference, why people might choose to attend the local Baptist church. The situation was to change when an Act of Parliament in 1824 authorised the building of nearly forty 'parliamentary churches' in the over-large parishes. These included some parishes in which Dugald Sinclair had itinerated with apparent success in gathering large congregations and included his home base at Lochgilphead. The provision of new established churches and ministers seemed a more

---

68 G.F. Nuttall, *The Significance of Trevecca College, 1768-1791*, (London: Epworth Press, 1968).
69 Lovegrove, *Established Church*, pp. 23-25.
70 *BHMS Report*, (Edinburgh: D.R. Collie & Son, 1856), pp. 18-19.

attractive proposition to many local people than the occasional visits of the itinerant preachers.[71] Even in Lochgilphead itself the Baptist cause was weakened by this advance in the fortunes of the established church, as Sinclair himself noted: 'The audience is considerably diminished, in consequence of a Government Church being lately opened in the neighbourhood.'[72] It may be that a change in Sinclair's theological views in his later years in Scotland contributed to the falling numbers at his meetings, but there was bound to be some diminution of his flock once the needs of the Highlanders were being addressed more adequately by the established church.[73] The despondency in the congregation is easy to understand in the light of the decision of many of his hearers to seek an alternative ecclesiastical home.

The Baptist mission churches also suffered in competition with other denominations. The preacher at Inveraray, John Campbell, suddenly lost most of his congregation in a very short period of time, partly through depopulation in that area but also because another denomination, the Secession Church, sent a preacher to the village.[74] William Tulloch, the Orkney Baptist pioneer, in a report from Westray two years later recorded a similar phenomenon: 'I know that my poor labours have led many to join the Secession; but if God is glorified in their salvation, angels rejoice, and the saints ought to give glory to God.'[75] However diminution of numbers did not always take place when a new denomination came into an area. Tulloch (junior) from Elgin reported in March 1845 that the Brethren were evangelising with great zeal in the area, but also recorded that his own congregation was on the increase.[76] Sometimes denominations 'shared' a congregation. John McPherson, at Breadalbane, reported that once a fortnight the church was crowded because there was no sermon that Sunday in the established church. His own congregation had grown in real terms by only two or three in the past few months.[77] This evidence was an important pointer as to what might happen if there was a major influx of evangelical Presbyterian clergymen into the Highlands.

The emergence of the Free Church of Scotland in the 1840s was more significant than the challenge posed by the presence of any other denomination. The accounts of the missionaries in the 1840s

---

71   Meek, 'Dugald Sinclair', pp. 76-77.
72   *BHMS Report*, 1829, p. 33.
73   Yuille (ed.), *Baptists in Scotland*, pp. 116-117.
74   *BHMS Report*, 1831, p. 9.
75   *BHMS Report*, 1833, p. 10.
76   *BHMS Report*, (Edinburgh: Thornton & Collie, 1845), p. 15.

all report significant upheavals in local communities at that time. Peter Grant in Grantown wrote:

> There is a great struggle going on between the two Churches of Scotland, as they call themselves. Our greatest difficulty is to draw the minds of the people from this fearful struggle, to the concerns of their precious souls.[78]

A similar picture was presented by Angus McNaughton from Islay:

> A great stumbling-block is cast in the people's way by the contentions of different parties. If the people of God were of one mind, striving together for the faith of the gospel, the fields were never more white to harvest, but in consequence of one pushing this way and another that, many halt between two opinions.[79]

The battle for the souls of the people was found all over Scotland. David Gibson, based in Auchencairn, Galloway, stated in his report in 1845: 'the people [were] much agitated, some about the Established and Free Churches, and others about the great doctrines of the Gospel.'[80] There appeared to be some legitimate concern that the battles for adherents between the churches might have the unintended consequence of providing opportunities for a growing number of Scots to avoid associating themselves with any of the churches.

This 'Christian competition' changed markedly the religious landscape of the Highlands. The 'Moderate' clergymen were a declining species, as James McQueen indicated in a report from Skye:

> Two years ago, hardly any meetings were held throughout the country, except by our people; now there are a number of weekly meetings for prayer and exhortation in many parts of the station, by people not connected with us, but favourable to us. I have seen the day which I often prayed for, and I trust it is the beginning of greater things.[81]

The Baptists were an established force on Skye in this period, but where their local presence was not as strong the battle could be intense. William Tulloch of Blair Atholl spoke of his delight at the easing of denominational tensions in his area. After noting that a meeting at Loch Tummel-side was attended by a much larger crowd

---

77 *BHMS Report*, 1829, p. 24.
78 *BHMS Report*, 1845, p. 13.
79 *BHMS Report*, (Edinburgh: Thornton & Collie, 1844), p. 15.
80 *BHMS Report*, 1845, p. 19.

than was expected, he gave the reason for his joy:
> There has not been such a meeting in that quarter since the Disruption. All parties seemed to give up their former strife, and came out as one man to hear the gospel. In another glen, where every means had been employed to prevent the people from hearing the Baptists, he preached one Sabbath evening, and the whole inhabitants of the glen turned out.[82]

William Tulloch, the Orcadian Baptist leader, had even greater joy on a tour of Orkney. He paid a visit to the island of Rousay during which he was invited to preach on the 'Lord's day' in the Free Church to almost all the church-attending people from the four denominations on the island: Free and Established Churches of Scotland; Secession and Independent churches. This was for him a picture of heaven to see Christians putting to one side their differences to rejoice in the same gospel message.[83] Church unity was always welcome, but the attractions of an evangelical Presbyterianism often seemed greater than that of the Baptists. In Lawers relations between the Baptists and the Free Church people were good, but the reports of Duncan Cameron indicated where the majority placed their allegiance. In 1848 he wrote, 'I am sorry to say that during the past year we have not had many additions, but we have had much unity among ourselves'.[84] The following year his report was similar in tone: 'The gospel is making its way amongst us, but its progress is slow; faith is the only antidote against discouragement; let us take courage in this day of small things…'[85] There was little change in the situation, as the reports in subsequent years indicate.[86] It was not a surprising step for Cameron to take when he accepted a call to the Baptist congregation in Breadalbane, Canada. His decision was tacitly supported by the BHMS when it decided not to appoint a successor in the near future. This left Donald McLellan of Glenlyon with the responsibility for the Baptist congregations from Lawers to Rannoch. Cameron was never replaced, despite the

---

81   BHMS Report, 1844, p. 12.
82   BHMS Report, 1845, p. 17. 'The Disruption' mentioned in this citation was the exodus from the Established Church of Scotland by over 450 ministers and a significant proportion of the congregations of this denomination, on Tuesday May 18, 1843, to form the Free Church of Scotland. See J. Baillie (ed.), *Proceedings of the General Assembly of the Free Church of Scotland*, (Edinburgh: W.P. Kennedy, 1843), pp. 1-8 for more details.
83   BHMS Report, 1845, p. 16.
84   BHMS Report, (Edinburgh: Thornton & Collie, 1848, p. 9.
85   BHMS Report, (Edinburgh: Thornton & Collie, 1849, p. 11.
86   BHMS Report, 1856, p. 15.

BHMS committee leaving their options open concerning the possibility of a future successor.[87] The comparative membership figures of the Baptist and Free Church congregations in this area reveal how dominant evangelical Presbyterianism had become. In 1843-1844 Lawers Baptist Church had thirty-eight members, Killin had twenty-two, Glenlyon had twelve and Aberfeldy twenty members.[88] In 1848 Lawers Free Church had eighty members, Killin had two hundred and seventy-one, Glenlyon had sixty and Aberfeldy two hundred and forty-nine.[89] There were now social pressures working against the Baptists in addition to their numerical weakness. 'In this place [Lawers], however, it is almost as difficult for one to join the Baptists as for the Hindoo to reject his caste. One young woman joined us lately, and endures much persecution.'[90] It was now clear that the Baptists would maintain a foothold in the Highlands and Islands of Scotland only where they had already established themselves. Any future progress would be slow and an uphill battle in the face of the success of evangelical Presbyterianism.

The reasons for the advances of evangelical Presbyterianism at the expense of the Baptists need to be considered. It is important to note that it was not just the Baptists that appeared to lose ground to the Free Church of Scotland. The Established Church had had a dramatic fall in its numbers from the 1830s to the 1850s. In Edinburgh it had declined from 44 to 16 % of churchgoers and in Glasgow from 41 to 20%. The overall decline from 1835/1836 to 1851 was from around 44% of church attenders to a low of 32%. The Free Church, formed in 1843, had attracted 33% of churchgoers in Edinburgh, 22% in Glasgow, and an overall figure of 32% by 1851. The Baptists had declined from 4 to 3% in Edinburgh, remained constant at 2% in Glasgow and their overall national attendance was 1% in 1851.[91] On the national scale, Baptists throughout this period were a tiny minority and as a result made at best only a modest impact in Scotland. The general warmth of relations between Baptists and other churches in the Highlands, especially the Free Church, was in part an acceptance that Baptists posed no threat to their hold on the loy-

---

87 *BHMS Report*, (Edinburgh: D.R. Collie & Son, 1857), pp. 6-7. Meek, 'Independent and Baptist Churches', pp. 292-293.
88 *First Yearly Report of the Baptist Union*, 1844, p. 20.
89 W. Ewing (ed.), *Annals of the Free Church of Scotland*, (2 Vols; Edinburgh: T. & T. Clark, 1914), II, pp. 131-132.
90 *BHMS Report*, (Edinburgh: D.R. Collie & Son, 1855, p. 26.

alties of the majority of churchgoers.

The success of the Free Church, in effect of evangelical Presbyterianism, in the Highlands and Islands of Scotland has been seen as the result of three complementary cultural influences.[92] The first two of these were indigenous developments. One was the spread of spiritual poetry in Gaelic. This type of poetry had begun in the mid-eighteenth century by vernacular poets like Dugald Buchanan. This devotional poetry was complemented by the singing of Psalms which had adopted the ballad metre for Gaelic praise. It was, however, an established feature of Baptist devotional exercises and congregational praise, and so the benefit of this development was shared with the Free Church. There was no better and more honoured example of this practice than Peter Grant, minister of Grantown-on-Spey Baptist Church, whose Gaelic compositions were in demand across the denominational boundaries.[93]

In view of the widespread use of spiritual poetry prior to the Disruption it cannot be enlisted as a sufficient reason for the success of the Free Church. The second and more important factor was the leadership of an evangelical lay elite (the men). These individuals, highly respected for their piety in their local communities, crucially chose to throw in their lot with the Free Church in 1843 and as a result carried large sectors of the Highland population with them. The third factor was the spread of Gaelic School Societies. The teachers employed in the Highland communities, especially in Skye and the Outer Hebrides, were often associated with the Evangelical Party in the Church of Scotland. They tended to reinforce the piety promoted by 'the men' and in combination with the evangelical clergy of the Church of Scotland ensured that there was a groundswell of popular support for the Disruption.[94] A further factor was the denominational rivalry between the large Presbyterian denominations that resulted in their seeking to be the dominant force in the land. Baptists were a minority body that suffered as a result of the battle between other competing denominations. James

---

91 Royal Commission on Religious Instruction, Parliamentary Papers, 1837, xxx, pp. 12-13, and 1837-1838, xxxii, p. 13; Census of Great Britain, 1851: Religious Worship and Education, Scotland, Parliamentary Papers, 1854, p. lix, cited by Brown, *Religion and Society in Scotland*, p. 45.

92 A.I. MacInnes, 'Evangelical Protestantism in Nineteenth-Century Highlands', in G. Walker & T. Gallagher, *Sermons and Battle Hymns*, (Edinburgh: Edinburgh University Press, 1990), pp. 43-68.

93 D.E. Meek, 'The Glory of the Lamb: The Gaelic Hymns of Peter Grant', in D.W. Bebbington (ed.), *The Gospel in the World*, (Studies in Baptist History and Thought, 1; Carlisle: Paternoster Press, 2002), pp. 129-164.

Paterson, minister of Hope Street Baptist Church, Glasgow, writing in 1863, captured something of the difficulties that had faced his colleagues in the Highlands during the previous two decades.

> The rise of the Free Church awakened a large amount of zeal in the other Presbyterian bodies in favour of earnest evangelical preaching. The efforts put forth by the three great sections of the Presbyterians of the North, since the events referred to [the Disruption], have been marked and decided...It will at once be seen, that this state of things presents a difficulty, not easily overestimated, in the way of a denomination so small and scattered as that of the Baptists. In the Presbyterian communities, their ministers have, in general, received a very competent education; their congregations, especially in the larger towns and cities, are respectable, influential, and frequently wealthy... To a fractional body of Baptists, consisting of a score or two, here and there; or in two or three of the larger towns, of several hundreds – this Presbyterian kingdom of the north does not present a field of easy conquest... In these circumstances, rapid progress, startling and crowning advance, on the part of the Baptists, is a calculation that could not at present be wisely entertained.[95]

If there had been any expectations of major advances against such large odds then it would have been destined to be disappointed. Baptists had, however, made modest progress in adverse religious conditions. It was, though, inevitable that some Scottish Baptists might suggest that greater success might be obtained by the BHMS if it operated in association with a union of Baptist Churches. Paterson makes reference to this matter in his article in *The Freeman*, the English Baptist newspaper: 'their [Free Church of Scotland] system of church-government works with seemingly greater smoothness than the pure democratic independency of the Baptist churches'.[96] A national body was needed. At that stage (1863) there was only a Scottish Baptist Association of individual members. Six more years were to elapse before the vision of a union of churches was to see the light of day.

The economic situation in Scotland also played its part. Periodic shortages of food had been a regular feature of Highland life in the early nineteenth century. The ongoing poverty of the Highland people meant that they would for many years be dependent on the BHMS paying the salaries of the missionaries.[97] This placed a strain on the tight budget of the BHMS, limiting the number of preachers it could employ. The financial support from England was vital, but

---

94   MacInnes, 'Evangelical Protestantism', p. 53.
95   *The Freeman*, 9 (May 27, 1863), p. 332.
96   *The Freeman*, (May 27, 1863), p. 332.

it was essential to recognise that the Scottish churches needed to be generous in their contributions to the work of the mission. There were rumours reaching English supporters, in 1839, that the Scottish churches were not supporting the BHMS in a generous manner, and thus raising questions about its stewardship. The issue was tackled in a letter from the joint secretaries, James and Robert Haldane, and the BHMS treasurer, Henry D. Dickie, to the Scottish Baptist Churches in November 1838.

> [The Society] has not received that countenance and support from the Baptist churches in Scotland which might have been expected...The apparent apathy with which it has been viewed by some of the churches at home, has formed a subject of complaint at a distance, and has tended to create a suspicion, either that the object of the Society is not so important as it appears, or that it is not conducted in such a manner as to secure the confidence of those who are best qualified to form an accurate judgement of its proceedings.[98]

This appeal managed to secure a 25% increase in the funds raised both north and south of the border, but though this level of giving was maintained in cash terms it did not allow for additional ministries to be undertaken. A careful analysis of the BHMS accounts reveals that the total giving to the mission had hardly gone up in real terms from the late 1830s to 1867. For example, the subscription income in 1837 and 1838 was £797 and £836. This had increased to £858 in 1864 and £853 in 1866. At the same time the salary bill for the missionaries was £913 in 1837 and £916 in 1838 and listed as £1,346 in 1864, but dramatically cut back to £738 in 1866.[99] Facing such financial restraint the BHMS was unable to maintain existing commitments and was, therefore, in no position to advance into new spheres of service.

The proportion of funds gathered amongst supporters at home can be compared with that provided by English contributors. When the subscription income for Scotland and England is separated and set out as in Appendices 3.4 to 3.6 it becomes apparent that there was a large drop in the financial support for the BHMS in England after 1850. This is masked in the total income figures by an almost equivalent increase in support in Scotland. There appeared to be a crisis of confidence in the value of united efforts amongst Baptists in England in the 1850s and 1860s that affected not only the English

---

97 *BHMS Report*, (Edinburgh: D.R. Collie, 1837), pp. 13-14.
98 *BHMS Report*, (Edinburgh: Thornton & Collie), 1839, p. 34.
99 *BHMS Report*, 1837, p. 47; 1838, p. 41; 1864, p. 34; (Edinburgh: D.R. Collie & Son, 1866), p. 36.

BHMS but also its Baptist Union. This lack of confidence in the Baptist Union resulted in the resignation of its secretary, John Howard Hinton, in 1866.[100] There was no evidence to suggest any particular diminution of enthusiasm for the work in Scotland; instead, a general spirit of apathy towards institutional efforts appeared to be prevalent. This transformation of fortunes north and south of the border in the 1860s may be as a result of the ministry of C.H. Spurgeon and the men he had trained for the pastoral ministry.[101] It is possible to suggest that part of the reason for the drop in funding was due to the lack of 'results' in the 1850s onwards in terms of conversions, baptisms and new members. There is also the possibility that the lack of unity between Scottish Baptists may have contributed to the modest financial contribution from English supporters during these years. The BHMS became dependent upon income from legacies to balance its books. There was no apparent benefit to the BHMS finances in the late 1850s and early 1860s from the so-called Second Evangelical Revival.[102] Any new funds generated by additional people coming into the churches must have been diverted into other causes. The society faced an annual deficit which was relatively small from 1859 to 1862. This deficit, though, would have reached the alarmingly high figures of £224 in 1863 and £562 in 1864 without the two legacies given in the financial year 1862-1863, and one in 1863-18[103]64.[104] The first legacy was from a Dr John Stewart who left £45 to the society. The second was from a Mr Wemyss, a deputy Commissary, who contributed the extraordinary sum of £1,050. It is probable that the man in question was William Wemyss Esq. from Edinburgh, but no other information is known about this person. The third legacy a year later in 1863-1864 came from Charles

---

100 Tidball, 'English Baptist Home Missions', pp. 140-147.
101 Tidball, 'English Baptist Home Missions', pp. 155-158. Chapter eight, pp. 300-307 discusses the influence of Spurgeon with regard to the 1869 Baptist Union of Scotland.
102 Information on this revival in the 1850s and 1860s, from a Scottish Baptist perspective can be found in contemporary articles in the Baptist periodical *The Freeman*. See also Chapter Eight, pp.296-298. Wider discussion of the impact of this awakening can be found in J.E. Orr, *The Second Evangelical Awakening in Britain*, (London: Marshall, Morgan & Scott, 1949), pp. 58-77. J.E. Orr, *The Light of the Nations*, (Exeter: Paternoster Press, 1965), pp. 132-139, and R. Carwardine, *Transatlantic Revivalism Popular Evangelicalism in Britain and America 1790-1865*, (Westport, Connecticut: Greenwood Press, 1978), pp. 159-197.

Robson, a member of Berwick Baptist Church, who had left £40 to the society. The encouragement received from these gifts could not hide the difficult decisions that lay ahead for the BHMS.

The situation on the island of Skye illustrated their dilemma. The economic situation was desperate with people utterly destitute after being cleared from their lands to be replaced by sheep. The Baptist congregation at Uig was also in urgent need of help in the midst of fears that the preaching station might be given up by the BHMS due to lack of funds. James McQueen, the missionary at Broadford, sent letters requesting assistance. In November 1854 he wrote:

> the people turn out well; it is my conviction, if there was a preacher, the people would attend well, especially when the meeting house is repaired, – it is in so ruinous a condition no person can enter it; it has been a meeting-house upwards of forty years. I have at present no place to preach but smoky houses, without comfort to myself or hearers.[105]

The next letter in December acknowledged the generosity of donors in Glasgow, Edinburgh and Tobermory who had paid for the restoration work on the church at Uig to be completed, but also pleaded for greater assistance from the Society in finding a preacher to be based there. McQueen's letter stated that, 'The people attended better than they have done for a number of years back...Uig should not be given up without giving it a fair trial'.[106] The report from the missionary on Skye (Alexander Macfadyen) in 1862 indicated the difficulties now facing the Society:

> The Skye people are not at all aware the committee are speaking of giving up Skye as a Missionary Station, or else they would be exceedingly sorry. They have great respect for the Baptists; for although they are few in number, and in poor circumstances, their conversation is as becometh the Gospel of Christ. Last summer as you are aware, I visited Ross, Iona, Mull, Colonsay and Islay; and in any of these places, I have not got such congregations, or seen such an appearance as I see in this place. I am sure, were it not that our chapel is in such a bad condition, – for some nights pools of water are on the floor, – it could not at all accommodate the vast congregations who would attend.[107]

The weakness of the churches could be seen as due, in part, to the

---

103 *BHMS Report*, (Edinburgh: D.R. Collie & Son, 1863), p. 41; 1864, p. 34.
104 *BHMS Report*, (Edinburgh: D.R. Collie & Son, 1860), p. 31; 1863, p. 41. *The Post Office Annual Directory for 1861-1862*, (Edinburgh: Ballantyne and Company, 1861), p. 287.
105 *BHMS Report*, (Edinburgh: D.R. Collie & Son, 1853), pp. 8-9.
106 *BHMS Report*, (Edinburgh: D.R. Collie & Son, 1854), p. 7.

lack of regular ministry from a missionary. The itinerating tours only served to highlight the great needs of the people and the inability of the missionaries to meet them. It was not a shortage of available Gaelic preachers, but a shortage of money that was at the bottom of this difficulty. The Society produced annual reports with less work being described in its pages and then less money was sent to improve the situation. The BHMS in its aims admitted to concentrating its ministries on the Highlands and Islands communities, but even here it was not achieving many of its objectives. The future for some stations was bleak, but the stewardship of resources by the BHMS could not have been questioned.

Another factor, though also related to the economic conditions, that had an even greater impact on Highland Baptist churches was emigration due to the clearances on Highland estates. The reports from missionaries showed a steady stream of people leaving Scotland in search of a better life in North America or Australia. William Fraser at Uig reported that ten or eleven members had emigrated to America in 1828.[108] In 1830 Fraser followed his flock to Canada with more of the membership, leaving only twenty-three members (though up to 300 hearers). The highest membership figure under Fraser's ministry, only a few years earlier, was around sixty, and so the size of the loss was considerable.[109] The 1832 report from the Uig missionary James Miller stated:'Our number is now very small; four dear brethren left us a few weeks ago for America, and our number is now reduced to nineteen.'[110] The number of hearers may not have diminished, but the core of the church, its membership, had been greatly weakened.

This was a common experience in the Highlands. Alexander Grant of Tobermory on a tour of Islay met one Sunday evening in June 1830 with the local Baptist congregation and their pastor Angus McNaughton in Port Charlotte. It was the final service on the island for one third of the congregation prior to emigration to America.[111] Duncan McDougald's report from Tiree in 1848 confirms the trend:

> In visiting a hamlet, where I formerly had a large congregation, but now a thin meeting, I asked how many had emigrated; the reply was sixty-one. It is a trying scene for me when passing the vacant houses now falling down, from which I learn many

---

107 *BHMS Report*, (Edinburgh: D.R. Collie & Son, 1862), pp. 15-16.
108 *BHMS Report*, 1829, p. 29.
109 *BHMS Report*, 1831, pp. 6-7. Meek, 'Independent and Baptist Churches', p. 336.
110 *BHMS Report*, (Edinburgh: J. & D. Collie, 1832), p. 10.

experimental lessons...As a church, we complain of not being so lively and zealous as in times past. Some of our best members have been removed to other countries. In consequence, some of our prayer meetings were given up, from the want of persons qualified to lead them.[112]

The experience of Alexander Grant, of Tobermory, in March 1848, in a tour of some mainland preaching stations raised questions about their viability in the future.

My next trip was by Torloisg, Ulva, and North Colonsay, where the few friends who still remain were very thankful for the visit. The population is fast diminishing. On Monday I crossed to North Colonsay, where only three families reside.[113]

James Miller, now the missionary at Islay and Colonsay, reported a similar story in his territory. 'The church at Bowmore [Islay] consists at present of about forty-five members, and in Colonsay of fifteen, – both much reduced by emigration'.[114] In view of the rapid depopulation of the Highlands and Islands, there were serious questions for the BHMS leadership to consider regarding the deployment of its limited resources.

It is also important to note the considerable migration of people from the Highlands and Islands to the towns and cities of Scotland to find work. The relocation of Alexander McLeod from Perthshire to a Gaelic-speaking congregation in South Portland Street, Glasgow, in 1820, and the earlier formation of a Gaelic-speaking congregation at Orangefield, Greenock, in 1806, with which the travelling representative of the BHMS Lachlan Mackintosh was associated from 1829 to 1832, pointed to a need that the BHMS attempted to address.[115] Mackintosh had been moved from Grantown to Dundee in 1827 to establish a home-mission church amongst the Highland migrants to that city.[116] The home mission also appointed John Frazer to work amongst the Gaelic-speaking migrants to Edinburgh in 1829.[117] The Established Church had provided Gaelic-speaking preachers for native Highlanders who had migrated to the Lowlands in the eighteenth century. The BHMS, as a Baptist body, therefore, was following an established practice in this matter.[118] This policy appeared to have had limited success in Dundee, as the church

---

111 *BHMS Report*, 1831, p. 18.
112 *BHMS Report*, 1848, p. 16.
113 *BHMS Report*, 1848, p. 15.
114 *BHMS Report*, 1854, p. 13.
115 Yuille (ed.), *Baptists in Scotland*, pp. 282-283.
116 P. Grant, 'Sketch of my own Life and Times', p. 7. *To the Baptist Churches in Scotland*, June 13 1827.

probably ceased to meet after Mackintosh's departure, and in Edinburgh, as the Society decided to terminate Frazer's ministry in 1830, after only one year, and despite its complete satisfaction 'with his zeal and qualifications'. Frazer, a fluent Gaelic preacher from Pitlochry, and a member of the Tabernacle Church, Edinburgh, had preached there from 1819 to crowds of up to 300 people.[119] The limited success of this attempt at ministering to Highlanders in a Lowland context may have reinforced the decision of the BHMS committee to continue placing the majority of its workers in the Highlands and Islands of Scotland.

There has recently come to light a series of documents associated with Hope Street Baptist Church, Glasgow, which gives some indication of the movement of church members from Highland churches to Lowland ones. Many of the letters are recommendations from the individual's pastor and are intended to enable them to transfer church membership to a sister church. The collection included a significant number of letters, from the late 1830s, from Robert Thomson, minister of Perth Baptist Church, to James Paterson, minister of Hope Street Church. One letter, dated May 27 1839, encapsulates the feelings some Highland ministers must have had as they saw their flock diminishing in numbers. The context of the letter was a recommendation of 'our sister widow McFarlane' to Paterson. In the second paragraph of the letter it states:

> Thus we send you one and another and if they continue to leave us as they have done of late I see no other way than that I must as a good shepherd just follow the flock and try to superintend them in your good town as I have done in the fair city!![120]

In view of the limited size of the congregations available in the Highlands and Islands and by contrast the vast crowds and the great needs of the urban areas of Scotland some Baptists began to question the wisdom of the strategy of the BHMS committee. If its ministry was primarily to the Highlands and Islands, then which Baptist body would give priority to the far greater and often untouched population inhabiting the towns and cities of Scotland? Similar questions were raised in England as a result of the 1851 cen-

---

117 *BHMS Report*, (Edinburgh: J. & D. Collie, 1830), p. 17.
118 C.W.J. Withers, *Urban Highlanders: Highland – Lowland Migration and Urban Gaelic Culture, 1700-1900*, (East Linton: Tuckwell Press, 1998), pp. 160-198.
119 *BHMS Report*, 1830, p. 17. J Brown, *Reminiscences of the late James Alex. Haldeane*, (Glasgow: James Brown, 1864), p. 20.
120 Robert Thomson to James Paterson, May 27 1839, Letter M, Hope Street Baptist Church documents, MS in the possession of Adelaide Place Baptist Church, Glasgow.

sus. In 1831 only 25% of the population of England and Wales lived in towns with a population of more than 20,000. In 1851 the percentage had risen to 44% and it would rise again to 59.5% by 1881. All the denominations noted the shifting population, but it was the Baptists who were among the first bodies to attempt to reach out to the urban masses after 1851.[121] In this period of time the English BHMS faced a severe financial crisis, resulting in the need to economise on its operations. It was recognised that the society could not now be responsible for both urban and rural ministry. It chose to concentrate on the country districts. This was a wise move as others, for example, the London Baptist Association (LBA) led by C.H. Spurgeon, took up the challenge of reaching the masses of the metropolis, though the work of the LBA did not begin until 1865.[122] Earlier attempts by English Particular Baptists to evangelise in the capital city in 1822 to 1825 had come to nothing as suitable preaching stations had been difficult to establish.[123] The Scottish BHMS had taken a greater interest in urban ministry than its English counterpart. This can be seen in the number of mission stations in Appendix 3.1 that are located in towns and cities as opposed to rural areas. Twenty seven per cent of home mission locations had been based in urban locations throughout Scotland, of which nine (12.5%) were located in central Scotland. There was, however, no doubt that the primary emphasis (73%) was upon rural communities, in line with the vision of the founders of the BHMS in 1827.

The organisation that took up the challenge of urban ministry in Scotland was the newly formed Baptist Union of Scotland.[124] One man in particular dominated the fresh thinking that was to emerge – Francis Johnston. He published a circular letter on behalf of the new union in 1843 in which he expressed his concern at the slowness of progress by Scottish Baptists in the task of evangelising Scotland. Johnston was especially critical of the strategies, or lack of them, in determining priorities in evangelism. He acknowledged the good work done by the BHMS in the Highlands and Islands, but insisted that this left many urban centres in Scotland untouched. He noted that there were 133 towns in Scotland with a population of over 2,000 people. Each of these towns should have a Baptist Church, yet only thirty-six of these towns had an established Baptist congregation. In fact these thirty-six towns had fifty-four Baptist Churches, leaving a further nineteen churches located in more rural

---

121 Tidball, 'English Baptist Home Missions', pp. 140-141.
122 Tidball, 'English Baptist Home Missions', pp. 140-147.
123 Lovegrove, *Established Church*, p. 153, n.32.
124 Chapter seven, pp. 233-237.

locations. There were, therefore, ninety-seven towns untouched by Baptist evangelists in the mid-nineteenth century. Why was this the case? Johnston had no doubts as to the reason:

> We have not resolved, as wisdom would dictate, first to attend to the populous towns, and then to the counties, till there be not a county or a town without a Baptist church. Our churches have been too much the offspring of chance; or in other words, just as there might happen to be a Baptist in a place who was wishful to spread his sentiments, and called for aid; there, something has been done, while many large towns and populous districts have been overlooked.[125]

This, he insisted, was not the strategy of the New Testament churches. They targeted the large urban centres first in their plans to spread the Christian faith throughout the Roman Empire. Here in Scotland the towns and cities had been largely neglected. The BHMS had supported a missionary at Grahamston (Falkirk) near to the Carron Iron Works in the early 1830s called Daniel Dunbar.[126] He had been working there, however, before the Society gave assistance to him, in response to his request, which ironically confirmed Johnston's point. Appendix 3.1 reveals that there had been missionaries based in Aberdeen, Dundee, Inverness, Stirling, Falkirk, South Portland Street, Glasgow, Stobhill, Greenock and Edinburgh. The home missionary society had not totally neglected the needs of the urban population. It had, however, failed to keep pace with the growing need for workers in these areas. What is more important was that there were Scottish Baptists who perceived the BHMS to have neglected the urban mission field. James Paterson, a committed supporter of this Society and a leader of the Scottish Baptist Association that had commenced in 1856,[127] insisted that:

> This Home Mission does nothing, or next to nothing, in the more populous districts of the south. In whatever way this fact is to be accounted for, that it is the simple fact cannot be denied. Hitherto it has aided little or nothing in establishing or extending Baptist churches in the more populous cities and towns of the kingdom.[128]

Resources for additional workers and stations were not forthcoming and it was therefore not surprising that with limited financial means at its disposal, the society decided to concentrate on maintaining the existing stations principally in the Highlands and

---

125 F. Johnston, *An Inquiry into the Means of Advancing the Baptist Denomination in Scotland*, (Cupar: G.S. Tullis, 1843), pp. 6-12.
126 *BHMS Report*, 1831, pp. 10-11.
127 Chapter Eight, pp. 298-299.
128 *The Freeman*, 9 (May 27, 1863), p. 332.

Islands. The work of the BHMS must continue, but the Baptist Union must rise to the challenge of raising extra money and labourers to reach the urban centres with the Christian gospel.[129] James Paterson's words were accurate and most Baptists would have acknowledged his point.

5.8 BHMS Activities that went beyond the Boundaries of a Baptist Union

In some aspects of the work of the BHMS it appeared to go beyond the boundaries of operations of a Baptist union of churches. One example of this was the decision to close down the work at Stobhill, a village near Glasgow. This was a mining community that had been initially responsive to the labours of the agent Robert Mackay. The description of the work in 1841 seemed to show promise for the future.[130] There was, however, a depression in the mining industry in the area shortly afterwards and the following gloomy report was presented in 1842:

> Mr Robert Mackay has been engaged in preaching both at Stobhill and in the neighbourhood; but in consequence of the state of matters, the Committee have judged it right to give up this station. £1 11s. 4d have been collected for the Society.

The abstract of the treasurer's accounts for 1842 reveals that the meeting-house at Stobhill was sold once the decision to give up the preaching station was taken.[131]

The decision to close down Stobhill preaching station was not typical of the decisions of the committee. It was more common to persevere with a situation hoping for better times. The 1831 report from Lochgilphead indicated that the ministry of Dugald Sinclair was not blessed with the same success as in former years and as a result he had decided to emigrate to Canada with sixteen of the members and some of the adherents. The Lochgilphead congregation had been reduced to thirteen members.

> They applied to the Society for another preacher; and although the prospects of usefulness have not for sometime past been so good at Lochgilphead as formerly, yet as there is an excellent field for preaching the gospel in the neighbourhood, Mr John Mackintosh of Stornoway, has proceeded to that station.[132]

The 1832 report indicated that the membership had increased to

---

129 *The First Yearly Report of the Baptist Union*, 1843, pp. 5-10.
130 *BHMS Report*, (Edinburgh: Thornton & Collie, 1841), p. 16.
131 *BHMS Report*, (Edinburgh: Thornton & Collie, 1842), pp. 22, 55.
132 *BHMS Report*, 1831, p. 6. Meek, 'Dugald Sinclair', pp. 79-82.

twenty-one.¹³³ The following year saw a further increase in membership and this led to great optimism for the future.

> When we recollect that thirty-three have been added to us in about eighteen months, we have reason to say, What hath God wrought? I hope these are only the first fruits of an abundant harvest to be gathered in this place.

The progress was confirmed by the decision to ordain and induct John Mackintosh as the pastor of this congregation in February 1833. Alexander Grant of Tobermory led the service with Lachlan Mackintosh, a former minister of the congregation, and now travelling representative of the BHMS. Lachlan Mackintosh conducted the formal ceremony and preached the charge to the minister. Angus McNaughton, the minister at Islay, preached the charge to the congregation.¹³⁴ The point illustrated by the example of Lochgilphead is the fact that the committee first of all took the decision to continue with the work at Lochgilphead. Then they decided to move the agent from Lewis, the only agent on the island at that time, to Lochgilphead. As a result of the success of his ministry he was then duly ordained and inducted to the pastorate of the church. The BHMS, in contrast to a Baptist Union, had the authority to close down its stations, and the society was also able to move staff around the country at short notice. The removal of the agent from Lewis effectively closed the door on a promising work on the island, but the strategic importance of Lochgilphead ensured that it had the prior claim to an agent. A Baptist union of churches would never have the control over affiliated churches that the BHMS exercised over its agents and mission stations. The large urban Baptist churches in particular would take steps to ensure that no committee would have control over their internal affairs.

A further factor that indicated that the BHMS had extended its control of Baptist church life beyond that of a Baptist union of churches concerned doctrinal controls. Agents and mission churches were expected to conform to a clear Calvinistic doctrinal pattern. The annual reports of the BHMS for the years 1831 and 1832 provide clear evidence of the 'guidance' provided, especially from the pen of James Haldane, one of the joint-secretaries. In 1831 after reports from the various missionaries, the secretary sought to summarise the content of the messages of the agents of the BHMS. There does not appear to be any logical order to the doctrinal statements made and may simply have been recorded as they came to the mind of the secretary. Haldane used the 'great commission' of Matthew

---

133 *BHMS Report*, 1832, p. 14.
134 *BHMS Report*, 1833, pp. 16-17.

28.19-20 to expound an evangelical Calvinistic understanding of the Christian faith. The secretary was determined to contrast the common faith of the Highland missionaries with the teaching of other preachers that his readers might have heard.

> Such is the doctrine promulgated by your Preachers. It has been the stay and support of the people of God in every age; it has animated them in life, and cheered them in death; and, amidst all the infidelity which prevails, there is a remnant who hold this doctrine; and however they may be despised, they are the salt of the earth, the light of a benighted world. It is the more necessary, at the present time, earnestly to contend for the faith once delivered to the saints, and to disseminate the unadulterated Gospel of Christ, because there are many winds of doctrine abroad with which the simple are carried away; and it is particularly necessary, when such zeal is shown in the dissemination of error, and when such strong appeals are made to the holy lives of those who are corrupting the Gospel of Christ.

The report went on to exhort the readers not to have any dealings with those people that were teaching these false doctrines.[135] The implications of his appeal seemed to suggest that the heresies he opposed were present within Baptist circles and gaining ground at the expense of what he believed was orthodox Christian theology. It would have been very surprising if there had been no response at all to such a stirring appeal.

The 1832 annual report gives some indication of the response of the society's supporters in England. This came in the report of the representative to the English churches, Lachlan Mackintosh. The comments he received were uniformly in favour of the doctrinal position set out by James Haldane. Mackintosh declared:'The statement of doctrine made in the last report gave general satisfaction'.[136] There may have been some suspicion on the part of some supporters in England and Scotland that the BHMS was weakening its doctrinal position, but this clear affirmation of its stance clarified this matter. In any case the Scotch Baptists routinely seemed to check up on sister churches' beliefs; hence the enquiry may have come from that part of the Baptist constituency. All of the preachers were expected to subscribe to orthodox Calvinist theology or risk expulsion from the BHMS This was not a major issue for leading Scottish Baptists in the early 1830s as they had something approximating to a consensus on this subject, but ten years later with the rise to prominence of Francis Johnston the situation was to change dra-

---

135 *BHMS Report*, 1831, pp. 20-24.
136 *BHMS Report*, 1832, p. 24.

matically. It is probable that prominent Scottish Baptist ministers in Glasgow and Edinburgh might be uneasy with the thought of their theology being 'checked' by leading members of the BHMS in the same way in which agents of the Society were advised. The negative reaction to Francis Johnston's militant crusades on behalf of Arminianism in the early 1850s appears to confirm this understanding of the situation.[137] A united front in doctrinal and practical matters had led to an increase over the years in the number of missionaries employed (Appendix 3.2) and in the amount of money raised (Apendices 3.3 to 3.6). In particular the income of the BHMS surged upwards in the years following the successful launch of the 1869 Baptist Union. Despite the ambivalence shown by many English Baptists towards their own Baptist Union it appears that they were in favour of a united front in Scotland.

The most obvious reason of all as to why the BHMS was not seen as a 'substitute union' is the simplest to state: there were three unsuccessful attempts to form a Baptist Union of Scotland prior to 1869 and a union that endured from that date. The Scottish Baptists involved in those attempts at union clearly felt that there were additional activities that Scottish Baptists should engage in that could not be covered by the remit of the BHMS; therefore there was a need for a union to cover those responsibilities. A letter in *The Baptist Magazine* in October 1836 from Donald Thomson (under the name Scotus), the minister of Orangefield Baptist Church in Greenock, picks up on this issue after speaking about the good work done by the BHMS:

> But it will sound strange...that the existence of this society should be supposed to be a sufficient reason for the non-existence of an Association, or that any should take alarm at the formation of an Association and refuse to give it their support, lest it should interfere with the prosperity of the Society already referred to; or that any of those supporting this and other kindred societies, should allege as an excuse for not co-operating in association, that for such things there is no scriptural precedent.[138]

Thomson rightly notes that in England the Home Missionary Society and the Union complemented each other in promoting Baptist witness, but his letter would have been insufficient to overcome the doubts of some of his Scottish Baptist colleagues regarding the SBA The example that he gave, however, would have encouraged advocates of Scottish Baptist union to persevere in their efforts. Sup-

---

137 Chapter seven, pp. 259-260, 265-273.
138 Scotus [Donald Thomson], in *The Baptist Magazine*, 28.10 (October, 1836), pp. 437-439.

port for the BHMS and a desire for a closer connection between the churches were not mutually exclusive. The *BHMS Report* for 1866 noted the growing conviction amongst their supporters in favour of a union of Scottish Baptist churches, and the hope that this desire would lead to greater prosperity for the society.

> The establishment of a monthly united prayer-meeting of the Baptist churches in Edinburgh, in connexion with the Society...is referred to in many of their letters as having afforded them peculiar satisfaction; and it was with much satisfaction that they heard of the social gathering of the same churches at the last new year, as indicative of an increased desire for union and fraternal cooperation, calculated, no doubt, to exert a reflex influence on the prosperity of the Society.[139]

Some Baptists, for example James Haldane,[140] felt that on balance there was no need for an additional national institution. Scottish Baptists in the 1840s onward who held to theological opinions outside the prevailing Calvinistic orthodoxy, believed that a more open theological climate might flourish in a union of churches that was less tightly structured than the BHMS.[141] A further group of Scottish Baptists led by men such as James Paterson believed that the need for ministerial theological training and for church-planting in the urban centres of the central belt of Scotland was more likely to be fulfilled under the auspices of a union.[142] There was no single factor of over-riding importance, but a combination of lesser factors that united to form a strong case for the establishment of a Baptist Union of Scotland.

In conclusion there were a number of considerations that seemed to suggest that the BHMS was acting as a substitute union in the period under discussion. The most prominent reason was the extraordinary success of this institution. Scottish Baptists comprised only 1% of the church-going population yet provided the funds, in association with Baptists in England, to cover the expenses of missionaries that covered most of the rural areas of their native land for a good proportion of the nineteenth century. In contrast to the apparent weakness of the English BHMS this society captured the affections of the Scottish Baptists from all three traditions in the land and maintained their loyalty when on so many other issues

---

139 *BHMS Report*, 1866, pp. 5-6.
140 Haldane, *Observations on the Association of believers*, pp. 9-16. Haldane, *View of the Social Worship*, p. 125. Chapter three, pp. 86-90.
141 Chapter seven, pp. 247-251.
142 Chapter eight, pp. 298-299, 315-316.

there were ongoing disputes and divisions. The society's preachers took responsibility for setting apart others as ministers. The organisational structure that enabled the BHMS to raise large sums of money in England was in part a recognition of the status of the BHMS in the eyes of Scottish and English Particular Baptists. This fact confirmed the belief of men such Christopher Anderson that Particular Baptists in England were part of the same denomination. Therefore it was a possibility that some Baptists in Scotland would see no need for an additional union of churches. In addition the provision of high calibre men as the home missionaries was the mainstay of the BHMS's success. The provision of training for these men was also the responsibility of the society.

There were, however, other factors that undermined the position of those who might see the BHMS as a substitute union. First of all the provision of extra Established Church buildings and ministers in some Highland parishes weakened the position of the Baptists in the communities concerned. The challenges faced by competition from other denominations, especially the Free Church after 1843, raised questions about the sustainability of the Baptist presence in several areas of the Highlands in the longer term. This point in turn raised the whole question about the focus of the mission being almost exclusively concentrated on the Highlands and Islands of Scotland. The interconnected issues of poverty, declining income in real terms, declining expectations of success from the 1850s onwards, and above all emigration and migration of ministers, members and hearers alike all brought great pressures to bear on the BHMS committee and workers. The BHMS to some degree appeared to exercise powers beyond that of a union of churches in its decisions concerning the opening and closing of causes and the deployment of personnel. This was also true in part in the maintenance of a clear theological position for all of its staff workers. It is possible that some Scottish Baptists feared that a Baptist Union might seek to impose even greater constraints on the churches than the BHMS These aspects of the BHMS ministry could, therefore, have hindered moves towards union. The most important issue, however, was the apparent lack of a strategy for reaching the majority of people in Scotland. Francis Johnston had been correct to point this out in his circular letter of 1843. His analysis of the situation in this respect was confirmed by the critique of the work of the BHMS by James Paterson in 1863. The needs of the urban masses above all other issues ensured the need for another national organisation amongst Scottish Baptists. The various attempts at forming a Baptist Union of Scotland from 1827 onwards are in part confirmation of this observation. The BHMS had in some respects the appearance of being a substitute union between 1827 and 1869. There was a small minority of Baptists who looked upon the Society in this way. The reality, however, was that the overwhelming majority of Scottish Baptists recognised the need for an adequate Baptist Union of Scotland even if it was to take them a long time before their hopes were realised.

CHAPTER 6

The Attempts to Form a Baptist Union of Scotland, 1827-1842

6.1 The Formation and Demise of the 1827 Baptist Union

The Process of Establishing the Baptist Union

The first attempt to promote the case for closer association amongst Scottish Baptist churches took place in March 1827.[1] This initiative was sponsored by a single congregation in Edinburgh. The response, however, from the wider Baptist constituency indicated that there was a significant proportion of its members in favour of the proposed venture. In a mere two months the Baptist Union of Scotland was constituted with the support of nearly half the churches,[2] as Appendix 4.2 reveals. There were, though, some congregations that were not convinced of the benefits of the new organisation and the criticism of the new body led to its ultimate demise, probably by the end of that decade. A proportion of the churches, including those from Highland Perthshire, were instrumental in the formation of the Scottish Baptist Association in 1835.[3] While this new body attracted modest support, it failed to engage the interest of the larger urban congregations of the central belt. Its slow but steady growth showed that an increased proportion of Baptist churches was convinced of the need for a union of churches. The arrival of the energetic and visionary leader Francis Johnston in 1842 gave a fresh impetus to this project which resulted in 1843 with the formation of the second Baptist Union of Scotland.[4] The majority of Scottish Baptists, though, chose not to associate with any of these three national organisations. This chapter will consider first the factors that promoted the impetus towards unity and then those factors that hindered the process of creating a formal union of churches.

---

1 Anonymous Circular, *To The Baptist Churches of Scotland*, March 18 1827, Bundle 8, Waugh Papers.
2 *To the Baptist Churches in Scotland*, June 13 1827.
3 Scottish Baptist Association Minutes, 1835.
4 *The First Yearly Report of the Baptist Union of Scotland*, 1844, pp. 18-22.

The circumstances in which this process began in 1827 were largely favourable to the new venture. The evidence for this is seen first of all in the growing desire of Scottish Baptists to work together in evangelism in Scotland. Baptists of all three groups, the Scotch Baptists, the Haldaneite Baptists and the 'English' Baptists, had seen the benefits of co-operation in this form of Christian service. The SIS, the mission agency of the 'English' Baptists led by George Barclay and Christopher Anderson, had merged with the Haldaneite workers in 1824. This new organisation was financially secure and was able to move forward with confidence. It revealed a very different picture from that of the serious deficits portrayed in the S.I.S. accounts for 1816-1824. The Society supported mainly by the Scotch Baptists, the Baptist Highland Mission, was to join forces with this new organisation, the Home Missionary Society for Scotland, in August 1827 to form the BHMS.[5] In addition the pastors and churches that promoted the united home missionary society were also prominent supporters of the process to unite churches in a Baptist union. They came from the three streams of Baptist traditions in Scotland. William Innes, pastor of Elder Street Chapel, Edinburgh, and Peter Grant from Stirling were associated with the Haldanes. George Barclay (Irvine), David Souter (Academy Street, Aberdeen), and Jonathan Watson (Cupar) were 'English' Baptists. David McLaren (North Portland Street, Glasgow), Charles Arthur (Kirkcaldy), and David Dewar (Dunfermline) were Scotch Baptists. The significance of these united efforts in evangelism cannot be underestimated in preparing the ground for a closer union of Baptist churches in Scotland. If Baptists were prepared to trust each other in this area of their labours, as they were, then it ought not to be a surprise that a call was soon to be made for a formal bond between them.

In the first half of 1827, at the same time as the formation of the BHMS, there were several well-attended meetings that aimed to create a union of Baptist churches in Scotland. The process began with an anonymous circular in March, though by James Farquharson. The first meeting called to consider the circular took place in William Innes's church at Elder Street in Edinburgh on April 19 that year. The minutes of the meeting record that several pastors and members from churches in different parts of Scotland gathered on this occasion. The speed with which this meeting had been called was astonishing. The appeal must have been sent to many Baptists who had already become convinced of the need for closer ties

---

5 *Address by the Committee of the Baptist Home Missionary Society for Scotland*, October 2 1827, p. 1.

between their congregations. The magnitude of this achievement increases when it is noted that all the members of the committee that sent the circular to the Baptist churches in Scotland came from one congregation in Edinburgh. It is evident that there were Baptists who had been predisposed towards such a call by their own experience. Scotch Baptists valued their links with colleagues in different parts of Britain and some 'English' Baptists were familiar with the importance of the associations in England amongst the Particular Baptists. Some, for example Christopher Anderson and George Barclay, regarded English Particular Baptists as fellow-members of the same denomination.[6] In Anderson's correspondence with Andrew Fuller, 'English' Baptists are referred to as 'Brother...' whereas other Baptists are mentioned as 'Mr...'[7] It must be stated, however, that these links could also have been a hindrance to a call for union in Scotland because, as we have seen, some churches, particularly among the Scotch Baptists, insisted on strict uniformity between churches in doctrine and ecclesiology when they were in formal association. The writer of the anonymous circular, James Farquharson, and some other members of Rose Street Baptist Church in Edinburgh, had resolved to meet every Wednesday evening at half past seven to spend an hour in prayer on this subject. They also had resolved to correspond with other Baptist churches in Scotland in the hope that they were not alone in their desire for unity.[8] It could be seen as surprising that there was such a quick response to their appeal. In addition to the above links between Baptist churches, it is also important to note that all three groups of Baptists in Scotland supported the work of the BMS. Archibald McLean, the leader of the Scotch Baptists, recorded the generous response to his appeal for support for the BMS in a letter sent to Andrew Fuller, the secretary of the BMS in April 1796.[9] The groundwork appeared to have been done in preparing the way for the establishment of a union of Baptist churches in Scotland.

The momentum which appeared to be bringing Baptists closer together in the 1820s was not unique to that group of Christians. In Britain since the 1790s there had been a groundswell of support for co-operation across denominational lines, as well as for the

---

6 Andrew Fuller to Christopher Anderson, February 16 1808, in Anderson, *Christopher Anderson*, pp. 183-184.
7 Anderson, *Christopher Anderson*, pp. 183-184 as above, and Anderson to 'a friend in England', December 1 1808', Anderson, *Christopher Anderson*, pp. 186-187.
8 *To The Baptist Churches of Scotland*, March 1827.
9 *The New Evangelical Magazine*, 2, (1816), p. 76.

strengthening of ties within the ranks of any particular constituency.[10] The establishment of the British and Foreign Bible Society in 1804, followed by its rapid growth in influence due to the support of both Churchmen and Dissenters, was one of a number of factors which contributed to the strengthening of ties between Christians of different denominations. An evangelical Anglican claimed in 1816 that the Bible Society had had the honour of commencing 'a new era in the Christian world'. 'They have roused the torpor of other religious institutions: they have thrown down the barriers which separated man from his brother, and united in one body the energies of the pious and the wise.'[11] There was, however, a time of serious controversy and division within the ranks of supporters of the Bible Society in the 1820s.[12] The controversies came to a head in Scotland during 1827 when forty of the forty-eight Scottish auxiliary societies that had been contributing to the parent society in 1825 ceased their association with that body.[13] In the Edinburgh auxiliary of the British and Foreign Bible Society there were those who, though supporting the viewpoint of their colleagues, did not wish to take the drastic step of secession and they decided in June 1827 to form a new auxiliary still connected with the parent society in London. There were in this latter group a number of Baptists including William Innes, Christopher Anderson and James Haldane, as well as representatives of the other denominations.[14] These Baptist leaders wished to resolve the problems by negotiation while at the same time retaining their ties with the parent organisation. If Baptists could co-operate with each other to help Christians from different denominations work together then it was not surprising that Innes and Anderson, amongst other Baptists, thought that the time was right to encourage closer co-operation between the different Baptist groups working in Scotland. It was in the same month, June 1827, that members of Anderson's and Innes' churches, along with other Scottish Baptists, were meeting to strengthen the ties between the

---

10 Martin, *Evangelicals United*, and Ward, *Religion and Society in England 1790-1850*, discuss the extent of this interdenominational co-operation.
11 *Christian Observer*, 15, (1816), p. 539, cited by Martin, *Evangelicals United*, p. 93.
12 Martin, *Evangelicals United*, pp. 99-146.
13 [21st and 24th] *Annual Report of the British and Foreign Bible Society*, for a comparison of Scottish patronage in 1825 and 1828, cited by Martin, *Evangelicals United*, p. 131.
14 'Bible Society Home Correspondence', H. Gray to Joseph Tarn (assistant secretary of the society), June 22 1827, cited by Martin, *Evangelicals United*, p. 130.

Baptist Churches in Scotland.[15] By the summer of 1827 the momentum in favour of a union of Baptist churches in Scotland appeared to be considerable.

The first committee of the proposed union had the advantage of strong ties between its members. These men were not only committed to a vision of union, but also prayed and worked together as members of one congregation, Charlotte Chapel in Rose Street, Edinburgh. The strength of their unity will be contrasted later with the inevitably weaker links between committee members after the establishment of the Baptist Union of Scotland in June 1827. Although anonymous, the first circular sent in March 1827 had indicated that all the original committee members had their membership in the same Edinburgh church. The minutes of the June 1827 committee meeting state that James Johnston, Archibald Wilson, James Farquharson, John Adam and William Fraser were members of that first committee.[16] It does not state that they were the only members and this may suggest that other people were involved in those early meetings in Charlotte Chapel. The five men listed were present at the June meeting that launched the 1827 Union as delegates of their church. The link between these individuals and Rose Street Baptist Church in Edinburgh is established from legal documents retained by that church. These documents, which date from 1824, reveal the names, addresses and occupations of some of the trustees of the church during the ministry of Christopher Anderson. James Johnston, James Farquharson and William Fraser were amongst the individuals named.[17] There was, however, no record of Archibald Wilson or John Adam serving as trustees of that congregation. The Edinburgh *Post Office Annual Directory* gives details of the occupations and addresses of these men. James Johnston was a ladies' shoemaker.[18] James Farquharson was a letter-carrier for the General Post Office.[19] Archibald Wilson was a spirit dealer up to 1828 then a wine and spirit dealer in subsequent years.[20] It is possible, though unlikely, that Wilson's occupation prevented him being

---

15 *Circular from the Committee of Proposed Baptist Union*, May 4 1827, and *To the Baptist Churches in Scotland*, June 13 1827.
16 *To the Baptist Churches in Scotland*, June 13 1827.
17 Charlotte Chapel documents listing the trustees up to 1848, MSS in the possession of Charlotte Baptist Chapel, Edinburgh.
18 *The Post Office Annual Directory for 1828-1829*, (Edinburgh: Ballantyne and Co., 1828), p. 92.
19 *The Post Office Annual Directory for 1826-1827*, (Edinburgh: James Ballantyne & Co., 1826), p. 58.

invited to serve in the 1830s as a trustee of Charlotte Chapel. Support amongst Scottish Baptists for the temperance movement grew rapidly in that decade and certainly in later years Baptists in Scotland did not always look favourably on members of their churches working in this industry. John Adam worked as a teacher in the city up to 1828, at which date his name ceases to be recorded in the directory.[21] This information is consistent with evidence that places Adam in Perth in the late 1820s.[22] It is known that Adam was minister of Perth Baptist Church in 1830, as the congregation under his leadership built a church in the town in South Street.[23] William Fraser worked in association with his father (who shared the same first name) as a dyer. The business was known as 'William Fraser & Co.' and based at in Market Street, Edinburgh.[24] Fraser Senior became a Burgess of Edinburgh in 1813, during his time employed as a dyer at 'Paul's Work'.[25] The younger Fraser entered Horton Baptist College, Bradford, in 1828, to train for the Baptist ministry. In subsequent years he served as the pastor of Baptist churches in Bolton (1830-1843) and Lambeth, London (1843-1850), until his death in 1850.[26] The strong ties that united these men in their vision for a union of Baptist churches enabled the early meetings for the proposed union to be a great success. The test would come in later months when they sought to incorporate into their ranks men of differing ideas and practices.

One factor that greatly strengthened this proposed union was the geographical spread of the participating churches. There were both

---

20 *The Post Office Annual Directory for 1827-1828*, (Edinburgh: Ballantyne and Co., 1827), p. 201. *The Post Office Annual Directory for 1828-1829*, 1828, p. 194.

21 *The Post Office Annual Directory for 1827-1828*, 1827, p. 1.

22 Robertson, *Perth Baptist Church*, p. 39.

23 Robertson, *Perth Baptist Church*, p. 39. Adam's predecessor as minister, James Campbell, had served both as minister of the congregation and as an itinerant preacher with the BHMS in tours of Lewis and Skye during 1828. It therefore seems probable that Adam took up the charge in 1828 or 1829, See *BHMS Report*, 1829, pp. 20-24.

24 *The Post Office Annual Directory for 1827-1828*, 1827, p. 65.

25 C.B. Boag-Watson (ed.), *The Burgesses and Guild Brethren of Edinburgh 1761-1841*, (Scottish Records Society; Edinburgh: J. Skinner and Company Ltd, 1933), p. 60.

26 *NBES Report*, 1828-1829, p. 17, (and subsequent reports on the ministries of former students). The Horton Report for 1829 refers to Fraser and one other student who had signed on for the course 'at their own expense'(page 17) which implies that this man had previously had a higher than average income.

urban and rural churches representing the north, west, east and south of Scotland. The map in Appendix 4.1 shows the strength of this union of churches. The north of Scotland was represented by Grantown-on-Spey Baptist Church, alongside Academy Street and John Street Baptist Churches in Aberdeen. Baptist churches from Eyemouth, Berwick-upon-Tweed and Hawick were the participants from the south of Scotland. The west Highlands contributed Lochgilphead and Tiree. There was also a good representation from Perthshire and Fife. Glasgow and Edinburgh, however, were the key to success, as a union of churches that did not contain the churches and leaders in these major urban centres would remain weak and ineffective. This union could begin from a position of strength with a good mixture of urban and rural congregations with a wide geographical spread, and legitimately claim the title The Baptist Union of Scotland.

It is important to examine the impact of the moves for union on the two major cities of Scotland. Glasgow had a maximum of four Baptist congregations in 1827, though only one was listed in the *Post Office Annual Directory* for that year. This congregation had a Scotch Baptist ecclesiology and had as its ministers Abraham Perrey and William Shirreff, a former Church of Scotland minister from Stirling.[27] Perrey had trained for the ministry at Bristol Baptist College prior to moving to Glasgow in 1819 with a view to church-planting.[28] The church was constituted in 1820 with Perrey apparently as sole minister for the next three years.[29] In 1823 William Shirreff, originally the minister of St Ninians Parish Church in the presbytery of Stirling, underwent a change of sentiment over the ordinance of baptism and was invited to serve as pastor of the congregation. This event took place soon after Shirreff's baptism that year in Edinburgh by William Innes.[30] Watts inaccurately states that this church was founded as late as 1823, shortly prior to Shirreff's arrival.[31] It seems likely that though Perrey remained in the church until 1828, Shirreff was unofficially accorded the position of senior pastor.[32] The only other known reference to this church comes in the 1821 report of the Horton Baptist College where Robert Thomson, in future

---

27 *The Glasgow Directory*, (Glasgow: W.Lang, 1827), Appendix, p. 31.
28 Hall, 'Scottish connections with Bristol Baptist College', p. 3.
29 Yuille (ed.), *Baptists in Scotland*, p. 281.
30 W. Shirreff, *Lectures on Baptism*, (London: Passmore and Alabaster, 1878), p. xvii.
31 D.W. Watts, 'Glasgow and Dumbartonshire', in Bebbington (ed.), *Baptists in Scotland*, p. 165.
32 *The Post Office Annual Directory* for Glasgow after 1827 lists Shirreff as the sole pastor of the church.

years a prominent Baptist minister in Perth, but then a new student at the college, is described as coming from 'Mr Perrey's church in Glasgow'.[33] The oldest Baptist congregation in the city was the Scotch Baptist church based in George Street. It was pastored by David Smith, Andrew Duncan and Walter Dick.[34] This congregation adhered strictly to Scotch Baptist ecclesiological views and sought no involvement in the moves towards union. Another more open-minded Scotch Baptist church located in (North) Portland Street, Glasgow, had as its leaders Charles Wallace and David McLaren.[35] Despite a critical and uncertain involvement in the process towards union, this congregation did decide to participate and identify with the fledgling movement. The fourth congregation in Glasgow, and the other one to join the Baptist Union, was the 'English' church that met in the Old Grammar School, which Alexander McLeod served as minister.[36] Glasgow, therefore, had two out of the four churches participating in this process. This was an encouraging start in the moves to bridge the barriers that had separated Scotch and 'English' Baptists in Scotland.

In 1827 Edinburgh had five Baptist congregations. There had been a sixth, a short-lived Scotch Baptist congregation based in Thistle Street and pastored by William Gray and Francis Sutherland, but it had disappeared from the *Post Office Directory* by 1825.[37] The main Scotch Baptist church in Edinburgh, originally founded by Archibald McLean, and now led by William Braidwood, William Peddie and Henry Dickie,[38] met at the Pleasance.[39] It had chosen to take no part in the moves towards union. Clyde Street Hall was a Scotch Baptist congregation that had broken away in 1824 from the Tabernacle Church, Edinburgh, after disagreements over the subject of 'forbearance'. It had two pastors, Andrew Ker and Archibald Smith, who was to be a leading member of the 1827 Baptist Union.[40] Smith was one of three men chosen in April 1827 to function as a

---

33 *NBES Report*, 1820-1821, (Rochdale: Joseph Littlewood,1821), p. 15.
34 *The Post Office Annual Directory for 1834-1835*, (Glasgow: John Graham, 1834), Appendix, p. 48.
35 *The Post Office Annual Directory for 1834-1835*, Glasgow, Appendix, p. 48.
36 *The Post Office Annual Directory for 1834-1835*, Glasgow, Appendix, p. 48. Details of this church are given in Chapter four, p. 125.
37 *The Post Office Annual Directory*, (Edinburgh: John Collie, 1824), Appendix, p. 31.
38 *The First Yearly Report of the Baptist Union of Scotland*, 1844, p. 19.
39 *The Post Office Annual Directory*, (Edinburgh: John Collie, 1825), Appendix, p. 42.

temporary union committee prior to the formal constitution of the Baptist Union of Scotland. He was appointed to serve as one of its secretaries dealing with correspondence from the churches.[41] The choice of Smith as a Baptist Union secretary was perceptive because he was an ideal candidate. His attention to detail and grasp of the key issues in a debate, as well as a sensitivity to people, are revealed in the Waugh Papers. This collection of nineteenth-century Baptist records principally consists of the documents preserved from the Clyde Street Hall, from the time when Smith served as one of its pastors. Elder Street Baptist Church, Edinburgh, was involved in the moves towards union from its inception. The crucial April and June 1827 meetings took place on its premises. William Innes, its minister, was unable to attend the latter event, and so two deacons, William Alexander and John Robertson, deputised for him.[42] The Leith Walk congregation pastored by James Haldane chose to take no part in the moves to establish a union of Baptist churches. It is possible that Haldane felt that he needed to concentrate his energies in re-establishing the ties between the Scottish churches and the British and Foreign Bible Society. In the spring of 1827 Christopher Anderson and William Innes were also engaged in that process which has been discussed earlier in this chapter. The relevance of that issue here is that the absence of Innes and Anderson from the union meetings was not because they were hostile to the process, but almost certainly because they believed the success of the union was assured. Rose Street Baptist Church, pastored by Anderson, had played the most important part in bringing Scottish Baptists together. The membership of the original group proposing union was exclusively from this congregation and the interim committee consisting of three persons set up in April 1827 contained two of its members, John Adam and James Farquharson.[43] As has been noted already, the Baptist Union committee after its constitution in June of that year had five out of its fourteen members from this congregation: John Adam, James Farquharson, Archibald Wilson, William Fraser, and James Johnston.[44] It is clear that though half the Glasgow Baptist churches had joined the new union, the centre of influence was in Edinburgh. Three out of the five Edinburgh churches were committed to this process and with the powerful backing of the

---

40 Bundle 8, Waugh Papers.
41 *Circular from the Committee of Proposed Baptist Union*, May 4 1827.
42 *Circular from the Committee of Proposed Baptist Union*, May 4 1827, p. 2. *To the Baptist Churches in Scotland*, June 13 1827, p. 2.
43 *Circular from the Committee of Proposed Baptist Union*, May 4 1827.
44 *To the Baptist Churches in Scotland*, June 13 1827, p. 2.

Rose Street and Elder Street churches it appeared to have a good chance of lasting success.

In addition to the geographical spread of participants represented in this process, the range of ecclesiological opinions contained within the movement was also an encouragement. The June 1827 meetings recorded the names of the men appointed to the Baptist Union committee. Representatives of all three Baptist traditions in Scotland were found on the list. Charles Spence was the one member associated with James Haldane in the Tabernacle Church. Archibald Smith and Adam Kirk, a pastor of the Scotch Baptist Church in Dunfermline, were the Scotch Baptist representatives. It may not be insignificant to note that both Scotch Baptists had previously been in fellowship with the Haldanes. Adam Kirk had been a member of the Haldaneite Independent Church in Dunfermline prior to joining the Scotch Baptist church in the town.[45] This meant that for them Baptist unity was not a step into the unknown. It is not surprising that men of the 'English' tradition dominated the places on the committee. It was after all from their ranks that the vision for union had first been expressed. Ten out of the fourteen members came from this constituency and besides the five men from Charlotte Chapel, Edinburgh, there were places for John Gilmour, Alexander McLeod, Jonathan Watson, George Barclay (the secretary) and David Souter. Alexander Nisbet, who was the Union treasurer, lived in Edinburgh. His church affiliation has not as yet been ascertained from the surviving documentary evidence. Although the leadership of the new Baptist Union was dominated by one tradition, the very fact that all three traditions were represented on its committee was a big step forward. Here was a strong position on which to build for the future.

In addition to the breadth of the committee membership, the total number of churches participating in the moves towards union suggested a groundswell of support for this body. The committee for proposed union received letters from twenty-three churches of which seventeen were favourable to the new venture. In addition, four of these churches, South Portland Street Baptist Church in Glasgow, Berwick-upon-Tweed Baptist Church, Auchtermuchty Baptist Church and Clyde Street Hall, Edinburgh, had also sent delegates to participate in the meetings to set up the Baptist Union. They had been joined by representatives from nine churches which were in favour, but had not sent a letter to indicate their approval. These nine churches were represented mainly by their pastors:

---

45   *The Evangelist*, 1.2 (August, 1846), p. 41.

Irvine (George Barclay); John Street, Aberdeen (John Gilmour); Academy Street, Aberdeen (David Souter); Lochgilphead and Tiree (Dugald Sinclair); Cupar (Jonathan Watson); Dunfermline (Adam Kirk); Eyemouth (William McLean); and Rose Street, Edinburgh, represented by the five prominent lay-members of the committee. This indicates that twenty-six churches were in favour of the new organisation.[46] In August 1827 a further letter of support was received from Charles Wallace and David McLaren, pastors of North Portland Street Scotch Baptist Church in Glasgow.[47] According to a thorough survey produced in 1844 there were sixty-two Baptist churches in existence in Scotland in 1827.[48] One other church, Elder Street Baptist Church in Edinburgh, could be assumed to be in favour as it provided the facilities for all the proposed union meetings and sent delegates to the gathering that constituted the union. There would, therefore, appear to have been twenty-eight out of sixty-two churches in support of the newly established union. The significance of this proportion of churches being involved in this process is revealed when it is noted that it was a higher figure than that attained by either the second or third attempts at uniting Scottish Baptists, as will be discovered in discussions of the 1835 to 1842 and the 1843 to 1856 bodies and noted in Appendix 4.2. Here there was the participation in attempts to unite Scottish Baptists of 45% of the Baptist churches in Scotland. This level of success at the first attempt was a most notable achievement.

The churches involved in this process had the advantage of unity in fundamental Christian doctrines. This point needs to be emphasised in the light of the growing diversity of beliefs between Scottish Baptists in the 1840s and 1850s that will be discussed in the next chapter. The doctrinal consensus that undergirded this venture was the strongest factor in its favour to the participating churches. These Baptists shared with most other Protestant churches the historic Reformed or Calvinistic view of theology and jealously guarded this common heritage. There were, in terms of ecclesiology, wide variations, and normally the emphasis in theological writings related to these differences, but the broad agreement in theology across the Protestant denominations was treasured. If this was true with regard to fellow Christians in the Presbyterian and Independent traditions, it was especially true in relation to fellow-Baptists. This

---

46 *To the Baptist Churches in Scotland*, June 13 1827, p. 2.
47 David McLaren to Archibald Smith, August 23 1827, Bundle 8, Waugh Papers.
48 *The First Yearly Report of the Baptist Union of Scotland*, 1844, pp. 18-24.

viewpoint comes out clearly in an anonymous circular sent out by some members of Rose Street Baptist Church in Edinburgh to the Scottish Baptist churches in March 1827. The letter begins by expressing sorrow at the level of disunity between different Christian churches. It emphasises that the Christian witness to the wider world has been hindered by disunity amongst professing Christians. This statement then presents a challenge to its readers.

> Deploring these evils, as many Christians in all denominations must do, what it should be asked, is to be done to remedy them? Should Christians remain contented with mere words of regret, without endeavouring to ascertain by what means they may rise from their degraded condition? 'Surely not', will be the reply of every lover of the Saviour.

The circular acknowledges that formal union across the spectrum of Protestant churches is impossible without a sacrifice of principle, but suggests that no such barrier divides the Baptist churches of Scotland:

> With regard to what are generally considered the essential doctrines of the Word of God, such as the Unity and Trinity of the Godhead, the essential Deity, Incarnation and Atonement of the Son of God – the necessity of the influence of the Holy Spirit – justification by faith – the sanctifying power of the belief of the truth as it is in Jesus – we are persuaded that the views of most of these Churches are the same; and they are known to be of one mind as to the *independency* of the Churches of Christ.

This selective statement of belief is not necessarily Reformed, but it was bound to cover the views of the various churches to which the circular was sent. It was in essence a reminder that they shared a common heritage about which there was no debate on these matters. The use of the word 'most' in line six is probably evidence of the caution of a group of Edinburgh laymen concerning the views of many Baptists in other parts of Scotland that they had never met rather than a belief that some Baptists held unorthodox beliefs. Scottish Baptists jealously guarded the independence of their local congregations. The promoters of this circular sought to reassure their readers that they had no plans to change this situation, which explains their reference to church polity in line eight.

There is a clear acknowledgement in this document that there are some differences between the church practices of the different types of Scottish Baptists. These differences are honestly acknowledged, but seen as insufficient to prevent a union of Baptist churches.

> These differences relate principally to the number of Elders or Pastors, and the exhortations of the brethren. May not the churches follow out their convictions on these and such like

points without standing aloof from each other and acting as if those holding different views on these things were 'aliens from the commonwealth of Israel'? Were a spirit of love diffused in the hearts of Christians, would they not forbear one another on these subjects? And would not there be a more likely means of bringing all to be more of one mind, with regard to the will of Christ, than a spirit of variance and indifference to each other can be? Surely it would.[49]

This is a clear appeal to the churches to focus on the things that unite them rather than their differences. There is no attempt to hide the distinctives of the different Baptist groups, but their significance is played down. It was a challenge to put their differences to one side for the sake of the gospel. It was not too surprising that there were churches willing both to hear and to act upon this appeal.

There were, therefore, strong grounds for optimism about the success of this union of churches, because of the strong theological base shared by the churches involved. Evidence for this is seen in an unidentified letter sent to the interim committee of the proposed Baptist Union in 1827.

We laid the circular before the church who most cordially approved of its great general object: but we know not the precise nature and full extent of the Union it contemplates. If mutually to receive each other's members with occasional fellowship, when from home, be all that is intended, we have for many years acted on this principle. The members of any Calvinistic Baptist Church, whether in England or Scotland, have been admitted by us, entirely irrespective of any difference of church-order which might obtain between us as churches, provided we were satisfied with them personally; and when any of our Members go from home, we never restrict them in their fellowship...

The original proposers of the Union and the colleagues that met with them at the meeting on April 19 evidently concurred with these sentiments as their circular records:'We give the following extract from one of the letters received, as the sentiments it contains so entirely correspond with those of the original proposers of the Union and the friends who met here on April 19.'[50] The same viewpoint was held by the delegates of twelve churches who met with the original committee and other friends interested in the proposed Union on June 13 that year.

Various resolutions were passed at the June meeting with the most care being taken over the second resolution: 'The doctrines

---

49 *To The Baptist Churches of Scotland*, March 1827.
50 *Circular from the Committee of Proposed Baptist Union*, May 4 1827.

specified in the second Resolution underwent the closest consideration, and are understood to be what are generally termed, by use of a distinction – Calvinistic'.[51] The uniformity of belief may be surprising to some modern Baptists, but only two Baptist churches in Scotland claimed to be of General or Arminian persuasion in the late 1820s or early 1830s. One was a church in Perth in the 1830s, led by William Taylor, that appealed in 1832 to the Old Connexion General Baptists of England 'for the support of a Unitarian preacher in Perth'; the second was a group in the same town that was led by the Rev. Jabez Burns from 1830 to 1835. It was an evangelical General Baptist church. The two churches, however, had both ceased to exist by 1841.[52] Doctrinal unity was a strong base on which to build the new Baptist Union, but accommodation needed to be made for differences in ecclesiology.

There have been claims that the Hope Street Church led by James Paterson was Arminian in its theology, 'heavily influenced by Methodism'.[53] This suggestion is probably based on the speculation of Yuille in his *History of the Baptists in Scotland*.[54] There is, however, evidence to the contrary which would suggest that Paterson and his congregation were in the 'English' Calvinistic tradition. *The Primitive Church Magazine*, the magazine of the party in Britain contending for the purity of church order, especially 'strict communion', in Particular Baptist churches, received support from Hope Street Baptist Church in Glasgow. The Hope Street church was not the only Baptist church in Glasgow whose minister and other members were subscribers to the cause. A comparison between the list of members in the Hope Street Church[55] and subscription lists in the magazine for the Baptist Evangelical Society (formed as the Strict Baptist Society in 1845 until 1856)[56] reveals some names in common including James Paterson, Howard Bowser and William Hodge.[57] The significance of this point is that this Society was formed to

---

51 *To the Baptist Churches in Scotland*, June 13 1827.
52 Robertson, *Perth Baptist Church*, pp. 39-40. Waugh, 'Converging Streams', pp. 64-65. A.H. Grant, 'Burns, Jabez, D.D.', in L. Stephen (ed.), *The Dictionary of National Biography*, VII, (London: Smith, Elder & Co., 1886), pp. 423-424.
53 Watts, 'Glasgow and Dumbartonshire', p. 165. This error is repeated by D.B. Murray, 'Paterson, James', in Lewis, (ed.), *DEB*, p. 858.
54 Yuille (ed.), *Baptists in Scotland*, p. 169.
55 Hope Street Baptist Church documents.
56 *The Primitive Church Magazine*, New Series, 13.5 (May, 1856), p. 122.
57 *The Primitive Church Magazine*, New Series, 15.12 (December, 1858), pp. 293-294.

unite Calvinistic Baptists who maintained that baptism by immersion was necessary before a person could be offered communion. Letters in the magazine revealed that individuals, and groups of churches, co-operated in seeking to support one another in this task. The resolutions of 'The Northern Brethren' (supporters of the Society in the North of England) in the January 1860 issue of the magazine reveal clearly the aims of participating churches. Resolution V included the following points:

> ...to report on the past and existing encroachment of the open communion system upon the doctrines, the discipline, and the property of Strict Baptist Churches in the United Kingdom, and to suggest plans for checking or avoiding those encroachments for the future; – to decide upon the best means of increasing the supply of faithful men of God as pastors over Strict Baptist churches; – and to lay down general plans of action (without encroaching at all on the independence of the churches) that shall be likely to secure a closer union and more regular and efficient co-operation among the Strict Baptists of Great Britain, than have hitherto existed among them.[58]

It may, therefore, be concluded that Paterson and members of his congregation would not have supported a Society whose theology was very different from their own. The evidence available seems to refute the notion that Hope Street Baptist Church was Arminian in its theology. It was, therefore, in the mainstream of 'English' Baptist churches in Scotland. The sharing of a common theological heritage amongst participating Scottish Baptist churches was a great encouragement in the moves towards establishing a Baptist Union of Scotland in 1827.

The leadership of the new Union had established an annual meeting of church deputies on the first Wednesday of June in Edinburgh. They had also suggested that the churches took up monthly collections to pay for the costs involved in the work of the Baptist Union of Scotland.[59] The new Union appeared to be firmly established, based both on a common theological base and a shared emphasis on evangelism in Scotland and overseas. It was, however, soon showing signs that this project would falter. The reasons for its failure need now to be examined.

---

58 *The Primitive Church Magazine*, New Series, 17.1 (January, 1860), pp. 68-69.
59 *To the Baptist Churches in Scotland*, June 13, 1827.

The Reasons for the Failure of this Baptist Union

The first stumbling block was Scotch Baptist fears of doctrinal and ecclesiological compromise. It was probably this kind of fear that led to the negative responses from the Scotch Baptist congregations in Dundee, Sanquhar and The Pleasance, Edinburgh, and can be assumed as the reason for the lack of a response from other Scotch Baptist congregations such as that meeting in George Street, Glasgow. The documents of this Union that have survived are mainly records of support for its operations. There were, however, some dissenting voices that were revealed by the printed circular sent out by the Baptist Union of Scotland committee in June 1827:'upwards of twenty letters were then read from the several churches, which, with the exception of six, expressed their most cordial and unqualified approval of such a Union as had been briefly intimated in the previous circular'.[60] The six churches that made the effort to state their objections no doubt were echoing the feelings of some of the other churches who did not bother to send in a reply. This state of affairs indicated that there was work to be done before some of the remaining Baptist churches could be persuaded to join the new Union.

One letter arrived too late to be read at the committee meeting in Edinburgh. The letter in question was from David McLaren and Charles Wallace, pastors of the North Portland Street Scotch Baptist Church in Glasgow. This church had intended to send a messenger to represent them at the June meeting, but had changed its position restricting its reply to a letter stating that it was in favour in principle of a Baptist Union, but not at the moment in practice. The letter spoke of ' strong fears [that] were entertained by some that the differences known to exist, would prevent any harmonious and Scriptural union'.[61] This kind of argument was powerful in Scotch Baptist circles where unanimity in doctrine and practice was not only desired but expected. It is ironic that the objections they raised were not against a Baptist church with a different ecclesiology, but against another Scotch Baptist Church. One of the reasons stated for opposition to the new venture was some remarks made by Andrew Ker, an elder at Clyde Street Hall, on the subject of forbearance. Ker had been discussing the limits of forbearance with respect to occasional communion with a visitor to his church. He stated:

Were a believer coming from a church tainted with Socinian

---

60 *To the Baptist Churches in Scotland*, June 13 1827.
61 David McLaren and Charles Wallace to the Committee for proposed Baptist Union, June 12 1827, Bundle 8, Waugh Papers.

errors, deploring them, and if he thought that he had not done his duty among them, (in warning them of their dangers in holding such errors), being fully satisfied myself of his holding the Faith, I will receive him and strengthen him and send him back to do his duty among them (and leave them if they repented not).[62]

This was an unfortunate choice of example as the Scotch Baptists had had a disputation over their understanding of God in the late eighteenth century. As we have seen the Sabellian heresy had been promulgated by Neil Stuart, a Scotch Baptist elder from Glasgow.[63] This conflict was settled by Archibald McLean, the leader of the Scotch Baptists, but it had involved serious (temporary) strains in relationships between the mother church in Edinburgh and the churches in Glasgow, Dundee and Montrose, where the heretical beliefs had been entertained. Wallace and McLaren wanted to have reassurance from the leaders of the Baptist Union of Scotland that this new body would be vigilant in maintaining orthodoxy.

This issue might have been settled quickly due to the strong friendship between Archibald Smith and David McLaren. They had been friends for over twenty years. This was a friendship 'unbroken by one harsh word or look on either side'. 'There are few persons in the circle of my Christian acquaintance to whom I have felt more strongly attached than yourself ', declared Smith to McLaren in a letter dated June 19.[64] He assumed that if Ker's words were put in their proper context an apology would be forthcoming and fellowship restored. This resolution did not take place because of another matter that had been raised in Wallace and McLaren's letter to the committee. This second issue concerned James Watson, an elder at Montrose Baptist Church, who had been received at a communion service in Clyde Street Hall. This man was the brother of Jonathan Watson, the minister at Cupar Baptist Church, a leading figure on the Baptist Union committee. McLaren was convinced that James Watson held some unorthodox (Arminian) views and, therefore, ought not to be welcomed to the Lord's Table in other Baptist churches. Smith made this comment on the incident:

> I freely admit that we acted inconsiderately and unwisely in admitting to our fellowship the individual referred to. That he was received 'cordially' amongst us is not the case. There were others besides myself who had misgivings on the subject, and before we parted he strengthened these misgivings and gave us

---

62 Andrew Ker to Archibald Smith, June 19 1827, explaining his comments at the meeting for proposed union on April 19 1827, Bundle 8, Waugh Papers.
63 Chapter two, pp. 62-63.
64 A. Smith to D. McLaren, June 19 1827, Bundle 8, Waugh Papers.

much room to fear that we had acted with precipitation in the business...but...we were in a great measure ignorant of his views.[65]

McLaren replied on June 22, only three days later, claiming that Alexander McLeod, an 'English' Baptist minister in Glasgow and strong supporter of the Union, had held to the same apparently erroneous opinions as Andrew Ker. In the summer of 1827 there was a constant exchange of letters between Smith and Mclaren which resulted in a triumph for Smith's persistence. A letter from McLaren, dated August 23,[66] finally admitted that the problems had been resolved and that another letter was on its way to the Baptist Union committee requesting to be put on the mailing list for future literature or intimations of meetings.[67] It appeared that the teething problems of the new Union were being resolved, but it was also a warning that problems of this nature could easily arise again. The prickly natures exhibited by many Scotch Baptists would ensure that a considerable period of time would need to elapse before some within their constituency would consider a Union containing Baptists of other ecclesiological principles.

An important issue to consider, which ironically was the one on which this Baptist Union foundered, was the contribution of the Watson family. The earliest association of this family in Baptist circles was with the Scotch Baptists. This family with ten children, of whom Jonathan was the youngest, lived in Montrose.[68] In the late eighteenth century, the Scotch Baptist connexion had been faced with some of the pastors and members of three of its churches in Glasgow, Dundee and Montrose holding to unorthodox views on the Trinity, as has been discussed in chapter two. The overwhelming majority of the dissidents were restored to the fold, but it is likely that they were treated with suspicion by their fellows. It is possible that some members of the Watson family were amongst those individuals holding the heterodox opinion in Montrose. Jonathan Watson was a Scotch Baptist pastor in Dundee prior to his move to Cupar in 1815. It was while resident in the Fife town that he became persuaded of the necessity of an educated and regularly ordained ministry and as a result he started an 'English' Baptist church in Cupar.[69] Details have apparently not survived to reveal whether

---

65 A. Smith to D. McLaren, June 19 1827.
66 D. McLaren to A. Smith, August 23 1827, Bundle 8, Waugh Papers.
67 D. McLaren to The Committee of The Baptist Union of Scotland, September 20 1827, Bundle 8, Waugh Papers.
68 *Scottish Baptist Magazine*, 4.12, (December 1878), p. 180.
69 *Scottish Baptist Magazine*, 4.12, (December 1878), p. 180.

James Watson was connected to the Scotch Baptists at this time, but the evidence discussed below seems to indicate a Scotch Baptist association in the 1820s. The reason for this is that he had been allowed to preach in the North Portland Street Scotch Baptist Church in Glasgow. It is unlikely that an outsider to the Scotch Baptist connexion would have been given such an honour at that time. It is probable, therefore, to place James Watson within the more liberal sector of the Scotch Baptist constituency in the third decade of the nineteenth century, though he may have been disfellowshipped by his fellow Scotch Baptists shortly prior to the establishment of the Baptist Union in 1827.[70]

What was the heresy of which James Watson was suspected? It is important to note that Watson's apparent error was in holding to Arminian doctrinal teaching, not Socinian beliefs as has been suggested.[71] David McLaren makes this clear in his correspondence with Archibald Smith. He referred to occasions when James Watson had been a guest preacher at McLaren's church in the past, 'whilst we were ignorant of his Arminian sentiments'. This is confirmed by the advice given to Smith, by McLaren, as a remedy for Clyde Street Hall's apparent error of judgement in inviting Watson as a guest preacher.

> I entertain the opinion that you should disavow to Mr W[atson] all further connection with him. This would be much better than a circular entertaining a statement of the sentiments of your church in opposition to the Arminian heresy.[72]

Doctrinal unity was thought essential to the success of this Baptist Union. It was, however, much harder for Smith to resolve this problem. Scotch Baptists would have had no problems dissociating themselves from a congregation suspected of holding erroneous views, but this was a much more difficult proposition for the 'English' Baptists. McLaren was asking the Clyde Street Hall, and by implication the Baptist Union of Scotland, to separate themselves from James Watson and the Montrose Church. Smith, as a Scotch Baptist, was probably willing to take this step to keep the Scotch Baptists on board, but others on the committee, not least the brother of the man in question, were unlikely to agree. The willingness of Jonathan Watson to adopt a generous attitude in his relationship with Christians of different ecclesiastical principles has already been noted.[73] Cupar Baptist Church was an open membership

---

70 D. McLaren to A. Smith, June 22 1827, Bundle 8, Waugh Papers.
71 Murray, 'Baptists in Scotland before 1869', p. 262.
72 D. McLaren to A. Smith, June 22 1827.
73 Chapter four, pp. 144-146.

church, that is, one that did not require baptism as a condition of membership.[74] This approach indicated a desire for fellowship with paedobaptists, but it also probably restricted Jonathan Watson's links with some of his fellow Scottish Baptists. The irony of this situation was that James Watson and his Montrose congregation had made no attempt to join this Baptist Union so they ought, therefore, in theory at least, to have been an irrelevance regarding the success or failure of the Union.

The tension resulting from such a dilemma proved too strong for the bonds of fellowship and Smith's subsequent resignation proved to be the turning point for the Union. The impact of Smith's withdrawal has been heightened by the lack of contemporary documentation. The papers relating to the 1827 Baptist Union in the Waugh collection came from those preserved by the Clyde Street elder. As a result, there is apparently no surviving written evidence for the remaining duration of this union. It is probable that it had ceased by 1830, but it certainly had dissolved before the formation of the 1835 Scottish Baptist Association. *The Baptist Magazine* provides no information regarding attempts at union by Scottish Baptists prior to 1835. The lack of information in this Particular Baptist magazine in 1827 regarding either the formation of the Baptist Union in June that year, or the mergers in Scotland to form the BHMS, in August 1827, suggests that its coverage of Scottish affairs was somewhat less than complete. It is, however, most improbable that the Baptist Union of Scotland and its committee had ceased to meet shortly after Smith's decision was taken. There was no question that the disputation in the committee in the autumn of 1827 was serious, but one man's resignation would have been insufficient to cause the dissolution of this national organisation. The letter of resignation from Archibald Smith, though, confirmed that not all of the committee supported his attempts to conciliate Scotch Baptist fears.

> I do not wish to conceal that the manner in which the church in Clyde Street Hall has been treated by some, at least, of the members of the committee, has tended to strengthen the resolution I have come to. While the feeling exists that has been manifested, there could be little cordiality in our acting together.[75]

It was clear that the basis of this union required a fundamental re-evaluation if it was to continue with any degree of success. Unanimity in belief on a wide range of theological issues, even if less rigorous than internal Scotch Baptist standards might dictate, could

---

74 *A Brief History of Cupar Baptist Church*, (Cupar: Cupar Baptist Church, 1936), pp. 8-9.
75 A. Smith to James Farquharson, November 1827, Bundle 8, Waugh Papers.

not be sustained.

Scottish Baptists had made significant steps of progress in their endeavours to associate more closely with each other in 1827, but the flexibility required to accommodate the views of James Watson was too large a step for the Scotch Baptists to take at that time. His Arminian views could not be tolerated without destroying the Calvinistic consensus that was the basis of this union in the first place. It was deemed easier to step back into the comfort of familiar associations rather than tackle the inevitable difficulties in need of resolution. The relations between the churches suffered a setback that was to last for a number of years before attempts could be made again towards union. Correspondence between James Haldane and Archibald Smith in October 1827 reveals a lack of warmth in their previously strong relationship at that time.[76] Likewise in the following year in correspondence with Christopher Anderson on the resignation of James Farquharson from membership at Charlotte Chapel and subsequent attendance at Clyde Street Hall, Smith forcefully points out the major differences between Scotch and 'English' Baptist churches. It revealed a very different tone from that shown in the co-operation between Baptists in the previous year.[77] Dissension in his own congregation in the late 1830s over the issue of 'open' versus 'closed' communion was to lead to Smith's forced resignation from Clyde Street Hall. His death a few months later marked a sad ending for this man who had sought to unite his fellow Baptists. His attempt, in association with a few other members, to request forbearance on the communion issue did, however, point forward to the kind of accommodation Scottish Baptists would have to offer to each other if a union of churches was to have any chance of lasting success.[78] A new attempt at union in the 1830s would have to wait for feelings to cool and thoughts to be more rational towards fellow-Baptists.

In the period following the demise of the 1827 Baptist Union, there were a number of Scottish Baptist ministers who wished to recommence formal fellowship between them. James Haldane took the lead in forming a new society whose annual meetings took place in Perthshire. This new organisation, simply called 'The Association', had one aim, that of fellowship between the churches and ministers. It was to last for a number of years in the early 1830s, but 'was given up from fear of Presbyterianising the churches and

---

76 A.Smith to J.A. Haldane, October 29 1827, Bundle 8, Waugh Papers.
77 A. Smith to C. Anderson, July 1 1828, Bundle 9, Waugh Papers.
78 Balmain, *Clyde Street Hall*, pp. 24-25.

clericalising the ministry'.[79] It is probable that this body ceased as a result of a failure to grasp the purpose of association between Scottish Baptist congregations. There was still too great a fear of losing the independence of local congregations. More years would have to elapse before a greater proportion of Scottish Baptists would recognise that greater mutual interdependence of churches did not threaten their autonomy.

6.2 The Formation and Establishment of the SBA, 1835-1842

The second major attempt to unite Baptists into a formal association of churches took place in the period 1835 to1842. It is probable that the reorganisation of the Baptist Union of Great Britain and Ireland (BUGBI) in 1832, with its revised constitution and greater inclusiveness, was influential in inspiring Baptists in Scotland to begin a second attempt at uniting themselves into a national organisation. The BUGBI prior to 1832 was self-consciously restricted to Particular Baptist churches, but now it was open also to evangelical General Baptists. This point was made by John Howard Hinton in a letter dated December 1841, to John Gregory Pike, the first General Baptist to be invited to hold the post of chairman at the annual BUGBI assembly. Hinton wished to assure Pike that 'the body of General Baptists...have been from the first [1832] a constituent part of the Union'.[80] If this model of Baptist union was to be followed in Scotland, as appears to have been the case, then a significant transformation of the theological climate needed to take place amongst Scottish Baptists in the period 1835 to 1842.

The first article of BUGBI's constitution is remarkably similar to the same point in the objects of the SBA of 1835. The 1832 Baptist Union constitution stated as its first aim: 'to extend brotherly love and union among the Baptist ministers and churches who agree in the sentiments usually denominated evangelical.'[81] The SBA's first resolution declared:

> that the objects contemplated by this association be the following;
> '1st. The increase of brotherly love and friendly intercourse among such Baptist Churches as agree in holding the sentiments usually termed evangelical.'[82]

---

79 W. Tulloch, 'President's Address', *The Fourteenth Annual Report of the Baptist Union of Scotland*, (Glasgow: The Baptist Union of Scotland, 1882), p. 40.
80 J.B. Pike and J.C. Pike (eds), *A Memoir and Remains of the late John Gregory Pike*, (London: Jarrold and Sons, 1855), p. 247.
81 E.A. Payne, *The Baptist Union: A Short History*, (London: Carey Kingsgate Press, 1959), pp. 60-61.
82 Scottish Baptist Association Minutes, 1835.

The other three objects of the two constitutions were extremely close in wording and sentiment. There is, therefore, no doubt that the Scottish Baptists who set up the SBA were directly influenced by events in BUGBI.

After the initial set-backs the desire for another attempt to unite Scottish Baptist churches resulted in the calling of a meeting of Baptist ministers and laymen at Tullymet on July 29 1835. This venue appears to be an unlikely setting for a national gathering of Baptist leaders in Scotland. The reason for a Perthshire location was probably due to the greatest pressure for the gathering coming from the churches in that area following on from their support for Haldane's Association. It is reasonable to ask why these particular churches had a special interest in re-establishing a Baptist Union of Scotland. In the period 1808-16 the Highland Perthshire Baptist churches, and their leaders, suffered great hardship when funds from the SPGH dried up, after Robert and James Haldane became Baptists and withdrew their formal support from this kind of work.[83] In practice there was a significant proportion of the Highland Baptist churches that received financial help from the Haldanes, but ad hoc arrangements were no substitute for formal ties. These Baptist churches, unlike the Perthshire churches that had remained as Independent churches, needed to find alternative means of guaranteed funding. The initial requests for support had led eventually to the formation of the BHMS in August 1827, as all three groups of Baptists in Scotland could see the benefits of working together in mission. This level of co-operation was as far as some of the larger central-belt Baptist churches wished to go, but by contrast, these smaller Highland

---

83 In Upper and Lower Canada (Ontario and Quebec) Canadian Baptist churches had enjoyed good fellowship with and support from American Baptist associations. However, after the War of 1812-1814 between the two countries, during which ties were greatly restricted, Canadian Baptists felt the need to set up their own independent support networks. The strength of these bonds of fellowship was clear. 'Before 1820 there was no such thing in Upper and Lower Canada as an "unassociated" Baptist Church.' An effective model of associating in the USA had been successfully transplanted into Canada. S. Ivison and F. Rosser, *The Baptists in Upper and Lower Canada before 1820*, (Toronto: Toronto University Press, 1956), pp. 62, 100 and 164. The Ottawa Baptist Convention organised in 1836, like the SBA above, was modelled on the BUGBI constitution. The later reorganised Canada Baptist Union of 1855 echoed these earlier Baptist bodies in the basis of its union. P.G.A. Griffin-Allwood, '"Baptist Unity in the Midst of Evangelical Diversity": Canadian Baptists and the 19th-Century Evangelical Debate over Christian Unity', in Priestly (ed.), *Memory and Hope*, pp. 130-132.

churches saw both the need for, and the benefits of, more formal links between the Baptist churches in Scotland. Others may have approved of union in principle and taken it no further, but these churches recognised the benefits of association and called for immediate action.

The BHMS reports in the period just prior to the launch of the SBA present a very encouraging picture. The introduction to the 1833 report included these words:'At no former period were the appearances in the Highlands more favourable'.[84] Alexander Grant, reporting on a tour through Tiree, Mull, Colonsay, and Islay, after describing a baptismal service on Tiree, stated: 'I trust this is but the first fruits of a large harvest of souls that will soon be gathered to Christ'.[85] Likewise the 1834 report is full of optimism about the work, sometimes side by side with difficulties, but the overall impressions follow on from the previous year. James Campbell, based in Aberdeenshire, is a good example of this optimism:'The prospects of [spiritual] good in this part of the country are as promising at present as they have been at any former period since I came to this place'.[86] This was a consistent pattern in the Highlands in the early 1830s. There was some emigration and hardship but its impact only began to be felt after the catastrophic failure of the potato crop in 1836-1837.[87] It can, therefore, be noted that the desire for Baptist union in Highland Perthshire arose at a time of great progress in terms of spiritual and numerical growth. It was not due to the hardship caused by economic difficulties or the discouragement that would happen in many churches at times of mass emigration. These problems may have reinforced the need for Baptist union amongst the Highland Perthshire Baptists, but they were not the initial catalyst that led to the establishment of the SBA. It was by contrast a desire to maximise the potential resources of Scottish Baptists to reach their fellow subjects with the Christian gospel.

The minutes of the first meeting in July 1835, after stating the purpose of the gathering, stressed the 'newness of the circumstances' and the 'importance of the object contemplated'.[88] There were ten churches that agreed to form the SBA: Tullymet, Kil-

---

84 *BHMS Report*, 1833, p. 5.
85 *BHMS Report*, 1833, p. 5.
86 *BHMS Report*, 1834, p. 10.
87 D.E. Meek, 'The Highlands', in Bebbington (ed.), *Baptists in Scotland*, p. 291. D.E. Meek, 'Evangelicalism and Emigration', in G.W. Maclennon (ed.), *Proceedings of the First North American Congress of Celtic Studies*, (Ottawa, University of Ottawa, 1988), p. 24.
88 Scottish Baptist Association Minutes, 1835.

mavionaig, Grantown-on-Spey, Lawers, Killin, Perth, Cupar, Orangefield Greenock, Millport and Campbeltown. The majority of this group of churches had been used to close co-operation through the work of the BHMS and knew that there was no danger of breaching the integrity and independency of local congregations. Cupar was the only church represented at this meeting that did not have Highland associations. It is important to state that seven of these churches were also involved in the previous attempt at union and, therefore, had previously been persuaded of the benefits of more formal association. Lawers, Breadalbane, Millport and Campbeltown were the four churches that did not participate in the earlier process. The reason for making this point here is that the churches which had had previous experience of the difficulties involved in setting up an association of churches would have had more realistic expectations of what could be achieved in the new organisation. It is significant that the name of the new body was not 'The Baptist Union of Scotland', but the more modest 'Scottish Baptist Association'. This is also a reflection on the fact that barely more than half the number of churches were involved in this meeting compared to 1827. In total fifteen out of the ninety-four churches in existence by 1842 chose to be linked with the SBA.[89] This stark statistic revealed that the proportion of participating churches had dropped from 45% to 16%. A more grandiose name for this collective body would have been an even starker reminder of how far they had fallen below their aspirations for a strong and vibrant union of Baptist churches in Scotland.

6.3 The Importance of Ministerial Training in Uniting Scottish Baptists

One issue which did concentrate the minds of Scottish Baptists in the late 1830s was the need for an educated ministry. It was probably the most important factor, after the work of the BHMS, in bringing Scottish Baptists together. The question of theological training for prospective ministers and evangelists had not arisen amongst the first generation of Scotch Baptists due to a significant number of men joining their ranks who had had a solid grounding in a Presbyterian college. Some examples of these included James Watt and David McLaren in Glasgow; Robert Carmichael, Charles Stuart and William Peddie in Edinburgh; and Charles Arthur in Kirkcaldy.[90] Robert Haldane had always placed a high value upon adequate preparation prior to Christian service and in his seminaries many

---

89 *The First Yearly Report of the Baptist Union of Scotland*, 1844, pp.18-22.
90 *Scottish Baptist Magazine*, 23.7 (July, 1897), p. 88.

Presbyterians had adopted a congregational ecclesiology and in some cases a Baptist understanding of the ordinance of baptism. There were two of the eight college tutors, William Stephens and Thomas Wemyss, whose adoption of Baptist principles in 1805 must have challenged the paedobaptist principles of their employer.[91] There were in addition, nine or ten of their agents who had left the SPGH by 1805 because of their new-found convictions.[92] After their own transfer to the Baptist fold the Haldanes continued to value theological education. In 1820 Lachlan Mackintosh, at Robert Haldane's expense, held classes for twenty men in preparation for their future service.[93] The level of training, however, was less rigorous than in a formal ministerial training institution and was in fact never intended to attain the same academic standards.[94] As a result 'English' Baptists who required a college education had to go to an English Baptist college. Arrangements had been made for them to study at Horton College, Bradford, with a view to them returning to serve Scottish Baptist churches. The 'English' Baptist tradition in Scotland had from the beginning in the first decade of the nineteenth century placed great importance upon formal academic training for its prospective pastors and evangelists. The first two Scottish students had been sent to Horton in 1806,[95] with a further twenty enrolled by 1837.[96] The value of this English college to Scottish Baptists was seen by the level of funding provided to that institution. In 1834, of the eleven churches listed in *The Northern Baptist Education Society Report* as donors to college funds, the total of Scottish churches was six, which gave £36, £1 more than from the named English churches.[97] Although Baptist churches in England did have to provide funding for other denominational colleges, the support base in England was potentially much greater than in Scotland. Scottish Baptists had shown, therefore, in this practical manner the level of importance they had placed on the possession of an educated ministry in their native land.

The importance of adequate preparation for pastoral ministry was underlined by the representative gathering of Scottish Baptists that met together in April 1836 to seek to enhance the facilities open

---

91 McNaughton, *Scottish Congregational Ministry*, p. 283.
92 Waugh, 'Converging Streams', pp. 52-53.
93 Yuille (ed.), *Baptists in Scotland*, p. 251.
94 D.B. Murray, *The Scottish Baptist College Centenary History 1894-1994*, (Glasgow: Scottish Baptist College, 1994), pp. 2-3.
95 *NBES Report*, 1805-1806, p. 57.
96 *NBES Reports*, 1805-1806 to 1837-1838.
97 *NBES Report*, 1833-1834, (Keighley: R. Aked, 1834), p. 56.

to prospective pastors and evangelists. This group included some Scotch Baptists who were in favour of an educated leadership. The impression is sometimes given that all Scotch Baptists opposed formal theological training, but this opinion was not representative of all parts of that constituency. There were individuals such as Ninian Lockhart of Kirkcaldy who had published his objections, and undoubtedly his views were shared by some others who held to the same ecclesiological views, but many others held a more favourable attitude.[98] A circular had been sent in 1836 to all the Baptist churches in Scotland from a group of men who wished to set up some form of formal training for prospective preachers and ministers. The group of men, led by the Haldane brothers and William Innes, included a number of Scotch Baptists including William Miller from Bristo Baptist Church, Edinburgh, John Paxton of Berwick-upon-Tweed, Robert Peddie of Stirling, James Blair of Saltcoats and Andrew Arthur of Kirkcaldy. The men appointed secretaries of the new society were to be William Miller and his fellow-elder Henry Dickie. The corresponding members of the committee included other Scotch Baptists including David Smith and David MacLaren from Glasgow.[99] David McLaren, an accountant and commission merchant based in Ingram Street, Glasgow, was one of the pastors of the North Portland Street congregation.[100] His contribution to this committee was cut short by his decision to accept his employer's offer in 1836 to become their South Australian Company's manager.[101] McLaren was then based in Adelaide, Australia. During his time in that city he was one of the main contributors, in association with George F. Angas, in the establishment of a Baptist church.[102]

---

98 Murray, *Scottish Baptist College*, pp. 1-2.
99 Meeting of Pastors and Members of Baptist Churches in Scotland, Friday April 29, 1836, pp. 1-3, Bundle 10, Waugh Papers.
100 *The Post Office Annual Directory for 1834-1835*, Glasgow, p. 161, and Appendix, p. 48.
101 *Scottish Baptist Magazine* 2.1 (January 1876), p. 25. McLaren had unwittingly involved his friend Angas in financial loss. His acceptance of the post in Australia was due to his determination to repay his obligations and recover his own fortunes. A. G. Price, *Founders and Pioneers of South Australia*, (Adelaide: Mary Martin Books, 1929), pp. 166-196.

The support of David Smith, a pastor of the George Street Scotch Baptist Church, Glasgow, for this venture reveals how strong the pro-college training sector of the Scotch Baptist constituency had become by 1836. This Glasgow congregation was the most conservative and traditional Scotch Baptist body within that city and only the Argyle Square congregation in Edinburgh retained more traditional opinions. When the importance of maintaining consensus views within their congregations as a point of principle is taken into account, Smith's involvement in this process suggests that he had the majority of his constituency behind him.[103] 'English' Baptists as expected were committed to this venture, with James Johnston of Charlotte Chapel, Edinburgh, David Souter of Aberdeen, John McIlvain and Donald Thomson of Orangefield, Greenock, James Paterson of Hope Street, Glasgow, Robert Thomson of Perth and George Barclay from Irvine the most prominent in 1836.[104] The provision of theological education was clearly, in 1836, a focus for Baptist unity in Scotland. It had not been stated as an aim in the objects of the 1835 Scottish Baptist Association,[105] but it was now at the forefront of the thoughts of many leading Baptists.

This cause was strengthened by the transformation of this committee into the Baptist Academical Society in 1837. The original committee had aimed to provide adequate theological training for young men 'as far as practical at their place of residence, and afterwards, if necessary, in Edinburgh'.[106] The Academical Society reaffirmed the aim of training its men in Scotland due to a fear of losing them to English churches, but it did not have the resources to carry this out in practice. There is some evidence that William Steadman, principal of Horton Baptist Academy, Bradford, from 1806 until a short time before his death in 1837, sought to keep good Scottish students in England. Steadman, in January 1820, had written to his good friend John Saffery, minister of Brown Street Baptist Church, Salisbury, including some comments about the Scottish students.

---

102 J.D. Bollen, *Australian Baptists: A Religious Minority*, (London: The Baptist Historical Society, 1975), p. 7. More details are given in H.E. Hughes, *Our First Hundred Years The Baptist Church of South Australia*, (Adelaide: South Australia Baptist Union, 1937), pp.17-28. Angas, a prominent Baptist businessman, was very influential in the establishment of the colony of South Australia. R. Linn, 'Angas, George Fife', in B. Dickey (ed.), *The Australian Dictionary of Evangelical Biography*, (Sydney: Evangelical History Association, 1994), pp. 7-8.
103 *The Post Office Annual Directory for 1834-1835*, Glasgow, Appendix, p. 48.
104 Meeting of Pastors and Members, p. 1.
105 *The Baptist Magazine* 27.9, (September, 1835), p. 387.
106 Meeting of Pastors and Members, pp. 1-2.

Five of them are bent on returning to Scotland, in June next, including [John] Gilmour and [David] Douglas. If they imbibe the Spirit, and tread in the footsteps of [Dugald] Sinclair I shall rejoice, though I feel some regret at their leaving England.[107]

The Horton principal had earlier made the following comment in his diary, in February 1806, concerning some of his Baptist ministerial colleagues.

Most of the ministers were illiterate, their talents small, their manner dull, and uninteresting, their systems of divinity contracted, their maxims of church discipline rigid, their exertions scarcely any at all.[108]

When these words about the Scottish students are combined with Steadman's strong criticism of the lack of education and training of many of his colleagues in Lancashire and Yorkshire Baptist causes, and his desire to provide a better quality of ministers for the churches, it is easy to understand how the Horton principal might have sought to place all his students in pastorates in the north of England. These Scottish Baptist leaders in the Academical Society recognised that they could not compete with the provision on offer at Horton because it provided a good college course that could be obtained at a much lower financial cost than they could provide in Scotland. Therefore the ongoing link with the Horton College was maintained, though students would have the option of attending any of the other English Baptist colleges.[109] A Baptist Union of Scotland report in 1846 noted that thirty men had been sent to the Bradford College since 1806. The records of the Horton College suggested that the total sent was thirty-three.[110] The college records present the fuller picture as they include Archibald McPhail who was expelled from the college for unspecified misconduct in 1823,[111] William McMillan who died in college in March 1838,[112] and Alexander Kirkwood who retired from the college due to poor health in 1843.[113] There were, however, only six Scots in total who had returned to minister in Scotland.[114] One of the few to do so was

---

107 W. Steadman to J. Saffery, January 7 1820, Letter R15/8, The Reeves Collection, Angus Library, Regent's Park College, Oxford.
108 T. Steadman, *Memoir of the Rev. William Steadman, D.D.*, (London: Thomas Ward and Co., 1838), pp. 227-228.
109 *First Report of the Committee of the Baptist Academical Society for Scotland*, 1840, pp. 3-4.
110 *NBES Reports*, 1805-1806 to 1842-1843.
111 *NBES Report*, 1822-1823, (Bradford: T. Inkersley, 1823), p. 24.
112 *NBES Report*, 1837-1838, (Bradford: W. & H. Byles, 1838), p. 19.
113 *NBES Report*, 1842-1843, (Leeds: John Heaton, 1843), p. 9.

James Stephen, a Scotch Baptist, who had been sent to Bristol (rather than Bradford) Baptist College on health grounds. He had been employed as an evangelist by Bristo Baptist Church, Edinburgh, with which he resumed employment after the completion of his studies.[115] The Academical Society members in Glasgow as early as 1839 were less than happy about the Edinburgh committee's attempts to rectify the loss of good potential ministers to English churches. The official minutes of the Society for the year 1840 to 1841 record the tension within this body's ranks.

> The friends of the Society in Glasgow, had grown impatient of its *apparent* [sic] inactivity; and before last year's Report was issued, they had resolved to stimulate your committee, by acting for themselves. They have formed a similar association in Glasgow, and are now engaged in promoting the same cause. Your committee cordially bid them God speed. In the meanwhile, the withdrawment of their support, narrows the means at the disposal of your committee.[116]

The frustrations within the membership of the Academical Society were evident, but until the Baptist Union of Scotland, formed in 1843, undertook to provide training for ministerial students after 1845, under the leadership of Francis Johnston, there were no other options open to either the Glasgow or Edinburgh committees of this body.[117] Quality candidates had been recruited, but new means needed to be found to bring these men back to their native land after training in England. This issue was a very important factor in uniting Scottish Baptists in the late 1830s, but the limited success of its proponents appeared to be in line with the slow progress of the SBA itself. It appeared that the case for a formal union of Baptist churches was now held with considerably less enthusiasm than in the late 1820s.

6.4 Reasons for the Lack of Success of the SBA

It is important to consider the reasons why the SBA did not develop as its founders had intended. One factor to note was the absence of the most prominent Scottish Baptist ministers and their churches. Appendix 4.3 records locations of the members of the SBA. The

---

114 'An Appeal on behalf of Ministerial Education in Scotland', *The Evangelist*, 1.6 (December, 1846), pp. 145-148.
115 Printed Circular Bristo Baptist Church, Edinburgh, to Beverley Church, February 9, 1838, MS Letters.
116 *Second Report of the Committee of the Baptist Academical Society for Scotland*, (Edinburgh: R. Marshall, 1841), pp. 5-6.
117 T. Stewart, 'Education for the Ministry', in Yuille (ed.), *Baptists in Scotland*, p. 252.

most glaring omissions from the list are the Glasgow and Edinburgh congregations. The 1827 Baptist Union had received the support of half the Glasgow congregations and three out of five Edinburgh churches, which had provided the majority of its leaders. Any Scottish Baptist organisation with claims to be a national body had to obtain the support of its most prominent leaders and churches. If even 'English' Baptist pastors such as George Barclay, Alexander McLeod, Christopher Anderson and William Innes could not be persuaded to join the new venture, then it was destined to obtain very limited success.

A second factor was the limited presence of the Scotch Baptists, the most conservative stream of Baptist witness in Scotland. In the previous Baptist Union, North Portland Street Scotch Baptist Church, Glasgow, and Clyde Street Scotch Baptist Church, Edinburgh, had been constituent members. Charles Arthur (Kirkcaldy) and David Dewar (Dunfermline) had recorded the support of their congregations for that venture by letter in June 1827. In the SBA there were two congregations from this group of Scottish Baptists, in Dunfermline and Kirkcaldy, which affiliated during its existence from 1835 to 1842.[118] The problems in Scotch Baptist ranks in 1834[119] may have hindered support in the mid-1830s, but it cannot have been the sole reason for the limited support for the association. It is probable that the majority of Scotch Baptists, like their 'English' colleagues, were unconvinced as to the viability of the SBA.

A third factor was the essentially rural and Highland support base for this body. The urban churches of the central belt of Scotland were conspicuous by their absence. Appendix 3.3 reveals that, apart from the blank in Edinburgh and Glasgow, none of the four Dundee Baptist churches was linked to the SBA. There were no churches from the south-west of Scotland or the east of Scotland south of Kinghorn in Fife. The north-west Highlands were also unrepresented. Aberdeen was the only north-eastern location to have a presence, and that by only one church in membership, the weak and fragile John Street Church, which barely survived the late 1830s.[120] In addition to this problem, the leadership of the Association had been largely by committee consensus. A dynamic leader with vision was needed to carry the work beyond what the SBA had achieved and enable other Scottish Baptists to identify with this project. There

---

118 Scottish Baptist Association Minutes, 1836.
119 Chapter two, pp. 68-70.
120 Minutes of the Proceedings of the Church Assembling in Crown Terrace Chapel, Aberdeen, Vol.1, 1821-1868, see the minutes from February 17 1837 to July 21 1839.

was, however, an attempt to overcome these weaknesses and to make a success of their venture. It is to these efforts that attention will now be given.

The challenge before these churches, mainly in the Highlands, was to find ways of encouraging other Baptists to join them and to raise the profile of this fledgling Association. It was natural for them to invite James Haldane to be the speaker at the first public meeting in July 1835. This was because it was through the work of the SPGH that Independent churches had begun to be established in Perthshire. The Haldane brothers were the most prominent leaders in the SPGH who became Baptists and a number of these small fellowships and their leaders had also become Baptist in the first decade of the nineteenth century. Tullymet, Kilmavionaig, Grantown, Breadalbane (Killin) and Lawers churches owed their origins to associates of the Haldanes.[121] The Perth church, a Scotch foundation, had gained a large number of new members from the Haldane Independent church after 1808, and they probably outnumbered the original congregation.[122] These churches would have been encouraged by the strong lead given by Robert and James Haldane in the work of the BHMS. It was natural to hope that James Haldane would put his considerable influence on Scottish Baptists behind their cause. His sermon was described in the SBA minutes for 1835 as 'excellent and impressive', implying that it was, at the very least, an encouragement to those present.[123] This account of the sermon was also published in *The Baptist Magazine*, in its September 1835 issue, which suggests confirmation of this understanding of the proceedings. This interpretation is at variance with those of Waugh[124] and Murray[125] who stated that James Haldane sought to dissuade these eleven churches from formally associating together in his sermon. The viewpoint Waugh and Murray express, however, appears to be inconsistent with Haldane's attendance at the gathering and with the official comments upon his sermon by the churches in the Association. There is apparently no surviving copy of the sermon, but it must have been expressing sentiments that were supportive to this gathering of church representatives in their new venture.

---

121 Meek, 'Independent and Baptist Churches', p. 276.
122 Robertson, *Perth Baptist Church*, p. 38.
123 Scottish Baptist Association Minutes, 1835.
124 P. Waugh, 'The Scotch Baptists and the First Baptist Union', in Yuille (ed.), *Baptists in Scotland*, p. 234.
125 Murray, 'Baptists in Scotland before 1869', p. 263.

In addition to the invitation to James Haldane, the minutes of that first Association meeting record that James Paterson, the minister of Hope Street Baptist Church in Glasgow, was one of the invited speakers for the next annual assembly in July 1836. If he was unable to accept the invitation then David McLaren, a Scotch Baptist minister in Glasgow, was suggested as a replacement. McLaren had been closely involved with William Tulloch of Aberfeldy in setting up the Baptist Highland Mission in 1816 in order to provide financial support to some of the Highland Perthshire churches and their ministers. Since no Scotch Baptist church had been involved at the inception of this attempt at union amongst Baptist churches, McLaren may well have been invited with a view to drawing Scotch Baptists into the SBA. If this was the aim then it had some limited success as the minutes for the July 1836 Association meeting reveal: 'It was unanimously resolved: 1 That the churches in Kirkcaldy, Kinghorn and Dumfermline, according to their request be received into this Association.'[126] At least two of these churches, those at Kirkcaldy and Dunfermline, were Scotch Baptist churches. The presence of the Dunfermline church is no surprise as it was previously associated with the Baptist Union, but its sister church in Kirkcaldy was now participating in such a venture for the first time. In addition to this, William Innes, the minister of Elder Street Church in Edinburgh, who had been associated with the 1827 Union, took a prominent role in the gathering, leading both the 7 a.m. prayer meeting and the 7 p.m. service. It could now be stated that though progress was slow, the cause of Baptist union was beginning to gather some momentum. Its leaders were mindful of the previous failure and did not want to assume the automatic success of their venture or its adoption by the majority of Baptist churches in Scotland, at least in the near future. This caution was certainly advisable, as future minutes indicate. At the end of the 1837 minutes the report ended by stating:

> The utmost harmony and love prevailed throughout the proceedings of the day; and though, by death and other causes, the clear increase during the year has not been great, the most cheering results are hoped for in the future from the influence of the Association.[127]

The 'clear increase', probably referred to the number of members in Association churches, but it was equally applicable to indicate the slow growth in churches linked with the Association. Minutes for 1838 and 1839 indicate further loss of momentum due to the need to

---

126 Scottish Baptist Association Minutes, 1836.
127 Scottish Baptist Association Minutes, 1837.

rearrange the dates of meetings. In 1838 the minutes began by stating:

> Circumstances of a prayerful kind, arising from the depression of the time and the connexion of the pastors at Kirkcaldy with secular affairs...it became necessary to postpone meeting there till some future and more suitable opportunity.

A hastily rearranged meeting took place in Killin on July 17 and 18 that year and in Perth at the end of July the following year. One new church joined in 1839, the 'English' Baptist church in Aberdeen. It had been involved in the previous attempt at union in 1827 when John Gilmour was minister. Alexander Stalker, who had graduated from the Bradford Academy and was familiar with English Particular Baptist Associations, was now the minister, but he stayed for only one year.[128] In 1840 another church was added to the total, the small fellowship at Montrose under the leadership of James Watson (1812-66). No dissent regarding the acceptability of the Montrose church and its Arminian minister has been recorded in the minutes of the SBA, but it is not too surprising as the churches most likely to object had never been associated with this organisation.[129] There was, therefore, a change of theological climate in Scotland in the decade since the formation of the previous Baptist Union. It is most likely that there was a growing tolerance of Arminianism amongst Scottish Baptists. James Watson had never paraded his views in front of others and this too may have contributed to his church's acceptance at this time. To some degree the reception accorded to the Montrose church did prepare the way for the presence of a greater number of Arminians in the next Baptist Union, though it was more likely to have been tolerance than acceptance that was being promoted at this time. There were no further additions in 1841.

In 1842, at a time when the Association was failing to make progress, a new man came to bolster its ranks, Francis Johnston, the new minister at Cupar. The resolutions of that meeting indicate his impact on the assembled delegates. The first resolution stated that the 1843 meeting of the Association would take place in Cupar. The third states:'that brother Johnston of Cupar be secretary to the fund...and brother [Robert] Thomson [the minister] of Perth be requested to cooperate with the secretary...'. The fourth resolution confirmed that Johnston would write the circular letter for the following year with the title, 'The best method of promoting the inter-

---

128 Yuille (ed.), *Baptists in Scotland*, p. 89.
129 Scottish Baptist Association Minutes, 1840.

ests of the Baptist denomination in Scotland'. The fifth and last resolution stated that the name of the Association was hereafter to be 'The Baptist Union of Scotland'.[130] This radical transformation in the Association indicates a new approach in the search for Baptist union that will be considered in chapter seven.

The SBA, in its seven-year history, 1835 to 1842, had overcome some major difficulties. First of all it had overcome the disappointment that had followed the failure of the 1827 attempt at union. It had also capitalised on the interest in wider fellowship shown by the un-named churches that joined James Haldane's Association. The reconstituting of the BUGBI on a more inclusive evangelical basis appeared to inspire the leaders of the SBA to establish a similar body in Scotland. It is to the credit of the small group of churches that formed the 1835 Association that they persevered in their endeavours, gradually increasing the numbers of co-operating churches. Secondly they had obtained the support of some Scotch Baptists. This was no mean feat after the 1834 division in Scotch Baptist ranks, a division, ironically, over the subject of Christian union between two Baptist churches in Aberdeen. Thirdly they had a dedicated group of leaders, especially Robert Thomson, the minister at Perth, who acted as secretary, and Jonathan Watson, the minister at Cupar, but the momentum was less than they had hoped for and the Association's profile was far too low. It was the arrival of Francis Johnston that was to make a major difference in the movement to establish a national union of Baptist churches.

This second attempt to form a Baptist Union of Scotland is usually merged with the body it became after the arrival of Francis Johnston in 1842. This analysis is partly due to its choice of name as an association rather than a union of churches, but also because progress is deemed to have been very limited in the period 1835 to 1842. There is, however, no justification for such an interpretation as the organisation changed beyond recognition after 1843 even if many of the participants were the same in each venture. The churches that were involved in this second attempt at union comprised a much smaller number than were involved in 1827. In addition they had the advantage of also working closely together in the BHMS. These points would have raised an obvious question in the minds of some Baptists: why is a union of these churches required? This question was not an issue in 1827 because a broader spectrum of churches was involved both from the different Baptist groups and from a wider geographical distribution in Scotland. Donald Thomson, minister of Orangefield Baptist Church, Greenock,

---

130 Scottish Baptist Association Minutes, 1842.

sought to address the root cause of disunity amongst the different Baptist groups in Scotland in a letter, under the pen-name Scotus, in the June 1836 issue of *The Baptist Magazine*. In that letter Thomson compares and contrasts Scotch and 'English' Baptists, casting both in an unfavourable light. The following extract will reveal the essence of his argument:

> first, I would call attention to the disjointed state of each party. There is no such thing as cordial union amongst either class. So much is this wanting and to such an extent it has become quite proverbial in Scotland, 'The Baptists are a mere rope of sand', there is no adhesion in their body; they make profession 'loud and long' of their being the most scriptural of all the churches in the order of their government, and yet they are of all others the farthest from what ought primarily to distinguish them, viz., scriptural union. I shall not, Mr Editor, attempt to deny the justice of these remarks, nor will anyone, I am convinced, at all acquainted with the state of the Denomination.[131]

The grounds for disunity amongst the two types of Scottish Baptists are not made clear in the June 1836 letter, but it is possible to make suggestions about what he is referring to. The Scotch Baptist connexion split in 1834 following the union of two Aberdeen congregations which had held opposing opinions in the 1810 division over the place of elders at the Lord's Table. A significant minority within their ranks refused to accept the validity of this merger. The effects were devastating, as we have already seen. There is less certainty about the cause of division amongst 'English' Baptists, but it is probable that it relates to the work of the Holy Spirit in conversion compared to the human agency in this process. Charles Finney and John Howard Hinton were two important contributors to this debate from outside Scotland while James Morison was the most prominent in Scotland. This issue will be considered further in chapter seven.

Thomson's letter was written out of frustration at the slow progress towards union by the majority of Baptist churches in Scotland, but it was not accepted as accurate by two correspondents in the same magazine. 'Z', a Scotch Baptist from Bristo Baptist Church in Edinburgh, probably Henry Dickie, one of its elders, accepts that there is room for improvement, but insists that the picture amongst liberal Scotch Baptists gives hope for future progress.[132] Robert Thomson, brother of Donald Thomson and the secretary of the SBA,

---

131 Scotus [Donald Thomson], in *The Baptist Magazine*, 28.6 (June, 1836), pp. 255-257.

was equally determined to give a more cheerful picture of the Scottish situation to Baptists in England. He stated: 'Things are, on the whole, looking well with the Baptists in Scotland at this time'. He proceeds to reject criticism of the Association and has a request to make to the editor:

> I entreat, Mr Editor, that you will suffer nothing to enter your pages respecting the Association in particular, or the denomination at large, in which any harshness of expression is found. Scotus is my brother, in a double sense, and I highly esteem and love him; but if he does not mind, I shall on behalf of the Association, be obliged to exclaim, 'Save me from my friends!'[133]

It is likely that a balanced assessment of the situation lay between the views expressed by the Thomson brothers. One of them was unduly pessimistic while the other was over-optimistic about the progress made by the Baptists in Scotland towards a union of churches. In reality the SBA failed to attract the support of central-belt churches, especially in the key urban centres of Glasgow and Edinburgh. This was linked with the lack of overt enthusiasm from the leading Baptist ministers in Scotland whose energies were concentrated on supporting the BHMS. Part of the reason for their failure to support the Association was that it appeared to be principally a Perthshire Baptist body and invited friends rather than being a truly national union of churches. This was not the fault of the Association, but in some cases was undoubtedly a reaction against the failure of the 1827 attempt at union. There was a desire for union in principle, but the motivation was lacking in practice. It was to take the arrival of a 'charismatic' figure, Francis Johnston, to bring the issue of Baptist union and its priority to the hearts and minds of Scottish Baptists.

In conclusion both of these two attempts to unite Baptist churches in Scotland failed to overcome the obstacles in their way. The 1827 attempt at union was initially successful in uniting Baptists from all three streams of Baptist life in Scotland in the one organisation, following on from their co-operation in the work of home mission. There were, though, personal suspicions in Scotch Baptist circles that led to the dispute with David McLaren and the issue which sealed its fate was the matter of fellowship with James Watson from Montrose. This first attempt at union came close to success, but too many Scottish Baptists accepted the need for union in principle but made too little effort in practice.

The 1835-42 SBA had the advantage of being a small group of

---

132 Z [H.D.Dickie], in *The Baptist Magazine*, 28.10 (October, 1836), pp. 435-437.
133 R.Thomson, in *The Baptist Magazine*, 28.12 (December, 1836), pp. 545-546.

principally Highland churches that had co-operated closely in the work of the BHMS. There was a strong sense of unity amongst these churches. The problem was that many Scottish Baptists saw this body as unlikely to succeed in its objectives and it failed to win support from key leaders and the large central-belt churches. Ministerial education was a cause that united Scottish Baptists in the late 1830s and early 1840s, though no benefits from this co-operation were passed on to the SBA This body did attract increasing numbers of churches to its ranks, but too many were still mindful of the previous failure in 1827 and so it never achieved its full potential. Once again Scottish Baptists agreed with the need for unity, but it was still a good number of years before the theory became a practical reality.

Chapter 7

The Third Attempt to Form a Baptist Union of Scotland, 1843-1856

7.1 The Religious Revolution in Scotland in the Early 1840s

The third attempt to form a union of Baptist churches in Scotland began in 1843. It is linked indissolubly with the name of Francis Johnston of Cupar Baptist Church, the minister who was the most influential figure in determining its theological direction and its ecclesiastical strategy. This chapter will look first at the importance of 1843 in the ecclesiastical history of Scotland during the nineteenth century in order to establish the context in which this third attempt to form a united organisation for Baptists in Scotland took place. It will then consider the evidence in favour of its progress and afterwards examine the reasons why it did not achieve its objectives.

The year 1843 is undoubtedly a key landmark in the church history of Scotland in the nineteenth century. The primary event that took place that year, on May 18, was the Disruption in the Church of Scotland. This event shook the religious establishment in Scotland. It called into question the dominant role formerly exercised in the country by the Church of Scotland. The English periodical, *The Evangelical Magazine,* reflected on the implications of this event in an article in June that year. It drew the following conclusions:

> The fact of so large a secession of good and great men, from the best national establishment extant, is an occurrence of which church history supplies no parallel. It must tend, in no ordinary degree, to awaken attention to the question of state patronage, and to lead men's minds afresh to the New Testament as the only legitimate source of information as to the genuine platform of the church of Christ.[1]

This major event undoubtedly overshadowed all other religious developments in Scotland in 1843. There was, however, another event, which did not make the headlines of the newspapers, that was to be theologically as significant as the emergence of the Free Church of Scotland, namely the formation of the Evangelical Union.

---

1   'Secession of the Nonintrusionists from the Church of Scotland, 18th May, 1843', *The Evangelical Magazine,* 21.6 (June, 1843), p. 306.

The reason for the formation of this new organisation had been the ejection of Robert and James Morison, Alexander Rutherford and John Guthrie from the United Secession Church. They had been deposed from their positions as ministers in this denomination due to their departure from the theological beliefs taught in the Westminister Confession of Faith, the subordinate standard of the United Secession Church. John Guthrie was minister of the Kendal congregation in Westmorland, Alexander Rutherford was pastor of the Falkirk church and Robert Morison was associated with the Bathgate congregation of this denomination. The leader of these men was James Morison, the minister of the United Secession Church in Kilmarnock. He had been charged with a number of alleged heresies such as a belief in universal atonement, a denial of the eternal generation of the Son of God, self-conversionism, teaching that noone ought to pray for grace to help him believe, and a faulty understanding of the nature of justification and repentance. They caused him to be put on trial before the synod of his denomination in 1841.[2] He was formally expelled from that body on June 14.[3] The expulsion of James Morison's colleagues was inevitable due to their protests at his removal from their ranks. After they had all been formally expelled it was agreed to form a new association of Christian individuals and churches. James Morison had anticipated the expulsion of Guthrie and Rutherford and had prepared a document that was to form the basis of the new union of Christians. It is significant to note the dates on which this new denomination was formed. The minute of the gathering records the following details in its opening paragraph:

> We, the undersigned Christian brethren, representatives of Christian Churches, and others, having met together at Kilmarnock, May 16th, 17th, and 18th, 1843, for the purpose of praying and conferring together about the best means of being useful in the service of our dear Redeemer, have agreed to form ourselves into an association under the designation of the 'Evangelical Union'.[4]

It is this 'disruption' in Presbyterian ranks that was to be most influential in Baptist circles in the remainder of the nineteenth century. Some of the links between the theological views of men associated with the Evangelical Union and Scottish Baptists in fel-

---

2   W. Adamson, *The Life of the Rev. James Morison*, (London: Hodder and Stoughton, 1898), pp. 124-132.
3   F. Ferguson, *A History of the Evangelical Union*, (Glasgow: Thomas Morison, 1876), p. 155.
4   Ferguson, *Evangelical Union*, p. 263.

lowship with Francis Johnston will be explored within this chapter.

One additional event of significance that was to influence Baptists in Scotland, in this era, was the formation of the Churches of Christ. The co-operative meeting of churches in Edinburgh in 1842 was regarded by members of that connexion as being the start of their formal association. Some Scottish Baptists were influenced by them through reading articles in the *Millennial Harbinger*, a periodical edited by London Scotch Baptist elder William Jones, or the Campbellite monthly magazine *The Christian Messenger and Family Magazine*, produced by the Church of Christ leader James Wallis, who was based in Nottingham.[5] There had been at least four Scottish Baptist congregations by 1843 that had adopted the teachings of Alexander Campbell, the founder of this new movement. These churches were located at Dumfries, at Stevenston and Newmills in Ayrshire, and at Auchtermuchty in Fife.[6] Reference will be made later in this chapter to the impact of this new religious sect on the Johnstonian Baptist Union of Scotland.

The era in which this third attempt to form a Baptist Union of Scotland took place can therefore be seen as one in which various key individuals led their colleagues along new ecclesiastical paths. It was an age of unparalleled religious changes and the actions of Johnston and his associates must be considered in this context. The particular focus and theological direction in which this Baptist Union progressed can be readily understood in the light of the religious influences of the day.

7.2 The Importance of Francis Johnston in the 1843-1856 Baptist Union

The key individual associated with this Baptist Union is Francis Johnston. He was born in Edinburgh on September 22 1810. His family had come to Edinburgh from Ayrshire and had had links with the Covenanting traditions of that part of Scotland. His father had been an office-bearer in Rose Street Baptist Church and afterwards in the Tabernacle, Leith Walk, in Edinburgh. Johnston was educated at the High School before entering Edinburgh University where he completed his course of studies before entering Bradford Baptist College to train for the ministry under the direction of William Steadman, the college principal. Steadman's zeal for evangelism may in part have contributed to a similar emphasis in the later ministry of this Scottish student. While ministering as a Baptist pastor in Broughton, Hampshire, in the 1790s, Steadman had been

---

5   Thompson, *Let Sects and Parties Fall*, pp. 22-28.
6   *The First Yearly Report of the Baptist Union of Scotland*, 1844, pp. 18-22.

invited by the English BHMS to lead their first preaching tour to Cornwall in the summer of 1796. The Hampshire minister, as a result of encouragement in this new venture, wrote to John Rippon, a prominent Baptist minister in London, with a view to similar work being conducted in other parts of England. The formation of The Baptist Society in London for the Encouragement and Support of Itinerant Preaching in 1797 was the start of the contribution of churches in the metropolis to itinerant preaching in rural areas of the United Kingdom. These evangelistic tours of Steadman in the south of England continued until his call to lead the work of the newly-formed Horton Baptist College, Bradford, in 1805.[7] Benjamin Godwin, assistant tutor to Steadman in the College, was often frustrated by his colleague's acceptance of preaching engagements for his students in preference to academic training. The president of the college insisted that his task was to train preachers not to educate scholars.[8] Johnston was called to his first charge in Yorkshire at the united church of Boroughbridge and Dishforth in May 1835. He was next invited to become the pastor of Carlisle Baptist Church in 1840, where he stayed only two years before returning to his native Scotland. The Baptist church in Cupar had invited him to become their pastor in that year and he served for three years until he planted another congregation that was to be located at Marshall Street in Edinburgh. His clerical successor in Edinburgh, and the writer of a biographical sketch of Johnston, Alexander Wylie, noted the significance of the changes in the religious climate in Scotland as part of the reasons for the return of Francis Johnston to his native land. Wylie made particular reference to James Morison and his colleagues in the Evangelical Union and stated the impact that their ideas had had on Johnston:

> Mr Johnston took the liveliest interest in these proceedings, welcomed the new views as a richer and fuller interpretation of the Gospel, and embraced them with the deepest conviction. His residence in England had widened his sympathies and prepared his mind to some extent for them, but their chief attraction lay in their consistency with the spirit of the Revival which he had imbibed in his early years at its pure fountainhead – the Haldane Tabernacle... He was above all things an Evangelical and because of this he held with such loyalty and tenacity to the universal

---

7 S. James, 'Revival and Renewal in Baptist Life – The contribution of William Steadman (1764-1837)', *Baptist Quarterly*, 37.6 (April, 1998), pp. 264-266.

8 J.H.Y. Briggs, *The English Baptists of the Nineteenth Century*, (A History of English Baptists, 3; Didcot: The Baptist Historical Society, 1994), pp. 76-77.

aspects of the Gospel. From this time Mr Johnston became the exponent and representative of these views in the Baptist denomination in Scotland.[9]

The extent of the acceptance by Johnston of Morisonian ideas will be discussed later in this chapter, but at this point it is important to note that, notwithstanding Wylie's contention, the theological convictions he held regarding religious revival were very different from the opinions propounded in the Leith Walk Tabernacle. His book, *The Work of God and the Work of Man in Conversion*, published in 1848, was a clear condemnation of any form of Calvinism and the traditional Reformed understanding of the work of the Holy Spirit. It is, though, unlikely that the mature opinions expressed in that book were held as early as 1843. It is probable that mutual interaction with Morisonians in Scotland in the 1840s led to his adoption of such radical views. Johnston, as the leader of the 1843 Baptist Union, had been willing to work with colleagues of Calvinistic opinions in the early years. This partnership had resulted in a remarkably successful first few years of the Baptist Union of Scotland in the mid-1840s.

The third attempt to form a union of Baptist churches in Scotland is to be dated between 1842 and 1856. These dates mark the arrival of Johnston in Cupar and his departure from Edinburgh to Cambridge in January 1856. In 1842 Johnston joined the SBA and had a profound impact on his very first annual assembly of that body, as outlined in the previous chapter. He was appointed the secretary of the Association and invited to write the circular letter for the following year. The circular letter, an opportunity to address one's fellow Baptists, was a tradition common amongst the English Associations[10] and may have been introduced to Scotland by Johnston. In addition, the Association was renamed as the Baptist Union of Scotland. The enthusiasm of a new leader with great organisational skills gave fresh hope of progress in the quest for a comprehensive union of Baptist churches in Scotland.

The resolutions from the first meeting of the Baptist Union of Scotland in July 1843 give some indication of Johnston's vision. Resolution One emphasised the need for evangelism and evangelistic literature as both by implication had been neglected in recent years. The next resolutions, while recognising the place of full-time evan-

---

9   A. Wylie (ed.), *A Short History of Marshall Street Baptist Church, Edinburgh, 1846-1896*, (Edinburgh: T. Adams, 1896), pp. 38-39.
10 T.S.H. Elwyn, 'Particular Baptists of the Northamptonshire Baptist Association as reflected in the Circular Letters 1765-1820', *Baptist Quarterly*, 36.8 (October, 1996), pp. 368-381.

gelists, asked all the Baptist churches in Scotland to consider releasing their minister for evangelistic tours during the next twelve months. A sub-committee of the Union would organise itineraries if that was required. Thirdly the Union was to concentrate its evangelistic activities in 'the large towns and populous districts'. This decision was no doubt a recognition that the BHMS was responsible for rural evangelism, especially in the north of Scotland, whereas it was not prominent in outreach in the densely populated urban areas in the central belt of Scotland. Peter Grant, Baptist minister in Grantown-on-Spey, was convinced of the need for the Baptist Union to undertake this emphasis in its evangelistic work. In a letter to his son William in March 1846 he made this point:

> I was confident that the Union had no intention to hurt the Society [BHMS], but rather to co-operate with it, and to supply what I thought a great deficiency, that is to supply some of the large towns and some districts of the Low country with Baptist preachers, for there is great need.[11]

The fourth resolution stated the aims of the Union: 'namely evangelistic labours, the support of a preacher, and the assistance of weak churches in the maintenance of their pastors'. For these purposes James Blair, pastor of the 'English' Baptist church in Dunfermline, Robert Thomson, and Francis Johnston were appointed to go round the churches to take collections for the work of the Union. This was a clever move as voluntary donations were small and personal visits would ensure greater financial support. Resolution Seven recognised the appointment of James Blair and Francis Johnston as denominational evangelists for the year and provided the means to support a preacher who would principally be engaged in evangelistic tours. The emphasis placed by Johnston on the ministry of evangelists, for example, was greater than was found in the Evangelical Union denomination.[12] One final resolution that will be mentioned is the sixth that recognized the duty of preparing young men for the ministry. Johnston was aware that Scots who went to England for their training were unlikely to return to their native land for settlement. This was not always a matter of personal choice

---

11 Peter Grant, Grantown, to William Grant, Edinburgh, March 30 1846, preserved in a collection of letters by J.A. Grant-Robinson, minister of Perth Baptist Church, 1890-1947, MS in the possession of Mrs Ann Tennyson of Elgin [Grant MS].

12 Ferguson, *Evangelical Union*, pp. 272-273, makes no reference to denominationally appointed evangelists, but does mention Alexander Forsyth, an evangelist employed by the Clerk's Lane Church, Kilmarnock, in 1843, to work both with it and the EU congregation at Catrine in Ayrshire.

as local churches near Baptist colleges were more likely than distant ones to offer opportunities for preaching and potential settlement. Johnston, himself, was a typical example when as a student at the Yorkshire college he was called and settled within the county. All Baptist churches in Scotland received copies of the resolutions of the Baptist Union so that none could be unaware of the proceedings. Johnston was a clear-thinking man who was able to translate his plans into action and who could persuade colleagues to join him in the execution of those objectives.

His circular letter for 1843 reveals the measure of care taken in the preparation of his plans. He believed that the level of progress made by Baptists in Scotland was unacceptable. There had been Baptists in Scotland since 1650, but the work was not firmly established until 1765 when Robert Carmichael and Archibald McLean began their labours. In Scotland there were 133 towns of over 2,000 inhabitants, but only thirty-six had a Baptist church, leaving ninety-seven without one, 'a tale enough to make every Baptist blush'. The omission was especially acute in Leith and Inverness that had populations of 26,000 and 9,000 respectively, and ten of Scotland's thirty-three counties did not have a single Baptist church. Scotland, Johnston found, was unfavourably represented compared with other parts of the United Kingdom in its numbers of Baptists. Wales, with 261 Baptist churches, had one Baptist for every 3,491 of the population; in England there were 1,310 Baptist churches with one to 11,446 of the population. Ireland had the worst figures, with only thirty-six Baptist churches and a ratio of 1:227,089 of the population. Scotland's figures revealed that there were seventy-three Baptist churches and one Baptist to 33,159 others in the population. Johnston believed that this weakness in Baptist numbers and churches in Scotland had arisen due to

> the evident want of system in the spread of our churches. We have not resolved, as wisdom would dictate, first to attend to the populous towns, and then to the Counties, till there be not a County or a town without a Baptist church. Our churches have been too much the offspring of chance.

He argued that too many churches were inward-looking and complacent rather than reaching out to the communities in which they had been placed. He stated, in addition, that there was too much despondency. This could be remedied if Baptists united and worked together both in church-planting and in the strengthening of existing churches. He went on to state that it was unacceptable that areas of Scotland did not need to be considered because other denominations were working there. He stated: 'If we believe our distinctive principles to be pure from the fountain of truth' then they ought to be established throughout the land. These distinctive principles were to be contrasted with false beliefs such as infant sprinkling, impure communion and a lack of emphasis on the need for personal conversion. Lastly, he argued that not only was home mission limited by Scottish Baptist numerical weakness, but the ability to contribute towards the work of foreign missions was also impaired.[13]

What practical points needed immediate attention amongst the Baptist churches in Scotland? The first object, Johnston said, 'is an immediate return to the primitive office of the Evangelist'. The denomination needed to look for new places to begin and then establish churches. This office of an evangelist was promoted in the new Churches of Christ in 1840, but it was not a fresh development.[14] Scotch Baptists had encouraged their preachers to itinerate in the late-eighteenth and early-nineteenth centuries. One example showing the extent of their employment of evangelists in the late 1830s comes from a letter sent by Robert Anderson of Bristo Baptist Church, Edinburgh, to James Everson of the Scotch Baptist Church in Beverley. The letter concentrates mainly on the work of James Stephen, a member of the Bristo church who was employed by them to engage in itinerant evangelism in Scotland. There is passing reference to the employment of an evangelist by a sister church in Berwick-upon-Tweed and to two evangelists employed by Scotch Baptists in Aberdeen to work in the north-east of Scotland.[15] James Blair, who was to be employed by the Baptist Union of Scotland in this capacity, had previously served in this way with the Scotch Baptist connexion. Blair, whose background had been in the Secession Church, married a Scotch Baptist lady and became associated in 1822 with the George Street congregation in Glasgow. He worked as a teacher until in 1829 the George Street congregation employed him to serve as an evangelist with the small Scotch Baptist congregation in Saltcoats. Blair was then employed by the BHMS from 1836 as an itinerant preacher in the south-west of Scotland.[16] His work was particularly successful in Ayr where a Baptist church was

---

13 F. Johnson, *An Inquiry into the means of advancing the Baptist Denomination in Scotland*, 1843, pp. 6-12.
14 *The Christian Messenger and Reformer*, 4, (1840-1841), pp. 37-38, 145, 240-242, and G.C. Reid, *Our First Evangelist*, (Southport, 1885), pp. 3-13, cited by Thompson, *Let Sects and Parties Fall*, p. 29.
15 *From the Baptist Church Meeting in Bristo Place, Edinburgh, to the Church in Beverley*, February 9 1838, MS Letters.

established by him in association with some 'English' Baptists. In this congregation Blair ministered as the sole pastor, and as a result his connection with the George Street congregation, Glasgow, was terminated. His most serious 'offence' was the association with 'English' Baptists in a local congregation that was not in formal fellowship with his supporting church.[17] Aggressive evangelism appeared to be successful in the cause of the Baptist Union of Scotland and complementary to the itinerant activities of the Scotch Baptists and the BHMS, but a lack of consultation with other Scottish Baptists regarding its home mission endeavours would later lead to strained relations.[18]

Secondly, in the list of objectives, those churches that were weak numerically or financially must be built up and firmly established. The responsibility of the Baptist Union of Scotland must be for the Lowland churches just as the BHMS had responsibility for churches in the Highlands and Islands. Thirdly an educated ministry was essential and that meant a Baptist Theological Institution in Scotland. Fourthly a building fund was needed to remove the debts on the Baptist places of worship. Literature also was essential both in terms of a periodical to convey 'intelligence regarding the progress of the gospel...to encourage greater liberality and zeal, largeness of heart and oneness of mind in extending our borders and regular tracts on various subjects'. Johnston's ability to marry inspiring rhetoric with a practical plan of action enabled many of his colleagues to believe that great progress could and would be made in strengthening the Baptist witness in Scotland.[19]

These forcefully argued points were an inspiration to his colleagues in Scotland, but also drew events north of the border to the attention of Baptists in England. The July 1844 Baptist Union minutes record a letter from the Lancashire and Cheshire Association of Baptist Churches which reveals details of their meeting in Stockport in May 1844, under the leadership of James Lister, the minister of Lime Street Baptist Church in Liverpool, formerly of the English Baptist Church in Glasgow. The minutes record that it was unanimously resolved:

---

16   D.B. Murray, 'Blair, James', in Lewis (ed.), *DEB*, I, pp. 106-107. For additional information on Blair see *The Scottish Evangelist The Life and Labours of the Rev. James Blair*, (Glasgow: George Gallie, 1860).
17   Andrew Duncan to James Everson, February 24 1837, MS Letters.
18   See pages 256-257.
19   *An Inquiry into the means of advancing the Baptist Denomination in Scotland, 1843*, pp. 6-12.

That the ministers and messengers now assembled have heard with much pleasure of the formation of a Baptist Union of Scotland, and avail themselves of this opportunity of assuring the ministers and churches thus associated of their fraternal sympathy and affection, and of their earnest desires for their spiritual welfare and prosperity.

The next resolution was a request to send a delegate, David Thompson of Chowbent, to represent them at the next assembly of the Scottish Baptist Union at Airdrie in July 1844. It is important to note that Francis Johnston had been the minister of Carlisle Baptist Church from 1840 to 1842, a congregation in membership with the Lancashire and Cheshire Association. Many of the delegates who had sent their best wishes would have known Johnston and thus their support is easier to understand. Likewise, the West Riding of Yorkshire Association sent a letter expressing its best wishes to the new Baptist Union of Scotland. Johnston would have been known by many of the churches in that Association due to his time spent in training at the Bradford College. It is likely that he had preached in a number of these churches during 1833 to 1835 whilst preparing for Baptist ministry.[20] This is the most tangible evidence of support received by Scottish Baptists in their attempts at union from the Baptists in England. There had been regular reports of home mission activities in Scotland printed in *The Baptist Magazine* since February 1817[21] and from 1835 there were reports on the SBA,[22] but this practical request concerning a delegate attending an assembly was evidence of greater interest in the work of the Scottish Baptist Union than before.

Another sign of progress was the increasingly healthy financial state of the Union. In 1844 the minutes record that funds had increased to £237.[23] The expenses must have increased considerably yet the accounts for the year to August 1845 reveal that the treasurer still had a balance of nearly £200. Work was not only being done, but seen to be done and Scottish Baptists were giving accordingly. The Baptists in England were now also donating money, especially in London, Newcastle-upon-Tyne and Bradford, where a regular supply of Scottish ministerial students had been trained at the Academy. The Baptists in England were also giving free supplies of tracts. J.F. Winks of Leicester, a General Baptist and editor of *The Baptist Reporter*, was the most generous contributor, closely followed by the

---

20   *NBES Report*, 1834-1835.
21   *The Baptist Magazine*, 8.2 (February, 1817), p. 79.
22   *The Baptist Magazine*, 27.9 (September, 1835), pp. 387-388.
23   *The First Yearly Report of the Baptist Union of Scotland*, 1844, p. 21.

Baptist Tract Society, though there were others who gave smaller amounts of literature. Johnston in expressing his thanks, hoped that the donations of tracts would continue to come in the future.[24] The support for the Baptist Union in Scotland by Winks was evidence of the growing convergence of opinions between many General and Particular Baptists in England in the 1830s and 1840s. Practical co-operation in Christian service was in evidence long before serious conversations took place about a formal merger later in the nineteenth century. Winks probably assumed that a similar working relationship between Baptists of differing theological opinions was taking place in Scotland.[25] The process of acceptance of both Arminian and Calvinistic opinions within the ranks of Scottish Baptists had not, however, proceeded at the same pace, though within the Baptist Union in the 1840s proponents of the two theological systems had worked harmoniously together.

The geographical spread of the Johnstonian Baptist Union, 1843 to 1856, quickly exceeded that of the SBA which had preceded it. The details of affiliated congregations are given in Appendix 5.1. The Shetland and Orkney Islands were represented for the first time. Dunrossness and Burra Isle represented the most northerly islands, with Westray, Eday and Burray Baptist churches the supporters from Orkney. Churches on Skye (two), Mull and Islay were new members from the Western Isles. The south of Scotland contributed two associated congregations in Galashiels and Hawick, with Dunbar, Leith, Bonyrigg and Edinburgh churches from the eastern part of central Scotland. There was one Glasgow congregation in membership alongside Airdrie Baptist Church and two of the Stirling fellowships that met in Spittal Street and the Guild Hall respectively. It was clear that this Baptist Union commanded support from churches all over Scotland, even if the total numbers were still less than 40% of the constituency. Its weakness, though, like the previous body, the SBA, was in failing to command the attention of the larger and more influential churches in Edinburgh and Glasgow. There were also no affiliated churches in Dundee. The total number of participating churches had increased from sixteen in 1842 to thirty-eight by 1850, as has been shown in Appendix 4.2. The growth in the numbers of Baptist churches in the intervening period, to ninety-eight by 1850, revealed that though the desire for union had increased it had not kept pace with the rise in the size of the Baptist constituency.

---

24 *The First Yearly Report of the Baptist Union of Scotland*, 1844, p. 6.
25 Briggs, *English Baptists of the Nineteenth Century*, pp. 101-105.

7.3 The Significance of the Temperance Movement

A further factor that contributed towards uniting Scottish Baptists in the middle of the nineteenth century was the temperance movement. This social phenomenon began in the 1830s in different parts of the United Kingdom and embraced people of all the major Protestant denominations and some important Roman Catholic leaders as well.[26] Religious controversies, including those noted at the start of this chapter, in the early 1840s, hindered the development of this cause for some years, but temperance gained a prominent place in the main Presbyterian denominations by the late 1840s. The United Secession Church established a ministers' society in 1845 which became a total abstinence society when that body merged with the Relief Church to form the United Presbyterian Church in 1847. The Free Church appointed a temperance committee in 1847, followed by the Church of Scotland in 1849.[27] The importance of this issue is its ecumenical character, in that it united people concerned about a social evil who would not otherwise have stood side by side on the same platform. Baptists of all streams in Scotland joined their fellow Christians in this moral crusade. The nature of the movement was stated most clearly by George Greig of Leeds, the Secretary of the British Temperance Association, in a public address in Liverpool in August 1841. He was speaking about the need for leaders of all denominations to unite against this evil as this was the only way to make headway against a powerful foe.

> If they wished to succeed they must all unite in this holy and good cause. They must not ask whether a man be a Catholic or a Protestant when he wished to enter their society. The men who conducted the affairs of the society ought to be good men, but the distinction of Catholic and Protestant should never be mentioned among them. They were to acknowledge no party, but to seek the interest and happiness of the community at large.[28]

This was not merely a pious hope, but an accurate description of

---

26 For a modern overview of this subject see B. Harrison, *Drink and the Victorians*, (Keele: Keele University Press, 1994), pp. 167-181. B. Harrison, 'The British Prohibitionists 1853-1872: A Biographical Analysis', *International Review of Social History*, (1970), pp. 375-467. For a contemporary analysis from a participant in Temperance work see D. Burns, 'Baptists and the Temperance Reform', in J. Clifford (ed.), *The English Baptists*, (London: E. Marlborough, 1881), pp.163-180. A specifically Scottish perspective is given in D.C. Paton, 'Drink and the Temperance Movement in Nineteenth Century Scotland', (PhD thesis, Edinburgh University, 1976).

27 S. Mechie, *The Church and Scottish Social Development 1780-1870*, (London: Oxford University Press, 1960), p. 93

what was happening in different parts of mainland Britain and Ireland.

In July 1841 there was an impressive sight in Glasgow. It was the occasion of a large demonstration on Glasgow Green in which the Independent Order of Rechabites appeared in full regalia with the intention of showing solidarity with Roman Catholic temperance advocates. It was important to note that the majority of those present were Roman Catholics. A similar gathering occurred later that summer on August 13 in honour of Father Theobald Matthew, the Irish priest who was one of the pioneers of the temperance movement in his native land,[29] and who had come for an extended visit to Scotland to spread the temperance message. On the evening of August 16 the executive of the Western Scottish Temperance Union (WSTU) gave a dinner in his honour and the main speech that evening was given by the Secretary of the WSTU, Robert Kettle.[30] Kettle, a member of Hope Street Baptist Church in Glasgow, was one of the most prominent Scottish Baptists in the temperance movement.[31] He first came to prominence in the cause in December 1830 when he became assistant treasurer of the Scottish Temperance Society. Kettle rose to become one of the secretaries in the following year.[32] He had come to Glasgow in 1815 after working as a clerk in Perth for the previous six years. Kettle was then employed by a company prominent in the cotton trade before setting up his own business as a cotton yarn merchant in Virginia Street, Glasgow, in 1834.[33] He had been in the 1820s an active member of Thomas Chalmers' congregation at the Tron in Glasgow and had risen to occupy the position of deacon. He had become convinced of the temperance cause after experiencing an accident while under the influence of alcohol. Kettle became President of the Glasgow Abstinence Society in December 1831, an office he held until March 1846. He was also the editor of the *Scottish Temperance Journal* from 1839 to 1847. The final senior office he held was the presidency of the

---

28 P.T. Winskill, *The Temperance Movement and its Workers*, (4 vols; Glasgow: Blackie & Son Ltd, 1893), II, p. 108.
29 P. Rogers, *Father Theobald Matthew Apostle of Temperance*, (Dublin: Browne and Nolan Ltd, 1943), is one of many biographies of this leading temperance figure. It provides good information on Matthew's work in Roman Catholic communities, but plays down the ecumenical importance of his work.
30 Winskill, *Temperance Movement*, II, p. 74.
31 Dawson, 'Baptists and the Temperance Reform', p. 168.
32 Winskill, *Temperance Movement*, I, p. 58.
33 *The Post Office Annual Directory for 1834-1835*, Glasgow, 1834, p. 116.

Scottish Temperance League from 1848 to 1852, a position he occupied until his death at the age of ninety-one.[34] Kettle joined Hope Street Baptist Church in the 1830s after a change of position over baptism. He had been acquainted with James Paterson through the work of the Glasgow City Mission. Kettle had been a director and Paterson an agent of the Mission. Kettle was one of two unnamed officials of the City Mission who had met with Paterson to discuss the latter's change of views on baptism and as a result of being unable to convince Paterson they felt it necessary to accept his resignation from the mission. The two City Mission officials joined Hope Street Church in the following year. This turn of events indicated the strength of Paterson's case on baptism and their personal respect for him.[35] Kettle and Paterson had also been associated in temperance work, with the latter noted as a prominent temperance lecturer.[36] These two men from the ranks of Scottish Baptists and Theobald Matthew in Roman Catholic circles were amongst those individuals who filled crucial leadership roles in promoting this cause. In the 1840s temperance principles were still held only by a small minority of Christians. The church leaders that espoused total abstinence were vital recruiters for this movement.

The younger Scottish Baptist ministers, and some Scotch Baptist elders, were quick to associate themselves with the temperance movement in the 1830s and early 1840s. Appendix 5.2 lists the known Baptist churches and their leaders that promoted this issue prior to 1842. The relevance of this issue for Baptist union is that the men who were quickest to associate with fellow Christians and others in moves to promote teetotalism also tended to be more prominent in the Baptist constituency amongst those people in favour of a closer association amongst the churches. There were at least twenty-three Baptist churches that were identified with total abstinence by 1842, of which only seven were not in favour of union. A proportion, therefore, of 70% of pro-temperance churches was in favour of moves to unite Scottish Baptists compared to the 17% of the wider constituency associated with the SBA in that year. The seven non-participating churches included five congregations of the more conservative variety of Scotch Baptists in Glasgow (two), Falkirk, Aberdeen and Paisley, and two other small congregations in Alloa and Stirling. It was not simply the temperance issue per se that revealed which Scottish Baptists were more likely to favour a

---

34 Winskill, *Temperance Movement*, II, p. 69.
35 H. Bowser, 'James Paterson, D.D. – A Biographical Sketch', *Scottish Baptist Magazine*, 23.8 (August, 1897), pp. 103-106.
36 Winskill, *Temperance Movement*, II, p. 67.

union of churches, but it gave an indication as to which leaders had a wider vision than the local affairs of their own congregation, in order to achieve common goals. The minister who identified with colleagues of other theological traditions in order to attain particular objectives was even more likely to work with others within his own religious community for the same kind of reasons. Amongst Scottish Baptists, for example, co-operation not only for the cause of a union of churches, but also in the work of the BHMS and in the provision of educational training for ministerial candidates marked these men who were involved in the propagation of temperance principles. This cause, therefore, was a kind of litmus test that gave a clear sign as to which Scottish Baptists were likely to be proponents of a union of Baptist churches in Scotland.

Baptists in the temperance movement in Scotland worked very closely with the denomination most committed to this cause, the Evangelical Union (EU). Leaders in the two denominations shared temperance platforms. This is not surprising in principle as some individuals had close links with both movements, but this co-operation extended to Baptists who would not on principle have joined Johnston's Baptist Union. Fergus Ferguson, an EU minister and the son of an EU minister of the same name, shared temperance platforms with Robert Kettle and James Paterson in 1849. This act has to be considered in the light of the prominence of members of Hope Street Baptist Church in the Scottish contingent who supported the Calvinistic strict communionist Baptist Evangelical Society at the time of the Johnstonian Baptist Union in Scotland. The significance, therefore, of Paterson's actions was that on non-doctrinal issues even Baptists of opposing doctrinal positions would willingly work with each other and with Christians of other denominations.[37]

There is evidence that indicates significant support by key Baptist leaders in the early years of this movement. Jabez Burns was the first Baptist minister in Scotland to promote this cause publicly. Burns was an Englishman born to Wesleyan Methodist parents in Oldham in 1805. He served as an itinerant minister with the Methodist New Connexion, working in the vicinity of York prior to joining the General Baptists at the age of twenty-four. Burns became minister of a General Baptist church in Perth in 1830 after spending a few months in evangelistic labours in Edinburgh and Leith, in 1829, for that Baptist body.[38] It was during his ministry there in the early 1830s that he espoused the temperance cause. He became an advocate of the Perth Temperance Society until his acceptance of a

---

37 Winskill, *Temperance Movement*, III, p. 18.

call to New Street General Baptist Church, London, in 1835. This Baptist preacher was one of the most prominent total abstinence advocates in Britain in the middle of the nineteenth century.[39]

George Barclay, minister of the Baptist Church in Irvine, an influential leader amongst the 'English' Baptists in Scotland, was also a prominent supporter of this movement. Barclay published a sermon on 'The Principles of Temperance Societies' as early as 1832.[40] Hope Street Baptist Church, Glasgow, was home to a number of key temperance leaders in Scotland in the 1830s. James Paterson, the minister, 'exerted a powerful influence as editor of the League's (Scottish Temperance League (STL)) early journals, *The Scottish Temperance Review*, which was succeeded by *The Scottish Review*, a monthly journal of social progress and general literature.'[41] *The Primitive Church Magazine*, an English Particular Baptist periodical promoting strict communion principles in that constituency and with which many Scottish Calvinistic Baptists associated themselves, had declared itself totally committed to promoting the cause of total abstinence from March 1853.

> We have lately felt it to be our duty to identify ourselves with the Total Abstinence cause. We believe it to be a cause which God has blessed in a high degree to the elevation of the working classes, and one to which Christian ministers and editors should give their cordial support.[42]

Robert Lockhart, the son of Ninian Lockhart, the prominent Baptist layman from Kirkcaldy, was another early temperance advocate.

> Mr Robert Lockhart early manifested that attachment to the temperance cause which has distinguished him through life, by joining the Kirkcaldy Total Abstinence Society on 21st January 1839, within little more than six years after the Total Abstinence movement had been inaugurated. From that early allegiance he has never wavered, and in the community in which he dwells [Dublin Street Baptist Church, Edinburgh] his name is prominently identified with social work on temperance lines.[43]

Lockhart, who had had a Scotch Baptist background, was one of four Baptist speakers at the STL anniversary services and meetings

---

38 A.H Grant, 'Burns Jabez', in L. Stephen (ed.), *Dictionary of National Biography*, (London: Smith, Elder & Co., 1886), 7, pp. 423-424.
39 Winskill, *Temperance Movement*, I, pp. 232-233.
40 *Adelaide Place Baptist Church 1829-1929*, (Glasgow: Adelaide Place Baptist Church, 1929), p. 11.
41 *Adelaide Place Baptist Church*, p. 11.
42 *The Primitive Church Magazine*, New Series, 10.3 (March, 1853), p. 90.

in July 1849. He was associated on that occasion with James Taylor of Glasgow and Francis Johnston of Edinburgh. These two men were key figures in the third attempt to establish a union of Baptist churches in Scotland. In September 1844 Peter Grant described Johnston, in a letter to his son William, as 'unconsciously zealous for the spread of the Gospel – for Baptist principles and for teetotalism'.[44] The other Baptist who spoke during the anniversary services was Robert Kettle. There was another influential advocate of temperance and the cause of Baptist union that needs to be mentioned. William Landels in his ministry at Cupar in the 1840s was as zealous for this cause as for Morisonian theology.[45] T.D. Landels, his son and biographer, noted his very active involvement in temperance work. He indicated that his father's views were very strong on this subject while at Cupar, but later they were 'modified considerably'. Landels had chosen deliberately to raise the temperance subject as his theme for anniversary soirees in this period. He was responsible for organising the Band of Hope amongst Cupar's children with more than 600 signed up as members. Landels, in addition, was involved in organising temperance gatherings in various parts of east central Scotland.[46]

The individuals noted above, and in Appendix 5.2, were opinion-formers and leaders amongst Scottish Baptists. Their names were prominent in the circles in which they moved and records have been kept of their views. It is probable that the numbers of Scottish Baptists in support of this movement in the 1840s was higher than the institutional records of the major temperance organisations would suggest. There were men such as James Malcolm, minister of Michael Street Baptist Church, Greenock, who never became prominent at a national level, but who were committed to promoting temperance work in their locality. On the occasion of his departure from Greenock to Aberdeen, Malcolm was entertained in his home town at a soiree organised by the Greenock Total Abstinence Society.[47] The key point to note here is that the men most closely identified with the temperance movement amongst Scottish Baptists were equally enthusiastic about plans for a union of Baptist churches. There is, of course, no formal link between the two issues, but the

---

43 'Mr Robert Lockhart', *Scottish Baptist Magazine*, 23.4 (April, 1897), p. 49.
44 Peter Grant to William Grant, September 23 1844, Grant MS.
45 *The Evangelist* 5.1 (January, 1850), pp. 13-17; 5.9 (September, 1850), pp. 202-203.
46 T.D. Landels, *William Landels, D.D.*, (London: Cassell and Company, 1900), p. 45.
47 *The Freeman*, 1 (October 3, 1855), p. 590.

ability to work with other Christians in the temperance cause marked out those individuals who were willing to co-operate with people of different views on other issues to achieve a common set of objectives. It was through that joint endeavour that they had considerable success in changing public attitudes to alcohol. A similar approach to working with fellow Baptists, from the different traditions, could also be fruitful in promoting their common cause.

7.4 The Place of Theological Education

The Baptist Union of Scotland led by Francis Johnston placed theological education high on its agenda alongside the need for evangelists and the support of pastors in small churches. *The Circular Letter of the Baptist Union of Scotland* for 1843, written by Johnston, stated:

> A third object of vital importance is the raising up of a thoroughly educated ministry in our churches. The furtherance of this object with spirit and resolution we believe to be indispensable to the welfare of Zion and the advancement of our principles...
>
> We are happy to say that not a few of our brethren and churches are fully alive to the importance of the subject, and that for some years committees for the education of a Baptist ministry have existed in Edinburgh and Glasgow, and that at the present they have young men under their auspices pursuing their studies...We regret the education of students in England; for, while there are some advantages connected with the plan, we believe they are more than counterbalanced by the fact, that the end in view, which is raising up pastors for our churches in Scotland, is not fully gained...
>
> We anxiously desire that the Edinburgh and Glasgow brethren, and all the churches, would combine to raise a Baptist Theological Institution in Scotland.[48]

Chapter six showed the strong consensus in favour of an educated ministry amongst Scottish Baptists and recorded the efforts made to establish appropriate training for the adopted candidates. Unfortunately Scottish Baptist churches had failed to gain much benefit from all the work undertaken by the Baptist Academical Society. A period of four years from 1842 to 1846 was to elapse before a new venture, the Baptist Theological Institute, commenced. On October 19 1846 the new body was constituted with James Taylor, minister of East Regent Place Baptist Church, Glasgow, as its chairman and two of his members serving as the secretary (William Pride) and treasurer (William McPhume). Francis Johnston, now

---

48 *An Inquiry into the means of advancing the Baptist Denomination in Scotland*, 1843, pp. 10-11.

resident in Edinburgh, was installed as the tutor.[49] Four students started the four-year course in December 1846, a total increased to six by the autumn of 1847.[50] A serious financial shortfall resulted in the student body being reduced to only three men in the academic year 1848 to 1849.[51] The generosity of the Baptist constituency allowed the work to expand to cover the costs of between nine and eleven students in the next three years, at which point the records apparently ceased though the work continued for a further three years until 1856.[52] A total of eighteen men were trained by Johnston with help from other part-time lecturers.[53] The breadth of support for the Baptist Theological Academy, unlike the previous Academical Society, was restricted to the minority of Baptists associated with the Baptist Union of Scotland. It had been correctly assumed that Johnston would seek to inculcate the newer ideas in theology into his students and as a result the majority of churches stood aloof from his efforts. Therefore, this cause around which the majority of Scottish Baptists identified in principle failed to contribute as expected in this period to the advancement of Baptist unity in Scotland.

7.5 The One Opportunity to Unite Scottish Baptists in the 1840s
The most promising opportunity to establish successfully the Baptist Union of Scotland in the 1840s was provided by the older Calvinistic ministers to their younger colleagues. In 1845, prior to the August annual meeting of the Baptist Union of Scotland a letter was received from the treasurer of the BHMS, Jonathan Watson, on behalf of that Society, 'pressing the homologating of the Union and that Society'.[54] Watson, a key member of the previous attempts at union, was a fitting person to try and bring the two groups of Scottish Baptists together. Watson had the full support of the conservative and Calvinistic ministers associated with the BHMS, yet he was also sympathetic to the Arminian Baptists, not least his own brother James, and therefore could appear as an approachable figure to Johnston and his colleagues. The Baptist Union appointed a subcommitee to draft a suitable reply. This was a fitting response to

---

49 *The Evangelist*, 1.6 (December, 1846), pp. 145-148.
50 *The Evangelist*, 2.3 (March, 1847), p. 219; 2.11 (November, 1847), p. 451.
51 *The Evangelist*, 5.9 (September, 1850), pp. 186-188.
52 *The Evangelist*, 5.6 (June, 1850), pp. 118-119; 6.5 (May, 1851), p. 97; 7.9 (September, 1852), p. 184.
53 D.B. Murray, *Scottish Baptist College Centenary History 1894-1994*, (Glasgow: Scottish Baptist College, 1994), p. 4.
54 Baptist Union of Scotland Minutes of Annual Meetings, Wednesday August 6 1845, MS in the possession of Bristo Baptist Church, Edinburgh.

Johnston's strong appeal in his 1843 address, *An Inquiry into the Means of Advancing the Baptist Denomination in Scotland*:

> The Baptist Union...is formed upon the principle that union is strength, that a threefold cord is not easily broken, and that two churches can do more than one, and a hundred more than ten; each church meanwhile retaining its own individual and scriptural independency. Our Union is formed upon the germinating principle, recognizing it to be one great design of the institution of the church, that the Christian in the family, the church in the world, and churches working together with churches should produce others, not ceasing the work till this rational and scriptural church extension scheme has covered the whole world...[55]

The committee met on August 7 and held what the minutes describe as 'a long conversation on the question of uniting with the Baptist Home Mission for Scotland'. This appears to suggest that there were differences of opinion concerning the response to the Home Mission. The meeting concluded unanimously that 'the Secretaries [Francis] Johnston and [Robert] Thomson...should do all in their power consistently with the avowed principles of the Union to meet the desire expressed in the letter received'. At the same meeting it was agreed that the committee would produce a series of tracts and start a periodical entitled *The Evangelist*. The man appointed as editor was James Taylor, the minister of Airdrie Baptist Church, and a man of moderate Arminian theological beliefs.[56] He was gifted in journalism. He edited *The Friendly Visitor*, an evangelistic periodical intended for free distribution, and *The Myrtle*, a Christian magazine for children. The Union adopted these two magazines and retained Taylor as editor of all three.[57] The committee also agreed to ask Taylor to leave the church at Airdrie and engage in church-planting work in Glasgow with a small company of Baptists who were already meeting in the city. They took the decision to pay for the financial implications of this new initiative. It was also agreed to start a church-plant on the 'English' model in Galashiels, as the Scotch Baptist congregation was deemed too tra-

---

55 *Inquiry into the Means of Advancing the Baptist Denomination in Scotland*, 1843, p. 12.

56 James Taylor, 'An Old Pastor's Reminiscences', 4,*The Victorian Freeman*, (April, 1881), pp. 92-93. I am indebted to Dr Ken Manley of Australia for providing copies of articles from this Australian periodical and for assistance in clarifying the developments in Taylor's theology. See also K.R. Manley, 'A Colonial Evangelical Ministry and a 'Clerical Scandal': James Taylor in Melbourne (1857-1868)', *Baptist Quarterly* 39.2 (April, 2001), pp. 56-79.

ditional in its practices. This decision seemed acceptable to Scottish Baptists at the time, but later on critical comments were received by the Union from churches not associated with it about the propriety of setting up another Baptist church in a town already containing a Baptist congregation.

The executive committee of the Baptist Union of Scotland met in October and December 1845. The minutes of these meetings imply that there was no action taken with regard to the proposal from the BHMS treasurer Jonathan Watson despite their agreement (October minutes) with the annual meeting's recommendation that the matter be approved 'without delay'.[58] It appears that the Union executive was not as enthusiastic for a merger at this stage. The decision, by inaction, to delay sending a reply must have been agreed by the four men on the executive. John Pullar (1803-1878) was a member of the famous family in Perth that was involved in the production of clothing, silk dying and scouring. Pullar was well known in the town and became a town Councillor and Lord Provost from 1867 to 1873. He was a very convinced Baptist and did not have much time for either the Church of Scotland or Roman Catholic denominations.[59] Robert Thomson, the minister of Perth Baptist Church, Francis Johnston from Cupar and Francis Macintosh, the pastor of the second Baptist church in Dunfermline, were the other members of the executive committee. One crucial difference between the October and December sessions was the presence of Johnston at the December function. This may explain the different attitude taken by the two meetings to Watson's proposal. The probable explanation is that Johnston persuaded his colleagues to reject the merger offer on both theological and practical grounds. The BHMS had a clear Calvinistic theological position for its workers. This viewpoint was constantly referred to both by mission workers and James Haldane, one of the mission secretaries, in the annual reports of the Home Mission.[60] The Baptist Union initially tolerated a broader view of theological opinions and employed both men acceptable to the BHMS and others, including Johnston, with Arminian theological beliefs. It is also likely that the Baptist Union secretary was convinced that the more conservative methodology and approach of the BHMS leaders would hinder the evangelistic thrust of the Baptist Union. He was of the opinion that the occasion of a more sub-

---

57 *Scottish Baptist Magazine* 12.3 (March, 1886), p. 74.
58 The Baptist Union of Scotland Executive Committee Minutes, October 1845, MS in the possession of Bristo Baptist Church, Edinburgh.
59 Robertson, *Perth Baptist Church*, pp. 44-45.

stantial union of Scottish Baptist work and witness was still a future ideal, rather than a practical proposition in the mid-1840s. Peter Grant had predicted the failure of potential merger talks between the BHMS and the Baptist Union as early as July 1845. In a letter to his son William he stated that some un-named Scottish Baptists believed 'that attempts will be made to join the Union and Society together, but I am afraid they are not ripe for it'.[61] This Highland preacher was unaware that the merger proposal was to be delivered less than one month after his letter had been written, but his assessment of the state of relationships between the Union and the Home Mission leaders proved to be accurate. It was, however, to be the last opportunity for the formation of a comprehensive Baptist Union during this period of Johnston's ministry in Scotland. In the autumn of 1845 it appeared that time was on the side of those who favoured a merger of the Baptist Union and the BHMS, but in reality this was not the case.

The formal reply from the Baptist Union was not sent until August 1846 and was taken after a vote at the annual meetings held in Perth. There was a lengthy discussion of the proposal sent to the Union by the BHMS in May 1845. James Taylor, of Glasgow, proposed the motion, Alexander Gregg of Perth was the seconder and it was unanimously adopted by those present. The motion stated that the committee and members of the Union viewed the proposal with great favour in principle:

> yet being persuaded that, by going forward as we have hitherto done, with brethren who are all of one mind on the subject, we shall be able more freely to carry forward the objects we have in view. And being also assured that our operations so far from injuring the Highland Mission will rather tend to strengthen it and to benefit its funds – these being better this year than ever – and that the members of this committee are willing as they have ever been to advance the interests of that institution, we are decidedly of the opinion, that by going on meanwhile with our various objects as formerly, we shall more effectively and rapidly advance the cause of God in the land.[62]

It seems probable that some Union members were concerned that they might not have the same freedom to express their theological opinions in their preaching and lectures if they were associated more formally with the ministers of stricter Calvinistic opinions. Others may have felt that the vision of the BHMS for spreading the

---

60   BHMS Reports for 1831 and 1832.
61   Peter Grant, Grantown, to William Grant, Edinburgh, July 6 1845, Grant MS.

Christian gospel across the nation was rather limited and unadventurous. In effect separate existence but with a measure of continued co-operation appeared to be the best policy for the immediate future.

This rejection of the BHMS proposal would have placed a strain upon the relationships of the individuals involved, but it did not preclude gestures of support for the work done for the Baptist cause in Scotland. One example occurred at the annual meetings of the BHMS in Bristo Baptist Church on May 1 1847. Robert Kettle, a deacon of Hope Street Baptist Church in Glasgow, during the course of a business session

> very kindly introduced to the notice of the meeting *The Evangelist* and warmly recommended it to the support of the denomination. This was kindly seconded by H.D. Dickie Esq, Chairman of the meeting, and Mr W. Robson, Baptist minister, Berwick.

The Evangelist article, quoted above, written in June 1847, continued with a statement revealing the response of the Union's leadership to such a gesture of friendship.

> We experienced great pleasure in attending the above meetings, and trust that now all the past will be forgotten and forgiven, and that, as a denomination, we shall be more united, more loving – in a word more Christ-like.[63]

The article also listed the names of the individuals who proposed or seconded motions during the meetings held from April 29 to May 1 1847. It is possibly significant that there were two prominent names listed from amongst the men who served on the Baptist Union Executive Committee, James Taylor, who held to moderate Arminian opinions, and Robert Thomson, who had retained Calvinistic theological views.[64] It is probable that these men had been favourable to the idea of a merger between the Union and the home mission agency, but drew back from advancing this cause when other colleagues held contrary opinions. There were no names given of the more vocal Arminian Baptists such as Francis Johnston or William Landels, who had only recently become a Baptist, having formerly been a pastor of an EU congregation in Ayrshire. He had been persuaded to change his views on baptism by the Calvinistic Baptist minister of Berwick Baptist Church, Archibald Kirkwood, who had vouched for his orthodoxy to Baptist colleagues.

---

62 Baptist Union of Scotland Minutes, August 1846.
63 *The Evangelist* 2.6 (June, 1847), pp. 289-290.
64 W. Landels, 'Denominational Reminiscences', *Scottish Baptist Magazine*, 12.3 (March, 1886), p. 74.

The Cupar Baptist Church where Landels was inducted as pastor in 1846 had been apprehensive concerning his orthodoxy, but had accepted the reassurances given by the Berwick minister. Landels was a fervent evangelist, an effective communicator with keen journalistic skills and a man destined for prominence in whatever ecclesiastical circles he was to mix.[65] He was, in the mid-1840s, fairly cautious about the promotion of his Morisonian beliefs, though it would not be too long before they received a prominent public exposition in the pages of *The Evangelist*[66] He freely admitted at a later date that when he had gone to Cupar it was with a view to propagating his Morisonian theological views.[67] The omission of the names of such ardent Arminian Baptist ministers from those who were present at the BHMS annual meetings in 1847 appears to suggest that they chose not to attend, fearing a less than warm welcome. It was, therefore, perceived as appropriate to refrain from any further steps of integrating Union and Home Mission work until relationships were strengthened.

The issue of uniting the Baptists of Scotland, who were affiliated to either the BHMS or the Baptist Union, was not brought up again in the surviving minutes of the Baptist Union before it ceased operations in 1856. It was unfortunate that this attempt at Union carried with it the seeds of its own destruction. The success of this Union, however, in the midst of its failure, was that Scottish Baptists were now beginning to realise that they ought to have a Baptist Union of Scotland.

7.6 Reasons for the Failure of the Johnstonian Baptist Union

It is now appropriate to consider the reasons for the failure of this attempt to unite Baptists in Scotland. There are a number of factors that contributed to this, but a major one was the decision to reject the 1845 offer of merger from Jonathan Watson on behalf of the BHMS. This decision and its implications will be discussed before the other issues are considered. The work of the BHMS and the Baptist Union had overlapped in the early 1840s and a merger proposal was therefore a sensible proposition. Initially there had been enthusiastic support from ordinary Union members at the annual meeting in August 1845, yet the executive committee repeatedly postponed making a decision on the offer until the December executive meeting that year at which the request was turned down. The

---

65 Landels, *William Landels*, pp. 31-35. D.E. Meek & D.B. Murray, 'The Early Nineteenth Century', in Bebbington (ed.), *Baptists in Scotland*, pp. 39-40.
66 *The Evangelist* 5.1 (January, 1850), pp. 1-6.
67 Landels, 'Denominational Reminiscences', p. 74.

decision may have been postponed until December due to the absence of Johnston at other meetings that autumn, but it was certainly he who was the decisive influence at the December 1845 executive committee meeting.[68] It is in the light of this decision that a controversy which erupted in the pages of *The Free Church Magazine* becomes more intelligible. In the January 1846 issue exception was taken to a tract issued in the name of 'The Baptist Union of Scotland' entitled *The Origin, Antiquity and Claims of the Baptists*. It was argued that this tract was offensive in its character and inaccurate in its content. This contribution would have passed without comment in Baptist Union circles had it not been for a letter in the February issue of *The Free Church Magazine* signed by nine of the leading Baptists from all three streams of Baptist ecclesiology. Their letter, dated January 21 1846, was *not* concerned about the tract that was condemned by the Free Church editor, but it was objecting to the implied claims of superiority on the part of Johnston and his colleagues. The letter included these lines:

> Now we have no knowledge of the tract in question, neither have we any connection with the said 'Union', but we owe it in justice to the older established Baptist Churches in Scotland to say, that it is but a mere fraction of their membership which has lately shot up into an association assuming this lofty appellation, calculated to lead the ignorant to conclude that the Baptists in Scotland have marshalled themselves under its banner, whereas the great body stand aloof from it, altogether disapproving of its proceedings.
>
> - We are, &c.
> J.A. Haldane,
> William Innes,
> H.D. Dickie,
> Christopher Anderson,
> Jonathan Watson,
> Andrew Arthur,
> John Leechman, Irvine,
> Alex. McLeod, Glasgow,
> James Paterson, Glasgow.[69]

There can be no doubt that it was the rejection of the merger proposal, instigated by the BHMS, that caused these men to react so angrily the following month in the letter to this Presbyterian magazine. Some previous studies of this controversy seem to be unaware of the main reason for the critical letter and not surprisingly find the

---

68 Baptist Union of Scotland Executive Committee Minutes, October and December 1845.

letter 'unjustifiable and inexplicable' if it is only a response to a popular tract.[70] This short Baptist handbill was in its substance largely acceptable to most Scottish Baptists. The offence was caused by the use of the corporate name, the 'Baptist Union', to represent only a select minority of the Baptist constituency. The content of the leaflet was standard Baptist propaganda which not surprisingly the editor of *The Free Church Magazine* could not accept. It was less than three years after the Disruption and the Free Church was on the defensive about its own ecclesiology. The editor of this Scottish periodical replied in a strongly worded propaganda article of his own, in the June 1846 issue, in which he helpfully printed the 'offensive' tract in full.[71]

The private correspondence, in 1846, between Peter Grant, the minister of the Baptist church in Grantown-on-Spey, and his son William, a student based in Edinburgh, sheds light on some aspects of this controversy. Peter Grant told his son that Robert Thomson, the minister of Perth Baptist Church, had written to him to explain that the letter by the nine men had had no connection with the tract, but the controversy in *The Free Church Magazine* had been used as an early opportunity to 'give a stab at the Union'. Thomson failed to explain why these nine men were so angry. It may be because he knew that Peter Grant would have supported the merger proposal. This interpretation is supported by a paragraph in a letter sent by Peter to William Grant on March 7 1846.

> My own opinion is that they [BHMS committee] should let the Union alone if they do not choose to join it. I am afraid that England will withdraw their support, for all the Baptists in England, America and throughout the world join in unions or associations. They have worked well for the last <u>300</u> years. And all know that the want of Union is the ruin of the Baptist cause in Scotland.[72]

The controversy deepened in March 1846 when a letter from James Haldane demanded that Grant state whether he wished to remain associated with the BHMS or with the Baptist Union of Scotland. Peter Grant enclosed a copy of his letter in reply to Haldane in a letter sent to his son on March 30 1846. Grant told his son that he had been informed that 'none of us could any longer remain connected with the union, and with the Baptist home missionary soci-

---

69   *The Free Church Magazine*, 26, (February 1846), pp. 60-61.
70   J. Scott, 'The Baptists in Scotland', (PhD thesis, Glasgow University, 1927), p. 94. Meek & Murray, 'The Early Nineteenth Century', pp. 41-42.
71   *The Free Church Magazine*, 30, (June, 1846), pp. 186-188.
72   Peter Grant to William Grant, March 7 1846, Grant MS.

ety'. Haldane had taken exception to the untrue claim from the Baptist Union circles that Peter Grant was on the Union committee. William was informed that his father had never even attended a meeting in support of the Baptist Union of Scotland though he was in favour of it in principle. The Grantown minister repeated his conviction that the lack of union amongst Baptists was the cause of so many of their problems.

> Having this conviction the committee [of the BHMS] need not wonder, that I should give my countenance to the men who were attempting to remedy the evils I so much deplored although their plans would not be altogether what I would wish, still I thought that they meant well. I thought I would remain in connection with both, as I was confident that the Union had no intention to hurt the society...

William Grant was concerned that funding for home mission work in Scotland from English Baptist churches would cease if the churches in Scotland were not united in a formal union. His father sought to reassure him in this lengthy letter that this was improbable. Peter Grant, however, indicated his opinion as to the likely outcome of the controversy between the Home Mission and the Union. 'I know that the weight of the Scottish Baptists are against the union, and under this weight the union may be crushed.'[73]

It is likely that all the individuals or churches supported by the BHMS were requested to withdraw their support from the Baptist Union of Scotland. The John Street Baptist Church in Aberdeen upon receiving their copy of the letter from James Haldane 'were in a terrible rage against the Society' and 'they have written to Edinburgh accordingly'. William Grant was advised by his father to 'keep yourself neutral, say nothing against the union or the society'.[74] The storm had subsided by the autumn of 1846. The correspondence between the Grants in December that year indicated a much improved relationship with James Haldane and the BHMS committee. Peter Grant reported that Haldane 'consults me in everything', with respect to the work of the Home Mission.[75] It is clear that ordinary Baptists like those in Aberdeen and the Grants did not wish to choose between the Union and the BHMS, wishing instead to support both organisations. It appears that some Baptists regarded the controversy as being the result of differences in methods of working, in addition to the theological disputation. The Grantown minister noted that 'Mr Johnston is the most active man

---

73 Peter Grant to William Grant, March 30 1846, Grant MS.
74 Peter Grant to William Grant, April 5 1846, Grant MS.

we have, but it is breaking out here and there that he is not sound in his views, but I give it no credit as yet. I think it arises from his manner of preaching'.[76] This perception may have changed later, but in 1846 the division between Baptists was not primarily between Arminian and Calvinistic theological beliefs.

The controversy was reported in some English Baptist periodicals including *The Baptist Reporter*. In the March issue of 1846 the editor noted the controversy and indicated that space would be devoted to it in future issues.[77] The April issue used the controversial tract as a commended article and later in that issue inserted in full the extract from the February issue of *The Free Church Magazine*.[78] The minutes of the executive of the Baptist Union of Scotland on May 19 1846 recorded a copy of the letter sent to their critics with a request for elucidation of the charges made against the Union.[79] Francis Johnston wrote a very important letter in the August issue of *The Baptist Reporter* that provides further helpful information concerning the private correspondence that followed the public exchange of views.[80] He records the Baptist Union's response to the criticisms of the nine ministers. There were two main criticisms: the first was the use of the name 'Baptist Union of Scotland', which it alleged was inappropriate for the use of a minority of Baptist churches. It is probable that behind this charge is the rejection of the formal merger request. The second criticism refers to the planting of new churches by the Baptist Union without consultation with the BHMS. Johnston in his letter refers to two examples, Galashiels and Glasgow, but fails to mention the one raised to the Union by the BHMS in the autumn of 1845. The minutes of the Union executive for December 1845 record the problem of the mission station at Auchterarder near Perth. Here the agent of the BHMS, a Mr Kirkwood, had applied to transfer his affiliation to the Union, with the assumption that the mission station would also have allegiance to the Union. His application was considered by the Baptist Union, but it withdrew its offer of support after the BHMS informed the Union executive member Francis MacIntosh that both the agent and the mission station 'had been not yet given up by that Society'. It was wise of the Union executive to withdraw gracefully, but this was an additional irritant to those Baptist leaders who felt that these

---

75   Peter Grant to William Grant, December 22 1846, Grant MS.
76   Peter Grant to William Grant, July 31 1845, Grant MS.
77   *The Baptist Reporter*, New Series, 3, (March, 1846), p. 148.
78   *The Baptist Reporter*, New Series, 3, (April, 1846), pp. 159-160, 175-176.
79   Baptist Union of Scotland Executive Committee Minutes, May 19 1846.
80   *The Baptist Reporter*, New Series, 3, (August, 1846), pp. 345-348.

younger men were interfering in already established work.[81] The two charges laid against the Union were thus understandable, but from the Union's perspective there was great frustration at the limited work being done by the BHMS in urban areas of Scotland and it was this that caused them to act unwisely.

Johnston's letter to *The Baptist Reporter* goes on to deal with the need for evangelistic outreach and church planting in the large towns and populous districts of Scotland which the Union was attempting in a more systematic way than the Home Mission. He held out an olive branch for the future: 'The time may come in which both will form but one society, but that time will not be hastened by injurious language or persecuting measures'.[82] This latter reference is to the exclusion in 1846 of Johnston, William Landels and one other Baptist Union official, from the committee of the BHMS.[83] It is possible that Johnston may have had second thoughts about the wisdom of rejecting the merger proposal in view of the further deterioration of relations between the BHMS and the Union, but the resulting conflict had definitely ruled it out for the near future. He may also have begun to realise that there were faults on both sides of the disputation and that nothing would be gained by further public wrangling. He had an unhealthy desire to confront his opponents in print as even his most devoted supporters, such as William Landels, admitted. Landels, in a tribute to Johnston after his death, made the following observation:

> His excessive zeal sometimes led him to forget – so engrossed was he in his work – that those who differed from him might not like to have their own beliefs assailed, and that the statement of his views at unsuitable times might justly give offence to those who were possibly as conscientious as himself.[84]

One further lengthy anonymous letter from a Union supporter appeared in *The Baptist Magazine* in July 1853, indicating that the BHMS still had not addressed the urgent need for evangelism in the major centres of population or updated its old-fashioned methods.[85] There are good grounds for believing that had the Baptist Union leadership exercised more patience with the BHMS in the early 1840s that co-operation rather than conflict might have been the outcome. It was obvious to all by the end of 1846 that great damage

---

81 Baptist Union of Scotland Executive Committee Minutes, December 18 1845.
82 *The Baptist Reporter*, New Series, 3, (August, 1846), p. 347.
83 *The Evangelist*, 5.1 (January, 1850), p. 19. *Evangelical Union Jubilee Conference Memorial Volume*, (Glasgow: T. Morison, 1892), p. 92.
84 *Scottish Baptist Magazine*, 12.10 (October, 1886), p. 268.

had been done to relationships between these two groups of Baptists. Evidence for this came from the minutes of the annual meetings of the Baptist Union of Scotland in August 1847 where both John Pullar, the Union treasurer, and Francis Johnston, the secretary, sought to resign their offices, but neither resignation was deemed acceptable to delegates.[86] Ordinary Union members had been in favour of joining forces with the BHMS, so it was not surprising that Johnston and other officebearers of the Union were blamed for causing the conflict with senior Baptist ministers, after their rejection of the merger proposal. In addition, the promised rise in the stipends paid to BHMS agents that year was not paid as the income to the Society was less than anticipated. This problem was revealed in a letter from Peter Grant to his son William in December 1846: 'I got a letter from Mr Haldane with the old salary, & no addition, I am sure this was not Mr James's fault nor several others'. Still we are struggling through, hitherto the Lord has helped'.[87] The people who had suffered the most from this conflict, the BHMS agents, had not been involved in the controversy. Here was a reminder to all the men involved in the disputation that no-one had benefited and some people were worse off.

Another factor that contributed to the divisions amongst Baptists, and as a result to the failure of the third attempt at Baptist union, was emigration from Scotland. The 1852 annual meetings heard discouraging reports from the churches. 'Most of the churches had suffered in numbers from emigration to Australia and America.'[88] This was not a new problem, but one that persistently discouraged Baptist churches in the mid-nineteenth century. Peter Grant in some remarks on the destitution of the West Highlands of Scotland, in November 1846, stated: 'yet it appears that few of them lay it to heart so as to turn to the Lord, but it will drive multitudes of them to America a land of plenty and liberty'.[89] The emigration was caused partly by famine and partly by the compulsory clearances instigated by landlords.[90] This problem meant that even when churches appeared to be growing their progress was arrested. The Tiree Baptist Church pastor, Duncan MacDougall, reported that his church membership total had grown from forty-four in 1842 to 100 in 1846, but added the following observation: 'It is probable that emigration will soon diminish our numbers'.[91] He was correct in his

---

85   *The Baptist Magazine*, 45.7 (July, 1853), pp. 451-452.
86   Baptist Union of Scotland Minutes, August 1847.
87   Peter Grant to William Grant, December 4 1846, Grant MS.
88   *The Evangelist*, 7.9 (September, 1852), p. 180.
89   Peter Grant to William Grant, November 10 1846, Grant MS.

observation because the membership of the church had fallen to thirty-two by 1851 as a result of departures abroad.[92] The BHMS committee and its supporters did not appear to understand that the removal of many thousands of people from all over the Highlands inevitably invited them to consider afresh their primary emphasis on work in the Highlands and Islands. An earlier plan in the late 1820s, discussed in chapter five, of putting BHMS personnel in Lowland cities to work amongst migrant Highlanders ought to have received further attention in the mid-1840s, but existing priorities appear to have been maintained. The Baptist Union committee, however, saw the greater urban population in the Lowlands as the principal concern for future evangelism. The declining Highland population, to them, indicated that less of a priority ought to be given to these Highland communities when resources were scarce. These younger leaders in the Union felt that their older colleagues in the Home Mission were set in their ways and needed encouragement to move forward in their thinking. Emigration was only a minor issue in their disputations, but it added an additional factor into the debate about evangelistic priorities.

The theological differences between the Scottish Baptist ministers had not been at the heart of disputes between the Baptist Union and the BHMS in the 1840s. Differences in methodology between men of different generations and personality conflicts had taken priority at that time. This was to change after August 1849 when the editorship of *The Evangelist*, transferred from James Taylor, a moderate Arminian, to William Landels, a Morisonian.[93] Taylor, a multi-talented man, had taken on too many responsibilities and as a result his health had broken down. He had to relinquish the editorship of *The Evangelist*. Under his editorship, the magazine had maintained a careful avoidance of controversial issues and a policy of co-operation between Baptists of different theological persuasions. The new editor, William Landels, had a very different approach. Noting that the Union had adopted *The Evangelist* as its publication, Landels decided that progress would be made most effectively by having a clear doctrinal position to advance. It was unfortunate that his doctrinal limits excluded the majority of Scottish Baptists. Landels was encouraged in this matter by Francis Johnston, the Baptist Union's inspirational leader, and Thomas Hughes Milner, who was to succeed Landels as editor of *The Evangelist*. The January 1850 editorial

---

90 Meek, 'Evangelism and Emigration', pp. 15-35.
91 *BHMS Reports*, 1842, pp. 25-26; (Edinburgh: Thornton & Collie, 1846), p. 26.
92 *BHMS Report*, 1854, p. 14.
93 *The Evangelist* 5.5 (May, 1850), pp. 99-100; 5.10 (September, 1850), p. 176.

address was a clear statement of the new public position of the Union. After noting that the formal decision was taken on this matter in April 1849 at the last annual meeting of the Baptist Union at Cupar, Landel's church, the following resolution was passed:

> That from January 1850, *The Evangelist* be taken under the sanction and management of the Union; and be recognised as the Union's organ. It will henceforth be employed in defending and propagating the three great scriptural doctrines, which the brethren in the Union generally are understood to hold – The love of God to – The death of Christ for – The influence of the Spirit on – all men. This doctrinal triplet we now adopt as our motto, and intend to inscribe on the front page of every future number, as an indication of its nature and design. We regard it as presenting the only consistent view of the character of the Triune God…And the better to secure this, we respectfully request our brethren to assist us, by contributing carefully written papers, in which these doctrines, in their bearings are explained, illustrated and applied, and shall refuse insertion to all such papers as do not harmonise therewith…[94]

The contrast between this theological stance and that presented by the committee of the 1827 Baptist Union is marked. In 1827 the Baptist Union committee could count on almost unanimous approval from Scottish Baptists for their doctrinal statement. The 1849 Union, by contrast, knew that this Arminian declaration of faith was a source of division. This small group of Baptist leaders had deliberately chosen to take this step knowing that it would lose them some of their existing supporters. There was, however, an honest admission that they knew what they were doing:

> We have counted the cost. Our principles we cannot renounce for friendship's sake…We calculate on the defection of those friends, with whom we differ in sentiment…The spread of truth, so important, is worthy of labour, of self- denial, and sacrifice…We ask no favour.[95]

Landels was editor of *The Evangelist* from September 1849 to May 1850. He was obliged to follow Taylor's conciliatory approach in the remaining issues of 1849, but became free to change that approach in the 1850 issues. He was asked to resign in April 1850 after receiving a call to a Baptist church in Birmingham. He at first refused to accede to this request, but upon the threat of the withdrawal of financial support from the Baptist Union he admitted defeat. The reason for requesting his resignation was that he would be living

---

94 *The Evangelist* 5.1 (January, 1850), p. 1.
95 W. Landels, 'Editorial Address', *The Evangelist*, 5.1 (January, 1850), pp. 1-2.

outside Scotland and this rendered his position as editor of a Scottish periodical untenable. Readers of the May issue of *The Evangelist* were given an opportunity to read about this unhappy incident.[96] It may also be pertinent to this decision to note that there was a significant and steady decline in the circulation figures for *The Evangelist* after the change of editorial policy in January 1850.[97] The readership of this denominational periodical, therefore, must have previously included a significant proportion of Calvinists who could not accept the new confrontational approach. The Baptist Union men were clearly prepared to lose their ties with Calvinistic brethren, but this issue indicated that they could not work in a satisfactory manner with each other.

Thomas Milner, a member of Francis Johnston's congregation in Edinburgh, was the new editor of this periodical. The minutes of the Baptist Union in July 1850 record Milner's rise to prominence in the Baptist Union. He had been appointed convenor of committees and editor of both the Union's magazines, *The Evangelist* and *The Myrtle*. He was also elected as secretary to the Baptist Theological Institution set up in response to Johnston's appeal in 1843.[98] It is appropriate to note the unhealthy concentration of power in the Baptist Union within one Edinburgh congregation that appears to indicate the weakness inherent in the Union. Johnston had kept a firm grip on the reins of power, delegating authority only to those who shared or tolerated his particular theological opinions. The new editor was just as zealous as his predecessor in beating the Arminian drum. No ammunition was spared in the attack on Scottish Baptists who dared to disagree with the 'new orthodoxy'. One of the targets of Milner's criticism in 1850 was Andrew Arthur, co-pastor with H.D.Dickie at Bristo Baptist Church in Edinburgh. There was, however, great embarrassment in that Arthur's 1849 sermon on Mark 4.10-12 entitled, *Spiritual Blindness the Result of Man's Voluntary Opposition to the Truth*, had been praised by William Landels on the grounds that it was contrary to the known views of Dickie, Arthur's co-pastor. Landels had wanted to take revenge on Dickie for excluding him from the committee of the BHMS in 1846 and used a review of these sermon notes as a pretext for this attack.[99] It was, however, doubtful whether his interpretation of Arthur's theology was correct. Arthur certainly believed he had been misrepresented and Mil-

---

96 *The Evangelist*, 5.5 (May, 1850), pp. 99-100.
97 Minute Book of the Executive Committee of the Baptist Union of Scotland and Theological Academy September 1850 to August 1855, February 11 1852, MS in the Scottish Baptist History Archive, Baptist House, Glasgow.
98 *The Evangelist*, 5.9 (September, 1850), pp. 173-174.

ner was happy to agree before suggesting in his reply that Arthur's theology was 'calculated to produce appalling effects' on its hearers.[100] The use of the denominational magazine to attack fellow-Baptists could only hinder the progress towards union between men of differing theological sentiments.

Thomas Milner and the Churches of Christ

One of the reasons for the weakness of the Baptist Union at this time was the loss of members to the Churches of Christ. *The Evangelist* reported in detail on Arminians from the Evangelical Union changing their position over baptism and then joining Baptist Union of Scotland congregations, but it for obvious reasons made no reference to those individuals who left to join other denominations.[101] Reference has already been made to the four churches that had abandoned the Baptist fold to join this new movement, but the Campbellite movement's biggest influence on Scottish Baptists came through a man who stayed on within Baptist circles to promote the 'advancement of Primitive Christianity'.[102] Thomas Hughes Milner, in partnership with his mother, worked as a silk mercer, draper and haberdasher in Edinburgh.[103] He had been converted and baptised at the age of seventeen through the witness of Bristo Baptist Church, Edinburgh, in 1842. Milner left Bristo to join an Evangelical Union congregation in Edinburgh and then rejoined the Baptists when Francis Johnston arrived from Cupar in 1846 to found a Baptist congregation in the city on Morisonian principles. In addition to his work commitments and duties in association with the Baptist Union and Theological Institution, this young man in his twenties was also a regular open-air preacher in the villages around Edinburgh. Milner had a strong dislike of any kind of clericalism and questioned the formal authority of pastors and elders. Increasing criticism of 'one-man' ministry in the Marshall Street Baptist congregation in Edinburgh during 1852 was probably instigated by Milner.[104] The disagreements in the Marshall Street church reached a climax at the time of an election of deacons in 1852. As a result twenty members led by Milner withdrew to form their own independent church.[105] The Milner family had been members of the

---

99 *The Evangelist*, 5.1 (January, 1850), p. 19.
100 *The Evangelist*, 5.7 (July, 1850), pp. 138-140; 5.8 (August, 1850), pp. 149-150.
101 *The Evangelist*, 6.6 (June, 1851), pp. 98, 116-119.
102 *The Evangelist*, 7.12 front cover (December, 1853), p. 265.
103 *Post Office Annual Directory 1849-1850*, (Edinburgh: Johnstone, Ballantyne & Co., 1849), p. 90.

Clyde Street Scotch Baptist Church prior to its merger with Bristo Baptist Church in the early 1840s.[106] Thomas Milner in 1852 had reunited with some other former members of Clyde Street Hall to form a new congregation meeting first in Nicholson Street, later Roxburgh Place, Edinburgh.[107] Milner and this church with which he was now associated formally separated from the Baptist Union of Scotland in June 1855.[108] Opposition within his own congregation must have decreased the energies of Johnston for the wider work of the Baptist Union. Milner's book *The Gospel Guide*, produced in 1853, revealed his adoption not only of avowed Arminian ideas,[109] but also denied the orthodox understanding of the work of the Holy Spirit in conversion, which he claimed comes about through instruction and teaching not through the direct influence of the Holy Spirit on the human heart. Scripture alone is the Spirit's voice and the sinner's heart is transformed by an act of human will, not through prayer.[110] It was no surprise that Calvinistic Baptists produced extremely critical reviews of this work, as for example, in *The Primitive Church Magazine*.[111] The prominence of a man holding such opinions in the Baptist Union of Scotland during the early 1850s ensured that there was no possibility of the vast majority of Calvinistic Baptists in Scotland joining in fellowship with this Union.

Milner's congregation after 1855 was associated with the Churches of Christ, with their leading member taking a prominent position in that constituency in Scotland.[112] Thomas Milner in January 1857 produced a new magazine, *The Christian Advocate*, in which he expressed his opinions on the work of the next attempt by Scottish Baptists to unite in the newly formed Baptist Association of Scotland set up by James Paterson and William Hodge from Hope Street Church, Glasgow, John Pullar from Perth and James Culross from Stirling.[113] Milner listed the following objections to the new organisation:

1. It is a piece of human legislation in the Church of God.

---

104 Thompson, *Let Sects and Parties Fall*, p. 51.
105 Wylie, *History of Marshall Street*, p. 25.
106 Balmain, *Clyde Street Hall*, p. 19.
107 Balmain, *Clyde Street Hall*, pp. 28-29.
108 Baptist Union of Scotland Executive Committee Minutes, 1850-1855, June 27 1855.
109 T.H. Milner, *The Gospel Guide*, (Edinburgh: E. Henderson, 1853), pp. 48-50, 56-58, 83-84, 95-99, 156-158, 174-175.
110 Milner, *Gospel Guide*, pp. 60-62, 83-84.
111 *The Primitive Church Magazine*, New Series, 17.3 (March, 1860), pp. 63-66.
112 Thompson, *Let Sects and Parties Fall*, pp. 51-54.

2. It implies the inefficiency of the church, as divinely constituted, to effect what God purposes by it.
3. It introduces a money qualification into the Christian church – the charge for membership being half a crown a year.
4. It leads the congregation to look for something without for 'the revival of spiritual religion'.
5. It reduces them to a kind of ecclesiastical pauperism.
6. It is essentially Sectarian alike by unavoidable coinage and circulation of unscriptural epithets, as 'Evangelical Baptists', by the avowed aim of mere denominationalism, and the forming of a party who adhere to the Association in contradistinction to those who cannot conscientiously do so.[114]

In the same article Milner rejected the Baptist view that men can be set apart as ministers, as he now believed there was no scriptural basis for such an office. In the February issue of *The Christian Advocate* there is a record of a gathering of representatives from the Scottish Churches of Christ in which they accepted a series of articles of faith as the basis of their co-operation. It is probable that Milner wrote the articles himself and it is noteworthy that there is no place for any formal union or association officially linking the churches together.[115] Even attempts towards co-operation between churches of his new connexion faced the determined opposition of the Edinburgh silk mercer.[116] It seems strange that his views had changed so rapidly, but there had been indications prior to his leaving the Baptist Union concerning the direction of his thinking. The change in the status of the Baptist Union at the August annual meetings of the Union in 1852 sounds very similar to Milner's later position. 'It will be noticed that...the Union, instead of consisting of churches, should be composed of individuals, members of Baptist churches, who are desirous and willing to co-operate for the extension of New Testament Christianity throughout Scotland'.[117] The name of the Baptist Union was changed to 'The Association' at the 1853 annual meetings.[118] It is likely that for Milner this development was not simply a recognition of a lesser vision for the new body, but was calling into question any ideas about a formal union of churches. This could not be further from Johnston's original vision in 1843. Milner was not alone in Britain in holding a leading position in a Baptist Union while at the same time wondering whether the very

---

113 *The Baptist Magazine* 48.10 (October, 1856), p. 628.
114 Milner, *The Christian Advocate* 1.1 (January, 1857), p. 19.
115 Milner, *The Christian Advocate* 1.2 (February, 1857), pp. 37-38.
116 Thompson, *Let Sects and Parties Fall*, p. 52.

concept was at all scriptural. John Howard Hinton, a leading member, and the first secretary, of the BUGBI was in a similar position. Hinton even debated as to whether it was scriptural to speak of such an organisation as 'the church'.[119] He certainly doubted whether a church could have any rules to guide the conduct of its members.[120] His resignation speech as secretary to the BUGBI in 1863 revealed the impact opinions like his own had had on English Baptists. He described the Union as 'a case of apparently morbid apathy' and that any 'Utopian attempts at working closer together would cause a highly combustible situation to explode'.[121] John Howard Hinton may have been a man of similar views on this subject to Milner, but he was not in as dominating a position in the BUGBI as Milner had obtained in 1852-53 in the Scottish Baptist Union. At this time voices advocating a significant role for a union of Baptist churches in Scotland were less influential than those of their opponents. It is no surprise that the Baptist Union of Scotland that existed from 1843 to 1856 was unable to succeed when one of the key leaders had such negative opinions as Milner. Even though it is accepted that his views were probably strengthened after he left Baptist circles, the negative tendencies were present a few years before he left to chart his own religious course.

7.7 Francis Johnston: His Methods and Theology

It is appropriate to consider last the man who had dominated the 1843-1856 Baptist Union of Scotland. His vision and dedication had revitalised the SBA that he had joined in 1842. It was, however, the same man in December 1845 who had rejected the BHMS merger proposal that would have combined the Union and the Home Missionary Society. Francis Johnston was a complex character who combined zeal for the promotion of the Baptist cause in Scotland with an equal zeal to put right the perceived faults of his fellow Baptists. His conflicts with three of his Scottish colleagues will illustrate why this attempt at union would ultimately founder. First of all it is important to consider his attitude to the Watson brothers, James, minister of Montrose Baptist Church, and Jonathan, co-pas-

---

117 Baptist Union of Scotland Minutes, *The Evangelist*, 7.9 (September, 1852), p. 180.
118 Baptist Union of Scotland Minutes, *The Evangelist*, 8.11 (November, 1853), pp. 258-267.
119 J.H. Hinton, 'The Church', in *The Theological Works of J.H. Hinton M.A.*, (7 Vols; London: Houlston & Wright, 1865), 5, pp. 490-491.
120 I. Sellers, 'John Howard Hinton Theologian', *Baptist Quarterly*, 33.3 (July, 1989), p. 119.
121 Sellers, 'John Howard Hinton', p. 119.

tor of Dublin Street Baptist Church, Edinburgh. Francis Johnston published a diary of his travels to the north of Scotland in the summer of 1850. He recorded his comments on the people and churches in various towns. James Watson, an Arminian, was the subject of a paragraph on Montrose. Johnston observed that the majority of the Baptists in the town attended the Independent Church due to their Calvinistic views. A proportion of the few who remained in the Baptist chapel appeared discontented with their situation according to Johnston:

> Some of the friends here anxiously long for the formation of a church by the Union, holding clear and enlarged views of the Gospel; and it is high time something of the kind were done, for here is a fine and beautiful town of 16,000 inhabitants where we are doing nothing to witness for God.[122]

The next place on the itinerary was St Andrews where Johnston met the founder pastor of Cupar Baptist Church, Jonathan Watson, who was now in 1850 based in Edinburgh. The diary entry recorded the following account of their conversation: 'I had also an interview with Mr Watson, who manifested an excellent spirit; but I was grieved to hear him speak of Universalism.'[123] This unjustified attack on a senior Baptist minister insinuating that he held unorthodox opinions could only harm Johnston's cause. Jonathan Watson was a committed Calvinistic Baptist whose views were remarkably similar to those of his colleague William Innes at Elder Street Church, Edinburgh. This type of personal criticism in the denominational periodical was both unwise and unhelpful and the quotations above reveal that it extended to his fellow Arminians as well as to Calvinistic brethren.

A further individual to face censure was Peter Grant, a lawyer and lay-pastor of an 'English' Baptist Church in Stirling. Grant had written a booklet entitled, *A Brief Review of a Recent Publication entitled, 'The Work of God and the Work of Man in Conversion'*, in response to this highly controversial book produced in 1848 by Francis Johnston. The Johnston book attracted criticism from many Scottish Baptists besides Peter Grant, but it is the Stirling pastor to whom Johnston responded in the pages of *The Evangelist*. There were five instalments in successive issues from August to December 1850. Johnston's manuscript would have been published earlier, but the editor of *The Evangelist* who first received it in the spring or summer of 1849, James Taylor, refused to publish it on the grounds that 'enough had been said on that subject'. This was a wise decision. A

---

122 *The Evangelist*, 5.7 (July, 1850), p. 135.
123 *The Evangelist* 5.7 (July, 1850), p. 135.

less discerning editor, Thomas Milner, was willing to publish his pastor's remarks.[124] It is important to ask why Johnston's book had caused so much alarm amongst his fellow Scottish Baptists. In order to answer this question it is appropriate to indicate the social context in which this theological debate was taking place.

Peter Grant, together with other Calvinistic Baptists, was concerned about the spread of new theological ideas in Scotland associated with James Morison and the Evangelical Union. Many of these new ideas had been taught by the American revivalist Charles Finney to whom Morison was greatly indebted. The Kilmarnock minister was so excited about his discoveries that he discussed their importance in a letter to his father Robert Morison, a United Secession Church minister, in 1838: 'I do strenuously advise you to get Finney's lectures on Revivals, and preach like him; I have reaped more benefit from the book than from all other human compositions put together'.[125] James Morison had had a similar doctrinal pilgrimage to Charles Finney. The two men had both been brought up in traditional Calvinistic Presbyterian circles and had begun their ministry believing in the doctrine of election before later discarding it.[126] The old ideas associated with the consequences of a belief in the doctrine of original sin were rejected by both men.[127] Likewise the necessity for a supernatural work of the Spirit in a person's heart before conversion was also rejected.[128] Finney, in his 1835 *Lectures on Revivals of Religion*, declared:'A revival is not a miracle, nor dependent on a miracle, in any sense. It is a purely philosophical result of the right use of the constituted means'.[129] James Morison had already drawn the attention of his peers to his independent mind when he had chosen to oppose his own denomination's belief in the eternal Sonship of Christ.[130] An article in *The Evangelist* in April 1851 also denied the validity of the traditional understanding of this doctrine.[131] In the earlier part of the nineteenth century the nature of Christ's Sonship was, as we have seen, a mark of heterodoxy or orthodoxy within Scotch Baptist circles.[132] A further parallel between Morison and the Scotch Baptists was concerning the nature

---

124 *The Evangelist* 5.8 (August, 1850), p. 150.
125 Adamson, *James Morison*, p. 55.
126 Adamson, *James Morison*, p. 79. G.W. Gale, *Autobiography of Rev. George Gale*, (New York: n.p., 1964), pp. 186, 274, cited by K.J. Hardman, *Charles Grandison Finney 1792-1875*, (Darlington: Evangelical Press, 1990 [1987]), p. 52.
127 Ferguson, *Evangelical Union*, p. 63. Hardman, *Charles Grandison Finney*, pp. 15-21.
128 Ferguson, *Evangelical Union*, p. 61.

of true faith. Morison, in his booklet *Saving Faith*, taught that faith is a simple act of belief in Christ which must not be confused with its effects, a view shared by Sandemanians. He referred to the disputations on this subject between Andrew Fuller[133] and Archibald McLean,[134] making it plain that he took the side of McLean on this matter.[135] Mainstream evangelical Calvinists like Peter Grant tended to follow Fuller's understanding of this subject. In 1827 Scottish Baptists had been in almost total agreement about theological matters, their disagreements being confined to ecclesiological matters. Now it appeared that the very foundational doctrines of the faith were being undermined. In such a context as this it is not surprising that Johnston's book aroused strong responses within the Scottish Baptist constituency.[136]

It is important to be aware that Johnston had completely rejected the Calvinistic understanding of God, humanity and salvation. Some modern writers, unlike his contemporaries, appear to underestimate the significance of this development.[137] Johnston in his debate with Peter Grant admits that he is an Arminian and that Grant is a Calvinist and that the traditional differences between these two systems regarding the doctrine of salvation are upheld in their writings.[138] Francis Johnston, however, is unwilling to accept the main charges brought by Grant against him. Grant's fundamen-

---

129 C.G. Finney, *Lectures on Revivals of Religion* (ed. W.G. McLoughlin, Cambridge: Harvard University, Belknap Press, 1960), p. 12, cited by Hardman, *Charles Grandison Finney*, p. 21.
130 Adamson, *James Morison*, pp. 41-43.
131 *The Evangelist*, 6.4 (April, 1851), p. 79.
132 Williamson, *Old Baptist Church Pleasance*, p. 15. See also Chapter two, pp. 63-64.
133 Belcher (ed.), *Andrew Fuller*, II, pp. 561-647.
134 Jones (ed.), *Works of Archibald McLean*, II, pp. 1-127.
135 J.Morison, *Saving Faith*, (Kilmarnock: J.Davie, 1842), pp. 50-51.
136 The ideas promoted in Johnston's book were very similar to an equally controversial book by John Kirk, *The Way of Life Made Plan*, published in 1842, (reprinted in J. Kirk, *The Complete Works*, (2 Vols; Glasgow: Lang and Tweed), 1859, I, pp. 1-113), that had caused division in the ranks of the Congregational Union churches. Kirk left his denomination to join the Evangelical Union in 1845. N.R. Needham, 'Kirk, John (1813-1886)', in Cameron (ed.), *Scottish Church History and Theology*, p. 460. Johnston would be fully aware of the contents of Kirk's book and the consequences of its publication. It is probable that he expected a polarisation of opinions in Scottish Baptist ranks also and was prepared for the consequences. The transformation of the Baptist Union from an inclusive to a largely exclusive Morisonian body, by 1849 at the latest, would be consistent with such a policy.

tal criticism refers to the apparent equality of roles in the process of conversion undertaken by man and God:

> in treating of the glorious work of the new creation, thus to place God and man side by side, and as being, as far as the terms go, compeers, and on a footing, is an exceeding violation of reverence and right feeling towards God...the doctrine of the lectures indicates views and feelings tending to the utter subversion of the grace of God.[139]

At the heart of the issue is the debate over the manner in which the Holy Spirit brings people to faith in Jesus Christ. Peter Grant assumed that Johnston followed Finney and Morison in denying the supernatural influence of the Holy Spirit in conversion as the determinative factor as to whether a person was brought to faith. The claim was denied by Johnston, though his book appeared to confirm the suspicions of his opponents. He argued that the Holy Spirit inspired the writers of Holy Scripture and they passed on the sacred writings to the members of the church who are commissioned to preach it to the world. 'It is thus that the Holy Spirit is at work for the conversion of man to God.'[140] The idea of the Holy Spirit working directly and actively on a human being in opening the mind and bringing it to respond to the gospel, as understood in Reformed theology, was decisively rejected. The effectual call of the Spirit

> is a doctrine of devils, a doctrine in which Satan and his angels and agents delight, as being so subservient to their hellish purposes in deceiving and destroying millions of souls. It behoves the people of God therefore to set their faces against it as a flint.[141]

Johnston appears to believe, echoing Finney, that if the right human methodology is used that there will be a mass turning of the people in the land to the Christian faith. 'Of one thing the writer is certain, that were the doctrines here stated universally preached, there would be a universal revival of religion in our churches.'[142]

Johnston also appears to imply a Campbellite view of baptism, suggesting that the reference to water in John 3.5 and the link between 'the laver of regeneration and the renewal of the holy Ghost' in Titus 3.5 inseparably link the two events.[143] Alexander

---

137 E.g. D.B. Murray, 'Johnstone, Francis', in Lewis (ed.), *DEB*, I, p.616.
138 F. Johnston, 'Reply to Mr Grant IV', *The Evangelist*, 5.11 (November, 1850), p. 221.
139 *The Primitive Church Magazine*, New Series 6.2 (February, 1849), pp. 67-68.
140 F. Johnston, *The Work of God and the Work of Man in Conversion*, (Edinburgh: W. Innes & Andrew Muirhead, 1848), p. 20.
141 Johnston, *Work of Man in Conversion*, pp. 112-113.

Campbell and his colleagues in the Churches of Christ taught that baptism by immersion was essential to conversion. In 1823 Campbell stated

> I contended that it was a divine institution designed for putting the legitimate subject of it into actual possession of the remission of his sins – that to every believing subject it did formally, and in fact, convey to him the forgiveness of sins. It was with much hesitation that I presented this view of the subject at that time, because of its perfect novelty.[144]

Opinions such as these expressed by Alexander Campbell and the rational, theologically Arminian position held by Charles Finney, James Morison and Francis Johnston were clearly distinct from orthodox Reformed teaching.

It was only to be expected that other Scottish Baptists besides Peter Grant would declare their opposition to Johnston's theology. Jonathan Watson in a public lecture in June 1852, given to the Tabernacle congregation in Edinburgh, spoke by contrast to Johnston of:

> the indispensable need of the Holy Spirit's influences for our personal establishment and general usefulness.' He exposed the modern views of the Spirit's work, and contended earnestly for the great truth, so plainly revealed in the Bible, that when Paul had planted, and Apollos watered, God must, for only he can, give the increase.[145]

Another prominent Baptist minister to speak out against the views propounded in Johnston's book was Alexander McLeod. After commending some churches for their orthodox faith McLeod then contrasts that with others known to him:

> are there not others of undisguised and undisguisable Pelagian opinions? And does not Pelagianism deny that it behoves 'the ungodly and sinners' to be illuminated and converted by the special operation of the Holy Spirit? While professing to admit 'the belief of truth' do they not stoutly deny 'the sanctification of the Spirit – the washing of regeneration – the renewing of the Holy Ghost?' of which the Lord himself said to Nicodemus, 'except a man be born of the Spirit he cannot see the kingdom of God?' Is this denial of the Holy Spirit less dangerous or less ungodly and pernicious than the rejection of our Lord's Divine glory and atoning sacrifice?[146]

---

142 Johnston, *Work of Man in Conversion*, p. 206.
143 Johnston, *Work of Man in Conversion*, pp. 132-133.
144 *The Christian Baptist* 5 (1828), p. 47, cited by E. Roberts-Thomson, *Baptists and Disciples of Christ*, (London: Carey Kingsgate Press, n.d., [1951]), p. 116.
145 *The Primitive Church Magazine*, New Series 9.8 (August, 1852), pp. 232-233.

Johnston had the opportunity to correct any mistakes in Grant's critique of his book on the work of the Spirit in conversion, but instead appeared to confirm his opponent's position. He admitted that 'Faith is the work of man as well as the gift of God',[147] and that the working of the Holy Spirit during the ministry of Jesus on earth was solely 'the Father drawing souls simply through Christ's doctrines and miracles. We ask, were not these the means through which God exerted or put forth that influence which alone could bring them to Christ?'[148] Far from reassuring fellow Baptists by his extended reply to Grant's accusations, Johnston only confirmed the suspicions of many that he had departed from the bounds of Christian orthodoxy. This understanding of the situation ensured that there was no possibility of the views of the various types of Scottish Baptists being contained in a single Baptist Union of Scotland in the 1850s.

This conclusion was reluctantly drawn by several Scottish Calvinistic Baptist ministers in the early 1850s after the separatist declaration of the Union's magazine, *The Evangelist*, in January 1850. A group of men led by Henry John Betts, the successor of James Haldane as pastor at the Tabernacle Church in Edinburgh, sought to have fellowship with like-minded English Calvinistic Baptists. They supported a little known society called 'The Baptist Evangelical Society', (BES)[149] and its magazine *The Primitive Church Magazine (PCM)*. The BES was never intended to form the basis of a separate denomination, as a declaration, dated April 1845, made plain: 'It was never contemplated that brethren or churches, uniting with it, should be expected to withdraw, in consequence of doing so, either from local organisations, or denominational institutions'.[150] This Society served the purpose of mutually encouraging Calvinistic Baptists in the upholding of the principle of strict communion and also in advocating the need for a Baptist college in England based upon its principles of belief. The college English Calvinistic Baptists in the Society had desired was opened in Bury in 1866. It was found a permanent home in Manchester in 1873. Charles Haddon Spurgeon formally opened the new facilities on October 9 1872. The BES ceased operations in 1866 after its main objectives had been

---

146 *The Primitive Church Magazine*, New Series 12.6 (June, 1855), pp. 169-172.
147 Johnston, 'Reply to Mr Grant chapter I', *The Evangelist*, 5.8 (August, 1850), p. 152.
148 Johnston, 'Reply to Mr Grant chapter IV', pp. 221-222.
149 G.R. Breed, *The Baptist Evangelical Society*, (Dunstable: The Fauconberg Press, 1988).
150 Breed, *Baptist Evangelical Society*, p. 10.

achieved.¹⁵¹ The Scottish backers of the Society included, from Glasgow, Alex and Richard McLeod of South Portland Street Baptist Church, James Paterson, Howard Bowser and William Hodge of Hope Street Church and John Shearer from John Street Baptist Church. The Baptists from Edinburgh included Jonathan Watson, Henry Dickie and Andrew Arthur, Christopher Anderson, and Henry Betts from the Tabernacle Church. John, Laurence and Robert Pullar (Perth), Thomas MacAlpine (Paisley), John McIlvain (Greenock), Peter Grant (Grantown-on-Spey) and Sinclair Thompson (Shetland) were also in favour of this cause. The subscription lists of supporters, for example in 1855-1858, include many of the leading Scottish Baptists.¹⁵² Henry Betts was the joint-editor from 1850 to 1851 and sole editor from 1851 to 1857.¹⁵³ In June 1857, a doctrinal basis was recorded that made plain that the *PCM* would continue to proclaim the traditional Calvinistic theology held historically by Particular Baptists.¹⁵⁴ A person who supported the work of this Society was never going to feel comfortable in the Baptist Union organised by Francis Johnston. An anonymous article by a Scottish supporter of the *PCM* hinted at the dissension in the ranks of the Baptist Union of Scotland as a result of the publication of Johnston's controversial book.

> All holding evangelical doctrine (and even some who are still of Mr J.[ohnston]'s party) are unanimous in pronouncing his book erroneous, insidious, and of evil tendency...Most sincerely do we regret the position of the theological tutor of the Baptist Union of Scotland. Some of the best supporters of his theological school, it is said, will support it no more.¹⁵⁵

One of Johnston's admirers who was a member of the BES, Peter Grant, had been concerned about the Cupar minister's theology in 1846, long before the damage caused by his 1848 treatise. In a letter to his son William, Peter Grant expresses his hopes and also his fears for Johnston's future:

> If the Lord preserves Johnston from erroneous views you will see that he will be one of the cleverest men of our denomination. I am

---

151 Breed, *Baptist Evangelical Society*, pp. 32-33.
152 *The Primitive Church Magazine*, New Series 12.2 (February, 1855), p. 63; 12.4 (April, 1855), p. 130; 14.4 (April, 1857), pp. 97-99; 14.12 (December, 1857), pp. 293-294; 15.1 (January, 1858), pp. 23-24; 15.12 (December, 1858), pp. 293-294.
153 *The Primitive Church Magazine*, New Series, 14.1 (January, 1857), Preface, pp. iii-iv. Breed, *Baptist Evangelical Society*, pp. 15-16, 22.
154 *The Primitive Church Magazine*, New Series, 14.6 (June, 1857), p. 151.
155 *The Primitive Church Magazine*, New Series, 6.3 (March, 1849), pp. 91-92.

not sorry that you cultivate acquaintance with him, I hope it will not offend anyone.[156]

The affairs of Baptists in Scotland received prominent coverage in the *PCM*. The Grant-Johnston debate was reported on at great length, predictably supporting Grant's allegations, much to the annoyance of Francis Johnston.[157] Betts, while editor of the *PCM*, strongly attacked an article on the atonement published in *The Evangelist* in May 1852. The Edinburgh Tabernacle minister received a blunt reply in the August issue of that periodical. The request from Betts for his letter to be published was delayed to the November issue of *The Evangelist*, but it was printed in the *PCM* in August 1852, at the same time as its reply from an unidentified supporter of *The Evangelist*.[158] The contrasting reviews given in the respective periodicals to Thomas Hughes Milner's book, *The Gospel Guide*, confirmed the distance between them.[159] It was easy and safe for these two groups of Baptists to attack each other in print, but it achieved only one objective and that was guaranteeing that instead of building 'bridges' they were erecting a 'wall' between them.

The arrival of Francis Johnston as minister of Cupar Baptist Church in 1842 was a turning point for the SBA. It now became the Baptist Union of Scotland, and had a name to match the new vision. Johnston was a leader who provided a vision that inspired many Scottish Baptists to give their time, money and skills to its cause and much good was done in terms of church-planting and the encouragement of some weaker churches. The Union, in contrast to the BHMS, had a more realistic strategy for evangelising Scotland and it was only its meagre resources that prevented new work from being done. It is important to note the support in terms of both finance and literature that came from England. The Scottish churches could no longer remain in splendid northern isolation if they wished to make progress. It is ironic that the strong personality of Johnston that enabled the Union to move forward was also its undoing.

The rejection by Johnston of the BHMS proposal for a merger with the Baptist Union at the December 1845 meeting of the execu-

---

156 Peter Grant to William Grant, November 17 1846, Grant MS.
157 *The Primitive Church Magazine*, New Series 5.11 (November, 1848), (apparently, as I have been unable to obtain a copy of this issue); 6.2 (February, 1849), pp. 67-68; 6.3 (March, 1849), pp. 87-92.
158 *The Evangelist*, 7.8 (August, 1852), pp. 145-148. *The Primitive Church Magazine*, New Series 9.8 (August, 1852), pp. 309-312.
159 *The Evangelist*, 8.4 (April, 1853), pp. 87-90. *The Primitive Church Magazine*, New Series 17.3 (March, 1860), pp. 63-66.

tive committee of the Union was the major reason for the failure of this attempt at union. A secondary reason was the conflict over strategy and sites between the two bodies that came to light at that same meeting. It was to be expected that there would be a negative response from the established Baptist leaders in Scotland to the rebuttal of this offer, though it was most unfortunate that it was within the pages of an unsympathetic magazine. It was also no surprise that Johnston would want the last word, but his confrontational approach, especially after 1850, ensured that barriers to union would increase rather than decrease in the Scottish Baptist constituency.

The Johnstonian Baptist Union which became openly Arminian in its sentiments in 1850 was to last only five more years. It came to an end with the departure of its leaders, Johnston, Milner and Landels. This failure was stark in comparison with the success of the Evangelical Union, the group led by James Morison out of the Secession Church. This new denomination experienced vigorous growth, eventually joining with the Congregationalists in 1896.[160] It is probable that the strength of the Evangelical Union delayed its merger with the Congregationalists in Scotland. The first indication of a possible union between these two paedobaptist bodies came in 1867, only two years later than the formal moves to unite Baptist churches in a national organisation in 1865.[161] Congregationalists appeared to favour the closer fellowship, but a powerful minority of Evangelical Union ministers opposed a merger on the grounds that Congregationalists were no nearer to accepting the 'three universalities' (the love of God to, the death of Christ for, the influence of the Spirit on, all men).[162] The 'three universalities', the doctrinal motto of Evangelical Unionists, had been given the same status in the Johnstonian Baptist Union.[163] Congregationalists finally agreed in 1896 to adopt the Evangelical Union's doctrinal tenet into the new denomination's constitution, providing that it would not be used as a theological test for any member or minister, as the Bible alone was to be regarded as the standard of faith and life.[164] The status of the Evangelical Union and its steady increase in its membership and numbers of churches in the mid-nineteenth century was in contrast with the weakness of the Johnstonian Baptists. This fact, when combined with their numerical and financial weakness, had ensured that this group of Scottish Baptists needed to work with

---

160 Escott, *Scottish Congregationalism*, pp. 172-176.
161 Yuille (ed.), *Baptists in Scotland*, p. 238.
162 Escott, *Scottish Congregationalism*, pp. 165-167.
163 *The Evangelist*, 5.1 (January, 1850), pp. 1-2.

Calvinistic Baptists from as early as 1856, the date of the founding of the SBA.

Emigration from Scotland, especially from some Highland communities, served to highlight the tensions between the old approach of the BHMS committee and the newer thinking of the Baptist Union men, though it was not a major factor. Baptists of all persuasions worked happily with members of other churches in the temperance movement, but it appeared to make little or no impact on their attitudes towards the Johnstonian Baptist Union in 1840s. Ministerial education was a key priority amongst Scottish Baptists in the 1830s, but the presence of Johnston as theological tutor, especially after 1848, ensured that Scottish Baptists outside the ranks of the Baptist Union had withdrawn their support for this work until he was replaced by James Paterson, a respected Calvinist, after Johnston's departure to England in 1856. Chapter eight will discuss these developments. The wider consequences of his actions, and those of his colleagues in the Baptist Union, appeared to be missed by Johnston.

Another key factor was the change in policy in the Baptist Union from being a theologically inclusive body at its inception to a militantly exclusive Morisonian body by January 1850. This decision sealed its fate. The reaction to Johnston's controversial book had revealed that he had lost the confidence of the majority of his colleagues. In addition the folly of provoking divisions amongst Scottish Baptists whilst at the same time calling them to unite was a sign of immaturity. Johnston, by the 1850s, had become an obstacle to the union so many Scottish Baptists desired. Calvinistic Baptists in Scotland sought fellowship for the time being with colleagues in England in the Baptist Evangelical Society. This decision was taken due to the lack of options at home in Scotland. Thomas Milner had the mentality of the strict party amongst the Scotch Baptists, from the early 1850s onwards, and it was inevitable that he would find his ecclesiastical home elsewhere. However in the year that the third attempt at Union failed, another group of Baptists arose to take up the challenge of forming a Baptist Union of Scotland. It was not incidental that Johnston had moved to a new pastorate in Cambridge. His later return to pastoral ministry in Scotland was as an older and wiser man and one who adopted an appropriately low national profile. The success of the three previous attempts to form a union of Baptist churches in the midst of this failure was to ensure that by the mid-1850s Scottish Baptists were largely persuaded of the need for

---

164 Escott, *Scottish Congregationalism*, pp.172-173.

a union of churches. Many individuals, such as Peter Grant of Grantown, heartily disapproved of the mud-slinging and doctrinal conflicts and were seeking an inclusive and welcoming union to all Scottish Baptists. The ease with which the next attempt would succeed revealed that the case for union had been established by the previous valiant failures.

CHAPTER 8

The Genesis of the 1869 Baptist Union

The Baptist Union of Scotland was formed in 1869. At its inaugural meeting in October 1869 William Tulloch, a leading Scottish Baptist minister and ardent advocate of union, proclaimed:

> the courting and wooing are all over, and the banns have been publicly proclaimed, in due order, none objecting, and none forbidding, and nothing now remains but the happy consummation of the too-long deferred Union.[1]

These words indicate something of his frustration that the process of combining Baptist churches in Scotland had taken so long.[2] The three previous attempts at union that had failed had been a reminder that for over forty years too few Scottish Baptists had been convinced of the need for a formal association of their congregations. This chapter will explore the reasons why the proposals for uniting Baptists in Scotland had been unsuccessful prior to 1869. It will also indicate those factors that were important in establishing the union formed through the work of the SBA which began in 1856.

The SBA was a body that comprised individual Scottish Baptists rather than being an association of churches. There was, therefore, a measure of continuity between the SBA and the previous Arminian organisation led by Francis Johnston, as that Baptist Union had been reduced from a union of churches to an association of personal members in its last three years of operations from 1853 to 1856. It was known in that period of time simply as 'The Association'.[3] The SBA, by contrast with the Johnstonian Union, did not attempt to

---

1   *First Report of the Baptist Union of Scotland*, (Edinburgh: John Lindsay, 1869), p. 7.
2   Tulloch, the first secretary of the 1869 Baptist Union of Scotland, had followed in the footsteps of his father who had been an ardent advocate of earlier attempts at union. As a Highlander with pastoral experience in Edinburgh and Elgin, he was an ideal choice for his post as secretary, as a man who could bring Baptists in the Highlands and Lowlands more closely into fellowship with each other. I am grateful to Prof. Donald Meek for his comments about William Tulloch in a private communication in July 1999.
3   Chapter seven, pp. 264-265.

take on more tasks than its resources could cover. Its leaders in 1856 made no attempt to engage in evangelistic tours or church-planting initiatives, concentrating instead on building up existing congregations, giving spiritual leadership to the wider fellowship of Baptist churches and providing training for young men preparing for the pastoral ministry.[4] The moves to form a new union of churches did not commence until 1865. There were doubts expressed by some unnamed individuals at the SBA annual meetings in 1865 and 1866, but those individuals in favour of the proposed venture continued to promote the cause until on October 21 1869 the Baptist Union of Scotland was formed in Hope Street Chapel, Glasgow.[5] The SBA by restricting its activities and achieving its limited goals had gained the confidence of a growing proportion of Scottish Baptists in the late 1850s and early 1860s. It was building, therefore, on a strong foundation when the plans to establish a union of churches began to be formulated in the mid-1860s.

8.1 Obstacles that had Hindered Attempts at Union

A number of obstacles had hindered previous attempts at union. The removal of these was necessary before the establishment of closer formal relationships between the Scottish Baptist churches could be effected. One obstacle had been the legacy of division that had been strengthened as a result of the militant Arminian doctrinal outlook of the Baptist Union of Scotland associated with Francis Johnston and Thomas Milner. It must have been clear even to its proponents that restricting membership of the Baptist Union of Scotland to those people whose views were in line with the secretary, Francis Johnston, was severely limiting the number of churches eligible for membership. In the later years of that union, in the early 1850s, it should have been obvious to the participants that Union leaders were not carrying fellow Baptists with them. There were some, like Thomas Milner, who were content to be a militant minority, but few shared his limited vision. The days of strict confessional orthodoxy amongst Baptists in Scotland were coming to an end. The theological climate in Baptist churches had been changing from the 1830s with the result that the boundaries of doctrinal orthodoxy were being extended. One example of this with regard to the divisions between Calvinists and Arminians comes from the career of James Malcolm. He had been the pastor of the Baptist church in Michael Street, Greenock, from 1853 to 1855 whilst also acting as the evangelist of the Baptist Union of Scotland. In order to

---

4   *The Freeman* 2 (September 17 1856), p. 553.
5   Yuille (ed.), *Baptists in Scotland*, pp. 238-239.

hold this appointment his theology must have been acceptable to Johnston and Milner. Yet he was called to the pastorate of the John Street Baptist Church, Aberdeen, in October 1855, a congregation holding to more traditional views.[6] Later, in June 1857, Malcolm accepted an invitation to pastor the Particular Baptist church at Maze Pond in London.[7] Maze Pond Chapel had been particularly noted for its evangelistic efforts in an era when many other Baptist congregations were also zealous in their public witness.[8] This was probably an unsuccessful ministry as he resigned his charge in December 1857. He did receive, however, another opportunity for ministry that December from the Dover Street Baptist Church, Leicester. This congregation was associated with the General Baptists of the New Connexion.[9] Malcolm is an example of a number of Baptists in both England and Scotland who wished to overlook the old differences between Christians who held to an evangelical view of their faith.

It must not be assumed that the most enthusiastic proponents of union amongst Scottish Baptists were those individuals who were indifferent to doctrinal orthodoxy. Hope Street Baptist Church, Glasgow, was the most prominent city church supporting union in 1856. Its minister, James Paterson, and a deacon, William Hodge, the first treasurer of the SBA,[10] were both supporters of the Baptist Evangelical Society in the 1850s.[11] This, as we have seen, had been a Particular Baptist body promoting strict communion principles amongst churches within BUGBI. An early meeting of English supporters of this cause passed the following resolution in April 1841:

> That since in the New Testament, the ordinance of baptism stands prior to admission into the church, and the observance of the Lord's Supper, it is the duty of churches invariably to maintain this precedence by admitting none but persons immersed upon profession of their faith, to the church, to the Lord's table, and other church privileges.[12]

---

6 *The Freeman* 1 (October 3, 1855), p. 590; 1 (October 17, 1855), p. 621.
7 *The Freeman* 3 (June 3, 1857) p. 313.
8 Briggs, *English Baptists of the Nineteenth Century*, p. 298.
9 *The Freeman* 3 (December 16, 1857), p. 762.
10 *The Freeman* 2 (September 17, 1856), p. 553.
11 *The Primitive Church Magazine*, New Series, 15.12 (December, 1858), p. 293.
12 *The Primitive Church Magazine*, New Series, 1.6 (June, 1841), pp. 129-135, cited by Breed, *Baptist Evangelical Society*, p. 5. The numbering of volumes of this periodical is confusing because there were two 'New Series'. See R. Taylor, 'English Baptist Periodicals, 1790-1865', *Baptist Quarterly* 27.2 (April, 1977), p. 66.

The declaration of principle enunciated by this gathering of Baptist leaders came from a group of men to whom doctrinal orthodoxy was very important. The Scottish supporters who were to join their English colleagues in maintaining strict Baptist distinctives,[13] were no less committed to their theological beliefs. Support for the Baptist Evangelical Society appeared to be one of the ties between the different types of Scottish Baptists who had been excluded from the Johnstonian Baptist Union. Paterson, Hodge and other Calvinistic Baptists in Scotland had sought another vehicle into which they could channel their co-operative vision amongst British Baptists. The new challenge for Scottish Baptists in the late 1850s was to enable Baptists with differing theological principles to work more closely together. Uniformity in ecclesiology was not required prior to united action. Scotch and 'English' Particular Baptists had co-operated successfully since 1827 in the work of the Baptist Home Missionary Society for Scotland. It was necessary, however, to extend from this Calvinistic base to include the moderate Arminian Baptists as well.

A second factor that was at the heart of the lack of unity amongst Scottish Baptists concerned mutual forbearance. John MacAndrew of Dublin Street Baptist Church, Edinburgh, read a paper at the 1868 SBA annual meetings in Rose Street Chapel, Edinburgh, on this subject. His title was:'What are the causes which hinder the more complete union of the Baptist churches in Scotland for practical purposes?' He made clear that 'the first cause of hindrance was the want of mutual forbearance'. The report of the meeting noted that his assertion resulted in applause from the gathering, indicating that his opinion was widely shared amongst the Baptist delegates.[14] The principle of forbearance towards fellow-Christians within or outside a particular denomination was easy to accept in theory, but more difficult to sustain in practice. There had been a split in the Tabernacle Church, Edinburgh, over this subject in 1824. On that occasion the debate concerned open or closed views on the relation of baptism to church membership.[15] The difficulties James Haldane encountered in seeking to put his principles into practice in that context is a good illustration of the greater challenges facing those individuals attempting to set up a union of Baptist churches. Scottish Baptist congregations had a variety of different shibboleths that needed to be overcome before such a vision could be transformed into reality.

---

13 Chapter seven, pp. 271-272.
14 *The Freeman*, 14 (October 30, 1868), pp. 863-864.
15 Balmain, *Clyde Street Hall*, pp. 24-25.

A more pressing subject was the debate between proponents of an open or closed table.[16] The traditional position amongst Particular Baptists was that only baptised believers could be invited to participate in the Lord's Supper. There were, however, some Baptists who were influenced by the growing trend in England amongst Particular Baptists to open the table to all believers regardless of their position on baptism. The presence of a growing proportion of ministers in Scottish Baptist churches from England ensured that some of them would raise this matter in their pastorates. This point was especially pertinent with reference to the Pastor's College as it had supplied most of the English-trained ministers in this period. The reason for this was that Spurgeon had been flexible on this question relating to the Lord's Supper.[17] He had made this clear in his address at the opening of the Strict Communion Baptist College, Manchester, in 1872.[18] When this subject was mentioned at SBA meetings it is noteworthy that the example given of a disputation on this subject concerned one of Spurgeon's former students,

---

16 The question of 'Open or Closed Membership' was less important to Scottish Baptists in the Nineteenth Century. A discussion of this subject in Scottish Baptist ranks can be found in K.B.E. Roxburgh, 'Open and Closed Membership among Scottish Baptists', in S.E. Porter & A.R. Cross (eds), *Baptism, the New Testament and the Church: Historical and Contemporary Studies in Honour of R.E.O. White* (JSNTSup, 171: Sheffield: Sheffield Academic Press, 1999), pp. 430-446. This issue was, by contrast, a significant problem for Victorian Baptists, Australia, in the period 1858-1861, and was one of a number of issues that led to the failure of the Baptist Association of Victoria in 1861. This setback, however, like the failure of the Johnstonian Baptist Union of Scotland in 1856, led to a greater determination to succeed with the next attempt at union in the following year, along similar lines to the establishment in Scotland of the 1869 Baptist union. B.S. Brown, *Members One of Another The Baptist Union of Victoria 1862-1962*, (Melbourne, Australia: The Baptist Union of Victoria, 1962), pp.21-36.
17 Spurgeon's views are discussed in T. George, 'Controversy and Communion: The Limits of Baptist Fellowship from Bunyan to Spurgeon', in D.W. Bebbington (ed.), *The Gospel in the World International Baptist Studies*, Studies in Baptist History and Thought Volume 1, (Carlisle: Paternoster Press, 2002), pp.55-57. M.J. Walker, *Baptists at the Table: The Theology of the Lord's Supper amongst English Baptists in the Nineteenth Century*, (Didcot: The Baptist Historical Society, 1992), is also helpful in its discussion of this subject.
18 C. Rignal, *Manchester Baptist College 1866-1916*, (Bradford: Wm Byles & Sons Ltd, 1916), pp. 63-64. Spurgeon's position was also noted in the *Primitive Church Magazine*, New Series, 25.5 (May, 1866), p. 116.

Thomas Medhurst[19]. The 1863 Association report refers to a preaching tour by Medhurst in the north of Scotland. He had been preaching at a small (un-named) Baptist church. The congregation would not allow him to receive the bread and wine during the celebration of communion because he held to open communion principles. It chose to disregard the fact that he was the minister of a church run on strict communion lines at North Frederick Street, Glasgow. Medhurst was, however, invited to pray prior to the reception of the elements.[20] This example was not representative of the majority of churches, but it illustrates the kind of issues that needed to be addressed before closer formal bonds between the churches could be established.

It was not, however, over any particular issue that Scottish Baptists found difficulty in forbearing with one another; rather it related more to the general principle of mutual forbearance. The 1859 Association report was written by John Williams, a Welshman from Pembroke Dock, who had trained for the Baptist ministry at Bristol Baptist College.[21] He had been the first Pembrokeshire Baptist to offer for service with the Baptist Missionary Society, working in Jamaica from 1840 to 1842.[22] After holding pastorates in Particular Baptist churches in Leeds and Walsall,[23] Williams had become the minister of North Frederick Street Baptist Church, Glasgow, in 1851.[24] His report deals with the issue of forbearance at length. A selection of comments from the printed report will make this plain.

> The tide of Christian love and union is rising, and overwhelming much of the evil that has long been the reproach of our denomination in the North. Alas, our unhallowed strifes and divisions have dishonoured our good name, and greatly hindered the prevalence of our principles. There has been much of the old Pharisee spirit abroad. More concern has been exhibited to uphold ceremonial and ecclesiastical practices, for which no clear and direct Scripture authority can be pleaded, than to preserve the weightier matters of the law, mercy, justice, and faith. Meddling, headstrong men -'conscientious believers in *trifles*'- have sought to invest some mean and insignificant crotchet with the dignity of a Scripture principle, and, by attempting to force it down the

---

19 Further information about Medhurst and his time in the Pastor's College can be found in M. Nicholls, *Lights to the World A History of Spurgeon's College 1856-1992*, (Harpenden: Nuprint, 1994), pp. 27, 60-62.
20 *The Freeman*, 9 (October 28, 1863), p. 864.
21 'John Williams', card in Alumni File, Bristol Baptist College.
22 T.M. Bassett, *The Welsh Baptists*, (Swansea: Ilston House, 1977), p. 167.
23 'John Williams', card in Alumni File.
24 Yuille (ed.), *Baptists in Scotland*, p. 173.

throat of everybody else, have rent and torn some of our churches with manifold and most mischievous divisions.[25]

The importance of this 1859 report consists in the public acknowledgement by a significant proportion of the Scottish Baptist constituency that there had been a major problem which needed to be addressed. This issue had been a source of controversy amongst the Scotch Baptists earlier in the century. It had also in a less formal manner afflicted the 'English' Baptist churches in Scotland. There was, however, a new determination to confront and resolve this matter.

The fourth anniversary meetings in October 1859 revealed a new spirit of optimism and determination to press ahead with plans for much closer co-operation between the churches. The report indicated that the desire for union was being expressed by a greater number of Scottish Baptists:

> There is one thing certain, that, as brethren get to know one another better, the spirit of mutual suspicion and distrust, too long the occasion of a widespread and protracted alienation among them, fast disappears. The old but not well- founded cry of heresy – [the] most fruitful source of brotherly estrangement – is quickly dying away.[26]

The 'cry of heresy' had been raised in the past over a variety of issues, but supremely over Arminian or Calvinistic opinions. Accommodation with other evangelical Christians had to be sought, but the resolution of long-standing grounds for conflict between Scottish Baptists would take some time to achieve.

The establishment of a union of Baptist churches in Scotland that would last for more than a decade had previously been beyond the capabilities of Scottish Baptists due to underlying differences between them. This Association of individuals had resolved to confront the underlying problems that separated Scottish Baptist churches prior to becoming a union of churches in 1869. It was this new approach in the context of a greater responsiveness to requests for union that was ultimately to succeed.

Another cause of previous failure concerned the unwillingness of the ministers from the large urban churches in the central belt of Scotland to participate in moves towards uniting Scottish Baptists. In the first and third attempts at union in the nineteenth century there had been some participants from Glasgow and Edinburgh, but an insufficient proportion to give momentum to this process.

---

25 *The Freeman*, 5 (November 2, 1859), p. 665.
26 *The Freeman*, 5 (November 2, 1859), p. 665.

The 1867 annual report of the SBA carefully noted the number of ministers who were present at the assembly in Glasgow. The host city provided ministers representing four churches: James Paterson of Hope Street; Richard Glover from Blackfriars Street; Thomas Medhurst from North Frederick Street; James Chamberlain from Bath Street Church.[27] This represents two thirds of the probably six Baptist churches in Glasgow at that time.[28] One of the other churches, South Portland Street, had been involved in two previous attempts at union since 1827 and thus can be assumed to have been in favour, even if it was not formally represented that year. It was, however, a small church in decline, with an aged minister whose remaining energies were focused on that congregation.[29] South Portland Street did not join the four previously mentioned churches in the 1869 Union prior to the church's demise in 1876.[30] John Street Scotch Baptist Church was the Glasgow congregation that had chosen not to join this process. Edinburgh provided only one representative: Samuel Newman, the minister of the Dublin Street Church.[31] This fact, however, does not give the whole picture, as in previous and subsequent years Charlotte Chapel, Duncan Street Baptist Church and Richmond Street Baptist Church were represented by their ministers in the SBA.[32] These four churches formally joined the Baptist Union constituted in 1869.[33] There were, therefore, four out of six Edinburgh Baptist churches associated with plans for the union of churches. It was the Scotch Baptist churches that chose at this stage to remain outside the SBA.[34] The tide had now turned in favour of union amongst the larger 'English' Baptist churches in the major cities of Scotland.

The Johnstonian Baptist Union, though largely based in Edinburgh, had prior to 1850 a key leader, James Taylor, based in Glasgow. After his departure to a church in Birmingham, the emphasis swung to the capital city and especially to Johnston's own congregation. The SBA was careful to avoid making the same mistakes in this matter. The Minutes of the first SBA meeting, held in September 1856, indicate the participants' desire to form a geographically inclusive body.

---

27 *The Freeman*, 13 (November 22, 1867), p. 928.
28 Yuille (ed.), *Baptists in Scotland*, pp. 169-189, 281-282.
29 Yuille (ed.), *Baptists in Scotland*, p. 282.
30 *First Report of the Baptist Union of Scotland*, 1869, p. 22.
31 *The Freeman*, 13 (November 22, 1867), p. 928.
32 *The Freeman*, 7 (October 30, 1861), p. 697.
33 *First Report of the Baptist Union*, 1869, p. 22.
34 Yuille (ed.), *Baptists in Scotland*, pp. 279-280.

On Tuesday a meeting of Baptists from various parts was held at Stirling, for the purpose of forming an Association for promoting spiritual religion in the denomination; for encouraging and aiding young men in preparing for the work of the ministry; and for affording to the smaller churches in maintaining the ordinances of religion. An excellent spirit prevailed, and resolutions were adopted as to the basis and operation of the Association. Mr W.B. Hodge, who presided, was chosen Treasurer, and Mr William Tolmie, Secretary. The headquarters of the committee will be Glasgow, but the annual conference will be held in various towns.[35]

The policy of rotating venues for the annual assembly was a useful way of drawing Baptists in different places into the work of the SBA. It ensured that the larger churches in the two major cities in Scotland were committed to the work of this body.

> The October Sacramental Fast-day happens to be observed on the same date in Edinburgh and Glasgow, and for some years past the annual meetings of the Baptist Association of Scotland, have been held on this day in these cities alternately.[36]

As a result of this decision the SBA was able to overcome some of the difficulties inherent in previous union attempts and create a solid base of support on which to build for the future.

In addition the premises of more than one Baptist congregation in Glasgow and Edinburgh were utilised in a given year. In Edinburgh during October 1861 the Rose Street and Dublin Street churches provided the venues.[37] Glasgow assemblies were based in North Frederick Street Baptist Church in 1863;[38] Blackfriars Street and Hope Street churches in 1865,[39] and Hope Street and Bath Street premises in 1867.[40] Evening dinner was provided during the assembly in a local hotel to encourage fellowship between delegates. At the 1863 Association meetings held in Glasgow the venue for the evening meal was the Waverley Temperance Hotel.[41] The policy of seeking to involve a number of churches from Scotland's two largest cities in the work of the SBA had the desired effect of increasing the base support for the cause.

A further extension of this policy was the invitation to a wide range of Baptist leaders to chair or speak at the various sessions of

---

35 *The Freeman*, 2 (September 17, 1856), p. 553.
36 *The Freeman*, 13 (November 22, 1867), p. 428.
37 *The Freeman*, 7 (October 30, 1861), p. 697.
38 *The Freeman*, 9 (October 28, 1863), p. 684.
39 *The Freeman*, 11 (November 1, 1865), p. 709.
40 *The Freeman*, 13 (November 22, 1867), p. 428.
41 *The Freeman*, 9 (October 28, 1863), p. 684.

annual meetings. The 1858 annual conference in Edinburgh (besides speakers from associated churches in Glasgow and Edinburgh) included John Pullar, Henry Dickie (Scotch Baptist, Edinburgh), E.B. Underhill (BMS, England), James Culross, and David Wallace (a former supporter of the Johnstonian Baptist Union from Paisley).[42] The 1860 gathering included as speakers William Grant from Grantown-upon-Spey and John Mansfield of Rothesay.[43] The involvement of a minister or layman from a variety of Baptist congregations throughout Scotland was likely to promote the work of the SBA in those churches.

Some churches had assumed in 1856 that this, the fourth attempt at union, would fail as had the previous attempts. Other churches had seen no benefit in the establishment of closer fellowship between Scottish Baptists. The 1861 annual report, though refusing to give details of churches in the above categories, indicated that their numbers were declining in line with the progress of the moves toward union.

> It is very pleasing to observe the steady progress which this institution is making. Five or six years ago when it started there were not wanting those who prognosticated failure, and some of the leading spirits of our denomination showed it but little favour or sympathy. Now, though some few of our brethren still stand aloof, the number of those who do so is becoming year by year smaller, and it is evident the Association is growing in the confidence and respect of the Baptists of Scotland generally.[44]

Although this quotation is a propaganda utterance issued with the intention of persuading more Scottish Baptists to unite with their brethren, there is no reason to doubt the accuracy of its statement. Greater care had been taken to ensure that this was an inclusive association of churches. This approach was to be vindicated when the formal establishment of the Baptist Union of Scotland took place in 1869.

Another reason for the lack of progress towards union amongst Scottish Baptist churches related to the pastoral office. John Macandrew in his address to the 1868 assembly of the SBA stated:

> It had been felt that one cause of the present low state of the churches was the erroneous views entertained as to the importance of the pastoral office, and of having men trained and thoroughly furnished to perform the important functions connected with that office.[45]

---

42   *The Freeman*, 4 (November 3, 1858), p. 668.
43   *The Freeman*, 6 (October 31, 1860), p. 696.
44   *The Freeman*, 7 (October 30, 1861), p. 697.
45   *The Freeman*, 14 (October 30, 1868), p. 864.

This point was a veiled attack on the Scotch Baptists, suggesting that their form of ecclesiology, in particular the rejection of specially trained 'sole' pastors in a church, had been a significant factor in the failure of Scottish Baptists to grow numerically and in their fellowship with one another. It was not without relevance to note that the Scotch Baptists had been reluctant to join the SBA. It would, however, be unfair to suggest that this was due to placing a low priority on Baptist unity. They would have countered any such suggestion with the response that it was because they placed such a high premium on unity within their own ranks that they were reluctant to unite in a formal structure with their 'English' Baptist colleagues. It is, therefore, appropriate to suggest that the differences in church structures between 'English' and Scotch Baptists had hindered progress towards a union of Baptist churches in Scotland.

The main reason for the delay in establishing a united body to co-ordinate Baptist work and witness in Scotland had been due to the lack of desire for such an organisation prior to the 1860s. It was ironically Francis Johnston, the leader of the third attempt at union, who declared at the 1868 Association assembly, in a speech giving reasons for the previous failures, that 'the third hindrance, and the great one, was the want of making a beginning'.[46] In earlier decades this aspiration had been the vision of a minority of individuals and churches who had sought to implement their visions in often contradictory ways. The leaders of the SBA that had commenced in 1856 recognised the need to prepare the ground before setting up a formally structured union of churches. It was as they had overcome this major obstacle to union that a bright future for their hopes was assured.

8.2 Factors that Assisted the Formation of a Union of Churches

The Importance of the SBA Leadership

It is appropriate next to consider the reasons for the success of this fourth attempt at union. The SBA differed from the three previous corporate Baptist bodies by being, until 1869, an association not of churches but of individuals. It is important, therefore, to consider the men who took up the challenge of forming the SBA in 1856. There were five men who attended the opening meeting to consider the possibility of forming a Scottish Baptist Association. Four of the men were well known Scottish Baptists: James Paterson and William Hodge from Hope Street, Glasgow, John Pullar from Perth,

---

46 *The Freeman*, 14 (October 30, 1868), p. 864.

and James Culross, the minister of Stirling Baptist Church. The other man was a Coal merchant and a former pastor[47] of the Stirling church, Thomas Muir (1814-1874).[48] The result of that meeting was that a circular, signed by all but Muir, was issued to Scottish Baptists notifying them of the aspirations of the signatories. The reason why Muir did not sign the circular is unclear, but it was not because he did not support the venture. This is evident from the SBA annual reports. Muir, for example, presided at one of the main meetings at the 1859 assembly.[49] *The Baptist Magazine*, in its October 1856 issue, gave a brief note about 'an important meeting that was held on the 9th of September':

> It appears that it has been thought desirable to establish a 'Baptist Union' in Scotland, and a meeting was called by a circular signed by James Paterson, John Pullar, James Culross, and W.B. Hodge. Twenty-seven ministers met at Stirling, and constituted themselves into the Baptist Association of Scotland; the objects being the revival of spiritual religion in the churches, the encouragement of young men in devoting themselves to the ministry, and pecuniary assistance to the support of the smaller churches. A harmonious spirit prevailed, and resolutions were adopted for carrying out these objects. A committee was appointed of eighteen representatives of eleven of the larger towns; the meetings to be held in Glasgow.[50]

The Baptist Magazine reference reveals some pertinent information. The most important point to note is the numbers of men present from the larger urban centres in Scotland. The failure of previous attempts at union, as already noted, was due in part to this factor. The Stirling link was important. Culross and Muir both took a prominent part in SBA annual assemblies. Culross was a regular speaker at these events, for example, in 1856 and 1858.[51] The Glasgow reference, however, is the most significant point. This is because of the domination of the SBA by Hope Street Baptist Church. The treasurer of the SBA from its inception had been

---

47 This information is given in an article preserved in the records of Stirling Baptist Church. 'Stirling Church Jubilee', in *The Stirling Observer* (May 25, 1904), pp.186-191, documents from this church are kept in the Stirling History Archive.
48 *Scottish Baptist Magazine*, 23.8 (August, 1897), p. 105. Muir's dates are given in Stirling Baptist Church Minute Book August 1852- July 1914, pp. 4, 22, MS in the possession of Stirling History Archive.
49 *The Freeman*, 5 (November 2, 1859), p. 665.
50 *The Baptist Magazine*, 48.10 (October, 1856), p. 628.
51 *The Freeman*, 2 (October 29, 1856), p. 649; 4 (November 3, 1858), p. 668.

William Hodge.[52] He had been a valuable member, and later deacon, of the church after joining that congregation from North Portland Street Scotch Baptist Church in October 1838.[53] The first secretary of the SBA, who held office from 1856 to 1865, was William Tolmie. He was also a member of the church, joining in December 1840 after a change of understanding on the subject of baptism. Tolmie had been a member of 'Mr Anderson's Relief Church, John Street, Glasgow'.[54] James Paterson was not only the chairman at the 1856 and 1857 SBA assemblies but was also given additional responsibilities in 1857. 'Dr Paterson, of Glasgow, had, at the unanimous request of the committee, undertaken the duties of theological tutor'.[55] It may have been seen as helpful for the SBA to have its senior office-bearers from one congregation, but the impression could have been conveyed that, like the previous union, in which in the early 1850s leading officials were mainly from Francis Johnston's church in Edinburgh, support for the cause was limited. It is probable, however, that the reason for this was not a lack of alternative volunteers, but a desire to streamline administrative procedures while the SBA was only an association of individuals.

Paterson, Tolmie, Hodge and Muir[56] had been involved in the Baptist Evangelical Society, the body that united strict communionist Particular Baptists in Britain during the time of the Johnstonian Union. These four 'English' Particular Baptists were prepared to work with Baptists who held different theological persuasions from themselves, but only on a basis of mutual acceptance. A lesson had been learnt from the failure of the third attempt to establish a national Baptist organisation in Scotland, namely, that to succeed it must welcome all evangelical Baptists to be participants. Any repetition of the policies of the first and third attempts at union, in this respect, would end once again in failure.

There were four names on the printed circular advocating the formation of the 1856 SBA. The two men mentioned in the previous paragraph, Paterson and Hodge, would have been excluded from the previous attempt at union, after 1850, because of their Calvinistic beliefs. The other individuals named on the circular, however, would have been associated with it, particularly John Pullar who

---

52 *The Freeman*, 13 (November 22, 1867), p. 928.
53 Hope Street Baptist Church Minute Book 1836-1841, October 28, 1838,n.p., MS in the possession of Adelaide Place Baptist Church, Glasgow.
54 Hope Street Baptist Church Minute Book 1836-1841, December 27, 1840, n.p..
55 *The Freeman*, 3 (October 29, 1857), p. 648.
56 *Primitive Church Magazine*, 4 (December 1, 1858), p. 294.

had been a member of the Baptist Union executive committee. James Culross had been in training for ministry during most of that period and thus would not have been eligible to act as a church representative at Baptist Union meetings. It is clear, therefore, that this circular would have been perceived in the Baptist community in Scotland as a bridge-building exercise between the Arminian and Calvinistic Baptists. John Pullar was by nature a bridge builder amongst Protestants. He was a convinced Baptist, but was involved in a whole range of religious activities. He gave lectures to the London Missionary Society,[57] backed a range of organisations from the Religious Tract Society to the Evangelical Protestant Deaconnesses' Institution, the Perth City Mission, the YMCA, and in addition he cleared the outstanding debt on the Evangelical Union chapel in Perth.[58] He was a committee member of the Perthshire Bible Society in 1828[59] and acted as an organiser of a series of lectures in 1873 by Robert Moffat, the famous missionary, who had served in southern Africa with the London Missionary Society.[60]

James Culross (1824-1899) had been brought up in the Presbyterian tradition in the Secession Church. He was a student at St Andrews University when he became convinced of Baptist principles under the preaching of Francis Johnston.[61] He was baptised by the lay pastor of St Andrews Baptist Church, John Somerville, on 7 March 1847.[62] Culross then studied with Francis Johnston with a view to Baptist ministry from 1846 to 1848. The church at Rothesay was his sphere of ministry from 1848 to1849, after which he spent a few months ministering in Cupar Baptist Church during the vacancy caused by the departure of William Landels to England. Stirling Baptist Church, in 1850, extended a call to Culross which he accepted, commencing a ministry that was to last until 1870. The Baptists in Stirling had gone through difficult days prior to Culross's arrival

---

57 *Perthshire Advertiser*, (December 15, 1867), cited by Albert W. Harding, *Pullars of Perth*, (Perth: Perth and Kinross District Libraries, 1991), p. 144.

58 *Perthshire Advertiser*, (November 2, 1871), and *Perth Courier*, (February 28, 1865), cited by Harding, *Pullars of Perth*, p. 144.

59 *Perthshire Advertiser*, (October 2, 1828), cited by Harding, *Pullars of Perth*, p. 144.

60 *Perthshire Advertiser*, (July 1, 1873), cited by Harding, *Pullars of Perth*, p. 144. See A.C. Ross, 'Moffat, Robert (1795-1883)' in Cameron (ed.), *Scottish Church History and Theology*, pp. 597-598. One of the additional biographies of Moffat, not listed by Ross, is W. Walters, *Life and Labours of Robert Moffat, D.D., Missionary in South Africa*, (London: Walter Scott, 1882).

61 *The Evangelist*, 2.4 (April, 1847), p. 244.

62 Yuille (ed.), *Baptists in Scotland*, pp. 157-158.

and, as a result, he had effectively begun a largely new congregation. It was likely, however, that many of the ninety-seven members present at his induction had attended the main Stirling church under its former Particular Baptist pastors. One former minister, Thomas Muir, had resigned the charge only in 1848 and had remained in the congregation.[63] This factor appears to suggest that Culross was more moderate in his theological persuasion than his tutor if he was acceptable both to the Stirling church and to Johnstonian Baptists.[64] This may, therefore have reduced the potential for differing views on church practices in the congregation. The men who issued the 1856 circular had clear convictions, but saw the need for an inclusive union of Scottish Baptists. All four individuals had experience of working with people from outside their own immediate constituency. This enabled them both to learn from previous attempts at union that had failed, and to be aware of what was needed to achieve their present objectives. It was for these reasons that this fourth attempt at union was more likely than its predecessors to succeed.

James Culross was representative of the new evangelical thinking in the second half of the nineteenth century. The formal Calvinistic doctrinal system inherited by the overwhelming majority of evangelicals was being discarded in favour of a more liberal and exclusively Bible-centred approach to theological endeavour.[65] James Acworth, the president of Horton Academy, around the middle of the nineteenth century, declared sentiments in line with this new emphasis. 'Make your own system' was his constant advice to ministerial students. This viewpoint was supported by the fact that he rarely gave any theological lectures, insisting that the students should directly read and understand 'the Words of God'.[66] Culross, in his published works, drew attention to devotional rather than controversial themes, emphasising evangelical views rather than Calvinistic or Arminian propositions. In his biography of William Carey, the Stirling minister avoided altogether terms such as 'hyper-Calvinism' or 'evangelical Calvinism', even when discussing the transformation of theological outlook from the former to the latter category amongst some English Particular Baptists in

---

63 Yuille (ed.), *Baptists in Scotland*, p. 230.
64 Yuille (ed.), *Baptists in Scotland*, pp. 145, 230.
65 D.W. Bebbington, 'Spurgeon and British Theological Education', in D.G. Hart & R.A. Mohler (eds), *Theological Education in the Evangelical Tradition*, (Grand Rapids: Baker, 1996), p. 217.
66 W. Medley, *Rawdon Baptist College Centenary Memorial*, (London: Kingsgate Press, 1904), p. 26.

the late eighteenth century.[67] Culross described this process of change in the following way: 'Through declension in preaching and life, however, they had been wasting away, while communities more distinctly evangelical gradually took their place'.[68] One of the main emphases covered when discussing Carey's work in India is the Serampore missionary's devotional life. 'Page after page might be filled with similar extracts, but these are sufficient. They illustrate the piety, humility and conscientiousness of the man'.[69] Culross, not only in his own charge, but in wider Baptist circles, was a promoter of pietistic Christianity. It was through this approach and theological understanding that Johnstonian Baptists felt able to associate with the SBA after 1856. The Stirling minister must be credited with this shift in emphasis amongst Arminian Baptists in Scotland.

This pietistic emphasis was not unique to Arminian Baptists. Across the range of evangelical theological traditions in the United Kingdom there was a new focus on personal holiness and the development of the 'inner life', in contrast to the perceived worldliness of many people within the churches.[70] In Scotland the Perth Conferences held from 1861 to 1868 under the able leadership of John Milne, a local Free Church of Scotland minister, promoted this new approach. The titles of the subjects for the morning 'Bible-readings' from 1863 to 1866 indicate the nature of these Scottish Christian conventions.

> In 1863, they were (1) Love to the Father, Son and Spirit, how promoted and how maintained; Love to the Saints; Love to a Lost World; (2) Searching the Scriptures daily; (3) The Believer's position in the world, accepted, working, waiting. In 1864, they were, Progress, Fruitfulness, Holiness; in 1865, Rejoicing, Working, Resting; in 1866, Peaceful, Hopeful, Watchful.[71]

This practical approach to Christian worship and service was carried over into Scottish Baptist circles in the 1860s. The basis of union for the Baptist Union of Scotland in 1869, for example, was not an Arminian or Calvinistic theological statement, but instead a declaration that the Union consisted of 'churches and individuals holding

---

67 R. Brown, *The English Baptists of the Eighteenth Century*, (A History of English Baptists, 2; London: The Baptist Historical Society, 1986), pp. 115-119.
68 J. Culross, *William Carey*, (London: Hodder & Stoughton, 1881), p. 18.
69 Culross, *William Carey*, pp. 74-78.
70 D.W. Bebbington, *Evangelicalism in Modern Britain*, (London: Unwin Hyman, 1989), pp. 151-180.
71 H. Bonar, *Life of the Rev. John Milne of Perth*, (London: James Nisbet & Co., 1869), pp. 337-340.

evangelical doctrines...and who agree to promote its objects and contribute to its funds'.[72] An undogmatic evangelicalism was gaining significant support amongst Scottish Baptists and appeared to be the most popular theological position at the end of the 1860s.

The SBA as an association of individuals had a more limited scope for activities than the Johnstonian Baptist Union. Its threefold purpose was directed at building up existing churches by seeking to stir up their spiritual zeal and by arranging for pecuniary assistance for 'comparatively feeble churches' in order to enable them to sustain 'the ordinances of the gospel'. The other focus was on the training of young men for the work of ministry and the encouragement of the skills of younger men new to the pastoral office.[73] The tone of the sermons delivered at the first annual assembly of the SBA emphasised the nature of this new organisation. 'Addresses of a practical character, bearing upon the objects of the association, were afterwards delivered by the Rev. Messrs [James] Martin, of Edinburgh; [James] Culross, of Stirling; and [John] Williams, of Glasgow.'[74] Unlike the previous union of churches, the new body made no appointment of evangelists or plans for a church extension scheme.[75] These issues would figure in later years, but in the 1850s James Paterson and his colleagues wished to ensure that the objectives of their corporate body could be carried out in full. In this respect the SBA was closer in format to the even more modest SBA that existed from 1835 to 1842.[76]

The Importance of Outside Influences

The climate for united efforts in the 1850s was more encouraging for Baptists than in previous decades. One of the reasons for this was the establishment of *The Freeman* as the national weekly Baptist newspaper. British Baptists of the different traditions subscribed to it, as was revealed by readers' comments listed in *The Freeman* in 1855. Andrew Arthur, one of the pastors at Bristo Scotch Baptist Church, Edinburgh, and Francis Johnston, the Arminian Baptist minister in the same city, were listed side by side.[77] In December 1858 this Baptist weekly newspaper published an article about 'Our Scottish Brethren' expressing concern at the ease with which they

---

72 *First Report of the Baptist Union of Scotland*,1869, p. 4.
73 *The Freeman*, 2 (October 29, 1856), p. 649.
74 *The Freeman*, 2 (October 29, 1856), p. 649.
75 Chapter seven, pp. 236-237.
76 Chapter six, pp. 212-225.
77 *The Freeman*, 1 (April 18, 1855), p. 195.

separated from each other. The article sought to encourage greater co-operation and fellowship between Scottish Baptists, in particular commending the work of the SBA.

> One great characteristic of the Baptists of Scotland has been their strong tendency to disunity and segregation...We are sure, however, we may suggest to our Scotch friends, the importance, in maintaining their individual convictions, of preserving also the unbroken unity of Christian fellowship, and of harmonising personal liberty with church order. We congratulate them on the fact that a more genial and unitive spirit has of late appeared amongst them, and we trust that that spirit will spread until their unity and charity are as marked as their sturdy integrity. Let the churches of Scotland be united, peaceful, and desirous of spiritual growth and increase, and they will find that...they will command and retain the services of ministerial brethren from other parts of the kingdom; while they may be certain that if the churches are divided and contentious their ministers will settle in England as surely as they did when educated there, and that English brethren will be slow to cross the border. We hope and believe that our denomination in Scotland is entering on a period of increased prosperity and progress, and trust the Association will greatly promote its advancement.[78]

There was a growing convergence of opinion between the different streams of Baptist witness in Scotland. Greater co-operation still was encouraged by this Baptist periodical that urged Scots not to rest on the modest progress achieved so far but to aim to attain a lasting bond of association amongst themselves.

When the SBA was set up in 1856 it had an evangelical Calvinistic basis. This statement of belief was mentioned in the 1859 assembly report. The SBA consisted of :

> Baptists who hold the doctrines of free, sovereign, unmerited grace; who view salvation as originating in God, carried forth and perfected by the Word of God made flesh, and effectually applied by the Holy Spirit.[79]

It is important to be aware that though the language is Calvinistic, revealing the doctrinal position of the most influential leaders, it did not exclude evangelical Arminians. The wording of this statement does appear to contrast with Francis Johnston's controversial book *The Work of God and the Work of Man in Conversion*,[80] but very few Scottish Baptists could have declined to agree with the stated propositions. This theological position was in line with that of the

---

78 *The Freeman*, 4 (December 1, 1858), p. 731.
79 *The Freeman*, 5 (November 2, 1859), p. 665.
80 Chapter seven, pp. 266-271.

1835-1842 SBA. It was also similar to a scheme for union devised by the Clyde Street Scotch Baptist Church in 1836.[81] Particular Baptists in England had followed a similar direction in their thinking about the basis of their union. The English Particular Baptist Union of 1812-1813 had been an exclusively Calvinistic one. This basis of union was modified in 1832 in order to provide a more inclusive union for English Baptists, in particular in order to enable the New Connexion General Baptists to associate with them. This was made possible by the withdrawal of the Calvinistic statement of faith and its replacement by an 'evangelical object'. This change was sufficient to allow the formal merging of the evangelical Arminian Baptists with the majority of their Calvinistic colleagues in England sixty years later.[82] Baptists in Scotland, like colleagues in the BUGBI, in the second half of the nineteenth century, sought inclusive rather than exclusive doctrinal statements.

The leaders of the SBA had held a meeting with the leaders of the Baptist Union from England in order to share fellowship together. The English Baptist churches had seen much growth in the 1860s following the revival at the beginning of the decade, but very little if any of the success was due to the minimal structures of the Baptist Union.[83] The meeting was intended to be a learning experience, though without any plans to copy slavishly the pattern set in place by English Particular Baptists. Charles Anderson, the chairman of the business session at the annual meetings of the SBA in 1866, noted that:

> The recent meeting which had taken place in connection with the English Baptist Union had been quite a success, and, although their Union was not of the same character, it was following in the same train, and he hoped it would meet with a like success.[84]

BUGBI, in the 1860s, was composed mainly of Particular Baptist churches, though a small number of New Connexion General Baptist congregations had also chosen to affiliate to this body.[85] The SBA had the task of uniting 'English' Particular Baptists, Scotch Baptists, and Arminian Baptists who had associated with the Johnstonian union. The fact that progress was undoubtedly made towards a

---

81 A. Smith to H.D. Dickie & W. Miller, May/June 1836, Bundle 10, Waugh Papers.
82 Payne, *Baptist Union*, pp. 60-61. J.H.Y. Briggs, 'Evangelical Ecumenism: The Amalgamation of General and Particular Baptists in 1891', *Baptist Quarterly* 34.3 and 34.4 (July-October, 1991), pp. 99-115, 160-179.
83 Tidball, 'Home Missions', pp. 148-154.
84 *The Freeman*, 12 (November 2, 1866), p. 428.
85 Briggs, *English Baptists of the Nineteenth Century*, p. 107.

union of Baptist churches in Scotland in this decade speaks volumes for the vision and dedication of its leaders. Mutual interaction of the English and Scottish Baptist leaders was bringing them closer together. There were still notable differences between the two bodies in that one was a union of individuals and the other a union of churches, but they were both going in the same theological direction, namely an inclusive Baptist evangelicalism that incorporated Calvinists with moderate Arminians.

Another way in which the bond of union between Scottish Baptists was strengthened was in the association of the SBA with the BMS. Scottish Baptists were involved in supporting the BMS in both a personal and collective capacity. It was natural, in the context of a national association of Scottish Baptists, to discuss activities which united them. At the 1857 assembly there was amongst the delegates Thomas F. Hands, who had worked with BMS from 1843 to 1852 in Jamaica,[86] and a Colonel Wakefield, who gave a talk on Baptist witness in India. He had been located for the past thirty-four years in the sub-continent.[87] The 1858 assembly heard an address by E.B. Underhill, one of the secretaries of the BMS, on the work in India. He spoke about the progress achieved since the arrival of pioneer missionaries such as William Carey. It is interesting to note that the Scotch Baptist Henry Dickie was chairing that session.[88] Scotch Baptists had supported the BMS since the 1790s.[89] The focus on BMS during SBA gatherings would act as a bridge to help Scotch Baptists in Scotland identify more closely with the work of the Association. The role of the BMS in bridging the differences between Scottish Baptists was important for the future development of the SBA.

One factor that transformed the spiritual life of many denominations was the 1859 revival.[90] Scottish Baptists were certainly among the beneficiaries. The connection between Baptists in Scotland and the revival was made plain in the 1859 annual report.

> The report, which was read at a business meeting, referred to the origin of the Association as having arisen out of an earnest desire on the part of members of the churches for a larger outpouring of

---

86 J. Clarke, *Memorial of Baptist Missionaries in Jamaica*, (London: Yates & Alexander, 1869).
87 *The Freeman*, 3 (October 29, 1857), p. 648.
88 *The Freeman*, 4 (November 3, 1858), p. 668.
89 Chapter two, pp. 51-52.
90 An excellent detailed study of the impact of this revival in one part of Scotland is found in K.S. Jeffrey, *When The Lord Walked The Land The 1858-62 Revival in the North East of Scotland*, (Studies in Evangelical History and Thought: Carlisle: Paternoster Press, 2002).

the Spirit of God, and to the coincidence that at the very time the same desire had taken possession of the hearts of Christians in America, Sweden, and elsewhere, which had been followed by actual Revival in these countries, and now in this. The report gratefully acknowledged that many of the churches connected with the Baptist denomination had participated in these tokens of God's mercy and grace.[91]

The revival reports in *The Freeman* during 1859 from John Williams, a Glasgow Baptist minister, indicate that it was a pan-denominational phenomenon. Prayer meetings in Glasgow, for example, were held under the auspices of the 'committee of the Glasgow Auxiliary of the Evangelical Alliance'. In Helensburgh Presbyterians, Baptists and Independents united in earnest prayer and formed a large crowd of people. Many individuals were converted and baptised by Baptist minister George Dunn in Drumclare near Airdrie.[92] 'A great awakening has taken place in the North of Scotland, embracing almost all the parishes between Aberdeen and Inverness – a distance upwards of 100 miles'. The impact in Thurso, a town of 3,000 people, resulted in 150 people being added to the membership of two unnamed local congregations. A large increase of this proportion had never been recorded in their previous history. Ayrshire had seen a significant change in social behaviour with a dramatic fall in the number of cases of public disorder for the police to handle. Maybole was singled out as a good example of a town affected by the revival.[93] Eyemouth in Berwickshire had seen 'a remarkable outpouring of the Holy Spirit'. The local population had been only 2,000 people, but almost every home had been affected by the revival. Every night of the week the four churches, Baptist, Methodist, Free Church and United Presbyterian, had been open for prayer meetings with seats quickly taken. 'The most cordial union exists among the ministers of the town, as well as among all Christians. Denominationalism is out of sight, and all are co-operating most heartily on behalf of Christ alone'.[94] Arminian and Calvinistic Baptists were united in favour of the 1859 Revival. The growth in the churches at this time would act as an incentive to further united efforts in prayer and evangelistic activity. The 1861 annual report declared that the SBA '…was designed to promote the cause of revivals'.[95] When the focus was on shared activities such as

---

91 *The Freeman*, 5 (November 2, 1859), p. 665.
92 *The Freeman*, 5 (October 26, 1859), pp. 649-650.
93 *The Freeman*, 5 (December 7, 1859), pp. 744-745.
94 *The Freeman*, 5 (December 21, 1859), p. 778.
95 *The Freeman*, 7 (October 30, 1861), p. 697.

prayer and evangelism, as mentioned in this context, the ties between Scottish Baptists were becoming more firmly established. The 1856 assembly of the SBA linked these two activities. It stated:

> The objects of the association were – first, to promote the revival of spiritual religion in the denomination...The chairman made several remarks on each of these objects, but dwelt particularly on the first, showing the necessity there was for increased earnestness and activity on the part of the ministers, deacons, and members. Addresses of a practical character...were afterwards delivered.[96]

In the context of revival blessings from God the theological differences between Baptists, and those between Baptists and other evangelical Christians, appeared to be much smaller than had previously been thought. William Tulloch, the president of the Baptist Union of Scotland in 1881, in his Presidential address, highlighted what he believed was one of the main sources of encouragement that strengthened ties between Baptists in Scotland.

> The Union was in fact born of a revival...Quickened souls in all the churches ...having been providentially led to co-operate in special efforts on behalf of the perishing, both ministers and people felt how good it was to work together for their common Lord. This excited in the minds of some of us a strong desire to see the body to which we belonged...take its part in so noble a work... The breath of heaven, which was then imparting new spiritual life to multitudes, could breathe on the Baptist churches too, and drawing together the scattered members of the body make them instinct with the life of God.[97]

Promoting the cause of the revival clearly brought many Scottish Baptists closer together and as a result it strengthened the support for the work of the SBA.

One of those shared objectives was the desire to see a greater emphasis on home missionary work in the urban centres of central Scotland. There was concern expressed at the unwillingness of the BHMS to devote more of its energies in this direction. The Johnstonian Baptist Union leadership had complained often about this matter. It had made urban church-planting one of its top priorities.[98] The attitude displayed by the SBA was revealed in a report drawn up after an unsuccessful meeting with the BHMS:

> It was suggested that the Home Mission direct its attention more

---

96 *The Freeman*, 2 (October 29, 1856), p. 649.
97 W. Tulloch, 'Presidential Address', *The Fourteenth Annual Report of the Baptist Union of Scotland*, (Glasgow: The Baptist Union of Scotland, 1882), p. 42.
98 Chapter seven, p. 235.

to the centres of population than it had done, and that efforts like that at Kilmarnock should be encouraged. This the Home Mission declines to do, and it remains with the friends of the association to carry out this recommendation.[99]

In the 1840s and early 1850s it had been primarily the Arminian Baptists that had laid the greatest stress on the need to reach the urban centres with the Christian gospel. Through the auspices of the Johnstonian Baptist Union they criticised the Calvinistic Home Mission for their flawed aims. Now with the SBA largely dominated by evangelical Calvinists, such as James Paterson and Jonathan Watson, there could be no claim that there was a theological reason behind the disputation. It was beyond doubt a matter of practical strategy. The best points from the strategy of the old Johnstonian Union were being carried on in the new organisation, enabling those associated with the former Baptist Union to see a measure of continuity with the previous regime. A policy of consensus was slowly emerging with the hope that one day most if not all Scottish Baptists would work together under the auspices of the SBA.

Some Scottish Baptists sought to work with other evangelical Christians. It is important to note those Baptist leaders from Scotland that had been involved in the process of setting up the Evangelical Alliance in the United Kingdom. In August 1845 a meeting of leaders from the Scottish evangelical churches met in Glasgow to co-ordinate a resolution to invite their counterparts from Ireland, England and Wales to unite more closely with them. All the Scottish Baptists involved in that meeting were evangelical Calvinists. In addition they had previously been involved in attempts to unite Calvinistic Baptists to work more closely together in their native land. James Paterson and Robert Kettle were from Hope Street Church, Glasgow. Alexander McLeod was minister of South Portland Street Baptist Church in the same city. William Innes represented Elder Street Baptist Church in Edinburgh.[100] It is notable that none of the leaders of the Johnstonian Baptist Union chose to be involved in this wider evangelical movement. It was, however, this broader vision of focussing on the principles that united evangelical Christians that enabled the leaders of the SBA in the 1850s and 1860s to prepare the way for the inclusive 1869 Baptist Union of Scotland.

---

99 *The Freeman*, 13 (November 22, 1867), p. 928.
100 *The Free Church Magazine*, 2.9 (September, 1845), pp. 313-314. See also I. Randall & D. Hilborn, *One Body in Christ: The History and Significance of the Evangelical Alliance*, (Carlisle: Paternoster Press, 2001), pp. 18-70, for further details.

A further factor that continued the process of building bridges between Scottish Baptists was the temperance movement. Scotch, 'English' and Arminian Baptists worked alongside each other in the company of other Christians to promote the cause of total abstinence.[101] We have already seen that the most important leaders in the three traditions were committed to this issue in the period from the 1830s to the 1850s. This pattern was in line with Nonconformist denominations in England where, in the 1850s and 1860s, the most prominent younger leaders were total abstainers, taking the pledge ahead of the majority of their contemporaries.[102] It is likely, however, that institutional records of the temperance societies do not present the whole picture. The records of the Scottish Temperance League for 1862 reveal that there were only sixteen Scottish Baptist ministers in membership. This total had risen to only seventeen by 1900. The same register noted, however, that a survey conducted in 1901 had indicated that all 117 Scottish Baptist ministers were teetotal though the overwhelming majority had not registered their position with a temperance organisation.[103] It is probable, therefore, that both grassroots and ministerial support for abstinence was higher than the formal records of temperance societies have indicated. This cause, however, was not as vital to the work of Baptist union in the late 1850s and the early 1860s as it had been in the 1830s and 1840s, because by the late 1850s Scottish Baptists had made greater efforts to overcome their differences.

English Particular Baptist Influences, with Special Reference to the London Baptist Association and the Pastor's College

The next factor for consideration is the possible influence of the Particular Baptist churches involved in the Baptist Union and the Baptist Associations in England. The leaders of attempts at union amongst Baptists in Scotland would have been aware that the Baptist Union in England had struggled to maintain its early momentum. There were many Baptist churches that were not in any kind of association for much of the century. John Howard Hinton, who had been the secretary to the Union through some difficult years, was called to the presidential office in 1863-1864. His address was a personal evaluation of the work of the union of churches and it was not a pleasant picture that he painted.

---

101 Chapter seven, pp. 240-246, and Appendix 5.2.
102 Harrison, *Drink and the Victorians*, 1994, p. 169.
103 *Scottish Temperance League Registers*, 1862-1913, cited by Paton, 'Drink and the Temperance Movement', pp. 348, 351.

Denominational union among Baptists, he said, has been slow in manifestation, and difficult of cultivation. We have long been a divided body, and we are so still; and if any progress at all has been made, it is unquestionable both that much remains to be done, and that the most recent efforts have met with little success...The Baptist denomination, while in name one, is in fact many. If it were an evil spirit it might say, 'My name is Legion...'

In the first place, it is divided into two by a difference of doctrinal sentiments, some churches holding the Calvinistic system, some the Arminian...Of these two bodies the larger, or the Particular Baptists, is itself divided by a doctrinal diversity, according as the Calvinistic system has been found capable of being modified into two forms, which have been called High and Moderate Calvinism.

The Particular Baptist body is further divided by a practical diversity on the subject of communion. It contains churches which restrict fellowship at the Lord's Table to persons who have made profession of their faith by baptism, and churches who admit to communion professed believers in Jesus, although unbaptized. These are called respectively Open-Communionists and Strict Communionists...we have then six parties.[104]

This was an unduly pessimistic utterance from an elder statesman of the Union but it was an indication that all was not well with BUGBI. It is apparent that the workings of this union of churches was unlikely to have provided much encouragement to those Scots seeking to establish their own Baptist union.

The heart of life amongst many English Baptists was their 'county' association. The Western Association and the Northamptonshire Association had been important in the late eighteenth, as well as the nineteenth, centuries.[105] There were, though, other associations that also played a prominent part in the lives of English Baptists in the nineteenth century. Brief consideration will be given to one, the London Baptist Association (LBA), that was formed in 1865. London Baptists were amongst the slowest in the Baptist constituency in England to succeed in organising themselves into a permanent association of churches. There had been various attempts to establish a united witness by the Particular Baptists, but all three of their associations that had been in existence in the early 1850s had ceased operations by 1856 due to divisions over high Calvinist issues. The parallel can be drawn with the situation in Scotland that year when new men were needed to advance the cause of united witness amongst Baptists. The 1865 LBA did not commence in a context of

---

104 Payne, *Baptist Union*, pp. 85-86.
105 Chapter four, p. 134.

high expectations, but it was able to overcome the apathy of many Baptists due to the leadership skills of its most prominent ministers. It is important to examine why this new association was successful when previous ones had failed because this could provide a key for understanding the success of other attempts for union amongst Baptists.[106]

The leaders of the LBA were amongst the most prominent in the metropolis. C.H. Spurgeon was the instigator of this project. He had been visiting James Mursell of Bradford and they had discussed the work carried out under the auspices of the Yorkshire Baptist Association. Spurgeon was particularly impressed by the Loan Fund for new church buildings. Here was a practical need that could be met in London by an association of Baptists.[107] It had been recognised by most London Baptists that the former associations had died out through a lack of aims and objectives, as was stated by *The Freeman* in an article in 1865. 'The old Association of Baptist Churches in the Metropolis...did some good, until at last, through sheer inanation, it died out; killed, because at length it ceased to find anything to do'.[108] Spurgeon had not been involved in a Baptist association of churches, but had now seen a successful model that could be copied. The colleagues that joined him in leadership of the LBA were men who had had some experience of association life. William Brock,[109] who had trained at the Stepney Academy, gained experience from his involvement in the Norfolk Baptist Association prior to commencing his ministry at Bloomsbury Baptist Church in London. William Landels[110], the minister of Regent's Park Baptist Chapel in London, had had greater experience in this matter. He had belonged, first of all, to the Evangelical Union denomination in Scotland. Landels then joined the Scottish Baptists associated with Francis Johnston, who were involved in the 1842-56 Baptist Union of Scotland. Landels probably was aware with hindsight that the Evangelical Union model of association amongst churches would not succeed amongst Baptists. An honest evaluation of the Johnstonian Union's policy of strict doctrinal conformity to its creed

---

106 W.T. Whitley, *The Baptists of London 1612-1928*, (London: The Kingsgate Press, 1928), pp. 58-64.
107 Whitley, *Baptists of London*, p. 80.
108 *The Freeman*, (no details), cited by G. Holden Pike, *The Life and Work of Charles Haddon Spurgeon*, (6 Vols; Edinburgh: Banner of Truth, 1991[1894]), 3, p. 139.
109 Information on the life of Brock can be found in C.M. Birrell, *The Life of William Brock, D.D.*, (London: James Nisbet & Co., 1878).
110 Information on Landels can be obtained from T.D. Landels, *William Landels, D.D.*, (London: Cassell and Company, 1900).

would have shown that it alienated many Baptists who would otherwise have been committed to the project. It was during his ministry in Birmingham that he would have had opportunity to observe the work of the Midland Baptist Association.[111] This body had been in operation for over two hundred years and it enabled Landels to see that Particular Baptists were as concerned about evangelism and church-planting as evangelical General Baptists. This range of experience enabled these leaders and other colleagues to take an inclusive approach in their attempts to unite London Baptists in 1865. This policy is evident from the first meeting of the LBA. *The Freeman* in its report stated:

> The brethren assembled represented well-nigh every shade of opinion amongst us, although, if any party predominated, we should say it was that of our strict communion brethren. Still, it was most apparent that the ruling wish of all present was to give as little place as possible to differences of opinion, and rather to find out the common basis on which they could practically agree.

The commentary by the newspaper affirmed its support for the inclusive nature of the LBA 'We are thankful, too, that the basis of this new Association is so broad...It does not rest on the technicalities of a creed, but simply on the wide basis of evangelical sentiment.'[112] The association had three primary aims: fellowship amongst Baptists, evangelism and church extension. On the last objective the LBA set itself a target of one new church to be erected every year. In the first decade of its existence eleven new chapels were built and one other cause saved from closure. This record was maintained for many years, with Spurgeon alone being instrumental in the foundation of over 200 churches in London.[113] This association was essentially a task-orientated body whose essence related more to what it was going to do than what they chose to believe as a group of churches. The significance of this for Scottish Baptists is that the first and third attempts at union related more to the latter emphasis whilst including the former. The 1835 to 1842 SBA, though it had made little progress in uniting Baptist churches, had had a practical emphasis from the start. This in part was due to the very limited resources of the small mainly Highland churches of which it chiefly consisted. It would, however, point forward to the best way to proceed for future attempts at union. The lessons that

---

111 Landels, *William Landels*, pp. 53-77.
112 Pike, *Charles Haddon Spurgeon*, 3, p. 140.
113 W.C. Johnson, *Encounter in London*, (London: Carey Kingsgate Press, 1965), p. 19. See also M. Nicholls, *C.H. Spurgeon The Pastor Evangelist*, (Didcot: The Baptist Historical Society, 1992), pp. 97-114.

were being learnt in London would act to reinforce the voices of those men in Scotland who had called for a similar basis of union.

A vital part of the LBA's success came about through the Pastor's College[114] that was established by Spurgeon in order to train men as preachers and pastors. In 1869 at the annual gathering Spurgeon declared his satisfaction that 285 students had been admitted to the institution since its inception in 1856, a number, he remarked, which 'is equal to what some colleges have received during a period of fifty years'. In addition 460 other men had attended the evening classes with a view to working as lay preachers or ministers in other denominations. In that year, 1869, 167 men were settled pastors and forty-three had formed new churches including the erection of twenty-two new buildings and eleven branch (mission-hall) congregations. The LBA in this period of thirteen years had grown to encompass 102 congregations, a major increase on the fifty-five churches involved in 1865.[115] Spurgeon's men contributed a significant proportion of the increase in the metropolis. He claimed, at the September LBA gathering in 1877, that his former students had built about forty chapels in London.[116] Spurgeon's College had trained almost 900 men at the time of his death in 1892. It had as early as 1866 one third of the students in the nine Baptist Colleges in the United Kingdom and one third of the income.[117] The college had trained ministers who were to accept calls from churches from all parts of the United Kingdom. In the north west of England, in the period 1860-76, there were twelve new churches brought to maturity by Spurgeon's men and there was a new enthusiasm for evangelism in many of the other churches. The new life in the south stirred up by the advent of Spurgeon to London had flowered in the Pastor's College, and the seed was now being scattered over the north. Students from this institution were in great demand. One example was the church at Tottlebank, in the Lake District, which requested a student to oversee a church it had planted nearby. Thomas Lardner was duly sent by Spurgeon and as a result the church at Ulverston was established.[118] The impact of C.H. Spurgeon

---

114 The name 'the Pastor's College' was retained until 1908-1909 when the institution took the name of its founder and became known as 'Spurgeon's College'. Nicholls, *Spurgeon's College*, p. 99.
115 Pike, *Charles Haddon Spurgeon*, 4, pp. 302-305.
116 Pike, *Charles Haddon Spurgeon*, 6, p. 202.
117 W.Y. Fullerton, *C.H. Spurgeon- A Biography*, (London: Williams and Norgate, 1920), p. 231.
118 W.T. Whitley, *Baptists of North West England*, (London: The Kingsgate Press, 1913), p. 213.

The Genesis of the 1869 Baptist Union

and the Pastor's College had transformed Baptist life not only in London but also in many other parts of England.[119]

Scotland too benefited from the presence of Spurgeon's men in its pulpits from 1859 onwards. John Crouch was called to be the founding pastor of Victoria Place Baptist Church in Paisley in 1866 by eighty-two former members of Storie Street congregation who had been affected by the 1859 revival.[120] James Chamberlain was called from the college to minister at Bath Street Church in Glasgow in February 1867.[121] John Alexander Wilson became the first pastor at Peterhead Baptist Church in 1867. He was inducted to his new position by Professor Rogers of the Pastor's College, a paedobaptist, in the presence of the ministers of other denominations in Peterhead.[122] Falkirk Baptist Church sought assistance from the Pastor's College after its numbers had been reduced to thirty by divisions within the congregation. John L. Spence was the student who accepted the call to that pastorate in 1868.[123] The most significant individual that came from the college to Scotland was Thomas Medhurst, Spurgeon's first student. He was invited in 1862 to pastor North Frederick Street Baptist Church, Glasgow, where he remained until 1869. The work advanced under his leadership, including the establishment of a branch-church in Govan. He found time, in addition to his other labours, for a preaching and lecturing tour to Dundee during which the Lochee Church was founded.[124] Medhurst was also strongly in favour of the establishment of a Baptist Union of Scotland. He was one of the ministers to whom credit is due for the decision to form the organisation in 1869. He had been the acting secretary at some of the meetings proposing union in the period prior to his removal to England.[125] The Pastor's College had contributed not only to the success of the LBA, but also to Scottish Baptist churches which received enthusiastic and well-trained men. The LBA had provided a successful model for union which others might follow.

---

119 Graduates of the Pastor's College were also prominent overseas, for example in Australia and New Zealand where 106 men served during the first ninety years of the college's existence. A figure apparently obtained from the Spurgeon's College records by Craig Skinner, cited by L.F. Rowston, *Baptists in Van Diemen's Land*, (Launceston, Tasmania: The Baptist Union of Tasmania, 1985), p.91.
120 Yuille (ed.), *Baptists in Scotland*, p. 203.
121 Yuille (ed.), *Baptists in Scotland*, p. 171.
122 Yuille (ed.), *Baptists in Scotland*, pp. 99-100,
123 Yuille (ed.), *Baptists in Scotland*, p. 228.
124 Yuille (ed.), *Baptists in Scotland*, pp. 160, 173-174.
125 Yuille (ed.), *Baptists in Scotland*, pp. 238-239.

The College had provided men with great zeal for evangelism and union amongst Baptists who would contribute to the process of establishing a Baptist union of churches in Scotland.

The extent to which the Pastor's College influenced events in Scotland in the period 1856- 1870 is seen by comparing the records of the settlements of the students from the English Baptist Colleges in Appendix 6.1. There were only three Regent's Park College students that chose to accept a call to a congregation in Scotland. John Pulsford settled briefly in Glasgow in 1840,[126] before spending three years at Portland Chapel, Southampton. After twenty years in Baptist ministry in Hull, 1843-1863, he moved to the Baptist church at Offord Road, London. His final ministry was in the Albany Street Congregational Church, Edinburgh, from 1867 to 1886.[127] James Brown transferred from a London charge prior to his induction at Anstruther in 1859.[128] In 1839 James Clark moved from his pastorate in Guilsborough in Northamptonshire to Edinburgh. He had no intention of pastoring a church, but became instrumental in the formation of an unknown Baptist church of which he was the minister from 1841 to 1851, prior to settling in Clifton near Bristol.[129] The Bury College was a new foundation designed to alleviate the shortage of ministers who held to strict communion principles in England. In the early years of its existence there was no surprise that its students all settled in England.[130] The Bristol College had received Scottish students on a regular basis after 1803, the year in which Christopher Anderson had commenced his studies there. The students who settled in Scotland did not play a prominent part in attempts at union, but three men were involved in the SBA which led to the formation of the Baptist Union of Scotland in 1869.[131] They were Thomas Holyoak, Bath Street Baptist Church, Glasgow, 1865 to 1866; William Rosevear, Blackfriars Street Baptist Church, Glasgow, 1869 to 1871; and John Williams, North Frederick Street Baptist Church, Glasgow, 1851 to 1862.[132] The two colleges which had a profound influence on Scottish Baptist churches were at Horton and

---

126 R.E. Cooper, *From Stepney to St Giles*, (London: Carey Kingsgate Press, 1960, p. 109.
127 *The Freeman*, 43, (May 28, 1897), p. 305.
128 A. McColl, *A Hundred Years of Baptist Witness 1860-1960*, (Anstruther: Anstruther Baptist Church, 1960, p. 1.
129 *The Baptist Handbook*, (London: J.Heaton and Son, 1863), p. 113.
130 Rignall, *Manchester Baptist College*, pp. 9-26.
131 Hall, 'Scottish Links with Bristol Baptist College'. N. Moon, *Education for Ministry*, (Bristol: Bristol Baptist College, 1979), p. 144.
132 Yuille (ed.), *Baptists in Scotland*, pp. 173, 181, 281.

the Pastor's College in London. Horton had five former students involved in either the SBA or in the early stages of the 1869 Baptist Union, but none had a leading position in the Association.[133] Francis Johnston and Robert Thomson had been prominent in previous attempts at union. The other three men and their churches were to affiliate with the new union in either 1869 or 1870; John Macfarlane (Elgin);[134] John Grant (Eyemouth); and J.K. Ashworth (North Frederick Street, Glasgow).[135] The honour of making the greatest numerical contribution to the process of union fell to the Pastor's College. In the period 1856-1870 fifteen out of twenty-three English-trained men came from that one college. Appendix 6.2 lists these former students and the churches they pastored at that time. It is also relevant to note that fourteen of these men came to Scotland shortly after the formation of the LBA.[136] Their experience of union amongst Baptists in London almost certainly influenced their decision to associate with the SBA in Scotland.[137] The presence of Spurgeon's men may have been the main factor that lay behind the decision to change the SBA from an association of individuals to a union of churches in the late 1860s.

8.3 From the SBA to the Baptist Union of Scotland

In the 1860s the Baptist laymen and ministers who took leading parts in the work of the SBA increased both in numbers and in the diversity of their theological beliefs. The solid foundation had been established by the five pioneers, Paterson, Hodge, John Pullar, Muir and Culross. Scottish Baptists had been too prone to fragmentation and division amongst themselves. When the SBA was set up in 1856 as an association of individuals this was because a more ambitious scheme was unlikely to win sufficient support from the churches. James Paterson gave the reason in an article written in 1863:'Partly diversity of opinion as to many things, and partly the instinctive love of perfect freedom on the part of the individual churches, rendered it inexpedient to attempt a union of churches'.[138] The climate probably changed in large measure due to an acknowledgement

---

133 *NBES Reports*, 1805/1806-1870/1871.
134 *First Report of the Baptist Union of Scotland*, 1869, p. 22.
135 *Second Annual Report of the Baptist Union of Scotland*, (Edinburgh: John Lindsay, 1870), p. 30.
136 'Spurgeon's College, Register of Students 1856-1871', MS in Spurgeon's College, London.
137 Contra Whitley, *Baptists in London*, p. 79, and in agreement with Nichols, *C.H. Spurgeon*, p. 102.
138 *The Freeman*, 9 (May 27, 1863), p. 332.

that a new basis for union amongst the churches had to be found for the future. Under the auspices of the SBA, supporters of the BES and the Arminians traditionally associated with Francis Johnston learned to co-operate with one another.

The first attempts to change the SBA into a union of churches came at the 1865 and 1866 annual meetings where serious discussion of the proposal resulted in the formation of a committee to look further into this matter. There appeared to be no further advances until 1868 when Richard Glover, minister of Blackfriars Street, Glasgow, proposed a motion that the assembled delegates accepted: 'That a meeting of all who are friendly to a more comprehensive union should be held in January following'. Hugh Rose, a leading Edinburgh Baptist layman, chaired the January 1869 meeting which produced the following resolution:

> That a union of the Evangelical Baptist Churches in Scotland is desirable and practical, and that its objects shall be to promote evangelical religion in connection with the Baptist denomination in Scotland, to cultivate brotherly affection, and to secure co-operation in everything relating to the interests of the associated churches, and generally to further every good work which from time to time may commend itself to the brethren as likely to be instrumental in the conversion of souls to the Saviour.

The decision was now taken to establish the new national body. Final details were worked out at a meeting of delegates during the time of the annual gathering of the BHMS, held that year in Edinburgh, in April 1869. The formal launch Union took place in October 1869.

The SBA that was founded in 1856 was primarily led by evangelical Calvinists, with the exception of James Culross, but prior to 1869 there were a number of men with more 'liberal' theological persuasions, including Oliver Flett of Storie Street Baptist Church in Paisley. He had studied with Culross under Johnston in 1846.[139] Flett, who had been exposed to the newer theological ideas taught by Johnston, had ministered in Baptist churches in Falkirk and Paisley that had had Scotch foundations. As a result of these experiences Flett would have been aware of what was involved in bringing Scottish Baptists of diverse backgrounds together in the SBA.[140] Richard Glover was one of the individuals in 1865 to 1867 who led the moves to press the case for the association of individuals to become a union of churches at each annual meeting.[141] Glover was a strong

---

139 Yuille (ed.), *Baptists in Scotland*, pp. 252-253.
140 *The Freeman*, 12 (November 2, 1866), p. 428.

believer in the cause of Baptist unions of churches. After his move to Tyndale Baptist Church, Bristol, in 1869,[142] he became involved in the affairs of BUGBI, emerging as the leading spokesman amongst those who recommended that all denominational societies should be absorbed by the Union.[143] His forceful leadership appeared to win the day in that body.[144] It does, therefore, suggest that his influence in the smaller Scottish society must have been considerable in favour of the cause of a union of churches. Richard Glover was persuaded to adopt Baptist principles by William Landels during his ministry at Regent's Park Chapel, London.[145] Glover, like Landels, strongly rejected any form of Calvinistic theology, counselling his hearers to 'avoid the darkness of Calvinism'.[146] He was also more than willing to accept the new developments in biblical criticism.[147] It is unsurprising, therefore, that when he moved to Scotland in 1861 that it was to the church recently vacated by Francis Johnston, the premier spokesman of Arminian theology. It was during his time at Blackfriars Street that he persuaded the church to adopt the practice of open communion.[148] The theological climate had indeed changed in Scotland if so liberal-minded a thinker as Richard Glover could act in association with the traditional Calvinistic Baptists.

There were a number of prominent laymen who supported the cause of union. Hugh Rose, an oil and colour merchant, was, in addition, a deacon at Dublin Street Baptist Church in Edinburgh.[149]

---

141 Yuille (ed.), *Baptists in Scotland*, p. 238.
142 Yuille (ed.), *Baptists in Scotland*, p. 282.
143 R. Glover, *The Desirability of a closer connexion between the Baptist Union and the leading Baptist Societies*, (London: Yates and Alexander, 1874), pp. 1-14. Given the history of Richard Glover's support for Baptist union initiatives it was unfair for J.H. Shakespeare, the General Secretary of the BUGBI, in January 1909, to refer to Glover as 'the champion of unbending Independency', *Baptist Times*, (January 22, 1909), cited by P. Shepherd, *The Making of a Modern Denomination: John Howard Shakespeare and the English Baptists 1898-1924*, (Carlisle: Paternoster, 2001), p. 65.
144 *The Freeman*, 23 (April 6, 1877), p. 157.
145 D.T. Roberts, 'Mission, Home and Overseas: Richard Glover of Bristol', *Baptist Quarterly*, 25.3 (July, 1993), p. 108.
146 Richard Glover, 'Lecture Notes on St Paul's Epistle to the Ephesians', 1883, p. 23, MS in the possession of Bristol Baptist College, cited by Roberts, 'Richard Glover', p. 109.
147 Roberts, 'Richard Glover', p. 109.
148 Yuille (ed.), *Baptists in Scotland*, p. 181.

Bailie John Walcot, following his return to business life in Edinburgh, worked for George Callum & Company, 'braiziers, template workers, plumbers, smiths and ironmonger'.[150] Walcot, a member of Charlotte Chapel, Edinburgh, was to be the lay president of the Union in 1881,[151] despite having served as minister of two Baptist churches in England following his attendance at Horton College, Bradford, from 1847 to 1850.[152] Thomas Coats, the sewing thread manufacturer who attended Storie Street Church in Paisley, took part in the annual assembly meetings,[153] later becoming Baptist Union president in 1873.[154] The Coats family, like many prominent Scottish Baptists, also supported the work of the BES.[155] Howard Bowser was another supporter of the BES, who, like his predecessor as secretary, William Tolmie, attended Hope Street Church in Glasgow.[156] Bowser held the post of secretary from 1865 to 1869,[157] and was the first lay president of the Union in 1871.[158] Earlier attempts at union had been organised almost exclusively by the ministers. By contrast, in this process in the 1860s, Baptist laymen made a far greater impact in offering leadership for Baptists at the national level.

When the Baptist Union of Scotland came into being in 1869, the two senior positions, that of Secretary and President were given to men long associated with the Baptist cause. Jonathan Watson, the first President, was the most appropriate man for that office as he had given unstinting service on this matter since the first Baptist Union of 1827. The full-time Secretary of the Baptist Union of Scot-

---

149 A.M. Baines, *History of Dublin Street Baptist Church, Edinburgh, 1858-1958*, (Edinburgh: McLagan and Cumming Ltd, 1958), p. 10.
150 *The Post Office Annual Directory 1869-1870*, (Edinburgh: Murray and Gibb, 1869), pp. 30, 219.
151 D.B. Murray, *The First Hundred Years*, (Glasgow: Baptist Union of Scotland, 1969), p. 61.
152 *NBES Reports*, 1846-1847, (Leeds: John Heaton, 1847) p. 26; 1849-1850, (Leeds: John Heaton, 1850), p. 28; 1854-1855, (Bradford: Firth & Field, 1855), p. 28.
153 C. Binfield, 'The Coats Family and Paisley Baptists', *Baptist Quarterly*, 36.1 (January, 1995), p. 29.
154 *Fifth Annual Report of the Baptist Union of Scotland*, (Edinburgh: John Lindsay, 1873), p. 3.
155 *Primitive Church Magazine*, New Series, 15.12 (December 1, 1858), p. 294.
156 *Primitive Church Magazine*, New Series, 15.12 (December 1, 1858), p. 293.
157 Yuille (ed.), *Baptists in Scotland*, pp. 201, 227, 236.
158 *Third Annual Report of the Baptist Union of Scotland*, (Edinburgh: John Lindsay, 1871), p. 3.

land when it commenced was William Tulloch, the son of William Tulloch of Blair Atholl. Tulloch Sr had done so much to unite Baptists in evangelism in the process that had led to the formation of the BHMS in 1827. He had also been prominent in the second attempt at Baptist union in the 1830s. His son had had pastorates in Elgin and Edinburgh prior to taking up this new appointment with the Baptist Union of Scotland.[159] Tulloch Jr, with experience of ministry both in the Highlands and the Lowlands, was an ideal candidate for the post of Union Secretary. Men from the two 'English' Baptist groupings, the Haldaneites and those individuals associated with Christopher Anderson, had united to form a viable unifying structure for the corporate life of Scottish Baptists.

There were fifty-one churches that covenanted together to form the Baptist Union of Scotland in 1869.[160] It is appropriate to consider which churches chose to join in fellowship in comparison with previous efforts. First of all this union comprised congregations from all parts of Scotland in contrast to the first two attempts at union.[161] The Johnstonian Baptist Union, the third corporate body, had managed to gain additional representatives from the Highlands and Islands as members,[162] but still only thirty-eight out of ninety-eight churches had affiliated (Appendix 4.2). The 1869 Baptist Union of Scotland was able to retain previously associated congregations as well as attract new members, as Appendix 6.3 reveals. It was able to strengthen the corporate presence in the northern mainland with the additions of Scarfskerry and Keiss, but the most obvious change came in the large urban centres of Scotland. Dundee provided two members, Bell Street Baptist Church in the city and Lochee Baptist Church on its outskirts. Glasgow increased its support for united witness from one congregation to four with Bath Street, Blackfriars Street, Hope Street and North Frederick Street congregations taking part. Edinburgh too increased its representation from one to four participating churches with Dublin Street, Duncan Street, Richmond Street and Rose Street Baptist congregations opting to join the united witness. The distinctive factor that ensured the success of this union was the presence of the large and influential congregations in Glasgow and Edinburgh. The ministers of these congregations had objected in 1846 to the Johnstonians calling their united body 'The Baptist Union of Scotland' because it represented only 39% of the Baptist churches in Scotland.[163] In 1869

---

159 Yuille (ed.), *Baptists in Scotland*, pp. 80-81.
160 *The First Report of the Baptist Union of Scotland*, 1869, pp. 22-23.
161 Appendices 4.1 and 4.3.
162 Appendix 5.1.

not only did the Union have affiliated congregations throughout Scotland, but also the concentration of churches in areas where the previous organisation had limited support had significantly increased. No-one could make an accusation such as the one of 1846 against this Baptist Union, though it still had commanded the allegiance of only 50% of the Baptist churches in Scotland.

Appendix 6.4 records that in 1879, ten years after it had been founded, there were eighty-three out of the ninety-two Baptist churches associating with the Baptist Union of Scotland. The remaining churches outside the Union included the Scotch Baptist congregations at John Street, Glasgow, Bristo Place, Edinburgh, Newburgh, Fife, the second Baptist church in Galashiels and Academy Street, Aberdeen. These congregations probably objected to the inclusive nature of this Baptist Union on both doctrinal and ecclesiological grounds. The other non-participating congregations were very small and it is probable that this, rather than theology, was the main reason for their failure to associate. A total of 90% of Scottish Baptist churches had formally identified with the national organisation by 1879.[164] Even in the congregations that chose to remain outside its ranks there were individuals who became personal members of the Union, for example, William Grant, a pastor at Bristo Place, Alexander Thomson, a pastor at the second church in Galashiels, and Alexander Grant, one of the pastors in John Street, Glasgow. Those individuals who had laboured so long could now rest assured that their dream had become a lasting reality. The need for a Baptist Union, and its continued existence, was now taken for granted. Ten years after the establishment of the 1869 Baptist Union its permanence was guaranteed, a notable achievement given the battles fought over this body in the previous fifty-two years since 1827.

8.4 Union for the Provision of Theological Education

The final and most important factor in the process that resulted in the 1869 Baptist Union of Scotland was the need to unite for the provision of theological education in order to train men for the Baptist ministry. The demand for a better education system had been felt throughout Scotland for the whole of the nineteenth century, culminating in 1872 with a government-controlled system of school edu-

---

163 Chapter seven, pp. 252-254 and Appendix 4.2.
164 *The Baptist Handbook*, (London: Yates and Alexander, 1879), pp. 234-236. *Eleventh Annual Report of the Baptist Union of Scotland*, (Glasgow: Baptist Union of Scotland, 1879), pp. 14-16.

cation.¹⁶⁵ The reasons for the rising standards were quite complex. One example of this was religious rivalry after 1843 between the Free Church of Scotland and the Church of Scotland. These two denominations both set up local schools as they strove to be not only the national church but also the best provider of schools for the people of Scotland.¹⁶⁶ The Free Church had the vision of achieving the ideal promoted by the sixteenth-century Scottish Reformers, as expressed in the *First Book of Discipline*, of educating each person up to their full potential, regardless of their ability to pay. This plan included, for males, university education with appropriate career opportunities to follow.¹⁶⁷ The style of training courses for potential ministers in Scotland became more academic as the century progressed, in line with the Presbyterian vision of an educated ministry.¹⁶⁸

British Baptists were also acutely aware of the need for educated ministers. One Baptist minister in the early nineteenth century, Thomas Lewis, who was conscious of his own lack of adequate training, declared 'I feel my great deficiencies, O, what an advantage is learning as the handmaid of religion! I cannot esteem it too highly. I bewail the lack.'¹⁶⁹ John Ryland, minister of Broadmead Baptist Church and President of the Bristol Education Society from 1792 to 1825, was convinced of the need for an educated ministry. 'It is highly expedient that every large body of Christians should possess some learned ministers and the greater their numbers and attainments the better', he said in an address at Stepney Academy in 1812. 'An illiterate, though pious ministry must be exposed to needless contempt.'¹⁷⁰ A thorough education, though, was not merely to aid the student in his future endeavours, for it was also essential if the respect of the congregation was to be gained and maintained. Isaac Mann, pastor of the Maze Pond Chapel in London,¹⁷¹ drew attention to this issue in 1829 when he argued that Baptists

---

165 R.D. Anderson, *Education and the Scottish People, 1750-1913*, (Oxford: The Clarendon Press, 1995), pp. 24-49.
166 R.D. Anderson, *Education and Opportunity in Victorian Scotland*, (Oxford: The Clarendon Press, 1983), p. 10.
167 S.J. Brown, 'The Disruption and the Dream: The Making of New College 1843-1861', in D.F. Wright & G.D. Badcock (eds), *Disruption to Diversity Edinburgh Divinity 1846-1996*, (Edinburgh: T. & T. Clark, 1996), pp. 33-34.
168 Wright & Badcock (eds), *Disruption to Diversity*, pp. 221-254.
169 J. Burrell, *Memoir of Rev. Thomas Lewis of Islington*, (London: Ward and Co., 1853), p. 24.
170 J. Ryland, *Advice to young ministers respecting their preparatory studies*, Bristol, 1812, cited by Moon, *Bristol Baptist College*, p. 28.

needed to keep up with trends in general education, otherwise their congregations would seek 'a more enlightened ministry'.[172] In the first half of the nineteenth century new Baptist colleges were opened at Horton and Stepney in England and Abergavenny and Llangollen in Wales, but the proportion of trained Baptist ministers in churches had reached only 45% between 1830 and 1859. There was, however, a significant increase to 67% for men who entered the ministry between 1850 and 1879.[173] Samuel Green, the President of Rawdon College,[174] was convinced by 1871 that debates over the education of ministers were to be centred only on the form, rather than on the principle, of theological training. At the autumnal session of the BUGBI that year he declared that

> There are questions which it is now unnecessary to re-open. Even those among us who most unfeignedly rejoice in the success of unlettered evangelists will not question the value of an educated ministry. It will not be maintained that there is anything in high mental training to make the preacher ineffective, the pastor careless, or the man undevout.[175]

If theological qualifications, however, were the mark of respectability then Baptist pastors still faced a serious shortfall, as a mere 10% of men entering college between 1870 and 1899 had obtained a degree, compared to 20% of Congregational ministers in the same period of time.[176] The Pastor's College, founded in 1856, however, had a different ethos regarding educational attainment, from that of Regent's Park College, formerly Stepney College, prior to 1856,[177] for example. Spurgeon made it plain that his institution was founded to train and equip 'a class of ministers who will not aim at lofty scholarship, but at the winning of souls – men of the people who might otherwise receive no training.'[178] The principle of the necessity of training for ministry was admitted by the vast majority of British Baptists. The debate centred on the nature of the

---

171 J.H.Y. Briggs, 'Mann, Isaac', in Lewis (ed.), *DEB*, II, p. 738.
172 D.M. Himbury, 'Training Baptist Ministers', *Baptist Quarterly*, 21.8 (October, 1966), p. 343.
173 Brown, *Nonconformist Ministry*, p. 67.
174 J.O. Barrett, *Rawdon College 1804-1954: A Short History*, (London: Carey Kingsgate Press, 1954), p. 56.
175 S.G. Green, *Education For The Ministry*, (London: Yates and Alexander, 1871), p. 4.
176 Brown, *Nonconformist Ministry*, p. 83.
177 Cooper, *Regent's Park College*, pp. 60-61.
178 Anon., *Charles Haddon Spurgeon: A Biographical Sketch*, (London, 1903), p. 139, cited by J.E.B. Munson, 'The Education of Baptist Ministers, 1870-1900', *Baptist Quarterly*, 25.7 (July, 1976), pp. 332-324.

courses that students would be expected to follow.

'English' and Haldaneite Baptists in Scotland had seen the need for an educated ministry since the beginning of the nineteenth century, and by the 1830s the majority of their Scotch colleagues had also indicated their support.[179] The main focus for discussion, though, amongst Scottish Baptists was regarding the proposal for a ministerial training college in their native land. This issue, however, was to take another quarter of a century before its resolution in 1894 with the establishment in Glasgow of the Baptist Theological College of Scotland.[180] The demand for an educated ministry, though, did not exclude spiritual qualities. An adequately trained Baptist minister, by the late 1850s, was expected to have both spiritual and scholarly qualifications before commencing his vocation.[181] The high educational standards in Scotland made Scottish Baptist ministers an attractive proposition to English congregations in the third quarter of the nineteenth century.[182] Scottish Baptists, however, had valued training and preparation for ministry throughout the nineteenth century even if their modest numerical strength had ensured that a permanent college would not be set up until almost the end of the century.

The SBA had as one of its main objectives 'the encouragement of young men in devoting themselves to the ministry'.[183] The leading promoter of this object was James Paterson, who was appointed as the sole tutor of Baptist ministerial students. The tuition was given on the premises of the Hope Street Church, in Glasgow. There were twenty-two men who were trained in this setting, including George Yuille who was later to become Secretary of the Baptist Union of Scotland. The great importance of this objective was taken over into the 1869 Baptist Union of Scotland. Its third object stated:'to aid young men of approved piety and talent in preparing for the work of the Christian ministry'. James Culross, at the opening meetings of the Baptist Union in 1869, delivered a powerful address on this subject. He was appointed the new tutor in place of James Paterson who wished to retire from this post at the age of sixty-seven.[184] Scottish Baptists had held to different theological systems and wor-

---

179 Chapter six, pp. 215-220.
180 Yuille (ed.), *Baptists in Scotland*, pp. 239-240, 253-259.
181 Bebbington, 'Spurgeon and British Evangelical Theological Education', pp. 1-3.
182 Brown, *Nonconformist Ministry*, pp. 46-47.
183 *The Baptist Magazine*, 48.10 (October, 1856), p. 628.

shipped in different traditions in the period 1836-1869, but a large number of them were convinced, throughout this period, of the necessity of providing opportunities for theological training. This issue served consistently to unite Scottish Baptists during decades of disagreement on other matters and continued to have that effect in the late 1850s and early 1860s. Other factors such as the impact of the evangelical revival and especially the presence of Spurgeon's men in post as ministers in a large minority of the churches in the mid to late 1860s may have been more influential later. But over a longer period concern for the training of ministers was probably the most important factor in uniting Scottish Baptists, so ensuring the success of the fourth and final attempt to establish a Baptist Union of Scotland.

In conclusion there had been many obstacles in the way of forming a union of Baptist churches in the period 1856 to 1869. Doctrinal differences between Calvinists and Arminians had caused the failure of the third attempt at union. This problem had been overcome partly by the removal of militant Arminians from Scottish Baptist circles in the mid-1850s, but also by the inclusive nature of the SBA. Its doctrinal statement, though Calvinistic, did not exclude evangelicals with broader views. Mutual forbearance on many issues such as open or closed communion and the nature of the pastoral office increased as Scottish Baptists were determined to maximise their unity for the common good. The failure of churches in the large towns to participate in attempts at union had been a problem in the past, though now they were supporting this venture. Indifference and an assumption that attempts to establish a union of churches would fail were overcome through careful preparation and a willingness to move forward at a pace that would carry the majority of churches with the leadership of the SBA.

Wider influences upon Scottish Baptists included involvement in the setting up of the Evangelical Alliance and participating in the after-effects of the 1859 revival. The regular features at SBA annual meetings of representatives or missionaries from the BMS enabled delegates to remember that they were part of a much wider Baptist family. The English Particular Baptists' basis of union in 1832 had prepared the way for evangelical Arminians to join in the union alongside their Calvinistic colleagues. The willingness of the leaders of the 1856 to 1869 SBA to welcome all evangelical Baptists into their midst ensured that the lesson had been learned from the mistakes of others. The Association was led in large measure by men

---

184 *First Report of the Baptist Union of Scotland*, 1869, pp. 4, 11-15. Yuille (ed.), *Baptists in Scotland*, pp.237-240. Murray, *Scottish Baptist College*, pp. 5-6.

who held strict communionist Particular Baptist views, but could also accommodate liberal-minded Arminians such as Richard Glover. That degree of comprehension at the level of leadership ensured that this co-operative venture would be inclusive of all Baptists who desired to take part.

It is instructive to note that even with an established Baptist Union, many English Baptists in this era were as reluctant as their Scottish counterparts to work closely with each other. The LBA served as a useful model of a successful union. The absence of an exclusive doctrinal basis and clear practical objects led many to join its ranks. The LBA was formed in 1865. It was soon making rapid progress in uniting London Baptists by engaging them in co-operative ventures such as church-planting. The Pastor's College provided not only extra ministers for the London area but also for the north of England and Scotland. The presence of so many Spurgeon's men in Scottish Baptist pulpits in the late 1860s was highly significant in the transformation of the SBA into the Baptist Union of Scotland. An association of individuals was changed into a union of churches. The individuals who had led the SBA since its foundation in 1856, however, were of greater importance. They had been able on the basis of mutual respect to unite Scottish Baptists, enabling a growing number of them to join in the union of churches.

The most important factor, however, deals with ministerial training. Scottish Baptists were divided on how best to train their prospective ministers, but were united in seeking to improve the opportunities for these men. It was crucial that there was a good contingent from each sector of the Baptist constituency in Scotland working on this problem. In each of the attempts to unite Scottish Baptists, after 1836, ministerial education was always one of the most important objectives. This consideration alone was not sufficient to guarantee the formation of the Baptist Union of Scotland, but it was the most important of the factors involved in this process in setting in place an Association on which a union of churches could be built. The presence of Spurgeon's men may have been decisive in the late 1860s, but their influence came to bear on a body of men already convinced of the benefits of mutual co-operation.

CHAPTER 9

Conclusions

This book has shown that many Scottish Baptists desired to belong to a common Baptist family in Scotland for the majority of the nineteenth century. In fact, conversations regarding unity between the different Baptist traditions had taken place as early as 1806, though a further sixty-three years were to elapse before a successful conclusion was reached. There were various obstacles that prevented closer fellowship between Baptists holding divergent understandings of Baptist principles. In conclusion we will consider both those issues that either hindered or helped the process towards union in the light of other studies of Scottish social and ecclesiastical history, as well as British Baptist developments in this period, prior to drawing some overall conclusions.

There were three ecclesiological traditions in the Baptist community in Scotland in the early part of the nineteenth century. The largest group consisted of the Scotch Baptists whose beliefs and practices were largely shaped by Archibald McLean, an inspirational leader who was the senior pastor of their Edinburgh congregation. The unity of that connexion largely revolved around his person. Prior to 1810 this group of churches saw much encouragement with new members and churches being established, but internal disputes over doctrinal and practical issues that had resulted in the division of 1810, followed by another split in 1834, caused a fatal weakening that hindered further growth. The main issue at the heart of their difficulties was the inability to exercise forbearance with each other on any doctrinal issue or church practice. It was evident, therefore, that even before any schemes for Baptist union amongst the churches had been proposed the Scotch Baptists would struggle with the necessity of being more flexible in their ecclesiology in order to arrive at any kind of agreement with their fellow Baptists.

The second group of Scottish Baptist churches was associated with Robert and James Haldane. This part of the Baptist community, like the Scotch Baptists, had strong leadership provided by these influential preachers who also provided the necessary pecuniary assistance to pay many of their pastors' salaries. The imposing presence of the Haldane brothers ensured that their colleagues were likely to keep in step with them. The Baptist constituency in Scotland grew by twenty-three churches in the years 1808 to 1810, after the adoption of Baptist principles by these two men. The total number of Scottish Baptist churches reached forty-eight by 1810. The fact that nearly half of the congregations had a close link to the Haldanes indicated that their voices would carry additional weight in any discussions about united Baptist ventures in Scotland.

Robert Haldane had been a strong proponent of uniting the churches that had been launched in association with the work of the SPGH at the end of the eighteenth century. The conflict between the elder Haldane and Greville Ewing led Robert Haldane after 1808 to revise his opinions on the nature of fellowship between Christian churches. He had come to the conclusion that there was little benefit in formal connexional structures. The undenominational 'catholic' Christianity so prominent at the end of the eighteenth and the beginning of the nineteenth centuries probably underlay his vision of the future for evangelical Christian churches.

James Haldane, the pastor of the Tabernacle congregation in Edinburgh, showed a greater awareness than his brother of the need for Baptists to work together in his native land. He did share, though, Robert's pan-evangelical vision as the ideal, but realised in practice the importance of co-operation between different congregations, especially in home mission. Unenthusiastic support sums up his approach to any scheme for a formal association of Baptist congregations. The significance of his position when combined with that of his brother, allied to the extreme caution of the Scotch Baptists, indicated that the prospects for a union of Scottish Baptist churches looked bleak in the early years of the nineteenth century.

The 'English' Baptists were by far the smallest sector of the Baptist constituency in Scotland from 1800 to 1820, but their vision and influence, and later their numbers, were to predominate in Scottish Baptist circles by the late 1830s. These Baptists identified with the English Particular Baptists due to a common understanding of theology and church practices. Christopher Anderson, their most prominent minister, had been impressed by association life amongst Calvinistic Baptists in England as early as 1805, but the weakness of the 'English' Baptist congregations in Scotland made it inevitable that any plans for an association of churches there would not be attempted for over twenty years.

One of the issues that provoked no disagreements between Scottish Baptists was the necessity for home mission work. All three Baptist streams had their schemes for the promotion of the Christian gospel, especially in the Highlands of Scotland. We have seen an outline of the early history of the three societies and the process by which they were united in one organisation, the BHMS, in August

Conclusions

1827. This society was extraordinarily successful in carrying out its work. The Baptists comprised a mere 1% of the Scottish population yet they provided the funds to cover the expenses for missionaries to cover nearly all the rural areas of the country with their evangelical message. In contrast to the limited support by English Particular Baptists of their own home mission organisation, the BHMS gained the affectionate support of its constituency. The success of the BHMS in raising funds to assist preachers and congregations in rural areas caused some Scottish Baptists to question the necessity of a Baptist Union of churches in addition to this body. There were, however, some weaknesses in the strategy of the BHMS, notably its lack of vision for the evangelisation of the urban masses. Francis Johnston and James Paterson were two of a number of Scottish Baptist ministers who at different times would raise this issue with their fellow Baptists. It was, therefore, no surprise that attempts would be made to strengthen the ties between Scottish Baptist congregations.

The first scheme proposing a formal union of Scottish Baptist churches was launched in the spring of 1827 at the same time as plans were being drawn up to unite the home mission organisations. The prospects for the success of the two projects appeared to be promising, but whereas the BHMS fulfilled its potential the Baptist Union of Scotland foundered within a short space of time. It is unfortunate that the only information that has survived about this body comes from the papers of one church, Clyde Street Hall, Edinburgh. This congregation was the first to withdraw from this venture when problems caused tension within the executive committee of the Baptist Union and, as a result, no documentation has apparently survived from the period after 1828. The stumbling-block that had led to the dissolution of this union was the request for admission by an Arminian Baptist, James Watson from Montrose. In the late 1820s it is probable that the majority of Scottish Baptists would have declined to allow the Montrose congregation and minister to affiliate to the Baptist Union. There were, however, others on the committee and in the constituency who took the opposing position, not least Watson's brother Jonathan Watson, the minister of Cupar Baptist Church. The Cupar minister was known to hold liberal views on a number of issues including support for an open communion table and open membership in Baptist churches, attitudes which his colleagues either accepted or tolerated. Accommodation with Arminians, however, was a step too far for many Scottish Particular Baptists. The issue of whether Arminians and Calvinists could be accommodated within the same union of churches would continue to be raised in successive attempts to bring together Baptist churches in Scotland. It was one of the major obstacles to be overcome in the middle of the nineteenth century.

The next attempt to unite Scottish Baptists took place between 1835 and 1842 with the formation of the SBA. The most obvious weakness of this body was the fact that a mere 16% of Scottish Baptist churches chose to affiliate with it. The majority of these churches were small Highland congregations based mainly in Perthshire. There was no interest from the larger congregations in Glasgow and Edinburgh; nor was much support forthcoming from the Scotch Baptist constituency. It was not surprising that this, the most conservative group of Scottish Baptists, had largely declined to participate in this venture because their own ranks had been decimated by the 1834 divisions. It is possible that disappointment from the failure of the previous Baptist Union had not sufficiently dissipated in order to give this association a chance to succeed. One thing was clear, however, an insufficient proportion of Scottish Baptists, in the 1830s and early 1840s, saw the need for a union of churches as a priority issue.

One man, Francis Johnston, was to dominate the Baptist Union of Scotland that existed from 1843 to 1856. His vision for closer ties amongst Scottish Baptists and above all for evangelistic enterprises amongst the urban communities of the central Lowlands was clear and inspiring to his colleagues. In the early years of his Baptist Union, 1843 to 1845, there was the potential to provide a framework that could have united a majority of Scottish Baptist congregations. Johnston, an Arminian Baptist, in these early years of his ministry in Cupar and as secretary of the Union, had sought to emphasize the bonds of unity between Scottish Baptists rather than highlight their differences. This conciliatory approach probably contributed to the decision by the Calvinistic leaders of the BHMS to offer to unite their operations with those of Johnston and his colleagues. The olive branch was rejected by the executive committee of the Baptist Union after months of reflection under the influence of its leader. This was the critical turning point in the fortunes of this Baptist Union of Scotland. Its numbers of affiliated churches may have continued to grow until in 1850 39% of the constituency had indicated their support, but its credibility was severely damaged. In 1827 through the auspices of the BHMS, the Haldaneite and 'English' Baptists had been brought together, leading them to share a common identity in the decades that followed. As a result of this development there were then only two Baptist streams in Scotland. The decision of the leaders of the Johnstonian Baptist Union to create a third constituency, parallel to the Evangelical Union, created a situation that appeared to place Baptist relationships in as weak a state as they had been in the early decades of the nineteenth century. Despite his good intentions, Johnston had set back the chances of a successful Baptist Union for another twenty years.

The polarising of the Scottish Baptist constituency not surprisingly led a significant number of Calvinistic Baptists to seek fellowship with like-minded colleagues in England, in particular with the strict communion Particular Baptists that united under the name of the Baptist Evangelical Society. In the 1850s the obstacles to union appeared to be even greater than prior to the 1827 Baptist Union of Scotland. The crucial difference on this occasion was that a clear majority of Scottish Baptists had been persuaded of the need for a union of churches. The problem to overcome was how to incorporate Baptists with different theological positions in the same organisation. The practical questions raised over the admission of James Watson in 1827 had re-emerged as a point of principle. The ability of the leaders of the next attempt at union to address this question successfully leads on to the factors that contributed to the formation of the Baptist Union of Scotland in 1869.

Scottish Baptists were involved in three unsuccessful attempts at resolving their differences prior to the establishment of the Baptist Union of Scotland in 1869. There were a number of factors that contributed to this process of building bridges between Scotch, 'English', and Johnstonian Baptists. First of all, they shared the same desire to support missionary activity at home and overseas. The Scotch Baptists had been generous supporters of the BMS since the 1790s and in their commitment they were followed by the other groups in later years. The merger of the home missionary societies in 1827 produced one of the strongest bonds between the three original streams in this constituency, resulting in closer ties of fellowship with each other, with the exception of the more conservative Scotch Baptists. The impact of the BHMS in uniting Scottish Baptists was, however, primarily felt in the 1820s to 1840s. After this time other factors were of greater importance.

The temperance cause in Scotland was wholeheartedly supported by the key younger leaders who were involved in moves towards union. The ability to work not only with fellow Baptists but with other Christians too would reveal the potential impact of union with others who shared the same aspirations for a union of Baptist churches in their own country. It is impossible to prove, and probably inaccurate to state, that all supporters of temperance work in the Baptist community in Scotland were in favour of a union of churches, but it was true that a great majority of their leaders had taken the pledge. George Barclay, James Paterson, Peter Grant, James Taylor, William Landels and Francis Johnston were amongst the most prominent temperance activists who were also public advocates of a union of Baptist churches. Temperance was of course only one of many causes in which evangelicals co-operated in the nineteenth century. This issue is a good example of a wider phenomenon in which those individuals who were most enthusiastic about participating with other Christians to advance different objectives were more likely to work with fellow-Baptists in the cause of a union of churches. Publications such as *The Edinburgh Almanac* reveal the hive of activities in which these men were engaged. These included Bible, missionary, religious tract, Gaelic School and anti-slavery societies; in addition, city mission activities and support for the Evangelical Alliance.[1] The ability to co-operate with Christians of different theological persuasions in order to achieve common objectives indicated the kind of flexibility required to set up a Scottish Baptist Union.

The commencement of *The Freeman* in 1855 as the national weekly Baptist newspaper provided an opportunity for Scottish Baptists to recognise that they were a part of a larger Baptist community in Britain. The proprietors of this newspaper, though, had clear opinions about their brethren in Scotland, in particular, concerning the ease with which they were willing to separate from one another. A clear message was communicated commending a united witness between the churches in order to realise the spiritual prosperity that would result from such a decision. Scottish Baptists would not be unaware of the closer ties in England between the New Connexion General Baptists and the Calvinistic Baptists since the 1832 reorganisation of the Baptist Union. The clearest sign of this new relationship was seen in the presidential office of BUGBI having been held twice by Arminian Baptists, namely J.G. Pike in 1842[2] and Jabez Burns in 1855.[3] Scottish Baptists on their own initiative were responsible for each of their attempts at union, but the English encouragement towards merger between the different types of Baptists in Scotland was now more evident in the late 1850s than it had ever been before.

An even greater English influence came from the London Baptist Association formed in 1865. It served as a model union showing how Calvinistic and Arminian Baptists could work together to

---

1   For example: *The Edinburgh Almanac for 1835*, (Edinburgh: Oliver & Boyd, 1835), pp. 443-453; *The Edinburgh Almanac for 1850*, (Edinburgh: Oliver & Boyd, 1850), pp. 506-510.
2   Payne, *Baptist Union*, p. 65.
3   J.H.Y. Briggs, 'Evangelical Ecumenism: The Amalgamation of General and Particular Baptists in 1891', *Baptist Quarterly*, 34.3 (July, 1991), p. 105.

achieve practical ends such as church-planting. It had an inclusive distinctive doctrinal basis that could incorporate both Charles Spurgeon, the champion of Particular Baptists, and William Landels, the advocate of Arminianism. The growing numbers of men trained in London at the Pastor's College who had settled in pastorates in Scotland brought with them that confidence in the importance of a united witness amongst Baptists. It was probably the presence of these men that provided the decisive momentum in the late 1860s behind the establishment of the Scottish Baptist Union.

The leadership of the 1856 SBA (of individuals) that guided the steps towards the establishment of a union of churches in 1869 must be given credit for their achievements. Their enthusiasm alone was insufficient to ensure success. It required a mature leadership taking their constituency with them at a pace it could accept. This association of pastors and lay-leaders had to build bridges after removing the barriers erected between Scottish Baptists in the later years of the Johnstonian Union. The extent of their achievement can be seen in the creation of a body that could accept both Scotch Baptists and the more liberally-minded Arminians such as Richard Glover. James Paterson and his fellow leaders enabled their colleagues to gain confidence in each other prior to inviting the churches to merge in another union. This policy may have taken thirteen years, but it ensured that the Baptist Union of Scotland began in 1869 on a solid foundation of support. There were fifty-one out of 101 churches that had affiliated to the new body at its inception, that is 50% of the constituency. Even more importantly, ten years later, in 1879, the figure had risen to eighty-three congregations that accounted for 90% of Scottish Baptists. In that decade a number of the small rural congregations had closed, thus accounting for the decline to ninety-two Baptist churches in Scotland. Support for the Baptist Union was maintained in the following ten years. In 1889 ninety-two out of ninety-seven congregations were affiliated to the national body.[4] The final decade of the century revealed the benefits of united witness with an increase of twenty-seven churches, of which 119 or 96% were Union-affiliated congregations.[5] There was, however, in 1869 a clear perception that the time had now come for Baptists to concentrate on what they had in common and on that basis to build a future together, leaving behind for good the era of fragmentation and division.

---

4   *The Twenty-Second Annual Report of the Baptist Union of Scotland 1889-1890*, (Glasgow: Baptist Union of Scotland, 1890), pp. 66-68.
5   *The Scottish Baptist Yearbook 1900*, (Glasgow: Baptist Union of Scotland, 1900), pp. 144-148.

The final and most important factor that brought Scottish Baptists together was the necessity to provide adequate provision for theological education. This conviction was held not only by the Haldaneite and 'English' Baptists, but also by the majority of Scotch Baptist pastors. Many of the ministers and lay leaders saw the need for a properly trained ministry. Students prior to 1842 were usually sent to England to prepare for ministry, but the limited number that returned to their native land had caused a reassessment of that policy. The control of theological education amongst Scottish Baptists by Francis Johnston in the 1840s and early 1850s caused some Calvinistic Baptists to lessen their support in practice, though not in principle, ensuring that this focus for unity had had a limited impact once Morisonian beliefs were aggressively promulgated by the Johnstonian Baptist Union. The 1856 SBA set as one of its main objectives the training of young men for the pastoral ministry. It was in reality the main purpose of this body in its early years. Baptists had now joined with Christians of other denominations in demanding higher standards of academic preparation for their preachers. If in the late 1850s Scottish Baptists had mixed views on plans for denominational unity, there was no hesitation expressed regarding this issue. They had consistently united in respect of support for ministerial training even when other theological issues had caused division. Other factors were needed to bring about the establishment of a union of churches in 1869, but theological education was a base around which to build a common future.

9.1 The Wider Social and Religious Context within Scotland

Scottish Baptists did not operate in a social vacuum. It is important to consider how they related to their social and ecclesiastical context within Scotland and in comparison with their Baptist colleagues in the rest of the United Kingdom. For this purpose the findings of this study will be compared with some of the major works in these fields. Alec Cheyne's *The Transforming of the Kirk* set out to explain a perceived religious revolution that took place in Victorian Scotland, especially amongst the Presbyterian churches. Developments amongst Scottish Baptists in this period do not provide comparable evidence for Cheyne's theory. This thesis has revealed that it was a slow evolution of growing support for a Baptist Union that led to the successful 1869 body, rather than a revolutionary development. Baptists did have fierce arguments on theological issues, but they tended to be the traditional issues such as the Calvinism-Arminianism debate. Many of the other controversial issues were ecclesiological, for example, how far local churches ought to be independent from or interdependent on each other – an issue at the heart of the debate over the place of a union of churches. Scotch Baptist disagreements reached their nadir over the manner in which the Lord's Supper was to be observed. Liturgical innovation over hymnody and communion was more readily accepted amongst most Baptists who had never formally espoused the austere worship patterns of some of their Presbyterian colleagues, though in the Highlands and Islands, where the Free Church held sway after the Disruption of 1843, psalmody and plain worship in Gaelic persisted throughout this period and beyond. The changes in the lives of Scottish Baptist churches in the period 1800 to 1870 could be described as more evolutionary than revolutionary. The Johnstonian Union from 1850 to1855 had tried to enforce a revolution, but its promoters had to acknowledge that it had failed.

Callum Brown's *Religion and Society in Scotland since 1707* describes the social impact of religion, in particular the Presbyterian form of Christianity, on Scotland over the last three centuries.[6] Baptists as one of the minor denominations were largely insignificant in social terms in the eighteenth and much of the nineteenth century. The highest density they achieved in terms of churchgoers was 4% in Edinburgh in 1835 to 1836.[7] This point was supported by James Paterson who stated in 1863 that their numbers were small and certainly no greater than 10,000 despite nearly doubling since 1843.[8] Brown in his descriptions of the fragmentation of Presbyterianism in the eighteenth and early nineteenth centuries refers to a phenomenon that was also experienced by Baptists in the period 1800 to 1856.[9] Arminianism, according to Brown, had become a cause of dissension in evangelical Presbyterianism from the 1750s onwards.[10] His claim is surely an exaggeration and the evidence on which it is based is weak. Brown uses a propaganda utterance of John McKerrow, in which the Secession minister is seeking to paint a very negative picture of the Established Church, with a view to its disestablishment. McKerrow, a strict Calvinist, writing on the eve of the Disruption in 1841, perceives any moderation of Reformed beliefs or practices as a sign of declension. He cites no examples of 'Arminianism' to support this claim, and it occurs in the conclusion of a section dealing with an alleged Socinian. It should be seen, therefore, as an

---

6   Brown extends his analysis to include other parts of Britain in his most recent book *The Death of Christian Britain*, (London: Routledge, 2001).
7   Brown, *Religion and Society in Scotland*, p. 45.
8   James Paterson, 'The Baptist Denomination in Scotland', *The Freeman*, 9 (27 May, 1863), p. 331.
9   Brown, *Religion and Society in Scotland*, pp. 17-31.
10 C.G. Brown, *The Social History of Religion in Scotland since 1730*, (London: Methuen, 1987), pp. 139-141.

overstatement in a time of religious conflict.[11] Brown also uses a quotation from Archibald McLean, the leading Scotch Baptist, concerning pastoral admonition to backsliders, which is taken out of context. Brown seeks to use the extract to imply that Scotch Baptists were weakening their stance regarding the eternal security of the elect, but the text cannot be forced to make such a point. McLean, however, had been proclaiming the strict conformity of his movement to Reformed soteriology. In the short citation used by Brown, the Edinburgh elder is simply referring to normal pastoral practice amongst the Scotch Baptists.[12] The 'Arminianism' that Brown describes became a serious issue in the 1840s, especially with reference to the trial of James Morison, though it was technically still a modified Calvinism as the source of inspiration came from the Finneyite version of New England Calvinistic theology.[13] Therefore it is unlikely that Arminianism was a significant factor in theological debate in Scottish Protestant denominations prior to the mid-1830s. The rise of formal Arminian opinions in Scottish Baptist circles was in line with similar development in other Protestant denominational bodies in the nineteenth century.

Orthodox Baptists had remained solidly Calvinistic into the 1830s, with only the Montrose congregation serving as an exception.[14] The major conflict over the extent of the atonement of Jesus did not begin in their ranks until 1846. The formally Arminian Baptist Union that emerged from the conflict in January 1850, led by Francis Johnston, survived for only five years and ended with the departure of its leaders, Johnston, Milner and Landels. This failure is in stark contrast to the trajectory of the Evangelical Union, the

---

11 J. McKerrow, *History of the Secession Church*, (Glasgow: A Fullarton & Co., 2nd edition, 1841), p. 371.

12 A. McLean, 'A Short Account of the Scots Baptists', in Rippon, *Baptist Annual Register*, 1795, pp. 374-375.

13 F.H. Foster, *A Genetic History of the New England Theology*, (Chicago: The University of Chicago Press, 1907). A more reliable guide to the declension from the Westminster standards in the eighteenth and nineteenth centuries is I. Hamilton, *The Erosion of Calvinist Orthodoxy*, (Edinburgh: Rutherford House Books, 1990).

14 There was, however, a Unitarian General Baptist church in Perth led by William Taylor from 1832-1841, some information is given on this church in Robertson, *Perth Baptist Church*, pp. 39-40. More details of this church in 1838 is found in the Appendix of the *Sixth Report of the Ecclesiastical Commission of Enquiry into the Opportunities of Public Religious Worship and Means of Religious Instruction, and the Pastoral Superintendence afforded to the People of Scotland*, (Edinburgh: W. & A.K. Johnston, 1838), 6, Appendix, pp. 184-185.

group led in 1843 by James Morison out of the United Secession Church. This new denomination experienced vigorous growth, eventually joining with the Congregationalists in 1896.[15] It is possible that the strength of the Evangelical Union delayed its merger with the Congregationalists. This strength is in contrast with the weakness of the Johnstonian Baptists that had ensured that they needed to work with their fellow Baptists in the Scottish Baptist Association of 1856. The trend in Scotland towards a moderated Calvinism that was experienced by various Presbyterian denominations in the mid to late nineteenth century was similar to the doctrinal changes in the same period amongst Scottish Baptists.

Scottish Presbyterianism in the late-eighteenth to mid-nineteenth century was marked by significant secessions from the Established Church and also within the ranks of the various seceding bodies. This practice was largely followed by a series of unions in the second half of the century, though the formation of the Free Presbyterian Church in 1893[16] and the continuing Free Church in 1900[17] were exceptions to this rule. There was, however, a modest reversal of the fissiparous trend by the union of the 'New Light' Burghers and Antiburghers to form the United Secession Church in 1820. This development was followed by the 1847 merger of the United Secession Church with the Relief Church to form the United Presbyterian Church, which in turn joined with the Free Church of Scotland to form the United Free Church in 1900. The main reasons for this reversal of disunity in Presbyterian ranks were the growing co-operation of these bodies in the nineteenth century in home and overseas evangelism, the work of Bible societies and other religious causes. The ability to co-operate in the advancement of so many non-denominational activities had convinced these Scottish Christians that they had much more in common than previously thought, and their differences were now perceived to be of limited importance, and too minor to prevent church union in the promotion of the Reformed faith. Scottish Baptists were also marked by a tendency to major on their differences with each other in the first two decades of the nineteenth century. Co-operation in the work of home mission, leading to the merger of the three home missionary societies in 1827, in addition to support of various other religious

---

15 Escott, *Scottish Congregationalism*, pp. 165-182.
16 A. McPherson (ed.), *History of the Free Presbyterian Church of Scotland*, (Inverness: Publications Committee of the Free Presbyterian Church of Scotland,1973), pp. 70-86.
17 J.D. MacMillan, 'Free Church of Scotland, post 1900', in Cameron (ed.), *Scottish Church History and Theology*, p. 338.

causes, led to the first attempt at Baptist union in 1827. The failure of this first body did not prevent further developments in this direction in 1835 and 1843. Even the fatally separatist tendencies of the Johnstonian Baptist Union, from 1850 to1855, served only to confirm the need for an inclusive union of Baptist churches in Scotland. The successful Baptist Union launched in 1869 was the culmination of a process that had begun in the late 1820s. It was, though, an evangelical non-confessional denomination. This position was not to be followed in Presbyterian circles until the United Free Church adopted this approach in 1906.[18] The tendency to fissiparity and later union in Scottish Baptist ranks was, therefore, broadly in line with similar developments in seceder Presbyterian circles.

The general decline in adherence to Calvinism in the nineteenth century in the English-speaking world was discussed in chapter one. It is important, though, here to place this development more firmly in the context of its impact on Baptists in Scotland. The body of men that comprised the leadership of the Scotch Baptists, the Haldaneite Baptists, the 'English' Baptists and the BHMS for Scotland, were all convinced Calvinists in the period prior to 1835. The doctrinal statement and in particular the pronouncements of the 1827 Baptist Union of Scotland assumed that all participating churches would hold to Reformed convictions. This Union of churches was probably influenced in this matter by the 1812 Particular Baptist Union in England, a body to which 'English' Baptists in Scotland felt some allegiance. There was a distinct change of emphasis in the 1835 to 1842 SBA. This new venture was inspired by the reorganisation of BUGBI in 1832 and the four objects of the constitution of the two bodies were almost identical. The significance of the change is that though the overwhelming majority of participating churches were of Calvinistic persuasion those congregations holding to Arminian sentiments were welcome to affiliate. In Scotland it was in 1840 that the Montrose Baptist Church and its Arminian minister applied for membership of the SBA. The minutes of the SBA indicate that the request was granted. This decision was proof of a change of theological climate in Scottish Baptist circles.

The Johnstonian Baptist Union from 1843 to 1849 continued with the inclusive policy of the SBA. In 1849 a decision had been taken to form, in January 1850, a Morisonian Baptist denomination in line with the Evangelical Union. It was assumed that many Calvinistic Baptists would withdraw their support from the Baptist Union, but

---

18 N.R. Needham, 'United Free Church', in Cameron (ed.), *Scottish Church History and Theology*, p. 838.

Conclusions

Johnston and his colleagues had expected that these individuals would be replaced by a greater number of incomers attracted by the new theology. The influence, ultimately, behind this policy had come from the modified Calvinism of Charles Finney, the American revivalist. He had been the inspiration for James Morison, the founder of Evangelical Unionism, who in turn had impressed Johnston, Landels and Milner, key leaders in the Baptist Union in the mid-nineteenth century.[19] Unlike the 1827 Baptist Union and the 1835-1842 SBA there was no known English influence on the theological opinions of the Johnstonian Baptist Union. The late 1840s saw a hardening of theological positions due to the crusading zeal of the Morisonian Baptists. Peter Grant, one of the most open-minded Calvinistic Baptist ministers in the 1840s, had expressed his fears about the future direction of the Johnstonian Union in a prophetic letter to his son William in February 1848.

> I thought that Morisonianism was dying away. When Johnston and the Union give them [Morisonian ideas] such countenance I am afraid that there must be a complete separation, that the Union will make up an Arminian body, and that all who are of these views through the churches will join them and that others will leave them, for they can hardly put up together.[20]

A month later the elder Grant had firmed up his opinions in his next letter to his son William.

> It is only just now that I got the two 'last' *Evangelists*. I am getting quite disgusted with the Union, for better that they would join into a body by themselves under the designation of General or Free Will Baptists.[21]

Grant, who was not party to the change in Baptist Union policies, had seen the direction in which Johnston was going. The 1840s was a decade of pioneers who were prepared to reject their original vision of the future for what they perceived to be a greater one. Johnston, in some respects, was similar to Thomas Chalmers. This Free Church minister had a great vision of the godly commonwealth encompassing the whole of society, but it was sacrificed at the Disruption in 1843 for a purer church purged of patronage and state interference. The ideal relationship that he had dreamed of

---

19 For a more detailed discussion of the influence of Charles Finney on Scottish church leaders see R. Carwardine, *Transatlantic Revivalism: Popular Evangelicalism in Britain and America, 1790-1865*, (London: Greenwood Press, 1978), pp. 94-101.
20 Peter Grant, Grantown, to William Grant, Edinburgh, 26 February 1848, Grant MS.
21 Peter Grant to William Grant, 28 March 1848.

between church and state would now disappear under the increasing secular control of the government over Scottish society. Johnston had aimed to produce a strong Arminian Baptist denomination that would see converts in the manner that Morrison and especially Finney had seen, but his vision was also unrealistic and less than five years after its inception it had demonstrably failed. Chalmers too realised the failure of his ambitions prior to his death in 1847.[22]

The inevitable collapse of the Johnstonian Union gave a new opportunity to commence afresh an inclusive approach to fellowship amongst Scottish Baptist ministers. Although the leaders of the next body to unite Scottish Baptists, the 1856 to 1869 SBA, were nearly all Calvinists, this association worked hard to bring all evangelical Baptists in Scotland together. The triumph, though, that was achieved in the formation of the Baptist Union of 1869 was of a very different kind of Union from the two previous organisations with that name. The 1827 Union was confessionally Calvinistic; the Johnstonian Union was strictly Arminian; the 1869 Union was open to all who professed to be evangelical. If the 1827 Union had been united regarding Calvinism, and the second Union destroyed because of it, the final body succeeded without final reference to it. Scottish Baptists in the mid to late 1860s had begun to promote a biblicism that deprecated confessionalism. It was, therefore, the end of the Calvinist ascendancy and the beginning of an era in which evangelical Arminianism would predominate.

The Congregational Union of Scotland was the denomination closest in doctrine and practices to Scottish Baptists. Congregationalists had had a union of churches since 1812, led by the inspirational Greville Ewing. Many of the churches in the connexion had large debts on their buildings and their main aim was to enable each other to survive the crisis of funding caused by the Haldanes' withdrawal from their ranks.[23] It was, however, a loose arrangement between the churches and individual members. The formal structures of the annual assembly were set in place only in 1887. Thus although their Union had been constituted many years earlier than the 1869 Baptist equivalent, it was nearly twenty years later before the Congregational body exercised the same functions in terms of its formal structure.[24] The other aim was the evangelisation of Scotland and, as a result, the Union functioned as a home missionary society.[25] Baptists meanwhile had established their own society for

---

22 S.J. Brown, *Thomas Chalmers and the Godly Commonwealth in Scotland*, (Oxford: Oxford University Press, 1982), pp. 337-349.
23 Escott, *Scottish Congregationalism*, pp. 94-95.
24 Escott, *Scottish Congregationalism*, p. 100.

home evangelisation, the BHMS, in 1827. It appeared that the inspirational leadership of Ewing had persuaded Congregationalists to form a union of churches quickly in 1812, but a wholehearted commitment to its operations, from this body, took a further generation to achieve. The majority of Scottish Congregationalists for a large part of the nineteenth century viewed their Union as little more than a church aid and home evangelisation society.[26] This perspective was in line with those Scottish Baptists who had settled for the BHMS as the one necessary bond of union in their own ranks.

The impact of the changing religious scene in the 1840s in Scotland affected Congregationalists in a similar way to the Baptists. The Disruption in the Church of Scotland, for example, had caused congregations in each to lose many of their hearers.[27] The views of James Morison regarding the work of the Holy Spirit in the conversion of the sinner, the proclamation of a universal atonement in association with a universal work of the Spirit influencing all men for salvation, were replicated in the theology of John Kirk, the pastor of the Congregational Church in Hamilton. Orthodox Calvinists led by Ralph Wardlaw, one of the most respected ministers in the Congregational Union, rejected the new views. The controversy that followed resulted in the expulsion of students from the Congregational Academy and some of the congregations, together with their ministers, including Kirk, leaving the Union. The number of individuals that had left was relatively small, but the dispute had caused a major upheaval amongst Congregationalists.[28] The position taken by John Kirk in his denomination was very similar to that of Francis Johnston amongst Scottish Baptists. Once Johnston had openly pronounced his apparently unorthodox opinions, Calvinistic Baptists were quick to attack the new theological system. The majority of Scottish Baptists, and especially Calvinistic Baptists, had no formal connection to the Johnstonian Union and so consequently they could neither resign nor ask Johnston to leave. Instead many chose to affiliate with the English strict communionist Calvinistic body, the Baptist Evangelical Society, until the Johnstonian Union had ceased its operations. Therefore in a parallel manner to the Congregationalists, proponents of the two theologies belonged to different associations of churches.

There were also parallels in the adoption of social issues such as

---

25 Escott, *Scottish Congregationalism*, p. 95.
26 Escott, *Scottish Congregationalism*, pp. 94-101.
27 Escott, *Scottish Congregationalism*, p. 106.
28 Escott, *Scottish Congregationalism*, pp. 109-115.

temperance. Congregationalists and their members who left to join the Evangelical Union both took an interest in promoting total abstinence prior to the establishment of a national temperance committee. The Congregational Union Total Abstinence Society was instituted in 1867, with the Evangelical Union society as late as 1879. The latter denomination's decision reveals that although its ministers and students for ministry were total abstainers in the 1840s, and drink-sellers were barred from the membership of EU churches, it was over thirty years later before a formal constitution outlined the EU's position.[29] The Baptist Union of Scotland set up its Total Abstinence Society in 1881,[30] though many of its leading members had been advocating the cause since the 1830s and 1840s. Institutional recognition of the temperance movement in Scottish denominations lagged a long way behind the practice of many individual churches. In the case of the Baptist Union of Scotland many of the key leaders had taken the pledge in excess of forty years earlier.[31]

The Congregational Union of Scotland was to merge with the Evangelical Union in 1896. Discussions about union between the two bodies had begun as early as 1867, but had been held up by members of the Evangelical Union, for example, William Adamson, pastor of Buccleuch E.U. Church, Edinburgh, who had insisted as late as 1884 that Congregationalists must accept the 'three universalities' of God's love for all people, Christ's death for all people and the Spirit's work in all people, before any union took place. As a result negotiations were lengthy and often produced little progress.[32] The contrast with Johnstonian Baptists in the 1850s could not be clearer. Their leaders Francis Johnston and William Landels had departed to English Baptist churches and Thomas Milner to the Churches of Christ. As a result the upper hand was held by the Calvinistic Baptists who decided to welcome their Arminian brethren, but on a basis that prevented old controversies dominating their association. The building of individual relationships from 1856 to 1869 led to a harmonious and united group of ministers and congregations that formed the Baptist Union of Scotland.

---

29 Escott, *Scottish Congregationalism*, pp. 127-128.
30 J.M. Gordon, 'The Later Nineteenth Century', in Bebbington (ed.), *Baptists in Scotland*, p. 53.
31 For example, the Rev. James Blair in 1829. *The Scottish Evangelist: The Life and Labours of the Rev. James Blair*, (Glasgow: George Gallie, 1860), pp. 9, 36.
32 Escott, *Scottish Congregationalism*, p. 167.

9.2 Developments amongst Baptists in England, Wales and Ireland

It is important to compare the progress towards union of Scottish Baptists with equivalent developments among their fellow Baptists in England. The General Union of English Particular Baptists was established in 1813.[33] Its articles of faith were Calvinistic, in fact similar in many respects to the doctrinal basis of the short-lived Baptist Union of Scotland constituted in 1827. This British Union was weak and made little progress before it was reconstituted in 1832, inviting Baptist ministers and churches to affiliate if they agreed with 'the sentiments usually denominated evangelical'.[34] The new British Union attracted support at its inception from a number of New Connexion General Baptists who played a full part in the life of the Union.[35] The English New Connexion General Baptists, who had participated in the life of the British Baptist Union and who held to some different theological views and church practices from Morisonian Baptists in Scotland,(though in a less marked way than the 'Old Connexion' General Baptists),[36] took a more conciliatory line in theological debates with Calvinistic colleagues and never caused the kind of difficulties instituted by Francis Johnston and his supporters in the 1840s and 1850s. This fact may be in part because they had retained membership in the New Connexion of General Baptists, the Arminian Baptist denomination in England, and thus were in a position to participate in the BUGBI as far as they felt able. The constructive contribution of General Baptists to the life of BUGBI since 1832 was, however, a factor in their favour, to which they drew attention when merger negotiations were taking place in the 1880s prior to the eventual merger of the two English Baptist denominations in 1891.[37] English Baptists engaged proportionately in less controversial debate over their corporate activities prior to 1870 than did their Scottish counterparts. Their support for the Union and its activities, however, was also more lukewarm than that of their brethren north of the border. In 1863 only thirteen of the thirty-seven Baptist Associations contributed to Union funds and out of the 1,270 affiliated churches only sixty sent in their subscriptions, allowing the Union to have an income that year of a mere £90

---

33 Payne, *Baptist Union*, p. 6.
34 Payne, *Baptist Union*, p. 61.
35 Briggs, 'Evangelical Ecumenism', p. 105.
36 For an explanation of the views and practices of the General Baptists in England see R. Brown, *The English Baptists of the Eighteenth Century*, (A History of the English Baptists, 2; London: Baptist Historical Society, 1986).
37 Briggs, *English Baptists of the Nineteenth Century*, pp. 123-124, 152-157.

pounds.[38] BUGBI had increased its income in 1874 to £352.[39] This figure compared unfavourably, though, with the Baptist Union of Scotland where the treasurer was able to make use of over £1069 that year.[40] The proportion of Baptist churches in England in membership with an association or the Union had risen to only 73% by 1883.[41] Scottish church affiliations to their Baptist Union, by contrast, had exceeded 90% as early as 1879. The British Union, prior to the commencement in 1863 of the secretaryship of J.H. Millard, minister at Huntingdon, had been extraordinarily weak and achieved very little.[42] The Johnstonian Union in the 1840s in Scotland had achieved greater successes proportionately in its denominational life than the corresponding body in England. It was in the 1860s that both the Scottish and British Baptist Unions came into their own and engaged the active support of a greater proportion of their constituencies. The Scots were much slower than the English to commence their Union, but once they had accepted the principle they showed greater enthusiasm for its different activities in the 1860s and 1870s.

Kenneth Dix in his *Strict and Particular: English Strict and Particular Baptists in the Nineteenth Century* has provided a thorough study of some of the most doctrinally and ecclesiologically conservative Baptists in England. Attempts to unite these Baptists were hindered by tensions over the nature of faith and religious experience, as well as other doctrinal and church practices. Various internal groups were identified by their support for particular periodicals produced by different parties within their ranks. There was, though, only limited support for a home missionary society. The Strict Baptist Mission, the overseas missionary agency of Strict Baptists, established in 1861, was also only partly successful in uniting this Baptist constituency.[43] It is noted that the greatest reason for the lack of progress in union between the churches and indeed any changes within their congregations was because, 'Strict Baptists were always averse to any kind of change, whether necessary or otherwise, which may explain their far greater success in the more conservative-minded rural areas,' in contrast to the larger urban areas outside of London.[44]

---

38   Payne, *Baptist Union*, p. 93.
39   Payne, *Baptist Union*, p. 106.
40   *Sixth Annual Report of the Baptist Union of Scotland*, (Edinburgh: John Lindsay, 1874), p. 48.
41   Payne, *Baptist Union*, p. 117.
42   Briggs, *English Baptists of the Nineteenth Century*, pp. 214-219.
43   Dix, *Strict and Particular*, pp. 204-208.
44   Dix, *Strict and Particular*, pp. 266-267.

There had been a similarly conservative minority of Scottish Baptists in the ranks of Scotch Baptists in the early nineteenth century who were resistant to any changes, but their secession to the Churches of Christ ensured that moves towards union amongst Scottish Baptist churches were aided by their departure.[45]

It is important next to consider the attitudes towards union amongst the Baptist Churches in Wales and Ireland. The Baptist Union of Wales was constituted in 1866. There had been associations of Baptist churches in Wales since the eighteenth century, revealing that the Baptist cause was in a much stronger position there than in Scotland in the first half of the nineteenth century. Welsh Baptists had, however, faced difficulties over language in their churches, with some using Welsh and others English. Another cause of division was a theological issue, namely open versus closed communion. These two issues often combined with the result that English-speaking churches practising open communion usually chose to affiliate with BUGBI and Welsh-speaking churches practising closed communion joined the Welsh Baptist Union. In Scotland the proportion of Baptist churches and ministers speaking Gaelic was small, probably no more than 10 to 15% of the total at the most, and their influence was limited, given that the majority of them were situated in the north-west of Scotland. There was, therefore, no formal conflict between English and Gaelic speakers in the Union. In Scotland the causes of division between Baptists were ecclesiological, between Scotch and 'English' Baptists, and theological, between Calvinistic and Morisonian Baptists. One area, though, where there was a similarity between Scotland and Wales concerned affiliation to the Union. In Wales the strongest Baptist associations were amongst the last to join the Union.[46] Some Baptist churches in Scotland that were amongst the largest and therefore the strongest were amongst the last to affiliate formally with their fellow Baptists.

The formation of the Irish Baptist Union was very different from the inception of the corresponding body in Scotland. The work amongst Baptists in Ireland had been seen in BUGBI as part of its home mission activities prior to 1862. When the Irish Baptist Association was formed in 1862 it became a constituent association of BUGBI with no thought at that stage of forming a separate union of churches. The Baptist Union of Ireland came into being as a reaction to the Downgrade controversy in BUGBI, in which Irish Baptists followed the opinions of Charles Spurgeon, who alleged that theological

---

45 Thompson, *Let Sects and Parties Fall*, pp. 26-28.
46 Bassett, *Welsh Baptists*, pp. 337-341.

liberalism had entered Union ranks. The formation of the Irish Baptist Union, therefore, was a statement of separation from this perceived theological downgrade in BUGBI.[47] Scottish Baptists, by contrast, formed their Baptist Union in 1869, and from a position of strength chose to consider affiliation to BUGBI in 1872. The offer from the British Union, however, was rejected by the Scottish body who desired to retain their independent identity.[48]

9.3 The Contribution of Scottish Baptist Historians, in particular the Work of Derek Murray

The final point of comparison is between the conclusions of this book and the standard histories of the Baptists in Scotland. For this purpose the various articles and books of Derek Murray[49] and *The Baptists in Scotland: A History* will be considered. Murray, the founding father of the critical study of Scottish Baptist history, laid the foundations for our understanding of it in his books and articles. The small number of criticisms below must be considered in the context of the broad acceptance of the contribution he has made to our understanding of Scottish Baptist history. This book, however, has sought to examine some aspects of his work, especially in relation to the formation of the Baptist Union of Scotland. He correctly distinguished the three streams of Baptist witness in the first three decades of the nineteenth century, discussed in chapters two to four. There were, however, some key individuals who were attributed either to the wrong tradition or whose theological position had been misunderstood. The prominent 'English' Baptist minister, Alexander McLeod, was incorrectly described as a 'Scotch Baptist pastor'.[50] James Paterson, the leader of the SBA that began in 1856, was described as a 'General Baptist' who had in 1829 'broadened his views'. Paterson was, however, a Particular Baptist and one of the Scottish supporters of the Baptist Evangelical Society, a society formed to promote strict communion principles amongst English

---

47 J. Thompson, *Century of Grace. The Baptist Union of Ireland: A Short History, 1895-1995*, (Belfast: Baptist Union of Ireland, 1995), pp. 6-8.
48 Briggs, *English Baptists of the Nineteenth Century*, is incorrect on this point. See Chapter One, pp. 17-18.
49 D.B. Murray, *The First Hundred Years- The Baptist Union of Scotland 1869-1969*, (Glasgow: Baptist Union of Scotland, 1969); Murray, 'Baptists in Scotland before 1869'; Murray, 'Scotch Baptist Tradition in Great Britain'; Murray, *Scottish Baptist College*; Murray, 'Johnstone, Francis' (Vol.1, p. 616) and 'Paterson, James', (Vol.2, p. 858), in Lewis (ed.), *DEB*. Murray and Meek, 'Early Nineteenth Century'.
50 Murray, 'Baptists in Scotland before 1869', p. 261. See Chapter four, pp. 124-126.

Particular Baptists.[51] It is important to grasp the correct theological views of Paterson in particular because he was one of the most important leaders in the Baptist community in Scotland prior to 1870.

The first major attempt to establish a union of Baptist churches in Scotland began in 1827. Murray, in an article in 1970, gave an outline description of the work of this Baptist Union, but some of the detail was still unclear.[52] The circulars issued by the individuals promoting this venture were issued anonymously. Chapter six reveals the names of the men responsible who were all in the membership of Charlotte Baptist Chapel, Edinburgh. As a result of discovering the names of the leading participants it has been possible to determine the level of support for this project by the members of the three Baptist traditions in Scotland. Churches from each part of the Baptist community participated, though the 'English' Baptists took the most prominent roles. In 1827 sixty-two Baptist congregations were in existence in Scotland, of which twenty-eight affiliated to the Baptist Union of Scotland. It was only in 1869 at the launch of the fourth Baptist fellowship of churches that more than 50% of churches supported the Union. The official history of the Baptist Union produced by Murray in 1969 omitted even to mention efforts to draw Scottish Baptists together in the late 1820s.[53] In a later study the impact of 1827 Union is summed up as 'being so premature as to be abortive'.[54] In contrast to that assessment, a more accurate understanding of this Baptist Union must conclude that it was of much greater significance than previous studies have acknowledged.

The length of time that this Baptist Union continued is a mystery. The only surviving records of the Union that have been preserved were those in the possession of Clyde Street Hall, Edinburgh. This congregation was, though, the first one to leave the Union in the autumn of 1827 and thus its records ceased at that point. It is important to note, however, that the Union was then fully functional and though it must have ceased before the start of the next attempt to

---

51 Murray, 'Paterson, James', p. 858. See Chapter seven, p. 272.
52 Murray, 'Baptists in Scotland before 1869', pp. 260-262. See also Murray & Meek, 'Early Nineteenth Century', pp. 40-41, for a similar understanding of this attempt at union.
53 Murray, *First Hundred Years*, pp. 14-15. Dr Murray in a private conversation explained that the Waugh Papers, our only primary source of information about the 1827 Baptist Union, had not been discovered until after his centenary history had been published.
54 Murray, 'Baptists in Scotland before 1869', p. 262.

unite Scottish Baptists in 1835, it is impossible in the present state of knowledge to determine the endpoint of this body. One vital point that probably determined the failure of this Baptist Union was the case of the application for membership by James Watson of Montrose. Murray refers to him as being probably 'tainted with Socinianism',[55] but surviving records describe the error as 'the Arminian heresy'.[56] This Scottish Baptist Union was a parallel to the British Particular Baptist Union instituted in 1813 and, as a result, contained only individuals and congregations who held firmly to the Calvinistic doctrinal basis. It is, therefore, inconceivable that James Watson would have been continuing in fellowship with Scotch Baptist churches in the 1820s had he been in any way teaching Socinianism. Watson, probably the first Scottish Baptist minister to espouse Arminianism, may have done so only in the late 1820s, thus accounting for his recent dismissal from Scotch Baptist ranks. If this is so then he is the pioneer of the new theological position amongst Scottish Baptists that gained new adherents in the 1830s and became dominant in Morisonian guise in the Johnstonian Union.

The next significant difference from Murray's findings relates to the other attempts at union discussed in chapters six and seven. He failed to note some of the important differences between the SBA, 1835 to 1842, and the Johnstonian Baptist Union of 1843 to 1856. The SBA was a new initiative deliberately modelled on the restructured British Baptist Union of 1832. Its four objects were expressed with the same sentiments and usually the same words as the other organisation. The key phrase comes in object 1:' holding the sentiments usually termed evangelical'.[57] In the 1832 Baptist Union statement the first object refers to Christians 'who agree in the sentiments usually denominated evangelical'.[58] The Scottish Association was clearly influenced by its counterpart in the change of theological direction. As in the British Union there were Arminian Baptists who sought membership, though in Scotland there were very few of them. This change of policy was in stark contrast to the previous Scottish Baptist Union which would not have accepted the Montrose minister. The Johnstonian Union continued the inclusivist policy of the SBA officially until the end of 1849. It was in January 1850 that William Landels' editorial in *The Evangelist* signalled the reconstituting of the basis for membership, in theory at least excluding anyone who did not sign up to the 'three Universals', as outlined in

---

55 Murray, 'Baptists in Scotland before 1869', p. 262.
56 David McLaren to Archibald Smith, June 22, 1827, Waugh Papers.
57 Minutes of the Scottish Baptist Association, July 29, 1835, p. 2.
58 Payne, *Baptist Union*, p. 61.

chapter seven. Johnston after having served as a pastor in England would have been aware of the New Connexion General Baptists. The success of that body at this time might have encouraged any ideas that he had about the setting up of a parallel Arminian denomination to the existing Calvinistic Baptist network of churches in Scotland. Murray's conclusion that Johnston 'reinvigorated the denomination' [59] was correct only for the first three or four years of his term as secretary of the Baptist Union of Scotland. After that time, by his own choice of an exclusivist vision of the future, he had become the architect of its certain failure.

Another area of disagreement with Murray's conclusions concerns the issue of theological education. This study regards the unifying force of this object as the main reason behind the drives for union amongst Scottish Baptists from the 1830s onwards. Murray, however, while correctly noting that some Scotch Baptists were opposed to theological training for pastoral ministry, failed to recognise that it was only members of the strictest party in Scotch ranks, after the 1834 division, that had maintained such a policy.[60] The fact that David Smith, one of the pastors at the most conservative Scotch Baptist congregation in Glasgow, was involved in 1836 in efforts to set up a society to co-ordinate ministerial training reveals the weakness of support for the opposing viewpoint. Instead of being a divisive issue, the efforts to provide financial assistance and opportunities for the training of young men for the pastoral ministry became the most prominent cause around which to unite from the late 1830s through to the 1860s. Divisions over the nature of the Johnstonian Union had closed its ranks to many Calvinists who had in turn, in the 1840s, withdrawn the opportunity for leading Union members to associate with the BHMS. There were still disagreements over the nature of this educational facility, but its necessity served the cause of union well, especially at the start of the 1856 SBA.

The Johnstonian Baptist Union from 1843 to 1845 had taken major steps to provide the kind of visionary and inspiring leadership that had been lacking from 1835 to 1842 in the earlier SBA. The first sign of problems ahead appeared to arise from a letter printed in *The Free Church Magazine* in February 1846. In his 1970 article Murray stated, 'What sort of jealousy and theological suspicion was involved here can only be guessed at'.[61] A clearer opinion had emerged in his 1988 article, co-written by Donald Meek, where it was noted that, 'the

---

59 Murray, 'Johnstone, Francis', p. 616.
60 Murray, *Scottish Baptist College*, pp. 1-2.
61 Murray, 'Baptists in Scotland before 1869', p. 264.

real reason may have been connected with theological differences'.[62] Chapter seven makes it plain that it was Johnston's rejection of the merger proposal at the executive committee of the Baptist Union of Scotland, in December 1845, that had caused the damaging split in Baptist ranks. As a result of this discovery the interpretation of the lasting effects of Johnston's ministry in Scotland from 1842 to 1856 can be reassessed. He has been described as 'the one man capable of arguing the case for co-operation'.[63] It must be accepted that Johnston had the skills to unite the majority of Scottish Baptists into a cohesive and effective union of churches, but when given the opportunity to put that inclusive vision into practice he had chosen to decline it. Instead he settled in 1850 for a smaller, more doctrinally pure and evangelistically zealous body, assuming that it would develop along the lines of the Evangelical Union denomination. The limited support for his new venture led to great discouragement in the ranks and after a mere two years a reversion in 1852 to an association of individuals. The decision of Johnston in 1856 to depart for a new ministry in England enabled him to make a fresh start and allowed other men with an inclusivist vision to begin to reunite the Scottish Baptist community. Murray's assessment of Johnston's ministry in the 1840s and 1850s contrasts sharply with the case argued here: 'To Francis Johnstone must be given pride of place, for he had the original vision, and refused to be discouraged'.[64] Surely pride of place, if it belongs to anyone in particular, must be given to Jonathan Watson who had sought to support wholeheartedly every attempt at union from 1827 until the Baptist Union of Scotland was established in 1869. The decision to appoint him as the first President of the Baptist Union of Scotland was sufficient testimony to the opinions of his colleagues on this subject.[65]

For Scottish Baptists, like the majority of other theological traditions in Scotland, the tendency to fissiparity overcame the desires for unity in the first half of the nineteenth century. This book has shown that the influence of English Baptists through the formation of their Unions helped to shape the direction of the bodies begun in 1827 and 1835. The presence of so many Spurgeon-trained men in the 1860s in Scottish Baptist churches helped to ensure that the association of individuals begun in 1856 became a union of churches in 1869. The importance of the 1827 Union and the sectarian nature of the later years of the Johnstonian Union have helped to explain why

---

62 Murray and Meek, 'Early Nineteenth Century', p. 41.
63 Gordon, 'The Later Nineteenth Century', p. 58.
64 Murray, *First Hundred Years*, p. 42.
65 *First Report of the Baptist Union of Scotland*, 1869, p. 3.

the moves towards union developed in the particular manner set out in chapters six to eight. The need to provide adequate training for ministerial students continued to provide a unifying force in the Baptist community whilst support for a union of churches appeared at time to ebb and flow. The support and leadership skills of men such as Jonathan Watson and James Paterson were crucial to give much needed direction, but ultimately, it was the wholehearted support of the Baptist community in Scotland, now convinced of the case for closer ties between the different congregations, that ensured that a successful union of churches would be established after 1869. In this development Scottish Baptists aligned themselves with other Christians in Scotland, because the second half of the nineteenth century was largely marked by a number of church unions. The conviction finally had dawned upon them, as with other Christians in other contexts, that the things they had in common were more than those issues over which they had been in disagreement.

Appendices

Appendix 1. The Attitude to Baptist Church Union amongst Haldaneite Baptists

	Church	Minister / Elder	Position on union
1.	Airdrie	John Calder	Against
2.	Anstruther	Alexander Hodge	Against
3.	Berwick-upon-Tweed	Alexander Kirkwood	In Favour
4.	Home Mission church, Dundee	Lachlan Mackintosh	In Favour
5.	Dunfermline Scotch Baptist	Adam Kirk	In Favour
6.	Charlotte Chapel, Edinburgh	Christopher Anderson	In Favour
7.	Clyde Street, Scotch Baptist, Edinburgh	Archibald Smith	In Favour
8.	Elder Street, Edinburgh	William Innes	In Favour
9.	South Portland Street, Glasgow	Alexander McLeod	In Favour
10.	Grantown-on-Spey	Peter Grant	In Favour
11.	Hawick	William Thorburn	In Favour
12.	Irvine	George Barclay	In Favour
13.	Kilmavionaig	William Tulloch	In Favour
14.	Lochgilphead & Tiree	Dugald Sinclair	In Favour
15.	Stirling	Peter Grant	In Favour
16.	Thurso	Edward McKay	Against

Sources:

R. Balmain, *Reminiscences of Clyde Street Hall and My Early Days* (Edinburgh: Private publication, 1893).
The Evangelist Magazine (1846-1847, 1850-1853).
The Waugh Papers, Baptist House, Glasgow.
G. Yuille (ed.), *History of the Baptists in Scotland* (1926).

Appendix 2. Scottish Baptists sent from Scotland to Horton Baptist College by 1837

Date of Entry		Name	Home Church [or church that sponsored their training]
1.	1806	Peter McFarlane	Kilwinning [Irvine]
2.	1806	Dugald Sinclair	Bellanoch [Lochgilphead]
3.	1807	John Edwards	Montrose
4.	1814	Peter Scott	Dunkeld
		[David Gibson, Kilwinning Church declined entry in 1815]	
5.	1816	David Douglas	Richmond Court, Edinburgh
		[Christopher Anderson's church]	
6.	1816	John Gilmore	Kilwinning
7.	1817	John Paul	Lochgilphead
8.	1817	John McKaog	Lochgilphead
9.	1819	James McPherson	Elder Street, Edinburgh
10.	1821	Archibald John McPhail	Lochgilphead
		[expelled from college 'for impropriety of conduct' in 1823]	
11.	1821	John McMillan	Lochgilphead
12.	1821	Robert Thomson	'Mr Perrey's church, Glasgow'
13.	1828	William Fraser	Charlotte Chapel, Edinburgh
		[Donald Thomson, brother of Robert, mentioned above was a Scot who entered Horton from Westgate Baptist Church, Bradford in 1830]	
14.	1831	Hugh Anderson	Charlotte Chapel, Edinburgh?
		[nephew of Christopher Anderson]	
15.	1832	Robert Alexander Johnstone	Orangefield, Greenock
16.	1833	Alexander Stalker	Perth
17.	1833	Francis Johnston	Leith Road, Edinburgh
18.	1835	John Girdwood	unknown, Edinburgh
19.	1835	David McKay	Thurso
20.	1836	William McMillan	Irvine
		[died due to a chill brought on by lack of heating in the College in 1838]	
21.	1837	Robert Cameron	unknown, Glasgow
22.	1837	Samuel Stone	unknown, Edinburgh

Sources

Northern Baptist Educational Society Reports, 1805-1806 to 1836-1837.

Appendix 3.1 Location of Baptist Home Missionaries in Scotland, 1800-1870

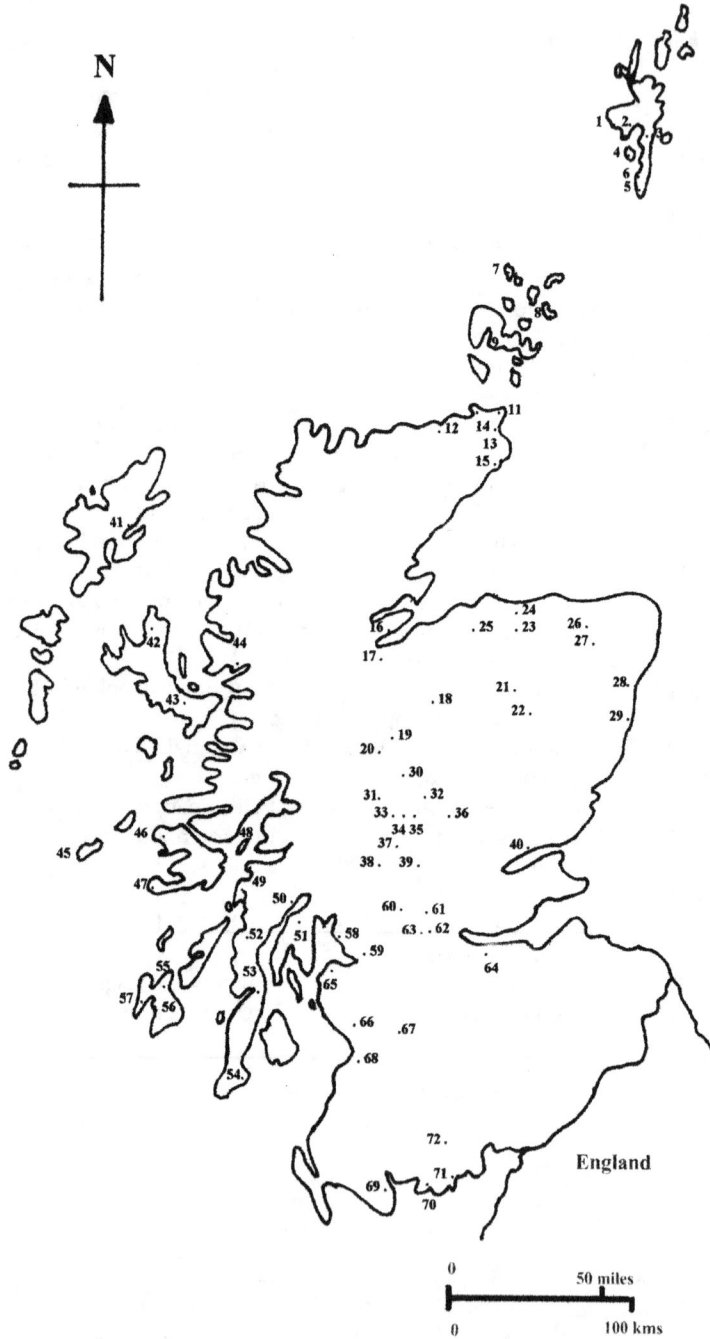

Appendix 3.1 Locations of Baptist Home Missionaries, 1800-1870

[All the listed places had a missionary based there for at least part of this time period.]

1. Sandsting (Shetland)
2. Semblister (Shetland)
3. Scalloway (Shetland)
4. Burra Isle (Shetland)
5. Dunrossness (Shetland)
6. Spiggie (Shetland)
7. Westray (Orkney)
8. Eday, Sandy (Orkney)
9. Kirkwall (Orkney)
10. Breckowall (Orkney)*
11. John O' Groats
12. Thurso
13. Keiss
14. Mey
15. Pultney Town (Wick)
16. Fortrose
17. Inverness
18. Grantown-on-Spey
19. Kingussie
20. Badenoch (near Kingussie)
21. Huntly
22. Insch
23. Elgin
24. Brandenburgh (Lossiemouth)
25. Forres
26. New Pitsligo
27. New Deer
28. Aberdeen
29. Stonehaven
30. Blair Atholl
31. Kinloch Rannoch
32. Tullymet
33. Glenlyon
34. Fortingal
35. Aberfeldy
36. Blairgowrie
37. Lawers
38. Crieff
39. Perth
40. Dundee
41. Long Island / Stornoway, Lewis
42. Uig (Skye)
43. Broadford (Skye)
44. Jeantown (Lochcarron)
45. Tiree
46. Tobermory (Mull)
47. Ross (Mull)
48. Lismore
49. Oban
50. Inverary
51. Cowal
52. Bellanoch
53. Lochgilphead
54. Campbeltown
55. Portaskaig (Islay)
56. Bowmore (Islay)
57. Port Charlotte (Islay)
58. Helensburgh
59. Stobhill (Glasgow)
60. Stirling
61. Tullibody
62. Grahamston
63. Falkirk
64. Edinburgh
65. Greenock
66. Kilwinning
67. Kilmarnock
68. Ayr
69. Wigtown
70. Kirkcudbright
71. Auchencairn
72. Castle Douglas

[* denotes a place whose exact location is uncertain and which is, therefore, not marked on the map]

Appendix 3.2 The Number of Baptist Missionaries Employed in Scotland, 1800-1879 (full- or part-time)

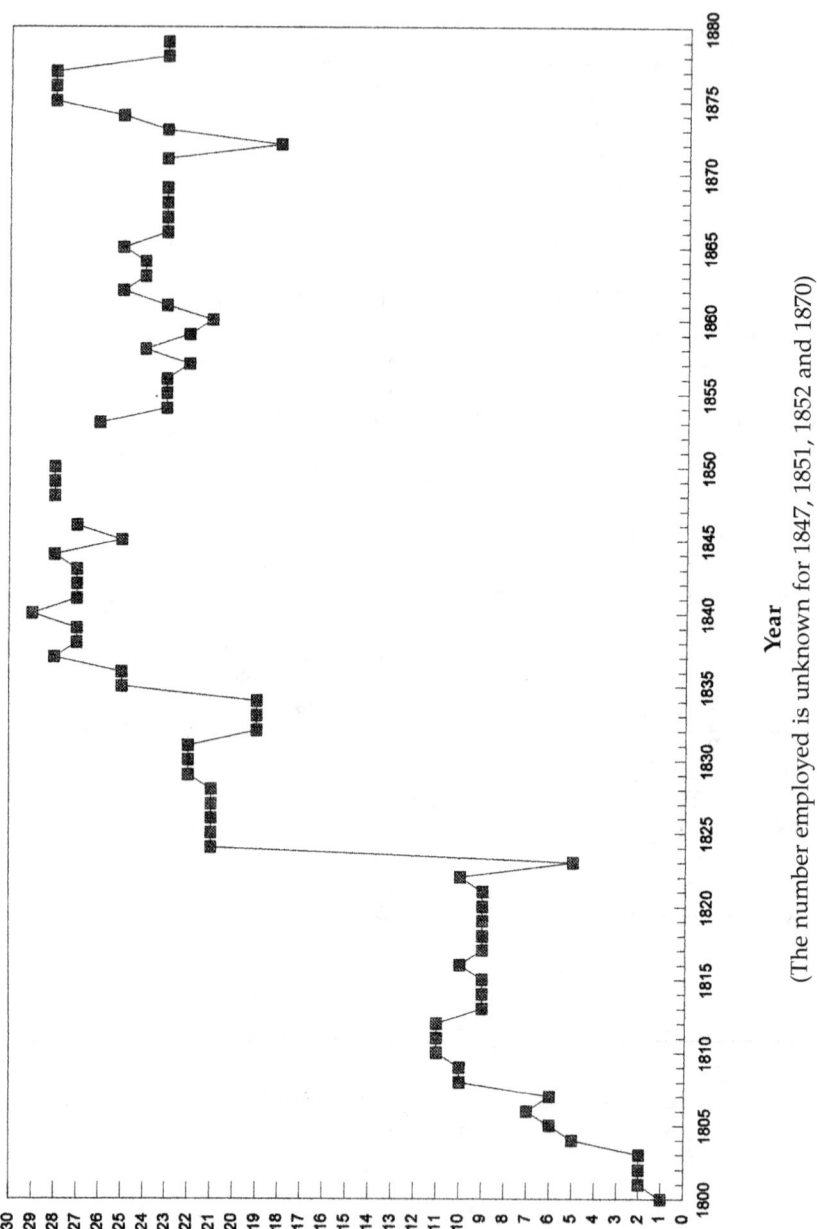

Number of Baptist Missionaries Employed in Scotland (full or part-time)
(Data incomplete 1800 to 1827; total given is the minimum number that year)

Appendices

Appendix 3.2 Home Missionaries in Scotland employed full- or part-time, 1800 to 1879

The data is incomplete. Records have apparently not survived in sufficient quantity to preserve all the required details.

The numbers given represent the minimum numbers of men employed in any given year. It is probable that in the years prior to 1824 that the figures should be slightly higher.

Organisations providing Funds for Missionaries

1. The home mission fund of the Scotch Baptists, administered by the Edinburgh Scotch Baptist church. Figures for this body are included up to 1827, at which point the majority of Scotch Baptists associated with the BHMS.
2. The Baptist Society in London for the Encouragement and Support of Itinerant Preaching. Figures for this society are included from extant minutes from 1797 to 1812.
3. The Scotch Itinerant Society, 1808-1823. It was led by Christopher Anderson and George Barclay.
4. The Tabernacle Baptist Church, Edinburgh. James Haldane, its minister, privately organised support through his congregation for a number of Highland preachers from 1808 to 1823.
5. The Baptist Highland Mission operated from 1816 to 1827. It was mainly supported by Scotch Baptists, but contributions from other Baptists were received. The Highland Mission was founded by North Portland Street Scotch Baptist Church, Glasgow, in association with some Baptists in Perth.
6. The Baptist Evangelical Society. This organisation was established in 1823 by the merger of (3) and (4). It was renamed 'The Home Missionary Society for Scotland' in 1824.
7. The Baptist Home Missionary Society for Scotland was constituted in 1827. It became the Scottish Baptist organisation responsible for itinerant evangelism in the years following 1827, after the merger of (5) and (6).

Sources:

An Account of Itinerant Exertions in different parts of the Highlands and Islands of Scotland from October 1822, till October 1823.
Baptist Home Missionary Society Reports, 1829-1868.
Minutes of The Baptist Society in London for the Encouragement and Support of Itinerant Preaching, 1797-1812.
Journal of Itinerating Exertions in some of the more destitute parts of Scotland, 6 Vols, 1814-1817.
G. Yuille (ed.), *History of the Baptists in Scotland*.

Appendix 3.3 Total Income of the Baptist Home Missionary Society in Scotland (including legacies and other extra donations in Scotland)

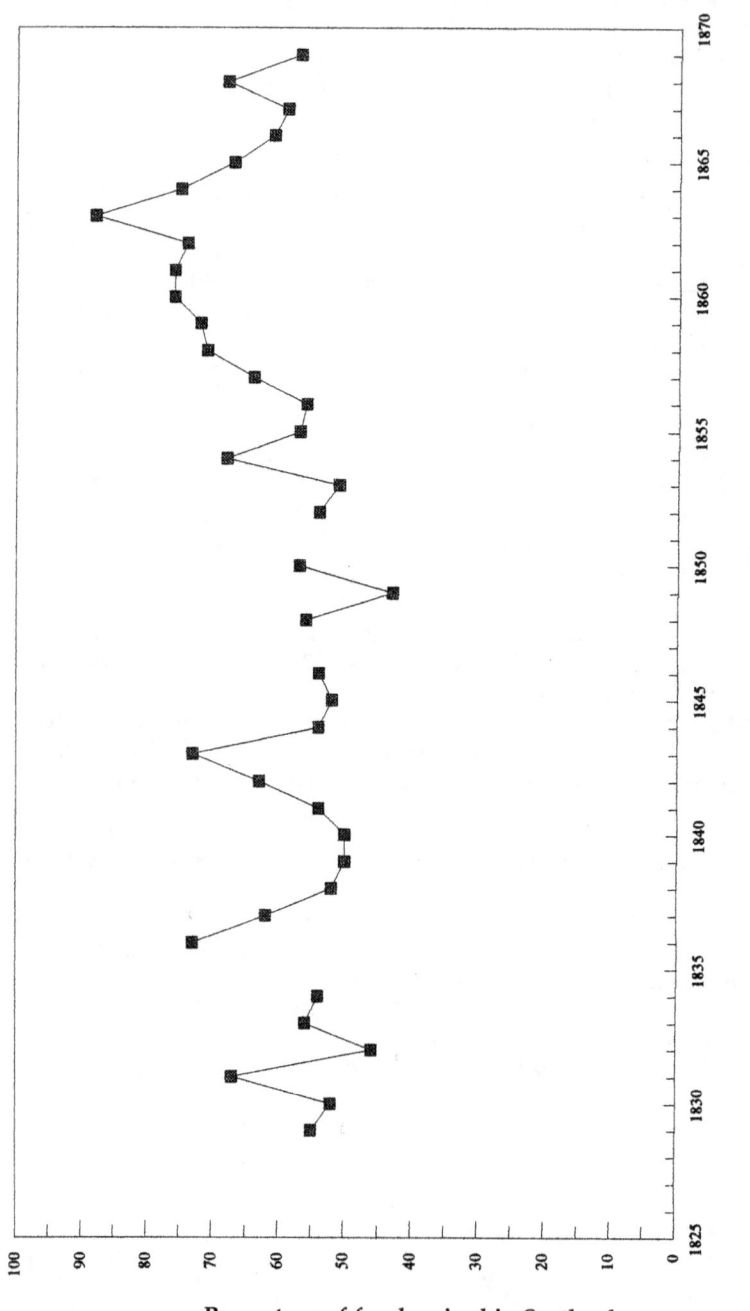

Appendix 3.4 Total Income of the BHMS, 1829-1870

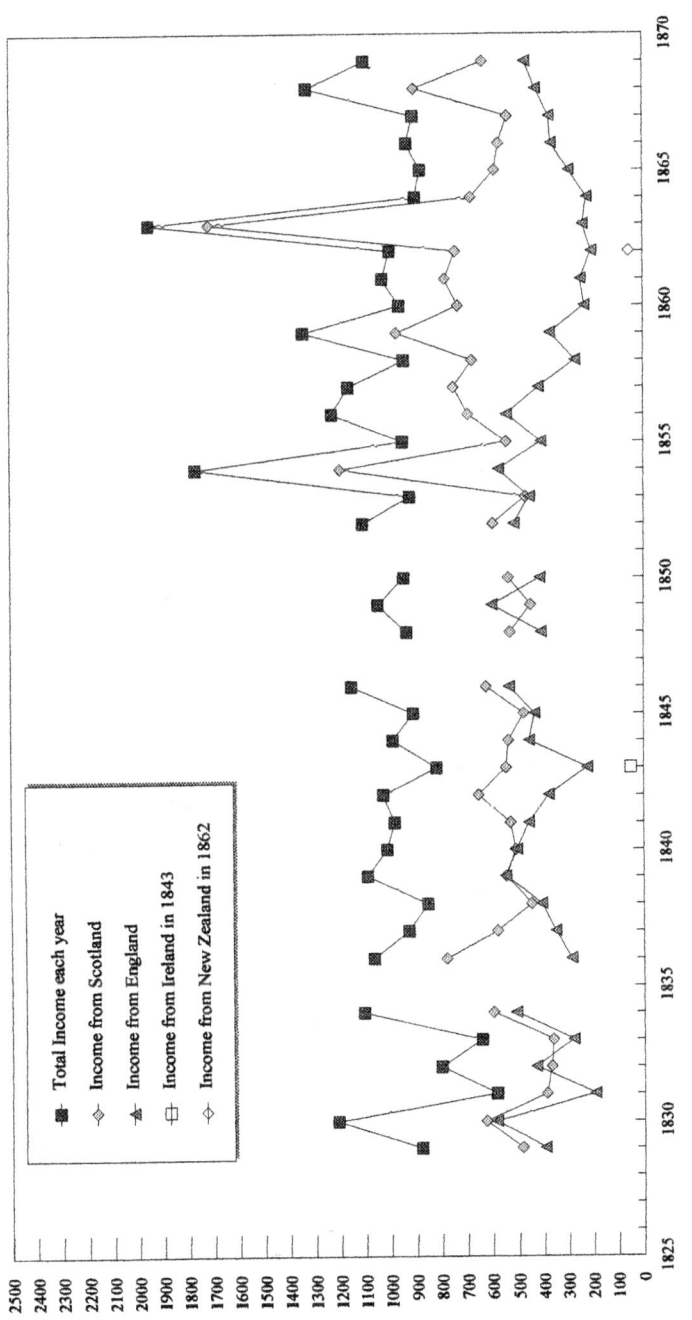

Appendix 3.5 BHMS Subscription Income from Scotland

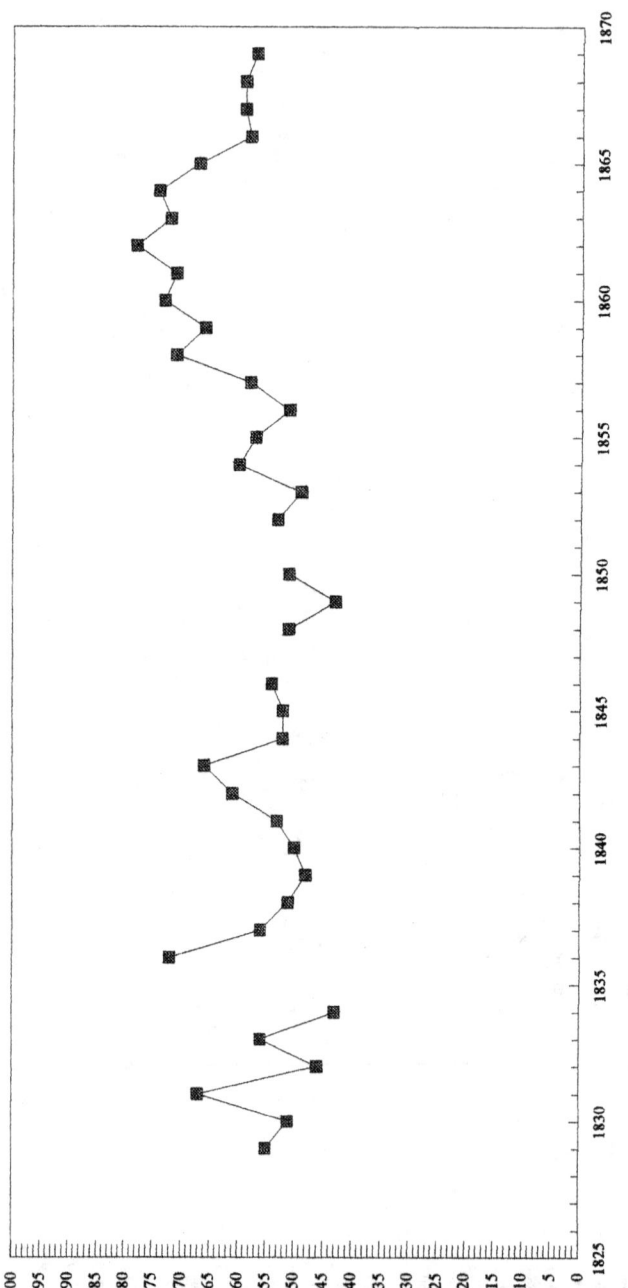

Year

(The details of BHMS income are missing from 1847 to 1851 and incomplete in 1865, 1867 and 1869 to 1898)

Percentages of Funds raised in Scotland

Appendix 3.6 The Trends in BHMS Subscription Income using a Four Year Moving Average

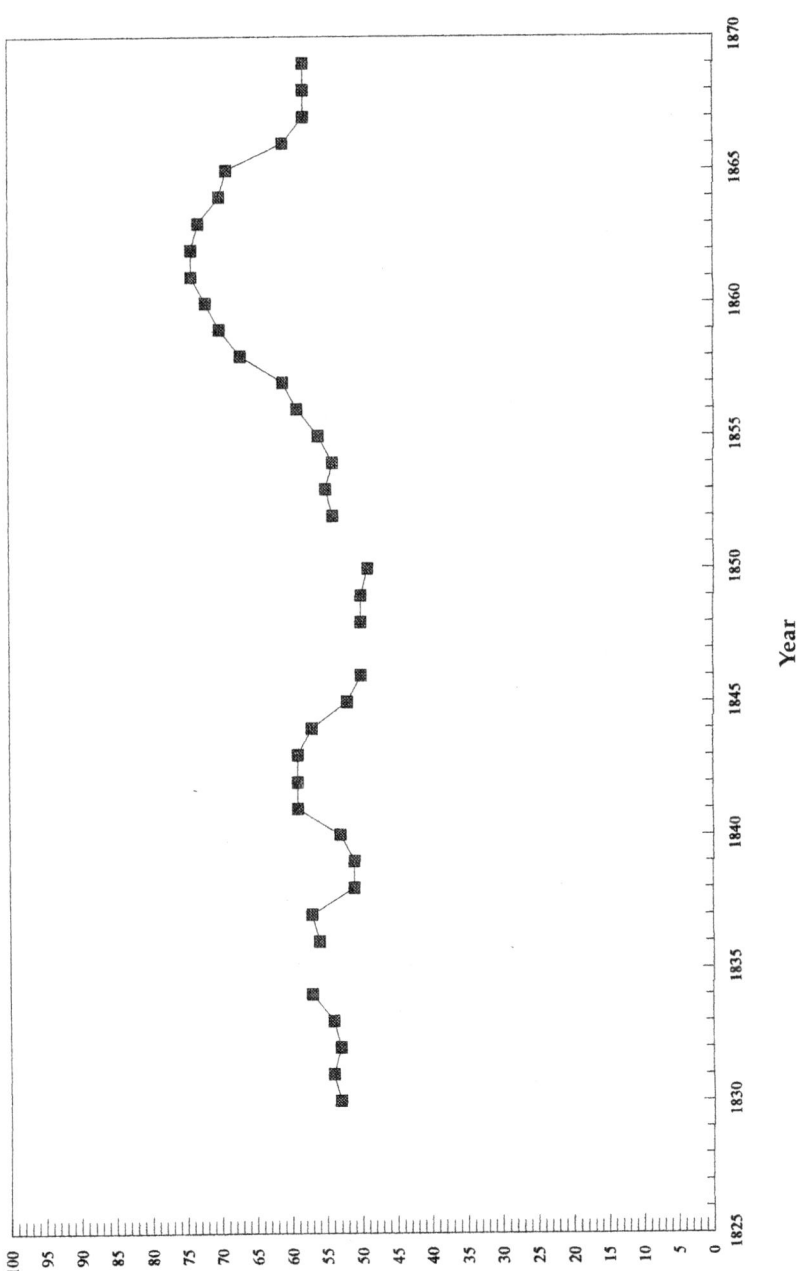

Appendix 4.1 The Baptist Union of Scotland, 1827

Appendices

Appendix 4.1 The Baptist Union of Scotland, 1827

A list of churches in membership with this Baptist Union.

1. John Street, Aberdeen
2. Academy Street, Aberdeen
3. Grantown-on-Spey
4. Kilmavionaig
5. Tullymet
6. Glenlyon
7. Cranoch [Rannoch]
8. Killin
9. Perth
10. Dundee [Home Mission Church]
11. Auchtermuchty
12. Cupar
13. Kirkcaldy
14. Dunfermline
15. Stirling
16. Bainsford, Falkirk
17. North Portland Street, Glasgow
18. South Portland Street, Glasgow
19. Orangefield, Greenock
20. Irvine
21. Lochgilphead
22. Tiree [fellowship not formally constituted yet]
23. Clyde Street, Edinburgh
24. Elder Street, Edinburgh
25. Rose Street, Edinburgh
26. Eyemouth
27. Berwick-upon-Tweed
28. Hawick

Appendix 4.2 The Proportion of Churches Affiliated to the Scottish Baptist Association or the Baptist Union of Scotland, 1827-1879

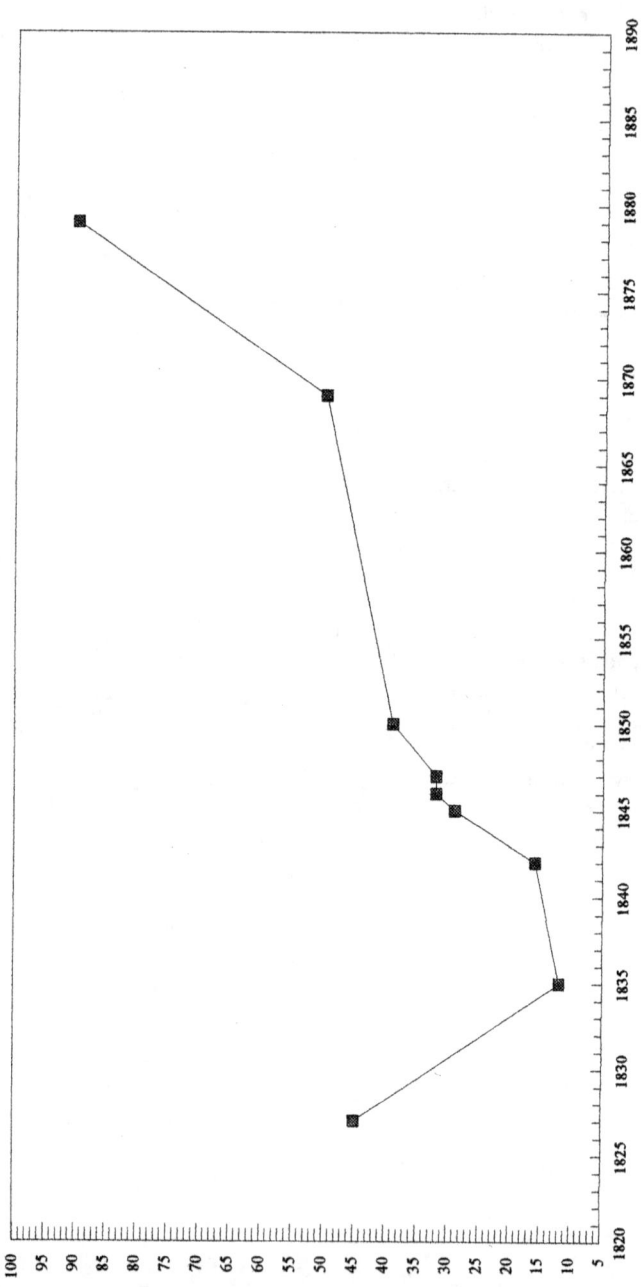

Percentage of Churches involved with the SBA or BU of Scotland

Appendix 4.2 The Proportion of Churches Affiliated to the Scottish Baptist Association or the Baptist Union of Scotland, 1827-1879

Year	Total Number of Baptist Churches in Scotland	Number involved in SBA or B.U.S.	Percentage of Churches involved
1827	62	28	45%
1835	80	10	12%
1842	94	15	16%
1845	94	27	29%
1846	93	30	32%
1847	93	30	32%
1850	98	38	39%
1869	101	51	50%
1879	92	83	90%

Sources:

The Waugh Papers for 1827 figures.
Minutes of the Scottish Baptist Association, 1835 to 1842.
The First Report of the Baptist Union of Scotland, Cupar, 1843.
A Manual of the Baptist Denomination, London, 1845, 1846 and 1847.
The Baptist Union of Scotland Annual Reports, 1869-1880.

Appendix 4.3 The Scottish Baptist Association, 1835–1842

Appendix 4.3 The Scottish Baptist Association, 1835–1842

A list of churches in membership with the SBA.

1. John Street, Aberdeen
2. Grantown-on-Spey
3. Montrose
4. Kilmavionaig
5. Tullymet
6. Lawers
7. Killin
8. Perth
9. Cupar
10. Kirkcaldy
11. Kinghorn
12. Dunfermline
13. Orangefield, Greenock
14. Millport, Great Cumbrae
15. Campbeltown

Appendix 5.1 The Baptist Union of Scotland, 1843–1856

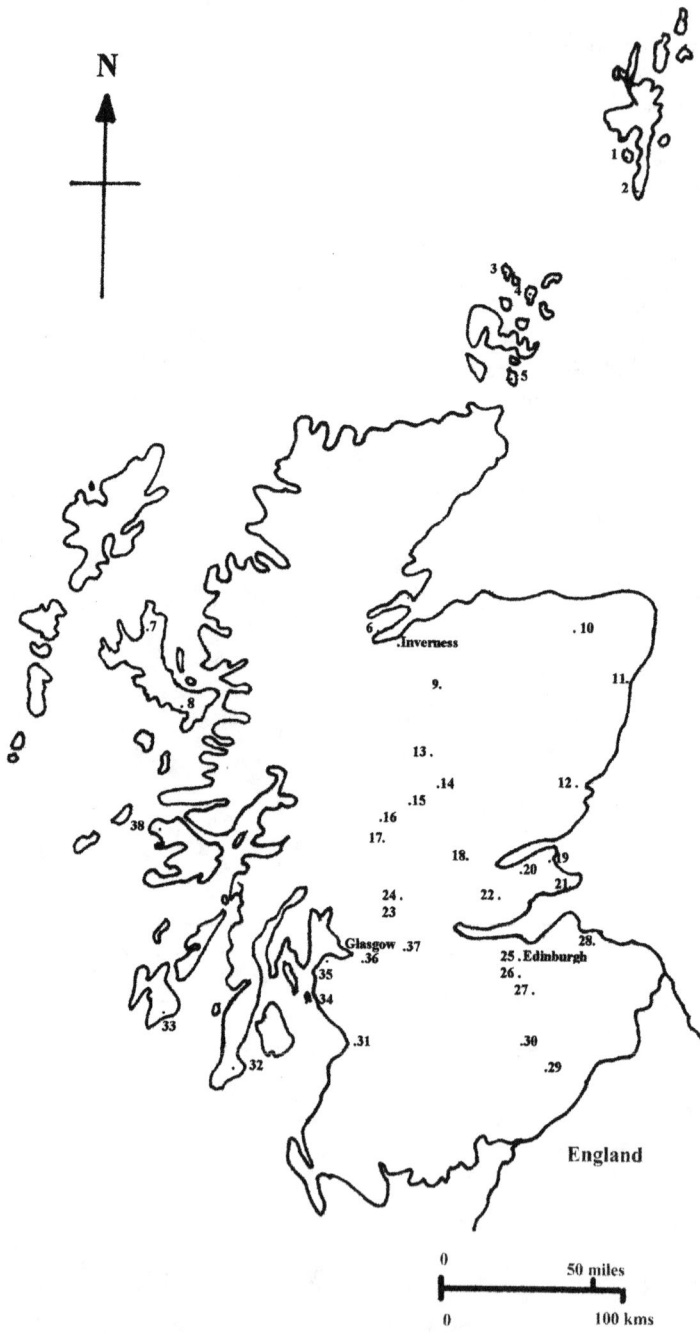

Appendices

Appendix 5.1 The Baptist Union of Scotland, 1843–1856

A list of churches in membership with this Baptist Union.

1. Burra Isle, Shetland
2. Dunrossness, Shetland
3. Westray, Orkney
4. Eday, Orkney
5. Burray, Orkney
6. Fortrose
7. Uig, Skye
8. Broadford, Skye
9. Grantown-on-Spey
10. New Pitsligo and New Deer, Aberdeenshire
11. John Street, Aberdeen
12. Montrose
13. Bridge of Tilt
14. Tullymet
15. Aberfeldy
16. Lawers
17. Killin
18. Perth
19. St Andrews
20. Cupar
21. Anstruther
22. Inglis Street, Dunfermline
23. Guild Hall, Stirling
24. Spittal Street, Stirling
25. Leith
26. Marshall Street, Edinburgh
27. Bonnyrigg
28. Dunbar
29. Hawick
30. Galashiels
31. Ayr
32. Campbeltown
33. Port Ellen, Islay
34. Millport, Great Cumbrae
35. Orangefield, Greenock
36. East Regent Street, Glasgow
37. Airdrie
38. Tobermory, Mull

Appendix 5.2 Scottish Baptist Churches, Ministers and Lay Leaders involved in the Total Abstinence Cause before 1842

	Name of Church (or church leader) other Temperance activity	Name of Minister Abstinence Society or	President of local Total
1.	John Street, Aberdeen		
2.	Silver Street Scotch Baptist, Aberdeen		
3	Airdrie	James Taylor	Temperance lecturer
4	Alloa		
5	Ayr	James Blair	Temperance lecturer
6	Berwick-upon Tweed	Alexander Kirkwood	Temperance lecturer
7	Dunfermline Scotch Baptist		
8	Dunrossness, Shetland	Sinclair Thomson	
9	Elder Street, Edinburgh	William Innes	
10	Falkirk Scotch Baptist	John Gillon	President of Falkirk T.A.S.
11	George Street Scotch Baptist, Glasgow	Walter Dick M.D.	Temperance lecturer
12.	Hope Street, Glasgow	James Paterson	Temperance lecturer and editor of *Scottish Temperance Review*, and later the *Scottish Review*, publications of the Scottish Temperance League.
		Robert Kettle	Vice-President of the Western Scottish Temperance Union in August 1841.
13	unknown Scotch Baptist, Glasgow	Thomas Brown	delegate to Annual meetings of the Western Scottish Temperance Union, June 1840 in Glasgow.
14	North Portland Street Scotch Baptist, Glasgow	Charles Wallace	Temperance lecturer
15	Grantown-on-Spey	Peter Grant	President of Grantown T.A.S.
16	St Michael's Street, Greenock	William Campbell Alexander Stevenson	
17	Irvine	George Barclay	Temperance writer (1832) and lecturer
		John Leechman	Temperance lecturer
18	Rose Street Scotch Baptist, Kirkcaldy	Robert Lockhart Ninian Lockhart jun.	Temperance lecturer Temperance lecturer
19	Lochgilphead	John McIntosh	Temperance lecturer

Appendices

20	Millport	James McKirdy	
21	Storie Street Scotch Baptist, Paisley	William Shanks	Committee member Paisley T.A.S.
	[Perth General B.C.]	Jabez Burns	Lecturer for Perth Temperance Society in the early 1830s. He took the T.A. pledge in London during May 1836.
22	Perth		
23	Port Street, Stirling	Mr Boyd	President of St Ninians T.A.S.

Sources:

The Scottish Temperance Herald, 1840-1842.
The Scottish Temperance Journal, Jan.1839 - Aug.1841.
P.T. Winskill, *The Temperance Movement and its Workers*,
(4 Vols), Glasgow, 1893.

Appendix 6.1 English Baptist Colleges and Scotland

Name of College	Scots training for ministry up to 1870	% Former students settled in Scotland by 1870	Former students settled in Scotland prior to 1870	Former students involved in the 1856 SBA.
Bristol 1800-1870	20/279	5%	13	3
Bury [Manchester] 1866-1870	0/9	0%	0	0
Horton [Rawdon] 1806-1870	43/303	7%	22	5
[Stepney] Regent's Park 1810-1870	7 / 236	0.1%	3	0
Pastor's 1856-1870	15 / 294	9%	25	15

Sources:

Regent's Park: R.E. Cooper, *From Stepney to St Giles*, pp.109, 135-137. *Stepney College Annual Reports*, 1830-1870.

Bury [Manchester]: C. Rignal, *Manchester Baptist College 1866-1916*, pp.247-266.

Bristol: *A Report of the Bristol Baptist College or Bristol Education Society*, 1875, pp.36-40.

S. Hall, 'The Scottish Links with Bristol Baptist College', private MS.

Horton [Rawdon]: *The Northern Baptist Educational Society Reports 1805-1806 to 1870-1871*.

Pastor's: Spurgeon's College, Register of Students 1856 to1871.

Appendices 365

Appendix 6.2 The Pastor's College Former Students involved in the Scottish Baptist Association or Baptist Union of Scotland by 1870

	Name	Church	Dates involved in SBA/B.U.S.
1.	Thomas Medhurst	North Frederick Street, Glasgow	1862-1869
2.	Clarence Chambers	Crown Terrace, Aberdeen	1866-1877
3.	Samuel Crabb	Aberchirder	1865-1869
		Rothesay	1869-1919
4.	Charles Hill	Viewfield, Dunfermline	1866-1875
		Stirling Street, Galashiels	1875-1881
5.	Alexander McDougall	Rothesay	1866-1868
		Islay	1869-1871
6.	John Crouch	Victoria Street, Paisley	1866-1896
7.	W.C. Dunning	Charlotte Chapel, Edinburgh	1867-1872
8.	James Chamberlain	Bath Street, Glasgow	1867-1868
9.	John Wilson	Peterhead	1867-1871
10.	J.O. Wills	Lochee, Dundee	1866-1869
		Bell Street, Dundee	1869-1873
11.	J. Scott	Forres	1867-1869
12.	John Spence	Falkirk	1868-1870
13.	Henry Moore	Bath Street, Glasgow	1869-1872
14.	J.D. Cameron	Lochee, Dundee	1870-1880
15.	Arthur Morgan	Grantown-upon Spey	1870-1872

Sources:

First Annual Report of the Baptist Union of Scotland, 1869.
Second Annual Report of the Baptist Union of Scotland, 1870.
Spurgeon's College Register of Students 1856 to 1871, MS in the possession of Spurgeon's College.
Yuille (ed.), *Baptists in Scotland*.

Appendix 6.3 The Baptist Union of Scotland, 1869

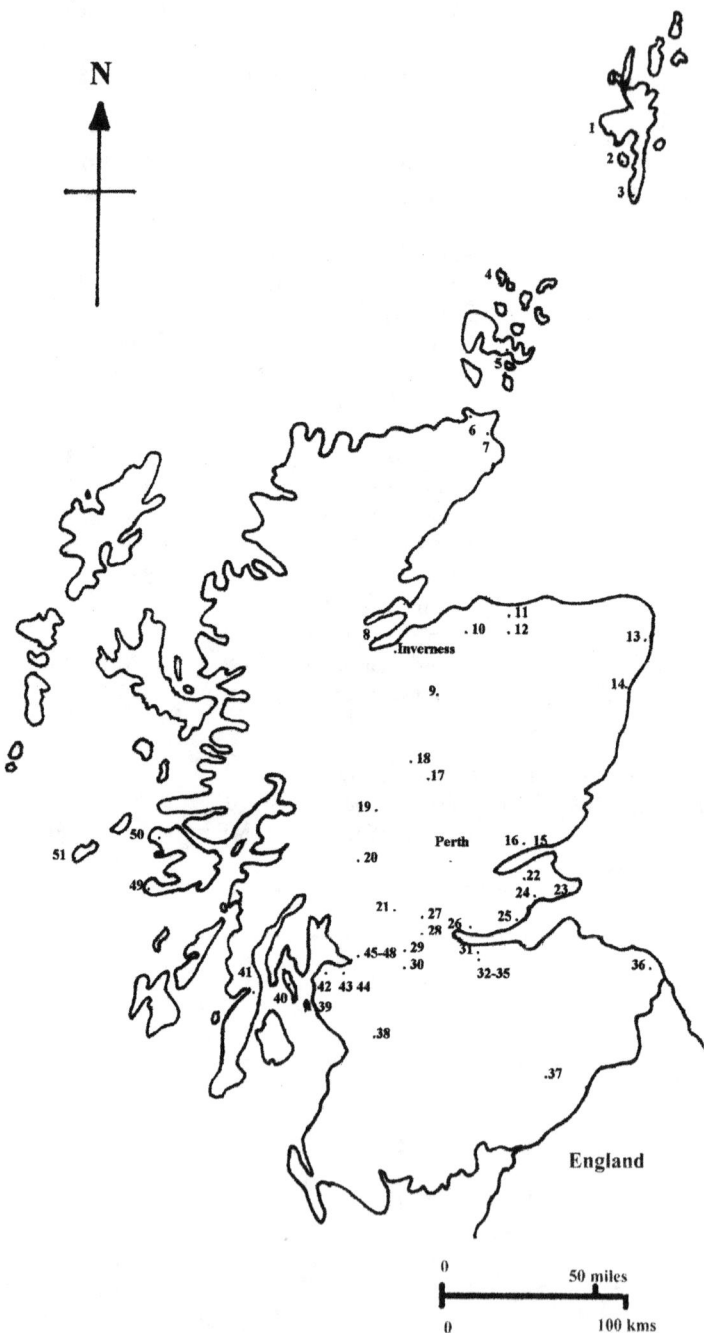

Appendices

Figure 6.3 The Baptist Union of Scotland, 1869

A list of churches in membership with this Baptist Union.

1	Sandsting, Shetland	27	Bainsford
2	Burra Isle, Shetland	28	Falkirk
3	Dunrossness, Shetland	29	Airdrie
4	Westray, Orkney	30	Coatbridge
5	Kirkwall, Orkney	31	Leith
6	Scarfskerry	32	Dublin Street, Edinburgh
7	Keiss	33	Duncan Street, Edinburgh
8	Fortrose	34	Richmond Street, Edinburgh
9	Grantown-on-Spey	35	Rose Street, Edinburgh
10	Forres	36	Eyemouth
11	Elgin	37	Hawick
12	Branderburgh	38	Kilmarnock
13	Peterhead	39	Millport, Great Cumbrae
14	John Street, Aberdeen	40	Rothesay
15	Bell Street, Dundee	41	Lochgilphead
16	Lochee, Dundee	42	Greenock
17	Blairgowrie	43	Storie Street, Paisley
18	Tullymet	44	Victoria Place, Paisley
19	Glenlyon	45	Bath Street, Glasgow
20	Crieff	46	Blackfriars Street, Glasgow
21	Stirling	47	Hope Street, Glasgow
22	Cupar	48	North Frederick Street, Glasgow
23	Anstruther	49	Ross, Mull
24	Largo	50	Tobermory, Mull
25	Kirkcaldy	51	Tiree
26	Dunfermline		

Appendix 6.4 The Baptist Union of Scotland, 1879

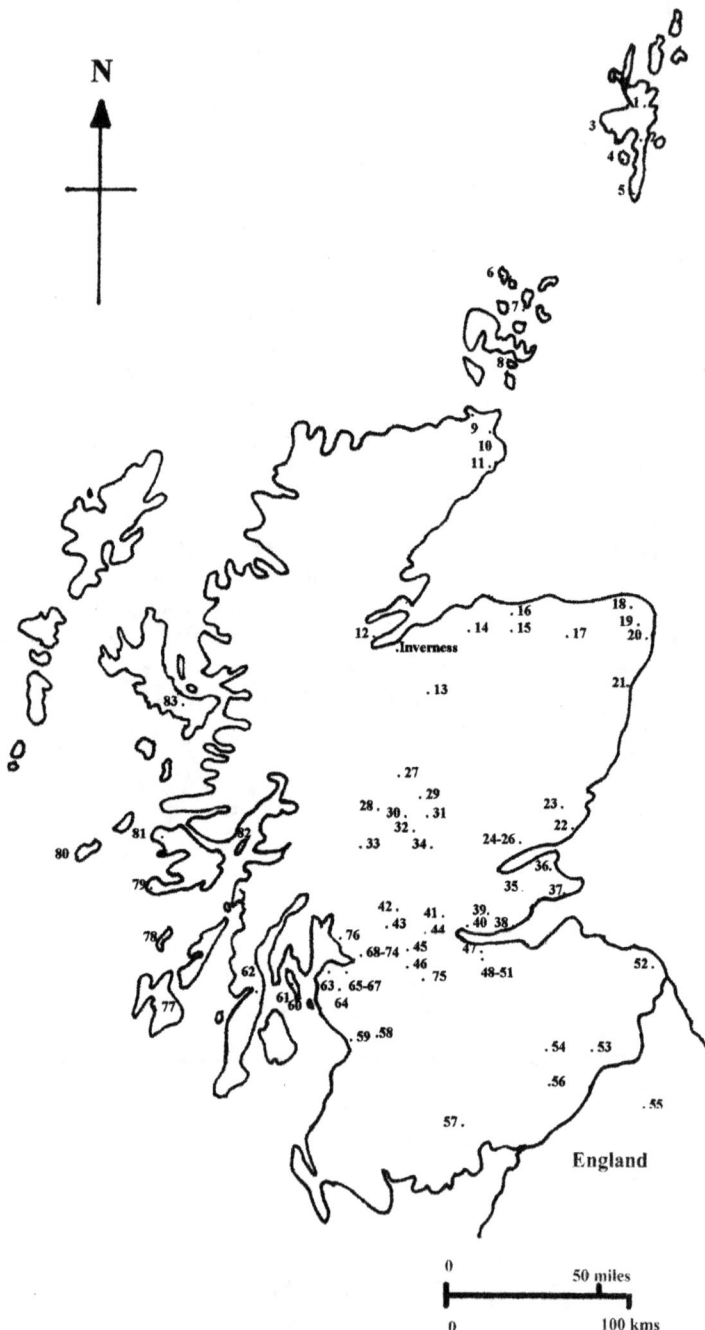

Appendix 6.4 The Baptist Union of Scotland, 1879

A list of churches in membership with this Baptist Union.

1. Lunnasting, Shetland
2. Lerwick, Shetland
3. Sandsting, Shetland
4. Burra Isle, Shetland
5. Dunrossness, Shetland
6. Westray, Orkney
7. Eday, Orkney
8. Burray, Orkney
9. Scarfskerry
10. Keiss and Stroma
11. Wick
12. Fortrose
13. Grantown-on-Spey
14. Forres
15. Elgin
16. Branderburgh
17. Aberchirder
18. Fraserburgh
19. St Fergus
20. Peterhead
21. Crown Terrace, Aberdeen
22. Arbroath B.C.
23. Forfar B.C.
24. Broughty Ferry, Dundee
25. Dundee
26. Lochee, Dundee
27. Blair Atholl
28. Rannoch
29. Tullymet
30. Glenlyon
31. Blairgowrie
32. Lochtayside [Lawers]
33. Crieff
34. Perth
35. Cupar
36. St Andrews
37. Anstruther
38. Kirkcaldy
39. Cowdenbeath
40. Dunfermline
41. Alloa
42. Stirling
43. St Ninians
44. Falkirk
45. Airdrie
46. Coatbridge
47. Leith
48. Dublin Street, Edinburgh
49. Duncan Street, Edinburgh
50. Marshall Street, Edinburgh
51. Rose Street, Edinburgh
52. Eyemouth
53. Kelso
54. Galashiels
55. Ford Forge, Northumberland
56. Hawick
57. Dumfries
58. Kilmarnock
59. Irvine
60. Millport, Great Cumbrae
61. Rothesay
62. Lochgilphead
63. Greenock
64. Johnstone
65. George Street, Paisley
66. Storie Street, Paisley
67. Victoria Place, Paisley
68. Adelaide Place, Glasgow
69. Cambridge Street, Glasgow
70. Gorbals, Glasgow
71. Govan, Glasgow
72. John Knox Street, Glasgow
73. North Frederick Street, Glasgow
74. Queens Park, Glasgow
75. Wishaw
76. Dumbarton
77. Bowmore, Islay
78. Colonsay
79. Ross, Mull
80. Tiree
81. Tobermory, Mull
82. Lismore
83. Broadford, Skye

Bibliography

Official Publications

Report of The Commission of Enquiry into the Opportunities of Public Religious Worship, and Means of Religious Instruction, and the Pastoral Superintendence afforded to the People of Scotland
Vol.1, London: House of Commons, 1837. 1837 (31.) xxi.19.
Vol.2, Edinburgh: W. & A.K. Johnston, 1837-38. 1837-38 [109.] xxxii.1.
Vol.3, Edinburgh: W. & A.K. Johnston, 1837-38. 1837-38 [113.] xxxiii.1.
Vol.4, Edinburgh: W. & A.K. Johnston, 1837-38. 1837-38 [122.] xxxiii.273.
Vol.5, Edinburgh: W. & A.K. Johnston, 1839. 1839 [152.] xxiii.1.
Vol.6, Edinburgh: W. & A.K. Johnston, 1839. 1839 [153.] xxiv.1.
Vol.7, Edinburgh: W. & A.K. Johnston, 1839. 1839 [154.] xxv.1.
Vol.8, Edinburgh: W. & A.K. Johnston, 1839. 1839 [162.] xxvi.1.
Vol.9, Edinburgh: W. & A.K. Johnston, 1839. 1839 [164.] xxvi.607.
Reference numbers are to copies held by the National Library of Scotland, Edinburgh.

Annuals

Annual Report of the Committee of the Baptist Home Missionary Society... of Great Britain for 1850, (London: John Haddon, 1850).
The Baptist Handbook, London: various publishers, 1861-1880.
Baptist Union of Scotland Annual Reports, (Edinburgh: John Lindsay, 1869-1875). (Glasgow: The Baptist Union of Scotland, 1876-1897).
Baptist Home Missionary Society Reports, (Edinburgh: Various Publishers, 1829-1868) (except 1847, 1851, 1865 and 1867).
Baptist Union of Scotland Annual Reports, (Edinburgh: John Lindsay, 1869-1875). (Glasgow: The Baptist Union of Scotland, 1876-1897).
The Edinburgh Almanac, (Edinburgh: Oliver & Boyd, 1835, 1850-1855).
Edinburgh Bible Society Annual Report, (Edinburgh: A. Balfour & Co., 1826, 1828-1831, 1833-1834).
Glasgow Post Office Directory, (Glasgow: Various Publishers, 1800-1870).
A Manuel of the Baptist Denomination, (London: Houlston and Stoneman, 1845-1856).
(Houlston and Wright, 1857-1860).
The Northern Baptist Education Society Reports 1805-1806 to 1870-1871, (Various Publishers and Locations, 1806-1871).
The Post Office Annual Directory, (Edinburgh: Various Publishers, 1790-1879).
A Report of the Bristol Baptist College, or Bristol Education Society for 1875, (Bristol: Hemmons, 1875).
Stepney (Regent's Park after 1856) Baptist College, Annual Reports, (London: Stepney Baptist College, 1830-1870).
Scottish Baptist Yearbook, Glasgow: W. Asher, 1899-1923).
Second Annual Report of the Edinburgh Total Abstinence Society, (Edinburgh: For the Society, 1839).

Newspapers and Journals

The Baptist Magazine, (London: Various Publishers, 1809-1864).
The Baptist Reporter, (London: Simpkin, Marshall & Co., 1842-1843, 1845-1848, 1850-1855).
The Christian Advocate, (Liverpool: William Jones, January 1809-January 1811).
The Christian Advocate and Scotch Baptist Repository, (March 1849-December 1849, January-December 1850, Beverley: James Everson, 1849-1850).
The Christian Advocate, (Edinburgh: J. Taylor, January 1857- December 1861). (Edinburgh: Kerr, 1865).
The Christian Repository, (Edinburgh: Balfour and Clarke, 1818).
The Church, (Leeds: John Heaton, 1846-1851, 1856). (London: J. Heaton & Son, 1863).
The Eclectic Magazine, (London: Various Publishers, 1818-1837).
Edinburgh Evangelical Magazine, (Edinburgh: John Turnbull, 1803-1805).
The Edinburgh Quarterly Magazine, (Edinburgh: J. Ritchie, 1798-1800).
The Evangelical Magazine, (London: Thomas Ward & Co., 1799-1847).
The Evangelist, Glasgow: G. Gallie, 1846-1847, 1850). (Edinburgh: E. Henderson, 1851-1853).
The Free Church Magazine, (Edinburgh: J. Johnstone, 1843-1846).
The Freeman, (London: Various Publishers, 1855-1879).
The Missionary Magazine, (Edinburgh: J.A. Pullans & Sons, 1797-1800).
The New Evangelical Magazine, (London: T. Tegg, 1815-1816, 1818-1824).
The New Theological Repository, (Liverpool: William Jones, 1800-1802).
The Primitive Church Magazine, (London: Arthur Hall & Co., 1843-1862). (London: Elliott Stock, 1863-1868).
Scottish Baptist Magazine, Various Locations and Publishers, 1875-2000).
The Scottish Temperance Herald, (Vols 1-3; Edinburgh: The East of Scotland Abstinence Union, 1840-1842).
The Scottish Temperance Journal, (Vol.1, January 1839 to August 1841; Glasgow: George Gallie, 1839-1841).
The Scottish Temperance Review, (Edinburgh: McDowell, Greig and Wahler, October 1845-December 1850).
The Scripture Magazine, (Vol.2; Edinburgh: J. Ritchie, 1810).
The Theological Repository, (Liverpool: William Jones, 1806-1808).
The Victorian Freeman (Australia), (January-October 1881 issues).
United Presbyterian Magazine, New Series, (Vol.2; Edinburgh: W. Oliphant, 1858).

Contemporary Printed Material

Address by the Committee of the Baptist Home Missionary Society for Scotland, 2 October 1827, Edinburgh, MS ref 1950.69 (20), National Library of Scotland, Edinburgh.
J. Aikman, *Observations on Exhortation in the Churches of Christ*, (Edinburgh: J. Ritchie, 1808).

Bibliography

An Account of Itinerant Exertions in different parts of the Highlands and Islands of Scotland from October 1822, till October 1823, MS ref QP 668/3, document in the possession of Edinburgh University Library..

An Account of the Proceedings of The Society for Propagating the Gospel at Home from their commencement December 28, 1797, to May 16, 1799, (Edinburgh: J. Ritchie, 1799).

W. Adamson, *The Life of Fergus Ferguson*, (Glasgow: Thomas Morison, 1900).

— *The Life of the Rev. James Morison*, (London: Hodder and Stoughton, 1898).

C. Anderson, *Brief Narrative of the Baptist Mission in India*, (London: Button and Son, 5th edition, 1819).

— *The Christian Spirit which is essential to the triumph of the Kingdom of God*, (London: B.J. Holdsworth, 1824).

— *A Discourse occasioned by the death of The Rev. William Carey DD of Serampore, Bengal*, (Edinburgh: Waugh and Innes, W. Whyte and Co., 1834).

— *The Domestic Constitution: or The Family Circle the Source and Test of National Stablility*, (Edinburgh: W.P. Kennedy, 1847).

— *Historical Sketches of the Native Irish and their Descendants*, (Edinburgh: Oliver and Boyd, 2nd edition, 1830).

— *Ireland - But still without the Ministry of the Word in her own Native Language*, (Edinburgh: Oliver and Boyd,1835).

— *Memorial on behalf of the Native Irish*, (London: Oliphant, Waugh and Innes, 1815).

— *Memorial respecting the Diffusion of the Sacred Scriptures throughout the United Kingdom*, (Edinburgh: Balfour and Clarke, 1819).

— *The Singular Introduction of the Bible into Britain*, (Edinburgh: W.P. Kennedy, 1849).

H. Anderson, *The Life and Letters of Christopher Anderson*, (Edinburgh: W.P. Kennedy, 1854).

Anonymous, *Hypocrisy Detected in a Letter to the late Firm of Haldane Ewing and Co., with a preface containing the narrative of Mr James Reid - A missionary sent by these gentlemen to Upper Canada*, (Aberdeen: J. Booth, 1812).

Anonymous, *A Letter to the Editor of the Evangelical Magazine containing a review of their Strictures on the Principles and Practices of the Baptists, in Sept. 1814*, (Dunfermline: John Miller, 1814).

J. Baillie (ed.), *Proceedings of the General Assembly of the Free Church of Scotland*, (Edinburgh: W.P. Kennedy, 1843).

R. Balmain, *Reminiscences of Clyde Street Hall and My Early Days*, (Edinburgh: Private publication, 1893).

J. Belcher (ed.), *The Complete Works of the Rev. Andrew Fuller*, (3 Vols; Harrisonburg: Sprinkle, 1988 [1844]).

J. Belcher and A.G. Fuller (eds), *The Baptist Irish Society: Its Origins, History and Prospects*, (London: Houlston and Stoneman, 1845).

J. Bennett, *Memoir of the Life of the Rev. David Bogue D.D.*, (London: Frederick Westley and A.H. Davis, 1827).

C.M. Birrell, *The Life of William Brock, D.D.*, (London: James Nisbet, 1878).

D. Bogue and J. Bennett, *The History of the Dissenters from the Revolution to the year 1808*, (4 Vols; London: Williams and Smith, 1808-1812).

D. Bogue, *Discourses on the Millennium*, (London: T. Hamilton, 1818).

D. Bogue, *Essay on the Divine Authority of the New Testament*, (London: Religious Tract Society, 2nd edition, 1804).
D. Bogue, *A Sermon preached at Salter's Hall, March 30th, 1792*, London: A. Strahan, 1793).
H. Bonar, *Life of the Rev. John Milne, M.A.*, (London: James Nisbet & Co., 1869).
W. Braidwood, *Purity of Christian Communion*, (Edinburgh: J. Guthrie, 1796).
J. Brown, *A Sketch of the life of the late Robert Primrose*, (Glasgow: William Gilchrist, 1861).
J. Burns, *The Christian's Sketch Book*, (Edinburgh: J. Burns, 1831).
J. Burrell, *Memoir of Rev. Thomas Lewis of Islington*, (London: Ward and Co., 1853).
W. Burton (ed.), *Essays and Correspondence, chiefly on Scriptural Subjects, by the late John Walker of Dublin*, (2 Vols; Dublin: E. Madden and R.M. Tims, 1846).
W. Carus, *Memoirs of The Life of the Rev. Charles Simeon, M.A.*, (London: J. Hatchard & Son, 1847).
V.J. Charlesworth, *Rowland Hill*, (London: Hodder & Stoughton, 1886).
J. Clifford (ed.), *The English Baptists: Who they are and what they have done*, (London: E. Marlborough & Co., 1881).
Condensed Report of Discussions by Delegates at the Conference, [Scotch Baptist], (Haggate: Private publication, 1872).
Conversation on Baptism in four parts, (The London Baptist Tract Society, October 15 1841, Tract no.85, London: Houlston and Stoneman, n.d). (apparently part four only extant).
F.A. Cox, *History of the Baptist Missionary Society from 1792-1842*, (Vol.1; London: T. Ward & Co., 1842).
J. Culross, *William Carey*, (London: Hodder & Stoughton, 1881).
R.W. Dale, *The Life and Letters of John Angell James*, (London: James Nisbet & Co., 1861).
Discourse addressed to the Baptist Church, Bristo Street, Edinburgh, on the occasion of the Death of Mr Andrew Arthur, One of the Pastors of the Church, September 16 1855, (Edinburgh: William Innes, 1855).
D. Douglas, *History of the Baptist Churches in the North of England*, (London: Houlston and Stoneman, 1846).
H.J. Ellison, *The Temperance Reformation Movement in the Church of England: Its Principles and Progress*, (London: S.W. Partridge,1865).
Evangelical Union Jubilee Conference Memorial Volume, (Glasgow: T. Morison, 1892).
G. Ewing, *Facts and Documents Respecting the Connections which have subsisted between Robert Haldane Esq and Greville Ewing*, (Glasgow: M. Ogle and J.& A. Duncan, 1809).
The Expulsion of Nine Students from the Glasgow Theological Academy, (Glasgow: G. Gallie, 1844).
F. Ferguson, *A History of the Evangelical Union*, (Glasgow: Thomas Morison, 1876).
C.G. Finney, *An Autobiography*, (London: Hodder and Stoughton, 1892).
— *Revivals of Religion*, (Chicago: Moody Press, 1962).
First Report of the Committee of the Baptist Academical Society for Scotland, (Edinburgh: R. Marshall, n.d. [1839]).

The First Yearly Report of the Baptist Union of Scotland, (Cupar: G.S. Tullis, 1843).
O. Flett, *Remarks on the Work of Ministerial Education carried on under the auspices of the Baptist Union of Scotland from 1869 till 1882*, (Edinburgh: R. Symon, 1883).
A. Fuller, *Memoirs of the late Rev. Samuel Pearce, A.M.*, (Clipstone: J.W. Morris, 1800).
W.Y. Fullarton, *C.H. Spurgeon: A Biography*, (London: Williams and Norgate, 1920).
J. Gill, *Gill's Commentary on the Whole Bible*, (6 Vols; Grand Rapids: Baker, 1980 [1852-1854]).
— *A Complete Body of Doctrinal and Practical Divinity*, (Paris, Arkansas: The Baptist Standard Bearer, 1987 [1839]).
D. Gilmour, *Reminiscences of The Pen' Folk*, (Paisley: Alex. Gardner, 3rd edition, 1889).
R. Glover, *The Desirability of a Closer Connexion between the Baptist Union and the leading Baptist Societies* , (London: Yates and Alexander, 1874).
G. Gogerly, *The Pioneers: A Narrative of Facts connected with the Early Christian Mission in Bengal, chiefly related to the operation of the London Missionary Society*, (London: John Snow & Co., 1843).
S.G. Green, *Education for the Ministry*, (London: Yates and Alexander, 1871).
A. Haldane, *The Lives of Robert and James Haldane*, (Edinburgh: Banner of Truth, 1990 [1853]).
J.A. Haldane, *An Address to the Church of Christ, Leith Walk, Edinburgh*, (Edinburgh: J. Ritchie, 1807).
— *The Crown of Righteousness*, (a Funeral sermon for Robert Haldane), (Edinburgh: Thornton and Collie, 1843).
— *The Doctrine of the Atonement with Strictures on Recent Publications*, (Edinburgh: W.P. Kennedy, 3rd edition,1862).
— *An Exposition of the Epistle to the Galatians*, (Edinburgh: William Whyte and Co., 1848).
— *The Foundation of the Observation of the Lord's Day and of the Lord's Supper Vindicated*, (Edinburgh: J. Ritchie, 1807).
— *The Importance of Hearing the Voice of God*, (Edinburgh: William Oliphant, 1824).
— *The Intimate Relation and Essential Difference between Judaism and Christianity*, (Edinburgh: William Whyte and Co., 1849).
— *Observations on Forbearance*, (Edinburgh: J. Ritchie, 1811).
— *Observations on The Association of Believers*, (Edinburgh: J. Ritchie, 1808).
— *Reasons for a Change of Sentiment and Practice on the Subject of Baptism*, (Edinburgh : J. Ritchie, 1809).
— *Remarks on Mr Jones's Review of Observations on Forbearance*, (Edinburgh: J. Ritchie, 1812).
— *A View of the Social Worship and Ordinances observed by the First Christians drawn from the Sacred Scriptures alone*, (Edinburgh: Ogle & Aikman and Guthrie & Tait, 1805).
J.A. Haldane, J. Aikman & J. Rate, *Journal of a Tour through the Northern Counties of Scotland and the Orkney Isles in Autumn 1797*, (Edinburgh: J. Ritchie, 1798).
R. Haldane, *Address to the Public concerning Political Opinions and Plans lately*

adopted to promote Religion in Scotland, (Edinburgh: J. Ritchie, 1800).
— *An Answer to Mr Greville Ewing's Pamphlet entitled Facts and Documents &c*, (Edinburgh: J. Ogle and A. Johnstone, 1810).
— *The Authenticity and Inspiration of the Holy Scriptures*, (Minneapolis: Klock & Klock, 1985 [1845 edition]).
— *A Letter to the Editor of the Edinburgh Christian Instructor: containing Strictures on Warburton, Lardner, Paley, Campbell and MacKnight*, (London: Waugh and Innes, 1820).
H. Harcus, *The History of The Orkney Baptist Churches*, (Ayr: David Hourston, 1898).
R.Hill, 'Glorious Displays of Grace' in *Sermons preached in London at the formation of the Missionary Society*, (London : T. Chapman, 1795).
J.H. Hinton, *The Theological Works of J.H. Hinton M.A.*, (7 Vols; London: Houlston & Wright, 1865).
— *The Work of the Spirit in Conversion*, (London: Holdsworth & Ball, 1830).
J. Horsburgh, *Pastoral Addresses*, (Edinburgh: John Bayne, 1869).
W. Innes, *Eugenio and Epenetus, or Conversations respecting the Evidence in support of Infant Baptism*, (Edinburgh: Oliphant and Balfour, 1811).
— *The Origin and Permanence of Christian Joy*, (London: The Religious Tract Society, 1839).
— *Reasons for Separating from the Church of Scotland*, (Dundee: Chalmers, Ray & Co, 1804).
— *Remarks on Christian Union*, (Edinburgh: Oliphant, Waugh & Innes, 1811).
id., *Sketches of Human Nature*, (Edinburgh: Waugh and Innes, 1823).
F. Johnston, *Baptism is Dipping, and Christian Baptism is Believers' Baptism*, (Edinburgh: John Hume, 1865).
F. Johnston, *The Gospel Roll*, (Glasgow: George Gallie, 1863).
F. Johnston, *Infant Baptism Not Christian Baptism*, (Edinburgh: Ebenezer Henderson, 1851).
F. Johnston, *The Work of God and the Work of Man in Conversion*, (Edinburgh: W. Innes & Andrew Muirhead, 1848).
S. Jones, *A Review of Mr J.A. Haldane's Late Publication entitled Observations on Forbearance*, (London: W. Jones 1812).
T.S. Jones, *The Life of The Right Honourable Willielma, Viscountess Glenorchy*, (Edinburgh: William Whyte And Co., 1824).
W. Jones, *Autobiography*, (edited by his son; London: John Snow, 1846).
— *Memoir of the Life, Ministry and Writings of the Rev. Rowland Hill M.A.*, (London: John Bennett, 1834).
— *The Miscellaneous Works of Archibald McLean*, (7 Vols; Elgin: Peter McDonald, 1847).
— *The Miscellaneous Writings of the late Mr William Braidwood*, (Edinburgh: William Oliphant and Son, 1838).
— *The Works of Mr Archibald McLean*, (2 Vols; Edinburgh: John Turnbull, 1805).
— *The Works of Mr Archibald McLean*, (6 Vols; London: William Jones, 1823).
Journal of Itinerating Exertions in some of the more destitute parts of Scotland, (6 Vols; Edinburgh: A. Balfour, 1814-1817).
Jubilee Handbook of Marshall Street Baptist Church, Edinburgh, (Edinburgh: T. Adams, 1896).

Bibliography

The Jubilee Memorial of the Scottish Congregational Churches, (Edinburgh: A. Fullarton & Co., 1849).
W. Keir, *The Baptist's Apology Vindicated*, (Irvine: E. MacQuistan, 1822).
R. Kinniburgh, *Fathers of Independency in Scotland*, (Edinburgh: A. Fullarton & Co., 1851).
J. Kirk, *The Complete Works of the Rev. John Kirk*, (2 Vols; Vol.1, Glasgow: Lang and Tweed, 1859; Vol.2, Glasgow: John Tweed, 1861).
T.D. Landels, *William Landels D.D.*, (London: Cassell and Company, 1900).
W. Landels, *The Gospel in various aspects*, (London: James Nisbet And Co., 1870, [1855]).
Letters (published) from an unknown book preserved separately in New College Library, Edinburgh. (Reference no. c.c./13.7)
G. Ewing, Glasgow, to Dr Ryland, Bristol, August 13 1816.
Dr Ryland to G. Ewing August 23 1816.
R. Haldane to Dr Ryland September 9 1816.
The Lifestory of William Quarrier, (Glasgow: R.L. Allan & Son, 4th edition, n.d.).
W. Logan, *Early Heroes of the Temperance Reformation*, (Glasgow: Scottish Temperance League, 1873).
J. McCurrey, *The Life of James McCurrey*, (London: S.W. Partridge & Co., n.d.).
J. McKerrow, *History of the Secession Church*, (Glasgow: A. Fullarton & Co., third edition, 1845).
A. McLean, *The Belief of the Gospel*, (London: William Jones, 1823).
— *A Sermon on the Promise that all nations shall be brought into subjection to Christ*, (Edinburgh: H. Inglis, 1796).
A. McLeod, *A View of Inspiration comprehending the Nature and Distinctions of the Spiritual Gifts and Offices of the Apostolic Age*, (Glasgow: George Gallie, 1827).
D. McRae, *A New View of the Old and New Way of Doctrine, Discipline and Government in the Churches of Christ*, (Inverness: J. Young, 1805).
J. Maguire, *Father Matthew: A Biography*, (London: Longman, Green, Longman, Roberts and Green [sic], 1864).
J.J. Matheson, *A Memoir of Greville Ewing*, (London: John Snow, 1843).
T. Milner, *The Gospel Guide*, (Edinburgh: E. Henderson, 1853).
— *The Messiah's Ministry*, (Edinburgh: J. Menzies, n.d. [1858]).
Ministerial Jubilee of the Rev. Principal Morison, D.D., (Glasgow: T.D. Morison, 1889).
J. Morison, *The Declaration, I pray not for the World*, (London: Ward & Co., 1845).
— *Remarks on the Doctrinal Errors condemned by the United Associate Synod, May 1842*, document in the possession of New College, Edinburgh.
— *Saving Faith*, (Kilmarnock: J. Davie, 1842).
— *The Way of Salvation*, (Kilmarnock: J. Davie, 1841).
R. Morison, *Defence of Christ's Truth*, (Glasgow: G. Gallie, 1842).
— *Review of Statement of Principles*, (Glasgow: G. Gallie, 1843).
J.W. Morris, *Memoirs of The Life and Writings of The Rev. Andrew Fuller*, (London: J.W. Morris, 1816).
J. Nicoll, *Diary of Public Transactions, 1650-1659*, (ed. D. Laing; Edinburgh: n.p., 1836; [Reference no.YDA 1854.650 in Edinburgh City Library]).
R. Philip, *The Life, Times and Missionary Enterprises of the Rev. John Campbell*, (London: John Snow, 1841).

T. Philips, *The Welsh Revival: Its Origins and Development*, (Edinburgh: Banner of Truth, 1989 [1860]).
G.H. Pike, *James Archer Spurgeon*, (London: Alexander & Shepheard, 1894).
— *The Life and Work of Charles Haddon Spurgeon*, (Edinburgh: Banner of Truth, 1991 [1894]).
J.B. Pike & J.C. Pike, *A Memoir and Remains of the late John Gregory Pike*, (London: Jarrold and Sons, 1855).
J.H. Pratt, *The Thought of the Evangelical Leaders*, (Edinburgh: Banner of Truth, 1978 [1856]).
L. Pullar, *Lengthening Shadows: Random Notes of a family history written in old age*, (Perth: L. Pullar, 1910).
G. Radford and J.A. James (eds), *The Autobiography of William Jay*, (Edinburgh: Banner of Truth, 1974 [1854]).
W. Reid, *The Temperance Cyclopedia*, Glasgow: Scottish Temperance League, 2nd edition, n.d., [1856].
— *Temperance Memorials of the late Robert Kettle Esq*, (Glasgow: Scottish Temperance League, 1853).
R. Richardson, *Memoirs of Alexander Campbell*, (Philadelphia: J.P. Lippincott & Co., Vol.1, 1868; Vol.2, 1870).
J. Rippon, *The Baptist Annual Register*, (4 Vols; London: Dilly, Button and Thomas, 1793-1802).
A. Rutherford, *Morisonianism examined and set aside*, (Glasgow: G. Gallie, 1850).
J. Ryland, *Life and Death of the Rev. Andrew Fuller*, (London: Button & Son, 1818).
Second Report of the Committee of the Baptist Academical Society for Scotland, (Edinburgh: R. Marshall, n.d. [1840]).
Sermons Preached in London at the formation of the Missionary Society September 22,23,24, (London: T. Chapman, 1795).
W. Shirreff, *Lectures on Baptism*, (London: Passmore and Alabaster, 1878).
O. Smeaton, *Principal James Morison*, (Edinburgh: Oliver & Boyd, 1901).
J.A. Smith, *Sinclair Thomson: The Shetland Apostle*, (Lerwick: Lerwick Baptist Church, 1969 [1867]).
T. Steadman, *Memoir of the Rev. William Steadman D.D.*, (London: Thomas Ward and Company, 1838).
W. Steadman, *The Utility of Associations*, (Bradford: J. Nicholson, 1807).
E. Steane, *Memoir of the Life of Joseph Gutteridge Esq*, (London: Jackson and Walford, 1850).
G. Struthers, *The History of the Rise, Progress and Principles of The Relief Church*, (Glasgow: A Fullarton And Co., 1843).
R. Wardlaw, *The Christian's Final Home*, (Edinburgh: A. Fullarton & Co., 1852).
J. Williamson, *Some Reminiscences of The Old Baptist Church Pleasance*, (Edinburgh: John Anderson, 1901).
P. Wilson, *The Origin and Progress of the Scotch Baptist Churches from their Rise in 1765 to 1834*, (Edinburgh: Fullarton And Co., 1844).

Secondary Sources

Adelaide Place Baptist Church 1829-1929: The Book of the Centenary, (Glasgow: Adelaide Place Baptist Church, 1929).

Bibliography

J.M. Anderson, *The Matriculation Roll of the University of St Andrews 1747-1897*, (Edinburgh: William Blackwood And Sons, 1905).

R.D. Anderson, *Education and Opportunity in Victorian Scotland*, (Oxford: The Clarendon Press, 1983).

— *Education and the Scottish People 1750-1913*, Oxford: The Clarendon Press, 1995.

D. Ansdell, *The People of The Great Faith: The Highland Church 1690-1900*, Stornoway: Acair Limited, 1998.

T. Armitage, *History of the Baptists*, (New York: Bryan Taylor & Co., 1887).

B. Aspinwall, *Portable Utopia: Glasgow and The United States 1820-1920*, (Aberdeen: Aberdeen University Press, 1984).

A.M. Baines, *History of Dublin Street Baptist Church, Edinburgh, 1858-1958*, (Edinburgh: McLagan and Cumming Ltd, 1958).

J.M. Banner, *Brae's O' Tullymet*, (Perth: Perth and Kinross District Libraries, 1994).

The Baptist Theological College of Scotland Jubilee 1894-1944, (Glasgow: The Baptist Theological College, 1944).

J. Barclay, *Bristo Place Mutual Improvement Society 1877-1932*, (Edinburgh: Macrae and Patterson, 1932).

J. Barr, *The United Free Church of Scotland*, (London: Allenson and Co., Ltd, 1934).

J.O. Barrett, *Rawdon College* 1804-1954, (London: Carey Kingsgate Press, 1954).

T.M. Bassett, *The Welsh Baptists*, (Swansea: Ilston House, 1977).

P. Beasley-Murray (ed.), *Mission to the World*, (Didcot: Baptist Historical Society, 1991).

J. Beattie, *The Haldanes: A Lecture*, (Edinburgh: Andrew Elliot, 1880).

D.W. Bebbingtoon, *Evangelicalism in Modern Britain: A History from the 1730s to the 1980s*, (London: Unwin Hyman, 1989).

— *The Nonconformist Conscience: Chapel and Politics 1870-1914*, (London: George Allen and Unwin, 1982).

— *Victorian Nonconformity*, (Bangor, Gwynedd: Headstart History, 1992.

D.W. Bebbington (ed.), *The Baptists in Scotland: A History*, (Glasgow: The Baptist Union of Scotland, 1988).

— *The Gospel in the World*, (Studies in Baptist History and Thought Volume 1; Carlisle: Paternoster, (2002).

C. Binfield, *George Williams and the Y.M.C.A.*, (London: Heinemann, 1973).

— *Pastors and People: The Biography of a Baptist Church Queen's Road, Coventry*, (Coventry: Queens Road Baptist Church, 1984).

J.D. Bollen, *Australian Baptists: A Religious Minority*, (London: The Baptist Historical Society, 1975).

C.B. Boog-Watson (ed.), *Roll of Edinburgh Burgesses and Guild Brethren 1761-1841*, (Scottish Record Society; Edinburgh: J. Skinner and Company Ltd, 1933.

The Book of the Old Edinburgh Club for the Years 1946-1947, (Edinburgh: T. and A. Constable Ltd, 1948).

W. H. Brackney (ed.), *The Believers' Church: A Voluntary Church*, (Kitchener, Ontario: Pandora Press, 1998).

G.R. Breed, *The Baptist Evangelical Society*, (Dunstable: The Fauconberg Press, 1988).

A Brief History of Cupar Baptist Church, (Cupar: Cupar Baptist Church, 1936).
Brierfield Baptist Church Centenary, 1886-1986, (Brierfield: Brierfield Baptist Church, 1986).
J.H.Y. Briggs, *The English Baptists of the Nineteenth Century*, (A History of the English Baptists, 3; Didcot: The Baptist Historical Society, 1994).
J.H.Y. Briggs & I. Sellers (eds), *Victorian Nonconformity*, (London: E. Arnold, 1973).
B.S. Brown, *Members One of Another The Baptist Union of Victoria 1862-1962*, (Melbourne, Australia: The Baptist Union of Victoria, 1962).
C.G. Brown, *Religion and Society in Scotland since 1707*, (Edinburgh: Edinburgh University Press, 1997).
— *The Death of Christian Britain: Understanding Secularisation 1800-2000*, (London: Routledge, 2001).
— *The People in the Pews*, (Glasgow: Economic and Social History Society of Scotland, 1993).
— *The Social History of Religion in Scotland since 1730*, (London: Methuen, 1987).
J. Brown, *The History of the Bedfordshire Union of Christians*, edited by D. Prothero, (London: Independent Press, 1946 [1896]).
K.D. Brown, *A Social History of the Nonconformist Ministry in England and Wales 1800-1930*, (Oxford: Clarendon Press, 1988).
R. Brown, *The English Baptists of the Eighteenth Century*, (A History of the English Baptists, 2; London: The Baptist Historical Society, 1986).
S.J. Brown, *Thomas Chalmers and the Godly Commonwealth in Scotland*, (Oxford: Oxford University Press, 1982).
S.J. Brown & M. Fry (eds), *Scotland in the age of Disruption*, (Edinburgh: Edinburgh University Press, 1993).
J.M. Bumstead, *The People's Clearances (1779-1815)*, (Edinburgh: Edinburgh University Press, 1982).
J.H.S. Burleigh, *A Church History of Scotland*, (London: Oxford University Press, 1960).
J. Burrell, *Memoir of the Rev. Thomas Lewis of Islington with extracts from his Diary and Correspondence*, (London: Ward and Co., 1853).
R. Butchart, *The Disciples of Christ in Canada since 1830*, (Toronto: Canadian Headquarters' Publications Churches of Christ, 1949).
A. Cameron, *The Haldane Brothers*, (Edinburgh: The Heralds Trust, 2001).
N.M. de. S. Cameron (ed.), *Dictionary of Scottish Church History and Theology*, (Edinburgh: T. & T. Clark, 1993).
R.H. Campbell, *The Rise and Fall of Scottish Industry 1707-1939*, (Edinburgh: John Donald, 1980).
G. Cantor, *Michael Faraday: Sandemanian and Scientist*, (Basingstoke: Macmillan, 1991).
J.T. Carson, *God's River in Spate: The Story of the Religious Awakening of Ulster in 1859*, (Belfast: Presbyterian Church in Ireland, 1958).
R. Carwardine, *Transatlantic Revivalism, Popular Religion in Britain and America, 1790-1865*, (London: Greenwood Press, 1978).
R. Chadwick, *Sacred Ground, High Tradition: Salendine Nook Baptist Church 1743-1993*, (Ardington: private publication, 1993).
O. Checkland, *Philanthropy in Victorian Scotland*, (Edinburgh: John Donald,

Bibliography

1980).
A.C. Cheyne, *Studies in Scottish Church History*, (Edinburgh: T. & T. Clark, 1999).
— *The Transforming of the Kirk*, (Edinburgh: The Saint Andrew Press,1983).
J. Clarke, *Memorial of Baptist Missionaries in Jamaica*, (London: Yates and Alexander, 1869).
A.S. Cook, *The Evolution of the Temperance Movement, 1837-1901*, (Aberdeen: n.p.,1901).
R.E. Cooper, *From Stepney to St Giles: The Story of Regent's Park College 1810-1960*, (London: Carey Kingsgate Press, 1960).
J. Cox, *The English Churches in a Secular Society: Lambeth 1870-1930*, (Oxford: Oxford University Press, 1982).
L.M. Cullen & T.C. Smout (eds), *Comparative Aspects of Scottish and Irish Economic and Social History 1600-1900*, (Edinburgh: John Donald, 1977).
G.J. Cumming and D. Baker (eds), *Councils and Assemblies*, (Cambridge: Cambridge University Press, 1984).
R.G.D., *History of Rattray Street Baptist Church 1769-1987*, (Dundee: Private publication, 1987).
T.M. Devine, *The Great Highland Famine*, (Edinburgh: John Donald, 1988).
— *The Scottish Nation 1700-2000*, (London: Penguin Books, 2000).
— *The Tobacco Lords*, (Edinburgh: John Donald, 1975).
T.M. Devine & R. Mitchison (eds), *People and Society in Scotland Vol.1, 1760-1830*, (Edinburgh: John Donald, 1988).
A. Digby and P. Searby, *Children, School and Society in Nineteenth Century England*, (London: The Macmillan Press Ltd, 1981).
K. Dix, *Strict and Particular: English Strict and Particular Baptists in the Nineteenth Century*, (Didcot: The Baptist Historical Society, 2001).
I.G. Docherty, *'Something Very Fine': A History of St Andrews Baptist Church*, (St Andrews: St Andrews Baptist Church, 1991).
A.L. Drummond, *The Churches in English Fiction*, (Leicester: Edgar Backus, 1950).
A.L. Drummond and J. Bulloch, *The Scottish Church 1688-1843*, (Edinburgh: The St Andrew Press, 1973).
— *The Church in Victorian Scotland 1843-1874*, (Edinburgh: The St Andrew Press, 1975).
— *The Church in Late Victorian Scotland 1874-1900*, (Edinburgh: The St Andrew Press, 1978).
V.E. Durkacz, *The Decline of the Celtic Languages*, (Edinburgh: John Donald, 1983).
T.S.H. Elwyn, *The Northamptonshire Baptist Association: A Short History 1764-1964*, (London: Carey Kingsgate Press, 1964).
H. Escott, *A History of Scottish Congregationalism*, (Glasgow: The Congregational Union of Scotland, 1960).
A. Everitt, *The Pattern of Rural Dissent: the Nineteenth Century*, (Leicester: Leicester University Press, 1972).
W. Ewing (ed.), *Annals of The Free Church of Scotland*, (2 Vols; Edinburgh: T. & T. Clark, 1914).
W. Ferguson, *Scotland: 1689 to the Present*, (Edinburgh: Mercat Press, 1990).
J.S. Fisher, *Impelled by Faith*, (Stirling: Scottish Baptist History Project, 1996).

E.R. Fitch, *The Baptists of Canada*, (Toronto: The Standard Publishing Company Limited, 1911).

M. Flynn (ed.), *Scottish Population History from the 17th Century to the 1930s*, (Cambridge: Cambridge University Press, 1977).

F.H. Foster, *A Genetic History of the New England Theology*, (Chicago: The University of Chicago Press, 1907).

W.H. Fraser & R.J. Morris (eds), *People and Society in Scotland Volume II, 1830-1914*, (Edinburgh: John Donald, 1990).

A. Gammie, *The Churches of Aberdeen: Historical and Descriptive*, (Aberdeen: Aberdeen Daily Journal Office, 1909).

A.D. Gilbert, *Religion and Society in Industrial England, 1740-1914*, (London: Longman, 1976).

G. Gordon & B. Dicks (eds), *Scottish Urban History*, (Aberdeen: Aberdeen University Press, 1983).

D.A. Gowland, *Methodist Secessions*, (Manchester: The Chetham Society, 1979).

R.L. Greenall, *The Kettering Connection: Northamptonshire Baptists and Overseas Mission*, (Leicester: University of Leicester, 1993).

C.E. Hambrick-Stowe, *Charles G. Finney and the Spirit of American Evangelicalism*, (Grand Rapids: Eerdmans, 1996).

I. Hamilton, *The Erosion of Calvinistic Orthodoxy: Seceders and Subscription in Scottish Presbyterianism*, (Edinburgh; Rutherford House Books, 1990).

J.E. Handley, *The Irish in Scotland 1798-1845*, (Cork: Cork University Press, 1945).

A.W. Harding, *Pullars of Perth*, (Perth: Perth and Kinross District Libraries, 1991).

K.J. Hardman, *Charles Grandison Finney 1792-1875*, (Darlington: Evangelical Press, 1990 [1987]).

J. Haroutunian, *Piety Versus Moralism: The Passing of the New England Theology*, (New York: Harper & Row, 1970 [1932]).

B. Harrison, *Drink and the Victorians*, (Keele: Keele University Press, 1994).

M.A.G. Haykin (ed.), *British Particular Baptists 1638-1910*, (Springfield, Missouri: Particular Baptist Press, Vol.1, 1998; Vol.2, 2000; Vol.3, 2003).

D.M. Himbury, *The South Wales Baptist College 1807-1957*, (Llandysul: J.D. Lewis, 1957).

J.D. Holmes, *More Roman than Rome: English Catholicism in the Nineteenth Century*, (London: Burns and Oats, 1978).

C.S. Horne, *The Story of the L[ondon] M[issionary] S[ociety] 1795-1895*, (London: London Missionary Society, 1895).

H.E. Hughes, *Our First Hundred Years The Baptist Church of South Australia*, (Adelaide: South Australia Baptist Union, 1937).

J. Hunter, *A Dance called America: The Scottish Highlands, The United States and Canada*, (Edinburgh: Mainstream Publishing, 1994).

— *The Making of the Crofting Community*, (Edinburgh: John Donald, 1995).

S. Ivison & F. Rosser, *The Baptists in Upper and Lower Canada before 1820*, (Toronto: University of Toronto Press, 1956).

D. Jamie, *John Hope Philanthropist and Reformer*, (Edinburgh: The Hope Trust, 1907).

E. Jay, *The Religion of the Heart*, (Oxford: Clarendon Press, 1979).

Bibliography 383

K.S. Jeffrey, *When The Lord Walked The Land The 1858-1862 Revival in the North East of Scotland*, (Studies in Evangelical History and Thought: Carlisle: Paternoster Press, 2002).
John Street Baptist Church [Glasgow] 1769-1969, (Glasgow: Private publication, 1969).
C. Johnson, *Developments in the Roman Catholic Church in Scotland 1789-1829*, (Edinburgh: John Donald, 1983).
D.A. Johnson, *The Changing Shape of English Nonconformity 1825-1925*, (Oxford: Oxford University Press, 1999).
W.C. Johnson, *Encounter in London*, (London: Carey Kingsgate Press, 1965).
E. Kaye, *For The Work of Ministry A History of Northern College and Its Predecessors*, (Edinburgh: T.& T. Clark, 1999).
E. King, *Scotland Sober and Free: The Temperance Movement, 1829-1979*, (Glasgow: Glasgow Museums and Art Galleries, 1979).
D. Kingdom, *Baptist Evangelism in 19th Century Ireland*, (Belfast: Baptist Union of Ireland, 1965).
R. Kinniburgh, *Fathers of Independency in Scotland*, (Edinburgh: A. Fullarton & Co., 1851).
J. Kirk (ed.), *The Church in the Highlands*, (Edinburgh: Scottish Church History Society, 1998).
A.S. Langley, *Birmingham Baptists: Past and Present*, (London: The Kingsgate Press, 1939).
A. Leaver, *Historical Fragments of Haggate Baptist Church*, (Burnley: A. Leaver, 1934).
Leith Baptist Church, Madeira Street 1845-1945, (Leith: Leith Baptist Church, 1945).
Leith Baptist Church, Madeira Street, 'These Fifty Years', (Leith: Leith Baptist Church, 1934).
B.P. Lenman, *An Economic History of Modern Scotland, 1660-1976*, (London: B.T. Batsford, 1977).
— *Integration, Enlightenment, and Industrialisation: Scotland 1746-1976*, (London: Edward Arnold, 1981).
I. Levitt and C. Smout, *The State of the Scottish Working Class in 1843*, (Edinburgh: Scottish Academic Press, 1979).
D.M. Lewis (ed.), *The Blackwell Dictionary of Evangelical Biography 1730-1860*, (2 Vols; Oxford: B. Blackwell, 1995).
F.G. Little and E.T.F. Walker (eds), *The Story of the Northern Baptists*, (Newcastle: Tyne Printing Works, 1945).
M. Lochhead, *Episcopal Scotland in the 19th Century*, (London: John Murray, 1966).
J. Love, *Falkirk Baptist Church: Some Notes on its History*, (Falkirk: Falkirk Baptist Church, 1906).
J. Love, *Falkirk Baptist Church: An Outline of its History*, (Falkirk: Falkirk Baptist Church, 1926).
D. Lovegrove, *Established Church, Sectarian People*, (Cambridge: Cambridge University Press, 1988).
W.L. Lumpkin, *Baptist Confessions of Faith*, (Valley Forge: Judson Press, 1969).
M. Lynch, *Scotland: A New History*, (London: Pimlico Publishing, 1992).

L. McBeth, *The Baptist Heritage*, (Nashville: Broadman Press, 1987).
A. McColl, *A Hundred Years of Baptist Witness: Anstruther Baptist Church 1860-1960*, (Anstruther: Anstruther Baptist Church, 1960).
J. MacInnes, *The Evangelical Movement in the Highlands of Scotland 1688-1800*, (Aberdeen: Aberdeen University Press, 1951).
J.R. McIntosh, *Church and Theology in Enlightenment Scotland: The Popular Party, 1740-1800*, (East Linton: Tuckwell Press, 1998).
H. McLachlan, *English Education under the Test Acts: being the history of the Non-Conformist Academies 1663-1820*, (Manchester: Manchester University Press, 1931).
A.A. MacLaren, *Religion and Social Class: The Disruption Years in Aberdeen*, (London: Routledge & Kegan Paul, 1974).
D.J. McLaren, *David Dale of New Lanark*, (Glasgow: Caring Books, 1999).
E.T. McLaren, *Dr McLaren of Manchester A Sketch*, (London: Hodder and Stoughton, 1911).
H. McLeod, *Class and Religion in the late Victorian City*, (London: Croom Helm, 1974).
— *Religion and the Working Class in Nineteenth Century Britain*, (London: Macmillan, 1984).
W.D. McNaughton, *The Scottish Congregational Ministry 1794-1993*, (Glasgow: The Congregational Union of Scotland, 1993).
A. McPherson (ed.), *History of the Free Presbyterian Church of Scotland*, (Inverness: Publications Committee of the Free Presbyterian Church of Scotland, 1973.
D. McRoberts (ed.), *Modern Scottish Catholicism 1878-1978*, (Glasgow: Burns, 1979).
G.I.T. Machin, *Politics and the Churches in Great Britain 1832-1868*, (Oxford: Clarendon Press, 1977).
M. Maison, *Search Your Soul Eustace*, (London: Sheed and Ward, 1961).
C. Malan, *The Life, Labours and Writings of Caesar Malan*, (London: James Nisbet & Co., 1869).
R.H. Martin, *Evangelicals United: Ecumenical Stirrings in Pre-Victorian Britain, 1795-1830*, (Metuchen, New Jersey: The Scarecrows Press, 1983).
S. Mechie, *The Church and Scottish Social Developments 1780-1870*, (London: Oxford University Press, 1960).
W. Medley, *Rawdon Baptist College: Centenary Memorial*, (London: Kingsgate Press, 1904).
D.E. Meek (ed.), *A Mind For Mission*, (Edinburgh: The Scottish Baptist History Project, 1992).
— *Island Harvest: A History of Tiree Baptist Church 1830-1988*, (Edinburgh: Tiree Books, 1988).
— *Sunshine and Shadow: The Story of the Baptists of Mull*, (Edinburgh: Tiree Books, 1991).
N. Moon, *Education for Ministry: Bristol Baptist College 1679-1979*, (Bristol: Bristol Baptist College, 1979).
J.N. Morris, *Religion and Urban Change: Croydon 1840-1914*, Suffolk: Boydell Press, 1992).
J. Munson, *The Nonconformists*, (London: S.P.C.K., 1991).

Bibliography

D.B. Murray, *The First 100 Years*, (Glasgow: The Baptist Union of Scotland, 1969).
— *The Scottish Baptist College Centenary History 1894-1994*, (Glasgow: Scottish Baptist College, 1994).
I.H. Murray, *Revival and Revivalism: The Making and Marring of American Evangelicalism 1750-1858*, (Edinburgh: Banner of Truth, 1994).
— *The Puritan Hope*, (Edinburgh: Banner of Truth, 1971).
T.J. Nettles, *By His Grace and for His Glory*, (Grand Rapids: Baker, 1986).
M. Nicholls, *A Light to the World: A History of Spurgeon's College, 1856-1992*, (Harpenden: Nuprint, 1994).
— *C.H. Spurgeon The Pastor Evangelist*, (Didcot: The Baptist Historical Society, 1992).
H. Nisbet, *Hawick Baptist Church*, (Hawick: private publication, 1983).
M. Noll, D.W. Bebbington, G.A. Rawlyk (eds), *Evangelicalism: Comparative Studies of Popular Protestantism in North America, The British Isles and Beyond 1700-1990*, (Oxford: Oxford University Press, 1994).
G.F. Nuttall, *The Significance of Trevecca College 1768-1791*, (London: Epworth Press, 1968).
J.E. Orr, *The Light of the Nations*, (Exeter: Paternoster, 1965).
— *The Second Evangelical Awakening in Britain*, (London: Marshall, Morgan & Scott, 1949).
I. Parker, *Dissenting Academies in England*, (New York: Octagon Books, 1969 [1914]).
G. Parsons et. al., *Religion in Victorian Britain*, (4 Vols; Manchester: Manchester University Press, 1988).
E.A. Payne, *The Baptist Union: A Short History*, (London: Carey Kingsgate Press, 1958).
— *Free Churchman, Unrepentant and Repentant and other papers*, (London: Carey Kingsgate Press Limited, 1965).
— *Studies in History and Religion*, (London: Lutterworth Press, 1942).
A. Peel, *These Hundred Years: A History of the Congregational Union of England and Wales 1831-1931*, (London: Congregational Union of England and Wales, 1931).
N.T. Phillipson and R. Mitchison, *Scotland in the Age of Improvement: Essays in Scottish History in the Eighteenth Century*, (Edinburgh: Edinburgh University Press, 1970).
H.M. Pickles, *Benjamin Ingham: Preacher amongst The Dales, Forests and Fells*, (Coventry: H.M. Pickes, 1995).
R. Polland, *I Will Build My Church A History of Falkirk Baptist Church*, (Falkirk: R. Polland, 1999).
S.E. Porter & A.R. Cross (eds), *Baptism, the New Testament and the Church: Biblical and Historical Studies in Honour of R.E.O. White*, (JSNTSup, 171: Sheffield: Sheffield Academic Press, 1999).
A.G. Price, *Founders and Pioneers of South Australia*, (Adelaide: Mary Martin Books, 1929).
D.T. Priestley (ed.), *Memory and Hope Strands of Canadian Baptist History*, (Waterloo, Ontario: Wilfred Laurier University Press, 1996).
G.A. Rawlyk and M. Noll (eds), *Amazing Grace: Evangelicalism in Australia,*

Britain, Canada, and the United States, (Grand Rapids: Baker, 1993).
M. Reeves, *Female Education and Nonconformist Culture 1700-1900*, (London: Leicester University Press, 1997).
— *SheepBell & Ploughshare*, (Bradford-on-Avon: Moonraker Press, 1978).
Register of The Society of Writers to Her Majesty's Signet, (Edinburgh: Clark Constable Ltd, 1983).
C. Rignal, *Manchester Baptist College 1866-1912*, (Bradford: W. Byles & Sons, 1916).
R.P. Roberts, *Continuity and Change: London Calvinistic Baptists and the Evangelical Revival 1760-1820*, (Wheaton, Illinois: Richard Owen Roberts, 1989).
E. Roberts-Thomson, *Baptists and Disciples of Christ*, (London: Carey Kingsgate Press, n.d., [1951]).
B. Robertson, *Perth Baptist Church The History The People*, (Perth: Strathfleet Publishing Company, 1994).
K. Robbins (ed.), *Protestant Evangelicalism: Britain, Ireland, Germany and America c.1750-c.1950*, (Oxford: B. Blackwell, 1990).
C.S. Rodd (ed.), *Foundation Documents of the Faith*, (Edinburgh: T. & T. Clark, 1987).
P. Rogers, *Father Theobald Matthew Apostle of Temperance*, (Dublin: Brown and Nolan Ltd, 1943).
D.M. Rosman, *Evangelicals and Culture*, (London: Croom Helm, 1984).
J. Ross, *A History of Congregational Independency in Scotland*, (Glasgow: James Maclehose & Sons, 1900).
G.M. Rossell and R.A.G. Dupuis (eds), *The Memoirs of Charles G. Finney*, (Grand Rapids: Academie Books, 1989).
H.H. Rowdon, *The History of the Brethren 1825-1850*, (London: Pickering and Inglis, 1967).
L.F. Rowston, *Baptists in Van Diemen's Land*, (Launceston, Tasmania: The Baptist Union of Tasmania, 1985).
A.P.F. Sell, *Church Planting: A Study of Westmorland Nonconformity*, (Eugene, Oregon: Wipf and Stock, 1998 [1986]).
— *Defending and Declaring the Faith*, (Exeter: Paternoster, 1987).
I. Sellers, *Nineteenth Century Nonconformity*, (London: E. Arnold, 1977).
W.J. Sheils and D. Wood (eds), *Voluntary Religion*, (Oxford: B. Blackwell, 1986).
P. Shepherd, *The Making of a Modern Denomination: John Howard Shakespeare and the English Baptists 1898-1924*, (Carlisle: Paternoster, 2001).
C.E. Shipley (ed.), *The Baptists of Yorkshire*, (Bradford: W. Byles & Sons Ltd, 1912).
R. Small, *History of the Congregations of the United Presbyterian Church 1733-1900*, (2 Vols; Edinburgh: David M. Small, 1904).
M.I. Smith, *A Short History of the First Baptist Church in Edinburgh, 1765-1965*, (Edinburgh: Bristo Baptist Church, 1965).
T.C. Smout, *A Century of The Scottish People 1830-1950*, (London: Collins, 1986).
— *A History of The Scottish People 1560-1830*, (Glasgow: Fontana, 1985).
D.C. Sparkes, *The Home Mission Story*, (Didcot: Baptist Historical Society, 1995).
B. Stanley, *The History of the Baptist Missionary Society 1792-1992*, (Edinburgh: T.& T. Clark, 1992).
L. Stephen (ed.), *Dictionary of National Biography*, 7, (London: Smith, Elder &

Co., 1886).

T.C.F. Stunt, *From Awakening to Secession: Radical Evangelicals in Switzerland and Britain, 1815-1835*, (Edinburgh: T. & T. Clark, 2000).

S. Taylor, *Baptists in Skye and the Hebrides Mission*, (Skye: S. Taylor, 2000).

A.B. Thomson, *Sketches of Some Baptist Pioneers in Scotland*, (2 Vols; Glasgow: W.Asher, 1901 and 1903).

D.M. Thompson, *Denominationalism and Dissent, 1795-1835: a question of identity*, (Friends of Dr Williams Library Thirty-Nineth Lecture; London: Dr Williams Trust, 1985).

— *Let Sects and Parties Fall*, (Birmingham: Berean Press, 1980).

— *Nonconformity in the Nineteenth Century*, (London: Routledge & Kegan Paul, 1972).

J. Thompson, *Century of Grace: The Baptists of Ireland: A Short History*, (Belfast: Baptist Union of Ireland, 1995).

R. Thompson, *Benjamin Ingham and the Inghamites*, (Kendal: R.W. Thompson & Co., 1958).

The Thomas Coats Memorial Church, Paisley, Jubilee Book, (Paisley: James Paton Limited, 1945).

D.P. Thomson, *Lady Glenorchy and Her Churches The Story of 200 Years*, (Crieff: The Research Unit,1967).

Two Hundred Years of Christian Witness, 1760-1960, (Haggate: Haggate Baptist Chapel, 1960).

A.C. Underwood, *A History of the English Baptists*, (London: The Kingsgate Press, 1947).

T.F. Valentine, *Concern For The Ministry: The Story of the Particular Baptist Fund 1717-1967*, (Teddington: Particular Baptist Fund, 1967).

H.C. Vedder, *A Short History of the Baptists*, (Philadelphia: The American Baptist Publication Society, 1907).

G. Walker and G.T. Gallagher (eds), *Sermons and Battle Hymns*, (Edinburgh: Edinburgh University Press, 1990).

M. Walker, *Baptists at the Table*, (Didcot: The Baptist Historical Society, 1992).

N.L. Walker (ed.), *Religious Life in Scotland from the Reformation to the Present Day*, (London: T. Nelson and Sons, 1888).

W.R. Ward, *Religion and Society in England 1790-1850*, (London: B.T. Batsford, 1971).

A. Watson, *The Angus Clan 1588-1950*, (n.p.: A.Watson, 1950).

A.C. Watters, *History of the British Churches of Christ*, (Birmingham: Berean Press, 1948).

M.R. Watts, *The Dissenters*, (2 Vols; Oxford: Clarendon Press, 1978 and 1995).

D.L. Weddle, *The Law as Gospel: Revival and Reform in the Theology of Charles G. Finney*, (Methuen, New Jersey: The Scarecrows Press, 1985).

W.T. Whitley, *The Baptists of London 1612-1928*, (London: The Kingsgate Press, 1928).

— *The Baptists of North West England*, (London: The Kingsgate Press,1913).

— *A History of British Baptists*, (London: Charles Griffiths & Company, 1923).

W. Whyte, *Revival in Rose Street: A History of Charlotte Baptist Chapel, Edinburgh*, (Edinburgh: Lindsay & Co. Ltd, n.d. [1973?])

D. Williamson, *The Life of Alexander McLaren*, (London: James Clark & Co.,

1910).
P.T. Winskill, *The Temperance Movement and its Workers*, (4 Vols; Glasgow: Blackie & Son Limited, 1893).
C.W.J. Withers, *Urban Highlanders: Highland-Lowland Migration and Urban Gaelic Culture, 1700-1900*, (East Linton: Tuckwell Press, 1998).
J. Wolfe, *The Protestant Crusade in Great Britain 1829-1860*, (Oxford: The Clarendon Press, 1991).
J. Wolfe (ed.), *Evangelical Faith and Public Zeal: Evangelicals and Society in Britian, 1780-1980*, (London: S.P.C.K., 1995).
D.F.Wright & G.D.Badcock (eds), *Disruption to Diversity: Edinburgh Divinity 1846-1996*, (Edinburgh: T.& T. Clark, 1996).
A. Wylie (ed.), *A Short History of Marshall Street Baptist Church, Edinburgh, 1846-1896*, (Edinburgh: T. Adams, 1896).
A.J. Youngson, *After The Forty-Five*, (Edinburgh: Edinburgh University Press, 1973).
C. Yrigoyen Jr & G.H. Bricker (eds), *Catholic and Reformed: Selected Theological Writings of John Williamson Nevin*, (Pittsburg: The Pickwick Press, 1978).
G. Yuille (ed.), *History of the Baptists in Scotland*, (Glasgow: Baptist Union Publications Committee, 1926).

Articles

Anon, 'Andrew Fuller and James Deakin, 1803', *Baptist Quarterly*, New Series, 7 (1934-1935).
Anon, 'Letters to James Deakin', *Baptist Quarterly*, New Series, 7 (1934-35).
Anon, 'An Index to Notable Baptists whose careers began within the British Empire before 1850', *Transactions of the Baptist Historical Society,*, 7 (1920-1921).
M.E. Aubrey, 'T.R. Glover Review and Reminiscence', *Baptist Quarterly*, 15 (1953-54).
D.W. Bebbington, 'The Baptist Conscience in the Nineteenth Century', *Baptist Quarterly*, 34.1 (1991).
— 'Baptist M.P.s in the Nineteenth Century', *Baptist Quarterly*, 29.1 (1981).
— 'Baptist Members of Parliament in the Twentieth Century', *Baptist Quarterly*, 31.6 (1986).
— 'Spurgeon and British Evangelical Theological Education', in D.G. Hart & R.A. Mohler (eds), *Theological Education in the Evangelical Tradition*, (Grand Rapids: Baker, 1996).
J. Bone, 'The Scottish Baptist Total Abstinence Society', *Scottish Temperance Annual*, (1901).
G.R. Breed, 'The London Association of Strict Baptist Ministers and Churches', *Baptist Quarterly*, 35.8 (1994).
J.H.Y. Briggs, 'C.H. Spurgeon and the Baptist Denomination in Nineteenth Century Britain', *Baptist Quarterly*, 31.5 (1986).
— 'Evangelical Ecumenism: The Amalgamation of General and Particular Baptists in 1891', *Baptist Quarterly*, 34.3 and 34.4, (1991).
C.G. Brown, 'The Cost of Pew-renting: Church Management, Church going and

Bibliography

Social Class in Nineteenth Century Glasgow', *Journal of Ecclesiastical History*, 38.3 (1987).

K.D. Brown, 'The Baptist Ministry of Victorian England and Wales: A Social Profile', *Baptist Quarterly*, 32.3 (1987).

— 'Patterns of Baptist Ministry in the Twentieth Century', *Baptist Quarterly*, 33.2 (1989).

S.J. Brown, 'The Disruption and Urban Poverty: Thomas Chalmers and the West Port Operation in Edinburgh, 1844-1847', *Records of the Scottish Church History Society*, 20 (1978-1980).

— 'Thomas Chalmers and the Communal Ideal in Victorian Scotland', in T.C. Smout (ed.), *Victorian Values*, (Oxford: Oxford University Press, 1992).

R.F. Calder, 'Robert Haldane's Theological Seminary', *Transactions of the Congregational History Society*, 13 (1937-1939), (Nendeln, Liechtenstein: Kraus Reprints, 1963).

R.H. Campbell, 'An Economic History of Scotland in The Eighteenth Century', *Scottish Journal of Political Economy*, 11 (1964).

R. Carwardine,' The Evangelist System: Charles Roe, Thomas Pulsford and the Baptist Home Missionary Society', *Baptist Quarterly*, 28.5 (1980).

L.G. Champion, 'Evangelical Calvinism and the Structures of Baptist Church Life', *Baptist Quarterly*, 28.5 (1980).

— 'The Theology of John Ryland: Its Sources and Influences', *Baptist Quarterly*, 28.1 (1979).

R.L. Child, 'Baptists and Disciples of Christ', *Baptist Quarterly*, 14 (1951-1952).

E.F. Clipsham,'Andrew Fuller and Fullerism: A Study in Evangelical Calvinism', *Baptist Quarterly*, 20.3 to 20.6 (1963-1964).

T.W. Davies, 'The Macleanist (Scotch) and Campbellite Baptists of Wales', *Transactions of the Baptist Historical Society*, 7 (1920-1921).

— 'A Scotch Baptist Circular', *Transactions of the Baptist Historical Society*, 5 (1916-1917).

N.D. Denny, 'Temperance and the Scottish Churches, 1870-1914', *Records of the Scottish Church History Society*, 23 (1988).

T.M. Devine, ' Highland Migration to Lowland Scotland, 1760-1860', *The Scottish Historical Review*, 62.174 (1983).

A.L. Drummond, 'Robert Haldane at Geneva (1816-1817)', *Records of the Scottish Church History Society*, 9 (1947).

T.S.H. Elwyn, 'Particular Baptists of the Northamptonshire Baptist Association as reflected in the Circular Letters 1765-1820', *Baptist Quarterly*, 36.8, 1996.

H. Foreman, 'Baptist Provision for Ministerial Education in the 18th Century', *Baptist Quarterly*, 27.8 (1978).

N.P. Hancock, 'Healing the Breach', *Baptist Quarterly*, 35.3 (1993).

R.B. Hannen, 'A Scottish Baptist Centenary', *Baptist Quarterly*, New Series, 11 (1942-1945).

E.B. Hardy, 'Association Life in Kent and Sussex, 1770-1950', *Baptist Quarterly* 27.4 (1977).

B. Harrison, 'The British Prohibitionists 1853-1872: A Biographical Analysis', *International Review of Social History*, (Assen, The Netherlands: Royal Van-gorcum, 1970).

F.M.W. Harrison, 'Nottinghamshire Baptists: Their Rise and Expansion', *Baptist*

Quarterly, 25.2 (1973).

E.W. Hayden. 'Joshua Thomas: Welsh Baptist Historian, 1719-1797', *Baptist Quarterly*, 23.3 (1969).

M.A.G. Haykin, 'Voluntarism in the Life and Ministry of William Fraser (1801-1883)', *Baptist Quarterly*, 39.6 (2002).

S.D. Henry, 'Baptist Church Growth in Fife from 1750 to the Present', *Baptist Quarterly*, 32.7 (1988).

P. Hillis, 'Presbyterianism and Social Class in Mid-Nineteenth Century Glasgow: a study of Nine Churches, *Journal of Ecclesiastical History*, 32.1 (1981).

D.M. Himbury, 'Training Baptist Ministers', *Baptist Quarterly*, 21.8 (1966).

J. Hunter, 'The Emergence of the Crofting Community: The Religious Contribution 1798-1843', *Scottish Studies*, 18 (1974).

S. James, 'Revival and Renewal in Baptist Life: The Contribution of William Steadman', (1764-1837)', *Baptist Quarterly*, 37.6 (1998).

A.H. Kirkby, 'Andrew Fuller- Evangelical Calvinist', *Baptist Quarterly*, 15 (1953-1954).

J. Lea, 'The Growth of the Baptist Denomination in Mid-Victorian Lancashire and Cheshire', *Transactions of the Historic Society of Lancashire and Cheshire*, 14 (1973).

D. Lovegrove, 'English Evangelical Dissent and the European Conflict 1789-1815', in W.J. Shiels (ed.), *The Church and War*, (Oxford: B. Blackwell, 1983).

— 'Particular Baptist Itinerant Preachers during the late 18th and early 19th Centuries', *Baptist Quarterly*, 28.3 (1979).

— 'A set of men whose proceedings threaten no small disorder': The Society for Propagating the Gospel at Home, 1798-1808', *The Scottish Historical Review*, 79.207, (April, 2000).

— 'Unity and Separation: Contrasting Elements in the Thought and Practice of Robert and James Haldane', in K.Robbins (ed.), *Protestant Evangelicalism: Britain, Ireland, Germany and America, c,1750-c.1950*, (Oxford: B. Blackwell, 1990).

— ' "The Voice of Reproach and Outrage": The Impact of Robert Haldane on French-Speaking Protestantism', in D.W.D. Shaw (ed.), *In Divers Manners*, (St Andrews: St Mary's College, St Andrews University, 1990).

V.A. McClelland, 'A Hierarchy for Scotland, 1868-1878', *Catholic Historical Review*, 56 (1970-1971).

I.F. Maciver, 'The Evangelical Party and the Eldership in General Assemblies, 1820-1843', *Records of the Scottish Church History Society*, 20 (1978-1980).

M. McHugh, 'The Religious Condition of the Highlands and Islands in the mid-Eighteenth Century', *Innes Review*, 35.1 (Spring, 1984).

A.A. MacLaren, 'Presbyterianism and the Working Class in a mid-Nineteenth Century city', *The Scottish Historical Review*, 46.141 - 46.142 (1967).

G.I.T. Machin, 'The Disruption and British Politics 1834-1843', *The Scottish Historical Review*, Vol.51.151 (1972).

K.R. Manley, 'A Colonial Evangelical Ministry and a 'Clerical Scandal': James Taylor in Melbourne (1857-1868)', *Baptist Quarterly*, 39.2, (2001).

— 'John Rippon and Baptist Historiography', *Baptist Quarterly*, 28.3 (1979).

— 'The Making of an Evangelical Baptist Leader', *Baptist Quarterly*, 26.6 (1976).

D.E. Meek, 'Baptists and Highland Culture', *Baptist Quarterly*, 33.4 (1989).

— 'Dugald Sinclair', *Scottish Studies*, 30 (1991).
— 'Evangelical Missionaries in the Early Nineteenth Century Highlands', *Scottish Studies*, 28 (1987).
— 'Evangelicalism and Emigration: Aspects of the Role of Dissenting Evangelicalism in Highland Emigration to Canada', in G.W. MacLennon (ed.), *Proceedings of the First North American Congress of Celtic Studies*, (Ottawa, 1988).
— '"The Fellowship of Kindred Minds": Some Religious Aspects of Kinship and Emigration from the Scottish Highlands in the Nineteenth Century', in *Hands Across The Water: Emigration from Northern Scotland to North America*, (Aberdeen: Aberdeen and North East Scotland Family History Society, 1995).
— 'The Independent and Baptist Churches of Highland Perthshire and Strathspey', *Transactions of the Gaelic Society of Inverness*, 61 (1991).
— 'The Preacher, the Press-gang and the Landlord: the impresment and vindication of the Rev. Donald MacArthur', *Records of the Scottish Church History Society*, 25.2 (1994).
R. Mitchison, 'The Highland Clearances', *Scottish Economic & Social* History, 1.1 (1981).
D.D.J. Morgan, 'Smoke, Fire and Light: Baptists and the Revitalisation of Welsh Dissent', *Baptist Quarterly*, 32.5 (1988).
A.T.N. Muirhead,' A Secession Congregation in its Community: The Stirling Congregation of the Rev. Ebenezer Erskine, 1731-1754', *Records of the Scottish Church History* Society, 22 (1986).
I.A. Muirhead, 'The Revival as a Dimension of Scottish Church History', *Records of the Scottish Church History Society*, 20 (1978-1980).
J.E.B. Munson, 'The Education of Baptist Ministers 1870 to 1900', *Baptist Quarterly*, 26.7 (1976).
D.B. Murray, 'Baptists in Scotland Before 1869', *Baptist Quarterly*, 23.6 (1970).
— 'The influence of John Glas', *Records of the Scottish Church History* Society, 22, (1986).
— 'The Scotch Baptist Tradition in Great Britain', *Baptist Quarterly*, 33.4 (1989).
M. Nicholls, 'Charles Haddon Spurgeon, Educationalist: Part 1, General Education Concerns', *Baptist Quarterly*, 31.8 (1986).
— 'Charles Haddon Spurgeon, Educationalist: Part 2, The Principles and Practice of Pastors' College', *Baptist Quarterly*, 32.2 (1987).
G.F. Nuttall, 'The Baptist Churches and their Ministers in the 1790s: Rippon's Baptist Annual Register', *Baptist Quarterly*, 30.8 (1984).
— 'Northamptonshire and the Modern Question: A Turning Point in Eighteenth Century Dissent', *Journal of Theological Studies*, 16.5 (1965).
J.A. Oddy, 'The Dissidence of William Richards', *Baptist Quarterly*, 27.3 (1977).
E.A. Payne, 'An 1820 Letter on Election', *Baptist Quarterly*, 24.4, (1971).
— 'Baptist Congregational Relations', *Congregational Quarterly*, 32.3 (1955).
— 'Carey and his Biographers', *Baptist Quarterly*, 19 (1961-62).
— 'The Development of NonConformist Theological Education in the Nineteenth Century with special reference to Regent's Park College', in E.A. Payne (ed.), *Studies in History and Religion*, (London: Lutterworth Press, 1942).
— 'The Diaries of John Dyer', *Baptist Quarterly*, 13.6 (1950).

— 'The Necrologies of John Dyer', *Baptist Quarterly*, 13.7 (1950).
— 'The Evangelical Revival and the Beginnings of the Modern Missionary Movement', *The Congregational Quarterly*, 21.3 (July, 1943).
S.J. Price, 'The Early Years of the Baptist Union', *Baptist Quarterly*, 4 (1928-1929).
G.P.R. Prosser, 'The Formation of the General Baptist Missionary Society', *Baptist Quarterly*, 22.1 (1967).
R. Reid, 'The Early History of the Temperance Movement in Scotland', *Scottish Temperance League Register and Abstainers' Almanac*, (1897).
D.T. Roberts, 'Mission, Home and Overseas: Richard Glover of Bristol', *Baptist Quarterly*, 25.3 (1993).
H. Sefton, '"Neu-Lights and Preachers Legall": some observations on the beginnings of Moderatism in the Church of Scotland', in N. MacDougall (ed.), *Church, Politics and Society: Scotland 1408-1929*, (Edinburgh: John Donald, 1983).
I. Sellers, 'John Howard Hinton Theologian', *Baptist Quarterly*, 33.3 (1989).
P. Shepherd, 'James Acworth and the Creation of Rawdon College', *Baptist Quarterly*, 39.6 (2002).
W. Speirs, 'An Old Scotch Baptist Church', *Baptist Quarterly*, 16 (1955-1956).
B. Stanley, 'C.H. Spurgeon and the Baptist Missionary Society 1863-1866', *Baptist Quarterly*, 29.7 (1982).
B.R. Talbot, 'Baptists and the Scottish Enquiry of Religion 1837-1839', *Baptist Quarterly*, 39.8 (2002).
— 'John Saffery, 1763-1825', in 'M.A.G. Haykin (ed.), *The British Particular Baptists 1638-1910*, (Vol. III; Springfield, Missouri: Particular Baptist Press, 2003).
— 'Unity and Disunity: The Scotch Baptists, 1765-1842', in R.Pope (ed.), *Religion and National Identity: Wales and Scotland c.1700-2000*, (Cardiff: University of Wales Press, 2001).
R. Taylor, 'English Baptist Periodicals 1790-1865', *Baptist Quarterly*, 27.2 (1977).
A.B. Thompson, 'Sketches of Some Pioneers in Scotland during the Eighteenth Century and the early years of the Nineteenth Century', *Scottish Baptist Magazine*, 25-49 (1899-1923).
R.W. Vaudry, 'The Constitutional Party in the Church of Scotland 1834-1843', *The Scottish Historical Review*, 62.173 (1983).
M. Walker, 'The Presidency of the Lord's Table among Nineteenth Century English Baptists', *Baptist Quarterly*, 32.5 (1988).
W.R. Ward, 'The Baptists and the Transformation of the Church, 1780-1830', *Baptist Quarterly*, 25.4 (1973).
G. Williams, 'Welsh Baptists in an Age of Revolution, 1776-1832', *Baptist Quarterly*, 33.5 (1990).
P.R. Wilson, 'Church and Community: Old School Baptists in Ontario, 1818-1901', in D.T. Priestly (ed.), *Memory and Hope Strands of Canadian Baptist History*, (n.p.: Wilfred Laurier University Press, 1996).
C.W.J. Withers, 'Highland Migration to Dundee, Perth and Stirling, 1753-1891', *Journal of Historical Geography*, 11.4 (1985).
D.J. Withrington, 'The 1851 Census of Religious Worship and Education: with a note on Church accommodation in mid-19th-Century Scotland', *Records of the Scottish Church History Society*, 18 (1973).
— 'The Disruption: a century and a half of historical interpretation', *Records of*

the *Scottish Church History Society*, 25, (1993).
— 'Non-Church-Going, c.1750 - c.1850: A Preliminary Study', *Records of the Scottish Church History Society*, 17 (1969-1971).
J. Wolffe, 'The Evangelical Alliance in the 1840s: An Attempt to Institutionalise Christian Unity', in W.J. Sheils and D. Wood (eds), *Voluntary Religion*, (Oxford: B. Blackwell, 1986).

Unpublished Theses and Essays

D.W. Bebbington,'The Dissenting Idea of a University: Oxford and Cambridge in Nonconformist Thought in the Nineteenth Century', (Hulsean Prize Essay, Cambridge University, 1973).
G.R. Breed, 'Strict Communion Organisations amongst the Baptists in Victorian England', (MA thesis, Keele University, 1991.
G. Carter, 'Evangelical Seceders from the Church of England c.1800-1850', (DPhil thesis, Oxford University, 1990).
R.E. Chadwick, 'Church and People in Bradford and District, 1880-1914: The Protestant Churches in an Urban Industrial Environment', (DPhil thesis, University of Oxford University, 1986).
D. Currie, 'The Growth of Evangelicalism in the Church of Scotland 1793-1843', (PhD thesis, St Andrews University, 1990).
R. Hayden, 'Evangelical Calvinism among Eighteenth-Century British Baptists', (PhD thesis, Keele University, 1991).
W.M. Kirkland, 'The Impact of the French Revolution on Scottish Religious Life and Thought with special reference to Thomas Chalmers, Robert Haldane and Niel Douglas', (PhD thesis, Edinburgh University, 1951).
C.E. Kirsch, 'The Theology of James Morison, with special reference to his theories of the Atonement', (PhD thesis, Edinburgh University, 1939).
J. Lea, 'Baptists in Lancashire, 1837-1887', (PhD thesis, Liverpool University, 1970).
N.D. Logan, 'Drink and Society: Scotland, 1870-1914', (PhD thesis, Glasgow University, 1983).
W.D. McNaughton, 'The Congregational Church in Kirkcaldy and other Congregational Churches in Fife', (ThD thesis, The American Congregational Centre, Ventura, California, 1989).
R.D. Mitchell, 'Archibald McLean 1733-1812, Baptist Pioneer in Scotland', (PhD thesis, Edinburgh University, 1950).
D.D.J. Morgan, 'The Development of the Baptist Movement in Wales between 1714-1815 with particular reference to the Evangelical Revival', (DPhil thesis, Oxford University, 1986).
D.B. Murray, 'The Social and Religious Origins of Scottish Non-Presbyterian Dissent from 1730-1800', (PhD thesis, St Andrews University, 1976).
R.W. Oliver, 'The Emergence of a Strict and Particular Baptist Community among the English Calvinistic Baptists, 1770-1850', (PhD thesis, C.N.A.A., 1981).
D.C. Paton, 'Drink and the Temperance Movement in Nineteenth Century Scotland', (PhD thesis, Edinburgh University, 1976).
D. Reeves, 'The Interaction of Scottish and English Evangelicals 1790-1810',

(MLitt thesis, Glasgow University, 1973).

F.W. Rinaldi, '"The Tribe of Dan". The New Connexion of General Baptists, 1770-1891: A Study from Revival Movement to Established Denomination', (PhD thesis, Glasgow University, 1996).

O.C. Robison, 'The Particular Baptists in England, 1760-1820', (DPhil thesis, Oxford University, 1963).

J. Scott, 'The Baptists in Scotland: A Historical Survey', (PhD thesis, Glasgow University, 1927).

K.E. Smith, 'The Community and the Believer: A Study of Calvinistic Baptist Spirituality in Some Towns and Villages of Hampshire and the Borders of Wiltshire, c.1730-1830', (DPhil thesis Oxford University, 1986).

K.J. Stewart, 'Restoring the Reformation: British Evangelicalism and the 'Reveil' at Geneva 1816-1849', (PhD thesis, Edinburgh University, 1992).

C. Terpstra, 'David Bogue D.D. 1750-1825, Pioneer and Missionary Educator', (PhD thesis, Edinburgh University, 1959).

D.J. Tidball, 'English Nonconformist Home Missions 1796-1901', (PhD thesis, Keele University, 1982).

J. Thompson, 'Baptists in Ireland 1792-1922: A Dimension of Protestant Dissent', (DPhil thesis, Oxford University, 1988).

D.E. Wallace, 'The Life and Work of James Alexander Haldane', (PhD thesis, Edinburgh University, 1955).

A.C. Watters, 'History of the Churches of Christ', (PhD thesis, Edinburgh University, 1940.

Index

A

Acworth, James 291
Adam, John 195
Adamson, William 334
Aikenhead, Robert 144
Aikman, John 93
Alexander, Lindsay 108
America 120, 121, 179, 213, 258
Anderson, Charles 295
Anderson, Christopher 22, 25, 73, 109, 115, 140, 142, 155, 193, 194, 195, 199, 211, 221, 253, 272, 311, 320
Anderson, Hugh 22
Anderson, John 104
Anderson, Magnus 80
Anderson, Robert 46, 52, 58, 59, 236
Angas, George F. 218
Ansdell, Douglas 11
Anstruther Baptist Church 111
Argyle Square Baptist Church 39, 52, 55, 70
Arminianism 8, 16, 26, 204, 205, 207, 209, 211, 239, 248, 250, 256, 260, 263, 269, 274, 277, 278, 280, 283, 290, 291, 292, 297, 309, 316, 321, 324, 328, 332, 334, 340
Arthur, Andrew 43, 253, 261, 272, 293
Arthur, Charles 158, 192, 215, 221
Ashworth, J.K. 307
Auchtermuchty Baptist Church 200
Australia 179, 217, 218, 248, 258, 281, 305
Ayr Baptist Church 60

B

Ballantyne, William 48, 78, 91, 92, 107
Baptist Academical Society 100, 149, 218, 246
Baptist Annual Register 37, 118
Baptist Bible Society 86
Baptist Evangelical Society 125, 204, 243, 271, 272, 273, 275, 279, 280, 289, 323, 333, 338.
Baptist Highland Mission 157, 192
Baptist Home Missionary Society 61, 82, 97, 102, 129, 257, 280, 296, 298, 316, 320
Baptist Irish Society 136, 162
Baptist Magazine 22, 46, 126, 128, 139, 156, 187, 210, 226, 238, 258, 288
Baptist Missionary Society 4, 48, 51, 115, 138
Baptist Reporter 239, 256, 257
Baptist Society in London for the Encouragement and Support of Itinerant Preaching 124, 153, 232
Baptist Theological Academy 247
Baptist Theological College of Scotland 315
Baptist Theological Institute 247
Baptist Tract Society 239
Baptist Union of Great Britain and Ireland 17, 67, 129, 148, 162, 212, 265, 279, 295, 301
Baptist Union of Ireland 18, 337
Baptist Union of Wales 18, 337
Barclay, George 25, 73, 109, 115, 123, 127, 138, 140, 149, 155, 156, 158, 192, 193, 200, 201, 218, 221, 244, 323
Bassett, T.M. 18
Bath Street Baptist Church, Glasgow 284, 305, 306
Bebbington, D.W. 10
Bedfordshire Union of Christians 81
Begg, George 49, 50, 62, 63
Berwick-upon-Tweed Baptist Church 178, 200, 252
Betts, Henry John 271, 272
Beverley Scotch Baptist Church 236
Bishop of Salisbury 81
Blackfriars Street Baptist Church, Glasgow 284, 306
Blair, James 60, 61, 217, 234, 236
Bogue, David 74, 81, 107, 133
Booth, Abraham 133

Bowser, Howard 204, 272
Braidwood, William 41, 53, 141, 198
Breed, Geoffrey 23
Briggs, J.H.Y. 17, 338
Bristo Baptist Church 23, 40, 43, 52, 70, 117, 220, 226, 236, 261, 262
Bristol Baptist College 197, 220, 306
British and Foreign Bible Society 79, 194, 199
British Temperance Association 240
Broadford Baptist Church, Skye 166
Brock, William 302
Brown, Callum 12, 327
Brown, James 306
Brown, Raymond 17
Bruce, Andrew 39
Buchan, James 46, 47, 157
Buchanan, Dr Walter 74, 79
Buchanan, Dugald 174
Bulloch, J. 11
Bunting, Jabez 38
Burleigh, J.H.S. 11
Burns, Jabez 204, 243, 324

C

Calvinism 15, 16, 26, 106, 185, 186, 201, 203, 211, 233, 239, 244, 247, 248, 256, 261, 263, 266, 267, 269, 271, 272, 275, 278, 280, 283, 289, 290, 291, 292, 295, 297, 299, 309, 316, 321, 324, 328, 332, 334
Cameron, Archibald 109
Cameron, Duncan 172
Campbell, Alexander 55, 57, 94, 95, 231, 270
Campbell, James 214
Campbell, John 92, 133, 170
Canada 29, 123, 150, 166, 173, 213
Carey, William 4, 131, 291, 296
Carmichael, Robert 30, 54, 215, 235
Chalmers, Thomas 241, 331
Chamberlain, James 284, 305
Charlotte Baptist Chapel, Edinburgh 115, 135, 195, 196, 199, 200, 202, 231, 280, 284, 310, 339
Charlton, John 42, 44
Chesser, George 60

Cheyne, A.C. 12, 326
Christian Advocate 21, 263, 264
Church of England 1, 81, 153
Church of Scotland 1, 75, 83, 173, 174, 229, 240, 249, 313
Churches of Christ 22, 24, 45, 71, 94, 231, 236, 262, 263, 270, 334
Clark, James 306
Clark, William 65
Cleghorn, John 78
Clift, Samuel 81
Clyde Street Hall Baptist Church, Edinburgh 23, 55, 58, 128, 198, 199, 200, 206, 207, 209, 211, 221, 263, 295, 321, 339
Coats, Thomas 310
Conder, Josiah 138
Congregational Union of Scotland 6, 8, 96, 97, 126, 274, 332, 334
Continental Society 85
Cowan, John 71
Cowie, George 80
Crouch, John 305
Crowe, Frederick 52
Culross, James 14, 264, 286, 288, 290, 293, 308, 315
Cupar Baptist Church 144, 209, 229, 321

D

Dale, David 30
Deakin, James 118, 119, 138
Dewar, David 158, 192, 221
Dewar, James 95
Dickie, Henry 42, 52, 58, 61, 69, 70, 117, 176, 198, 217, 226, 251, 253, 261, 272, 286, 296
Disciples of Christ 123
Dix, Kenneth 336
Doddridge, Philip 106
Douglas, David 219
Downgrade controversy 19, 337
Drummond, A.L. 11
Dublin Street Baptist Church, Edinburgh 146, 280, 284, 310
Dunbar, Daniel 183
Duncan Street Baptist Church,

Edinburgh 284
Duncan, Andrew 44, 60, 66, 80, 198
Duncan, James 46
Dundee Tabernacle Church 95
Dunfermline Scotch Baptist Church 200
Dunn, George 297
Dunrossness Baptist Church 126
Dyer, John 131

E

East India Company 82
East Regent Place Baptist Church, Glasgow 247
Edinburgh Almanac 324
Edinburgh Auxiliary Bible Society 100
Edinburgh City Mission 99
Edinburgh Tabernacle Church 55, 58, 82, 87, 92, 93, 99, 113, 156, 200, 271, 272, 273, 280
Edwards, Jonathan 15
Elder Street Baptist Church, Edinburgh 99, 100, 132, 138, 146, 192, 199
Elgin Tabernacle 91
Elizabeth, Charlotte 137
emigration 179, 214, 258
English BHMS 162, 167, 177, 189, 232
English Particular Baptists 2, 37, 182, 316
Escott, Harry 10, 96, 154
Essex Baptist Association 165, 167
Eternal Sonship of Christ 63, 268
Evangelical Alliance 99, 297, 299, 316, 324
Evangelical Magazine 139, 140, 229
Evangelical Union 6, 16, 230, 232, 243, 262, 267, 274, 302, 329, 330, 334
Everson, James 20, 35, 39, 45, 52, 57, 59, 66, 70, 236
Ewing, Greville 10, 75, 90, 93, 96, 97, 98, 107, 320, 332

F

Farquharson, James 192, 193, 195, 199, 211
Ferguson, Duncan 166
Ferguson, Fergus 243
Ferguson, William 14
Fernie, David 48
Ferrier, Dr William 50
Finney, Charles 16, 226, 267, 270, 331
Fisher, J.S. 10
Flett, Oliver 308
Fraser, A. 42
Fraser, William 108, 149, 165, 166, 179, 195
Frazer, John 180
Free Church Magazine 253, 254, 256, 341
Free Church of Scotland 6, 7, 171, 173, 175, 229, 240, 292, 297, 313, 329
Free Presbyterian Church 329
Fuller, Andrew 4, 5, 15, 17, 34, 48, 64, 109, 119, 124, 131, 154, 268

G

Gaelic School Societies 174
Garie, James 107
Gaussen, Louis 84
General Baptists 243
General Union of Particular Baptist Churches in England 135, 335
Geneva 84
George Street Scotch Baptist Church, Glasgow 60, 198, 206
Gibson, David 155, 171
Gilbert, John 57
Gilmour, John 146, 148, 200, 201, 219, 224
Glas, John 29, 30, 33, 34
Glasgow 'English' Baptist Church 117, 118, 138
Glasgow Abstinence Society 242
Glasgow City Mission 242
Glasgow Scotch Baptist Church 62
Glasgow Tabernacle Church 90
Glasite movement 29, 33, 93
Glover, Richard 284, 308, 309, 317,

325
Godwin, Benjamin 148
Gordon, D. 57
Graham, William 48
Grant, Alexander 156, 166, 168, 179, 180, 185, 214, 312
Grant, John 307
Grant, P.W. 14
Grant, Peter 10, 22, 105, 108, 171, 174, 234, 245, 250, 254, 255, 258, 272, 273, 276, 323, 331
Grant, Peter (Stirling) 158, 192, 266, 267, 268, 269
Grant, William 22, 245, 250, 254, 255, 258, 273, 286, 312, 331
Grantown-on-Spey Baptist Church 105, 107, 174, 197
Gray, William 198
Green, Samuel 314
Greenock Total Abstinence Society 245
Grieve, George 35, 54, 64
Gutteridge, Joseph 131

H

Haggate Baptist Church, Burnley 35
Haldane, Alexander 89, 91
Haldane, James Alexander 3, 4, 21, 24, 45, 47, 48, 58, 73, 133, 138, 142, 155, 176, 185, 186, 188, 194, 211, 222, 225, 249, 253, 255, 271, 280, 319, 320
Haldane, Robert 3, 4, 13, 17, 24, 47, 48, 73, 138, 155, 176, 215, 319, 320
Hampshire Association of Independent Churches 75
Hands, Thomas F. 296
Hill, James 167
Hill, Rowland 75, 76, 133
Hine, John 45
Hinton, James 139
Hinton, John Howard 177, 212, 226, 265, 300
Hodge, William 204, 264, 272, 279, 288, 289
Holyoak, Thomas 306

Home Missionary Society for Scotland 156, 192
Hope Street Baptist Church, Glasgow 149, 159, 175, 181, 204, 205, 244, 272, 278, 288, 310, 315
Hope, Samuel 131
Horsburgh, John 39, 69
Horton Baptist College, Bradford 122, 123, 147, 148, 169, 196, 198, 216, 218, 219, 232, 291, 307, 310
Hutchison, William 102, 109, 156
Hynd, William 64, 67

I

Inglis, Henry David 41, 54
Innes, William 21, 58, 74, 75, 89, 93, 99, 100, 108, 127, 138, 158, 192, 194, 197, 199, 217, 221, 223, 253, 266, 299
Ireland 128, 136
Irish Baptist Association 19

J

James, John Angell 113
Jay, William 106
John Street Baptist Church, Aberdeen 148, 255
John Street Scotch Baptist Church, Glasgow 272, 284
Johnston, Francis 6, 9, 16, 20, 22, 23, 149, 159, 183, 186, 187, 189, 191, 220, 224, 225, 227, 229, 231, 234, 245, 246, 247, 248, 252, 256, 258, 262, 265, 270, 272, 273, 277, 278, 287, 290, 293, 294, 307, 308, 309, 322, 323, 328, 333, 334, 335
Johnston, James 195, 218
Johnstone, Robert 149
Jones, J. Idwal 20, 65, 69
Jones, Samuel 87
Jones, William 21, 31, 51, 56, 57, 65, 67, 69, 70, 231

K

Kemp, Daniel 43
Ker, Andrew 198, 206
Kettle, Robert 241, 243, 245, 251, 299

Index 399

Kilwinning Baptist Church 115, 123, 244
Kirk, Adam 111, 159, 200, 201
Kirk, John 333
Kirkcaldy Total Abstinence Society 244
Kirkwood, Alexander 111, 219
Kirkwood, Archibald 252

L

Lady Glenorchy's Chapel 75
Lancashire and Cheshire Association of Baptist Churches 237
Landels, T.D. 245
Landels, William 16, 24, 245, 252, 257, 259, 290, 302, 309, 323, 325, 334, 340
Leechman, John 130, 131, 253
Liddel, Andrew 45, 57, 70
Lister, James 118, 122, 134, 237
Livingstone, Archibald 169
Lochgilphead Baptist Church 123, 185
Lockhart, Ninian 217, 244
Lockhart, Robert 244
London Baptist Association 182, 300, 301, 324
London Missionary Society 75, 138, 290
Lord's Supper 2, 32, 56, 64, 67, 69, 88, 90, 91, 117, 142, 281, 327
Lord's Table 9, 57, 226, 301
Lothian, William 145
Lynch, Michael 15

M

MacAlpine, Thomas 272
MacAndrew, John 280, 286
MacDougall, Duncan 259
Macfadyen, Alexander 178
Macfarlane, Duncan 168
Macfarlane, John 66, 307
MacInnes, John 12
MacIntosh, Francis 257
Macintyre, Duncan 166
Mackay, Edward 42, 109, 111, 158

Mackay, Robert 184
Mackintosh, John 184
Mackintosh, Lachlan 102, 105, 107, 109, 156, 163, 166, 180, 185, 186, 216
MacLaren, Allan 13
Macrae, David 42, 158
Malcolm, James 245, 278
Mann, Isaac 314
Mansfield, John 286
Marshall Street Baptist Church, Edinburgh 263
Marshman, John 142
Martin, James 293
Matthew, Father Theobald 241, 242
McArthur, Donald 120
McCulloch, William 15
McDougald, Duncan 180
McFarlane, Frederick 120
McFarlane, Peter 123, 147
McIlvain, John 149, 218, 272
McKay, David 149
McKerrow, John 7, 327
McLaren, David 46, 47, 157, 158, 192, 198, 201, 206, 207, 215, 217, 223, 227
McLean, Archibald 3, 9, 21, 30, 33, 35, 38, 41, 48, 55, 62, 71, 117, 138, 141, 193, 207, 235, 268, 319, 328
McLean, William 201
McLellan, Donald 173
McLeod, Alexander 124, 146, 155, 160, 180, 198, 200, 208, 221, 254, 270, 299, 338
McLeod, Richard 272
McMillan, John 148
McMillan, William 219
McNaughton, Angus 171, 179, 185
McPhail, Archibald 219
McPherson, John 170
McQueen, James 108, 166, 171, 178
McVicar, Donald 109, 119
Medhurst, Thomas 282, 284, 305
Meek, D.E. 10, 19, 342
Methodists 38, 65, 81, 127, 204, 243, 297
Midland Baptist Association 167, 303

Millard, J.H. 336
Millennial Harbinger 56, 231
Miller, James 160, 179, 180
Miller, William 217
Milne, John 292
Milner, Thomas 16, 22, 260, 261, 262, 263, 267, 273, 275, 278, 334
Missionary Magazine 81
Moffat, Robert 290
Montrose Baptist Church 207, 330
Moodie, William 83
Moravian 81
Morison, James 16, 226, 230, 232, 267, 268, 270, 274, 329, 331, 333
Morison, Robert 16, 267
Morisonian 8, 9, 16, 20, 259, 326, 330, 331, 337, 340
Muir, Thomas 288, 291
Munro, Walter 104, 156, 165
Murray, Derek 19, 338
Murray, James 66
Mursell, James 302

N

New Connexion General Baptists 295, 324, 335, 341
New Evangelical Magazine 21, 69
New Theological Repository 21
New Zealand 305
Newton, John 133
Nicol, Isaac 47
Niddry Street Baptist Church, Edinburgh 54, 55
Nisbet, Alexander 200
Norfolk Baptist Association 302
North Frederick Street Baptist Church, Glasgow 282, 284, 305, 306
North Portland Street Scotch Baptist Church, Glasgow 104, 198, 201, 206, 209, 221, 289
Northamptonshire Baptist Association 131, 134, 167, 301
Northern Baptist Education Society Report 216

O

Old Connexion of English General Baptists 33, 204
Old Scotch Independents 30, 66, 93, 133
Oncken, Johann 52
open or closed communion 18, 59
open or closed table 281
Orangefield Baptist Church, Greenock 103, 149, 187, 226
Orr, James 12

P

Pastor's College 300, 304, 305, 307, 314, 317
Paterson, James 147, 149, 159, 175, 181, 183, 184, 188, 189, 204, 218, 223, 242, 243, 244, 254, 264, 272, 275, 279, 284, 287, 289, 293, 299, 307, 315, 323, 325, 327, 338, 343
Paterson, Mr 160
Pattison, William 39, 66, 69
Paxton, John 217
Payne, E.A. 17
Pearce, Samuel 169
Peddie, Robert 217
Peddie, William 198, 215
Perrey, Abraham 197
Perth Baptist Church 181, 196
Perth Temperance Society 244
Peterhead Baptist Church 305
pietistic Christianity 292
Pike, J.G. 212, 324
Primitive Church Magazine 23, 126, 204, 244, 263, 271
Pullar, John 249, 258, 264, 272, 286, 288, 290
Pullar, Robert 47
Pulsford, John 306

R

1859 revival 296
Rainy, Robert 11
Rate, Joseph 78
Rawdon College 314
Regent's Park College 306, 314
Relief Church 6, 7, 80, 93, 240
Religious Tract Society 290

Index 401

Richmond Court 'English' Baptist Chapel, Edinburgh 124
Richmond Street Baptist Church, Edinburgh 284
Rippon, John 37, 53, 118
Robe, James 15
Robison, Prof. John 83
Robson, Charles 178
Robson, W. 251
Roman Catholics 1, 133, 136, 153, 240, 241, 242, 249
Rose, Hugh 308, 310
Rosevear, William 306
Ross, Hugh 80
Ryland, John Jr 131, 139, 313

S

Saffery, John 128, 132, 169, 218
Saltcoats Scotch Baptist Church 60
Sandeman, Robert 34
Sandemanianism 33, 59, 129, 268
Scotch Baptists 208
Scotch Itinerant Society 122, 124, 128, 140, 148, 150, 155
Scott, Andrew 65
Scottish Temperance Journal 242
Scottish Temperance League 242, 244, 300
Scottish Temperance Review 244
Scottish Temperance Society 241
Secession Church 6, 8
Selina, Countess of Huntingdon 107
Selly, John 42
Serampore Baptist College, India 130, 142
Shearer, John 168, 272
Shirreff, William 74, 138, 197
Simeon, Charles 74, 75, 76
Sinclair, Dugald 10, 109, 121, 147, 148, 165, 170, 184, 201, 219
Smith, Archibald 58, 111, 128, 141, 198, 200, 207, 210, 211
Smith, David 46, 198, 217, 341
Smith, James 33
Smout, T.C. 13
Society for Propagating the Gospel at Home 5, 75, 78, 156

Society in Scotland for Propagating Christian Knowledge 79
Society of Irish Church Missions 136
Socinianism 206, 209, 340
Somerville, John 290
Souter, David 158, 192, 200, 201, 218
South Portland Street Baptist Church, Glasgow 111, 122, 125, 200, 272
Spence, Charles 200
Spence, John L. 305
Spurgeon, C.H. 19, 177, 182, 272, 281, 302, 303, 305, 325, 337
Stalker, Alexander 149, 224
Stalker, John 47
Steadman, William 148, 169, 218, 231
Stephen, James 43, 220, 236
Stephens, William 108, 109, 216
Stepney Academy 302, 313
Stirling Baptist Church 288, 290
Storie Street Baptist Church, Paisley 308, 310
Struthers, Gavin 7, 93
Stuart, Dr Charles 35, 53, 54, 64, 124, 127, 138, 215
Stuart, Neil 62, 63, 207
Sutcliff, John 15
Sutherland, Francis 198
Swan, Samuel 35, 39
Swan, Thomas 142

T

Taylor, James 245, 247, 248, 250, 251, 259, 267, 284, 323
Taylor, Nathaniel W. 16
Taylor, William 204
Temperance Movement 240
The Association 104, 111, 211, 265
The Evangelist 9, 22, 248, 251, 252, 259, 260, 261, 262, 267, 268, 271, 340
The Fife Home Missionary Association or Itinerating Society 145, 167
The Freeman 126, 175, 293, 297, 302, 324
The Friendly Visitor 248

The Myrtle 248, 261
The Scottish Review 244
The Strict Baptist Mission 336
The Theological Repository 21, 31, 69
theological education 106, 147, 215, 246, 312, 326
Thompson, David 238
Thompson, Joshua 18
Thompson, Sinclair 272
Thomson, Alexander 312
Thomson, Donald 149, 187, 218, 226, 227
Thomson, Robert 149, 181, 198, 218, 224, 225, 227, 234, 248, 249, 251, 254, 307
Thomson, Sinclair 126
Thomson, William 39
Thurso Baptist Church 111
Tiree Baptist Church 259
Tolmie, William 289, 310
Trevecca College 107, 169
Tulloch, William 47, 103, 109, 157, 172, 223, 277, 298, 311
Tulloch, William (Orkney) 170, 172
Turnbull, William 142

U

Uig Baptist Church 166
Underhill, E.B. 286, 296
Unitarian 204
United Free Church 6, 8, 329
United Presbyterian Church 6, 8, 240, 297, 329
United Secession Church 6, 7, 230, 240, 329
Universalism 266
Urquhart, John 14

W

Wakefield, Colonel 296

Walcot, John 310
Walker, John 97
Walker, Robert 53, 54, 63
Wallace, Charles 198, 201, 206
Wallace, David 286
Wallis, James 45, 56, 231
Ward, William 5, 153
Wardlaw, Ralph 333
Watson, James 207, 209, 210, 211, 224, 227, 266, 321, 340
Watson, Jonathan 58, 144, 146, 149, 158, 192, 200, 201, 207, 208, 210, 225, 247, 249, 252, 253, 266, 270, 272, 299, 310, 321, 342, 343
Watt, Dr James 4, 12, 41, 46, 47, 67, 70, 117, 157, 215
Waugh, Percival 21
Welch, George 106
Wemyss, Thomas 108, 216
Western Baptist Association 134, 166, 301
Western Scottish Temperance Union 241
Whitefieldite Tabernacles 83
Whitfield, Charles 167
Williams, John 282, 293, 297, 306
Williamson, James 63
Wilson, Archibald 149, 195
Wilson, John Alexander 305
Wilson, Patrick 9, 29
Winks, J.F. 239
Withers, C.W.J. 14
Wylie, Alexander 232
Wylie, David 49

Y

YMCA 290
Yorkshire Baptist Association 302
Young, James 141, 142
Young, John 109
Yuille, George 9

Studies in Baptist History and Thought

(All titles uniform with this volume)
Dates in bold are of projected publication
Volumes in this series are not always published in sequence

David Bebbington and Anthony R. Cross (eds)
Global Baptist History
(SBHT vol. 14)

This book brings together studies from the Second International Conference on Baptist Studies which explore different facets of Baptist life and work especially during the twentieth century.
2005 / 1-84227-214-4

David Bebbington (ed.)
The Gospel in the World
International Baptist Studies
(SBHT vol. 1)

This volume of essays from the First International Conference on Baptist Studies deals with a range of subjects spanning Britain, North America, Europe, Asia and the Antipodes. Topics include studies on religious tolerance, the communion controversy and the development of the international Baptist community, and concludes with two important essays on the future of Baptist life that pay special attention to the United States.
2002 / 1-84227-118-0 / xiv + 362pp

Damian Brot
Church of the Baptized or Church of Believers?
A Contribution to the Dialogue between the Catholic Church and the Free Churches with Special Reference to Baptists
(SBHT vol. 26)

The dialogue between the Catholic Church and the Free Churches in Europe has hardly taken place. This book pleads for a commencement of such a conversation. It offers, among other things, an introduction to the American and the international dialogues between Baptists and the Catholic Church and strives to allow these conversations to become fruitful in the European context as well.
2006 / 1-84227-334-5 / approx. 364pp

Dennis Bustin
Paradox and Perseverence
Hanserd Knollys, Particular Baptist Pioneer in Seventeenth-Century England
(SBHT vol. 23)

The seventeenth century was a significant period in English history during which the people of England experienced unprecedented change and tumult in all spheres of life. At the same time, the importance of order and the traditional institutions of society were being reinforced. Hanserd Knollys, born during this pivotal period, personified in his life the ambiguity, tension and paradox of it, openly seeking change while at the same time cautiously embracing order. As a founder and leader of the Particular Baptists in London and despite persecution and personal hardship, he played a pivotal role in helping shape their identity externally in society and, internally, as they moved toward becoming more formalised by the end of the century.

2006 / 1-84227-259-4 / approx. 324pp

Anthony R. Cross
Baptism and the Baptists
Theology and Practice in Twentieth-Century Britain
(SBHT vol. 3)

At a time of renewed interest in baptism, *Baptism and the Baptists* is a detailed study of twentieth-century baptismal theology and practice and the factors which have influenced its development.

2000 / 0-85364-959-6 / xx + 530pp

Anthony R. Cross and Philip E. Thompson (eds)
Recycling the Past or Researching History?
Studies in Baptist Historiography and Myths
(SBHT vol. 11)

This collection of essays examines the issues of historiography and myths in Baptist history and theology: these include the idea of development in Baptist thought, studies in the church, baptismal sacramentalism, community, spirituality, soul competency, women, Baptist bishops, creeds and the Bible, and overseas missions.

2005 / 1-84227-122-9

Anthony R. Cross and Philip E. Thompson (eds)
Baptist Sacramentalism
(SBHT vol. 5)

This collection of essays includes biblical, historical and theological studies in the theology of the sacraments from a Baptist perspective. Subjects explored include the physical side of being spiritual, baptism, the Lord's supper, the church, ordination, preaching, worship, religious liberty and the issue of disestablishment.

2003 / 1-84227-119-9 / xvi + 278pp

Anthony R. Cross and Philip E. Thompson (eds)
Baptist Sacramentalism 2
(SBHT vol. 25)

This second collection of essays exploring various dimensions of sacramental theology from a Baptist perspective includes biblical, historical and theological studies from scholars from around the world.

2006 / 1-84227-325-6

Paul S. Fiddes
Tracks and Traces
Baptist Identity in Church and Theology
(SBHT vol. 13)

This is a comprehensive, yet unusual, book on the faith and life of Baptist Christians. It explores the understanding of the church, ministry, sacraments and mission from a thoroughly theological perspective. In a series of interlinked essays, the author relates Baptist identity consistently to a theology of covenant and to participation in the triune communion of God.

2003 / 1-84227-120-2 / xvi + 304pp

Stanley K. Fowler
More Than a Symbol
The British Baptist Recovery of Baptismal Sacramentalism
(SBHT vol. 2)

Fowler surveys the entire scope of British Baptist literature from the seventeenth-century pioneers onwards. He shows that in the twentieth century leading British Baptist pastors and theologians recovered an understanding of baptism that connected experience with soteriology and that in doing so they were recovering what many of their forebears had taught.

2002 / 1-84227-052-4 / xvi + 276pp

November 2004

Michael A.G. Haykin (ed.)
'At the Pure Fountain of Thy Word'
Andrew Fuller as an Apologist
(SBHT vol. 6)

One of the greatest Baptist theologians of the eighteenth and early nineteenth centuries, Andrew Fuller has not had justice done to him. There is little doubt that Fuller's theology lay behind the revitalization of the Baptists in the late eighteenth century and the first few decades of the nineteenth. This collection of essays fills a much needed gap by examining a major area of Fuller's thought, his work as an apologist.

2004 / 1-84227-171-7 / xxii + 276pp

Michael A.G. Haykin
Studies in Calvinistic Baptist Spirituality
(SBHT vol. 15)

In a day when spirituality is in vogue and Christian communities are looking for guidance in this whole area, there is wisdom in looking to the past to find untapped wells. The Calvinistic Baptists, heirs of the rich ecclesial experience in the Puritan era of the seventeenth century, but, by the end of the eighteenth century, also passionately engaged in the catholicity of the Evangelical Revivals, are such a well. This collection of essays, covering such things as the Lord's Supper, friendship and hymnody, seeks to draw out the spiritual riches of this community for reflection and imitation in the present day.

2005 / 1-84227-149-0

Brian Haymes, Anthony R. Cross and Ruth Gouldbourne
On Being the Church
Revisioning Baptist Identity
(SBHT vol. 21)

The aim of the book is to re-examine Baptist theology and practice in the light of the contemporary biblical, theological, ecumenical and missiological context drawing on historical and contemporary writings and issues. It is not a study in denominationalism but rather seeks to revision historical insights from the believers' church tradition for the sake of Baptists and other Christians in the context of the modern–postmodern context.

2005 / 1-84227-121-0

Ken R. Manley
From Woolloomooloo to 'Eternity'
A History of Baptists in Australia
(SBHT vol. 16)

From their beginnings in Australia in 1831 with the first baptisms in Woolloomooloo Bay in 1832, this pioneering study describes the quest of Baptists in the different colonies (states) to discover their identity as Australians and Baptists. Although institutional developments are analyzed and the roles of significant individuals traced, the major focus is on the social and theological dimensions of the Baptist movement.

2005 / 1-84227-194-6

Ken R. Manley
'Redeeming Love Proclaim'
John Rippon and the Baptists
(SBHT vol. 12)

A leading exponent of the new moderate Calvinism which brought new life to many Baptists, John Rippon (1751–1836) helped unite the Baptists at this significant time. His many writings expressed the denomination's growing maturity and mutual awareness of Baptists in Britain and America, and exerted a long-lasting influence on Baptist worship and devotion. In his various activities, Rippon helped conserve the heritage of Old Dissent and promoted the evangelicalism of the New Dissent

2004 / 1-84227-193-8 / xviii + 340pp

Peter J. Morden
Offering Christ to the World
Andrew Fuller and the Revival of English Particular Baptist Life
(SBHT vol. 8)

Andrew Fuller (1754–1815) was one of the foremost English Baptist ministers of his day. His career as an Evangelical Baptist pastor, theologian, apologist and missionary statesman coincided with the profound revitalization of the Particular Baptist denomination to which he belonged. This study examines the key aspects of the life and thought of this hugely significant figure, and gives insights into the revival in which he played such a central part.

2003 / 1-84227-141-5 / xx + 202pp

Peter Naylor
Calvinism, Communion and the Baptists
A Study of English Calvinistic Baptists from the Late 1600s to the Early 1800s
(SBHT vol. 7)

Dr Naylor argues that the traditional link between 'high-Calvinism' and 'restricted communion' is in need of revision. He examines Baptist communion controversies from the late 1600s to the early 1800s and also the theologies of John Gill and Andrew Fuller.

2003 / 1-84227-142-3 / xx + 266pp

Ian M. Randall, Toivo Pilli and Anthony R. Cross (eds)
Baptist Identities
International Studies from the Seventeenth to the Twentieth Centuries
(SBHT vol. 19)

These papers represent the contributions of scholars from various parts of the world as they consider the factors that have contributed to Baptist distinctiveness in different countries and at different times. The volume includes specific case studies as well as broader examinations of Baptist life in a particular country or region. Together they represent an outstanding resource for understanding Baptist identities.

2005 / 1-84227-215-2

James M. Renihan
Edification and Beauty
The Practical Ecclesiology of the English Particular Baptists, 1675–1705
(SBHT vol. 17)

Edification and Beauty describes the practices of the Particular Baptist churches at the end of the seventeenth century in terms of three concentric circles: at the centre is the ecclesiological material in the Second London Confession, which is then fleshed out in the various published writings of the men associated with these churches, and, finally, expressed in the church books of the era.

2005 / 1-84227-251-9 / approx. 230pp

Frank Rinaldi
'The Tribe of Dan'
A Study of the New Connexion of General Baptists 1770–1891
(SBHT vol. 10)

'The Tribe of Dan' is a thematic study which explores the theology, organizational structure, evangelistic strategy, ministry and leadership of the New Connexion of General Baptists as it experienced the process of institutionalization in the transition from a revival movement to an established denomination.

2006 / 1-84227-143-1 / approx. 330pp

Peter Shepherd
The Making of a Modern Denomination
John Howard Shakespeare and the English Baptists 1898–1924
(SBHT vol. 4)

John Howard Shakespeare introduced revolutionary change to the Baptist denomination. The Baptist Union was transformed into a strong central institution and Baptist ministers were brought under its control. Further, Shakespeare's pursuit of church unity reveals him as one of the pioneering ecumenists of the twentieth century.

2001 / 1-84227-046-X / xviii + 220pp

Karen Smith
The Community and the Believers
A Study of Calvinistic Baptist Spirituality in Some Towns and Villages of Hampshire and the Borders of Wiltshire, c.1730–1830
(SBHT vol. 22)

The period from 1730 to 1830 was one of transition for Calvinistic Baptists. Confronted by the enthusiasm of the Evangelical Revival, congregations within the denomination as a whole were challenged to find a way to take account of the revival experience. This study examines the life and devotion of Calvinistic Baptists in Hampshire and Wiltshire during this period. Among this group of Baptists was the hymn writer, Anne Steele.

2005 / 1-84227-326-4 / approx. 280pp

Martin Sutherland
Dissenters in a 'Free Land'
Baptist Thought in New Zealand 1850–2000
(SBHT vol. 24)

Baptists in New Zealand were forced to recast their identity. Conventions of communication and association, state and ecumenical relations, even historical divisions and controversies had to be revised in the face of new topographies and constraints. As Baptists formed themselves in a fluid society they drew heavily on both international movements and local dynamics. This book traces the development of ideas which shaped institutions and styles in sometimes surprising ways.

2006 / 1-84227-327-2 / approx. 230pp

Brian Talbot
The Search for a Common Identity
The Origins of the Baptist Union of Scotland 1800–1870
(SBHT vol. 9)

In the period 1800 to 1827 there were three streams of Baptists in Scotland: Scotch, Haldaneite and 'English' Baptist. A strong commitment to home evangelization brought these three bodies closer together, leading to a merger of their home missionary societies in 1827. However, the first three attempts to form a union of churches failed, but by the 1860s a common understanding of their corporate identity was attained leading to the establishment of the Baptist Union of Scotland.

2003 / 1-84227-123-7 / xviii + 402pp

Philip E. Thompson
The Freedom of God
Towards Baptist Theology in Pneumatological Perspective
(SBHT vol. 20)

This study contends that the range of theological commitments of the early Baptists are best understood in relation to their distinctive emphasis on the freedom of God. Thompson traces how this was recast anthropocentrically, leading to an emphasis upon human freedom from the nineteenth century onwards. He seeks to recover the dynamism of the early vision via a pneumatologically-oriented ecclesiology defining the church in terms of the memory of God.

2005 / 1-84227-125-3

Linda Wilson
Marianne Farningham
A Plain Working Woman
(SBHT vol. 18)

Marianne Farningham, of College Street Baptist Chapel, Northampton, was a household name in evangelical circles in the later nineteenth century. For over fifty years she produced comment, poetry, biography and fiction for the popular Christian press. This investigation uses her writings to explore the beliefs and behaviour of evangelical Nonconformists, including Baptists, during these years.

2006 / 1-84227-124-5

Other Paternoster titles relating to Baptist history and thought

George R. Beasley-Murray
Baptism in the New Testament
(Paternoster Digital Library)
This is a welcome reprint of a classic text on baptism originally published in 1962 by one of the leading Baptist New Testament scholars of the twentieth century. Dr Beasley-Murray's comprehensive study begins by investigating the antecedents of Christian baptism. It then surveys the foundation of Christian baptism in the Gospels, its emergence in the Acts of the Apostles and development in the apostolic writings. Following a section relating baptism to New Testament doctrine, a substantial discussion of the origin and significance of infant baptism leads to a briefer consideration of baptismal reform and ecumenism.

2005 / 1-84227-300-0 / x + 422pp

Paul Beasley-Murray
Fearless for Truth
A Personal Portrait of the Life of George Beasley-Murray
Without a doubt George Beasley-Murray was one of the greatest Baptists of the twentieth century. A long-standing Principal of Spurgeon's College, he wrote more than twenty books and made significant contributions in the study of areas as diverse as baptism and eschatology, as well as writing highly respected commentaries on the Book of Revelation and John's Gospel.

2002 / 1-84227-134-2 / xii + 244pp

David Bebbington
Holiness in Nineteenth-Century England
(Studies in Christian History and Thought)
David Bebbington stresses the relationship of movements of spirituality to changes in their cultural setting, especially the legacies of the Enlightenment and Romanticism. He shows that these broad shifts in ideological mood had a profound effect on the ways in which piety was conceptualized and practised. Holiness was intimately bound up with the spirit of the age.

2000 / 0-85364-981-2 / viii + 98pp

November 2004

Clyde Binfield
The Country a Little Thickened and Congested?
Nonconformity in Eastern England 1840–1885
(Studies in Evangelical History and Thought)
Studies of Victorian religion and society often concentrate on cities, suburbs, and industrialisation. This study provides a contrast. Victorian Eastern England—Essex, Suffolk, Norfolk, Cambridgeshire, and Huntingdonshire—was rural, traditional, relatively unchanging. That is nonetheless a caricature which discounts the industry in Norwich and Ipswich (as well as in Haverhill, Stowmarket, and Leiston) and ignores the impact of London on Essex, of railways throughout the region, and of an ancient but changing university (Cambridge) on the county town which housed it. It also entirely ignores the political implications of such changes in a region noted for the variety of its religious Dissent since the seventeenth century. This book explores Victorian Eastern England and its Nonconformity. It brings to a wider readership a pioneering thesis which has made a major contribution to a fresh evolution of English religion and society.
2005 / 1-84227-216-0 / approx. 274pp

Christopher J. Clement
Religious Radicalism in England 1535–1565
(Rutherford Studies in Historical Theology)
In this valuable study Christopher Clement draws our attention to a varied assemblage of people who sought Christian faithfulness in the underworld of mid-Tudor England. Sympathetically and yet critically he assess their place in the history of English Protestantism, and by attentive listening he gives them a voice.
1997 / 0-946068-44-5 / xxii + 426pp

Anthony R. Cross (ed.)
Ecumenism and History
Studies in Honour of John H.Y. Briggs
(Studies in Christian History and Thought)
This collection of essays examines the inter-relationships between the two fields in which Professor Briggs has contributed so much: history—particularly Baptist and Nonconformist—and the ecumenical movement. With contributions from colleagues and former research students from Britain, Europe and North America, *Ecumenism and History* provides wide-ranging studies in important aspects of Christian history, theology and ecumenical studies.
2002 / 1-84227-135-0 / xx + 362pp

Keith E. Eitel
Paradigm Wars
The Southern Baptist International Mission Board
Faces the Third Millennium
(Regnum Studies in Mission)
The International Mission Board of the Southern Baptist Convention is the largest denominational mission agency in North America. This volume chronicles the historic and contemporary forces that led to the IMB's recent extensive reorganization, providing the most comprehensive case study to date of a historic mission agency restructuring to continue its mission purpose into the twenty-first century more effectively.
2000 / 1-870345-12-6 / x + 140pp

Ruth Gouldbourne
The Flesh and the Feminine
Gender and Theology in the Writings of Caspar Schwenckfeld
(Studies in Christian History and Thought)
Caspar Schwenckfeld and his movement exemplify one of the radical communities of the sixteenth century. Challenging theological and liturgical norms, they also found themselves challenging social and particularly gender assumptions. In this book, the issues of the relationship between radical theology and the understanding of gender are considered.
2005 / 1-84227-048-6 / approx. 304pp

David Hilborn
The Words of our Lips
Language-Use in Free Church Worship
(Paternoster Theological Monographs)
Studies of liturgical language have tended to focus on the written canons of Roman Catholic and Anglican communities. By contrast, David Hilborn analyses the more extemporary approach of English Nonconformity. Drawing on recent developments in linguistic pragmatics, he explores similarities and differences between 'fixed' and 'free' worship, and argues for the interdependence of each.
2005 / 0-85364-977-4

Mark Hopkins
Nonconformity's Romantic Generation
Evangelical and Liberal Theologies in Victorian England
(Studies in Evangelical History and Thought)
A study of the theological development of key leaders of the Baptist and Congregational denominations at their period of greatest influence, including C.H. Spurgeon and R.W. Dale, and of the controversies in which those among them who embraced and rejected the liberal transformation of their evangelical heritage opposed each other.

2004 / 1-84227-150-4 / xvi + 284pp

Galen K. Johnson
Prisoner of Conscience
John Bunyan on Self, Community and Christian Faith
(Studies in Christian History and Thought)
This is an interdisciplinary study of John Bunyan's understanding of conscience across his autobiographical, theological and fictional writings, investigating whether conscience always deserves fidelity, and how Bunyan's view of conscience affects his relationship both to modern Western individualism and historic Christianity.

2003 / 1-84227- 151-2 / xvi + 236pp

R.T. Kendall
Calvin and English Calvinism to 1649
(Studies in Christian History and Thought)
The author's thesis is that those who formed the Westminster Confession of Faith, which is regarded as Calvinism, in fact departed from John Calvin on two points: (1) the extent of the atonement and (2) the ground of assurance of salvation.

1997 / 0-85364-827-1 / xii + 264pp

Donald M. Lewis
Lighten Their Darkness
The Evangelical Mission to Working-Class London, 1828–1860
(Studies in Evangelical History and Thought)
This is a comprehensive and compelling study of the Church and the complexities of nineteenth-century London. Challenging our understanding of the culture in working London at this time, Lewis presents a well-structured and illustrated work that contributes substantially to the study of evangelicalism and mission in nineteenth-century Britain.

2001 / 1-84227-074-5 / xviii + 372pp

Stanley E. Porter and Anthony R. Cross (eds)
Semper Reformandum
Studies in Honour of Clark H. Pinnock

Clark Pinnock has clearly been one of the most important evangelical theologians of the last forty years in North America. Always provocative, especially in the wide range of opinions he has held and considered, Pinnock, himself a Baptist, has recently retired after twenty-five years of teaching at McMaster Divinity College. His colleagues and associates honour him in this volume by responding to his important theological work which has dealt with the essential topics of evangelical theology. These include Christian apologetics, biblical inspiration, the Holy Spirit and, perhaps most importantly in recent years, openness theology.

2003 / 1-84227-206-3 / xiv + 414pp

Meic Pearse
The Great Restoration
The Religious Radicals of the 16th and 17th Centuries

Pearse charts the rise and progress of continental Anabaptism – both evangelical and heretical – through the sixteenth century. He then follows the story of those English people who became impatient with Puritanism and separated – first from the Church of England and then from one another – to form the antecedents of later Congregationalists, Baptists and Quakers.

1998 / 0-85364-800-X / xii + 320pp

Charles Price and Ian M. Randall
Transforming Keswick

Transforming Keswick is a thorough, readable and detailed history of the convention. It will be of interest to those who know and love Keswick, those who are only just discovering it, and serious scholars eager to learn more about the history of God's dealings with his people.

2000 / 1-85078-350-0 / 288pp

Jim Purves
The Triune God and the Charismatic Movement
A Critical Appraisal from a Scottish Perspective
(Paternoster Theological Monographs)

All emotion and no theology? Or a fundamental challenge to reappraise and realign our trinitarian theology in the light of Christian experience? This study of charismatic renewal as it found expression within Scotland at the end of the twentieth century evaluates the use of Patristic, Reformed and contemporary models (including those of the Baptist Union of Scotland) of the Trinity in explaining the workings of the Holy Spirit.

2004 / 1-84227-321-3 / xxiv + 246pp

Ian M. Randall
Evangelical Experiences
A Study in the Spirituality of English Evangelicalism 1918–1939
(Studies in Evangelical History and Thought)
This book makes a detailed historical examination of evangelical spirituality between the First and Second World Wars. It shows how patterns of devotion led to tensions and divisions. In a wide-ranging study, Anglican, Wesleyan, Reformed and Pentecostal-charismatic spiritualities are analysed.
1999 / 0-85364-919-7 / xii + 310pp

Ian M. Randall
One Body in Christ
The History and Significance of the Evangelical Alliance
In 1846 the Evangelical Alliance was founded with the aim of bringing together evangelicals for common action. This book uses material not previously utilized to examine the history and significance of the Evangelical Alliance, a movement which has remained a powerful force for unity. At a time when evangelicals are growing world-wide, this book offers insights into the past which are relevant to contemporary issues.
2001 / 1-84227-089-3 / xii + 394pp

Ian M. Randall
Spirituality and Social Change
The Contribution of F.B. Meyer (1847–1929)
(Studies in Evangelical History and Thought)
This is a fresh appraisal of F.B. Meyer (1847–1929), a leading Free Church minister. Having been deeply affected by holiness spirituality, Meyer became the Keswick Convention's foremost international speaker. He combined spirituality with effective evangelism and socio-political activity. This study shows Meyer's significant contribution to spiritual renewal and social change.
2003 / 1-84227-195-4 / xx + 184pp

Geoffrey Robson
Dark Satanic Mills?
Religion and Irreligion in Birmingham and the Black Country
(Studies in Evangelical History and Thought)
This book analyses and interprets the nature and extent of popular Christian belief and practice in Birmingham and the Black Country during the first half of the nineteenth century, with particular reference to the impact of cholera epidemics and evangelism on church extension programmes.
2002 / 1-84227-102-4 / xiv + 294pp

November 2004

Alan P.F. Sell
Enlightenment, Ecumenism, Evangel
Theological Themes and Thinkers 1550–2000
(Studies in Christian History and Thought)

This book consists of papers in which such interlocking topics as the Enlightenment, the problem of authority, the development of doctrine, spirituality, ecumenism, theological method and the heart of the gospel are discussed. Issues of significance to the church at large are explored with special reference to writers from the Reformed and Dissenting traditions.

2005 / 1-84227330-2 / xviii + 422pp

Alan P.F. Sell
Hinterland Theology
Some Reformed and Dissenting Adjustments
(Studies in Christian History and Thought)

Many books have been written on theology's 'giants' and significant trends, but what of those lesser-known writers who adjusted to them? In this book some hinterland theologians of the British Reformed and Dissenting traditions, who followed in the wake of toleration, the Evangelical Revival, the rise of modern biblical criticism and Karl Barth, are allowed to have their say. They include Thomas Ridgley, Ralph Wardlaw, T.V. Tymms and N.H.G. Robinson.

2006 / 1-84227-331-0

Alan P.F. Sell and Anthony R. Cross (eds)
Protestant Nonconformity in the Twentieth Century
(Studies in Christian History and Thought)

In this collection of essays scholars representative of a number of Nonconformist traditions reflect thematically on Nonconformists' life and witness during the twentieth century. Among the subjects reviewed are biblical studies, theology, worship, evangelism and spirituality, and ecumenism. Over and above its immediate interest, this collection provides a marker to future scholars and others wishing to know how some of their forebears assessed Nonconformity's contribution to a variety of fields during the century leading up to Christianity's third millennium.

2003 / 1-84227-221-7 / x + 398pp

Mark Smith
Religion in Industrial Society
Oldham and Saddleworth 1740–1865
(Studies in Christian History and Thought)
This book analyses the way British churches sought to meet the challenge of industrialization and urbanization during the period 1740–1865. Working from a case-study of Oldham and Saddleworth, Mark Smith challenges the received view that the Anglican Church in the eighteenth century was characterized by complacency and inertia, and reveals Anglicanism's vigorous and creative response to the new conditions. He reassesses the significance of the centrally directed church reforms of the mid-nineteenth century, and emphasizes the importance of local energy and enthusiasm. Charting the growth of denominational pluralism in Oldham and Saddleworth, Dr Smith compares the strengths and weaknesses of the various Anglican and Nonconformist approaches to promoting church growth. He also demonstrates the extent to which all the churches participated in a common culture shaped by the influence of evangelicalism, and shows that active co-operation between the churches rather than denominational conflict dominated. This revised and updated edition of Dr Smith's challenging and original study makes an important contribution both to the social history of religion and to urban studies.
2005 / 1-84227-335-3 / approx. 300pp

Martin Sutherland
Peace, Toleration and Decay
The Ecclesiology of Later Stuart Dissent
(Studies in Christian History and Thought)
This fresh analysis brings to light the complexity and fragility of the later Stuart Nonconformist consensus. Recent findings on wider seventeenth-century thought are incorporated into a new picture of the dynamics of Dissent and the roots of evangelicalism.
2003 / 1-84227-152-0 / xxii + 216pp

Haddon Willmer
Evangelicalism 1785–1835: An Essay (1962) and Reflections (2004)
(Studies in Evangelical History and Thought)
Awarded the Hulsean Prize in the University of Cambridge in 1962, this interpretation of a classic period of English Evangelicalism, by a young church historian, is now supplemented by reflections on Evangelicalism from the vantage point of a retired Professor of Theology.
2005 / 1-84227-219-5

Linda Wilson
Constrained by Zeal
Female Spirituality amongst Nonconformists 1825–1875
(Studies in Evangelical History and Thought)

Constrained by Zeal investigates the neglected area of Nonconformist female spirituality. Against the background of separate spheres, it analyses the experience of women from four denominations, and argues that the churches provided a 'third sphere' in which they could find opportunities for participation.

2000 / 0-85364-972-3 / xvi + 294pp

Nigel G. Wright
Disavowing Constantine
Mission, Church and the Social Order in the Theologies of John Howard Yoder and Jürgen Moltmann
(Paternoster Theological Monographs)

This book is a timely restatement of a radical theology of church and state in the Anabaptist and Baptist tradition. Dr Wright constructs his argument in dialogue and debate with Yoder and Moltmann, major contributors to a free church perspective.

2000 / 0-85364-978-2 / xvi + 252pp

Nigel G. Wright
New Baptists, New Agenda

New Baptists, New Agenda is a timely contribution to the growing debate about the health, shape and future of the Baptists. It considers the steady changes that have taken place among Baptists in the last decade – changes of mood, style, practice and structure – and encourages us to align these current movements and questions with God's upward and future call. He contends that the true church has yet to come: the church that currently exists is an anticipation of the joyful gathering of all who have been called by the Spirit through Christ to the Father.

2002 / 1-84227-157-1 / x + 162pp

Paternoster
9 Holdom Avenue
Bletchley
Milton Keynes MK1 1QR
United Kingdom
Web: www.authenticmedia.co.uk/paternoster

November 2004

www.ingramcontent.com/pod-product-compliance
Lightning Source LLC
Chambersburg PA
CBHW071226290426
44108CB00013B/1303